Writing First

PRACTICE IN CONTEXT

WITH READINGS

Writing First

PRACTICE IN CONTEXT

WITH READINGS

Second Edition

Laurie G. Kirszner
University of the Sciences in Philadelphia

Stephen R. Mandell
Drexel University

with additional teaching tips and ESL tips by
Linda Mason Austin
McLennan Community College

Bedford/St. Martin's
Boston ■ New York

For Bedford/St. Martin's

Developmental Editor: Mikola De Roo
Senior Production Editor: Harold Chester
Senior Production Supervisor: Joe Ford
Marketing Manager: Brian Wheel
Art Direction and Cover Design: Lucy Krikorian
Text Design: Wanda Kossak and Wanda Lubelska
Copy Editor: Alice Vigliani
Photo Research: Alice Lundoff
Cover Photos: (left to right) Tom Stewart/CORBIS Stock Market; David Young-Wolff/PhotoEdit; David Frazier/Photo Researchers; Esbin-Anderson/The Image Works; Paul Barton/CORBIS Stock Market
Composition: Monotype Composition Company, Inc.
Printing and Binding: RR Donnelley & Sons Co.

President: Joan E. Feinberg
Editorial Director: Denise B. Wydra
Editor in Chief: Nancy Perry
Director of Marketing: Karen R. Melton
Director of Editing, Design, and Production: Marcia Cohen
Managing Editor: Erica T. Appel

Library of Congress Control Number: 2002107341

Manufactured in the United States of America.

8 7 6 5 4 3
f e d c b a

For information, write: Bedford/St. Martin's, 75 Arlington Street, Boston, MA 02116   (617-399-4000)

ISBN: 0-312-39974-X (Instructor's Annotated Edition)
      0-312-39802-6 (Student Edition with Readings)
      0-312-39801-8 (Student Edition)

Acknowledgments

Acknowledgments and copyrights appear at the back of the book on pages 658–59, which constitute an extension of the copyright page.

Preface for Instructors

In college, writing comes first. In fact, as soon as students set foot in a classroom, they are asked to write—to take notes, to complete assignments, to write papers, to take exams. But writing is also crucial outside the classroom. In the community and in the workplace, writing empowers students, enabling them to participate more fully in every aspect of their lives. For all these reasons, writing also comes first in *Writing First: Practice in Context*, where our organization and emphasis reflect our priorities as teachers as well as the importance of writing in college and in the wider world.

In *Writing First*, writing comes first chronologically: the book begins with thorough coverage of the writing process, and most chapters begin with writing prompts. Writing is also first in importance: extensive writing practice is central to the grammar chapters as well as to the writing process chapters. In addition to an abundance of practice exercises, each grammar chapter includes a unique three-step sequence of writing and editing prompts (Writing First/Flashback/Revising and Editing) that guides students in applying the chapter's concepts to a piece of their own writing. One thing our years in the classroom have taught us is that students learn writing skills best in the context of their own written work. Here, by moving from their own writing to workbook-style mastery exercises and back to their own work, students learn more effectively and more purposefully.

Our goals in this edition of *Writing First* remain the same as they have been from the start: to motivate students to improve their writing for college and for everyday life, and to give them the tools they need to do so. It is our hope that by practicing these skills in the context of their own writing, students will come to see writing as something at which they can succeed. To achieve our goals, we worked hard in this revision to keep the text flexible enough to support a variety of teaching styles and to meet the needs of individual students. We wrote this book for adults—our own interested, concerned, hardworking students—and we tailored the book's approach and content to them. Consequently, we avoid exercises that present writing as a seemingly dull, pointless, and artificial activity, and we do our best to offer fresh, contemporary examples, writing assignments, and student passages. In the book's style and tone, we try to show respect for our audience—to treat college students as adults who can take responsibility for their own learning and for their development as writers.

Organization

Writing First: Practice in Context has a flexible organization that permits instructors to teach various topics in the order that works best for them and their students. The book is divided into three sections: "Writing Paragraphs and Essays," "Revising and Editing Your Writing," and "Becoming a Critical Reader." The first section provides a comprehensive discussion of the writing process. The second section presents a thorough review of sentence skills, grammar, punctuation, mechanics, and spelling. The third section introduces students to critical reading skills and includes nineteen professional essays, each illustrating a particular pattern of development. Finally, two appendixes—Appendix A, "Strategies for College Success," and Appendix B, "Writing a Research Paper"—provide help with skills that students will need in other courses. Appendix A helps students develop effective study strategies for taking notes, completing homework, taking exams, managing their time well, and using the Internet. Appendix B gives a brief overview of the research process, illustrates and explains MLA documentation style, and includes an annotated, fully documented student research paper.

Features

Central to *Writing First* is our "student writing first" philosophy, which is supported by innovative features designed to make students' writing practice meaningful, productive, and enjoyable.

The text's process approach guides students step by step through the writing process, providing comprehensive coverage in a flexible format. Eleven chapters on paragraph development (Units One and Two) feature many examples of student and professional writing, with separate chapters on each method of paragraph development. A comprehensive treatment of essay writing (Unit Three) starts with Chapter 12, "Writing an Essay." Chapter 13, "Introductions and Conclusions," offers guidance rarely found in developmental writing texts. In Chapter 14, "Patterns of Essay Development," each pattern is illustrated by a student essay.

Unique "practice in context" activities let students apply each new concept to their own writing. Most chapters begin with a *Writing First* activity, a writing prompt accompanied by a photo or other visual. Then, a series of *Flashback* exercises encourages students to practice skills introduced in the chapter in the context of their Writing First response. At the end of the chapter, a *Revising and Editing* activity guides students through a final look at their Writing First responses.

***Writing First* makes information easy to find and use.** The engaging full-color design supports the text's pedagogy and helps students find information quickly. *Focus boxes* highlight key concepts and important information, *quick-reference corner tabs* make the book easy to navigate, and *marginal cross-references* to other parts of the text help students find and review key information. *Writing Tips* in the margins provide additional information, address common problem areas, and make connections between academic and everyday writing situations. *Computer Tips* give helpful advice for students writing with computers. For students who need additional practice with specific skills, *marginal cross-references to the* Exercise Central *online exercise collection* have been added to the text.

Both native and nonnative writers get the grammar help they need. Thorough, accessible grammar explanations are complemented by clear, helpful examples. The book also offers stronger ESL coverage than any competing text: Chapter 30, "Grammar and Usage Issues for ESL Writers," discusses concerns of special interest to nonnative writers, and *ESL Tips* in the *Instructor's Annotated Edition* guide instructors in helping ESL students get the most out of the text.

Each chapter offers numerous opportunities for practice and review. Easy-to-grade *Practices* following each section of every chapter form a strand of workbook-style mastery exercises that let students hone specific skills. (These Practices can supplement or replace the Writing First strand, depending on an instructor's preference.) *Visual writing prompts* in Chapter 14's essay assignments serve as additional sources of inspiration for writing. *Self-Assessment Checklists* in the paragraph and essay chapters show students how to revise and edit their own writing. Three kinds of *Chapter Review* activities provide additional practice opportunities: an *Editing Practice* featuring a passage of student writing gives students an opportunity to edit to eliminate a specific writing problem; *Collaborative Activities* offer creative options for student-centered classroom learning; and a *Review Checklist* recaps the main points of each chapter for quick review. Finally, *Answers to Odd-Numbered Exercise Items* at the end of the book let students check their own work as they practice and review.

Writing First helps students make the connection between reading and writing. Chapter 35, "Reading for College," guides students step by step through the reading process and includes a sample annotated reading. Chapter 36, "Readings for Writers," contains nineteen professional readings that illustrate the patterns of development covered in the paragraph and essay chapters of the book. Questions following each reading test comprehension, help build vocabulary skills, and offer topics for student writing.

Writing First respects students as serious writers. The text has more student writing than any other developmental textbook: numerous paragraph-length examples as well as thirty-three complete essays provide realistic models. *Student Voices* in the margins evoke the experiences of actual students working to master the topic at hand. The tone and level of explanatory material, as well as the subject matter of examples and exercises, acknowledge the diverse interests, ages, and experiences of developmental writers.

Two appendixes cover skills that students can also use in other courses. Appendix A, "Strategies for College Success" (unique in books of this type), gives students practical strategies they can use throughout their college careers. Appendix B, "Writing a Research Paper," teaches students the basics of researching and writing a paper and citing and documenting sources. The chapter includes an annotated sample student paper in MLA style.

New to this Edition

In revising *Writing First,* our goal was to expand and improve upon the features that users of the first edition found most helpful, at the same time adding features to make the book more appealing and more useful to both students and teachers.

Over 70 new exercises. In addition to replacing certain Practices to provide new content, we have written many additional exercises. As in the first edition, these exercises give students opportunities to practice skills as they learn them; in this edition, we have worked to achieve a better balance of subject matter in exercises focusing on everyday life, the world of work, academics, and historical and cultural topics.

Visual texts complementing all chapter-opening writing prompts. Each Writing First activity is now accompanied by a photo or some other image. These visual texts, designed to help stimulate student thinking and writing, have particular appeal to students who are visual learners.

Expanded coverage of topic sentences, thesis statements, and outlining. In Unit One, Focus on Paragraphs, we have expanded our treatment of topic sentences, adding explanatory material and new exercises to help students understand the role of the topic sentence in structuring the paragraph. This unit also includes a new student paragraph-in-progress on the topic of required community service for college students. In Unit Three, Focus on Essays, we have expanded coverage of the thesis statement and also added material that explains and illustrates the process of preparing a formal outline.

A new appendix on developing effective academic study skills, "Strategies for College Success." This unique feature offers students numerous practical strategies for approaching note-taking, homework, exams, and time management, as well as tips for adjusting to college life. A comprehensive section on Internet strategies includes essential information on evaluating Web sites as well as explanations of how to use the Internet to find information for assignments, for improving writing skills, and for enhancing everyday life.

A new vocabulary enhancement strand in every chapter. Marginal Word Power boxes beside each Writing First prompt introduce two or three words (along with their definitions) that students might use in their responses. This feature enables students to expand their vocabularies in a nonthreatening way—in the context of their own writing—and encourages them to practice using words that may already be in their speaking or reading vocabularies.

Expanded ESL coverage in Chapter 30. This comprehensive chapter, addressing concerns of special interest to nonnative writers, has been expanded to include over a dozen new exercises.

New readings and student essays. Nearly half of the professional essays in Chapter 36 are new to this edition. New selections continue to focus on timely topics likely to be of interest to students—for example, the relationship between "wife-beater" T-shirts and domestic violence, and the debate over requiring Americans to carry national ID cards. In addition, new student essays are featured in Chapter 14, "Patterns of Essay Development," as well as in many of the Chapter Reviews.

Ancillaries

Writing First is accompanied by a comprehensive teaching support package that includes the following items:

- The *Instructor's Annotated Edition* includes answers to the Practice exercises as well as numerous teaching tips and ESL tips in the margins.
- *Classroom Resources for Instructors Using WRITING FIRST* includes helpful teaching suggestions, sample syllabi, and additional teaching materials.
- *Teaching Developmental Writing: Background Readings* offers more than two dozen professional articles on topics of interest to developmental writing instructors, accompanied by suggestions for practical applications to the classroom.
- **Exercise Central,** the largest collection of grammar exercises available with any writing text, includes multiple-exercise sets on every grammar topic to give students all the practice they need. This software can be accessed via the World Wide Web at <bedfordstmartins.com/exercisecentral>.
- *Diagnostic and Mastery Tests to Accompany WRITING FIRST* offers diagnostic and mastery tests complementing the topic coverage in *Writing First*. This volume's perforated pages enable instructors to copy the material and distribute it to students.
- *Supplemental Exercises to Accompany WRITING FIRST* offers additional grammar exercises (including material from the Exercise Central online exercise collection). Like *Diagnostic and Mastery Tests*, this book is offered as a workbook with perforated pages to make it easier for instructors to copy and distribute the exercises to students.
- *Writing Guide Software for WRITING FIRST* supports students as they work on paragraph and essay assignments. This software is available for Windows and Macintosh platforms.
- *Transparency Masters to Accompany WRITING FIRST*, including editable student writing samples from the text, are available as a printed package and as files downloadable from the Web site.
- The *Writing First* **Web site** <bedfordstmartins.com/writingfirst> offers downloadable teaching aids and links to other useful materials.

Acknowledgments

In our work on *Writing First,* we have benefited from the help of a great many people.

Franklin E. Horowitz of Teachers College, Columbia University, drafted an early version of Chapter 30, "Grammar and Usage Issues for

ESL Writers," and his linguist's insight continues to inform that chapter. Linda Stine and Linda Stengle of Lincoln University devoted energy and vision to the preparation of *Classroom Resources for Instructors*. Linda Mason Austin of McLennan Community College drew on her extensive teaching experience to contribute teaching tips and ESL tips to the *Instructor's Annotated Edition*. Susan Bernstein's work on the compilation and annotation of *Teaching Developmental Writing* reflects her deep commitment to scholarship and teaching. We are very grateful for their contributions.

We thank Judith Lechner for her work on Exercise Central and the accompanying exercise book. Carol Sullivan and Mark Gallaher, longtime friends and colleagues, made valuable contributions to the book's exercises, and we thank them as well.

Writing First could not exist without our students, whose words appear on almost every page of the book, whether in sample sentences, paragraphs, and essays, or as Student Voices. Our thanks go to Lis Bare, Kevin Bey, Dan Brody, Susan Burkhart, Michelle Cooper, Daniel Corey, Shannon Cornell, Mark Cotharn, Sutapa Das, Megan Davia, Demetrius Davis, Andrea DeMarco, Kim DiPialo, Jerry Doyle, Ann Duong, Thaddeus Eddy, Mohamad Faisal, John Fleeger, Richard Greene, Linda Grossman, Monica Han, Catherine Hartman, Beth Haurin, Russ Hightower, Keith Jackson, Nisha Jani, Panhej Jolanpretra, Willa Kincaid, Nicholas Kinlaw, Serge Komanawski, Meredith Krall, Peter Likus, George Lin, Jennifer Loucks, Dan Lynn, Krishna Mahajan, Toni-Ann Marro, Felicia May, Jeremy McDonald, Matt McDonald, Michael McManus, Timothy E. Miles, Kelly Miller, Kristin Miller, Hiro Nakamura, Miniinah Neal, Samantha Nguyen, Rob O'Neal, Karoline Ozols, Nirav Patel, Doreen Queenan, James Ramos, Linda Richards, Cheri Rodriguez, Allison Rogers, Christina Rose, Terry Simons, Todd Slunt, Rizwana Syed, Deborah Ulrich, Lisa Van Hoboken, Jason Varghese, Jason Walsh, Jen Weber, Scott Weckerly, Kristin Whitehead, Janice Williams, Teren Williams, Tom Woller, Alisha Woolery, Mai Yoshikawa, and Jessica Zimmerman.

Instructors throughout the country have contributed suggestions and encouragement at various stages of the book's development. For their collegial support, we thank Linda Austin, McLennan Community College; Susan Brant, College of the Canyons; Vilma Chemers, Roosevelt University; Helen Chester, Milwaukee Area Technical College; Eileen Eliot, Broward Community College; Jacqueline Gray, St. Charles Community College; Johanna Grimes, Tennessee State University; Deanne Gute, University of Northern Iowa; Adam Heidenreich, Roosevelt University; Carra Leah Hood, Southern Connecticut State University; Robin Ikegami, Sacramento City College; Enid Leonard, Lane Community College; Janene Lewis, Huston-Tillotson College; Jane Long, Southwestern Oklahoma State University; Donna Maurer, North Shore Community College; Samuel McLeary, Southeastern Community College; David Merves, Miami-Dade Community College; Ronald Miazga, Kalamazoo Valley Community College; Katherine Ellen Perrault, University College of the Fraser Valley; Michael Ritterbrown, Glendale College; Meredith Anne Serling, Southeastern Community College; Joyce Stoffers, Southwestern Oklahoma State University; Rebecca Suarez, University of Texas–El Paso; Janet Turk, Lamar University; Linda Varvel, Anoka-Ramsey Community College; Margaret Whalen, Mt. San Antonio College; and Jayne Williams, Texarkana College.

At Bedford/St. Martin's, we thank founder and former president Chuck Christensen and president Joan Feinberg, who believed in this project and gave us support and encouragement from the outset. We thank Nancy Perry, editor in chief and our longtime friend, who continues to earn our respect as well as our affection. We also thank Greg Johnson, associate editor, for his diligent work in revising the book's ancillaries; Joanna Imm, editorial assistant, for helping with numerous tasks, big and small; Erica Appel, managing editor, and Harold Chester, senior project editor, for guiding the book ably through production; Lucy Krikorian, art director, for overseeing the beautiful and innovative design; Nick Carbone, director of New Media, for overseeing the production of the *Writing Guide Software;* and New Media editors Harriet Wald and Coleen O'Hanley for their work on the *Writing First* Web site. Thanks also go to Joe Ford, senior production supervisor; Karen Melton, director of marketing; and Brian Wheel, marketing manager. Our biggest thanks go to our editor, Mika De Roo, who took over the project in this edition without missing a beat. Her insights, energy, and thoroughness have gone a long way toward making this book as good as it could possibly be.

We are grateful, too, for the continued support of our families—Mark, Adam, and Rebecca Kirszner and Demi, David, and Sarah Mandell. Finally, we are grateful for the survival and growth of the writing partnership we entered into in 1975, when we were graduate students. We had no idea then of the wonderful places our collaborative efforts would take us. Now, we know.

Laurie G. Kirszner
Stephen R. Mandell

Contents

REVISING AND EDITING YOUR WRITING   211

UNIT SEVEN   Understanding Punctuation, Mechanics, and Spelling   477

A Student's Guide to Using Writing First

What *Writing First* Can Do for You

It is no secret that writing will be very important in most of the courses you take in college. Whether you write lab reports or English papers, midterms or final exams, your ability to organize your thoughts and express them in writing will help to determine how well you do. In other words, succeeding at writing is the first step toward succeeding in college. Perhaps even more important, writing is a key to success outside the classroom. On the job and in everyday life, if you can express yourself clearly and effectively, you will stand a better chance of achieving your goals and making a difference in the world around you.

Whether you write as a student, as an employee, as a parent, or as a concerned citizen, your writing almost always has a specific purpose. For example, when you write an essay, a memo, a letter, or a research paper, you are writing not just to complete an exercise but to give other people information or to tell them your ideas or opinions. That is why, in this book, we do not ask you simply to do grammar exercises and fill in blanks; in each chapter, we also ask you to apply the skills you are learning to a piece of your own writing.

As teachers—and former students—we know how demanding college can be and how hard it is to juggle assignments with work and family responsibilities. We also know that you do not want to waste your time or money. That is why in *Writing First* we make information easy to find and use and provide many different features to help you become a better writer.

The following sections describe the key features of *Writing First*. If you take the time now to familiarize yourself with these features, you will be able to use the book more effectively later on.

Teaching Tip
Go over this guide with students on the first day of class. Once they have looked through the book and located some of its helpful features, they are more likely to use the book as a resource during the semester.

XXV

How *Writing First* Makes Information Easy to Find and Use

Brief table of contents   Inside the front cover is a brief table of contents that summarizes the topics covered in this book. This feature can help you find a particular chapter quickly.

Detailed table of contents   The table of contents that starts on page xiii provides a detailed breakdown of the book's topics. Use this table of contents to find a specific part of a particular chapter.

Index   The index, which appears at the back of the book starting on page 661, enables you to locate all the available information about a particular topic. The topics appear in alphabetical order; so, for example, if you wanted to find out how to use commas, you would find the *C* section and look up the word *comma*. (If the page number following a word is **boldfaced,** that tells you that on that page you can find a definition of the word.)

List of Self-Assessment Checklists   On page xxx is a list of checklists designed to help you write, revise, and fine-tune the paragraphs and essays you compose. Use this list to help you find the checklist that is most useful for the particular writing assignment you are working on.

A handy cross-referencing system   Often, an *italicized marginal cross-reference* will point you to another section of the book (for example, "*See 28A and 28B*"). At the tops of most pages of *Writing First,* you will find *quick-reference corner tabs* consisting of green-and-blue boxes, each containing a number and a letter. This information tells you which chapter you have turned to and which section of that chapter you are looking at. Together, the cross-references and the tabs help you find information quickly. For example, if a cross-reference in the text suggests, "*See 10A for more on classification,*" you can use the tabs to help you locate section 10A.

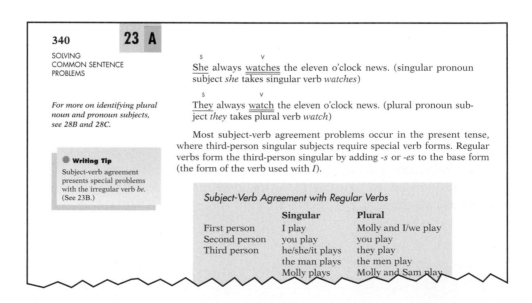

How *Writing First* Can Help You Become a Better Writer

Preview boxes   Each chapter starts with a list of key concepts that will be discussed in the chapter. Looking at these boxes before you skim the chapter will help you get an overview of the chapter.

PREVIEW

In this chapter, you will learn

■ to recognize parallel structure (19A)

■ to use parallel structure (19B)

Word Power
enlighten   to give insight to; to educate

Writing First activities   Most chapters include a three-part writing activity that helps you apply specific skills to your own writing. Each chapter starts with a *Writing First* assignment that asks you to write about a particular topic. (An accompanying photograph or other visual is included to stimulate your writing.) Beside each assignment, a Word Power box lists two or three vocabulary words (and their definitions) that you might find useful as you write your response. Throughout the chapter, *Flashback* exercises help you analyze your Writing First response so you can identify and correct specific writing problems. Finally, a *Revising and Editing* exercise asks you to fine-tune your writing. (See, for example, pages 213, 216, and 222 in Chapter 15.)

Focus boxes   Throughout the book, boxes with the word *Focus* in a red banner highlight useful information, identify key points, and explain difficult concepts.

FOCUS   *There Is* and *There Are*

In a sentence that begins with *there is* or *there are,* the subject comes after the form of the verb *be.* (*There* can never be the subject.)

        v   s
There <u>are</u> nine <u>justices</u> on the Supreme Court.

        v   s
There <u>is</u> one chief <u>justice</u> on the Court.

Self-Assessment Checklists   Chapters 1, 3–12, and 14 include Self-Assessment Checklists that give you a handy way to check your work and measure your progress. Use these checklists to help you revise your writing before you hand it in.

> ☑ SELF-ASSESSMENT CHECKLIST:
> Writing an Exemplification Paragraph
>
> *Unity*
>
> ▪ Does your topic sentence state a general idea that can be supported with examples?
>
> ▪ Is your topic sentence specifically worded?
>
> ▪ Do all your examples support your topic sentence?
>
> *Development*
>
> ▪ Do you need to find additional examples that more clearly support your topic sentence?

Marginal notes   In the margins of *Writing First,* you will find several kinds of notes that give you additional information in an easy-to-read format. *Writing Tips* offer practical information and helpful hints, including definitions and examples. *Computer Tips* help you make effective use of your computer as you write. *Student Voices* present the words of real students telling what works and doesn't work for them when they write. *Word Power* boxes define words you might choose to include in your Writing First response. Finally, if you need additional practice with specific skills, *marginal cross-references to the* Exercise Central *online exercise collection* have been added to the text.

> ● **Writing Tip**
>
> Use a transitional phrase such as *for instance* or *for example* to let readers know you are going to use an example. (See 2D.)

> ▪ **Computer Tip**
>
> Try boldfacing or underlining the topic sentence of a paragraph before you start to revise the paragraph. (See 2D.)

> ▼ **Student Voices**
>
> *At my job, I often have to write paragraphs telling people how to do something.*
> Liz Bare

> **Word Power**
>
> **primary**   most important
>
> **aspiration**   a strong desire for high achievement; an ambitious goal

Review Checklists   Each chapter ends with a summary of the most important information in the chapter. Use these checklists to review material for quizzes or to remind yourself of the main points in the chapter you have been studying.

> ☑ REVIEW CHECKLIST:
> Achieving Sentence Variety
>
> ■ Vary sentence types, using an occasional question or exclamation. (See 18A.)
>
> ■ Vary sentence openings. (See 18B.)
>
> ■ Combine sentences. (See 18C.)
>
> ■ Vary sentence length. (See 18D.)

Answers to Odd-Numbered Exercise Items   Starting on page 647, you will find answers for some of the Practice items in the book. When you need to study a topic independently or when your instructor has you complete a Practice but not hand it in, you can consult these answers to see if you are on the right track.

How *Writing First* Can Help You Succeed in Other Courses

In a sense, this whole book is all about succeeding in other courses. After all, as we said earlier, writing is the key to success in college. But *Writing First* also includes specific sections at the end of the book that you may find especially useful in courses you take later on in college. We have designed these sections so you can use them on your own as well as with your instructor's help.

Appendix A, "Strategies for College Success"   This practical guide offers specific, useful information on a wide variety of important topics, such as note-taking, study skills, time management, and using the Internet.

Appendix B, "Writing a Research Paper"   This appendix gives a short overview of the research process and shows how to document sources and create a list of works cited. A student paper complete with helpful marginal notes is also included.

List of correction symbols   The chart inside the back cover lists marks that many instructors use when evaluating and marking student papers. Becoming familiar with these symbols will help you get the most out of your instructor's comments on your work.

Self-Assessment Checklists for Writing Paragraphs and Essays

Units 1–3 of *Writing First* include a number of Self-Assessment Checklists designed to help you write, revise, and fine-tune your paragraphs and essays. You can use these checklists both in your writing course and in other courses that include written assignments. The following list shows the page number for each checklist.

Writing First

PRACTICE IN CONTEXT

WITH READINGS

UNIT ONE

Focus on Paragraphs

Writing a Paragraph

◼ WRITING FIRST

What do you think is the primary purpose of college—to give students a general education, or to prepare them for careers? Look at the picture above, and think about this question carefully as you read the pages that follow. This is the topic you will be writing about as you move through this chapter.

Writing is not just something you do to get a grade in school; writing is a life skill. If you can write clearly, you can express your ideas convincingly to others—in school, on the job, and in the community. Writing tasks take many different forms. In college, you might write a single paragraph, an essay exam, a short paper, or a long research paper. At work, you might write a memo, a proposal, or a report. In your daily life as a citizen of your community, you might write a letter asking for information, explaining a problem, or complaining about a service. Writing is important. If you can write, you can communicate; if you can communicate effectively, your writing is likely to get a response.

1 B

A Understanding Paragraph Structure

This chapter takes you through the process of writing a **paragraph**. A paragraph can be part of a longer piece of writing, as it is in an essay, or it can stand alone, as it does in a one-paragraph classroom exercise or an exam answer. Because paragraphs play a part in almost every writing task, learning to write a paragraph is an important step in becoming a competent writer.

A paragraph is unified by a single main idea. The **topic sentence** states the main idea, and the rest of the sentences in the paragraph **support** the main idea. Often a final **concluding statement** gives readers a summary of the paragraph's main idea.

Paragraph

Topic sentence

Support

Concluding statement

A paragraph consists of a **topic sentence** and **support**. The topic sentence states the main idea of the paragraph. This idea unifies the paragraph. The other sentences in the paragraph provide support. These sentences present details, facts, and examples. At the end of the paragraph is a final **concluding statement**, a sentence that sums up the paragraph's main idea. Many paragraphs follow this general structure.

Note that the first sentence of a paragraph is **indented**, starting about one-half inch (five spaces) from the left-hand margin. Every sentence begins with a capital letter and, in most cases, ends with a period.

◆ PRACTICE 1-1

Bring two paragraphs to class: one from a newspaper or magazine and one from a textbook. Compare your paragraphs with those brought in by other students. What features do all your paragraphs share? How do the paragraphs differ from one another?

B Focusing on Your Assignment, Purpose, and Audience

In college, a writing task usually begins with an assignment that gives you a topic to write about. Instead of plunging in headfirst and starting to write, take time to consider some questions about your **assignment** (*what* you are expected to write), your **purpose** (*why* you are writing), and your **audience** (*for whom* you are writing). Finding out the answers to these questions at this point will save you time in the long run.

▼ **Student Voices**
As soon as I get a writing assignment, I choose a time to set aside distractions and concentrate on my paper.
Jason Varghese

Questions about Assignment, Purpose, and Audience

Assignment

- What is your assignment?
- Do you have a word or page limit?
- When is your assignment due?
- Will you be expected to complete your assignment at home or in class?
- Will you be expected to work on your own or with others?
- Will you be allowed to revise after you hand in your assignment?

Purpose

- Are you expected to express your personal reactions—for example, to tell how you feel about a piece of music or a news event?
- Are you expected to present information—for example, to answer an exam question, describe a process in a lab report, or summarize a story or essay you have read?
- Are you expected to argue for or against a position on a controversial issue?

Audience

- Who will read your paper—just your instructor, or other students, too?
- Do you have an audience beyond the classroom—for example, your supervisor at work or your landlord?
- How much will your readers know about your topic?
- Will your readers expect you to use formal or informal language?

◆ PRACTICE 1-2

Each of the following writing tasks has a different audience and purpose. Think about how you would approach each task. (Use the Questions about Assignment, Purpose, and Audience listed above to help you decide on the best strategy.) On the lines following each task, write some notes about your approach. Discuss your responses with your class or in a small group.

1. For the other students in your writing class, describe your best or worst educational experience.

   Answers will vary. Students will include personal experiences and will

   probably use informal language.

   _____

   _____

2. For the instructor of an introductory psychology course, discuss how early educational experiences can affect a student's performance throughout his or her schooling.

   Answers will vary. Students will probably use fairly formal language and

   may include facts and findings from studies.

Teaching Tip
Some students may be reluctant to write their answers in this book because they are afraid of making mistakes. (They will also have been told in high school never to write in a textbook.) Encourage them to write directly in the text where it is required.

Teaching Tip
Get volunteers to share experiences or ideas about each of the four topics listed. Hearing ideas from others often helps students who have trouble generating their own ideas.

ESL Tip
Make sure at least one student from another culture shares his or her experience or idea. Nonnative speakers often feel isolated because of the language barrier. You may have to draw them in each time you have a class discussion.

3. Write a short letter to your community's school board in which you try to convince members to make two or three specific changes that you believe would improve the schools you attended or those your children might attend.

Answers will vary. Students will probably use formal language and include

both personal experiences and objective information.

4. Write a letter to a work supervisor—either past or current—telling what you appreciate about his or her supervision and how it has helped you develop and grow as an employee.

Answers will vary. Students may use either informal or formal language

and will include personal experiences.

C Using Invention Strategies

Once you know what, why, and for whom you are writing, you can begin to experiment with different invention strategies. **Invention**—sometimes called *prewriting* or *discovery*—is the process of finding material to write about. This process is different for every writer.

Stella Drew, a student in an introductory writing course, was given this assignment.

Write a paragraph that answers the following questions: Should community service—unpaid work in the community—be a required part of the college curriculum? Why or why not?

Before she drafted her paragraph, Stella used a variety of invention strategies to help her come up with ideas. The pages that follow illustrate the four strategies she used: *freewriting, brainstorming, clustering,* and *journal writing*.

Freewriting

When you **freewrite**, you write for a set period of time—perhaps five minutes—without stopping, even if what you are writing doesn't seem to have a point or a direction. Your goal is to relax and let ideas flow without worrying about whether or not they are logical. You can freewrite without a topic in mind, but sometimes you will focus your attention on a topic. This strategy is called **focused freewriting**.

When you finish freewriting, read what you have written, and underline any ideas you think you might be able to use. If you find an idea you want to explore further, freewrite again, using that idea as a starting point.

Here is Stella's focused freewriting on the topic of whether or not community service should be a required part of the college curriculum.

▪ Computer Tip

Try doing "invisible freewriting" by turning off your monitor and writing without looking at the screen. When you have finished, turn on the monitor to see what you have written.

> Community service. Community service. Sounds like what you do instead of going to jail. Service to the community—service in the community. Community center. College community—community college. Community service—I guess it's a good idea to do it—but when? In my spare time—spare time—that's pretty funny. So after school and work and all the reading and studying I also have to do <u>service</u>? Right. And what could I do anyway? Work with kids. Or homeless people. Old people? Sick people? Or not people—maybe animals. Or work for a political candidate. Does that count? But when would I do it? Maybe other people have time, but I don't. OK idea, could work—but not for me.

Freewriting

▼ Student Voices

I get ideas by clearing my mind and writing until I come up with something I like. If I have trouble, I walk away and come back to my writing later.

Felicia May

◆ PRACTICE 1-3

Reread Stella's freewriting on the topic of community service for college students. If you were advising her, what ideas would you suggest she explore further? Underline these ideas in her freewriting and then recopy them on the lines below.

Answers will vary.

_____

_____

_____

_____

_____

_____

_____

_____

1 C

◆ PRACTICE 1-4

Now it is time for you to begin the work that will result in a finished paragraph. (You already have your assignment from the Writing First box on page 3: to write about whether the primary purpose of college is to educate students or to prepare them for careers.) Your first step is to freewrite about your topic. Use a blank sheet of lined paper, and write for at least five minutes without stopping. If you have trouble thinking of something to write, keep recopying the last word you have written until something else comes to mind.

◆ PRACTICE 1-5

Reread the freewriting you did for Practice 1-4. Underline any ideas you think you might use in your paragraph. Then, choose one of these ideas, and use it as a starting point for another focused freewriting exercise.

Brainstorming

When you **brainstorm**, you record all the ideas about your topic that you can think of. Unlike freewriting, brainstorming is often scattered all over the page. You don't have to use complete sentences; single words or phrases are fine. You can underline, star, or box important points. You can also ask questions, list points, and draw arrows to connect ideas.

Stella's brainstorming on the topic of community service appears on the next page.

FOCUS **Collaborative Brainstorming**

You often brainstorm on your own, but at times you may find it helpful to do **collaborative brainstorming**, working with other students to find ideas. Sometimes your instructor may ask you and another student to brainstorm together. At other times, the class might brainstorm as a group while your instructor writes ideas on the board that the class can later evaluate. However you brainstorm, your goal is the same: to come up with as much material about your topic as you can.

◆ PRACTICE 1-6

Reread Stella's brainstorming on community service (page 9). How is it similar to her freewriting on the same subject (page 7)? How is it different? If you were advising Stella, which ideas would you suggest that she cross out as she continues to explore her subject? Write your suggestions on the lines that follow on the next page.

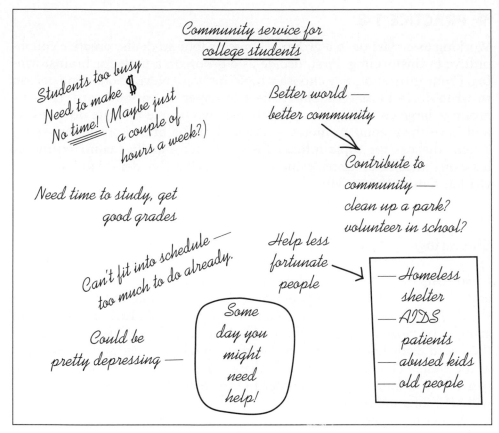

Brainstorming

Answers will vary.

_____

_____

_____

_____

_____

_____

_____

_____

◆ PRACTICE 1-7

On a piece of *unlined* paper, brainstorm about your assignment: What do you think is the primary purpose of college—to give students a general education or to prepare them for careers? (Begin by writing your topic, "The purpose of college," at the top of the page.) Write quickly, without worrying about using complete sentences. Try writing on different parts of the page, making lists, and drawing arrows to connect related ideas. When you have finished, look over what you have written. Which ideas are the most interesting? Did you come up with any new ideas as you brainstormed that you did not discover while freewriting?

◆ PRACTICE 1-8

Working as a class or in a group of three or four students, practice collaborative brainstorming. First, decide as a group on a topic for brainstorming. (Your instructor may choose a topic for you.) Next, choose one person to write down ideas on a blank sheet of paper or on the board. (If your group is large enough, you might choose two people to write down ideas and have them compare notes at the end of the brainstorming session.) Then, discuss the topic informally, with each member contributing at least one idea. After fifteen minutes or so, review the ideas that have been written down. As a group, try to identify interesting connections among ideas and suggest ideas that might be explored further.

Clustering

Clustering, sometimes called *mapping,* is another useful invention strategy. When you cluster, you begin by writing your topic in the center of a sheet of paper. Then, you branch out, writing related ideas on the page in groups, or clusters, around the topic. As you add new ideas, you circle them and draw lines to connect the ideas to one another and to the topic at the center. (These lines will look like spokes of a wheel or branches of a tree.) As you move from the center to the corners of the page, your ideas will get more and more specific.

Sometimes, one branch of your exercise will give you all the material you need; at other times, you may decide to write about the ideas from several branches—or to choose one or two from each branch. If you find you need additional material after you finish your first cluster exercise, you can cluster again on a new sheet of paper, this time beginning with a topic from one of the branches.

Stella's clustering on the topic of community service for college students appears on the next page.

◆ PRACTICE 1-9

Reread Stella's clustering on community service (next page). How is it similar to her brainstorming on the same subject (page 9)? How is it different? If you were advising Stella, which branches of the cluster diagram would you say seem most promising? Why? Can you add any branches? Can you extend any of her branches further? Write your suggestions on the following lines. Then, discuss them with your class or in a small group.

Answers will vary.

_____

_____

_____

_____

◆ PRACTICE 1-10

Try clustering on the Writing First assignment: What do you think is the primary purpose of college—to give students a general education or to

> ● **Writing Tip**
> Although you may fill a page with branches and ideas, you will probably not be able to use all of them in your paragraph.

> **Teaching Tip**
> Tell students that for a short paragraph, where they will not be expected to go into much detail, they may not move very far from the center of their cluster diagram in selecting ideas. For longer, more complex writing assignments, however, they will need to use the more specific material generated as they moved out from the center.

prepare them for careers? Begin by writing the topic in the center of a blank sheet of unlined paper. Circle the topic, and then branch out with specific ideas and examples, continuing to the edge of the page if you can. When you have finished, look over what you have written. What are the most interesting ideas in your cluster diagram? Which branches seem most promising as the basis for further writing? What new ideas have you come up with that your freewriting and brainstorming did not suggest?

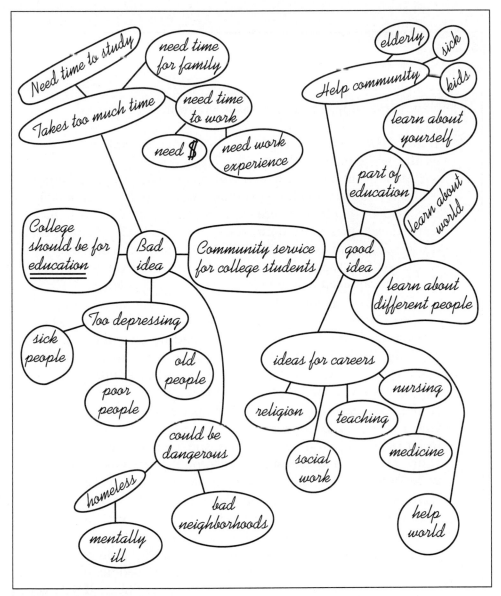

Clustering

Journal Writing

A **journal** is a notebook in which you keep an informal record of your thoughts and ideas. In a journal, you can reflect, question, summarize, or even complain. When you are involved in a writing project, your journal is a place where you jot down ideas to write about and think on paper about your assignment. Here you can try to resolve a problem, restart a stalled project, argue with yourself about your topic, or critique a draft. You can

■ Computer Tip

Try keeping a journal on your computer by making entries at the same time every day—when you check your e-mail, for example.

also try out different versions of sentences, keep track of details or examples, or keep a record of potentially useful things you read, see, or hear.

Once you have started making regular entries in your journal, take the time every week or so to go back and reread what you have written. You may find material you want to explore in further journal entries—or even an idea for a paper.

FOCUS **Journals**

Here are some subjects you can write about in your journal.

- *Your school work* You can use your journal to explore ideas for writing assignments. When you get a specific assignment, you can write a journal entry in which you record your thoughts about it and try to decide what you might write about. Your journal can also be a place where you think about what you have learned, ask questions about concepts you're having trouble understanding, and examine new ideas and new ways of seeing the world. Writing regularly in a journal about what you're studying in school can even help you become a better student.

- *Your job* In your journal, you can record job-related successes and frustrations, examine conflicts with coworkers, or note how you handled problems on the job. Reading over these entries can help you understand your strengths and weaknesses and become a more effective employee. As an added bonus, you may discover work-related topics to write about in school.

- *Your ideas about current events* Expressing your opinions in your journal can be a good way to explore complex ideas or just to let off steam. Your entries may spur you to write letters to your local or school newspaper or to public officials—and even to become involved in community projects or political activities.

- *Your impressions of what you see around you* Many professional and amateur writers carry their journals with them everywhere so they can record any interesting or unusual things they observe in the course of their daily lives. Rather than relying on memory, they jot down images of memorable people, places, or events as soon as possible after they observe them. If you get into the habit of recording such impressions, you can later incorporate them into stories or other pieces of writing.

- *Aspects of your personal life* Although you may not want to record the intimate details of your life if your instructor plans to collect your journal, such entries are the most common of all in a private journal. Writing about relationships with family and friends, personal problems, hopes and dreams—all the details of your life—can help you reach a better understanding of yourself and others.

Here is Stella's journal entry on the topic of community service for college students.

> *I'm not really sure what I think about community service. I guess I think it sounds like a good idea, but I still don't see why we should have to do it. I can't fit anything else into my life. I guess it would be possible if it was just an hour or two a week. And maybe we could get credit and a grade for it, like a course. Or maybe it should just be for people who have the time and want to do it. But if it's not required, will anyone do it?*

Journal Entry

◆ PRACTICE 1-11

Buy a notebook to use as a journal. (Your instructor may require a specific size and format, particularly if journals are going to be collected at some point.) Set a time to write for fifteen minutes or so in your journal—during your lunch break, for example, or before you go to bed. Make entries daily or several times a week, depending on your schedule and your instructor's suggestions. For your first journal entry, write down your thoughts about the topic you have been working on in this chapter: the primary purpose of college.

D   Identifying Your Main Idea and Choosing Supporting Points

When you think you have enough material to write about, you can move on to the next stage of the writing process: finding a main idea to develop into a paragraph and selecting and organizing the points that will support that idea most effectively.

Identifying Your Main Idea

Begin by looking over what you have already written. As you read through your freewriting, brainstorming, clustering, and journal entries, look for your **main idea**—the central point that your material seems to support. The sentence that states this main idea and gives your paragraph its focus will be the paragraph's **topic sentence**.

Stella Drew thought her notes supported the idea that community service requires time and commitment but is basically worthwhile. She stated this idea in a sentence.

> Community service takes time, but it is so important that college students should be required to do it.

● **Writing Tip**

If at any stage of the writing process you run out of ideas, return to the invention strategies you found most helpful and use them to find more material.

For more on topic sentences, see 2A.

Choosing Supporting Points

After you identify your main idea, review your notes again. This time, look for the specific points (facts, reasons, and examples) that provide **support** for your main idea. Write or type the topic sentence that states this main idea at the top of a blank page. As you review your notes, list all the supporting points you think you might be able to use.

Stella chose the following points from her notes to support her paragraph's main idea.

```
Main idea: Community service takes time, but it is
so important that college students should be required
to do it.
```

- Community service helps people.
- Community service can help the world.
- Community service helps the community.
- College students are busy, and community service takes a lot of time.
- Community service can teach students about careers and about life.
- Community service can be upsetting or depressing.

Ordering Supporting Points

● Writing Tip

You can arrange your points in time order, spatial order, or logical order. (See 2D.)

Once you have made a list of points you can use, arrange them in the order in which you plan to present them, as Stella did in the following list.

```
Main idea: Community service takes time, but it is
so important that college students should be required
to do it.
```

Teaching Tip
Remind students that they will need specific examples to support their main ideas. Have two or three students who have done community service talk about their experiences.

- Community service takes a lot of time.
- Students need time for family and friends, for studying, and for working.
- Community service can be depressing and upsetting.
- Community service helps the community.
- Community service can be part of a student's education.
- Community service can make the world a better place.

◆ PRACTICE 1-12

In Practices 1-4, 1-7, and 1-10, you practiced freewriting, brainstorming, and clustering. Now, you are ready to write a paragraph about your topic. Look over the invention exercises you have done, and try to find one main idea that your material can support. Write a sentence that expresses this idea on the following lines.

Answers will vary.

_____

_____

_____

Now, reread your invention exercises, and list the points you believe will support your main idea most effectively. Also, list any new points you think of.

Answers will vary.

_____

_____

_____

_____

_____

Look over the material you listed above, making sure each point supports your main idea. Arrange your points below in the order in which you plan to write about them.

1. *Answers will vary.*
   _____

2. _____

3. _____

4. _____

5. _____

6. _____

7. _____

E   Drafting Your Paragraph

Once you have found a main idea for your paragraph, selected the points you will discuss, and arranged them in the order in which you plan to write about them, you are ready to write a first draft.

In a first draft, your goal is to get your ideas down on paper. Begin with a topic sentence stating your paragraph's main idea. Then, keeping an eye on the list of points you plan to discuss, write or type without worrying about correct wording, spelling, or punctuation. If a new idea—one that is not on your list—occurs to you, write it down. Don't worry about where it goes or whether it fits with the other ideas. Your goal is not to produce a perfect piece of writing but simply to create a working draft. When you revise, you will have a chance to rethink ideas and rework sentences.

Because you will revise this first draft—adding or crossing out words and phrases, reordering ideas and details, clarifying connections between ideas, and rephrasing—you should leave plenty of room for revision. Leave wide margins, triple-space, and leave extra space in places where you might need to add material. Feel free to be messy and to cross out; remember, the only person who will see this draft is you.

When you have finished your first draft, don't start revising right away. Take a break and think about something—anything—else. Then, return to your draft, and read it with a fresh eye.

Here is the first draft of Stella's paragraph on the topic of community service for college students.

Why Community Service Should Be Required

Community service takes time, but it is so important that college students should be required to do
it. When college students do community service, they
volunteer their time to do good for someone or for
the community. Working in a soup kitchen, raking
leaves for senior citizens, and reading to children
are all examples of community service. Community service can require long hours and take time away from
studying and jobs. It can also force students to deal
with unpleasant situations, but overall it is rewarding and helpful to others. Community service is good
for the community and can be more fulfilling than
playing sports or participating in clubs. Community
service can also be an important part of a college
education. Students can even discover what they want
to do with their lives. Community service can also
make the world a better place.

First Draft

◆ PRACTICE 1-13

Reread Stella's draft paragraph. If you were advising her, what would you suggest that she change in the draft? What might she add? What might she cross out? Write your suggestions on the following lines. Then, discuss your ideas with your class or in a small group.

Answers will vary.

_____

_____

_____

_____

◆ PRACTICE 1-14

Using the material you came up with for Practice 1-12, draft a paragraph about your topic that states your main idea and supports it with specific points. Be sure to leave wide margins and skip lines. (If you type your draft, you can triple-space.) When you are finished, give your paragraph a title.

F Revising and Editing Your Paragraph

Revision is the process of reseeing, rethinking, reevaluating, and rewriting your work. Revision involves much more than substituting one word for another or correcting a comma here and there. Often, it means moving sentences, adding words and phrases, and even changing the direction or emphasis of your ideas. To get the most out of the revision process, begin by carefully rereading your draft with a critical eye, using the checklist below to guide your revision.

✓ SELF-ASSESSMENT CHECKLIST:
Revising Your Paragraph

- Have you stated your main idea clearly in your topic sentence?
- Do you have enough points to support your paragraph's main idea, or do you need to look back at your notes or try another invention strategy to find additional supporting material?
- Do you need to explain anything more fully or more clearly?
- Do you need to add more examples or details?
- Should you cross out any examples or details?
- Does every sentence say what you mean?
- Can you combine any sentences to make your writing smoother?
- Should you move any sentences?
- Are all your words necessary, or can you cut some?
- Should you change any words?
- Does your paragraph end with a sentence that sums up its main idea?

▼ **Student Voices**
When I revise, I look to see if everything flows and if there are any out-of-place ideas, weird sentences, or odd words.

Felicia May

FOCUS Editing

Don't confuse revision with editing. Revision often involves extensive rewriting and rearranging, and it can be hard work. Editing comes after revision.

When you **edit**, you concentrate on the surface features of your writing, checking for clarity and for correct grammar, punctuation, mechanics, and spelling. You proofread carefully for typographical errors that a computer spell checker may not identify.

(continued on the following page)

● **Writing Tip**
When you edit your paragraph, be sure you have indented the first sentence, and check to make sure every sentence begins with a capital letter and ends with appropriate punctuation.

> *(continued from the previous page)*
>
> Although editing is a lot less comprehensive than revision, it is a vital last step in the writing process. Many readers will not take your work seriously if it contains grammatical or mechanical errors. Correctness goes a long way toward establishing your competence and authority with your audience.

Guided by the Self-Assessment Checklist on page 17, Stella revised her paragraph, writing her changes in by hand on her typewritten draft.

Why Community Service Should Be Required

Community service takes time, but it is so important that college students should be required to do it. When college students do community service, they ~~volunteer their time to~~ do good for someone or for the community. *For example, they work* ~~Working~~ in a soup kitchen, ~~raking~~ *rake* leaves for senior citizens, ~~and reading~~ *or read* to children. *These activities* ~~are all examples of community service. Community service~~ can require long hours and take time away from *important things like* ~~studying and jobs. It can also force students to deal with unpleasant situations, but overall it is rewarding and helpful to others.~~ *However, community service is worth the time it takes.* Community service ~~is good for the community and~~ can be more fulfilling *for students* than playing sports or participating in clubs, *other college activities, such as* Community service can also be an important part of a college education. Students can *learn about themselves, about their communities, and about their world,* even discover what they *and* want to do with their lives. *Finally,* ~~C~~ommunity service can *they can* ~~also~~ make the world a better place. *For all these reasons, community service should be a required part of the college curriculum.*

Revised Draft

When she revised, Stella didn't worry about being neat. She crossed out, added material, and made major changes in her words, sentences, and ideas. Then, she edited her paragraph, checking punctuation, mechanics, and spelling and looking for typos. The final typed version of Stella's paragraph appears below.

```
        Why Community Service Should Be Required
```
```
        Community service takes time, but it is so impor-
    tant that college students should be required to do
    it. When college students do community service, they do
    good for someone or for the community. For example, they
    work in a soup kitchen, rake leaves for senior citizens,
    or read to children. These activities can require long
    hours and take time away from important things, like
    studying and jobs. However, community service is worth
    the time it takes. Community service can be more ful-
    filling for students than other college activities, such
    as playing sports or participating in clubs. Community
    service can also be an important part of a college edu-
    cation. Students can learn about themselves, about their
    communities, and about their world, and they can even
    discover what they want to do with their lives. Finally,
    community service can make the world a better place.
    For all these reasons, community service should be a
    required part of the college curriculum.
```

◆ PRACTICE 1-15

Reread the final draft of Stella's paragraph about community service for college students (above), and compare it with her first draft (page 16). What kinds of changes did she make? Which do you think are her most effective changes? Why? Note your thoughts on the lines below. Then, with your class or in a small group, discuss your reaction to the revised paragraph.

Answers will vary.

_____

_____

_____

_____

◆ PRACTICE 1-16

Use the Self-Assessment Checklist on page 17 to evaluate the paragraph you drafted for Practice 1-14. What additions can you make to support your main idea more fully? Should anything be crossed out because it doesn't support your main idea? Can anything be stated more clearly? On the following lines, list some of the changes you might make in your draft.

1 F

_____

_____

_____

_____

_____

_____

_____

▼ **Student Voices**

When I revise, I look to see if everything is related to the topic and if transitions are where they should be. I also see if I contradicted myself or strayed from my topic.

Monica Han

Now, revise your draft. Cross out unnecessary material and material you want to rewrite, and add new and rewritten material between the lines and in the margins. After you finish your revision, edit your paragraph, checking grammar, punctuation, mechanics, and spelling—and look carefully for typos. When you are satisfied with your paragraph, print out a clean copy, and hold onto it for the Writing First exercise that opens Chapter 2.

✔ **REVIEW CHECKLIST:**
Writing a Paragraph

- Learning to write a paragraph is an important step in becoming a competent writer. (See 1A.)

- Before you start to write, consider your assignment, purpose, and audience. (See 1B.)

- Use invention strategies—freewriting, brainstorming, clustering, and journal writing—to find ideas. (See 1C.)

- Identify your main idea and choose supporting points; then, arrange them in a logical order. (See 1D.)

- Write a first draft. (See 1E.)

- Revise your draft. (See 1F.)

- Edit your draft. (See 1F.)

Fine-Tuning Your Paragraph

PREVIEW

In this chapter, you will learn

■ to write effective topic sentences (2A)

■ to write unified paragraphs (2B)

■ to write well-developed paragraphs (2C)

■ to write coherent paragraphs (2D)

■ WRITING FIRST

Make a copy of the final draft of the paragraph that you wrote and revised in Chapter 1. You will continue to work on your paragraph as you go through this chapter.

Word Power
pragmatic   practical; active rather than passive

A   Writing Effective Topic Sentences

As you learned in Chapter 1, a paragraph is a group of related sentences that develops one central idea. Every paragraph includes a topic sentence that states the paragraph's main idea. This topic sentence helps guide readers, and it also helps keep writers on track as they write.

The Topic Sentence in the Paragraph

The topic sentence is the most general sentence of your paragraph. The rest of the sentences in your paragraph support the topic sentence with

21

details, facts, and examples. Many paragraphs also include a concluding statement that sums up the paragraph's main idea.

Topic sentence

Support (details, facts, examples)

Concluding statement

Although most people do not know it, the modern roller coaster got its start in Coney Island in Brooklyn, New York. The first economically successful roller coaster, the first high drop, and the first circuit coaster were all pioneered in Coney Island. In 1888, the Flip Flap Railway, which featured a circular loop, was built. This coaster was the first to go upside down, but it had a habit of injuring people's necks. In 1901, the Loop-the-Loop, which provided a safer ride than the Flip Flap Railway, was built. From 1884 through the 1930s, over thirty roller coasters were constructed in Coney Island. The most famous coaster in history, the Cyclone, was built at a cost of $100,000 in 1926. Although it opened in 1927, it is still the standard by which all other roller coasters are measured. It has steep drops, lots of angular momentum, and only a lap belt to hold riders in their seats. Still in operation, the Cyclone is the most successful ride in Coney Island history. It is also the last survivor of the classic wooden roller coasters that once drew crowds to Coney Island. Because of the innovations that took place there, Coney Island made possible the many high-tech roller coasters in amusement parks today.

Revising Topic Sentences

▼ **Student Voices**
The biggest problem I have is making sure my paragraphs make sense.

Terry Simons

The first step toward writing a good paragraph is learning to write an effective topic sentence. When you revise, keep in mind the following three characteristics of effective topic sentences.

1. *A topic sentence should be a complete sentence.* Like any sentence, it must contain a subject and a verb and state a complete thought. Remember that there is a difference between a **topic** and a **topic sentence**. The *topic* is what the paragraph is about; the *topic sentence* is the sentence that presents the paragraph's **main idea**—the idea the paragraph will develop.

Topic	Topic Sentence
Television violence	Violent television shows have a negative effect on my younger brother.
Animal testing	One reason not to buy products tested on animals is that most animal testing is not necessary.
Heroes	My heroes are people who take action instead of waiting for others to act.

2. *A topic sentence should be more than just an announcement of what you plan to write about.* It should make a point about the topic the paragraph discusses.

Announcement	Topic Sentence
In this paragraph I will write about the problems my first credit card caused.	When I got my first credit card, I had no idea of the problems it would cause.

3. ***A topic sentence should present an idea that you can discuss in a
single paragraph.*** If your topic sentence is too broad, you will not be
able to discuss it in just one paragraph. If your topic sentence is too
narrow (for example, if it is a statement of fact), you will not be able
to say much about it.

TOPIC SENTENCE   Students with jobs have special needs.
TOO BROAD

TOPIC SENTENCE   The tutoring center closes at 5 p.m.
TOO NARROW

EFFECTIVE TOPIC   Because many students have jobs, the tutoring center
SENTENCE   should remain open until 9 p.m.

FOCUS **Placing Topic Sentences**

A topic sentence can appear anywhere in a paragraph—at the beginning, in the middle, or at the end. For the time being, however,
you should place your topic sentences at the beginning of your
paragraphs. This strategy will keep you on track as you write. In addition, by telling readers what your paragraph will be about, it will
help readers follow your ideas.

◆ PRACTICE 2-1

Underline the topic sentence in each of the following paragraphs.

1.   Genetically modified crops, created by adding a desired trait from one
plant to another, can be very beneficial. "Golden rice," for example, was
created when scientists took genes from daffodils and other small plants
and put them into a strain of rice. These genes gave the rice a golden color.
More important, the new genes enabled the rice to produce beta-carotene,
or vitamin A. The Swiss scientist who created golden rice wanted to produce a product containing this vitamin because he knew that about three
hundred million people in China suffer from vitamin A deficiencies. The
lack of vitamin A can cause a person to become sick easily or even to go
blind, but in China vitamins are not easily available, and they are expensive.
So, if the rice the Chinese people depend on already contains a vitamin that
they need, eating the rice might solve a number of medical problems.

2.   Perseverance is a handy quality to have if you want to publish a novel.
J. K. Rowling, author of the Harry Potter books, first began writing the
books in 1990. By 1993, she was the divorced mother of a young daughter.
Rowling couldn't afford day care on the money she received in public assistance from the British government, and she couldn't get a job without
paying someone to watch her child. As a result, she could only write when
her daughter was asleep. When Rowling finished her first book five years
later, she wanted to send a copy to publishers and keep a copy for herself,
but she couldn't afford to make photocopies. She didn't give up, though.

Instead, she typed copies on her old typewriter. In 1997, *Harry Potter and the Philosopher's Stone* was bought by a publisher, and critics called Rowling an overnight sensation. They didn't know how long that "night" had been.

3.   In the mid-nineteenth century, steamboats were an important means of transportation in America. Initially, these boats carried cargo and passengers between river towns. In some towns, passengers were met at the wharf by stage coaches that carried them to their final destinations. In other towns, a railroad line came within walking distance of the wharf. Americans were pleased with this new type of transportation. Trips that had taken weeks by horse and carriage could now be completed in days.

4.   During the American Civil War, a notorious camp was built at Andersonville, Georgia, to house prisoners of war. The Confederates selected the site because it was far from Richmond, Virginia, their capital, and near fresh water and a railroad. Although the prison was built to house 10,000 prisoners, the number of inmates grew to over 32,000. There was no shelter from the weather, no source of fresh water (except for a small stream that ran through the camp and was also used as a sewer), no clothing other than what the prisoners arrived in, and no fruit or vegetables. Many simply dug holes in the ground to live in. Because of these conditions, nearly a third of the prisoners died of disease. Today, the Andersonville National Historic Site, built on the land occupied by the old prison, is a monument to all Americans who have been prisoners of war.

5.   Many experts believe that space travelers will not be able to fly to Mars until four medical obstacles have been overcome. The first obstacle is the problems caused by a lack of gravity, which can lead to loss of bone strength, dizziness, and an inability to walk. And, because we cannot yet create gravity on a spaceship, the astronauts who land on Mars might be unable to do their jobs once they arrive. Second, science cannot protect the astronauts from the cosmic rays they would encounter in deep space. Exposure to these rays would make the astronauts more likely to become ill or to develop serious diseases, such as cancer. Third, the astronauts would have very little help if they did become ill. They would not have access to the doctors and technology used to treat such diseases here on earth. Finally, astronauts might develop psychological problems because of their isolation from society for the length of time it would take to get to Mars. Until science can conquer these problems, going to Mars will remain a dream.

◆ PRACTICE 2-2

Rearrange the following sentences into a coherent paragraph by placing a *1* in front of the topic sentence, a *2* in front of the next sentence, and so on.

___6___ By the end of the war, the game had spread throughout the country, and standard rules had been established.

___1___ The first official baseball game was played in New York City in 1846.

___2___ In that game, the Knickerbocker Baseball Club played a team made up of its own members.

_5_ Soldiers even played baseball behind their own lines and in prisoner-of-war camps.

_3_ Between 1846 and the start of the Civil War, interest in the game grew slowly.

_7_ Several years after the war, in 1871, the first professional baseball league was formed.

_4_ During the war, however, the popularity of the game increased enormously.

◆ PRACTICE 2-3

Read the following items. Put a check mark next to each one that has all three characteristics of an effective topic sentence.

Examples:

The common cold. _____

Many people are convinced that large doses of vitamin C will prevent the common cold. _✔_

1. Global warming, a crisis for our cities._____

2. If something is not done soon, the city of New Orleans may be under water by the year 2010. _✓_

3. In this paragraph, I will discuss global warming. _____

4. Computers and college students. _____

5. Colleges should make sure that every student has access to a computer.
    _✓_

◆ PRACTICE 2-4

Decide whether each of the following statements could be an effective topic sentence for a paragraph. If a sentence is too broad, write "too broad" in the blank following the sentence. If the sentence is too narrow, write "too narrow" in the blank. If the sentence is an effective topic sentence, write "OK" in the blank.

Example: Thanksgiving always falls on the fourth Thursday in November. _too narrow_

1. Computers are changing the world._____ too broad _____

2. There are five computer terminals in the campus library._ too narrow _

3. The computer I use at work makes my job easier._____ OK ____

4. Soccer is not as popular in the United States as it is in Europe.

_____too broad_____

5. Americans enjoy watching many types of sporting events on television.

_____too broad_____

6. There is one quality that distinguishes a good coach from a mediocre

one. _____OK_____

7. Vegetarianism is a healthy way of life. _____too broad_____

8. Uncooked spinach has fourteen times as much iron as steak does.

_____too narrow_____

9. Fast-food restaurants are finally beginning to respond to the growing

number of customers who are vegetarians. _____OK_____

10. There are many different kinds of cars to choose from. _____too broad_____

◆ PRACTICE 2-5

The following paragraphs do not have topic sentences. Think of a topic
sentence that expresses each paragraph's main idea, and write it on the
lines above the paragraphs.

> **Example:** Possible answer: Early rock and roll was a creation of both
>
> black and white performers.

Early 1950s African-American musicians included performers such as
Johnny Ace, Big Joe Turner, and Ruth Brown. Groups like the Drifters
and the Clovers were also popular. By the mid-1950s, white performers such as Bill Haley and the Comets, Jerry Lee Lewis, and Elvis Presley imitated African-American music. Although their songs did not
have the heavy back beat and explicit lyrics that most black music had,
their music appealed to a white audience. Eventually, this combination
of black and white musical styles became known as rock and roll.

1. Possible answer: For most Americans, television is the major source of

information, entertainment, and relaxation.

Most Americans own televisions. In fact, more people watch television
than read magazines and newspapers. Television has even replaced
going to the movies as the most popular form of entertainment. Not
surprisingly, recent surveys have shown that most Americans get their
news from television. Moreover, as anyone in the book industry knows,
the best way for a book to become a best seller is for it to be promoted
on a popular television show. For example, a book that was endorsed
by Oprah Winfrey was almost sure to become an instant best seller.
Finally, Americans spend many hours a day staring at their televisions,
just trying to unwind.

2. *Possible answer: Applying for a job can be difficult, but the process can be made easier and more rewarding if you follow a few simple steps.*

First, you have to find a suitable job to appy for. Once you decide to apply, you have to type your résumé and send it to your prospective employer. Then, when you are invited in for an interview, you need to decide what you are going to wear. At the interview, you need to speak slowly and clearly and answer all questions directly and honestly. After the interview, you need to send a note to the person who interviewed you, thanking him or her. Finally, if everything goes well, you will get a letter or a telephone call offering you the job.

3. *Possible answer: A lot of questions remain about Native Americans who were living in North America when the Europeans arrived.*

There are no written records left by the Native Americans themselves. Most of the early settlers were more interested in surviving than in writing about the Native Americans. In addition, as the westward expansion took place, the Europeans encountered the Native Americans in stages, not all at once. Also, the Native Americans spoke at least fifty-eight different languages, which made it difficult for the Europeans to communicate with them. Most important, by the time scholars decided to study Native American culture, many of the tribes no longer existed. Disease and war had wiped them out.

■ WRITING FIRST: Flashback

Look back at the paragraph you wrote for the Writing First exercise on page 21. Does your paragraph have an effective topic sentence? Write that sentence on the lines below. If necessary, revise the topic sentence so that it states the main idea of your paragraph more clearly. (If your paragraph does not have a topic sentence, write one on the lines below.)

_____

_____

B   Writing Unified Paragraphs

An effective paragraph focuses on a single main idea. A paragraph is **unified** when all its sentences support the main idea stated in the topic sentence.

2 B

Understanding Unity

To write a unified paragraph, state your main idea clearly in the topic sentence. Then, make sure the rest of the sentences in your paragraph relate directly to this idea.

Topic sentence

> The population problem is one of the biggest causes for concern for scientists. In 1900, there were 1.6 billion people on earth, a quarter of today's population. In 1900, the average life expectancy was also much shorter than it is now. In some places, it was only twenty-three years. By the year 2000, the world's population had grown to over 6 billion. Today, average life expectancy worldwide is almost sixty-five years. This means that billions of people are living longer and using more of the earth's resources. The low death rate, combined with a high birth rate, is adding the equivalent of one new Germany to the world's population each year. According to a United Nations study, if present trends continue, by 2050 the world's population will be so large (between 7.3 and 10.5 billion) that most people in the world will be malnourished or starving.

The paragraph above is unified. The topic sentence states the paragraph's main idea, and the rest of the sentences present specific details to support the main idea.

Revising Paragraphs for Unity

A paragraph lacks unity when its sentences wander from the main idea. When you revise, you can make sure your paragraphs are unified by rewriting or deleting sentences that do not support the main idea that your topic sentence states.

Paragraph Not Unified

Topic sentence

> The changing economic picture has led many people to move away from the rural Pennsylvania community where I was raised. Over the years, farmland has become more and more expensive. Years ago, a family could buy each of its children twenty-five acres on which they could start farming. Today, the price of land is so high that the average farmer cannot afford to buy this amount of land. I am tired of seeing my friends move away. After I graduate, I intend to return to my town and get a job there. Even though many factories have moved out of the area, I think I can get a job. My uncle owns a hardware store, and he told me that after I graduate, he will teach me the business. I think I can contribute something to the business and to the town.

■ **Computer Tip**

Try boldfacing or underlining the topic sentence of a paragraph before you start to revise the paragraph. (See 2D.)

This paragraph is not unified. After presenting one reason why people are moving away, the writer wanders from his paragraph's main idea, instead complaining about his friends and discussing his own future plans. These digressions do not support the topic sentence.

The following revised paragraph is unified. It discusses only what the topic sentence promises: the reasons why people have moved away from the writer's hometown.

Paragraph Unified

<u>The changing economic picture has led many people to move away from the rural Pennsylvania community where I was raised.</u> Over the years, farmland has become more and more expensive. Years ago, a family could buy each of its children twenty-five acres on which they could start farming. Today, the price of land is so high that the average farmer cannot afford to buy this amount of land, and those who choose not to farm have few alternatives. They just cannot get good jobs anymore. Factories have moved out of the area and have taken with them the jobs that many young people used to get after high school. As a result, many eighteen-year-olds have no choice but to move to Pittsburgh to find employment.

Topic sentence

◆ PRACTICE 2-6

The following paragraphs are not unified because some sentences do not support the topic sentence. Cross out any sentences in each paragraph that do not belong.

Teaching Tip
Before doing Practice 2-6, read aloud a paragraph (humorous if possible) that clearly lacks unity. Let students explain why the paragraph is not unified.

1. The one possession I could not live without is my car. In addition to attending school full time, I hold down two part-time jobs that are many miles from each other, from where I live, and from school. Even though my car is almost twelve years old and has close to 120,000 miles on it, I couldn't manage without it. ~~I'm thinking about buying a new car, and I always check the classified ads, but I haven't found anything I want that I can afford. If my old car breaks down, I guess I'll have to, though. I couldn't live without my portable tape recorder because I use it to record all the class lectures I attend. Then I can play them back while I'm driving or during my breaks at work.~~ Three nights a week and on weekends, I work as a counselor at a home for teenagers with problems, and my other job is in the tire department at Sam's. Without my car, I'd be lost.

2. Studies conducted by Dr. Leonard Eron over the last thirty years suggest that the more television violence children are exposed to, the more aggressive they are as teenagers and adults. In 1960, Eron questioned parents about how they treated their children at home, including how much television their children watched. ~~There is more violence on television today than there was then.~~ Ten years later, he interviewed these families again and discovered that whether teenage sons were aggressive depended less on how they had been treated by their parents than on how much violent television programming they had watched as children. Returning in 1990, he found that these same young men, now in their thirties, were still more likely to be aggressive and to commit crimes. ~~Researchers estimate that a child today is likely to watch 100,000 violent acts on television before finishing elementary school.~~

3. Libraries today hold a lot more than just books. Of course, books still outnumber anything else on the shelves, but more and more libraries are expanding to include other specialized services. For example, many libraries now offer extensive collections of tapes and compact discs, ranging from classical music to jazz to country to rock. Many have also increased their holdings of videotapes, both instructional programs and

popular recent and vintage movies. Some libraries also stock DVDs. ~~However, most people probably still get more movies from video stores than from libraries.~~ In addition, the children's section often has games and toys young patrons can play with in the library or even check out. Most important, libraries are offering more and more computerized data services, which can provide much more detailed and up-to-date information than printed sources. These expanding nonprint sources are the wave of the future for even the smallest libraries and will allow patrons access to much more information than books or magazines ever could. ~~People who don't know how to use a computer are going to be out of luck.~~

■ WRITING FIRST: Flashback

Look back at the paragraph that you wrote for the Writing First exercise on page 21. Review your paragraph for unity. Cross out any sentences that do not support the topic sentence. If necessary, rewrite sentences so they support your main point.

C Writing Well-Developed Paragraphs

A paragraph is **well developed** when it contains enough details, facts, and examples to support the topic sentence. A paragraph is not well developed when it lacks the support readers need to understand or accept its main idea.

Supporting the Topic Sentence

To determine the amount and kind of support you need, ask yourself two questions:

1. *How complicated is your main idea?* A complicated main idea will need more support than a relatively simple one. A relatively straightforward topic sentence—for example, "During the first week of school, registration is a nightmare"—would require only two or three well-chosen examples. A more far-reaching topic sentence—"Our community has to do much more to accommodate the physically challenged," for example—would call for a lot more support.

2. *How much do your readers know about your main idea?* If you know that your readers have regularly eaten food served in your school's cafeteria, you do not need to give them many examples to convince them that the food leaves much to be desired. If you think that your readers are not familiar with the food at your school, however, you have to supply more examples and possibly definitions (explaining what you mean by "mystery meat," for example) to support your point.

Revising Paragraphs for Development

A well-developed paragraph provides the support readers need to understand its points and to accept the statement the topic sentence makes. If your paragraph contains only general statements, it is not well developed. When you revise, be sure to support your general statements with details, facts, and examples.

Undeveloped Paragraph

> Although pit bulls were originally bred to fight, they can actually make good pets. Today, many people are afraid of pit bulls. These dogs are sometimes mistreated. As a result, they become more aggressive. For this reason, they are misunderstood and persecuted. In fact, some cities have taken action against them. But pit bulls do not deserve their bad reputation. Contrary to popular opinion, they can make good pets.

The preceding paragraph is not well developed. It consists of a series of general statements that leave the writer's points unclear and therefore do not provide adequate support for the main idea.

Well-Developed Paragraph

> Although pit bulls were originally bred to fight, they can actually make good pets. It is true that their powerful jaws, short muscular legs, and large teeth are ideally suited to fighting, and they were used extensively for this purpose in the rural South and Southwest. It is also true that some pit bulls—especially males—can be aggressive toward other dogs. However, most pit bulls like human beings and are quite friendly. Owners report that pit bulls are affectionate, loyal, and good with children. When pit bulls behave viciously, it is usually because they have been mistreated. As a recent newspaper article pointed out, the number of reported bites by pit bulls is no greater than the number of bites by other breeds. In fact, some dogs, such as cocker spaniels, bite much more frequently. The problem is that whenever a pit bull attacks a person, the incident is reported in the paper. But pit bulls do not deserve their reputation. Contrary to popular opinion, they can make good pets.

The paragraph is now well developed. Because general statements are clarified by examples or details, readers are more likely to accept the idea that pit bulls can make good pets.

> **■ Computer Tip**
>
> Hit the Enter or the Return key after your topic sentence and after each sentence that follows it. By isolating each detail and example, you can evaluate the amount and kind of support you have used.

> **● Writing Tip**
>
> Length alone is no guarantee that a paragraph is well developed. A paragraph that consists of one generalization after another can be long and yet still not be well developed.

◆ PRACTICE 2-7

Read the following paragraphs, and then write an appropriate topic sentence for each.

Answers will vary.

1. *Possible answer: Good drivers have three ways to deal with road rage.* The first—and simplest way—is to move out of the way of the enraged driver. If the good driver does not do this, the angry driver will probably honk the horn, flash the lights, or tailgate the slower driver. Next, when the angry driver tries to get the good driver's attention, the defensive driver should avoid making eye contact. This lessens the chance that the furious driver

will try to insult the good driver and make things worse. Finally, once the angry driver has passed, the good driver must consider whether or not to call the police.

2. _Possible answer: Some singers are more famous after death than before._
For example, Jim Morrison, lead singer of the Doors, has been the subject of a big-budget movie and several books since his death in July 1971. His grave in France is visited around the clock by fans, including many who were not even born when he was alive. Kurt Cobain, who committed suicide in 1994, is now the subject of several books, and his group, Nirvana, has an album that continues to sell well even though it is almost ten years old. Another example is Tupac Shakur. He was killed in 1996, but his albums still sell well, and his poetry has been collected and published. Probably the biggest sign that all three singers are still remembered fondly is the number of Web sites that try to prove they are still alive.

3. _Possible answer: Patients are trying a variety of new methods to deal with their medical problems._ Some people who once turned to allergy shots now prefer to try vitamins and supplements. Others, who suffer with back problems, are trying to give up their pain relievers by visiting acupuncturists and chiropractors. Still other patients prefer to see if physical therapy can help them deal with a health problem instead of scheduling surgery. Some people also attend yoga classes to relieve stress instead of taking a prescription medication. Obviously, many patients are willing to try nontraditional methods to help them deal with their ailments.

◆ PRACTICE 2-8

Underline the supporting details, facts, and examples in each of the following paragraphs.

1. Hearing people have some misconceptions about the deaf community First, some hearing adults might assume that everyone who is deaf considers himself to be a disabled individual who would trade anything not to be "handicapped." These people do not realize that many deaf people do not consider themselves handicapped and are very proud to be part of the deaf community. They have their own language, customs, and culture. Second, many hearing people assume that all deaf people read lips, so there is no need to learn sign language to communicate with the deaf. Lip reading—or speech reading, as many deaf people call the practice—is difficult. Not all hearing people say the same words in the same way, and facial expressions can also change the meaning of the words. If hearing people make more of an attempt to understand the deaf culture, communication between them will improve.

2. In 1996, the National Basketball Association (NBA) decided to approve a women's professional basketball league. Within fifteen months, eight teams had been formed, four in the Eastern Conference and four in the Western Conference. Next, the teams began to draft players for these teams and to select a logo and uniforms. The final logo selected, a red, white, and blue shield, showed the silhouette of a woman player dribbling the ball, with the letters "WNBA" above her. The uniforms consisted of

shorts and jerseys in the colors of the different teams. That first season, games were played in the summer when the television sports schedule was lighter so they could be televised during prime time. At the end of that season, the Houston Comets became the first WNBA champions. Today, the WNBA consists of sixteen teams that play 256 regular season games televised to audiences worldwide.

3.   A hurricane is a storm with winds of seventy-three miles per hour or greater that blow in a circle around the center, or eye, of the storm. These storms form near the Equator and move along a curved path at anywhere from five to fifty miles per hour. To help weather forecasters talk about hurricanes to the general public, the storms are given names. Often, more than one storm will be active at a time, so the names help people understand which storm is being discussed. Since 1979, storms in the Atlantic have been given common men's and women's names beginning with all the letters of the alphabet except q, x, y, and z. In the Pacific, the practice was the same until recently, when names common to the people in that area began to be used. So, while the second storm in the Atlantic in 2002 was named Bertha, the second in the Pacific Northwest was named Boris.

4.   Turtles, among the oldest and most adaptable living reptiles, have been present on earth since even before the dinosaurs. They can live on land or in the water and are found everywhere in the world except Antarctica. In spring and summer, turtles search for food, including insects, fish, berries, and water plants. In winter, they hibernate in the mud of lakes or creeks or under piles of leaves and brush. Turtles range in size from several inches to as large as eight feet, which is the average length of a sea turtle called the leatherback. Unfortunately, pollution and population growth are now threatening the existence of these fascinating and harmless creatures.

5.   One of the largest celebrations of the passage of young girls into womanhood occurs in Latin American and Hispanic cultures. This event is called La Quinceañera, or the fifteenth year. It acknowledges that a young woman is now of marriageable age. The day usually begins with a Mass of Thanksgiving. The young woman wears a full-length white or pastel-colored dress and is attended by fourteen friends and relatives who serve as maids of honor and male escorts. Her parents and godparents surround her at the foot of the altar. When the Mass ends, other young relatives give small gifts to those who attended, while the Quinceañera places a bouquet of flowers on the altar of the Virgin. Following the Mass is an elaborate party, with dancing, cake, and toasts. Finally, to end the evening, the young woman dances a waltz with her favorite escort.

◆ PRACTICE 2-9

Provide two or three supporting details for each of the following topic sentences.

Answers will vary.

1. A sport utility vehicle (SUV) has advantages over a minivan.

2. Candles can help make an occasion special.

3. Home security systems protect families in several ways.

4. Conducting a successful garage sale requires organization.

5. Shopping online can save time.

◆ PRACTICE 2-10

The following two paragraphs are not well developed. On the lines that follow each paragraph, write three questions or suggestions that might help the writer develop his or her ideas more fully.

1. Other than my parents, the biggest influence on my life was probably my Aunt Sylva. When I was little, she used to baby-sit for me every day, and she always found interesting and educational things for us to do, either at home or on trips downtown. She had lived in Mexico City for many years, and I always admired her exotic looks. As a teenager, I tried to copy the way she walked, talked, and even dressed. Even today, I often think of her when I catch myself putting on the sort of outfit she might have worn. Tragically, she died just before my eighteenth birthday.

Answers will vary. Students might suggest supplying more details about the

activities done with Aunt Sylva, her appearance and dress, or her death.

2. Computerized special effects have made a big difference in movies over the last ten years. Science fiction films are more spectacular than ever, and filmmakers are able to take moviegoers to places they've never been before. New special-effects techniques can also create fierce monsters, more terrifying than anything seen on the screen before. Other effects have been used in comedies to create hilarious visual jokes. It is likely that the future will bring even more impressive effects for the enjoyment of movie audiences.

Answers will vary. Students might suggest supplying titles of movies, names of

monsters, or specific visual jokes.

■ WRITING FIRST: Flashback

Look back at the paragraph you wrote for the Writing First exercise on page 21. Is your paragraph well developed? On the lines below, list the details, facts, and examples that you used to support your main idea. Then, list suggestions for revision, noting the kinds of facts, examples, and details you might add.

Facts, examples, and details:

Answers will vary.

(continued on the following page)

(continued from the previous page)

_____

_____

_____

_____

Suggestions for revision:

Answers will vary.

_____

_____

_____

_____

_____

D Writing Coherent Paragraphs

A paragraph is **coherent** if all its sentences are arranged in a clear, sensible order. You can make a paragraph coherent by arranging details carefully and by supplying transitional words and phrases that show the connections between sentences.

Arranging Details

In general, you can arrange the details in a paragraph according to *time order, spatial order,* or *logical order.*

Paragraphs that are arranged in **time order** present events in the order in which they occurred. Stories, historical accounts, and instructions are generally arranged in time order.

The following paragraph presents events in time order. Specific dates as well as the words *before, once, then, finally, later,* and *after* indicate the sequence of events in the paragraph.

> In 1856, my great-great-great-grandparents, Anne and Charles McGinley, came to the United States to start a new life. Before they left Ireland, their English landlords had raised the taxes on their land so high that my ancestors could not afford to pay them. It took them three years to save the money for passage. Once they had saved the money, they had to look for a ship that was willing to take them. Then my great-great-great-grandparents were on their way. They and their ten children spent four long months on a small ship. Storms, strong tides, and damaged sails made the trip longer than it should have been. Finally, in November of 1856, they saw land, and two days later they

See p. 38 for a list of transitions that signal time order.

sailed into New York Harbor. <u>After</u> they were admitted to the United States, they took a train to Baltimore, Maryland, where some cousins lived.

Paragraphs that are arranged in **spatial order** present details in the order in which they are seen—from top to bottom, from near to far, from right to left, and so on. Spatial order is central to paragraphs that describe something—for example, what an object, place, or person looks like.

The following paragraph presents events in spatial order. Notice how the phrases *directly in front of, next to, behind, in between, on top of, inside,* and *in the center of* help establish the order—from far to near—in which readers will view the details of the scene.

See p. 38 for a list of transitions that signal spatial order.

The day I arrived at the Amish school I knew it was unlike any other school I had seen before. A long, tree-lined dirt road led to the small wooden schoolhouse. <u>Directly in front of</u> the school was a line of bicycles and metal scooters. A small baseball diamond had been carved into the dirt in the yard <u>next to</u> the schoolhouse. <u>Behind</u> the school, two little outhouses stood next to each other with a green water pump <u>in between</u>. The schoolhouse itself was a small one-story structure. White paint curled off its clapboard siding, and a short steeple, holding a brass bell, sat firmly <u>on top of</u> the roof. <u>Inside</u> the open door, a long line of black hats hung on pegs. <u>In the center of</u> the small schoolhouse was an iron potbellied stove surrounded by the children's desks.

Paragraphs that are arranged in **logical order** present ideas in a sequence that indicates why one idea logically follows another. For example, a paragraph may move from least important to most important, from general to specific, or from most familiar to least familiar.

The following paragraph presents ideas in logical order. Here, the phrases *the first rule, an even sillier rule,* and *the most ridiculous rule* establish the order in which the rules are presented—from least to most silly—and thus help readers move from one point to another.

See p. 38 for a list of transitions that signal logical order.

My high school had three rules that were silly at best and ridiculous at worst. <u>The first rule</u> was that only seniors could go outside the school building for lunch. In spite of this rule, many students went outside to eat because the cafeteria was not big enough to accommodate all the school's students at the same time. Understanding the problem, the teachers and the principal looked the other way as long as we returned to school before the lunch period was over. <u>An even sillier rule</u> was that we had to attend 95 percent of the classes for every course. This rule meant that a person could miss only about six days of class every semester. Naturally, this rule was never enforced because if it had been, half the students would have failed. <u>The most ridiculous rule</u>, however, was that students could not throw their hats into the air during graduation. At one point in the past—no one seems to know when —a parent had complained that a falling hat could poke someone in the eye. As a result, graduating classes were told that under no circumstance could they throw their hats. Naturally, on graduation day we did what every previous graduating class had done—ignored the rule and threw our hats into the air.

◆ **PRACTICE 2-11**

Read each of the following topic sentences carefully. If you were writing a paragraph introduced by the sentence, how would you arrange the supporting details—in time order, spatial order, or logical order? Write your answer in the blank following the topic sentence.

Example: It is important to keep several things in mind when shopping for a new stereo. _logical order_

1. My first week at my new job began badly but ended better than I ever could have expected. _time order_

2. People would get along better if everyone practiced a few important rules of common courtesy. _logical order_

3. My son's bedroom reflects his many different interests and hobbies. _spatial order_

4. The Mustangs are a stronger team than the Bobcats for three reasons. _logical order_

5. Babies develop in amazing ways during the first three months of life. _time order_

6. When you interview for a job, keep in mind that most employers look for the same qualities in a prospective employee. _logical order_

7. Dressing for success means looking your best from the hair on your head to the shoes on your feet. _spatial order_

8. I had always felt safe in my neighborhood until last year, when something happened that changed my attitude completely. _time order_

9. To protect yourself on campus after dark, you should always take the following precautions. _logical order_

10. The new Southern Trust Bank in Gaston is one of the ugliest buildings in town. _spatial order_

Using Transitional Words and Phrases

Within a paragraph, **transitional words and phrases** often indicate the relationships among sentences. By establishing the time order, spatial order, and logical order of the ideas in a paragraph, these words and phrases enable readers to see the connections among ideas.

■ **Computer Tip**

Keep a list of transitional
words and phrases in a separate file. When you revise,
consult this file to see if you
have used the most appro-
priate transitions.

Transitional Words and Phrases

Some Words and Phrases That Signal Time Order

after	finally	dates (for example, "In June")
afterward	later	
at first	next	
before	now	
during	soon	
earlier	then	
eventually	today	

Some Words and Phrases That Signal Spatial Order

above	in front	on the left
behind	in the center	on the right
below	inside	on top
beside	near	over
in back	next to	under
in between	on the bottom	

Some Words and Phrases That Signal Logical Order

also	last
although	moreover
consequently	next
first . . . second . . . third	not only . . . but also
for example	one . . . another
for instance	similarly
furthermore	the least important
in addition	the most important
in fact	therefore

Revising Paragraphs for Coherence

▼ **Student Voices**
*I usually spend a lot of time
revising my paragraphs.*
Meredith Krall

Because transitional words and phrases establish **coherence**, a paragraph
without them is difficult to understand. You can correct this problem
when you revise by including all the words and phrases that are needed to
link the ideas in your paragraph.

Paragraph without Transitional Words and Phrases

During his lifetime, Jim Thorpe faced many obstacles. Thorpe was
born in 1888, the son of an Irish father and a Native American mother.
He was sent to the Carlisle Indian School in Pennsylvania. "Pop"
Warner, the legendary coach at Carlisle, discovered Thorpe when he
saw him jump more than six feet while he was wearing street clothes.
Thorpe left Carlisle to play baseball for two seasons in the newly
formed East Carolina minor league. Thorpe returned to Carlisle,
played football, and was named to the All-American team. Thorpe
went to the Olympic games in Stockholm, where he won two gold
medals. Thorpe's career took a dramatic turn for the worse when a
sportswriter who had seen him play baseball in North Carolina exposed him as a professional. The Amateur Athletic Union stripped him
of his records and medals. The International Olympic Committee returned Thorpe's Olympic medals to his family.

The above paragraph is not coherent because it does not include the transitional words and phrases needed to establish how the events in Jim Thorpe's life relate to one another.

Paragraph with Transitional Words and Phrases

     During his lifetime, Jim Thorpe faced many obstacles. Thorpe was born in 1888, the son of an Irish father and a Native American mother. In 1904, he was sent to the Carlisle Indian School in Pennsylvania. The next year, "Pop" Warner, the legendary coach at Carlisle, discovered Thorpe when he saw him jump more than six feet while he was wearing street clothes. Thorpe left Carlisle in 1909 to play baseball for two seasons in the newly formed East Carolina minor league. In 1911, Thorpe returned to Carlisle, played football, and was named to the All-American team. In 1912, Thorpe went to the Olympic games in Stockholm, where he won two gold medals. The next year, however, Thorpe's career took a dramatic turn for the worse when a sportswriter who had seen him play baseball in North Carolina exposed him as a professional. As a result, the Amateur Athletic Union stripped him of his records and medals. After years of appeals, the International Olympic Committee returned Thorpe's Olympic medals to his family in 1982.

The paragraph is now coherent. It contains transitional words and phrases—*in 1912, the next year,* and *after years of appeals,* for example—that establish the time order of the events in Thorpe's life.

◆ PRACTICE 2-12

Underline the transitional words and phrases in each of the following paragraphs. Then, decide what order—time order, spatial order, or logical order—the writer has chosen for arranging details in each paragraph. Write your answers in the blanks provided.

1. Alarmed that teenage girls today get only half as much exercise as boys, researchers are trying to find out why. One reason, they say, is the amount of television girls watch. But this is not an adequate explanation because boys generally watch as much television as girls do. A more important reason is that many girls do not have available to them the sorts of organized athletic programs that are available to boys. Furthermore, because both parents often work now, girls are more likely than boys to have responsibilities at home that leave them less free time to pursue physical activity. Most important, though, may be the lingering attitude that boys aren't attracted to girls who are athletic. Being "feminine," for many girls, means avoiding anything that might mess up their hair or make them sweat. Unless these habits and attitudes change, the current generation of teenage girls may grow into a generation of women plagued by serious health problems.

Order: *logical order* _____

2. The high school I attended is unusual because, instead of being a single building, it is actually a campus consisting of six separate buildings located on a small hill. The building in front, which faces the street, houses

administrative offices, the library, and the cafeteria. <u>Beside</u> the adminis-tration building is a large structure that contains the gym, a swimming pool, and rehearsal rooms for band and chorus. <u>In back of</u> the adminis-tration building is a parallel building where English and foreign language classes are held. <u>Behind</u> this is a large grassy space flanked by two build-ings that run at right angles to the English building. The building <u>on the right</u> is for political science and history courses, and the building <u>on the left</u> is for math and the sciences. <u>At the far end</u> of the grassy space is a small A-frame building containing the art studio and the shop. <u>Between</u> the buildings are covered cement walkways. Changing classes requires going from building to building, and this is usually a nice break—except in the dead of winter, when people freeze as they pass from class to class.

Order: _spatial order_

3.   The Caribbean island of Puerto Rico has a complex history. <u>Before the 1400s</u>, the island's inhabitants for centuries were the native Arawak Indi-ans. <u>In 1493</u>, Christopher Columbus and his crew were the earliest Euro-peans to reach the island. <u>Fifteen years later</u>, Ponce de Leon conquered the island for Spain, and the Spanish subjected the Arawaks to virtual slavery to develop a sugar industry. <u>Finally</u>, these native people were annihilated completely, slaughtered by the sword and by European diseases to which they had no immunity. The Arawaks were <u>soon</u> replaced by African slaves as a European plantation culture flourished. <u>In 1898</u>, after the Spanish-American War, the island was ceded to the United States. <u>The next year</u>, the United States designated Puerto Rico a colony under an American governor. <u>Later</u>, in 1917, Puerto Ricans were granted U.S. citizenship, and the country became a U.S. commonwealth in 1952. <u>Since then</u>, Puerto Ricans have debated this status, with some arguing for statehood and oth-ers for independence. <u>For now</u>, the island remains a commonwealth, and its citizens share most of the rights and obligations of U.S. citizenship.

Order: _time order_

■ WRITING FIRST: Flashback

Look back at the paragraph you wrote for the Writing First exercise on page 21. Are all its sentences arranged in a clear, sensible order? Is this order time, spatial, or logical? List below the transitional words and phrases that signal this order to readers.

Answers will vary.

_____   _____

_____   _____

_____   _____

_____   _____

Now, add to your paragraph any transitions you think are needed, and rearrange your sentences if necessary.

■ WRITING FIRST: Revising and Editing

Review the work you did for the Flashback exercises on pages 27, 30, 34, and 40. Then, revise your paragraph for unity, development, and coherence, incorporating changes and corrections from your Flashback exercises.

CHAPTER REVIEW

◆ EDITING PRACTICE

Read the following paragraphs, and evaluate each in terms of its unity, development, and coherence. First, underline each topic sentence. Then, cross out any sentences that do not support the topic sentence. Add transitional words and phrases where needed. Finally, discuss in class whether additional details and examples could be added to each paragraph.

Teaching Tip
Assign groups of three or four students to rewrite two of the Editing Practice paragraphs, adding details and examples.

1.   In 1979, a series of mechanical and human errors in Unit 2 of the nuclear generating plant at Three Mile Island, near Harrisburg, Pennsylvania, caused an accident that profoundly affected the nuclear power industry. A combination of stuck valves, human error, and poor decisions caused a partial meltdown of the reactor core. *Therefore, large* Large amounts of radioactive gases were released into the atmosphere. The governor of Pennsylvania immediately evacuated pregnant women from the area. People *soon* panicked and left their homes. The nuclear regulatory agency *later* claimed that the situation was not really dangerous and that the released gases were not a health threat, but activists and local residents disputed this. The reactor itself remained unusable for more than ten years. Massive demonstrations followed the accident, including a rally of more than 200,000 people in New York City. Some people came because the day was nice. By the mid-1980s, new construction of nuclear power plants in the United States had stopped.

2 D

2.   A survey of cigarette commercials shows how tobacco companies have consistently encouraged people to continue smoking. One of the earliest television ads showed two boxes of cigarettes dancing to an advertising jingle. The approach in this ad was simple: create an entertaining commercial, and people will buy your product. ~~Many people liked these ads. Other~~ *Later, other* commercials were more subtle. Some were aimed at specific audiences. Marlboro commercials, with the rugged Marlboro man, targeted men. Virginia Slims made an overt pitch to women by saying, "You've come a long way, baby!" Salem, a mentholated cigarette, showed rural scenes and targeted people who liked the freshness of the outdoors. Kent, with its "micronite filter," appealed to those who were health conscious by claiming that Kent contained less tar and nicotine than any other brand. ~~This claim was not entirely true. Other brands had less tar and nicotine.~~ *During the 1980s, cigarette* ~~Cigarette~~ companies responded to the national decline in smoking by directing advertising at young people. Camel *, for example,* introduced the cartoon character Joe Camel, which was aimed at teenagers and young adults. *Finally,* Merit and other high-tar and high-nicotine cigarettes used commercials that were specifically directed at minorities.

3.   Cities created police forces for a number of reasons. The first reason was status: after the Civil War, it became a status symbol for cities to have a uniformed police force. *Second, a* ~~A~~ police force provided a large number of political jobs. This meant that politicians were able to promise jobs to people who would work to support them. *Third, police* ~~Police~~ forces made people feel safe. *For example, police* ~~Police~~ officers helped visitors find their way. *In addition, they* ~~They~~ took in lost children and sometimes fed the homeless. They *also* directed traffic, enforced health ordinances, and provided other services. *Finally, police* ~~Police~~ officers kept order. Without a visible,

uniformed police force, criminals would have made life in nineteenth-century cities unbearable.

◆ COLLABORATIVE ACTIVITIES

1. Working in a group, list the reasons why you think students decide to attend your school. After working together to arrange these reasons from least to most important, write a topic sentence that states the main idea suggested by these reasons. Finally, on your own, draft a paragraph in which you discuss the factors that lead students to attend your school.

2. In a newspaper or magazine, find an illustration or photograph that includes a lot of details. Then, write a paragraph describing what you see in the photograph. (Include enough support—details, facts, and examples—so that readers will be able to "see" it almost as clearly as you can.) Decide on a specific spatial order—from top to bottom, from left to right, or another arrangement that makes sense to you. Use that spatial order to organize the details in your draft paragraph. Finally, trade paragraphs with another student, and offer suggestions that could improve his or her paragraph.

3. Bring to class a paragraph from a newspaper or a magazine. Working in a group, decide whether each of your paragraphs is unified, well developed, and coherent. If any paragraph does not conform to the guidelines outlined in this chapter, try as a group to rewrite it to make it more effective.

ESL Tip
Collaborative Activity 2 is an excellent exercise for bringing out students' creativity. Assign it as a group project, being sure to pair nonnative speakers with native speakers.

✔ REVIEW CHECKLIST:
Fine-Tuning Your Paragraph

- ☐ A topic sentence states the main idea of your paragraph. (See 2A.)

- ☐ A paragraph is unified when it focuses on a single main idea. (See 2B.)

- ☐ A paragraph is well developed when it contains enough details, facts, and examples to support the main idea. (See 2C.)

- ☐ A paragraph is coherent if its sentences are arranged in a clear, logical order and it includes all necessary transitional words and phrases. (See 2D.)

Teaching Tip
Have students work in pairs to make up twenty test questions that Chapter 2 could answer. Discuss suggested questions (and how they might be answered).

Teaching Tip
Give an unannounced open-book test asking ten questions about the chapter's content. Allow the students to consult their notes as well as the text.

UNIT TWO

Patterns of Paragraph Development

Exemplification

PREVIEW

In this chapter, you
will learn to write
an exemplification
paragraph.

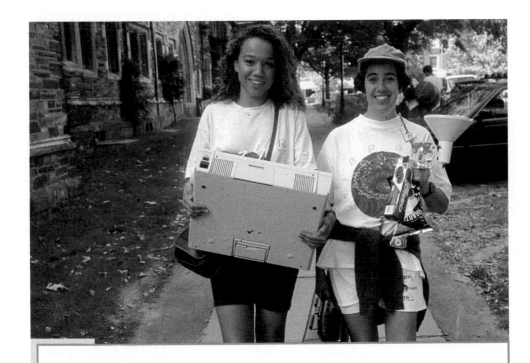

■ WRITING FIRST

What could your school do to make it easier for new students to
adjust to college life? Look at the picture above, and then write a
paragraph in which you answer this question. Make sure you review the strategies discussed in Chapter 1 before you begin.

Word Power

adapt to adjust to new surroundings

mentor an experienced
and trusted adviser

facilitate to make easy

▼ Student Voices
*Examples, examples: my in-
structor is always telling me
to use more examples.*
Nicholas Kinlaw

In Chapters 1 and 2, you learned how to write paragraphs. In Chapters 3
through 11, you will become acquainted with the options you have for
organizing ideas within paragraphs. As you write, you will see that your
ideas tend to develop in ways that reflect how your mind works to make
sense of information and communicate it to others: you give examples, tell
what happened, describe physical characteristics, explain how something
operates, identify causes or predict effects, identify similarities and differences, classify information into categories, define, or persuade. These
methods of arranging ideas correspond to specific patterns of paragraph
(and essay) development: *exemplification, narration, description, process,*

cause and effect, comparison and contrast, classification, definition, and *argument.* Recognizing these patterns and understanding how they help you organize your ideas will help you become a more confident writer.

A Understanding Exemplification

An example is a specific illustration of a general idea. **Exemplification** is writing that explains a general statement by offering one or more specific examples. In an **exemplification paragraph,** you state a general idea in the topic sentence and then use examples to illustrate and explain it. Thus, an example is always more specific than the topic sentence of the paragraph. To be effective, examples must be *appropriate* (that is, they must support or explain your point), and they must be *specific* (that is, they must be precise).

You can use a number of short examples to support your topic sentence, or (if one example is particularly vivid or compelling) you can use a single extended example. The following paragraph about the 1969 Woodstock festival uses a series of short examples.

Writing Tip

Use a transitional phrase such as *for instance* or *for example* to let readers know you are going to use an example. (See 2D.)

Topic sentence

Series of short examples

Teaching Tip

To help students understand the concept of exemplification, ask them to put brackets around all the specific examples in this paragraph. What is left? Discuss how specific examples enrich a paragraph.

> In most respects, after all, Woodstock was a disaster. To begin with, it rained and rained for weeks before the festival, and then, of course, it rained during the festival. The promoters lost weeks of preparation time when the site had to be switched twice. They rented Yasgur's field less than a month before the concert. The stage wasn't finished, and the sound system was stitched together perilously close to the start of the show. As soon as the festival opened, the water- and food-delivery arrangements broke down, the gates and fences disintegrated, and tens of thousands of new bodies kept pouring in. (One powerful lure was the rumor that the revered Bob Dylan was going to perform; he wasn't.) In response to an emergency appeal for volunteers, fifty doctors were flown in. The Air Force brought in food on Huey helicopters, and the Women's Community Center in Monticello sent thirty thousand sandwiches. One kid was killed as he was run over by a tractor, one died of appendicitis, and another died of a drug overdose.
>
> Hal Espen, "The Woodstock Wars"

Writing Tip

Many everyday tasks call for exemplification. For example, in a letter to your local paper, you might give examples of quality-of-life improvements that need to be made in your neighborhood.

The writer of this paragraph piles on a series of examples, one after the other, to support his paragraph's main idea. Each example gives a specific illustration of how Woodstock was a disaster: it rained, the promoters had to switch sites, water and food were not delivered as planned, and so on.

The next paragraph uses a single extended example to support its main idea—that fear can move people to take action.

Topic sentence

Single extended example

> Sometimes, fear can be a great motivator. Once, when I was in high school, I tried out for a part in the school play. I was surprised and thrilled when I was given one of the leads. Never for a moment, however, did I consider how long my part was or how hard I would have to work to memorize it. All I could think of was how much attention I was getting from my friends. I even ignored the warnings of the play's director, who told me I would be in trouble if I did not begin to mem-

orize my lines. The reality of my situation finally sank in during our first dress rehearsal when I stumbled all over my lines and the rest of the cast laughed at me. That night, and for the two weeks leading up to the play, I spent hours going over my lines. Miraculously, I got through the first night of the play without missing (at least obviously missing) many of my lines. As a result of that experience, I learned two things: first, that I could do almost anything if I was frightened enough, and second, that I would never try out for another play.

Jerry Doyle (student)

Here, a single extended example supports the topic sentence.

> ● **Writing Tip**
> Often, a personal experience like this one can be an interesting and effective way of illustrating your main idea.

For information on how to write an exemplification essay, as well as a list of transitions suitable for exemplification paragraphs and essays, see 14A.

FOCUS   Exemplification

How many examples you need in a paragraph depends on your topic sentence. A complicated, far-reaching statement might require many supporting examples to convince readers that it is reasonable. A simple, more straightforward statement would require fewer examples.

B   Writing an Exemplification Paragraph

◆ PRACTICE 3-1

Read this exemplification paragraph; then, follow the instructions on page 50.

Youthful Style?

As a teenager in the late 1960s and early 1970s, I was always pretty tolerant of radical clothing styles, but more and more today I find myself asking, "Why do these kids want to look so weird?" (For example,) I do not understand why a boy would wear a baseball cap backwards on his head. To me, this just looks weird, like something a person would do and then talk in a really stupid voice to make his friends laugh. Under the backwards cap, the boy probably has his hair in a buzz cut, except for one long strand of hair reaching halfway down his back. I can't imagine who thought up this hairstyle, unless it was an ex-monk. (Furthermore,) every boy I see today seems to be wearing a T-shirt that looks ten sizes too big for him and comes down below his knees, or, if not that, he's got all his clothes on inside out or backwards or both! (Then) there are the girls. Who decided that it was attractive to combine a white T-shirt and a long, sheer, flowing skirt with

a pair of huge black jackboots? I'm so confused. It all
just makes me nostalgic for the days of frayed bell-
bottoms, tie-dyed tank tops, strands of hippie beads,
and headbands circling heads of long, stringy hair.

Willa Kincaid (student)

1. Underline the topic sentence of the paragraph.

2. List the specific examples the writer uses to support her topic sentence. The first example has been listed for you.

boys wearing baseball caps backwards

buzz-cut hair with one long strand

oversize T-shirt

clothes inside out

_____

_____

3. Circle the transitions that the writer uses to connect ideas in the paragraph.

◆ PRACTICE 3-2

Teaching Tip
Give students a few minutes to work on Practice 3-2. Before they finish, get some of them to share what they have written so far.

ESL Tip
Check the *-ed* and *-ing* endings of verbs as students work on this exercise.

Following are four possible topic sentences for exemplification paragraphs. List three examples you could use to support each topic sentence. For example, if you were writing a paragraph about how difficult the first week of your new job was, you could mention waking up early, getting to know your coworkers, and learning new routines.

1. I have a number of reasons for liking my neighborhood.

Answers will vary.

_____

_____

2. Summer jobs provide valuable opportunities for young people by allowing them to develop their interests and test their abilities.

Answers will vary.

_____

_____

3. Some rules and regulations are unfair.

Answers will vary.

_____

_____

4. Many television programs insult the intelligence of their audiences.

Answers will vary.

_____

_____

_____

◆ PRACTICE 3-3

Choose one of the topics below (or one of your own choice) as the subject of an exemplification paragraph. Then, on a separate sheet of paper, use one or more of the invention strategies described in 1C to help you think of as many examples as you can for the topic you have chosen.

Effective (or ineffective) teaching	Weight training
Qualities that make a song popular	Terrible dates
Successful movies	The importance of recycling
Challenges that older students face	Role models
Why people watch reality shows	Rude behavior
Unattractive clothing styles	Politicians
Peer pressure	Acts of bravery
The benefits of e-mail	Lying

◆ PRACTICE 3-4

Review your notes from Practice 3-3, and list the examples that can help you develop a paragraph on the topic you have chosen.

Answers will vary.

_____

_____

_____

_____

◆ PRACTICE 3-5

Reread your list of examples from Practice 3-4. Now, draft a topic sentence that introduces your topic and communicates the main idea your paragraph will discuss.

Answers will vary.

_____

_____

◆ PRACTICE 3-6

Arrange the examples you listed in Practice 3-4 in a logical order—for example, from least important to most important.

1. *Answers will vary.* _____

2. _____

3 B

3. _____

4. _____

◆ PRACTICE 3-7

On a separate sheet of paper, draft your exemplification paragraph. Then, using the Self-Assessment Checklist below, revise your paragraph for unity, development, and coherence.

◆ PRACTICE 3-8

On a separate sheet of paper, type a final, edited draft of your exemplification paragraph.

ESL Tip
You might want to give students a proofreading exercise focusing on verb forms, verb endings, prepositions, and articles. Prepare this exercise ahead of time by keeping track of frequent errors in students' writing.

■ WRITING FIRST: Revising and Editing

Look back at your response to the Writing First exercise on page 47, and evaluate it for unity, development, and coherence. Then, prepare a final, edited draft of your paragraph.

☑ SELF-ASSESSMENT CHECKLIST:
Writing an Exemplification Paragraph

Unity

☐ Does your topic sentence state a general idea that can be supported with examples?

☐ Is your topic sentence specifically worded?

☐ Do all your examples support your topic sentence?

Development

☐ Do you need to find additional examples that more clearly support your topic sentence?

☐ Should you use one of the invention strategies discussed in 1C to help you come up with more ideas?

Coherence

☐ Are your examples arranged in an order that makes sense?

☐ Do you need to add transitional words or phrases?

Narration

PREVIEW

In this chapter, you will learn to write a narrative paragraph.

■ WRITING FIRST

Look at the picture above, which illustrates a scene from *The Three Little Pigs*. Then write a paragraph in which you retell a fairy tale or child's story that you know well. Make sure that your topic sentence states the point of the story.

Word Power
memorable worth remembering

moral a lesson of a fable or story

A Understanding Narration

Narration is writing that tells a story. In a **narrative paragraph**, you relate a sequence of events. A narrative paragraph usually has a topic sentence that tells readers what the point of the paragraph is—that is, why you are telling this particular story. The rest of the paragraph develops this point, with ideas arranged in time order.

In the following paragraph, writer Ron Kovic tells how he celebrated his birthday when he was a child.

▼ Student Voices
When I write narratives, I get to tell my own story.
                        Amy Neal

53

Topic sentence

Events presented in time order

● **Writing Tip**

Because narrative para-
graphs tell what happened,
they often rely on transitional words and phrases
that indicate time, such as
after, before, now, and *then.*
(See 2D.)

*For information on how to
write a narrative essay, as well
as a list of transitions suitable
for narrative paragraphs and
essays, see 14B.*

● **Writing Tip**

Many everyday writing tasks
call for narration. For example, in a complaint letter,
you might summarize, in
chronological order, the
problems you had with a
particular product.

Teaching Tip

Bring to class a magazine
photograph that shows two
people talking. Ask students
to guess what the people are
saying and to write out the
conversation in dialogue format. Then, have the students
exchange papers to check
each other's work. Explain
that dialogue enriches narrative writing.

When the Fourth of July came, there were fireworks going off all over the neighborhood. It was the most exciting time of year for me next to Christmas. <u>Being born on the exact same day as my country I thought was really great</u>. I was so proud. And every Fourth of July, I had a birthday party and all my friends would come over with birth-day presents and we'd put on silly hats and blow these horns my dad brought home from the A&P. We'd eat lots of ice cream and water-melon and I'd open up all the presents and blow out the candles on the big red, white, and blue birthday cake and then we'd all sing "Happy Birthday" and "I'm a Yankee Doodle Dandy." At night everyone would pile into Bobby's mother's old car and we'd go down to the drive-in, where we'd watch the fireworks display. Before the movie started, we'd all get out and sit up on the roof of the car with our blankets wrapped around us watching the rockets and Roman candles going up and ex-ploding into fountains of rainbow colors, and later after Mrs. Zimmer dropped me off, I'd lie on my bed feeling a little sad that it all had to end so soon. As I closed my eyes I could still hear strings of firecrack-ers and cherry bombs going off all over the neighborhood.

Ron Kovic, *Born on the Fourth of July*

In this paragraph, all events and activities are related to the topic sentence, and transitional words and phrases—*at night, later,* and *as I closed my eyes*—clearly identify the order in which the events occurred.

B **Writing a Narrative Paragraph**

◆ **PRACTICE 4-1**

Read this narrative paragraph; then, follow the instructions on page 55.

The Trip to a Brand-New Life

When I was seven, my family took a trip that changed our entire lives--the trip to America. Leaving our native Vietnam illegally, we (first) traveled three days in a small boat with about fifty other people. We (soon) ran out of food and supplies, and I thought we would never make it, but (at last) we reached Malaysia. The people who met us on shore led us to a campsite where there were hundreds of other Vietnamese refugees. (For nine months,) my family stayed there, living in a shelter consisting of logs covered with thick plastic. (During this time,) we were called in to pre-sent our situation to representatives from a variety of countries so they could process our documents and decide whether to accept us as immigrants. We were among the for-tunate ones accepted by the United States. (Next,) we were transferred to a camp in the Philippines, where the houses were more stable and the floors were cement instead of dirt. (For three months,) we continued to study English; (then,) the happy moment came when we learned that we would be leaving for America. (A few days later,) we were headed for New York, changing planes in several countries before reaching our destination. (As the last plane landed,) I was overwhelmed by the realization that my family and I had (finally) reached the land of our dreams. I knew that my first step on the ground would lead me to a new future and a completely new life. I was scared, but I did not hesitate.

Ann Duong (student)

1. Underline the topic sentence of the paragraph.

2. List below the major events of the narrative. The first event has been listed for you.

   The family left Vietnam and spent three days on the water.

   When they reached Malaysia, they entered a refugee camp.

   For nine months, they waited to be accepted by another country.

   After being accepted by the United States, they moved to the Philippines for three months.

   Finally, they were flown to New York to begin their new life.

3. Reread the narrative, circling the transitional words and phrases the writer uses to link events in time.

◆ PRACTICE 4-2

Below are four possible topic sentences for narrative paragraphs. After each topic sentence, list four events that could support the main idea. For example, if you were recalling a barbecue that turned into a disaster, you could tell about burning the hamburgers, spilling the soda, and forgetting to buy paper plates.

1. One experience made me realize that I was no longer as young as I thought.

   Answers will vary.

Teaching Tip
Discuss dialogue (punctuation, format, etc.). Show students how to indent each time the speaker changes.

2. The first time I _____, I got more than I bargained for.

Answers will vary.

_____

_____

_____

3. Even though the accident lasted only a few seconds, it seemed to last much longer.

Answers will vary.

_____

_____

_____

4. I remember my reaction to one particular news event very clearly.

Answers will vary.

_____

_____

_____

◆ PRACTICE 4-3

Choose one of the topics below (or one of your own choice) as the subject of a narrative paragraph. On a separate sheet of paper, use one or more of the invention strategies described in 1C to help you recall events and details about the topic you have chosen.

A difficult choice	An embarrassing situation
A frightening situation	A surprise
A time of self-doubt	A sudden understanding
A success	Something funny a friend did
An act of violence	Unexpected good luck
A lesson learned	A conflict with authority
Your happiest moment	An event that changed your life
An instance of injustice	An important decision

◆ PRACTICE 4-4

List the events you recalled in Practice 4-3 that can help you develop a narrative paragraph on the topic you have chosen.

Answers will vary.

_____

_____

_____

_____

_____

_____

◆ PRACTICE 4-5

Reread your list of events from Practice 4-4. Then, draft a topic sentence that introduces your topic and communicates the main idea your paragraph will discuss.

Answers will vary. _____

_____

_____

◆ PRACTICE 4-6

Write down the events you listed in Practice 4-4 in the order in which they occurred.

1. _Answers will vary._ _____

2. _____

3. _____

4. _____

5. _____

Teaching Tip
Stop here and have students share their ideas with the class.

◆ PRACTICE 4-7

On a separate sheet of paper, draft your narrative paragraph. Then, consulting the Self-Assessment Checklist on page 58, revise your paragraph for unity, development, and coherence.

◆ PRACTICE 4-8

On a separate sheet of paper, write a final, edited draft of your narrative paragraph.

Teaching Tip
For a quiz on dialogue, photocopy a comic strip and have students rewrite the conversation in dialogue format.

ESL Tip
Remind students to copy the conversation exactly as it appears in the comic strip. Check to make sure their sentences are grammatical and complete.

■ WRITING FIRST: Revising and Editing

Look back at your response to the Writing First exercise on page 53, and evaluate your paragraph for unity, development, and coherence. Then, prepare a final, edited draft of your paragraph.

✓ SELF-ASSESSMENT CHECKLIST:
Writing a Narrative Paragraph

Unity

☐ Does your topic sentence tell readers what the point of the paragraph is?

☐ Is your topic sentence specific enough?

☐ Do all details and events support your topic sentence?

Development

☐ Should you add more events or details to make your narrative clearer or livelier?

Coherence

☐ Does your narrative proceed clearly from an earlier time to a later time?

☐ Do you need to add transitional words or phrases?

Description

PREVIEW

In this chapter, you
will learn to write a
descriptive paragraph.

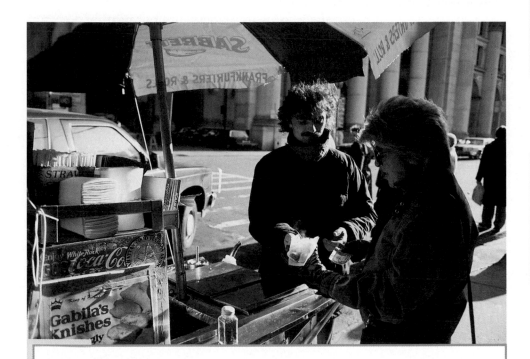

● **Writing Tip**

Many everyday writing tasks
call for description. At work,
for example, you might
write a memo describing a
piece of equipment you
would like your department
to purchase.

■ WRITING FIRST

Look at the picture above. Then, write a paragraph in which you
describe a person you encounter every day—for example, a street
vendor, a bus driver, or a worker in your school cafeteria. Before
you begin writing, decide what general impression you want to
convey about the person you are describing.

Word Power
disregard   to ignore; to
neglect

distinctive   distinguishing;
typical of its kind

A   Understanding Description

Teaching Tip
Before starting this chapter,
write several "dead verbs"
on the board and ask stu-
dents to give variations of
each verb in "living verb"
form. (For example, instead
of *The snake moved* they
might say *slithered* or
wriggled.)

Description is writing that paints a word picture of a person, place, or
thing. In a **descriptive paragraph**, you use description to enable readers
to see what you see, hear what you hear, smell what you smell, taste what
you taste, and feel what you feel. Details in a descriptive paragraph are
usually arranged in *spatial order*—that is, from top to bottom, near to far,
front to back, and so on.

5 A

When you write a descriptive paragraph, you try to create a single
dominant impression—a mood or feeling that you want to communicate
to readers. For example, if you were describing an old house in your neighborhood and wanted to leave readers with the impression that it was
mysterious, your topic sentence would convey this idea: *The old house
stands dark and alone, with just one window lit.* The rest of the sentences
in the paragraph would reinforce this dominant impression.

In general, there are two kinds of descriptive paragraphs: *objective* and
subjective. Writers use **objective description** to describe something without conveying their own emotions or opinions. This kind of description is
used in technical or scientific writing but can also be used in other kinds
of writing. In the following paragraph, the writer uses precise language
and specific details to describe a scene to readers, but her writing does not
indicate any special meaning the scene may have for her.

> Just south of Delaware Bay, where the land juts out and curves
> down the east coast, is a small town called Bethany Beach, Delaware.
> <u>One look at the beach at Bethany shows the effect of construction on
> the shoreline.</u> On the Atlantic side of Bethany, the white beach slopes
> gradually up from the ocean. In back of the beach are low rippling
> dunes that gradually blend into higher mounds of sand that have been
> planted with several types of beach grass and stubby green shrubs. The
> town council hoped that these plants would stabilize the dune struc-
> ture and stop the erosion that threatens the beach every time there is
> a storm. Arching over the dunes are narrow gray boardwalks that pro-
> tect the fragile dunes from the human traffic that eventually would de-
> stroy them. Behind the dunes, however, nature seems to stop. Along
> the Atlantic coast, as far south as Virginia Beach, the land has been
> divided into sandy plots, each with its own beach house or apartment.
> The natural flow of the beach has been interrupted by geometrical
> structures of shining glass and weathered gray wood.
>
> Kim DiPialo (student)

Because the writer's purpose is to help readers picture the scene she describes, her description is primarily objective. The topic sentence presents
the main idea of the paragraph. Then, the writer describes the beach, the
dunes, and finally the area behind the dunes. Transitional words and
phrases emphasize the spatial arrangement of details—*in back of the
beach, arching over the dunes,* and *behind the dunes*—and connect various
parts of the description. Specific visual details such as *stubby green shrubs,
narrow gray boardwalks,* and *weathered gray wood* give readers a clear picture of the scene.

Writers use **subjective description** primarily to convey their feelings
and opinions about a person, place, or thing, but subjective descriptions
also contain specific details, just as objective descriptions do. In the following paragraph, the writer describes her impression of a building that
has strong emotional associations for her.

Topic sentence

> <u>The school building was not a welcoming sight for someone used
> to the bright colors and airiness of tropical architecture.</u> The building
> looked functional. It could have been a prison, an asylum, or just what
> it was: an urban school for the children of immigrants, built to with-

stand waves of change, generation by generation. Its red brick sides rose to four solid stories. The black steel fire escapes snaked up its back like exposed vertebrae. A chain link fence surrounded its concrete playground. Members of the elite safety patrol, older kids, sixth graders mainly, stood at each of its entrances, wearing their florescent white belts that criss-crossed their chests and their metal badges. No one was allowed in the building until the bell rang, not even on rainy or bitter-cold days. Only the safety patrol stayed warm.

Judith Ortiz Cofer, *Silent Dancing: A Partial Remembrance of a Puerto Rican Childhood*

Specific details

> **Teaching Tip**
> This descriptive paragraph works well with a minimum of transitional words and phrases. As an exercise, ask students to add some transitions to this paragraph.

In this paragraph, the topic sentence conveys the paragraph's dominant impression. The details of the paragraph are arranged in spatial order, starting with the school itself, moving to the chain link fence that surrounded the school, and ending with the children standing outside. The paragraph includes enough specific details to give readers a clear picture of the school; at the same time, it also communicates the writer's strong negative response to the building she is describing.

For information on how to write a descriptive essay, as well as a list of transitions suitable for descriptive paragraphs and essays, see 14C.

B   Writing a Descriptive Paragraph

◆ PRACTICE 5-1

Read this descriptive paragraph; then, follow the instructions on the next page.

> ● **Writing Tip**
> Most descriptive paragraphs mix objective and subjective description. Although one kind of description may dominate, the other will probably be present as well.

Camaro Joe

When I was growing up, my older sister Roxanne invariably managed to come up with the greasiest lowlifes for boyfriends, generally characterized by their lip-snarling, cigarette-smoke-trailing, "I-just-might-die-tomorrow-and-I-might-as-well-take-someone-with-me" attitude. Usually named Mitch or Jake, these guys would hoist my delicate sister onto the backs of their black, chrome-laden motorcycles and tear off in a cloud of dirt and exhaust fumes. <u>I particularly remember the one we called Camaro Joe, Roxanne's boyfriend the summer I was twelve.</u> When he first squealed into our driveway in a sputtering dirty-gold Camaro with a thumping stereo that shook the trees, we knew my sister had picked another winner. Joe's cowboy boots swung from his car onto the gravel of our driveway, and we watched as he launched his massive beer belly from the low seat. His waddle up to the house reminded me of a penguin. Joe was short and stocky with beady, black eyes and a thin, fuzzy mustache. He wore his black hair slicked back with grease, and a Camel cigarette hung from his lower lip as if it had

> **ESL Tip**
> Have students copy the passage to help strengthen their understanding of sentence structure before they go on to work on their own descriptions.

been glued there. Like any good Neanderthal, he communi-
cated mostly in grunts. My father eventually laid down the
law and insisted that Roxanne stop seeing Joe, and, much to
Dad's satisfaction, she did. Of course, it wasn't long
before Joe was replaced by another Mitch--or was it Jake?

Susan Burkhart (student)

1. Underline the topic sentence of the paragraph.

2. In a few words, summarize the dominant impression the writer wants to give of her subject, Camaro Joe.

   Joe is a greasy, unattractive lowlife.
   _____

3. What are some of the details the writer uses to create this dominant impression? The first detail has been listed for you.

   drives a dirty Camaro

   big beer belly

   waddles

   thin, fuzzy mustache

   slicked-back hair

   grunts

◆ PRACTICE 5-2

Each of the four topic sentences below states a possible dominant impression for a paragraph. After each topic sentence, list three details that could help convey this dominant impression. For example, to support the idea that sitting in front of a fireplace is relaxing, you could describe the crackling of the fire, the pine scent of the smoke, and the changing colors of the flames.

1. After the rainstorm, everything in the city seemed clean and new.

   Answers will vary.
   _____

   _____

2. The bus was at least twenty years old and looked shabby.

   Answers will vary.
   _____

   _____

3. I could see the toll that living on the streets had taken on him.

Answers will vary.

_____

_____

_____

4. One of the most interesting stores I've seen sells used (or, as they say, "recycled") clothing.

Answers will vary.

_____

_____

_____

◆ PRACTICE 5-3

Choose one of the topics below (or one of your own choice) as the subject of a descriptive paragraph. On a separate sheet of paper, use one or more of the invention strategies described in 1C to help you come up with specific details about the topic you have chosen. If you can, observe your subject directly and write down your observations.

A favorite place from childhood   A favorite article of clothing
A place you felt trapped in   An interesting object
A quiet spot on campus   A pet
An unusual person   A building you find interesting
A place you find comforting   Your car or truck
A family member or friend   A scenic spot
A work of art   A statue or monument
A valued possession   Someone you admire
Your workplace

◆ PRACTICE 5-4

List the details you came up with in Practice 5-3 that can best help you develop a descriptive paragraph on the topic you have chosen.

Answers will vary.

_____

_____

_____

_____

_____

_____

◆ **PRACTICE 5-5**

Reread your list of details from Practice 5-4. Then, draft a topic sentence that summarizes the dominant impression you want to convey in your paragraph.

Answers will vary.

_____

◆ **PRACTICE 5-6**

Teaching Tip
Put a section of a descriptive piece of writing (Maya Angelou's "Summer Picnic Fish Fry" or Esmeralda Santiago's "Guavas" from Chapter 36, for example) on an overhead. Have students model their descriptions and sentence patterns on the sample.

Arrange the details you listed in Practice 5-4 in spatial order. You might arrange them in the order in which you are looking at them—for example, from left to right, near to far, or top to bottom.

1. *Answers will vary.* _____

2. _____

3. _____

4. _____

5. _____

6. _____

7. _____

◆ **PRACTICE 5-7**

On a separate sheet of paper, draft your descriptive paragraph. Then, consulting the Self-Assessment Checklist on page 65, revise your paragraph for unity, development, and coherence.

◆ **PRACTICE 5-8**

On a separate sheet of paper, write a final, edited draft of your descriptive paragraph.

■ **WRITING FIRST: Revising and Editing**

Look back at your response to the Writing First exercise on page 59, and evaluate your paragraph for unity, development, and coherence. Then, prepare a final, edited draft of your paragraph.

✓ SELF-ASSESSMENT CHECKLIST:
Writing a Descriptive Paragraph

Unity

- ☐ Does your topic sentence express the dominant impression you want to communicate?

- ☐ Do all the details in your paragraph support your topic sentence?

- ☐ Do all the details help to convey the dominant impression stated in your topic sentence?

Development

- ☐ Do you need to include more objective description to help readers see your subject?

- ☐ Do you need to add more subjective description to help readers understand your feelings and opinions about your subject?

Coherence

- ☐ Are your details arranged in a spatial order that makes sense?

- ☐ Do you need to add transitional words or phrases?

Process

PREVIEW

In this chapter, you will learn how to write a process paragraph.

LEFT FOOT   RIGHT HAND

LEFT HAND   RIGHT FOOT

Word Power

compete to work against another in pursuit of a goal

objective a purpose or goal

penalty a punishment or loss of advantage

Teaching Tip
To help students understand the concept of process, photocopy the operating instructions for an appliance or electronic device. (Students could also be asked to bring instruction booklets or operating manuals to class.) Have students take turns reading steps aloud, and ask the class to supply any missing transitions.

■ WRITING FIRST

Look at the picture above, and then write a paragraph in which you explain how to play your favorite board (or other indoor) game. Assume that your readers know nothing about the game.

A Understanding Process

A **process** is a series of steps, presented in chronological order, leading to a particular result. In a **process paragraph**, you explain how something works or tell how to do something. The topic sentence of your paragraph should identify the process (for example, "Frying chicken is easy" or "The typical job interview has three stages") and communicate the point you want to make about it. The rest of the paragraph should discuss the steps in the process, one at a time, in the order in which they occur.

In general, there are two kinds of process paragraphs: *process explanations* and *instructions*. In a **process explanation**, the writer's purpose is simply to help readers understand a process, not perform it. The following paragraph is a process explanation.

> <u>Once asleep, we go through four distinct stages.</u> The first stage of sleep is marked by an easing of muscle tension and a change in brain-wave activity. This transitional stage is especially light and typically lasts about twenty minutes, during which time you may be easily awakened. In stage two, brain waves slow and slumber grows deeper. Even with the eyes taped open, we are quite literally blind during this phase and would be incapable of seeing anything—even a hand passing over the face—since the eye-brain connection has been shut off. More than half of the time devoted solely to sleep is spent in stage two, and no dreaming occurs. Stages three and four are marked by even slower brain waves, but the deepest sleep occurs in stage four. Mysteriously, the highest levels of the body's growth hormone are released during this sleep stage. After cycling back for a few minutes of stage-two sleep, dreaming begins. The first dream phase, lasting only a few minutes, is the shortest of the night. When dreaming is over, the sleeper retraces all the stages back to lighter sleep and then repeats the deep-sleep stages back to dreaming.
>
> Mark McCuchen, *The Compass in Your Nose and Other Astonishing Facts about Humans*

Topic sentence
Stage 1

Stage 2

Stages 3 and 4

The topic sentence identifies the process, and the rest of the paragraph presents the steps in strict chronological order. Throughout the paragraph, transitional words and phrases—*the first stage*, *in stage two*, and *stages three and four*—clearly identify individual steps in the process.

Other process paragraphs present **instructions**. Here, the writer's purpose is to give readers the information they need to actually perform a task or activity. The following paragraph gives instructions for checking a pair of in-line skates before beginning to skate.

> <u>Now that you are the proud owner of in-lines, you must be sure your skates are fine-tuned and road-worthy, so before you roll, be sure to do the following.</u> First, sit down and place your blades between your legs, wheels facing up. Make certain they are clean so you won't get dirty. Next, wiggle each wheel, making certain there is no lateral play (side-to-side). If bolts are loose, tighten them with the Allen, socket, or crescent wrench supplied by the manufacturer. Then, spin each wheel so they all spin smoothly and evenly. Feel and listen for any grinding. If this occurs, the bearings may need to be cleaned or replaced. After checking the wheels, look at your brake. Some stoppers screw on, while others have bolts on the side or through the center. Jiggle the stopper, and if it's loose, tighten it. If it is worn, replace it. It is best to replace your brake before you start to wear it down to the metal, or you might strip the threads of the bolt and have to saw off the brake, a time-consuming and difficult process. Finally, check your laces or buckles for any wear and tear. Properly serviced, a pair of

Topic sentence

Step 1

Step 2

Step 3

Step 4

Step 5

skates will have a long life span and allow you to roll more easily and smoothly.

Joel Rappelfeld, *The Complete Blader*

For information on how to write a process essay, as well as a list of transitions suitable for process essays and paragraphs, see 14D.

Because the writer of this process paragraph expects readers to follow his instructions, he addresses them directly, using commands to tell them what to do (for instance, "Sit down and place your blades between your legs"). He uses clear transitional words and expressions—*next, then, after checking the wheels*—to help readers see the exact sequence in which the steps are to be performed. He even includes cautions and reminders ("Make certain they are clean so you won't get dirty") and explains the purpose for some steps, such as replacing a worn brake.

● **Writing Tip**

Many everyday writing tasks call for outlining a process. For example, you might write a set of instructions telling your family members what to do in case of a fire.

FOCUS Process

Like narrative paragraphs, process paragraphs present a sequence of events. Unlike narrative paragraphs, however, process paragraphs describe a sequence that occurs—or should occur—in exactly the same way every time.

B Writing a Process Paragraph

◆ **PRACTICE 6-1**

Read this process paragraph; then, follow the instructions on page 69.

ESL Tip

Have students write a process paragraph using one of the sample paragraphs on page 67 as a model for sentence structure and style. Then, have them write a process essay (directed at an American audience) about a practice unique to their culture.

An Order of Fries

I had always enjoyed the french fries at McDonald's and other fast-food restaurants, but I never realized just how much work goes into making them until I worked at a potato processing plant in Hermiston, Oregon. The process begins with freshly dug potatoes being shoveled from trucks onto conveyor belts leading into the plant. During this stage, workers must sort out any rocks that may have been dug up with the potatoes because these could damage the automated peelers. After the potatoes have gone through the peelers, they travel on a conveyor belt through the "trim line." Here, workers cut out any bad spots, being careful not to waste potatoes by trimming too much. Next, the potatoes are sliced in automated cutters and then fried for about a minute. After this, they continue along a conveyor belt to the "wet line." Here, workers again look for bad spots, discarding any rotten pieces. At this point, the

potatoes go to a second set of fryers for three minutes
before being moved to subzero freezers for ten minutes.
Then, it's on to the "frozen line" for a final inspection.
The inspected fries are weighed by machines and then sealed
into five-pound plastic packages, which are weighed again
by workers who also check that the packages are properly
sealed. The bags are then packed into boxes and made ready
for shipment to various McDonald's and other restaurants
across the western United States. This process goes on
twenty-four hours a day, to bring us consumers the tasty
french fries we all enjoy so much.

Cheri Rodriguez (student)

1. Underline the topic sentence of the paragraph.

2. Is this a process explanation or instructions? _process explanation_

   How do you know? _Verbs are not commands._

3. List the steps in the process. The first step has been listed for you.

   The potatoes are unloaded, and the rocks are sorted out.

   They are peeled and carried to the "trim line."

   They are sliced and fried for a minute.

   They are carried to the "wet line."

   They are fried again and then frozen.

   They get a final inspection on the "frozen line."

   They are weighed, packaged, and boxed for shipment.

◆ PRACTICE 6-2

Following are four possible topic sentences for process paragraphs. After
each topic sentence, list three or four steps that explain the process the
sentence identifies. For example, if you were explaining the process of getting a job, you could list preparing a résumé, looking at the classified ads,
writing a job application letter, and going on an interview. Make sure each
step follows logically from the one that precedes it.

1. There are four major steps in the process of making the perfect sandwich.

   a. _Answers will vary._

   b. _____

   c. _____

   d. _____

2. Before you begin the semester, you should take the time to set up a study schedule.

a. _Answers will vary._ _____

b. _____

c. _____

d. _____

3. Before you start any fitness program, set up a workout routine.

a. _Answers will vary._ _____

b. _____

c. _____

d. _____

4. Discouraging unwanted attention from a coworker is a delicate process.

a. _Answers will vary._ _____

b. _____

c. _____

d. _____

◆ PRACTICE 6-3

Choose one of the topics below (or one of your own choice) as the subject of a process paragraph. Use one or more of the invention strategies described in 1C to help you come up with as many steps as you can for the topic you have chosen, and list these steps on a separate sheet of paper.

Making a major purchase
Strategies for winning an
  argument
How to be popular
Buying a book or CD online
Your typical work or school day
How to discourage telemarketers
How to drop a class
Your morning routine
How to break up with someone

How to program a VCR
How to perform a particular
  household repair
Installing a computer program
How to apply for financial aid
A process involved in a hobby of
  yours
Painting a room
How to scramble eggs

◆ PRACTICE 6-4

Review your notes on the topic you chose in Practice 6-3, and decide whether to write a process explanation or a set of instructions. Then, on the lines below, choose the steps from the list you wrote in Practice 6-3 that can best help you develop a process paragraph on your topic.

Answers will vary.

_____   _____
_____   _____
_____   _____
_____   _____

◆ PRACTICE 6-5

Reread your list of steps from Practice 6-4. Then, draft a topic sentence that identifies the process you will discuss and communicates the point you will make about it.

Answers will vary.
_____

_____

_____

◆ PRACTICE 6-6

Review the steps you listed in Practice 6-4. Then, write them down in chronological order, moving from the first step to the last.

1. *Answers will vary.*   4. _____

2. _____   5. _____

3. _____   6. _____

◆ PRACTICE 6-7

On a separate sheet of paper, draft your process paragraph. Then, consulting the Self-Assessment Checklist on page 72, revise your paragraph for unity, development, and coherence.

◆ PRACTICE 6-8

On a separate sheet of paper, write a final, edited draft of your process paragraph.

Teaching Tip
Students have a tendency to use short sentences in process paragraphs. Take this opportunity to do a sentence-combining exercise.

ESL Tip
Check drafts for correct use of articles and prepositions. (Nonnative speakers tend to omit these parts of speech or to use them incorrectly.) Have students circle articles and prepositions so you can check them quickly.

■ WRITING FIRST: Revising and Editing

Look back at your response to the Writing First exercise on page 66, and evaluate your paragraph for unity, development, and coherence. Then, prepare a final, edited draft of your paragraph.

☑ SELF-ASSESSMENT CHECKLIST:
Writing a Process Paragraph

Unity

☐ Does your topic sentence identify the process you will discuss? Does it state your main idea—the point you will make about the process?

☐ Is your topic sentence specifically worded?

☐ Have you eliminated information that does not relate directly to the process?

Development

☐ Have you included all the steps that readers need to know in order to understand the process?

☐ Do you need to explain any steps in greater detail?

☐ If your paragraph is a set of instructions, do you need to include any cautions or reminders?

Coherence

☐ Is your process explained in chronological order, or do you need to rearrange the steps?

☐ Do you need to add transitional words or phrases?

Cause and Effect

PREVIEW

In this chapter, you will learn to write a cause-and-effect paragraph.

Teaching Tip
To help students understand the concept of cause and effect, have them write a one-paragraph summary of a newspaper column or editorial that deals with the causes and/or effects of a particular action or event.

■ WRITING FIRST

Look at the picture above. Then, write a paragraph in which you describe the impact of a particular electronic appliance or gadget on your life or the life of your family—for example, an ATM machine, a cell phone, or a television remote control. Be sure that your topic sentence identifies the item and that the rest of the paragraph discusses how it affects you or your family.

Word Power

gadget a small, specialized mechanical or electronic device

impact the effect of one thing on another

simplify to make easier

A   Understanding Cause and Effect

A **cause** is what makes a particular thing happen. An **effect** is what results from a particular cause: a situation, activity, or behavior. You write **cause-and-effect paragraphs** when your purpose is to help readers understand why something happened or is happening, or when you want to show

73

Topic sentence: effect

First (minor) cause: paper costs

Second (major) cause: illiteracy

readers how one thing affects something else. You can also use cause-and-effect writing to speculate about future events.

The main difficulty you may have when planning a cause-and-effect paragraph is making sure that a **causal relationship** exists—that one event actually *caused* another event and did not just come before it in time. Another problem is considering all possible causes and effects, not just the most obvious ones. As you write, consider the importance of the causes or effects you discuss; don't make a particular cause or effect seem more significant than it actually is, just to strengthen your case.

A cause-and-effect paragraph can focus on causes or on effects. The following paragraph examines causes.

> Newspapers are folding. Paper costs are high, but loss of literate readers is much higher. Forty-five percent of adult citizens do not read newspapers. Only 10 percent abstain by choice. The rest have been excluded by their inability to read. Even the most distinguished daily papers are now written at an estimated tenth-grade level. Magazines such as the *Nation, New Republic, Time, Newsweek,* and the *National Review* are written at a minimum of twelfth-grade level. Circulation battles represent a competition for the largest piece of a diminished pie. Enlargement of that pie does not yet seem to have occurred to those who enter these increasingly unhappy competitions. The only successful major paper to be launched in the last decade, *USA Today*, relies on a simplistic lexicon, large headlines, color photographs, and fanciful weather maps that seek to duplicate the instant entertainment on TV.
>
> Jonathan Kozol, *Illiterate America*

The topic sentence identifies the problem the paragraph will discuss. After mentioning one relatively minor cause of the problem (the cost of paper), the paragraph goes on to analyze the primary cause of the problem—illiteracy.

The paragraph below discusses effects.

Topic sentence: cause

First effect: pain disappears

Second effect:
muscle damaged further

> Professional athletes are sometimes severely disadvantaged by trainers whose job it is to keep them in action. The more famous the athlete, the greater the risk that he or she may be subjected to extreme medical measures when injury strikes. The star baseball player whose arm is sore because of a torn muscle or tissue damage may need sustained rest more than anything else. But his team is battling for a place in the World Series; so the trainer or team doctor, called upon to work his magic, reaches for a strong dose of butazolidine or other powerful pain suppressants. Presto, the pain disappears! The pitcher takes his place on the mound and does superbly. That could be the last game, however, in which he is able to throw a ball with full strength. The drugs didn't repair torn muscle or cause the damaged tissue to heal. What they did was to mask the pain, enabling the pitcher to throw hard, further damaging the torn muscle. Little wonder that so many star athletes are cut down in their prime, more the victims of overzealous treatment of their injuries than of the injuries themselves.
>
> Norman Cousins,
> "Pain Is Not the Ultimate Enemy"

The topic sentence identifies the cause of the problem the paragraph will consider. The paragraph then goes on to discuss two effects—the second more important than the first—of the trainer's actions.

For information on how to write a cause-and-effect essay, as well as a list of transitions suitable for cause-and-effect paragraphs and essays, see 14E.

For more on commonly confused words, see 34E.

FOCUS   **Cause and Effect**

Be careful not to confuse the words *affect* and *effect*. *Affect* is a verb meaning "to influence." *Effect* can be a verb meaning "to bring about" or a noun meaning "result."

B   **Writing a Cause-and-Effect Paragraph**

◆ PRACTICE 7-1

Read this cause-and-effect paragraph; then, follow the instructions on page 76.

follow the instructions on page 76.

        The Ultimate High

     <u>Some people associate running only with panting, sweating, and plain and simple torture, but for me and other experienced runners the effect of running is pure pleasure.</u> When I run, it may look as though I'm in agony, with my gaping mouth, soaked brow, and constantly contracting leg muscles. In fact, my daily half-hour run represents a time of complete physical and mental relaxation. As I begin my run, my lungs are immediately refreshed by the clean, open air. The daily tensions built up in my body ease as my muscles stretch and pump, releasing all feelings of anger or frustration. I mentally dive into my run and feel as though I am lifting my feet from the pavement and ascending into the air. My mind wanders and I seem to float, daydreaming about wherever my thoughts take me. I take pride in my effort, signified by the perspiration that trickles down my face and body. After I complete my run and cool down with long, deep breaths, my body tingles and feels energized, as if I had just come off a roller coaster. I am more alert, my concentration is sharper, and my state of mind is relaxed and peaceful. I feel alive. Beginning runners initially experience soreness and fatigue

rather than this kind of "high." They should be patient,
however. As their bodies build up strength and tolerance,
they will no longer equate running with pain but rather
with relief from tension and with greater emotional well-
being.

Scott Weckerly (student)

1. Underline the topic sentence of the paragraph.

2. Does this paragraph deal mainly with the causes or the effects of running? _____*effects*_____ How do you know? *The topic sentence says the*

   paragraph will focus on the "effect of running."

   _____

3. List some of the effects the writer describes. The first effect has been
   listed for you.

   His lungs are refreshed with clean air.

   Tension and frustrations are released.

   He escapes into another world.

   He feels proud of his effort.

   He feels energized afterward, alert and relaxed at the same time.

   _____

◆ **PRACTICE 7-2**

Following are four possible topic sentences for cause-and-effect paragraphs. After each topic sentence, list the effects that could result from the
cause identified in the topic sentence. For example, if you were writing a
paragraph about the effects of excessive drinking on campus, you could
list low grades, health problems, and vandalism.

1. Studying at the last minute can cause a number of problems.

   Answers will vary.

   _____

   _____

2. Learning a second language has many advantages.

   Answers will vary.

   _____

   _____

3. Walking can have some important benefits.

   Answers will vary.

   _____

   _____

4. Impulse buying can have negative effects on a person's finances.

   Answers will vary.

   _____

   _____

◆ **PRACTICE 7-3**

List three causes that could support each of the following topic sentences.

1. The causes of teenage pregnancy are easy to identify.

   Answers will vary.

   _____

   _____

2. Chronic unemployment can have many causes.

   Answers will vary.

   _____

   _____

3. Why is college tuition so expensive?

   Answers will vary.

   _____

   _____

4. Athletes' high salaries can be explained by the principle of supply and demand.

   Answers will vary.

   _____

   _____

5. People own pets for a variety of reasons.

   Answers will vary.

   _____

   _____

◆ PRACTICE 7-4

Choose one of the following topics (or one of your own choice) as the subject of a paragraph that examines causes or effects. Then, on a separate sheet of paper, use one or more of the invention strategies described in 1C to help you think of as many causes or effects as you can for the topic you have chosen.

Why a current television show or movie is popular
Some causes (or effects) of stress
Why so many young Americans do not vote
The negative effects of credit cards
Why teenagers (or adults) drink
The reasons you decided to attend college
The effects of a particular government policy
How becoming a vegetarian might change (or has changed)
    your life
The benefits of home cooking
Why a particular sport is so popular
How an important person in your life influenced you
The effects of violent song lyrics on teenagers
The benefits of e-mail
Why some people find writing so difficult
The effects of a new baby on a household
The major reasons that high school or college students drop out
    of school
How managers can get the best (or the worst) from their
    employees

◆ PRACTICE 7-5

*For more on creating a cluster
diagram, see 1C.*

Review your notes on the topic you chose in Practice 7-4, and create a cluster diagram. Write the topic you have chosen in the center of the page, and draw arrows branching out to specific causes or effects.

◆ PRACTICE 7-6

Choose a few of the most important causes or effects from the cluster diagram you made in Practice 7-5, and list them here.

Answers will vary.
_____

_____

_____

_____

_____

◆ PRACTICE 7-7

Reread your list of causes or effects from Practice 7-6. Then, draft a topic sentence that introduces your topic and communicates the point you will make about it.

Answers will vary.

_____

_____

_____

◆ PRACTICE 7-8

List the causes or effects you will discuss in your paragraph, arranging them in an effective order—for example, from least to most important.

1. *Answers will vary.* _____

2. _____

3. _____

4. _____

◆ PRACTICE 7-9

On a separate sheet of paper, draft your cause-and-effect paragraph. Then, consulting the Self-Assessment Checklist on page 80, revise your paragraph for unity, development, and coherence.

◆ PRACTICE 7-10

On a separate sheet of paper, write a final, edited draft of your cause-and-effect paragraph.

■ WRITING FIRST: Revising and Editing

Look back at your response to the Writing First exercise on page 73, and evaluate your paragraph for unity, development, and coherence. Then, prepare a final, edited draft of your paragraph.

ESL Tip
Do not just mark students' errors; write in corrections and have them rewrite the material. You can decide when to start asking them to make corrections on their own (maybe toward the end of the semester, depending on how often they receive graded assignments).

☑ SELF-ASSESSMENT CHECKLIST:
Writing a Cause-and-Effect Paragraph

Unity

- Does your topic sentence clearly identify the cause or effect on which your paragraph will focus? Does it state your paragraph's main idea?

- Does all your information relate directly to the causes or effects you are discussing?

Development

- Do you need to add other important causes or effects?

- Does your audience need more information about any causes or effects you have included?

Coherence

- Are your causes and effects arranged in a logical order—for example, from least to most important?

- Do you need to add transitional words or phrases?

Comparison and Contrast

PREVIEW

In this chapter, you will learn to write a comparison-and-contrast paragraph.

■ WRITING FIRST

Look at the picture above, which depicts a scene from the 1950s television family sitcom classic *Father Knows Best*. Then, write a comparison-and-contrast paragraph in which you explain how you think your life is different from (or the same as) the lives of the children in the picture.

Word Power

diverge to go in different directions; to differ

generation a group of individuals born and living about the same time

tradition a practice passed down from one generation to another

● **Writing Tip**

Sometimes, your purpose in a comparison-and-contrast paragraph is to analyze two subjects in order to clarify what makes each unique. At other times, your purpose may be to evaluate two subjects in order to determine which has greater merit or worth.

A   Understanding Comparison and Contrast

A **comparison** tells how two things are similar. A **contrast** tells how they are different. A **comparison-and-contrast paragraph** can either examine just similarities or differences, or it can examine both.

Before two things can be compared and contrasted, they need to have a **basis of comparison**—that is, they have to have enough in common so

81

the comparison makes sense. Without at least one significant element in common, there can be no basis of comparison. For example, you would have a difficult time comparing people and bananas. (They do not share any significant characteristics.) You could, however, compare people and chimpanzees: both are mammals, both live in complex social groups, and both are capable of communication.

In general, there are two kinds of comparison-and-contrast para-graphs: *subject-by-subject* and *point-by-point comparisons*. In a **subject-by-subject comparison**, you first discuss all your points about one subject and then all your points about the other subject. When your points about the subjects correspond closely—and they often will—they should be presented in the same order. A subject-by-subject comparison has the following structure.

Subject-by-subject comparison

    Subject A _____

        Point 1 _____

        Point 2 _____

        Point 3 _____

        Point 4 _____

    Subject B _____

        Point 1 _____

        Point 2 _____

        Point 3 _____

        Point 4 _____

The following paragraph is an example of a subject-by-subject comparison.

Topic sentence
Subject 1 (women's conversations)

    <u>First, it is important to note that men and women regard conver-sation quite differently.</u> For women it is a passion, a sport, an activity even more important to life than eating because it doesn't involve weight gain. The first sign of closeness among women is when they find themselves engaging in endless, secretless rounds of conversation with one another. And as soon as a woman begins to relax and feel comfortable in a relationship with a man, she tries to have that type of conversation with him as well. However, the first sign that a man is feeling close to a woman is when he admits that he'd rather she please quiet down so he can hear the TV. A man who feels truly intimate with a woman often reserves for her and her alone the precious gift of one-word answers. Everyone knows that the surest way to spot a success-ful long-term relationship is to look around a restaurant for the table where no one is talking. Ah . . . now *that's* real love.

Subject 2 (men's conversations)

Merrill Markoe, *Men, Women, and Conversation*

This paragraph begins with a topic sentence that states the main idea of the paragraph and indicates that the paragraph will focus on differences between men and women. The writer then discusses women's ideas about conversation and men's ideas about conversation separately. The transition *however* signals the writer's shift from one subject to the other.

In a **point-by-point comparison**, you discuss each point for *both* subjects before going on to the next point. A point-by-point comparison has the following structure.

Point-by-point comparison

    Point 1 _____
        Subject A _____
        Subject B _____
    Point 2 _____
        Subject A _____
        Subject B _____
    Point 3 _____
        Subject A _____
        Subject B _____
    Point 4 _____
        Subject A _____
        Subject B _____

● **Writing Tip**

Many everyday writing tasks call for comparison and contrast. For example, you might write a paragraph comparing the qualifications of two people applying for the same job at your workplace.

The following paragraph is an example of a point-by-point comparison.

After being a fan of both football and baseball for years, I have begun to understand how different these games really are. Football is much more violent than baseball. In football, the object is to tackle the opponent. The harder the hit, the better the tackle. As a result, many football players are injured each year. In baseball, however, violence is not the object of the game. If a player gets hurt, it is usually because of an accident, such as two players running into each other or a batter being hit by a pitch. The language used to describe each game is also different. The language of football is like the language of war: linemen "blitz," quarterbacks "throw bombs," tacklers "crush" receivers, and games end in "sudden-death" overtime. The language of baseball, however, is peaceful: hitters "bunt" or "pop up," runners "slide," and pitchers throw curves or sliders. Finally, the pace of each game is different. Football is played against the clock. When the clock runs down, the game ends, and the side with the most points wins. In baseball, however, the game does not end until nine innings have been completed or a tie has been broken. Theoretically, a game could go on for days—or even forever. Even though football and baseball are so different, I like them both. When I want to let off steam, I prefer football, and when I want to relax and sit in the sun, I like baseball.

Trent Patterson (student)

Topic sentence

Point 1 (level of violence is different)

Point 2 (language is different)

Point 3 (pace is different)

Concluding statement

Like a subject-by-subject comparison, this point-by-point comparison begins with a topic sentence that states the main idea of the paragraph and indicates whether the paragraph will focus on similarities or on differences. The rest of the paragraph discusses three points of contrast, with each point made about both subjects—first for football and then for baseball—before the writer moves on to the next point. Shifts from one subject to another are signaled by the transition *however* and the words *football* and *baseball*.

For information on how to write a comparison-and-contrast essay, as well as a list of transitions suitable for comparison-and-contrast paragraphs and essays, see 14F.

FOCUS Comparison

A subject-by-subject comparison works well if you are discussing relatively few points for each subject and if you can be sure that readers can keep these points in mind as they read. A point-by-point comparison is best for a paragraph in which you discuss many points because it enables readers to identify the individual points of the comparison as they proceed.

B **Writing a Comparison-and-Contrast Paragraph**

◆ **PRACTICE 8-1**

Read this comparison-and-contrast paragraph; then, follow the instructions on the next page.

Comparing the British and
American Education Systems

The British system of education is very different from the American system. First, most American children have only one year of kindergarten, beginning at age five. Under the British system, children begin kindergarten at age four and then go on to another year of more advanced kindergarten called "preparatory" or "prep," which is comparable to American first grade. Starting in seventh grade, most American students study basic subjects separately, devoting a semester to algebra, for example, and another semester to geometry. However, under the British system, algebra, geometry, and trigonometry are taught together in a single course that is then repeated at a higher level in each grade. Also, in American high schools some classes, particularly electives, may include sophomores, juniors, and seniors. In schools run according to the British system, students at different levels, or "forms," are not mixed in classes; each form attends all its classes together. Finally, American students generally graduate after their twelfth year of school, and senior year is just another year of course work. British students, on the other hand, finish everything they need to learn in secondary school during the first term of their eleventh year of school. During the second term, they study for comprehensive final exams that cover everything they have learned

for the last three and a half years. These exams, which
include three separate tests for every subject, are taken
during the final term.

Lisa Van Hoboken (student)

1. Underline the topic sentence of the paragraph.

2. Does this paragraph deal mainly with similarities or differences?

_____differences_____ How do you know? _The topic sentence points_

to differences.

3. Is this paragraph a subject-by-subject or point-by-point comparison?

_____point-by-point_____ How do you know? _Discussion of points_

alternates between American and British systems.

4. List some of the contrasts the writer describes. The first contrast has
been listed for you.

American students start kindergarten at age five, while students in

British schools start kindergarten at age four.

American students study subjects separately, but in the British system

students study all branches of a subject in one course.

American classes may include students in different grades, but in the

British system, classes do not mix levels.

American students don't prepare for comprehensive tests in their final year

as students in the British system do.

◆ PRACTICE 8-2

Following are four possible topic sentences. List three similarities or differences for the two subjects being considered in the topic sentence. For
example, if you were writing a paragraph comparing health care provided
by a local clinic with health care provided by a private physician, you
could discuss cost, the length of waiting time, the quality of care, and the
frequency of follow-up visits.

1. My mother (or father) and I are very much alike (or different).

Answers will vary.

2. My friends and I have similar views on _____.

Answers will vary.

_____

_____

3. Democrats and Republicans have two very different ways of trying to solve the country's problems.

Answers will vary.

_____

_____

4. Two of my college instructors have very different teaching styles.

Answers will vary.

_____

_____

◆ **PRACTICE 8-3**

Choose one of the topics below (or one of your own choice) as the subject of a paragraph exploring similarities or differences. On a separate sheet of paper, use one or more of the invention strategies described in 1C to help you think of as many similarities and differences as you can for the topic you have chosen. (If you use clustering, create a separate cluster diagram for each of the two subjects you are comparing.)

Two popular television or radio talk-show hosts
Dog owners versus cat owners
A common perception of something versus its reality
How you act in two different situations (home and work, for example) or with two different sets of people (such as your family and your friends)
Two ads for similar products directed at different audiences
Two different bosses
Men's and women's attitudes toward dating, shopping, or conversation
Your goals when you were a child versus your goals today
Public school education versus home schooling
Two competing consumer items, such as two car models, two computer systems, or two types of cell phones
Two relatives who have very different personalities
Two different kinds of vacations
Two generations' attitudes toward a particular issue or subject (for example, how people in their forties and people in their teens view religion or politics)

◆ PRACTICE 8-4

Review your notes on the topic you chose in Practice 8-3, and decide
whether to focus on similarities or differences. On the following lines, list
the similarities or differences that can help you develop a comparison-and-
contrast paragraph on the topic you have selected.

Answers will vary.

◆ PRACTICE 8-5

Reread your list of similarities or differences from Practice 8-4. Then, draft
a topic sentence that introduces your two subjects and suggests your
purpose for comparing or contrasting them.

Answers will vary.

◆ PRACTICE 8-6

In the space below, outline a plan for your paragraph. If you plan to use a
subject-by-subject comparison, decide which subject you will discuss first.
If you plan to use a point-by-point comparison, decide on the order in
which you will present your points—for example, from least important to
most important.

Subject-by-subject comparison

    Subject A ___*Answers will vary.*___

        Point 1 _____

        Point 2 _____

        Point 3 _____

        Point 4 _____

    Subject B ___*Answers will vary.*___

        Point 1 _____

        Point 2 _____

        Point 3 _____

        Point 4 _____

Point-by-point comparison

    Point 1 ___*Answers will vary.*___

        Subject A _____

        Subject B _____

8 B

Point 2 _____ *Answers will vary.* _____

    Subject A _____

    Subject B _____

Point 3 _____ *Answers will vary.* _____

    Subject A _____

    Subject B _____

Point 4 _____ *Answers will vary.* _____

    Subject A _____

    Subject B _____

◆ PRACTICE 8-7

On a separate sheet of paper, draft your comparison-and-contrast paragraph. Then, consulting the Self-Assessment Checklist below, revise your paragraph for unity, development, and coherence.

◆ PRACTICE 8-8

On a separate sheet of paper, write a final, edited draft of your comparison-and-contrast paragraph.

ESL Tip

Pay special attention to students' sentence structure and to their use of articles and prepositions. You might also spot-check verb forms. These areas often cause difficulty for nonnative speakers.

■ WRITING FIRST: Revising and Editing

Look back at your response to the Writing First exercise on page 81, and evaluate your paragraph for unity, development, and coherence. Then, prepare a final, edited draft of your paragraph.

☑ SELF-ASSESSMENT CHECKLIST:
Writing a Comparison-and-Contrast Paragraph

Unity

    ◻ Does your topic sentence indicate whether you are stressing similarities or differences? Does it state your paragraph's main idea?

    ◻ Does all your information relate directly to the similarities or differences between your two subjects?

(continued on the following page)

(continued from the previous page)

Development

- Is there a basis of comparison between your two subjects?

- Do you need to include more similarities? More differences?

Coherence

- Have you used a subject-by-subject or a point-by-point comparison? Is this type of comparison appropriate for your subject?

- Would arranging points in a different order be more effective?

- If your paragraph is a subject-by-subject comparison, have you treated the points for the second subject in the same order as the points for the first subject?

- Do you need to add any transitional words or phrases?

9

Classification

Word Power

enthusiastic having or
showing great excitement or
interest; eager

fanatic someone who has
extreme enthusiasm for a
cause

■ WRITING FIRST

Look at the picture above, and then write a paragraph in which you
discuss the various types of fans of a particular sport.

A Understanding Classification

Classification is the activity of sorting items (people, things, ideas) into
categories. In a **classification paragraph**, you tell readers how a collection of items can be sorted into categories. Each of the categories into
which you classify information must be *distinct:* an item cannot fit into more
than one category. For example, you would not classify novels into mysteries, romance novels, and paperbacks because a mystery or romance
novel could also be a paperback.

The topic sentence of a classification paragraph identifies the subject (the group of items being discussed) and the categories into which items will be sorted. The rest of the paragraph considers the categories in the order in which they are mentioned in the topic sentence. The following is an example of a classification paragraph.

Topic sentence

I can classify my friends into three categories: those who know what they want out of life, those who don't have a clue, and those who are searching for goals. In the first category are those who know what they want; they are the most mature. They know exactly what they want to do for the rest of their lives. Although these friends will most likely be successful, they are the most predictable and therefore the most boring. In the second category are those who don't have a clue; they are the most immature. They seem to live for the minute and do not think much about the future. If there is a party the night before a big test, they will go to the party and then try to study when they get back. Although these friends can be a bad influence, they are the most fun. In the third category are those who are searching for goals; they are somewhere between the other two types when it comes to maturity. They do not know exactly what they want to do with their lives, but they realize that they should be trying to find a goal. Although these friends can sometimes be unpredictable, their willingness to try new things makes them by far the most interesting.

Category 1

Category 2

Category 3

Daniel Corey (student)

The topic sentence clearly identifies the paragraph's subject—friends—and the three categories into which individual friends will be sorted. The rest of the paragraph discusses these three categories, one at a time. The shift from one category to another is signaled by the transitional phrases *the first category*, *the second category*, and *the third category*.

For information on how to write a classification essay, as well as a list of transitions suitable for classification paragraphs and essays, see 14G.

FOCUS **Classification**

Before you can classify information, you must decide what your focus will be when you choose your categories. For example, instructors can be classified according to their knowledge or their teaching ability, and computers can be classified according to their speed at processing information or their ease of use.

B   Writing a Classification Paragraph

◆ PRACTICE 9-1

Read this classification paragraph; then, follow the instructions below it.

9 B

Three Kinds of Shoppers

Shoppers can be broken into three categories. (The first category) is made up of pragmatic shoppers; they shop because they need something. Pragmatic shoppers are pur-poseful. You can recognize them because they go right to the item they are looking for in the store and then leave. They do not waste time browsing or walking aimlessly from store to store. For them, shopping is definitely a means to an end. (The next category) is made up of recreational shop-pers; they shop for entertainment. Recreational shoppers usually have too much time on their hands. For them, shop-ping is like going to the movies or out to dinner. They do it because it is fun. They will spend hours walking through stores looking at merchandise. More often than not, they will not buy anything. For recreational shoppers, it is the activity of shopping that counts, not the purchase itself. (The third category) is made up of professional shoppers; they shop because they have to. Professional shoppers are on a mission. For them, shopping is a serious business. You can see them in any mall, carrying four, five, or even six shopping bags. Frequently, an exhausted spouse who carries even more merchandise follows them. For merchants and for credit card companies, professional shoppers are a dream come true.

Kimberly Toomer (student)

1. Underline the topic sentence of the paragraph.

2. What is the subject of the paragraph? _categories of shoppers_
   What three categories of the subject does the writer describe?

   pragmatic shoppers

   recreational shoppers

   professional shoppers

3. Circle the phrases the writer uses to introduce the three categories.

◆ PRACTICE 9-2

Classify the following groups of items into categories.

1. All the items on your desk

   Answers will vary.

2. Buildings on your college campus

Answers will vary.

_____   _____

_____   _____

_____   _____

3. Magazines or newspapers you read

Answers will vary.

_____   _____

_____   _____

_____   _____

4. The various parts of a piece of equipment you use for a course or on the job

Answers will vary.

_____   _____

_____   _____

_____   _____

◆ PRACTICE 9-3

Choose one of the topics below (or one of your own choice) as the subject of a classification paragraph. On a separate sheet of paper, use one or more of the invention strategies described in 1C to help you classify the members of the group you have chosen into as many categories as necessary.

Your friends   Popular music
Drivers   Fitness routines
Commuters on public transportation   Popular Web sites
Television shows   Part-time jobs
Employees or bosses   Teachers
Parents or children   Popular movies
Types of success   T-shirt slogans
Radio stations

◆ PRACTICE 9-4

Review the information you came up with for the topic you chose in Practice 9-3. On the following lines, list three or four categories you can develop in your paragraph.

Category 1: *Answers will vary.* _____

Category 2: _____

Category 3: _____

Category 4: _____

◆ PRACTICE 9-5

Reread the list you made in Practice 9-4. Then, draft a topic sentence that introduces your subject and the categories you will discuss.

Answers will vary.

_____

_____

_____

◆ PRACTICE 9-6

List below the categories you will discuss in your classification paragraph in the order in which you will discuss them.

1. *Answers will vary.* _____

2. _____

3. _____

4. _____

◆ PRACTICE 9-7

On a separate sheet of paper, write your classification paragraph. Then, consult the Self-Assessment Checklist on page 95, revise your paragraph for unity, development, and coherence.

◆ PRACTICE 9-8

On a separate sheet of paper, write a final, edited draft of your classification paragraph.

■ WRITING FIRST: Revising and Editing

Look back at your response to the Writing First exercise on page 90, and evaluate your paragraph for unity, development, and coherence. Then, prepare a final, edited draft of your paragraph.

☑ SELF-ASSESSMENT CHECKLIST:
Writing a Classification Paragraph

Unity

- ☐ Does your topic sentence identify the categories you will discuss? Does it state your paragraph's main idea—the point your classification paragraph makes?

- ☐ Does all your information support your topic sentence or relate to your subject and its categories?

Development

- ☐ Do you need to include additional categories?

- ☐ Do you need to include more examples or more specific information for any category?

Coherence

- ☐ Do you need to rearrange categories (or details within categories)?

- ☐ Do you need to add transitional words or phrases?

Teaching Tip
Divide the class into pairs, and have students use the checklist to help them critique each other's paragraphs.

Definition

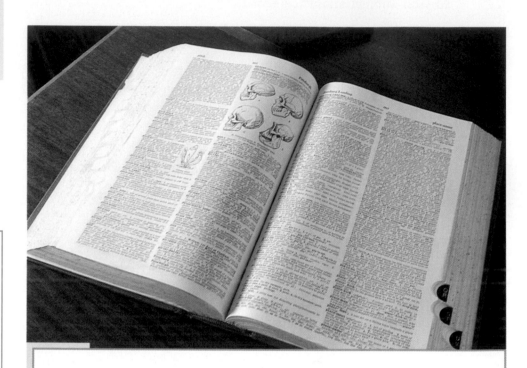

■ WRITING FIRST

Look at the picture above. Then, write a one-paragraph definition of a word you learned in one of your college courses. Assume that your readers are not familiar with the term you are defining.

A Understanding Definition

A **definition** explains what a term means. When you want your readers to know exactly how you are using a certain term or an unfamiliar concept, you use definition.

When most people think of definitions, they think of the one- or two-sentence **formal definitions** they see in a dictionary. These definitions have a three-part structure that includes the term to be defined, the general class to which the term belongs, and the characteristics that make the term different from all other terms in that class.

Term	Class	Differentiation
A pineapple	is a tropical fruit	that has large swordlike leaves and yellow edible fruit.
Basketball	is a game	played between two teams in which the object is to put a ball through an elevated basket on the opponent's side of a rectangular court.

A single-sentence formal definition may not be enough to define an abstract concept (*envy* or *democracy,* for example), a technical term, or a complex subject. In such cases, you may need to expand this definition by writing a **definition paragraph**. A **definition paragraph** usually includes the three components of a formal definition, but it does not follow a particular pattern of development. It may define a term or concept by using examples, by outlining a process, or by using any of the other patterns discussed in this text. A definition paragraph may even define a term by using **negation**, telling what the term is not—for example, that a bicycle is *not* a motorized vehicle.

In a definition paragraph, the topic sentence identifies the term to be defined (and may briefly define it as well). The rest of the paragraph develops the definition by means of one or more of the patterns of development discussed in Chapters 3–11. The following paragraph defines the term *business casual.*

Many businesses allow business casual dress on Fridays; others permit it all the time. As a result, more and more people are finding themselves asking, "What is business casual?" <u>Broadly speaking, business casual means dressing professionally but also looking relaxed.</u> For women, this usually means wearing a skirt or slacks with a blouse or sweater. For men, it means no tie—and certainly no suit. Khakis and a short-sleeved knit shirt are popular in the summer; in other seasons, men wear a jacket over a shirt left open at the collar. Business casual, however, is not a license for being sloppy or dressing inappropriately. In other words, it does not mean wearing shorts, low-cut shirts, tank or halter tops, sandals, flip-flops, jeans, or T-shirts.

Melissa Morris (student)

Topic sentence

Series of examples

Negation

The topic sentence introduces the term the paragraph will define. The paragraph goes on to define the term, using several short examples to illustrate the definition. The paragraph ends with negation—telling what the term *business casual* does not mean.

For information on how to write a definition essay, as well as a list of transitions suitable for definition paragraphs and essays, see 14H.

Topic sentence

History and background:
comparison and contrast

Explanation of current function:
process

The following paragraph defines a piece of gymnastics equipment—
the pommel horse.

<u>The pommel horse is of ancient origin.</u> The Romans used it for the
very practical purpose of training soldiers to mount horses. Some suggest it was used even earlier, by the bull dancers of Minoan Crete.
Jumping over the bulls by doing springs off the animals' horns, these
dancers surely must have practiced on something a little tamer than a
live bull. Today, the pommel horse events are less exciting. The gymnast performs intricate leg-swinging movements while supporting his
weight on his hands, which are either grasping the pommels or lying
flat on the leather of the horse. As he swings his legs so that one
follows, or "shadows," the other, the gymnast demonstrates strength,
balance, and timing. Exercises such as single or double leg circles and
scissors must be done continuously and in both directions. The pommel horse is difficult to master and not a favorite among gymnasts;
they call it "the beast."

Ford Hovis, *The Sports Encyclopedia*

Here, the writer defines an object in terms of its history and its current
function, using comparison and contrast and process to develop his
definition.

FOCUS **Definition**

In general, avoid including a dictionary definition in your definition
paragraph. After all, readers can look up a term themselves. Your
definition paragraph should show how *you* define a term—not how
a dictionary does.

B **Writing a Definition Paragraph**

◆ **PRACTICE 10-1**

Read this definition paragraph; then, follow the instructions on page 99.

Writer's Block

Have you ever sat staring at a blank notebook page
or computer screen, searching your brain for words and
ideas, fidgeting with frustration, and longing to be anywhere else? If so, you probably want to know more about
writer's block, a condition that afflicts ten out of
ten writers at some point during their lives. <u>Simply</u>

stated, writer's block is the inability to start a piece of
writing. For nonprofessionals, writer's block almost
always involves assigned writing, such as a paper for
school or a report for work. (People rarely feel blocked
when they are writing simply for pleasure.) Sometimes
writer's block is caused by poor preparation: the writer
has not allowed enough time to think and make notes that
will pave the way for the actual writing of a draft. However, even prepared writers with many ideas already on
paper can experience writer's block. It is comparable to
being tongue-tied, only this kind of writer's block is more
like being brain-tied. All the ideas keep bouncing around
but will not settle into any order, and the writer cannot
decide what to say first. When the agony of writer's block
strikes, often the only cure is to give up and find another time to start.

Thaddeus Eddy (student)

1. Underline the topic sentence of the paragraph.

2. What is the subject of this definition? _writer's block_

3. What is the writer's one-sentence definition of the subject?

   Simply stated, writer's block is the inability to start a piece of writing.

4. List some of the specific information the writer uses to define his subject. The first piece of information has been listed for you.

   It causes fidgeting and a desire to escape.

   It usually involves assigned writing.

   It can be caused by poor preparation.

   It's like being "brain-tied."

5. What patterns of development does the writer use in his definition?
   List them here.

   uses description of writer's block

   uses examples of writer's block

   uses cause and effect to explain cause of writer's block

◆ PRACTICE 10-2

Following are four possible topic sentences for definition paragraphs.
Each topic sentence includes an underlined word. In the space provided,
list two possible patterns of development that you could use to expand a
definition of the underlined word. For example, you could define the word
feminist by giving examples and by telling a story.

1. During the interview, the job candidate made a <u>sexist</u> comment.

    Possible strategy: _Answers will vary._

    Possible strategy: _Answers will vary._

2. <u>Loyalty</u> is one of the chief characteristics of golden retrievers.

    Possible strategy: _Answers will vary._

    Possible strategy: _Answers will vary._

3. More than forty years after President Johnson's Great Society initiative, we have yet to eliminate <u>poverty</u> in the United States.

    Possible strategy: _Answers will vary._

    Possible strategy: _Answers will vary._

4. The problem with movies today is that they are just too <u>violent</u>.

    Possible strategy: _Answers will vary._

    Possible strategy: _Answers will vary._

◆ **PRACTICE 10-3**

Teaching Tip
Encourage students to
choose a topic from one of
their other courses, if they
wish. By doing so, students
can see how strategies they
learn in this course can be
helpful in other disciplines.

Choose one of the topics below (or one of your own choice) as the subject of a definition paragraph. On a separate sheet of paper, use one or more of the invention strategies described in 1C to help you define the term you have chosen to discuss. Name the term, and then describe it, give examples of it, tell how it works, explain its purpose, consider its history or future, compare it to other similar things; in short, do whatever works best for defining your specific subject.

> A negative quality, such as envy or dishonesty
> An ideal, such as the ideal friend or neighborhood
> A type of person, such as a worrier or a show-off
> A social concept, such as equality, opportunity, or discrimination
> An important play in a particular sport or game
> A hobby you pursue or an activity associated with that hobby
> A technical term or specific piece of equipment that you use in your job
> An object (such as an article of clothing) that is important to your culture or religion
> A basic concept in a course you are taking
> A particular style of music or dancing
> A controversial subject whose definition not all people agree on, such as affirmative action or date rape
> A goal in life, such as success or happiness

◆ **PRACTICE 10-4**

Review your notes for the topic you chose in Practice 10-3. On the following lines, list the details that you think you can use to develop a definition paragraph.

Answers will vary.

_____

_____

_____

_____

_____

_____

◆ PRACTICE 10-5

Reread your notes from Practice 10-4. Then, draft a topic sentence that summarizes the main point you want to make about the term you are going to define.

Answers will vary.

_____

_____

_____

_____

◆ PRACTICE 10-6

List the ideas you will discuss in your paragraph, arranging them in an effective order.

1. *Answers will vary.* _____

2. _____

3. _____

4. _____

5. _____

◆ PRACTICE 10-7

On a separate sheet of paper, write your definition paragraph. Then, using the Self-Assessment Checklist on page 102, revise your paragraph for unity, development, and coherence.

◆ PRACTICE 10-8

On a separate sheet of paper, write a final, edited draft of your definition paragraph.

Teaching Tip
Explain the difference between "revising and editing"
and proofreading. On the
board, show students some
commonly used proofread-
ers' marks, such as the caret
and the delete mark.

Teaching Tip
Have students revise
once more using the Self-
Assessment Checklist.

■ **WRITING FIRST: Revising and Editing**

Look back at your response to the Writing First exercise on
page 96, and evaluate your paragraph for unity, development, and
coherence. Then, prepare a final, edited draft of your paragraph.

☑ SELF-ASSESSMENT CHECKLIST:
Writing a Definition Paragraph

Unity

- Do you define your term clearly in your topic sentence?

- Does your topic sentence state your paragraph's main idea—
the point you want to make about the term you are defining?

- Does all your information support your topic sentence?

Development

- Do you use an appropriate pattern (or patterns) of development in your paragraph?

- Would a different pattern of development be more effective?

- Should you use negation to help you define your term?

- Do you need to include more information about your term?

Coherence

- Would arranging the information in a different order make it
clearer or more interesting to readers?

- Do you need to add transitional words or phrases?

Argument

PREVIEW

In this chapter, you
will learn to write an
argument paragraph.

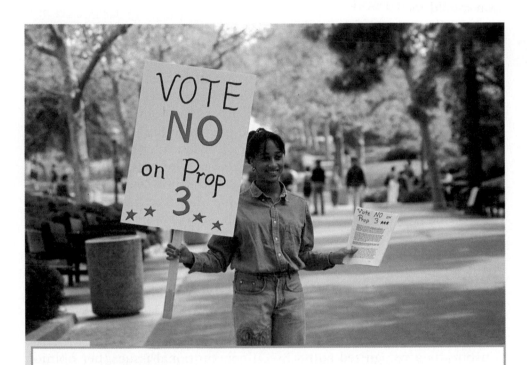

■ WRITING FIRST

Write a paragraph in which you argue for or against one of the
following policies:

- Censoring the Internet
- Putting drunk drivers in jail for their first offense
- Requiring a license for all handguns
- Reinstituting the military draft in the United States
- Enabling people to vote in federal elections on their home
  computers

Include examples from your experience or from your reading to
support your position.

Word Power

controversy a dispute between two parties holding
opposing views

debate to discuss or argue
about

refute to prove false

Teaching Tip
To help students understand
the concept of argument,
photocopy a newspaper editorial or letter to the editor,
and review it in class.

103

Topic sentence

Facts and examples

A **Understanding Argument**

An **argument** takes a position on a debatable subject. When you write an
argument paragraph, your purpose is to persuade readers that your particular position has merit. The topic sentence states your position. In the
rest of the paragraph, you support the points you make with **evidence**—
facts, examples, and *expert opinions.* The paragraph ends with a conclusion
that sums up your position.

A **fact** is information that can be verified. For example, it is a fact that
A comes before G in the alphabet and that the Canadian ice hockey team
won a gold medal in the 2002 Olympics. If you make the point that students are less prepared for college today than they were twenty years ago,
you should support it with facts—for example, by citing SAT scores and
college dropout rates. Avoid sweeping statements that are not supported
by facts from encyclopedias, newspapers, or other reliable sources.

An **example** is a specific illustration of a general statement. To be
convincing, an example should relate clearly to the point you are making.
For example, to support a point that the quality of life in your neighborhood has improved recently, you could discuss a number of new businesses that have opened and several neighbors who have spent time and
money improving their properties. Make sure, however, that your examples are typical, not exceptional. For instance, the fact that one new
business has opened is not enough to establish that your neighborhood is
improving.

An **expert** is someone who is generally recognized as knowledgeable
about a particular subject. The opinion of an expert who supports your
view on a subject can be very persuasive. For example, if you wanted to
argue that censoring the Internet would undercut people's freedom of
speech, you could quote an expert on constitutional law such as Ruth
Bader Ginsburg, a justice of the United States Supreme Court. Because
Ginsburg is a recognized authority on constitutional issues, her opinion
carries a great deal of weight. Remember, though, that an expert in one
field is not necessarily an expert in another field. For instance, Ginsburg's
personal opinion about stem-cell research would have less value than the
opinion of someone who has spent most of his or her life studying this
subject.

The following paragraph argues against the use of Astroturf surfaces
in sports stadiums.

Sports stadiums built during the 1960s and 1970s use Astroturf
because it requires little maintenance and creates a uniform playing
surface. But recently it has become clear that Astroturf has caused so
many injuries that it should be eliminated from all pro sports stadiums. Anyone who follows baseball or football knows that Astroturf
causes many knee and ankle injuries. The main reason for this situation is that it does not absorb impact the way a natural grass surface
does. Astroturf consists of a layer of rough artificial grass on top of a
layer of padding. Beneath these layers is a cement pad. Players who fall
on Astroturf or, in the case of football, are thrown down onto it, risk
serious injury. The New York Giants, for example, lost tight end Mark
Bavaro to knee injuries caused by his falling on the artificial surface of

the Meadowlands Stadium. And the Astroturf surface in Philadelphia's Veterans Stadium, long known by players to be the worst in the country, has caused the Eagles to lose a number of key players. As sports columnist Bill Lyon points out, when you sit in the stands of Veterans Stadium, you can see the gaps where sections of the Astroturf do not meet properly. When a player catches a foot in these gaps, the result can be a painful sprain or worse. The situations in Philadelphia and New Jersey are not unique. You can see the same problems in every stadium that has an Astroturf playing surface. For this reason, players, owners, and fans should insist that stadiums remove Astroturf and restore natural grass surfaces.

Toni-Ann Marro (student)

The paragraph begins with a sentence that gives some background. The topic sentence then states the writer's position. After stating that Astroturf causes injuries, the paragraph presents facts, examples, and comments by experts that support the writer's position. The paragraph ends with a conclusion based on the evidence presented. Throughout the paragraph, transitional words and phrases—*the main reason, for example,* and *for this reason*—lead readers through the argument.

For information on how to write an argument essay, as well as a list of transitions suitable for argument paragraphs and essays, see 14I.

FOCUS Audience

In addition to presenting evidence to support your argument, you need to consider the effect of your argument on your audience. Before you write, try to determine whether your readers are likely to be hostile, friendly, or neutral to your position. Let your analysis of your audience determine the approach you use.

For example, if you suspect your audience may not be receptive to your position, you might mention their possible objections in your topic sentence before stating your position. In your paragraph, you can **refute** (argue against) those objections.

> Although some people may argue that students will be shortchanged [possible objection], a core curriculum will actually benefit most students at Baker County Community College [position].

You can also address possible audience objections in the paragraph itself, stating the major argument against your position and then refuting it by showing that it is incorrect, shortsighted, or illogical. For example, for the argument outlined above, you could say that people who object to a core curriculum fail to understand that students should receive a well-rounded education, not just training for a particular job.

● **Writing Tip**

Many everyday writing tasks call for argument. For example, in a letter to your local school board, you might argue against raising class size in the elementary school.

Teaching Tip

Point out the importance of being open-minded enough to include opposing arguments.

B   **Writing an Argument Paragraph**

◆ PRACTICE 11-1

Read this argument paragraph; then, follow the instructions below.

Big Brother in the Workplace

<u>Employers should not routinely monitor the computer
use of their employees.</u> First of all, monitoring computer
use violates an employee's privacy. Every day, employees
use their computers for work-related tasks, and every
keystroke they make is recorded. In addition, companies
routinely read employees' private e-mail files as well
as monitor the sites they visit on the Internet. This
monitoring creates an unpleasant work environment because
employees feel that someone is always watching them. At
some companies, employees have even been fired for sending
personal e-mails or for sending humorous pictures to one
another. Of course, companies that believe computers should
be used only for work-related tasks have a point. After
all, the company pays for both the computers and the
employees' time. The problem with this line of thinking,
however, is that it ignores the fact that workers need to
feel secure in order to work effectively. It therefore
makes sense that a limited use of computers for personal
reasons (to send e-mails to friends, for example) should be
allowed--just as coffee breaks are. Unless the company has
reason to suspect misuse of company computers, it should
not routinely monitor all employees' computers. Putting an
end to this type of surveillance would not only create a
more relaxed workplace, but it would also make it possible
for employees to work more efficiently.

Scott Rathmill (student)

1. Underline the topic sentence of the paragraph.

2. What controversial subject is the writer dealing with?

   personal privacy for computer use at work

   What is the writer's position?

   Employers should not routinely monitor the computer use of their

   employees.

3. What points does the writer use to support his topic sentence?

   Monitoring computer use violates an employee's privacy.

   Monitoring computer use creates an unpleasant work environment.

4. List some of the evidence that the writer uses to support his points. The first piece of evidence has been listed for you.

Every keystroke an employee makes is recorded.

Companies routinely monitor personal e-mails as well as other uses.

Some companies have fired employees for sending personal e-mails or

humorous pictures to one another.

5. What evidence (facts, examples, expert opinion) does the writer use to support his points?

He uses facts and examples.

6. What other evidence could the writer have used?

He could have presented statements by experts about the effects of

monitoring employees' personal use of computers. He also could have

presented additional factual information in the form of statistics. Finally,

he could have given specific examples of workers who were fired.

7. What opposing argument does the writer address?

Computers should be used only for work-related tasks.

8. How does the writer refute this argument?

He shows how it is shortsighted because it ignores the fact that workers

need to socialize sometimes.

◆ PRACTICE 11-2

Following are four topic sentences for argument paragraphs. For each topic sentence, list two or three points that could support the topic sentence. For example, if you were arguing in support of laws requiring motorcycle riders to wear safety helmets, you could say they cut down on medical costs and save lives.

1. Marijuana use for certain medical conditions should be legalized.

Answers will vary.

2. All student athletes should be paid a salary by their college or university.

Answers will vary.

3. College students caught cheating should be expelled.

Answers will vary.

_____

_____

_____

_____

4. The government should provide free health care for all senior citizens.

Answers will vary.

_____

_____

_____

_____

◆ PRACTICE 11-3

Choose one of the topic sentences from Practice 11-2. Then, list two pieces of evidence that could support each point you listed. For example, if you said that wearing safety helmets saves lives, you could list accident statistics and statements by emergency room physicians.

Answers will vary.

_____

_____

_____

◆ PRACTICE 11-4

Choose one of the topics below (or one of your own choice) as the subject of an argument paragraph. Then, on a separate sheet of paper, use one or more of the invention strategies described in 1C to help you focus on a specific issue to discuss in an argument paragraph.

An issue related to your school

Grading policies
Required courses
Entrance requirements
Attendance policies
Course offerings

Financial aid
Student activity fees
Childcare facilities
Sexual harassment policies
The physical condition of classrooms

A community issue

The need for a traffic signal, a youth center, or something else you
think would benefit your community
An action you think local officials should take, such as changing
school hours, cleaning up a public eyesore, or improving a specific
service

A new law you would like to see enacted
A current law you would like to see repealed
A controversy you have been following in the news

◆ PRACTICE 11-5

Once you have chosen an issue in Practice 11-4, write a journal entry about your position on the issue. Consider the following questions: Why do you feel the way you do? Do you think many people share your views, or do you think you are in the minority? What specific actions do you think should be taken? What objections are likely to be raised against your position? How might you respond to these objections?

◆ PRACTICE 11-6

Review your notes for the topic you chose in Practice 11-4, and select the points that best support your position. List these points below. (You may also want to list the strongest objections to your position.)

Answers will vary.

Supporting points: _____

_____

Objections: _____

_____

◆ PRACTICE 11-7

Draft a topic sentence that clearly expresses the position you will take in your paragraph.

Answers will vary.

_____

_____

◆ PRACTICE 11-8

In the space provided, arrange the points that support your position in an order that you think will be convincing to your audience.

1. *Answers will vary.*

2. _____

3. _____

4. _____

5. _____

◆ **PRACTICE 11-9**

In the space provided, list the evidence (facts, examples) that you could use to support each of your points.

Answers will vary.

Evidence for point 1: _____

_____

Evidence for point 2: _____

_____

Evidence for point 3: _____

_____

◆ **PRACTICE 11-10**

On a separate sheet of paper, draft your argument paragraph. Then, consulting the Self-Assessment Checklist below, revise your paragraph for unity, development, and coherence.

◆ **PRACTICE 11-11**

On a separate sheet of paper, write a final, edited draft of your argument paragraph.

Teaching Tip
Because argument paragraphs can be hard to organize, you might require students to write outlines before they begin.

■ WRITING FIRST: Revising and Editing

Look back at your response to the Writing First exercise on page 103, and evaluate your paragraph for unity, development, and coherence. Then, prepare a final, edited draft of your paragraph.

Teaching Tip
Hold a class debate. Divide the class into two groups, and have the groups take opposing positions on a controversial topic. Record their responses on the board under Arguments, Possible Objections, and Refutations.

☑ SELF-ASSESSMENT CHECKLIST:
Writing an Argument Paragraph

Unity

☐ Does your topic sentence clearly state your position?

☐ Is all your information directly related to your topic sentence?

☐ Do you need to revise your topic sentence to accommodate new ideas?

(continued on the following page)

(continued from the previous page)

Development

- [ ] Have you made enough points to support your topic sentence?

- [ ] Do you need more facts or other evidence to convince your audience to accept any of your points?

- [ ] Have you mentioned the major arguments against your position?

- [ ] Have you refuted these arguments?

- [ ] Do you need to use one or more of the invention strategies discussed in 1C to help you come up with more ideas?

Coherence

- [ ] Would arranging ideas in a different order make your argument more convincing to readers?

- [ ] Do you need to add transitional words or phrases?

UNIT THREE

Focus on Essays

Writing an Essay

PREVIEW

In this chapter, you will
learn:

■ to understand essay
structure (12A)

■ to decide on a topic
(12B)

■ to use invention
strategies (12C)

■ to state a thesis
(12D)

■ to arrange ideas
(12E)

■ to draft an essay
(12F)

■ to revise and edit
your essay (12G)

■ WRITING FIRST

What was the worst job you ever had? Look at the picture above, a
famous scene from an episode of *I Love Lucy* in which Lucy and
Ethel go to work at a candy factory, and think about this question
carefully as you read the pages that follow. This is the topic you will
be writing about as you move through this chapter. (If you have
never had a job, you may write about a specific task that you dis-
liked or a bad job that a friend or a relative has had.)

Word Power

dehumanize to deprive of
human qualities

exploit to make use of
selfishly

Most of the writing you do in school will be longer than a single paragraph. Often, you will be asked to write an **essay**—a group of paragraphs
on a single subject. When you write an essay, you follow the same process
you do when you write a paragraph: you move from invention to selecting
and arranging ideas and then to drafting, revising, and editing. Chapters
12 through 14 will show you how to apply the paragraph skills you learned
in Chapters 1 through 11 to writing essays.

*For a discussion of writing
paragraphs, see Chapter 1.*

115

12 A

A   Understanding Essay Structure

Many essays have a **thesis-and-support** structure. The first paragraph of the essay—the **introduction**—begins with opening remarks and ends with a **thesis statement**, which presents the essay's main idea. The **body** of the essay is made up of several paragraphs that support the thesis. Each of these body paragraphs begins with a topic sentence that states the paragraph's main idea and goes on to develop it with details, facts, and examples. The last paragraph—the **conclusion**—restates the thesis in different words and offers the writer's concluding thoughts on the subject.

Essay

Opening remarks introduce the subject to be discussed.

The **thesis statement** presents the main idea of the essay, usually in the last sentence of the first paragraph.

Introduction

Topic sentence (first point)

Support (details, facts, examples)

Topic sentence (second point)

Support (details, facts, examples)

Topic sentence (third point)

Support (details, facts, examples)

Body paragraphs

The **restatement of the thesis** summarizes the essay's main idea.

Closing remarks present the writer's last thoughts on the subject.

Conclusion

◆ **PRACTICE 12-1**

Following is an essay based on the diagram on page 116. Read the essay, and then answer the questions that follow it.

More and more smokers today are aware of the serious risks smoking poses both for themselves and for the nonsmokers around them. Many of them would like to quit but just do not think they can. However, several strategies can help smokers achieve this goal.   Introduction

Thesis statement

The first and easiest strategy is substituting something for the cigarette that they have gotten used to holding. Some people use a pencil, a straw, or a coin. I have a friend who started using a Japanese fan. There are even special products available to keep people's hands busy, such as worry beads and small rubber balls. Almost any small object can work.

Next, people who quit smoking need to substitute something for the stimulation they get from cigarettes. They might chew a strongly flavored sugarless gum, for example, or take fast, short breaths. Other people splash their faces with ice cold water or do some light exercise. Some even claim that standing on their heads has helped. The point is to find something that gives a physical jolt to the system.

A third strategy is to change habits associated with smoking. For example, people who associate cigarettes with drinking coffee might temporarily switch to tea or another beverage with caffeine, while people who generally smoke while on the telephone might try using e-mail instead of making long-distance calls. Unfortunately, some smoking-associated activities are difficult to eliminate. People who associate smoking with being in their cars obviously cannot give up driving. The point, though, is to alter as many habits as possible to eliminate times when one would normally reach for a cigarette.   Body paragraphs

Finally, most people who successfully quit smoking prepare themselves to resist temptation in moments of stress or discomfort. Rather than reaching for a cigarette, they have another sort of treat ready for themselves. Some people, understandably, choose candy or sweets of some kind, but these are not the best alternatives, for obvious reasons. A better idea is to use the money saved by not buying cigarettes to purchase something to pamper oneself with, such as expensive cologne or a personal CD player.

No one would say that it is easy to quit smoking, but this fact should not keep people from recognizing that they can kick the habit. These four antismoking strategies have worked for many ex-smokers, who recommend them highly.   Conclusion

12 B

1. What is the essay's thesis? Write it below in your own words.

   Several strategies can help people learn to stop smoking.

2. What point does the first body paragraph make?

   Substituting another object for the cigarette they have gotten used to

   holding can help smokers quit.

3. What point does the second body paragraph make?

   People also need to substitute something for the stimulation they get

   from cigarettes.

4. What point does the third body paragraph make?

   People who want to stop smoking need to change habits associated

   with smoking.

5. What point does the fourth body paragraph make?

   People who want to quit smoking have to be ready to resist temptation

   when they are under stress.

6. At what point in the conclusion does the writer restate the essay's thesis?

   The last sentence restates the essay's thesis.

◆ PRACTICE 12-2

How does the writer of the essay on page 117 develop the points made in
the body paragraphs?

   Body paragraph 1: Examples of substitutes for holding cigarettes.

   Body paragraph 2: Examples of substitutes for the stimulation of cigarettes.

   Body paragraph 3: Examples of ways to break habits and advice for

   doing so.

   Body paragraph 4: Examples of treats to help resist smoking.

B   Deciding on a Topic

Most of the essays you will write in college begin as an **assignment** given
to you by your instructor. The following assignments are typical of those
you might be given in your composition class.

A. Discuss some things you would like to change about your school.

B. What can college students do to improve the environment?

C. Describe something you do outside of school that contributes to your education.

Because these assignments are so general, it would be difficult—if not impossible—to write about them. What specific things would you change? Exactly what could you do to improve the environment? Which activity outside of school should you write about? Answering these questions will help you narrow these assignments into **topics** that you can write about.

Assignment	*Topic*
Discuss some things you would change about your school.	Three things I would change to improve the quality of life at Jackson County Community College
What can college students do to improve the environment?	The campus recycling project
Describe something you do outside of school that contributes to your education.	The advantages of having a part-time job in college

For each assignment you are given, try to list several possible topics so that you have choices. For example, if you were assigned to write a four-hundred-word essay about an activity you do outside of school that contributes to your education, you could make the following list of topics.

A. The advantages of having a part-time job in college

B. Volunteering at the neighborhood community center

C. Building houses for the homeless during spring break

D. My week helping at Meals on Wheels

E. My summer job at Disney World

After you make your list, review each topic and choose the one that you can write the best essay about. (The more you know about a topic, the more you will have to write about.) If you have difficulty coming up with a list of topics, try freewriting or brainstorming for a short period of time. If you still have difficulty, brainstorm with some of your classmates or make an appointment with your instructor.

For more on freewriting and brainstorming, see 1C and 12C.

◆ PRACTICE 12-3

Decide whether the following topics are suitable for an essay of four or five paragraphs. If a topic is suitable, write *OK* in the blank. If it is not, write in the blank a revised version of the same topic that is narrow enough for a brief essay.

Examples: Successful strategies for quitting smoking _____ *OK* _____

Horror movies _____ *1950s Japanese monster movies* _____

1. Violence in American public schools _Answers will vary._

   Example: the need to ban weapons in a local high school

2. Ways to improve your study skills _OK_

3. Using pets as therapy for nursing-home patients _OK_

4. Teachers _Answers will vary._

   Example: qualities of an effective teacher

5. Safe ways to lose weight _OK_

6. Clothing styles _Answers will vary._

   Example: the influence of MTV on teenagers' clothing styles

7. Parent-child relationships _Answers will vary._

   Example: strategies for communicating with your child

8. Reasons children lie to their parents _OK_

9. College education _Answers will vary._

   Example: the benefits of going to college

10. Television's impact on children _Answers will vary._

    Example: the influence of violent cartoons on children's behavior

■ WRITING FIRST: Flashback

Look back at the Writing First assignment on page 115. To narrow the topic to one you can write about, you need to decide which job to focus on. On the lines below, list all the possible jobs you could discuss.

_____

_____

_____

_____

C   Using Invention Strategies

Before you start writing about a topic, you have to discover what you have to say about it. Once you have done this, you will be ready to decide on a thesis for your essay. Sometimes, ideas may come to you easily. More often, you will have to use one or more **invention strategies**, such as *freewriting* or *brainstorming*, to help you come up with ideas about your topic.

For a full discussion of invention strategies, see 1C.

Freewriting

When you **freewrite**, you write (or type) for a fixed period of time without stopping. When you engage in **focused freewriting**, you write with a specific topic in mind. Then, you read what you have written and choose the ideas you think you can use. Following is an example of focused freewriting by a student, Kevin Coleman, on the topic *"the advantages of having a part-time job in college."*

▼ **Student Voices**
Deciding what I want to say is my favorite part of the writing process.
                    Todd Slunt

> Working in college. I never really wanted to work, but my parents told me that I'd have to pick up some of my expenses. I got a student loan, but it didn't cover everything--movies, food, etc. I began working during my second semester. I had a bunch of part-time jobs. Waiter. Library. Pizza truck. Some were fun--others were pretty bad. I hated driving that pizza truck. But there were some advantages. One was that I didn't have to ask my parents for money all the time. That made them happy. Paid half of my tuition. Working also made me happy. I began to feel independent. Yeah--my Declaration of Independence. I saw that if things got tough, I could make it. (Not a bad thing to know about yourself.) I wonder if my parents knew this all along. Or is this something that just happened? Maybe working taught me some lessons that I didn't learn in school. I guess I'll never know. It's not like I can really ask them. I'm running out of things to say. The end.

◆ PRACTICE 12-4

Reread Kevin Coleman's freewriting. If you were advising Kevin, which ideas would you suggest that he explore further? Why? Write your answers below.

Answers will vary.

■ WRITING FIRST: Flashback

Choose two of the jobs you listed for the Flashback exercise on page 120. Freewrite about each of them on separate sheets of paper. Which job gave you the most interesting material? On the lines below, write the name of the job, followed by the ideas that you would like to develop further.

Job: _____

_____

Ideas: _____

_____

_____

_____

Brainstorming

When you **brainstorm** (either individually or in collaboration with others), you write down (or type) all you can think of about a particular topic. After you have recorded as much material as you can, you look over your notes to figure out which ideas are useful and which ones are not. Here is Kevin Coleman's brainstorming on the advantages of part-time jobs for college students.

```
              Advantages of a Part-Time Job
    Working ever since my second year of college
    Bad jobs
         Waiter--library--pizza truck driver (good tips)
    Gained confidence
    Helped pay tuition
    Got independence
    Bought lots of clothes
    Bought photography supplies
    Got a lot of satisfaction
    Felt like an adult--had my own money
    Brother going to college next year
    Sometimes not enough time
    Final exams--papers
    Not enough free time
    Did grades suffer? Did social life?
    Always found time
    Things you learn
         Responsibility
         Business
         About independence, survival skills
```

◆ **PRACTICE 12-5**

Reread Kevin Coleman's brainstorming. Which ideas would you advise him to explore further? Write them on the lines below.

Answers will vary.

_____

_____

_____

_____

■ WRITING FIRST: Flashback

Review the freewriting you did in the Flashback exercise on page 122. Now, brainstorm about the job for which you have found the most interesting ideas. What ideas about the job did you get from brainstorming that you did not get from freewriting? Write your response on the following lines.

_____

_____

_____

_____

D **Stating Your Thesis**

After you have used invention strategies to gather information about your topic, you have to decide exactly what you want to say about it. By choosing and rejecting ideas and by identifying connections among the ideas you keep, you can decide on the point you want your essay to make. You can then express this point in a **thesis statement**: a single sentence that clearly expresses the main idea that you will discuss in the rest of your essay.

Topic	Thesis Statement
Three things I would change about Jackson County Community College	If I could change three things to improve Jackson County Community College, I would expand the food choices, decrease class size in first-year courses, and ship some of my classmates to the North Pole.
The campus recycling project	The recycling project recently begun on our campus should be promoted more actively.

12 D

Topic	Thesis Statement
The advantages of having a part-time job.	A part-time job is a valuable part of any college student's education.

For more on topic sentences, see 2A.

Like a topic sentence, a thesis statement tells readers what to expect. An effective thesis statement has two important characteristics.

1. *An effective thesis statement makes a point about a topic or takes a stand on an issue; for this reason, it must do more than state a fact or announce what you plan to write about.*

STATEMENT OF FACT Many college students work.

ANNOUNCEMENT In this essay, I would like to present my opinion about whether college students should work.

EFFECTIVE THESIS STATEMENT A part-time job is a valuable part of any college student's education.

Teaching Tip
Spend extra time on writing effective thesis statements and on their placement. Remind students not to make an announcement and not to state the thesis in their essay's first sentence.

A statement of fact is not an effective thesis statement because it takes no position and gives you nothing to develop in your essay. After all, how much can you say about the *fact* that many college students work? Likewise, an announcement of what you plan to discuss gives readers no indication of the position you will take on your topic. An effective thesis statement takes a stand. It could say, for example, that a part-time job is a valuable part of a college education.

2. *An effective thesis statement is clearly worded and specific.*

VAGUE THESIS STATEMENT Television commercials are not like real life.

EFFECTIVE THESIS STATEMENT Television commercials do not accurately portray women or minorities.

The vague thesis statement above says little about the ideas that the essay will discuss or how it will present those ideas. It does not say, for example, *why* television commercials are not realistic. The effective thesis statement is more focused. It signals that the essay will give examples of television commercials that present unrealistic portrayals of women and minorities.

FOCUS Stating Your Thesis

You can sometimes revise a vague thesis statement by including in it a list of the specific points that it will discuss. Revised in this way, the thesis acts as a road map, telling readers what to expect as they read.

VAGUE THESIS STATEMENT Raising tropical fish is a good hobby.

(continued on the following page)

● **Writing Tip**
Keep in mind that at this stage of the writing process, your thesis statement is not definite but *tentative*. You will almost certainly change it as you write and revise your essay.

(continued from the previous page)

EFFECTIVE THESIS   Raising tropical fish is a good hobby because it is
STATEMENT   inexpensive, interesting, and educational.

The vague thesis statement above gives readers little information about the essay to follow. The effective thesis statement, however, lays out the plan of the essay and gives readers a clear idea of what the rest of the essay will discuss.

◆ **PRACTICE 12-6**

In the space provided, indicate whether each of the following items is a statement of fact (*F*), an announcement (*A*), a vague statement (*VS*), or an effective thesis (*ET*).

Examples:

My commute between home and school takes more than an hour each way. ___*F*___

I hate my commute between home and school. ___*VS*___

1. Students who must commute a long distance to school are at a disadvantage compared to students who live close by. ___*ET*___

2. In this paper, I will discuss cheating and why students shouldn't cheat. ___*A*___

3. Schools should establish specific policies that will discourage students from cheating. ___*ET*___

4. Cheating is a problem for both students and teachers. ___*VS*___

5. Television commercials are designed to sell products. ___*F*___

6. I would like to explain why some television commercials are funny. ___*A*___

7. Single parents have a rough time. ___*VS*___

8. An article in the newspaper says that young people are starting to abuse alcohol and drugs at earlier ages than in the past. ___*F*___

9. Alcohol and drug abuse are major problems in our society. ___*VS*___

10. Families can use several strategies to help children avoid alcohol and drugs. ___*ET*___

◆ PRACTICE 12-7

A list of broad topics for essays follows. Select five of these topics, narrow them, and generate a thesis statement for each.

Answers will vary.

1. Vacations

2. Reality television

3. Tattoos

4. Music

5. Chocolate

6. Required Courses

7. Computer Games

8. Disciplining Children

9. X Games

10. Footwear

◆ PRACTICE 12-8

Label each of the following thesis statements *VS* if it is too vague, *F* if it is factual, *A* if it is an announcement, or *ET* if it is an effective thesis. On a separate sheet of paper rewrite those that are not effective thesis statements.

Answers to rewrites will vary.

1. Different types of amusement parks appeal to different types of people. __VS__

2. To encourage more people to vote, Election Day should be a national holiday. __ET__

3. Every fourth year, on the first Tuesday in November, the United States elects a new president. __F__

4. My paper will prove that DVDs are better than videotapes. __A__

5. The largest fish in the sea is the whale shark. __F__

6. Forty years ago, scientists believed that the dinosaurs were killed off by the arrival of a new Ice Age. __F__

7. NASCAR drivers should be forced to drive at safer speeds. __ET__

8. This paper will discuss the increase in the number of women in the military since the 1970s. __A__

9. Movies provide great entertainment. _VS_

10. Computers have made it easier for teachers and their students to communicate. _ET_

◆ PRACTICE 12-9

Rewrite the following vague thesis statements.

Example: My relatives are funny.

Rewrite: _My relatives think they are funny, but sometimes_

their humor can be offensive.

Answers will vary.

1. Camping can be dangerous.

2. Photography is an interesting hobby.

3. Athletes are paid too much.

4. Many people get their identities from their cars.

5. A community college education has many advantages.

■ WRITING FIRST: Flashback

Review your freewriting and brainstorming from the Flashback exercises on page 122 and page 123. Then, draft a thesis statement for your essay on the lines below.

Answers will vary.

_____

_____

_____

_____

E   Arranging Ideas

Once you have decided on a thesis statement, look over your freewriting and brainstorming again, this time to find the points that best support your thesis. Then, make a list of these points. Here is Kevin Coleman's list of supporting points about the advantages of part-time jobs for college students.

```
Job makes parents happy
Job gives satisfaction
Job provides an income
Able to buy photography supplies
Don't have to ask parents for money
Paid half of my tuition
Feel like an adult
Buy clothing
Brother going to college next year
Gained confidence
```

■ **Computer Tip**

Indent items in your list of points with the Tab key to show how they are related.

After you have selected the points you think will best support your thesis, arrange them in the order in which you will discuss them (for example, from general to specific, or from least important to most important). This orderly list of points can serve as a rough outline to guide you as you write. Kevin listed his points in the following order.

```
Job provides steady income
   Buy clothing
   Able to buy photography supplies
Job helps pay tuition
   Makes parents happy
   Brother going to college next year
   Paid half of my tuition
Job gives satisfaction
   Feel like an adult
   Gained confidence
```

◆ PRACTICE 12-10

Look over Kevin's list of points above. Do you think his arrangement is effective? Can you suggest any other ways he might have arranged his points? Write your answer on the lines below.

Answers will vary.

FOCUS Preparing a Formal Outline

The rough outline discussed above is all you need to plan most of your essays. However, some writers—especially when they are planning longer, more detailed essays—like to use a more formal outline. **Formal outlines** contain a combination of numbered and lettered headings and use roman numerals, capital letters, and

(continued on the following page)

(continued from the previous page)

arabic numerals (and sometimes lower-case letters) to show the relationships among ideas. For example, the most important (and most general) ideas are assigned a roman numeral; the next most important ideas are assigned capital letters. Each level develops the idea before it, and each new level is indented. Here is a formal outline of the points that Kevin planned to discuss in his essay.

> *Thesis statement:* A part-time job is a valuable part of any student's college education.
>
> I. Job gives me steady income
>   A. Can buy clothing
>   B. Can buy photography supplies
> II. Job helps pay tuition
>   A. Makes parents happy
>   1. Sets example for brother
>   2. Helps parents pay for brother's tuition
>   B. Helps me pay expenses
>   1. Provides half of college tuition
>   2. Provides money for living expenses
> III. Job gives me satisfaction
>   A. Feel like an adult
>   1. Earn respect
>   2. Invest in my future
>   B. Have more confidence

Teaching Tip
Take this opportunity to explain to students that all headings in a formal outline are stated in parallel terms. You might want to refer students to Chapter 19, Using Parallelism.

■ WRITING FIRST: Flashback

On the lines below, write the thesis statement you drafted in the Flashback exercise on page 127.

Answers will vary.

_____

_____

Now, review your freewriting and brainstorming again, and list below the points you plan to use to support your thesis statement.

Answers will vary.

_____

_____

_____

_____

(continued on the following page)

(continued from the previous page)

Finally, arrange these points in an order in which you could write about them. Cross out any points that do not support your thesis statement.

1. *Answers will vary.* _____

2. _____

3. _____

4. _____

5. _____

F   Drafting Your Essay

For a discussion of introductions and conclusions, see Chapter 13.

After you have decided on a thesis for your essay and have arranged your points in the order in which you will discuss them, you are ready to draft your essay. At this stage of the writing process, you should not worry about spelling or grammar or about composing a perfect introduction or conclusion. Your main goal is to get your ideas down so you can react to them. Remember that the draft you are writing will be revised, so leave room for your changes: write on every other line, and triple-space if you are typing. Follow your rough outline, but don't hesitate to depart from it if you think of new points or if your ideas take an interesting or unexpected turn as you write.

For a discussion of thesis and support, see 12A.

As you draft your essay, remember that it should have a **thesis-and-support** structure—that is, it should state a thesis and support it with details, facts, and examples. (Because this structure enables you to present your ideas clearly and persuasively, it will be central to much of the writing you do in college.) Regardless of the specific **pattern of development** you use to shape a particular essay, each of your essays should follow this basic structure.

For a discussion of patterns of essay development, see Chapter 14.

Notice how Kevin Coleman uses a thesis-and-support structure in the first draft of his essay.

Working

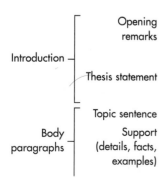

Ever since I began college, I have been working. While some of my friends sat around wasting time, I have managed to hold down several part-time jobs. I have gained a lot by working. <u>A part-time job is a valuable part of any college student's education.</u>

The first reason to work is that a job provides income. I've had a number of part-time jobs, and I didn't like them all, but they did have their uses. When

I want to buy books or clothes, I usually can. If an unexpected expense comes up, I can usually increase my hours so I can earn more. Last year, for example, I unexpectedly had to buy supplies for a photography course I was taking.

Another reason for working is that a job helps pay tuition. Both my parents work, and they are able to make ends meet. My mother is a teacher, and my father works for an insurance company. Their jobs are demanding, and they are usually tired at the end of the day. Even so, they don't have the money to pay all my tuition. My brother will be going to college next year, and they have to save for him. Every summer, I try to earn enough money to pay part of my tuition. The jobs I hold during the year pay for most of my weekly expenses. This past year, I was able to pay almost half my tuition and almost all of my living expenses.

The third reason for working is that a job gives me satisfaction. By working, I feel that I am earning the respect of my parents. I am not a drain on the family, and I set a good example for my brother. I would feel horrible if I had to run to my parents every time I needed money. I would also feel like a kid, not an adult. By working, I am developing the confidence I will need when I graduate and enter the work force. Because I have been able to earn my own way, I know I can support myself no matter what happens.

I would advise any student to consider getting a part-time job. Working supplements income and helps pay tuition, and it also provides a great deal of satisfaction.

Topic sentence

Support (details, facts, examples)

Body paragraphs

Topic sentence

Support (details, facts, examples)

Restatement of thesis
Closing remarks

Conclusion

◆ PRACTICE 12-11

Reread Kevin Coleman's first draft. What changes would you suggest he make? What might he add? What might he delete? Write your suggestions on the lines below.

Answers will vary.

_____

_____

_____

_____

_____

_____

_____

> ■ WRITING FIRST: Flashback
>
> On a separate sheet of paper, write a draft of an essay about the job you chose in the Flashback exercise on page 122. Be sure to include the thesis statement you developed in the Flashback exercise on page 127 as well as the points you listed in the Flashback exercise on page 129.

G   Revising and Editing Your Essay

When you **revise** your essay, you resee, rethink, reevaluate, and rewrite your work. Some of the changes you make—such as adding, deleting, or rearranging several sentences or even whole paragraphs—will be major. Others will be small—for example, adding or deleting words or phrases.

Before you begin revising, put your paper aside for a time. This "cooling-off" period allows you to put some distance between yourself and what you have written so you can view your draft more objectively. (Keep in mind that revision is usually not a neat process. When you revise, feel free to write directly on your draft: draw arrows, underline, cross out, and write above lines and in the margins.)

When you **edit** your essay, you check grammar and sentence structure. Then, you look at punctuation, mechanics, and spelling.

As you revise and edit, think carefully about the questions in the two Self-Assessment Checklists that follow.

■ **Computer Tip**

Revise and edit by hand on a hard copy of your essay before you type in your changes.

■ **Computer Tip**

When you remove material from your draft, move it to the end of the draft or to a separate file. Do not delete it until you are sure you do not need it.

For a discussion of how to write paragraphs that are unified, well developed, and coherent, see Chapter 2.

> ☑ SELF-ASSESSMENT CHECKLIST:
> Revising Your Essay
>
> ☐ Does your essay have an introduction, a body, and a conclusion?
>
> ☐ Does your essay have a clearly worded thesis statement?
>
> ☐ Does your thesis statement make a point about your topic?
>
> ☐ Does each body paragraph have a topic sentence?
>
> ☐ Does each topic sentence reinforce the thesis?
>
> ☐ Does each body paragraph contain enough details, facts, or examples to support the topic sentence?
>
> ☐ Are the body paragraphs unified, well developed, and coherent?
>
> ☐ Do you restate your thesis or summarize your main points in your conclusion?
>
> *(continued on the following page)*

(continued from the previous page)

☐ Have you varied sentence type, structure, and length? (See Chapter 18.)

☐ Have you used effective parallel structure in your sentences? (See Chapter 19.)

✔ SELF-ASSESSMENT CHECKLIST:
Editing Your Essay

Editing for Common Sentence Problems

☐ Have you avoided run-ons and comma splices? (See Chapter 21.)

☐ Have you avoided sentence fragments? (See Chapter 22.)

☐ Do your subjects and verbs agree? (See Chapter 23.)
Have you avoided illogical shifts? (See Chapter 24.)

☐ Have you avoided dangling and misplaced modifers? (See Chapter 25.)

Editing for Grammar

☐ Are your verb forms and verb tenses correct? (See Chapters 26 and 27.)

☐ Have you used nouns and pronouns correctly? (See Chapter 28.)

☐ Have you used adjectives and adverbs correctly? (See Chapter 29.)

Editing for Punctuation, Mechanics, and Spelling

☐ Have you used commas correctly? (See Chapter 31.)

☐ Have you used apostrophes correctly? (See Chapter 32.)

☐ Have you used capital letters where they are required? (See Chapter 33.)

☐ Have you used quotation marks correctly where they are needed? (See Chapter 33.)

☐ Have you spelled every word correctly? (See Chapter 34.)

■ Computer Tip

Use the Search function to find spelling errors that you commonly make but that the spell checker will not catch—using *there* instead of *their*, for example.

When he typed the first draft of his essay about the advantages of having a part-time job in college, Kevin triple-spaced so he could write more easily in the space between the lines. Here is his draft, with his handwritten revision and editing changes.

Working

Ever since I began college, I have been working.

While some of my friends sat around wasting time, I have
Even though there have been times when I wished I didn't have to work,
managed to hold down several part-time jobs. I have

gained a lot by working. A part-time job ~~is~~ *can be* a valuable

part of any college student's education ~~,~~ *; I know it has been for me.*

The first reason to work is that a job provides
a steady source of money for day-to-day expenses.
~~income.~~ I've had a number of part-time jobs, and I

Because I have a steady salary, when
didn't like them all, but they did have their uses. ~~When~~

I want to buy books or clothes, I usually can. If an
along,
unexpected expense comes ~~up,~~ I can usually increase my

hours so I can earn more. Last year, for example, I

unexpectedly had to buy supplies for a photography
At first I thought I would have to drop the course because I
course I was taking. *couldn't afford the supplies. After talking to my boss,*

however, I was able to arrange to work a few extra hours and earn enough to buy the supplies I needed.

Even though my parents have never said anything to me, I know that paying my tuition is a hardship for them.

Another reason for working is that a job helps pay

tuition. Both my parents work, and they are able to make

ends meet. ~~My mother is a teacher, and my father works~~

~~for an insurance company. Their jobs are demanding, and~~

~~they are usually tired at the end of the day. Even so,~~
But even with loans, we   *In addition, my*
~~they~~ don't have the money to pay all my tuition. ~~My~~

brother will be going to college next year, and they

have to save for him. Every summer, I try to earn

enough money to pay part of my tuition. ~~The jobs I hold~~

~~during the year pay for most of my weekly expenses.~~ This

past year, I was able to pay almost half my tuition. ~~and~~

~~almost all of my living expenses.~~
most important
The ~~third~~ reason for working is that a job gives me

satisfaction. By working, I feel that I am earning the

respect of my parents. I am not a drain on the family,

and I set a good example for my brother. I would feel

horrible if I had to run to my parents every time I

needed money. I would also feel like a kid, not an

adult. By working, I am ^also developing the confidence I will

need when I graduate and enter the work force. Because I

have been able to pay my own way, ^so far I know I can support

myself no matter what happens.

I would advise any student to consider getting a

part-time job. Working ~~supplements~~ *not only provides needed* income and helps pay

tuition, ~~and it~~ *but* also ~~provides a great deal of~~ *offers* satisfac-

tion. *In my case, a job has given me the insight and the confidence I will need to succeed after I graduate.*

◆ PRACTICE 12-12

What material did Kevin Coleman add to his draft? What did he delete?
Why did he make these changes? Write your answers on the following
lines.

Answers will vary. Students might suggest that Kevin added more explanation

about the importance of money for day-to-day expenses, expanded the example

about the unexpected expense of the photography course, added a concluding

sentence, and deleted personal information about his parents because it was

irrelevant.

When his revisions and edits were complete, Kevin proofread his essay
to be sure he had not missed any errors. The final revised and edited version of his essay appears below.

Working

Ever since I began college, I have been working.
While some of my friends sat around wasting time, I have
managed to hold down several part-time jobs. Even though
there have been times when I wished I did not have to
work, I have gained a lot by working. A part-time job
can be a valuable part of any college student's education; I know it has been for me.

The first reason to work is that a job provides a
steady source of money for day-to-day expenses. I have
had a number of part-time jobs, and even though I did
not like them all, they did have their uses. Because
I have a steady salary, when I want to buy books or
an item of clothing, I usually can. If an unexpected

expense comes along, I can usually increase my hours so I can earn more. Last year, for example, I unexpectedly had to buy supplies for a photography course I was taking. At first, I thought I would have to drop the course because I could not afford the supplies. After talking to my boss, however, I was able to arrange to work a few extra hours and earn enough to buy the supplies I needed.

Another reason for working is that a job helps pay tuition. Even though my parents have never said anything to me, I know that paying my tuition is a hardship for them. Both my parents work, and they are able to make ends meet. But even with loans, they do not have the money to pay all my tuition. In addition, my brother will be going to college next year, and they have to save for him. Every summer I try to earn enough money to pay part of my tuition. This past year, I was able to pay almost half my tuition.

The most important reason for working is that a job gives me satisfaction. By working, I feel that I am earning the respect of my parents. I am not a drain on the family, and I set a good example for my brother. I would feel horrible if I had to run to my parents every time I needed money. I would also feel like a kid, not an adult. Furthermore, by working, I am developing the confidence I will need when I graduate and enter the work force. Because I have been able to pay my own way so far, I know I can support myself no matter what happens.

I would advise any student to consider getting a part-time job. Working not only provides needed income and helps pay tuition but also offers satisfaction. In my case, a job has given me the insight and the confidence I will need to succeed after I graduate.

◆ PRACTICE 12-13

Reread the final draft of Kevin Coleman's essay. Do you think this draft is an improvement over his first draft? What other changes could Kevin have made? Write your ideas here.

Answers will vary.

_____

_____

_____

_____

_____

_____

■ WRITING FIRST: Flashback

Using the Self-Assessment Checklist for revising your essay on page 132 as a guide, evaluate the essay you wrote for the Flashback exercise on the same page. What points can you add to support your thesis more fully? What points can you delete? Can any ideas be stated more clearly? (You may want to get feedback by exchanging essays with another student.) On the following lines, describe any changes you think you should make to your draft.

Answers will vary.

_____

_____

_____

_____

_____

■ WRITING FIRST: Revising and Editing

Now, revise the draft of your essay, writing in new material between the lines or in the margins. Then, edit this revised draft, using the Self-Assessment Checklist for editing your essay on page 133 to help you find errors in grammar, sentence structure, punctuation, mechanics, and spelling. When you have finished, prepare a final draft of your essay.

CHAPTER REVIEW

◆ EDITING PRACTICE

After reading the following student essay, write an appropriate thesis statement on the lines provided. (Make sure your thesis statement clearly communicates the essay's main idea.) Then, fill in the topic sentences for the second, third, and fourth paragraphs. Finally, restate the thesis in different words in the conclusion.

```
            Preparing for a Job Interview

    I have consulted a lot of books and many Web sites

that give advice on how to do well on a job interview.
```

Some recommend practicing your handshake, and others sug-gest rehearsing answers to typical questions. This advice is useful, but not many books tell how to get mentally prepared for an interview. [Thesis statement:] _Answers will vary._

_____

_____

[Topic sentence for the second paragraph:] _____
Answers will vary.

_____

Feeling good about how I look is important, so I usually wear a jacket and tie to an interview. Even if you will not be dressing this formally on the job, try to make a good first impression. For this reason, you should never come to an interview dressed in jeans or shorts. Still, you should be careful not to overdress. For example, wearing a suit or a dressy dress to an interview at a fast-food restaurant might make you feel good, but it could also make you look as if you do not really want to work there.

[Topic sentence for the third paragraph:] _____
Answers will vary.

_____

Going on an interview is a little like getting ready to participate in an important sporting event. You have to go in with the right attitude. If you think you are not going to be successful, chances are that you will not be. So before I go on any interview, I spend some time building my confidence. I tell myself that I can do the job and that I will do well in the interview. By the time I get to the interview, I am convinced that I am the right person for the job.

[Topic sentence for the fourth paragraph:] _____
Answers will vary.

_____

Most people go to an interview knowing little or nothing about the job. They expect the interviewer to tell them

what they will have to do. Once, an interviewer told me
that he likes a person who has taken the time to do his or
her homework. Since that time, I have always done some
research before I go on an interview--even for a part-time
job. (Most of the time, my research is nothing more than
a quick look at the company Web site or a call to a person
who has a job where I want to work.) This kind of research
really pays off. At my last interview, for example, I was
able to talk in specific terms about the job's duties and
indicate which shift I would prefer. The interviewer must
have been impressed because she offered me the job on the
spot.

[Restatement of thesis:] _____

Answers will vary. _____

_____

_____

Of course, following my suggestions will not guarantee that
you get a job. You still have to do well at the interview
itself. Even so, getting mentally prepared for the interview will give you an advantage over people who do almost
nothing before they walk in the door.

◆ COLLABORATIVE ACTIVITIES

1. On your own, find a paragraph in a magazine or a newspaper about a controversial issue that interests you. Working in a group, select one of the best paragraphs. Choose three points about the issue discussed that you could develop in a short essay, and then brainstorm about these points. Finally, write a sentence that could serve as the thesis statement for an essay.

2. Working in a group, come up with thesis statements suitable for essays on three of the following topics.

Professional sports	Gun safety
The Internet	Dressing well on a budget
Safe driving	College entrance exams
Parenthood	Bad habits
Honesty	How to prepare for a test

3. Exchange your group's three thesis statements with those of another group. Choose the best one of the other group's thesis statements. A member of each group can then read the thesis statement to the class and explain why the group chose the thesis statement it did.

For information on stating a thesis, see 12D.

☑ REVIEW CHECKLIST:
Writing an Essay

- Most essays have a thesis-and-support structure: the thesis statement presents the main idea, and the body paragraphs support the thesis. (See 12A.)

- Begin by deciding on a topic (See 12B.)

- Use invention strategies to narrow your focus and find ideas to write about. (See 12C.)

- Develop an effective thesis statement. (See 12D.)

- List the points that best support your thesis, and arrange them in the order in which you plan to discuss them. (See 12E.)

- As you write your first draft, make sure your essay has a thesis-and-support structure. (See 12F.)

- Revise your essay. (See 12G.)

- Edit the final draft of your essay. (See 12G.)

Introductions and Conclusions

PREVIEW

In this chapter, you will learn:

■ to write an introduction (13A)

■ to choose a title (13A)

■ to write a conclusion (13B)

■ WRITING FIRST

Look at the picture above, in which Charlie Chaplin, in the film *Modern Times* (1936), is sucked into a factory machine. Then, make a copy of the essay you wrote for Chapter 12. As you go through this chapter, you will continue to work on the introduction and conclusion of this essay.

Word Power
monotonous repetitious; lacking in variety

robotic mechanical

routine a standard procedure; to be followed regularly

When you draft an essay, you usually concentrate on the **body** because it is the largest single section and because it is the section in which you develop your ideas. A well-constructed essay, however, is more than a series of body paragraphs. It also includes an **introduction** and a **conclusion**, both of which contribute to the overall effectiveness of your writing.

▼ **Student Voices**
When I write an introduction, I try to start with something that will surprise my readers.

Kelly Miller

● **Writing Tip**
Remind students that the introduction should be a full paragraph.

Teaching Tip
Find two introductory paragraphs (one that is catchy and one that is dull), and read each one to the class. After you read each introduction, ask the class whether they would like to hear the rest of the essay—and why or why not.

A   Introductions

An introduction is the first thing people see when they read your essay. If your introduction is interesting and effective, it is likely to draw readers into your essay and make them want to read further. If it is not, readers may get bored and stop reading.

Your introduction should prepare readers for your essay by giving them the information they need to follow your discussion. For this reason, the introduction should include a **thesis statement** that presents the main idea of your essay. This statement usually appears at the end of the introductory paragraph. (In each of the examples on pages 143–45, the thesis statement is underlined.)

Here are some options you can experiment with when you write your introductions.

FOCUS   What to Avoid in Introductions

■ Do not begin your essay by announcing what you plan to write about.

Phrases to avoid

This essay is about . . .

Today I will talk about . . .

In my essay I will discuss . . .

■ Do not apologize for your ideas.

Phrases to avoid

Although I don't know much about this subject . . .

I might not be an expert but . . .

Beginning with a Direct Approach

▼ **Student Voices**
The hardest thing about writing introductions is saying something original.

Doreen Queenan

The simplest way to start an essay is to present a few opening remarks and then list the points you will discuss. This straightforward approach moves readers directly to the central concerns of your essay. (Once you feel comfortable with this strategy, you can experiment with other approaches.)

Television sitcoms are a part of most people's lives. Almost everyone watches these shows at one time or another. In addition to providing entertainment, sitcoms often show characters struggling with real-life situations. By doing so, these characters convey ideas about what is right and wrong and what is acceptable and not acceptable. Unfortunately, some viewers, especially young ones, are overly influenced by what they see. That is why it is disturbing to see how many sitcoms convey unrealistic images of men and women. These stereotypes not only misrepresent reality, but they also teach distorted values that make it almost impossible for real men and women to relate to one another.

Thesis statement

                                        Amy Donohue (student)

Beginning with a Narrative

You can begin an essay with a narrative drawn from your own experience or from a current news event. If your story is interesting, it will involve readers almost immediately. Notice how the narrative in the following introduction sets the stage for an essay in which the writer discusses his experiences as a volunteer firefighter.

On September 11, 2001, the unthinkable happened: terrorists crashed two commercial airplanes into the twin towers at the World Trade Center. Ignoring the possibility that the two one-hundred-and-ten-story towers were in danger of falling, hundreds of firefighters rushed inside the buildings to try to save as many lives as possible. Their selfless actions enabled thousands of people to get out, but half the firefighters—over three hundred—died when the twin towers collapsed. Although I have never faced a catastrophe like the one in New York, as a volunteer firefighter I am ready—day or night whenever an alarm sounds—to deal with a dangerous situation.

Thesis statement

                                        Richard Pogue (student)

Beginning with a Question (or a Series of Questions)

Using one or more questions at the beginning of your essay is an effective introductory strategy. Because readers expect you to answer the questions in your essay, they will want to read further. Notice how two questions in the following introduction catch the reader's eye.

> ▼ **Student Voices**
> *I like to begin with a question. It makes the reader want to read more.*
> *Jen Weber*

Imagine this scene: A child is sitting under a Christmas tree opening her presents. She laughs and claps her hands as she gets a doll, a pair of shoes, and a sweater. What could spoil this picture? What information could cause the child's parents to feel guilt? The answer is this: that children from developing countries probably worked long hours in substandard conditions so this American child could receive her gifts.

Thesis statement

                                        Megan Davia (student)

Beginning with a Definition

A definition at the beginning of your essay can give valuable information to readers. Such information can explain a confusing concept or clarify a complicated idea, as the following paragraph demonstrates.

Thesis statement

The term *good parent* is not easy to define. Some things about being a good parent are obvious—keeping your children safe, taking them to the dentist for regular checkups, helping them with their homework, being there for them when they want to talk, and staying up at night with them when they are sick, for example. Other things are not so obvious, however. I found this out last year when I became a volunteer at my daughter's middle school. Up until that time, I never would have dreamed that one morning a week could do so much to improve my daughter's attitude toward school.

Russ Hightower (student)

FOCUS **Beginning with a Definition**

Do not introduce a definition with a tired opening phrase such as "According to *Webster's* . . ." or "*The American Heritage Dictionary* defines . . ."

Beginning with a Background Statement

A background statement can provide an overview of a subject and set the stage for the discussion to follow. As the following introduction illustrates, a background statement can also help prepare readers for a surprising or controversial thesis statement.

▼ **Student Voices**
The kind of introduction I like to write includes a short summary of the rest of the paper.

Linda Richards

ESL Tip
Ask students why one might think English is "crazy."

Thesis statement

English is the most widely spoken language in the history of our planet, used in some way by at least one out of every seven human beings around the globe. Half of the world's books are written in English, and the majority of international telephone calls are made in English. English is the language of over sixty percent of the world's radio programs, many of them beamed, ironically, by the Russians, who know that to win friends and influence nations, they're best off using English. More than seventy percent of international mail is written and addressed in English, and eighty percent of all computer text is stored in English. English has acquired the largest vocabulary of all the world's languages, perhaps as many as two million words, and has generated one of the noblest bodies of literature in the annals of the human race. Nonetheless, it is now time to face the fact that English is a crazy language.

Richard Lederer, "English Is a Crazy Language"

Beginning with a Quotation

An appropriate saying or an interesting piece of dialogue can immediately draw readers into your essay. Notice how the quotation below creates interest and leads smoothly and logically into the thesis statement at the end of the introduction.

> According to the comedian Jerry Seinfeld, "When you're single, you are the dictator of your own life. . . . When you're married, you are part of a vast decision-making body." In other words, before you can do anything, you have to discuss it with someone else. These words kept going through my mind as I thought about asking my girlfriend to marry me. The more I thought about Seinfeld's words, the more I hesitated. <u>I never suspected that I would pay a price for my indecision.</u>   Thesis statement
>
> Dan Brody (student)

Beginning with a Surprising Statement

You can begin your essay with a surprising or unexpected statement. Because your statement takes readers by surprise, it catches their attention. Notice in the following paragraph how a rather startling opening statement leads readers to the essay's thesis.

> Some of the smartest people I know never went to college. In fact, some of them never finished high school. Even so, they know how to save twenty percent on the price of a dinner, fix their own faucets when they leak, get discounted prescriptions, get free rides on a bus to Atlantic City, use public transportation to get anywhere in the city, and live on about twenty-two dollars a day. These are my grandparents' friends. Some people would call them old and poor. <u>I would call them survivors who have learned to make it through life on nothing but a Social Security check.</u>   Thesis statement
>
> Sean Ragas (student)

Beginning with a Contradiction

You can begin your introduction with an idea that many people believe to be true. Then, as the following paragraph does, you can capture readers' attention by demonstrating why this idea is untrue or questionable.

> Drugs and crime are so thoroughly intertwined in the public mind that to most people a large crime problem seems an inevitable consequence of drug use. But the historical link between the two is more a product of drug laws than of drugs. There are four clear connections between drugs and crime, and three of them would be much diminished if drugs were legalized. <u>This fact doesn't by itself make the case for legalization persuasive, of course, but it deserves careful attention in the emerging debate of whether prohibition of drugs is worth the trouble.</u>   Thesis statement
>
> Ethan A. Nadelmann, "Legalize Drugs"

FOCUS Titles

Every essay should have a **title** that suggests the subject of the essay and makes people want to read it.

Before you choose a title, reread your essay (especially your thesis statement) carefully. Then, jot down several possible titles and select the one you like the best. When you write your title, be sure to follow these guidelines.

- Capitalize all words except for articles (*a, an, the*), prepositions (*at, to, of, around,* and so on), and coordinating conjunctions (*and, but,* and so on), unless they are the first or last word of the title.
- Do not underline your title or enclose it within quotation marks.
- Center the title at the top of the first page. Double-space between the title and the first line of your essay.

As you consider a title for your paper, think about the following options.

- A title can highlight a key word or term.

    Guavas

    Dyslexia

    Liars

- A title can be a straightforward announcement.

    Thirty-Eight Who Saw Murder Didn't Call the Police

    The "Black Table" Is Still There

- A title can be a question.

    Who Killed the Bog Men of Denmark? And Why?

    Why Fear National ID Cards?

- A title can set a scene.

    Summer Picnic Fish Fry

- A title can establish a personal connection with readers.

    The Men We Carry in Our Minds

    I Have a Dream

(continued on the following page)

> ● **Writing Tip**
> Do not underline your title, and do not put quotation marks around it unless you are directly quoting a source. For more on punctuating titles, see 33C.

(continued from the previous page)

■ A title can offer an unusual perspective.

The New Prohibitionism

■ A title can be a familiar saying or a quotation from your essay itself.

Men Are from Mars, Women Are from Venus

Slice of Life

■ A title can relate to the pattern of development used in the essay.

For more information on patterns of essay development, see Chapter 14.

Three Ways to Make Your Neighborhood Better (exemplification)

The Rise and Fall of Doo-Wop (narrative)

My Grandfather (description)

How to Write an Effective Résumé (process)

Why the *Titanic* Sank (cause and effect)

Four-Year vs. Two-Year Colleges (comparison and contrast)

Types of Sports Fans (classification)

What It Means to Be Happy (definition)

Let's Stop Persecuting Smokers (argument)

◆ **PRACTICE 13-1**

Look at the student essays in Chapter 14, locating one introduction you think is particularly effective. On the lines below, explain the strengths of the introduction you chose.

Answers will vary.

_____

_____

_____

_____

◆ **PRACTICE 13-2**

Using the different options for creating titles discussed above, write two titles for each of the essays described below.

Answers will vary.

1. A student writes an essay about three people who disappeared mysteriously: Amelia Earhart, aviator; Ambrose Bierce, writer; and Jimmy

Hoffa, union leader. In the body paragraphs, the student describes the circumstances surrounding their disappearances.

_____

_____

2. A student writes an essay arguing against doctors' letting people select the sex of their babies. In the body paragraphs, she presents reasons why she thinks it is unethical.

_____

_____

3. A student writes an essay to explain why America is ready to elect a woman president. In the body paragraphs, the writer gives reasons for his beliefs.

_____

_____

4. A student writes an essay describing the harmful effects of steroids on student athletes. In the body paragraphs, he shows the effects on the heart, brain, and other organs.

_____

_____

5. A student writes an essay explaining why she joined the Navy. In the body paragraphs, she discusses her need to earn money for college tuition, her wish to learn a trade, and her desire to see the world.

_____

_____

■ WRITING FIRST: Flashback

Look back at the essay you reprinted for the Writing First exercise on page 141. Evaluate your introduction. Does it prepare readers for the essay to follow? Does it include a thesis statement? Is it likely to interest readers? On a separate sheet of paper, draft a different opening paragraph using one of the options presented in 13A. Be sure to include a clear thesis statement. In the space provided, indicate the kind of introduction you have drafted.

After you have finished drafting a new introduction, think of a new title that will attract your readers' attention. (Use one of the options listed in the Focus box on pages 146–47.) In the space provided, write your new title, and then indicate the option you used.

(continued on the following page)

(continued from the previous page)

Option used for new introduction: _Answers will vary._

New title: _Answers will vary._

Option used for new title: _Answers will vary._

B Conclusions

Because your **conclusion** is the last thing readers see, they often judge your entire essay by its effectiveness. For this reason, conclusions should be planned, drafted, and revised with care.

Your conclusion should give readers a sense of completion. One way you can accomplish this is by restating the essay's thesis. Keep in mind, however, that a conclusion is more than a word-for-word restatement of the thesis. If you return to your thesis here, you should summarize it, expand on it, and make some general concluding remarks; then, try to end with a sentence that readers will remember.

▼ **Student Voices**
I like my conclusions to be powerful and not just repeat what has already been written.
Jason Walsh

Teaching Tip
Remind students that the conclusion should be a full paragraph.

FOCUS **What to Avoid in Conclusions**

■ Do not introduce any new ideas. Your conclusion should summarize the ideas you discuss in your essay, not open up new lines of thought.

■ Do not apologize for your opinions, ideas, or conclusions. Apologies will undercut your reader's confidence in you.

Phrases to avoid

I may not be an expert . . .

At least that's my opinion . . .

I could be wrong, but . . .

■ Do not use overused phrases to announce your essay is coming to a close.

Phrases to avoid

In summary . . .

In conclusion . . .

● **Writing Tip**
In essay exams, when time is limited, a one-sentence restatement of your thesis is often enough for a conclusion. Likewise, an essay exam may require just a one- or two-sentence introduction.

13 B

Here are some options you can experiment with when you write your conclusions.

Concluding with a Restatement of Your Thesis

This no-nonsense conclusion reinforces your essay's most important ideas by restating your thesis in different words and reviewing the main points of the discussion.

> It is unfortunate that television sitcoms do not show men and women relating to each other in a meaningful way. The simplistic plots, the reliance on humor—especially sexual humor—to resolve complicated problems, and the use of male and female stereotypes do little to educate viewers. At best, television sitcoms teach viewers that sex can make any problem disappear. At worst, they reinforce behavior patterns that make it almost impossible for men and women to relate to each other. A more realistic response from characters would show viewers that honest communication could do more to resolve conflicts between men and women than stereotypical behavior can.
>
> Amy Donohue (student)

Concluding with a Narrative

A narrative conclusion can bring an event discussed in the essay to a logical, satisfying close. The following conclusion uses a narrative to tie up the essay's loose ends.

> After twenty years, the tree began to bear. Although Grandfather complained about how much he lost because pollen never reached the poor part of town, because at the market he had to haggle over the price of avocados, he loved that tree. It grew, as did his family, and when he died, all his sons standing on each other's shoulders, oldest to youngest, could not reach the highest branches. The wind could move the branches, but the trunk, thicker than any waist, hugged the ground.
>
> Gary Soto, "The Grandfather"

Concluding with a Question (or a Series of Questions)

By ending with a question, you leave readers with something to think about. However, the question should build on the thesis statement and not introduce any new issues. Notice how the conclusion below asks a series of questions before restating the essay's thesis.

> Why is it that when the sun or the moon or the stars are out, they are visible, but when the lights are out, they are invisible, and that when I wind up my watch, I start it, but when I wind up this essay, I shall end it? English is a crazy language.
>
> Richard Lederer, "English Is a Crazy Language"

Concluding with a Prediction

This type of conclusion not only sums up the thesis but also looks to the future. The following conclusion uses this technique to paint a troubling picture of the future of American cities.

> On that little street were the ghosts of the people who brought me into being and the flesh-and-blood kids who will be my children's companions in the twenty-first century. You could tell by their eyes that they couldn't figure out why I was there. They were accustomed to being ignored, even by the people who had once populated their rooms. And as long as that continues, our cities will burst and burn, burst and burn, over and over again.
>
> Anna Quindlen, "The Old Block"

Concluding with a Recommendation

Once you think you have convinced readers that a problem exists, you can make recommendations in your conclusion about how the problem should be solved. Notice how the following paragraph makes a series of recommendations about a cancer drug made from the Pacific yew tree.

> Every effort should be made to ensure that the yew tree is made available for the continued research and development of taxol. Environmental groups, the timber industry, and the Forest Service must recognize that the most important value of the Pacific yew is as a treatment for cancer. At the same time, its harvest can be managed in a way that allows for the production of taxol without endangering the continual survival of the yew tree.
>
> Sally Thane Christensen, "Is a Tree Worth a Life?"

Concluding with a Quotation

Frequently, a well-chosen quotation—even a brief one—can add a lot to your essay. In some cases, quoted speech or writing can add authority to your ideas. In others, as in the following paragraph, it can reinforce the main point of the essay.

> It was 4:25 a.m. when the ambulance arrived to take the body of Miss Genovese. It drove off. "Then," a solemn police detective said, "the people came out."
>
> Martin Gansberg, "Thirty-Eight Who Saw Murder Didn't Call the Police"

▼ **Student Voices**
I like to end my essays with a quotation from a book I'm writing about.
Meredith Krall

◆ PRACTICE 13-3

Look at the student essays in Chapter 14, locating one conclusion you think is particularly effective. On the lines below, explain the strengths of the conclusion you chose.

Answers will vary.

● **Writing Tip**
You should draft the body paragraphs before you spend too much time writing the introduction or conclusion. Once you see the direction in which your essay has developed, you can revise your introduction and conclusion so they fit in with the rest of your essay.

■ WRITING FIRST: Flashback

Look back at your response to the Writing First exercise on page 141. Evaluate your conclusion. Is it suitable for your topic and thesis? Does it bring your essay to a clear and satisfying close that will leave a strong impression on readers? On a separate sheet of paper, try drafting a different concluding paragraph using one of the options presented in 13B. In the space provided, indicate what kind of conclusion you have drafted.

Option used for new conclusion: _Answers will vary._

■ WRITING FIRST: Revising and Editing

Reread your responses to the Flashback exercise above and the one on page 148. Are the new paragraphs you wrote more effective than the introduction and conclusion of the essay you wrote in Chapter 12? If so, substitute them for the opening and closing paragraphs of that essay.

CHAPTER REVIEW

◆ EDITING PRACTICE

The following student essay has an undeveloped introduction and conclusion. Decide what introductory and concluding strategies would be most appropriate for the essay. Then, on a separate sheet of paper, rewrite both the introduction and the conclusion to make them more effective. Finally, add an interesting title for the essay.
Answers will vary.

Possible title: Justice — by and for Women

Although women got the right to vote in 1919, no woman had ever served on the U.S. Supreme Court until the 1980s.

However, President Reagan was determined to fulfill his campaign promise of appointing women to positions of power in his administration. So, in 1981, he nominated Sandra Day O'Connor, a relatively unknown judge from Arizona, to fill the vacancy left by retiring Associate Justice Potter Stewart. O'Connor, who had graduated with honors from Stanford law school in 1952, was unable to find a position as a lawyer because she was a woman. So she married and raised three sons. Later on, she found a position in the Arizona Attorney General's office. From that point on, she moved into increasingly responsible political and legal positions, including first an appointment and later election to the Arizona senate. After she was nominated to the Supreme Court, O'Connor was confirmed by the U.S. Senate by a vote of 99-0, quite a vote of confidence for someone who had been unable, at first, to practice her profession.

In 1993, President Clinton nominated a second woman to the Supreme Court. This woman was Ruth Bader Ginsburg, whose path to the Court was similar to O'Connor's. She, too, graduated from law school with honors yet was unable to find employment as a lawyer. She did, however, find work as a law professor and eventually became the first tenured woman law professor at Columbia. Throughout her career, Ginsburg worked hard to end discrimination against women. In fact, she argued six cases before the Supreme Court on women's rights before her own appointment.

Although O'Connor is seen as conservative and Ginsburg as moderate, both women fight hard for the rights of women and children.

◆ COLLABORATIVE ACTIVITIES

1. Bring to class several copies of an essay you wrote for another class. Have each person in your group comment on your essay's introduction and conclusion. Revise the introduction and conclusion in response to your classmates' suggestions.

2. Find a magazine or newspaper article that interests you. Cut off the introduction and conclusion and bring the body of the article to class.

Ask your group to decide on the best strategy for introducing and concluding the article. Then, collaborate on writing new opening and closing paragraphs and an interesting title.

3. Working in a group, think of interesting and appropriate titles for essays on each of the following topics. Try to use as many of the different options outlined in the Focus box on pages 146–47 as you can.

The difficulty of living with a roommate
The evils of gambling
The need for regular exercise
The joys of living in the city (or in the country)
The responsibility of having a pet
Things that make life easier
Job interviews
The obligation to vote
Celebrating the holidays
Parents (or being a parent)
Public transportation

✔ REVIEW CHECKLIST:
Introductions and Conclusions

- The introduction of your essay should prepare readers for the ideas to follow and should include a thesis statement. It should also create interest. (See 13A.) You can begin an essay with any of the following options.

A direct approach	A definition
A narrative	A background statement
A question	A quotation
A surprising statement	A contradiction

- Your title should suggest the subject of your essay and make people want to read further. (See 13A.)

- The conclusion of your essay should restate the thesis and make some general concluding remarks. (See 13B.) You can conclude an essay with any of the following options.

A restatement of the thesis	A prediction
A narrative	A recommendation
A question	A quotation

Patterns of Essay Development

PREVIEW

In this chapter, you will learn to organize your essays according to different patterns of development:

- ■ exemplification (14A)

- ■ narration (14B)

- ■ description (14C)

- ■ process (14D)

- ■ cause and effect (14E)

- ■ comparison and contrast (14F)

- ■ classification (14G)

- ■ definition (14H)

- ■ argument (14I)

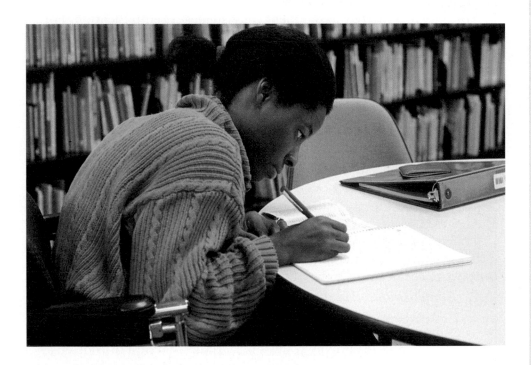

As you learned in Chapters 3 through 11, writers have a variety of options for developing ideas within a paragraph. These options include *exemplification, narration, description, process, cause and effect, comparison and contrast, classification, definition,* and *argument.* When you write an essay, you can use these same strategies to help you organize your material.

In your college courses, different assignments and writing situations call for different patterns of essay development. For instance, if an exam question asked you to compare two systems of government, you would use *comparison and contrast* to structure your essay. If your lab manual asked you to explain the stages of a particular chemical reaction, you would use *process.* If an English composition assignment asked you to tell about a childhood experience, you would use *narration.* If a section of a research paper on environmental pollution called for examples of dangerous waste disposal practices, you would use *exemplification.*

Each section in this chapter defines and explains one pattern of essay development, gives examples of how it is used in typical college writing assignments, provides several options for organizing an essay, and includes a list of useful transitions. A student essay illustrates each pattern, and a list of writing topics and a Self-Assessment Checklist give you opportunities for practice and review.

155

*For information on writing an
exemplification paragraph, see
Chapter 3.*

A Exemplification

Exemplification illustrates a general statement with specific examples that support it. An **exemplification essay** uses specific examples to support a thesis.

Teaching Tip
For each pattern of development, you can assign an
appropriate reading from
Chapter 36 and have stu-
dents answer some of the
questions that follow it.

Teaching Tip
For examples of exemplification essays by professional
writers, see 36A.

● Writing Tip
Many everyday writing tasks
call for exemplification. For
example, in a parent com-
mittee report for your child's
day-care center, you might
present examples of environmental hazards in the school
building.

FOCUS Topics for Exemplification

The wording of your assignment may suggest exemplification. For example, you may be asked to *illustrate* or to *give examples*.

Assignment	*Thesis Statement*
Education Should children be taught only in their native languages or in English as well? Support your answer with examples of specific students' experiences.	The success of students in a bilingual third-grade class suggests the value of teaching elementary-school students in English as well as in their native languages.
Literature Does William Shakespeare's *Othello* have to end tragically? Illustrate your position with references to specific characters.	Each of the three major characters in *Othello* contributes to the play's tragic ending.
Composition Discuss the worst job you ever had. Include plenty of specific examples to support your thesis.	My summer job at a fast-food restaurant was my all-time worst job because of the endless stream of rude customers, the many boring and repetitive tasks I had to perform, and my manager's insensitive treatment of employees.

In an exemplification essay, each body paragraph can develop a single example or discuss several related examples.

Teaching Tip
Make sure students know
that ¶ is the symbol for a
paragraph.

Options for Organizing Exemplification Essays

One Example per Paragraph	**Several Related Examples per Paragraph**
¶1 Introduction	¶1 Introduction
¶2 First example	¶2 First group of examples
¶3 Second example	¶3 Second group of examples
¶4 Third example	¶4 Third group of examples
¶5 Conclusion	¶5 Conclusion

Regardless of how many examples you select, each one should relate to your thesis, and your essay's topic sentences should make clear just how each example supports the thesis statement. In addition, transitional words and phrases should introduce each example and indicate the relationship between one example and another.

FOCUS **Transitions for Exemplification**

Also	Furthermore	The most impor-
Besides	In addition	tant example
Finally	Moreover	The next example
First	One example . . .	
For example	Another example	
For instance	Specifically	

The following student essay, "Fighting Fire with Fire Safety Education" by Timothy E. Miles, uses a series of examples to illustrate the need to educate children about fire safety. Some paragraphs group several brief examples together; others develop a single example. Notice how Timothy uses clear topic sentences and helpful transitions to introduce his examples and link them to one another.

Fighting Fire with Fire Safety Education

Since young children suffer more fire-related   1
injuries and fatalities than most others do, fire safety
education must be introduced at an early age. This can
be done both by parents and by local fire departments.
Fire safety for young children is an ongoing concern, and
adults must take the responsibility for educating and protecting them.

What should small children be taught? First, they   2
should understand what matches are and what the consequences of playing with them can be. In addition, they
should be taught that matches are not toys and that they
can cause great damage. Children should also be taught how
to avoid contact burns from stove burners, hot liquids, and
electrical appliances.

Another essential part of fire safety education for   3
children is learning how to extinguish fires when their
own clothing ignites. Many children are burned by their own
clothing. The chance of injury can be prevented if they are
taught how to "Stop, Drop, and Roll." One way of teaching
this is for the adult to cut out a "flame" from paper and
tape it lightly to the child. When the child actually
stops, drops, and rolls on the ground, the "flame" will
fall off, thereby "extinguishing" the "fire."

Exit drills in the home can <u>also</u> save lives. These **4**
drills need to include information such as how to crawl
low to escape smoke, how to feel for hot doors, and how
to place towels or clothing under doors to stop smoke from
coming into a room. (Children should also understand that
smoke and fumes, not the fire itself, cause most deaths.)
Deciding on a meeting place where all family members can be
accounted for is perhaps the most important.

Making sure children know the fire department phone **5**
number is <u>another</u> way to reduce fire-related injuries
and deaths. It is very important that children know the
correct number because not all areas have a 911 system.
The numbers of all emergency services should be prominently
posted near each phone. Children should know how to dial
these numbers and should know the address from which they
are calling. To practice reporting a fire, a child can
use a toy phone, with an adult assuming the role of the
operator.

<u>Finally,</u> children should be aware of what fire- **6**
fighters look like in their equipment. Some children,
particularly very young ones, are afraid of firefighters
because of their unfamiliar appearance. During a visit
to any local firehouse, children can meet firefighters
who can answer questions and demonstrate and explain their
equipment and gear. If children are familiar with firefighters and their equipment, they will not run away from
them or hide.

Of course, educating children is not enough in itself **7**
to ensure fire safety; parents and other adults must <u>also</u>
educate themselves about what to do (and what not to do)
if a fire actually occurs. For example, do not go back
into a fire for any reason. Have a meeting place where
family members can be accounted for. Do not try to put out
a fire; instead, have someone notify the fire department
immediately. <u>In addition</u>, adults should take the responsibility for getting children involved in fire prevention.
Many children learn best by example. Handouts, displays,
and videotapes are especially helpful. Demonstration and
practice of exit drills in the home and of "Stop, Drop,
and Roll" are <u>also</u> useful, particularly during special fire
hazard periods such as Halloween and Christmas. Participating in drawing escape plans and making inspections of the
home for potential problems <u>also</u> make children feel they
are helping. In fact, children can sometimes see things
that adults overlook.

By keeping these points in mind, children and their **8**
parents can join together to avoid potential disaster. If
family members learn about fire safety and if they practice

and review what they have learned on a regular basis, lives
will be saved.

◆ PRACTICE 14-1

1. Underline the thesis statement of "Fighting Fire with Fire Safety Education." Restate it below in your own words.

Adults should teach young children about fire safety.

2. (a) List the examples Tim uses to support his thesis. (b) Which examples does he group together? Why? (c) Which examples does he develop in paragraphs of their own? Why?

(a) Young children should be taught the consequences of playing with matches, stove burners, hot liquids, and electrical appliances; how to extinguish fires; how to conduct exit drills in the home; the fire department phone number; to be aware of how firefighters look in their equipment.

(b) Tim groups matches together with other burn-producing household items because they are all commonly found around the house, and because teaching children not to use them as toys is the first step in fire prevention.

(c) Tim develops full paragraphs on how to extinguish clothing fires, how to conduct exit drills, knowing the fire department phone number, and being aware of what firefighters look like in their equipment. He also includes a full paragraph on adults' responsibilities. Each of these examples requires some explanation because they deal with what to do if a fire occurs.

3. How does Tim link his examples to one another? Underline some of the transitional words that serve this purpose.

Tim uses transitional words such as first, another, also, and finally to link examples and connect all his ideas to his thesis.

4. Is the straightforward introduction effective? How else might Tim have opened his essay?

Answers will vary.

5. Is the conclusion effective? How else could Tim have ended his essay?

Answers will vary.

6. What is this essay's greatest strength? What is its greatest weakness?

Strength: _____ *Answers will vary.* _____

Weakness: _____ *Answers will vary.* _____

◆ PRACTICE 14-2

Following the writing process outlined in Chapter 12, write an exemplification essay on one of the following topics.

> Advantages (or disadvantages) of starting college right after high school
> The three best things ever invented
> Who (or what) should appear on U.S. postage stamps? Why?
> Advantages (or disadvantages) of being a young parent
> Athletes who really are role models
> Four items students need to survive in college
> What messages do various hip-hop artists send to listeners?
> Study strategies that work
> Traits of a good employee
> News events that concerned, troubled, or shocked you

◆ PRACTICE 14-3

On a separate sheet of paper, write an exemplification essay explaining how this advertisement appeals to its target audience. Is it effective? Why or why not? Begin by identifying the ad, the product it promotes, and the audience you think it hopes to reach. Then, state your thesis. After briefly describing the ad, give examples to support your thesis.

Word Power

manipulate to use dishonest or devious behavior in order to exert influence

entice to attract by appealing to hope or desire; to lure

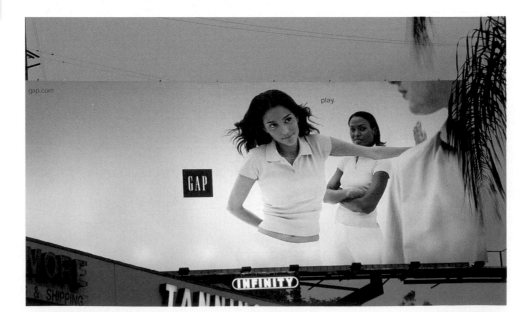

☑ SELF-ASSESSMENT CHECKLIST:
Writing an Exemplification Essay

☐ Does your introduction give readers a clear idea of what to expect? If not, revise your introduction to clarify your essay's goals.

☐ Does your essay include a clearly stated thesis? If not, revise your thesis statement to clarify your essay's main idea.

☐ Do all your examples support your thesis? Eliminate any irrelevant examples.

☐ Do you have enough examples to support your thesis? Add examples where necessary.

☐ Is each example clearly related to the essay's thesis? If not, reword your topic sentences to clarify the connection.

☐ Do transitional words and phrases clearly link your examples to one another? Add transitions where necessary.

☐ Does your conclusion sum up the main idea of your essay? If not, revise the conclusion to make this idea clear to readers.

☐ What problems did you experience in writing your essay? What would you do differently next time?

B   Narration

Narration tells a story, usually presenting a series of events in chronological (time) order, moving from beginning to end. A **narrative essay** can tell a personal story, or it can recount a recent or historical event or a fictional story.

For information on writing a narrative paragraph, see Chapter 4.

FOCUS Topics for Narration

The wording of your assignment may suggest narration. For example, you may be asked to *tell, trace, summarize,* or *recount.*

Assignment	Thesis Statement
Composition Tell about a time when you had to show courage even though you were afraid.	Sometimes a person can exhibit great courage despite being afraid.

(continued on the following page)

Teaching Tip
For examples of narrative essays by professional writers, see 36B.

● **Writing Tip**

Many everyday writing tasks call for narration. For example, in a job application letter, you might summarize your previous work experience.

14 B

(continued from the previous page)

Assignment	Thesis Statement
American history Summarize the events that occurred during President Franklin Delano Roosevelt's first one hundred days in office.	Although many thought they were extreme, the measures enacted by Roosevelt during his first one hundred days in office were necessary to fight the effects of the economic depression.
Political science Trace the development of the Mississippi Freedom Democratic Party.	As the Mississippi Freedom Democratic Party developed, it found a voice that spoke for equality and justice.

When you write a narrative essay, you can discuss one event or several in each paragraph of your essay.

Options for Organizing Narrative Essays

One Event per Paragraph	**Several Events per Paragraph**
¶1 Introduction	¶1 Introduction
¶2 First event	¶2 First group of events
¶3 Second event	¶3 Second group of events
¶4 Third event	¶4 Third group of events
¶5 Conclusion	¶5 Conclusion

Sometimes, to add interest to your narrative, you may decide not to use exact chronological order. For example, you might begin with the end of your story and then move back to the beginning to trace the events that led to this outcome. However you arrange the events, carefully worded topic sentences and clear transitional words and phrases will help readers follow your narrative.

FOCUS   Transitions for Narration

After	First . . . Second . . .	Soon
As soon as	Third	Then
At the same time	Immediately	Two hours (days,
Before	Later	months, years)
Earlier	Meanwhile	later
Eventually	Next	
Finally	Now	

The following student essay, "Swing Shift" by Mark Cotharn, is a narrative that relates the events of a day in the life of a police officer. Notice that Mark uses present tense to make his dramatic, emotional story more immediate. (Paragraph 3, which moves back in time to summarize events that occurred earlier in the week, uses past tense.) Transitional words and phrases help link events in chronological order, and the mention of specific days and times also helps keep readers on track.

Swing Shift

I'm home <u>now</u>, safe within familiar walls. Surrounded by my wife and children, I sit at my kitchen table drinking a cold beer, trying to wake up. <u>After the week I've had</u>, I wonder why I keep this job.

<u>Today</u> is Thursday, and I've got to pull myself together long enough for one more shift. It's eleven o'clock in the morning, and I've got one hour to prepare mentally for work. This was such a crazy week, I'm not sure if I can.

<u>Monday</u> it was the guy on Weeping Willow who was cut up like a side of beef by two parolees. <u>Later</u> that evening, there was that seventeen-year-old boy who was stabbed to death by his friend. <u>Tuesday</u> brought a father angry at me for giving his kid a citation. The kid didn't tell his old man I threw a bag of dope away, to give him a second chance. <u>Wednesday</u> was the triple gangland execution on Holley. I will never forget the way Teto Gomez looked with most of his head gone or the way his brains decorated the yellow rose bush. But the worst part of that case was doing CPR on Robert Berassa, who had been shot fourteen times. He was wearing a white T-shirt that was turning crimson. Every time I compressed on his chest, my shirt turned crimson, too. It was too late; Robert was dead.

<u>Soon</u> I finish my beer and make my way to the station. Only God can know what the day's events will bring, but I really hope it won't be much.

After a short briefing, I begin my shift on patrol. <u>Almost immediately</u>, I find myself in pursuit of an armed robbery suspect carrying several handguns and some dynamite. I chase him through the city for almost twelve minutes, at speeds exceeding a hundred miles per hour, before his van quits running and comes to a stop.

I stop my unit behind his van. <u>Then</u>, with shotgun in hand, I make my way to within twenty feet of his door. I repeat commands for him to put his hands up, but he won't listen to me. Instead, he opens his door and charges at me. I see that he has something in his hand, but I can't tell what it is. <u>Before</u> I know it, I hear two loud booms. The suspect falls to the ground in a pool of blood. Confused, I feel the rotorwash of a helicopter twenty feet over my head and hear the wail of approaching police cars. Still, I don't understand why

1

2

3

4

5

6

Word Power

swing shift a work shift between the day and night shifts (for example, 4 p.m. to midnight)

Teaching Tip
Because the student is telling the story in his own voice, this essay includes many contractions. Remind students that contractions are generally not acceptable in college writing.

ESL Tip
This essay contains many colloquial expressions. You may need to explain them to nonnative speakers.

the suspect dropped so suddenly until I see smoke rising
from the barrel of my shotgun. The suspect is dead,
clutching a stick of dynamite.

Unable to let go of my professionalism in public, I   7
immediately detach myself from all emotions or feelings.
Many fellow officers come to me and call me Stud,
Killer, Ice Man, Exterminator; others come to me and
congratulate me on a job well done.

Later, heading back to the station, I turn off the   8
radio and listen to the silence of my thoughts. I know
when I get there I will be read my rights and interviewed like a common crook. What did I do wrong?

As I expected, I'm met at the door by a shooting   9
team from Internal Affairs. These guys are serious about
their job. If the team can find a reason to convict me,
they will. The interrogation is lengthy; I'm exhausted.
Eventually, I realize that twelve hours or so have
gone by and the questions are still coming. I recognize
the interrogation technique because it's the same one
I use.

It's three o'clock in the morning. The shooting   10
team is done with me, and I'm headed out the door for
home when my chief tells me to go upstairs and talk to
the department shrink. Why? I don't need a shrink; I
need sleep.

The shrink is asking me stupid questions like "How   11
do you feel?" and "Are you going to be OK?" What am I
supposed to say? No? I tell her I'm just fine and that
I'll be back to work in two days.

Finally, on my way home, alone in my car, I come   12
to. My palms sweat; my chest constricts; my pulse ham-
mers. My mind races back to the intersection of Citrus
and Arrow. I can see his face; he's laughing at me. I
hear two crisp booms and see him fall.

◆ PRACTICE 14-4

1. Underline the thesis statement of "Swing Shift." Restate it below in
   your own words.

   After a terrible week at work, Mark wonders why he doesn't just quit his

   job.

2. Underline the specific transitional words and phrases and the references to days and times that Mark uses to link events in chronological
   order.

3. Where does Mark mention specific days and times?

   Mark mentions specific days and times in paragraph 2; when he describes what happened during the past work week (paragraph 3); and in para-

graph 10.

4. What specific events and situations support Mark's thesis? List as
   many as you can.

   Answers will vary. Paragraph 3 recounts a series of violent incidents;

   paragraphs 5 and 6 describe the shooting.

5. Do you think Mark's essay should have a longer, more fully developed
   opening paragraph, or do you like the introduction he has? Why?

   Answers will vary. The introduction is brief, but it does set the scene,

   establish the tone, and present the essay's thesis statement.

6. Do you think Mark's conclusion should summarize the events his essay
   discusses, or is his conclusion effective? Why?

   Answers will vary.

7. What is this essay's greatest strength? What is its greatest weakness?

   Strength: *Answers will vary.*

   Weakness: *Answers will vary.*

◆PRACTICE 14-5

Following the writing process outlined in Chapter 12, write a narrative
essay on one of the following topics.

   The story of your education
   An ideal day
   The plot summary of a terrible book or movie
   A time when you had to make a split-second decision
   Your first confrontation with authority
   An important historical event
   A day everything went wrong
   A story from your family's history
   Your employment history, from first to most recent job
   A biography of your pet

◆ PRACTICE 14-6

On a separate sheet of paper, write a narrative essay that tells the story behind the picture on the following page.

Word Power

peril   imminent danger;
risk of harm

menacing   threatening

Scene from a movie from the early 1900s in which the heroine narrowly escapes from a variety of perilous situations.

✔ SELF-ASSESSMENT CHECKLIST:

Writing a Narrative Essay

☐ Does your introduction make the purpose of your narrative clear to readers? Does it set the scene and introduce important characters? Develop your opening paragraph further if you need to.

☐ What is your essay's thesis? If necessary, revise your thesis statement to make your main idea clear.

☐ Have you included all the specific events you need? Tell about additional incidents, if necessary.

☐ Are all the events you discuss clearly related to your thesis statement? If necessary, revise your essay to clarify the relationship of each event to your essay's main idea; delete any irrelevant events.

☐ Are the events you discuss arranged in clear chronological order? Rearrange events if necessary to reflect the order in which they occurred.

☐ Do topic sentences and transitional words and phrases make the sequence of events clear? Revise if necessary to clarify this sequence.

(continued on the following page)

(continued from the previous page)

■ Does your conclusion remind readers why you have told them your story? If necessary, revise your conclusion to make your purpose clear.

■ What problems did you experience in writing your essay? What would you do differently next time?

C Description

Description tells what something looks, sounds, smells, tastes, or feels like. A **descriptive essay** uses details to give readers a clear, vivid picture of a person, place, or object.

For information on writing a descriptive paragraph, see Chapter 5.

FOCUS Topics for Description

The wording of your assignment may suggest description. For example, it may ask you to *describe* or to *tell what an object looks like*.

Assignment	Thesis Statement
Composition Describe a room that was important to you when you were a child.	Pink-and-white striped wallpaper, tall shelves of cuddly stuffed animals, and the smell of Oreos dominated the bedroom I shared with my sister.
Scientific writing Describe a piece of scientific equipment.	The mass spectrometer is a complex instrument, but every part is ideally suited to its function.
Art history Choose one modern painting and describe its visual elements.	The disturbing images crowded together in Picasso's *Guernica* suggest the senselessness of war.

Teaching Tip
For examples of descriptive essays by professional writers, see 36C.

● **Writing Tip**
Many everyday writing tasks call for description. For example, in a statement to your insurance company after an automobile accident, you might describe the damage to your car.

When you plan a descriptive essay, you focus on selecting details that help your readers see what you see, feel what you feel, and experience what you experience. Your goal is to create a single **dominant impression**, a central theme or idea to which all the details relate. This dominant impression unifies the description and gives readers an overall sense of what the person, object, or scene looks like (and perhaps what it sounds, smells, tastes, or feels like). Sometimes—but not always—your details will support a thesis, making a point about the subject you are describing.

You can arrange details in a descriptive essay in many different ways. For example, you can move from least to most important details (or vice versa), from top to bottom (or from bottom to top or side to side), or from far to near (or near to far). Each of your essay's body paragraphs may focus on one key characteristic of the subject you are describing or on several related descriptive details.

Options for Organizing Descriptive Essays

Least to Most Important	Top to Bottom	Far to Near
¶1 Introduction	¶1 Introduction	¶1 Introduction
¶2 Least important details	¶2 Details at top	¶2 Distant details
¶3 More important details	¶3 Details in middle	¶3 Closer details
¶4 Most important details	¶4 Details on bottom	¶4 Closest details
¶5 Conclusion	¶5 Conclusion	¶5 Conclusion

When you describe a person, object, or scene, you can use **objective description**, reporting only what your senses of sight, sound, smell, taste, and touch tell you ("The columns were two feet tall and made of white marble"). You can also use **subjective description**, conveying your attitude or your feelings about what you observe ("The columns were tall and powerful looking, and their marble surface seemed as smooth as ice.") Many essays combine these two kinds of description.

FOCUS **Figures of Speech**

Descriptive writing, particularly subjective description, is frequently enriched by *figures of speech*—language that creates special or unusual effects.

■ A **simile** uses *like* or *as* to compare two unlike things.

Her smile was like sunshine.

■ A **metaphor** compares two unlike things without using *like* or *as*.

Her smile was a light that lit up the room.

■ **Personification** suggests a comparison between a nonliving thing and a person by giving the nonliving thing human traits.

The sun smiled down on the crowd.

As you write, use transitional words and expressions to guide readers through your description. (Many of these transitions are prepositions or other words and phrases that indicate location or distance.)

FOCUS **Transitions for Description**

Above	In front of	Outside
Behind	Inside	Over
Below	Nearby	The least
Between	Next to	important
Beyond	On	The most
In	On one side . . . On	important
In back of	the other side	Under

The following student essay, "African Violet" by Alisha Woolery, uses description to create a portrait of a family member. By combining subjective and objective description and using specific visual details, Alisha conveys a vivid impression of her great-grandmother as physically frail yet emotionally spirited.

African Violet

The black-and-white picture of my great-grand-parents is a picture I often bring into my mind when I have decided to look at the "big picture" of life and think all the "deep thoughts." I see their faces, etched into the contrasting grays, so young, so hopeful for their new lives together. My mind then shifts to a more recent picture of my great-grandma with her small, frail body, which in the end gave her more pain than she could handle. At this point, I realize how much she taught me about life and death--and about everything in between.   1

My great-grandfather died when I was quite young, and I have only a faint memory of riding his foot like a horse while he recited "Banbury Cross." I have to create an image of him from my relatives' fond memories. Fortunately, however, I knew my great-grandma well, and the conversations we had are among my favorite memories of her. Often, I picture her sitting with me in her parlor, telling me one of the numerous stories of her youth.   2

"One time I was getting to be about sixteen years old, and there was this boy who asked me on a picnic." Her eyes brightened as she told her story. "He was older than me, and he had a horse and buggy! And whoowee! That was really something."   3

The look of astonishment on my face must have been apparent because we laughed until I thought we would keel over. There she was, ninety years old, with absolutely no teeth, telling me how hot this boy who had asked her out was. It was then I realized that the eyes looking out from her aging face were the same brown eyes that had flirted with boys, had fallen in love, and had seen her children and her children's children's children. She had years of experience, and I had very little, but on that warm summer evening, as we sat in her living room, her story bridged the gap between generations.   4

When I don't picture my great-grandma telling stories, I see her on her sunporch, engaged in her one true passion: caring for her plants. She loved them all, but her favorites were small plants with dark green leaves and purple blossoms, African violets. I didn't inherit her green thumb, so the miracles she worked with plants were a constant wonder to me. Stems and leaves seemed to thrive under her gentle touch. Plants were her pride and joy, and until she was in her mid-eighties I often saw her, on hands and knees, digging around in the dirt in her front yard.   5

No, Grandma didn't resign herself to age and let life pass her by; she rode it for all it was worth. In fact, when I picture her, I often see her outside, behind the wheel of her car. The woman was a traffic hazard, not because she poked along as so many older folks do but because she was a speed demon! Poised for action, Grandma strapped herself into her brown 1972 Nova and sped out toward destinations unknown, with one foot on the gas and the other on the brake. I suppose, by all laws of nature, her driving escapades should have done her in, but Grandma died a peaceful death with quiet resolution and acceptance. In fact, she probably had a better outlook on the whole thing than anyone else in the family. I was only fifteen, and she was the closest person to me to die, so it was especially difficult for me to accept that our talks were simply over.   6

It wasn't until recently that I realized that even by her dying, Grandma was continuing to teach me about life. Now, when I picture her, I see not just her lively stories, caring hands, and daredevil spirit, but also her courage: I see how bravely she dealt with the increasing pain in her legs as her body deteriorated.   7

The memories of my great-grandma are very important to me, and sometimes it scares me when a detail escapes my mind because remembering our time together and what I've learned from her is all I have left of her. It is   8

virtually impossible to communicate the impact she has
had on me. The only way I feel I can repay her is by
telling her stories to my own grandchildren and great-
grandchildren someday, keeping her memory alive.

◆ PRACTICE 14-7

1. What dominant impression of her great-grandmother does Alisha convey to readers?

   Wise, high-spirited, strong, funny, and brave

2. List the specific visual details Alisha uses to convey her essay's dominant impression. What other details could she have included?

   Answers will vary. They might include her great-grandmother talking about

   a boy who asked her to go on a picnic, digging in the dirt in her front yard,

   speeding in her brown 1972 Nova.

3. What determines the order in which details are presented in this
essay? How else might Alisha have arranged details?

   The settings for Alisha's memories of her great-grandmother determine

   the order. She moves from indoors (the parlor) to the sunporch to the

   open road.

4. Is this essay primarily a subjective or an objective description?

   subjective

5. What is this essay's greatest strength? What is its greatest weakness?

   Strength: *Answers will vary.*

   Weakness: *Answers will vary.*

◆ PRACTICE 14-8

Following the writing process outlined in Chapter 12, write a descriptive
essay on one of the following topics.

An abandoned building   A street, road, or highway
Your supervisor   A painting or photograph
A person or character who   A historical site or monument
   makes you laugh (or   An advertisement
   frightens you)   An object you cherish
Your room (or your closet   Someone whom everyone notices
   or desk)

◆ **PRACTICE 14-9**

On a separate sheet of paper, write a real-estate brochure for the house pictured here, using your imagination to describe its setting, exterior, and interior in detail. Your goal in this descriptive essay is to provide enough positive details to interest a prospective buyer.

Word Power

mansion   a large, stately house

lush   characterized by luxuriant growth

☑ SELF-ASSESSMENT CHECKLIST:
Writing a Descriptive Essay

◻ Does your introduction identify the subject of your description and convey your essay's dominant impression? Revise your introduction if necessary to clarify your essay's focus.

◻ Do you describe every significant aspect of your subject in detail? If necessary, add specific visual details to create a more complete, more vivid picture.

◻ Do all the details in your essay support your dominant impression? Eliminate any irrelevant details.

◻ Are your details arranged in a definite order within your essay and within paragraphs? Would another order be more effective? Rearrange the details if necessary.

◻ Do topic sentences and transitional words and phrases move readers smoothly from one part of your subject to another? Reword topic sentences and add transitions where necessary.

(continued on the following page)

(continued from the previous page)

■ Does your conclusion leave readers with a clear sense of your essay's purpose? Revise if necessary to reinforce the dominant impression you want your description to convey.

■ What problems did you experience in writing your essay? What would you do differently next time?

D Process

A **process** is a series of chronological steps that produces a particular result. **Process essays** explain the steps in a procedure, telling how something is (or was) done. A process essay can be organized as either a *process explanation* or a set of *instructions*.

For information on writing a process paragraph, see Chapter 6.

FOCUS Topics for Process

The wording of your assignment may suggest process. For example, you may be asked to *explain a process, give instructions, give directions,* or *give a step-by-step account.*

Assignment	Thesis Statement
American government Explain the process by which a bill becomes a law.	The process by which a bill becomes a law is long and complex, involving numerous revisions and a great deal of compromise.
Pharmacy practice Summarize the procedure for conducting a clinical trial of a new drug.	To ensure that drugs are safe and effective, scientists follow strict procedural guidelines for testing and evaluating them.
Technical writing Write a set of instructions for applying for a student internship in a state agency.	When applying for a government internship, students must follow several important steps.

Teaching Tip
For examples of process essays by professional writers, see 36D.

● **Writing Tip**
Many everyday writing tasks describe a process. For example, in a training manual for new employees at your place of work, you might explain how to operate a piece of equipment or what to do in an emergency.

If your purpose is simply to help readers understand a process, not actually perform it, you will write a process explanation. **Process explanations,** like the first two examples in the Focus box above, often use present tense verbs ("Once a bill *is* introduced in Congress" or "A scientist first *submits* a funding application") to explain how a procedure is generally carried out. However, when a process explanation describes a specific procedure that was completed in the past, it uses past tense verbs ("The next thing I *did*").

14 D

● **Writing Tip**

Instructions also usually
include a list of necessary
materials or equipment as
well as cautions and re-
minders readers might need
to know when performing
the process.

If your purpose is to enable readers to actually perform the steps in a process, you will write instructions. **Instructions**, like the last example in the Focus box on page 173, always use present tense verbs in the form of commands to tell readers what to do ("First, *meet* with your adviser").

Whichever kind of process essay you write, you can either devote a full paragraph to each step of the process or group a series of minor steps together in a single paragraph.

Options for Organizing Process Essays

One Step per Paragraph	**Several Steps per Paragraph**
¶1 Introduction	¶1 Introduction
¶2 First step in process	¶2 First group of steps
¶3 Second step in process	¶3 Second group of steps
¶4 Third step in process	¶4 Third group of steps
¶5 Conclusion	¶5 Conclusion

As you write your process essay, discuss each step in the order in which it is performed, making sure your topic sentences clearly identify the function of each step or group of steps. If you are writing instructions, be sure to include any warnings or reminders you think are necessary.

Transitions are extremely important in process essays because they enable readers to follow the sequence of steps in the process and, in the case of instructions, to perform the process themselves.

FOCUS **Transitions for Process**

After that	Later	The first (second,
As	Meanwhile	third) step
As soon as	Next	The last step
At the same time	Now	Then
Finally	Once	The next step
First	Soon	When
Immediately	Subsequently	While

The following student essay, Mai Yoshikawa's "Under Water," explains the process of scuba diving. Because Mai did not think her readers would be likely to have the opportunity to try scuba diving, she did not write her essay in the form of instructions. Instead, she wrote a process explanation, using present tense verbs. Notice how clear transitions move readers smoothly through the steps of the process.

```
                    Under Water

      For most people, their first scuba-diving experi-     1
   ence in the ocean does not turn out to be a very good
   one, and so it was with me. Because I rushed to see the
   beauty of the seascape, I wasted oxygen and didn't pay
```

much attention to the instructor. Unexpected dangers lie under water, and most first-time divers, like me, are unaware of the risk they are taking when they enter this other world. Now, as a more experienced diver, I have learned that I need to protect myself from trouble by having the right equipment and knowing how to use it correctly.

To ensure a safe dive, the first thing everyone   2
needs to do is to assemble some basic equipment: an air tank, fins, snorkel, mask, life vest, nylon socks, weight belt, gloves, regulator, pressure and depth gauges, and, occasionally, a wetsuit. The weight belt maintains the diver's neutral buoyancy; therefore, the number of weights a person carries will vary. (The lighter the diver, the more weights he or she needs.) While I am floating under water, the weight belt and the air pressure work together to enable me to stay at a certain depth without moving up and down. The nylon socks keep my fins from slipping and help me avoid foot injuries. The pressure and depth gauges are connected to the tank where I can easily reach them and check to make sure the numbers on the two instruments correspond. The gauges are set to notify me how deep I can swim with the amount of oxygen left in my tank. Once I get all this equipment and check it, I plan the day's activities and routes with the instructor. The instructor, at that point, becomes my "buddy."

The next step--a thorough, careful equipment   3
check--is extremely important. If there are more than two divers, each person pairs up with another person. Usually someone who has had a lot of experience and knows the importance of the inspection, such as an assistant instructor or the owner of the dive shop, is available to help the amateur divers get set up. Using the buddy system, I check my partner's equipment and make sure every part is in gear, and she checks mine as well. First, I make sure that the mask fits my buddy's face and that no hair is caught in the rubber lining because any space will allow water to enter. Next, I pull the string on her life vest, examine the jacket as the air inflates, and listen to make sure it holds the air with no leak. Then, I place the regulator in my mouth, and I try breathing for a while as the oxygen from the tank flows into me each time I inhale. Finally, I open the valve of the tank to its fullest so that my partner will get enough oxygen as she dives.

As I check to make sure my equipment is working, I   4
get tense and nervous, thinking about possible accidents that, in the worst situation, could kill me. Once this

serious phase is finished, however, I am ready for
the main event of the day: the dive itself. Usually,
the group dive lasts for two or three separate periods,
each consisting of approximately twenty to forty minutes. Changing diving spots after every swim gives me
the opportunity to enjoy different scenery. On lucky
days, I can see rare, enormous fish that I never dreamt
of viewing except on the television screen. In most
cases, the instructors give us permission to feed these
fish.

Scuba diving is an exciting, breathtaking sport,   5
but I have learned that no matter how many times I experience it, I have to be very careful and responsible
about the actions I take both before and after I enter
the water. But once I start swimming deep into the
ocean, I feel so small, yet so free. The fear and panic
disappear from my mind with the bubbles of oxygen that
flow out from my regulator, and my own rhythmic breathing echoes in my ears.

◆ PRACTICE 14-10

1. List the major steps in the process of scuba diving. Does the writer
   present them in strict chronological order?

   assembling basic equipment, checking equipment, the dive itself

   Yes, the steps are presented in strict chronological order.

2. What identifies Mai's essay as a process explanation rather than a set
   of instructions?

   Verbs are not commands.

3. Underline some of the transitional words and phrases that link the
   steps in the process. Are any other transitions needed?

   Answers will vary.

4. Underline Mai's thesis statement. Restate it below in your own words.

   Divers must protect themselves by having proper equipment and using it

   correctly.

5. Why does Mai open her essay with a negative experience? Is this an effective opening strategy?

Answers will vary. Students may suggest that it is an effective strategy because Mai points out from the beginning that scuba diving can be potentially dangerous and that divers must be careful to follow certain procedures.

6. What is the essay's greatest strength? What is its greatest weakness?

Strength: *Answers will vary.*

Weakness: *Answers will vary.*

◆ PRACTICE 14-11

Following the writing process outlined in Chapter 12, write a process essay on one of the following topics. (Note: Before you begin, decide whether a process explanation or a set of instructions will be more appropriate for your purpose.)

An unusual recipe
College registration
Finding an apartment
Applying for a job
Getting dressed for a typical Saturday night
A religious ritual or cultural ceremony
A task you often do at work
A do-it-yourself project that didn't get done
Your own writing process
A self-improvement program (past, present, or future)
How to find something on the Internet

◆ PRACTICE 14-12

List the steps involved in planning the perfect party. Then, use this list to help you write a process essay that gives step-by-step instructions in the order in which they need to be done. (Hint: You can devote separate paragraphs to tasks to be done the week before, the day before, the morning of the party, and so on.) Be sure to include cautions and warnings to help your readers avoid problems.

Word Power

priorities most important tasks

optimum the most favorable condition for a particular situation

John Belushi, as John "Bluto" Blutarsky, in the infamous toga party scene from Animal House *(1978).*

☑ SELF-ASSESSMENT CHECKLIST:
Writing a Process Essay

☐ Does your introduction identify the process you will discuss and indicate its purpose? Revise your introduction if necessary to clarify your purpose.

☐ Is your essay a process explanation or a set of instructions? If your strategy is not appropriate for your essay's purpose, rewrite the essay using a different strategy.

☐ Does your thesis statement present an overview of the process? If not, revise the statement to make it as clear and specific as you can.

☐ Do you include every important step in the process? If not, add steps that will help readers understand (or perform) the process.

☐ Are all the steps you present necessary? Delete any irrelevant or unimportant ones.

☐ Are the steps in the process presented in strict chronological order? Rearrange any that are out of order.

☐ Are related steps grouped in individual paragraphs? If not, revise to make each paragraph unified.

(continued on the following page)

(continued from the previous page)

■ Do topic sentences clearly identify major stages in the process? Do they clarify the function of each step or group of steps? Revise topic sentences as necessary.

■ Do transitional words and phrases clarify the relationship between steps? If necessary, add transitions to make connections clear.

■ Have you included all necessary warnings or reminders? Add cautions or clarifications as needed.

■ Does your conclusion effectively sum up your process? Revise as necessary to clarify your purpose.

■ What problems did you experience in writing your essay? What would you do differently next time?

E Cause and Effect

A **cause** makes something happen; an **effect** is a result of a particular cause or event. **Cause-and-effect essays** identify causes or predict effects; sometimes they do both.

For information on writing a cause-and-effect paragraph, see Chapter 7.

FOCUS Topics for Cause and Effect

The wording of your assignment may suggest cause and effect. For example, the assignment may ask you to *explain why, predict the outcome, list contributing factors, discuss the consequences,* or tell what *caused* something else or how something is *affected* by something else.

Assignment	Thesis Statement
Women's studies What factors contributed to the rise of the women's movement in the 1970s?	The women's movement of the 1970s had its origins in the peace and civil rights movements of the 1960s.
Public health Discuss the possible long-term effects of smoking.	In addition to its physical effects, smoking may also have long-term social and emotional consequences.
Media and society How has television affected the lives of those who have grown up with it?	Television has created a generation of people who learn differently from those in previous generations.

● **Writing Tip**

Many everyday writing tasks involve discussing causes and effects. For example, in a letter to your community's zoning board, you might discuss possible consequences of building a road, mall, or multiplex.

Teaching Tip

For examples of cause-and-effect essays by professional writers, see 36E.

A cause-and-effect essay can focus on causes or on effects. When you write about causes, be sure to examine *all* pertinent causes. You should emphasize the cause you consider the most important, but do not forget to consider other causes that may be relevant to your topic. Similarly, when you write about effects, consider *all* significant effects of a particular cause, not just the first few that you think of.

If your focus is on finding causes, as it is in the first assignment in the Focus box on page 179, your introductory paragraph should identify the effect (the women's movement). If your focus is on predicting effects, as it is in the second and third assignments listed there, you should begin by identifying the cause (smoking, television). In the body of your essay, you can devote a full paragraph to each cause (or effect), or you can group several related causes (or effects) together in each paragraph.

Options for Organizing Cause-and-Effect Essays

Identifying Causes	**Predicting Effects**
¶1 Introduction (identifies effect)	¶1 Introduction (identifies cause)
¶2 First cause	¶2 First effect
¶3 Second cause	¶3 Second effect
¶4 Third (and most important) cause	¶4 Third (and most important) effect
¶5 Conclusion	¶5 Conclusion

Transitions are important in cause-and-effect essays because they establish causal connections, telling readers that A caused B and not the other way around. They also make it clear that events have a *causal* relationship (A *caused* B) and not just a *sequential* one (A *preceded* B). Remember, when one event follows another, the second is not necessarily the result of the first.

FOCUS **Transitions for Cause and Effect**

Accordingly	For this reason	The most important cause
Another cause	Since	
Another effect	So	The most important effect
As a result	The first (second, third) cause	
Because		Therefore
Consequently	The first (second, third) effect	
For		

The following student essay, "How My Parents' Separation Changed My Life" by Andrea DeMarco, examines the effects of a significant event on the writer and her family. Andrea begins by identifying the cause—the separation—and then goes on to explain its specific effects on her family and on herself. Notice how transitional words and phrases make Andrea's causal connections clear to her readers.

How My Parents' Separation Changed My Life

Until I was ten, I lived the perfect all-American
life with my perfect all-American family. I lived in a
suburb of Albany, New York, with my parents, my sister
and brother, and our dog, Daisy. We had a ping-pong
table in the basement, a barbecue in the backyard, and
two cars in the garage. My dad and mom were high school
teachers, and every summer we took a family vacation.
Then, it all changed. <u>My parents' separation made everything different</u>.

One day, just before Halloween, when my sister was
twelve and my brother was fourteen (Daisy was seven),
our parents called us into the kitchen for a family conference. We didn't think anything was wrong at first;
they were always calling these annoying meetings. We
figured it was time for us to plan a vacation, talk
about household chores, or be nagged to clean our rooms.
As soon as we sat down, though, we knew this was different. We could tell Mom had been crying, and Dad's
voice cracked when he told us the news. They were sepa-
rating--they called it a "trial separation"--and Dad was
moving out of our house.

I hardly remember what else we talked about that
day. But I do remember how things changed right after
that. Every Halloween we always had a big jack-o'-
lantern on our front porch. Dad used to spend hours at
the kitchen table cutting out the eyes, nose, and mouth
and hollowing out the insides. That Halloween, <u>because</u>
he didn't live with us, things were different. Mom
bought a pumpkin, and I guess she was planning to carve
it up. But she never did, and we never mentioned it. It
sat on the kitchen counter for a couple of weeks, getting soft and wrinkled, and then it just disappeared. I
suppose Mom threw it out.

Other holidays were also different <u>because</u> Mom and
Dad were not living together. Our first Thanksgiving
without Dad was pathetic. I don't even want to talk about
it. Christmas was different, too. We spent Christmas Eve
with Dad and our relatives on his side, and Christmas
Day with Mom and her family. Of course, we got twice as
many presents as usual. I realize now that both our parents were trying to make up for the pain of the separation. The worst part came when I opened my big present
from Mom: Barbie's Dream House. This was something I had
always wanted. Even at ten, I knew how hard it must
have been for Mom to afford it. The trouble was, I had
gotten the same thing from Dad the night before.

The worst <u>effect</u> of my parents' separation on all
three of us was not the big events but the disruption

Teaching Tip
Because the student is telling the story in his own voice, this essay includes many contractions. Remind students that contractions are generally not acceptable in college writing.

1

2

3

4

5

in our everyday lives. Dinner used to be a family time, a chance to talk about our day and make plans. But after Dad left, Mom seemed to stop eating. Sometimes she would just have coffee while we ate, and sometimes she would not eat at all. She would microwave some frozen thing for us or heat up soup or cook some hot dogs. We didn't care--after all, now she let us watch TV while we ate--but we did notice.

Other parts of our routine changed, too. <u>Because</u> Dad didn't live with us anymore, we had to spend every Saturday and every Wednesday night at his apartment, no matter what else we had planned. Usually he would take us to dinner at McDonald's on Wednesdays, and then we would go back to his place and do our homework or watch TV. That wasn't too bad. Saturdays were a lot worse. We really wanted to be home, hanging out with our friends in our own rooms in our own house. Instead, we had to do some planned activity with Dad, like go to a movie or a hockey game.

6

My parents were separated for only eight months, but it seemed like forever. By the end of the school year, they had somehow worked things out, and Dad was back home again. That June, at a family conference around the kitchen table, we made our summer vacation plans. We decided on Williamsburg, Virginia, the all-American vacation destination. So things were back to normal, but I wasn't, and I'm still not. Now, eight years later, my mother and father are all right, but I still worry they'll split up again. And I worry about my own future husband and how I will ever be sure he's the one I'll stay married to. <u>As a result</u> of what happened in my own family, it is hard for me to believe any relationship is forever.

7

◆ PRACTICE 14-13

1. Underline Andrea's thesis statement. Restate it below in your own words.

Everything changed for Andrea after her parents separated.

_____

_____

2. What specific effects of her parents' separation does Andrea identify?

changes in holiday celebrations

changes in dinner routine

visits to father

3. Underline the transitional words and phrases that make the causal connections in Andrea's essay clear to her readers.

4. Is Andrea's relatively long concluding paragraph effective? Why or why not? Do you think it should be shortened or divided into two paragraphs?

Answers will vary.

_____

_____

_____

5. Is Andrea's straightforward title effective, or should she have used a more creative or eye-catching title? Can you suggest an alternative?

Answers will vary.

_____

_____

_____

6. What is this essay's greatest strength? What is its greatest weakness?

Strength: ___*Answers will vary.*_____

Weakness: ___*Answers will vary.*_____

◆ PRACTICE 14-14

Following the writing process outlined in Chapter 12, write a cause-and-effect essay on one of the following topics.

A teacher's positive (or negative) effect on you
Why you voted a certain way in a recent election (or why you chose not to vote)
Why the popularity of soap operas has been steadily declining
How your life would be different if you dropped out of school (or quit your job)
How a particular invention (for example, the cell phone) has changed your life
Why e-mail is so popular
A movie or book that changed the way you look at life
How a particular season (or day of the week) affects your mood
How having a child would change (or has changed) your life
How a particular event made you grow up

◆ PRACTICE 14-15

Imagine you have won a multi-million-dollar lottery. How would your life change? Write a cause-and-effect essay that discusses specific ways in which your life would be different.

☑ SELF-ASSESSMENT CHECKLIST:
Writing a Cause-and-Effect Essay

- Does your introduction identify the particular cause or effect on which your essay will focus? Revise your introduction if necessary to zero in on your topic.

- Does your essay focus on causes or effects? Does your thesis statement accurately convey this emphasis to readers? If not, revise your thesis statement to identify the key causes or effects that you will emphasize.

- Do you identify all causes or effects relevant to your topic? If not, revise to include all significant causes or effects.

- Do you discuss any irrelevant causes or effects? If necessary, revise to eliminate them.

- Which cause or effect is most important? Arrange causes or effects to indicate their relative importance.

- Does each body paragraph identify and explain one particular cause or effect (or several closely related causes or effects)? Revise where necessary to unify each body paragraph.

- Do your transitional words and phrases make causal connections clear? If not, revise to clarify the relationships between causes and effects.

(continued on the following page)

(continued from the previous page)

■ Does your conclusion reinforce the causal relationships you discuss? Revise to make your emphasis clearer.

■ What problems did you experience in writing your essay? What would you do differently next time?

F Comparison and Contrast

Comparison identifies similarities; **contrast** identifies differences. **Comparison-and-contrast essays** explain how two things are alike or how they are different; sometimes, they discuss both similarities and differences.

For information on writing a comparison-and-contrast paragraph, see Chapter 8.

FOCUS Topics for Comparison and Contrast

The wording of your assignment may suggest comparison and contrast—for example, by asking you to *compare, contrast, discuss similarities,* or *identify differences.*

Assignment	Thesis Statement
Philosophy What basic similarities do you find in the beliefs of Henry David Thoreau and Martin Luther King Jr.?	Although King was more politically active, both he and Thoreau strongly supported the idea of civil disobedience.
Nutrition How do the diets of native Japanese and Japanese Americans differ?	As they become more and more assimilated, Japanese Americans consume more fats than their native Japanese counterparts do.
Literature Contrast the two sisters in Alice Walker's short story "Everyday Use."	Unlike Maggie, Dee—her more successful, better-educated sister—has rejected her family's heritage.

● **Writing Tip**
Many everyday writing tasks call for comparison and contrast. For example, in a report to your supervisor at work, you might compare the merits of two procedures or two suppliers.

Teaching Tip
For examples of comparison-and-contrast essays by professional writers, see 36F.

When you organize a comparison-and-contrast essay, you can choose either a *point-by-point* or a *subject-by-subject* arrangement. A **point-by-point** comparison alternates between the two subjects you are comparing or contrasting, moving back and forth from one subject to the other. A **subject-by-subject** comparison treats its two subjects separately, first fully discussing one subject and then moving on to consider the other subject. In both kinds of comparison-and-contrast essays, the same points are discussed in the same order for both subjects.

● **Writing Tip**
In a comparison, your points must match up. If you discuss the appearance and behavior of one breed of dog, you should discuss the same two points for the other breeds you are writing about.

Options for Organizing Comparison-and-Contrast Essays

Point-by-Point Comparison	**Subject-by-Subject Comparison**
¶1 Introduction (identifies subjects to be compared or contrasted)	¶1 Introduction (identifies subjects to be compared or contrasted)
¶2 First point discussed for both subjects	¶¶2–3 First subject discussed
¶3 Second point discussed for both subjects	¶¶4–5 Second subject discussed
¶4 Third point discussed for both subjects	¶6 Conclusion
¶5 Conclusion	

The transitional words and phrases you use in a comparison-and-contrast essay tell readers whether you are focusing on similarities or differences. Transitions also help move readers through your essay from one subject to the other and from one point of similarity or difference to the next.

FOCUS Transitions for Comparison and Contrast

Although	Likewise
But	Nevertheless
Even though	On the contrary
However	On the one hand . . . On the other hand
In comparison	Similarly
In contrast	Unlike
Like	Whereas

The following student essay, "Another Ordinary Day" by Nisha Jani, contrasts teenage boys and girls by going through a typical day in the lives of "Johnny" and "Jane." A point-by-point comparison, Nisha's essay alternates between her two subjects, treating the same points in the same order for each. Notice that topic sentences identify the part of the day under discussion in each paragraph and clearly signal shifts from one subject to the next.

Another Ordinary Day

"Boys are from Jupiter and get stupider/Girls are   1
from Mars and become movie stars/Boys take a bath and
smell like trash/Girls take a shower and smell like a
flower." As simple playground songs like this one suggest, the two sexes see themselves very differently.

Even though as adults, men and women have similar goals, values, and occupations, as children and teenagers, boys and girls often seem to belong to two different species. In fact, from the first moment of the day to the last, the typical boy and girl live very different lives.

The sun rises, and the alarm clock signals the beginning of another day for Johnny and Jane, two seventh-grade classmates. Johnny, an average thirteen-year-old boy, wakes up late and has to hurry. He throws on his favorite jeans, a baggy T-shirt, and a baseball cap. Then, he goes into the kitchen, has a hearty high-cholesterol breakfast, and runs out of the house to school, usually forgetting some vital book or homework assignment. Jane, unlike Johnny, wakes up early. She takes a shower, blow-dries her hair, and puts on her make-up. Then, there is the moment of truth: What should she wear today? Getting dressed can be a very difficult process, one that often includes taking everything out of her closet and calling friends for advice. After she makes her decision, she helps herself to some food (probably low- or no-fat) and goes off to school.

School is a totally different experience for Johnny and Jane. Johnny will probably sit in the back of the classroom with a couple of guys, throwing paper airplanes and spitballs. These will be directed at the males they do not like and the females they think are kind of cute. (However, if their male friends ever ask the boys about these girls, they will say girls are just losers and deny that they like any of them.) On the opposite side of the classroom, however, is Jane, focused on a very different kind of activity. At first it looks as if she is vigorously copying the algebra notes that the teacher is putting on the board, but these notes have absolutely nothing to do with algebra. In actuality, she is writing about boys, clothes, and other topics that are much more important to her than the square root of one hundred twenty-one. Then, she proceeds to fold the note into a box or other creative form, which can often put origami to shame. As soon as the teacher turns around, the note is passed and the process begins all over again.

Lunch, a vital part of the school day, is also very different for Johnny and Jane. On the one hand, for Johnny and his friends, it is a time to compare baseball cards, exchange sports facts, and of course tell jokes about every bodily function imaginable. In front of them on the table, their trays are filled with pizza, soda, fries, and chips, and this food is their main focus. For

Jane, <u>on the other hand</u>, lunch is not about eating; it is a chance to exchange the latest gossip about who is going out with whom. The girls look around to see what people are wearing, what they should do with their hair, and so on. Jane's meal is quite a bit smaller than Johnny's: it consists of a small low-fat yogurt and half a bagel (if she feels like splurging, she will spread some cream cheese on the bagel).

After school, Johnny and Jane head in different   5
directions. Johnny rushes home to get his bike and meets up with his friends to run around and play typical "guy games," like pick-up basketball or touch football. Johnny and his friends play with every boy who shows up, whether they know them or not. They may get into physical fights and arguments; however, in the end it is all a game, and they plan to meet up again the next day. <u>In contrast</u> to the boys, Jane and her friends are very selective. Their circle is a small one, and they do everything together. Some days, they go to the mall (they will not necessarily buy anything there, but they will consider the outing productive anyway because they have spent time together). Most days, though, they just talk, with the discussion ranging from school to guys to lipstick colors. When Jane gets home, she will most likely run to the phone and talk for hours to the same three or four girls.

At the age of thirteen or fourteen, boys and girls   6
do not seem to have very much in common. Given this situation, it is amazing that boys and girls grow up to become men and women who coexist and interact as neighbors, friends, and coworkers. What is even more amazing is that so many grow up to share lives and raise families together, treating each other with love and respect.

◆ PRACTICE 14-16

1. Underline Nisha's thesis statement. Restate it below in your own words.

   Boys and girls are very different in their daily routines.

   _____

2. Does Nisha's opening paragraph identify the subjects she will discuss? Will she focus on similarities or on differences?

   Yes. She indicates that she will focus on differences.

   _____

_____

3. Nisha's essay is a point-by-point comparison. What four points does she discuss for each of her two subjects?

   difference in morning routine, school behavior, lunch routine, and after-

   school activities

   _____

   _____

4. Underline some transitional words and phrases Nisha uses to move readers from one subject (Johnny) to the other (Jane).

5. Reread Nisha's topic sentences. What do they contribute to the essay?

   The topic sentences remind readers that the essay's focus is on con-

   trasting Johnny and Jane.

   _____

   _____

6. What is this essay's greatest strength? What is its greatest weakness?

   Strength: _*Answers will vary.*_____

   Weakness: _*Answers will vary.*_____

◆ PRACTICE 14-17

Following the writing process outlined in Chapter 12, write a comparison-and-contrast essay on one of the following topics.

   Two coworkers
   Two movie heroes
   How you expect your life to be different from the lives of your parents
   Men's and women's ideas about their body images
   Two ways of studying for an exam
   Risk-takers and people who play it safe
   Library research and Internet research
   Country and city living (or you can compare suburban living with either)
   Two popular magazines (features, ads, target audiences, pictures)
   Two professional athletes

◆ PRACTICE 14-18

On a separate sheet of paper, write an essay in which you compare the following two photographs, considering both what the monuments look like and their emotional impact on you.

Word Power
symbol something that represents something else

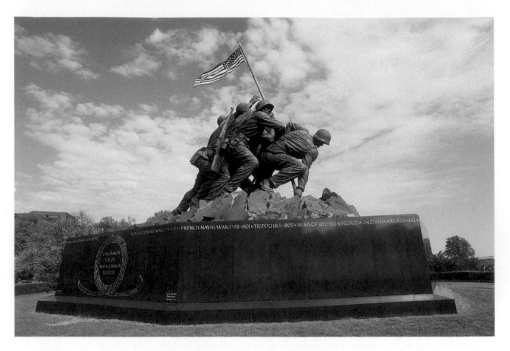

Iwo Jima memorial statue at Arlington National Cemetery.

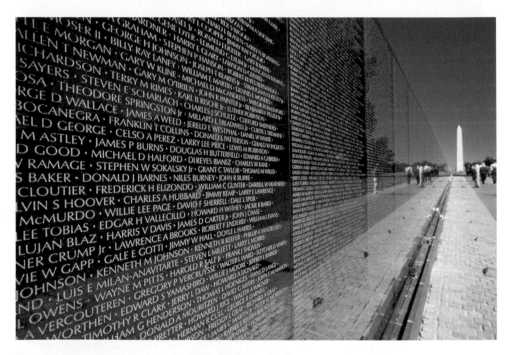

Vietnam Veterans Memorial in Washington, D.C.

☑ SELF-ASSESSMENT CHECKLIST:
Writing a Comparison-and-Contrast Essay

- Does your introduction identify the two subjects you will compare and contrast? If not, revise to make the focus of your essay clear.

(continued on the following page)

(continued from the previous page)

- Does your essay examine similarities or differences? If necessary, revise your thesis statement to make your emphasis clear.

- Have you discussed all significant points of comparison or contrast that apply to your two subjects? Develop your discussion further if necessary.

- Are any points insignificant or irrelevant? If necessary, revise to eliminate any similarities or differences that do not support your thesis.

- Have you treated the same points for both of your two subjects? Revise if necessary to make your discussion balanced.

- Is your essay a point-by-point comparison or a subject-by-subject comparison? If necessary, revise to make your organization consistent with one of these two ways of organizing material.

- Does each topic sentence clearly identify the subject and the point of comparison or contrast being discussed? If necessary, revise topic sentences to clarify each paragraph's focus.

- Do transitional words and phrases move readers from one subject or point to another? Add transitions where necessary.

- Does your conclusion remind readers what your two subjects are and whether you have focused on similarities or differences? If not, revise to reinforce your essay's focus.

- What problems did you experience during the process of writing your essay? What would you do differently next time?

G   Classification

Classification is the act of sorting items into appropriate categories. **Classification essays** divide a whole (your subject) into parts and sort various items into categories.

For information on writing a classification paragraph, see Chapter 9.

FOCUS   **Topics for Classification**

The wording of your assignment may suggest classification. For example, you may be asked to consider *kinds, types, categories, components, segments,* or *parts of a whole.*

(continued on the following page)

● **Writing Tip**

Many everyday writing tasks call for classification. For example, if you coach a youth sports team, you might write a recruitment flyer classifying player requirements by age, grade, and level of experience.

Teaching Tip
For examples of classification essays by professional writers, see 36G.

(continued from the previous page)

Assignment	Thesis Statement
Business What kinds of courses are most useful for students planning to run their own businesses?	Courses dealing with accounting, management, interpersonal communication, and computer science offer the most useful skills for future business owners.
Biology List the components of the blood, and explain the function of each.	Red blood cells, white blood cells, platelets, and plasma have very distinct functions.
Education Classify elementary school children according to their academic needs.	The elementary school population includes special-needs students, students with reading and math skills at or near grade level, and academically gifted students.

As a rule, each paragraph of a classification essay examines a separate category—a different part of the whole. For example, a paragraph could focus on one kind of course in the college curriculum, one component of the blood, or one type of child. Within each paragraph, you discuss the individual items that you have assigned to a particular category—for example, accounting courses, red blood cells, or gifted students. If you consider some categories less important than others, you may decide to discuss those minor categories together in a single paragraph, devoting full paragraphs only to the most significant categories.

Options for Organizing Classification Essays

One Category in Each Paragraph	Major Categories in Separate Paragraphs; Minor Categories Grouped Together
¶1 Introduction (identifies whole and its major categories)	¶1 Introduction (identifies whole and its major categories)
¶2 First category	¶2 Minor categories
¶3 Second category	¶3 First major category
¶4 Third category	¶4 Second (and more important) major category
¶5 Conclusion	¶5 Conclusion

In a classification essay, topic sentences identify the category or categories discussed in each paragraph. Transitional words and phrases signal movement from one category to the next and may also tell readers which categories you consider most and least important.

FOCUS Transitions for Classification

One kind . . .	The first (second,	The most impor-
Another kind	third) category	tant component
The final type	The last group	The next part

The following student essay, "Selling a Deam" by Rob O'Neal, classifies American car names into categories on the basis of the kind of message they communicate to consumers. Notice that Rob discusses one category in each of his body paragraphs, using clear topic sentences to identify and define each kind of car name and relate each category to the group as a whole.

Selling a Dream

The earliest automobiles were often named after the men who manufactured them--Ford, Studebaker, Nash, Olds, Chrysler, Dodge, Chevrolet, and so on. More recently, however, American car makers have been competing to see what kinds of names will sell the most cars. Many car names seem to be chosen simply for how they sound: Alero, Corvette, Neon, Probe, Caprice. Many others, however, are designed to sell specific dreams to consumers. Americans always seem to want to be, do, and become something different. They want to be tough and brave, to explore new places, to take risks. With the names that auto manufacturers choose for their cars, they appeal to Americans' deepest desires. 1

Some American cars are named for places people dream of traveling to. Park Avenue, Malibu, Riviera, Seville, Tahoe, Yukon, Aspen, and Durango are some model names that suggest escape--to New York City, California, Europe, the West. Other place names--Sebring, Daytona, and Bonneville, for example--are associated with the danger and excitement of car racing. And then there is the El Dorado, a car named for a fictional paradise: a city of gold. 2

Other car names convey rough and tough, even dangerous, images. Animal names fall into this category, with models like Ram, Bronco, and Mustang suggesting powerful, untamed beasts. (Cars named after animals, such as Mercury's Cougar, Lynx, and Bobcat and Pontiac's Impala, convey speed as well as power.) Other cars in the "rough and tough" category include those that suggest the wildness of the Old West: Wrangler and Rodeo, for example. Because the American auto industry is centered near Detroit, Michigan, where many cities have 3

Indian names, cars named for the cities where they are manufactured have inherited these names. Thus, cars called Cadillac, Pontiac, and Cherokee recall the proud history of Indian nations, and these too might suggest the excitement of the untamed West.

The most interesting car names in terms of the dream they sell, however, are those that suggest exploration and discovery. Years ago, some car names honored real explorers, like DeSoto and LaSalle. Now, model names only sell an abstract idea. Still, American car names like Blazer, Explorer, Navigator, Mountaineer, Expedition, Caravan, and Voyager (as well as the names of foreign cars driven by many Americans, such as Nissan's Pathfinder and Quest and Honda's Passport and Odyssey) have the power to make drivers feel they are blazing new trails and discovering new worlds--when in fact they may simply be car pooling their children to a soccer game or commuting to work.

4

Today, the car is an ordinary piece of machinery, a necessity for many people. Clearly, the car is no longer seen as the amazing invention it once was. Despite the fact that most people take the existence of cars for granted, however, manufacturers still try to make consumers believe they are buying more than just transportation. But whether we drive a Malibu, Mustang, Cherokee, or Expedition--or even a "royal" LeBaron or Marquis--we eventually realize that we are driving cars, not magic carpets.

5

◆ PRACTICE 14-19

1. What three categories of car names does Rob discuss in his essay?

Rob discusses names that suggest exciting destinations, names that

suggest danger, and names that suggest exploration.

2. Is Rob's treatment of the three categories similar? Does he give the same kind of information for each kind of car name?

Yes. In each of his three body paragraphs, Rob identifies a category of

car name, explains the dream with which it is associated, and gives a

series of examples.

3. How do Rob's topic sentences move readers from one category to the next? How do they link the three categories?

The topic sentence of each body paragraph repeats the words car names

("Some American cars are named . . ."; "Other car names . . ."; "The most

interesting car names . . .") to link the three categories and move readers
from one category to the next.

4. Underline Rob's thesis statement. Restate it below in your own words.

   Car manufacturers select model names to appeal to Americans' dreams

   and desires.

5. Should Rob have included additional examples in each category?
   Should he have included any additional categories?

   Answers will vary. Students will probably be able to suggest additional

   examples for each category, and they may suggest additional categories

   as well.

6. What is this essay's greatest strength? What is its greatest weakness?

   Strength: _____ *Answers will vary.* _____

   Weakness: _____ *Answers will vary.* _____

◆ PRACTICE 14-20

Following the writing process outlined in Chapter 12, write a classification
essay on one of the following topics.

Types of teachers (or bosses)   Traits of oldest children, middle
Ways to lose (or gain) weight   children, and youngest children
Things that you hang on your   Kinds of desserts
  walls   Workers you encounter in a typi-
Kinds of stress   cal day
How students dress   Popular music
Kinds of stores in your com-
  munity shopping district or
  mall

◆ PRACTICE 14-21

Look at the picture on page 196. Then, on a separate sheet of paper, write
an essay in which you classify the food you eat. The categories you create
can classify the food according to convenience, ease of preparation,
healthfulness, where it is consumed, and so on.

Word Power
binge to experience a
period of uncontrolled self-
indulgence

☑ SELF-ASSESSMENT CHECKLIST:
Writing a Classification Essay

- Does your introduction give readers an overview of the subject whose categories you will discuss? If necessary, revise to clarify the subject of your classification.

- Does your thesis statement identify the categories you will discuss? If not, revise your thesis statement to clarify your essay's focus.

- Does each body paragraph discuss a single category or a related group of minor categories? If not, revise to create unified paragraphs.

- Are any categories insignificant or irrelevant? Revise to eliminate any categories that are not central to your essay's purpose.

- Does each topic sentence identify and define the category or categories the paragraph discusses? If necessary, revise your topic sentences to clarify the focus of each paragraph.

- Have you treated each major category similarly and with equal thoroughness? If not, revise to make your discussion balanced.

- Do transitional words and phrases clearly lead readers from one category to the next? If not, revise to make your essay flow more smoothly.

(continued on the following page)

(continued from the previous page)

◻ Does your conclusion review the major categories your essay discusses? If necessary, revise to sum up the categories and their relationships to your subject.

◻ What problems did you experience in writing your essay? What would you do differently next time?

H   Definition

Definition explains the meaning of a term or concept. A **definition essay** presents an *extended definition*, using other patterns of development to move beyond a simple dictionary definition.

For information on writing a definition paragraph, see Chapter 10.

FOCUS   Topics for Definition

The wording of your assignment may suggest definition. For example, you may be asked to *define* or *explain* or to answer the question *What is x?* or *What does x mean?*

Assignment	Thesis Statement
Art Explain the meaning of the term *performance art*.	Unlike more conventional forms of art, *performance art* extends beyond the canvas.
Biology What did Darwin mean by the term *natural selection?*	*Natural selection*, popularly known as "survival of the fittest," is a good deal more complicated than most people think.
Psychology What is *attention deficit disorder?*	*Attention deficit disorder* (ADD), once narrowly defined as a childhood problem, is now known to affect adults as well as children.

Teaching Tip
For examples of definition essays by professional writers, see 36H.

● **Writing Tip**
Many everyday writing tasks call for definition. For example, in a letter of complaint to a neighborhood business, you might define what you mean by terms like *excessive noise* and *rude behavior*.

Teaching Tip
Tell students that when they write a definition, the term being defined should be underlined.

As the thesis statements above suggest, definition essays can be developed in various ways. For example, you can define something by telling how it occurred (narration), by describing its appearance (description), by giving a series of examples (exemplification), by telling how it operates (process), by telling how it is similar to or different from something else (comparison and contrast), or by discussing its parts (classification).

Some definition essays use a single pattern of development; others combine several patterns of development, perhaps using a different one in each paragraph.

Options for Organizing Definition Essays

Single Pattern of Development	Combination of Several Different Patterns of Development
¶1 Introduction (identifies term to be defined)	¶1 Introduction (identifies term to be defined)
¶2 Definition by example	¶2 Definition by description
¶3 Additional examples	¶3 Definition by example
¶4 Additional examples	¶4 Definition by comparison and contrast
¶5 Conclusion	¶5 Conclusion

The kinds of transitions used in a definition essay depend on the specific pattern or patterns of development in the essay. (In addition to the transitional words and expressions listed in the following Focus box, you may also use those appropriate for the particular patterns you use to develop your definition essay. These transitions are listed in Focus boxes throughout this chapter.)

FOCUS **Transitions for Definition**

Also	One characteristic . . . Another
For example	characteristic
In addition	One way . . . Another way
In particular	Specifically
Like	

The following student essay, "Street Smart" by Kristin Whitehead, defines the term *street smart*. In the essay's introduction, Kristin defines her term briefly; in the essay's body paragraphs, she expands her definition. Notice that the topic sentences of Kristin's three body paragraphs repeat a key phrase to remind readers of her essay's subject.

Street Smart

I grew up in a big city, so I was practically born   1
street smart. I learned the hard way how to act and
what to do, and so did my friends. To us, <u>street smart</u>
meant having common sense. We wanted to be cool, but we
needed to be safe, too. Now I go to college in a big
city, and I realize that not everyone here grew up the
way I did. Lots of students are from suburbs or rural

areas, and they are either terrified of the city or totally ignorant of city life. The few suburban or rural kids who are willing to venture downtown are not street smart--but they should be. Being street smart is a vital survival skill, one that everyone should learn.

For me, being street smart means knowing how to protect my possessions. Friends of mine who are not used to city life insist on wearing all their jewelry when they go downtown. I think this is asking for trouble, and I know better. I always tuck my chain under my shirt and leave my gold earrings home. Another thing that surprises me is how some of my friends wave their money around. They always seem to be standing on the street, trying to count their change or stuff dollars into their wallets. Street-smart people make sure to put their money safely away in their pockets or purses before they leave a store. A street-smart person will also carry a backpack, a purse strapped across the chest, or no purse at all. A person who is not street smart carries a purse loosely over one shoulder or dangles it by its handle. Again, these people are asking for trouble.

Being street smart also means protecting myself. It means being aware of my surroundings at all times and looking alert. A lot of times I have been downtown with people who kept stopping on the street to talk about where they should go next or walking up and down the same street over and over again. A street-smart person would never do this. It's important that I look as if I know where I am going at all times, even if I don't. Whenever possible, I decide on a destination in advance, and I make sure I know how to get there. Even if I am not completely sure where I am headed, I make sure my body language conveys my confidence in my ability to reach my destination.

Finally, being street smart means protecting my life. A street-smart person does not walk alone, especially after dark, in an unfamiliar neighborhood. A street-smart person does not ask strangers for directions; when lost, he or she asks a shopkeeper for help. A street-smart person takes main streets instead of side streets. When faced with danger or the threat of danger, a street-smart person knows when to run, when to scream, and when to give up money or possessions to avoid violence.

So how does someone get to be street smart? Some people think it is a gift, but I think it is something almost anyone can learn. Probably the best way to learn how to be street smart is to hang out with people who know where they are going.

◆ **PRACTICE 14-22**

1. Underline Kristin's thesis statement. Restate it below in your own words.

   Everyone should learn how to be street smart.

2. In your own words, define the term *street smart*. Why does this term require more than a one-sentence definition?

   Answers will vary.

3. Where does Kristin use examples to develop her definition? Where does she use comparison and contrast?

   Answers will vary. Students may suggest that Kristin contrasts herself

   with people who are not street smart, giving examples of her behavior and

   theirs.

4. What phrase does Kristin repeat in the topic sentences to tie her three body paragraphs together?

   Being street smart means . . .

5. Kristin's conclusion is quite a bit shorter than her other paragraphs. What, if anything, do you think she should add to this paragraph?

   Answers will vary.

6. What is this essay's greatest strength? What is its greatest weakness?

   Strength: *Answers will vary.*

   Weakness: *Answers will vary.*

◆ **PRACTICE 14-23**

Following the writing process outlined in Chapter 12, write a definition essay on one of the following topics.

Fear	Success	Surprise
Upward mobility	Responsibility	Happiness
Peer pressure	Procrastination	
Competition	Security	

◆ **PRACTICE 14-24**

On a separate sheet of paper, write an essay in which you define *family*. In what ways do the family groups shown on the following page fit or not fit into your definition?

Word Power

nuclear family a family unit made up of a mother and father and their children

14 **I**

For more on the patterns of paragraph development, see Chapters 3–11.

☑ SELF-ASSESSMENT CHECKLIST:
Writing a Definition Essay

☐ Does your introduction identify the term that your essay will define and provide a brief definition? If not, revise to make the scope of your essay clear.

☐ Does your thesis statement indicate why you are defining the term? If not, revise to clarify your purpose.

☐ What pattern or patterns of development do you use to develop your definition? Try exploring other options.

☐ Do topic sentences clearly introduce the different aspects of your definition? If necessary, revise to clarify the relationships between paragraphs.

☐ Are all your ideas clearly related to the term you are defining? If not, revise to eliminate any irrelevant ideas.

☐ Do transitional words and phrases clearly link your ideas? If necessary, add transitions to help guide readers through your essay.

☐ Does your conclusion sum up your essay's main points? Does it remind readers why you are defining the term? If necessary, revise to make your conclusion consistent with the rest of your essay.

☐ What problems did you experience in writing your essay? What would you do differently next time?

I Argument

For information on writing an argument paragraph, see Chapter 11.

Argument takes a stand on a debatable issue. An **argument essay** uses different kinds of evidence—facts, examples, and expert opinion—to persuade readers to accept a position.

● **Writing Tip**

Many everyday writing tasks call for argument. For example, in a letter to the editor of a newspaper, you might take a stand on a political, social, economic, religious, or environmental issue affecting your family or community.

FOCUS **Topics for Argument**

The wording of your assignment may suggest argument. For example, you may be asked to *debate, argue, consider, give your opinion, take a position,* or *take a stand.*

(continued on the following page)

Teaching Tip
For examples of argument essays by professional writers, see 36I.

▼ **Student Voices**
The paper I most enjoyed writing was about the injustices suffered by women in modern society. I liked the powerful feeling I put into it.
Felicia May

(continued from the previous page)

Assignment	Thesis Statement
Composition Explain your position on a current social issue.	People who contribute to Social Security should be able to invest some of their money in the stock market.
American history Do you believe that General Lee was responsible for the South's defeat at the Battle of Gettysburg? Why or why not?	Because Lee refused to listen to the advice given to him by General Longstreet, he is largely responsible for the South's defeat at the Battle of Gettysburg.
Ethics In your opinion, should physician-assisted suicide be legalized?	Although many people think physician-assisted suicide should remain illegal, I believe it should be legal in certain situations.

An argument essay can be organized *inductively* or *deductively*. An **inductive argument** moves from the specific to the general—that is, from a group of specific observations to a general conclusion based on these observations. An inductive argument responding to the first topic in the Focus box above, for example, could begin with a series of facts, examples, and opinions about the benefits of investing in the stock market and end with the conclusion that people should be able to invest part of their Social Security money.

A **deductive argument** moves from the general to the specific. A deductive argument begins with a **major premise** (a general statement that the writer believes his or her audience will accept) and then moves to a **minor premise** (a specific instance of the belief stated in the major premise). It ends with a **conclusion** that follows from the two premises. For example, an essay that responds to the last topic in the Focus box above could begin with the major premise that all terminally ill patients who are in great pain should be given access to physician-assisted suicide. It could then go on to state and explain the minor premise that a particular patient is both terminally ill and in great pain, offering facts, examples, and the opinions of authorities to support this premise. The essay could conclude that this patient should, therefore, be allowed the option of physician-assisted suicide. In this way, the deductive argument goes through three steps.

MAJOR PREMISE   All terminally ill patients who are in great pain should be allowed to choose physician-assisted suicide.

MINOR PREMISE   John Lacca is a terminally ill patient who is in great pain.

CONCLUSION   Therefore, John Lacca should be allowed to choose physician-assisted suicide.

Before you present your argument, think about whether your readers will be hostile to, neutral toward, or in agreement with your thesis. Once you understand your audience, you can decide which points to make in support of your argument.

As you write your argument essay, begin each paragraph with a topic sentence that clearly relates the discussion to the previous paragraph or to your thesis statement. Throughout your essay, try to include specific examples that will make your arguments persuasive. Keep in mind that arguments that rely just on generalizations are not as convincing as those that include vivid details and specific examples. Finally, strive for a balanced, moderate tone, and avoid name-calling or personal attacks.

In addition to presenting your case, you should also briefly identify arguments *against* your position and **refute** them (that is, prove them false) by identifying factual errors or errors in logic. If an opposing argument is particularly strong, concede its strength—but try to point out some weakness as well. Dealing with the opposing point of view in this manner will help you overcome any objections your audience might have and will establish you as a fair and reasonable person.

Options for Organizing Argument Essays

Induction	Deduction
¶1 Introduction	¶1 Introduction
¶2 First point (supported by facts, examples, and expert opinions)	¶2 Major premise stated and explained
¶3 Second point	¶3 Minor premise stated and explained
¶4 Third point	¶4 Evidence supporting minor premise presented
¶5 Identification and refutation of opposing arguments	¶5 Opposing arguments identified and refuted
¶6 Conclusion	¶6 Conclusion

Transitions are extremely important in argument essays because they not only signal the movement from one part of the argument to another but also relate specific points to one another and to the thesis statement.

FOCUS **Transitions for Argument**

Accordingly	However	On the one hand
Admittedly	In conclusion	. . . On the other
Although	Indeed	hand
Because	In fact	Since
But	In summary	Therefore
Certainly	Meanwhile	Thus
Consequently	Moreover	To be sure
Despite	Nevertheless	Truly
Even so	Nonetheless	
Granted	Of course	

The following student paper, "Why Isn't Pete Rose in the Hall of Fame?" by John Fleeger, is an argument essay. John takes a strong stand, and he supports his thesis with specific facts and examples. The deductive argument that underlies John's essay moves from the major premise ("Qualified players who do not violate major-league rules should be inducted into the Hall of Fame") to the minor premise ("Pete Rose is a qualified player who did not violate major-league rules") to the conclusion ("Therefore, Pete Rose should be inducted into the Hall of Fame").

Why Isn't Pete Rose in the Hall of Fame?

The year 1992 was the first year Pete Rose would have been eligible for the National Baseball Hall of Fame. Not only was he not elected, his name did not even appear on the ballot. Why? Has he not established himself as the all-time best hitter in baseball? Was he not a member of two championship teams with the Cincinnati Reds and one with the Philadelphia Phillies? Did he not help build the foundation for the 1990 championship Reds team? Has he not set or tied several major-league and team records during his career? The answer to all of these questions is yes. His dedication to and enthusiasm for the game of baseball earned him the nickname "Charlie Hustle," but they did not earn him his rightful place in the Hall of Fame. This situation is unfair and should be changed.

In the late summer of 1989, Pete Rose was banned from professional baseball. The legal agreement reached between major-league officials and Pete Rose does not offer any evidence that Rose bet on any baseball games, and Rose himself does not say that he did. Despite the lack of any confirmation, A. Bartlett Giamatti, Commissioner of Baseball at that time, publicly stated that Rose bet not only on baseball but also on his own team. Betting on baseball is a violation of major-league rules and is punishable by lifetime banishment from baseball. This was the sentence Pete Rose received.

In 1991, the Hall of Fame Committee along with Fay Vincent, who was then Commissioner of Baseball, decided that as long as a player is banned from baseball, he is ineligible for Hall of Fame selection. This action was taken just a few weeks before Rose's name could have been placed on the ballot, and many believe that Vincent encouraged it specifically to make sure Rose could not be considered for selection. Several of the baseball writers who voted for the Hall of Fame candidates voiced their disapproval of this policy by writing in Rose's

1

2 *[handwritten: each criteria
1. legal
2. didn't admit]*

3. *[handwritten: Commissioner
integrity]*

3

name on the ballot. Unfortunately, write-in votes are not counted.

Rose's only hope of making the Hall of Fame depends on his being readmitted to baseball. The commissioner would have to review Rose's application and approve his reinstatement. Chances are not good, however, that this will happen. In fact, in recent years, new charges have surfaced. Someone who calls himself a confidant of Rose's now accuses him not only of having bet on baseball but also of having people forge his signature on baseball memorabilia. However, at this time none of these charges has been proven. 4

Meanwhile, on the strength of circumstantial evidence and the testimony of convicted felons, baseball has convicted Pete Rose of betting on baseball. He has admitted to betting on horse races and football games but denies ever betting on the sport he loves. He has also admitted that his gambling was a problem and that he has spent time in counseling. Why is a player who once gambled any worse than the many players who have tested positive for drugs? Those players are suspended from the game for a period of time and are given one or more chances to recover and return to the major league. Why are gamblers not treated the same way as drug abusers? 5

Many people mistakenly believe that Pete Rose went to prison for betting on baseball and that, for this reason, he should be kept out of the Hall of Fame. The fact is, however, that Rose went to prison for tax-law violations. He failed to pay income tax on his gambling winnings and on the money he made at baseball-card shows. Even so, when has the Hall of Fame ever been reserved for perfect people? Babe Ruth was an adulterer and a serious drinker, but he still holds a place in the Hall. Mickey Mantle and Willie Mays were barred from baseball for being employees of an Atlantic City casino (an obvious gambling connection), but even this decision was eventually overturned. 6

Granted, Pete Rose has made some serious mistakes in his life, but this is no reason to keep him out of the Hall of Fame. His contributions to the game and his accomplishments as a player are all that should be considered, and these more than qualify him to occupy a place beside the greats of the game. Baseball should, in all fairness, let Pete Rose take his rightful place in the Hall of Fame. 7

◆ PRACTICE 14-25

1. What position does John take in his essay?

    He argues that Pete Rose should be in the Hall of Fame.

2. List the facts and examples John uses to support his thesis. Can you think of any that he doesn't mention?

    The Hall of Fame Committee may have intentionally discouraged Rose's

    selection. Rose has been convicted of betting on baseball only on the

    strength of circumstantial evidence and the testimony of convicted felons.

    Rose has admitted that his gambling was a problem but denies betting on

    baseball. Drug-addicted players are allowed to return to the game, and so

    should players who gamble. Other Hall of Famers had problems but were still

    allowed to play baseball.

3. Underline the transitional words and phrases John uses to move his argument along.

4. John's opening paragraph includes a series of questions he does not expect his readers to answer. Is this an effective opening strategy? Why or why not?

    Answers will vary. Some students may argue that it is effective because

    John proceeds to list facts that answer the questions for us.

5. Throughout his essay, John acknowledges Pete Rose's problems and shortcomings. Do you think this is a good idea? Why or why not?

    Answers will vary.

6. Where does John address opposing arguments? What other arguments should he have addressed?

    John addresses opposing arguments when he talks about Rose's conviction.

    He could have gone into more detail about Rose's gambling and tax problems,

    but that might lessen the strength of his own argument.

7. What is this essay's greatest strength? What is its greatest weakness?

    Strength: *Answers will vary.*

    Weakness: *Answers will vary.*

14 1

◆ PRACTICE 14-26

Following the writing process outlined in Chapter 12, write an argument essay on one of the following topics.

> The United States should (or should not) have an "open door" immigration policy, with no restrictions.
>
> Teenagers who commit serious crimes should (or should not) be tried as adults.
>
> All citizens without criminal records should (or should not) be permitted to carry concealed weapons.
>
> Welfare recipients with preschool children should (or should not) be required to work.
>
> Human beings should (or should not) be used in medical research experiments.
>
> Parents should (or should not) be permitted to use government vouchers to pay private school tuition.
>
> College financial aid should (or should not) be based solely on merit.
>
> Government funds should (or should not) be used to support the arts.
>
> Public high schools should (or should not) be permitted to distribute condoms to students.
>
> The minimim wage should (or should not) be raised to ten dollars an hour.

◆ PRACTICE 14-27

Many states are considering a ban on cell phone use by drivers in moving vehicles. Do you agree that this is a good idea, or do you believe that the convenience of cell phones outweighs the possible risk (which some consider remote) of accidents?

Word Power

multitasking doing several tasks at the same time.

hazardous dangerous

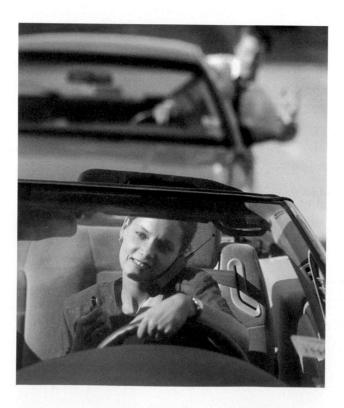

☑ SELF-ASSESSMENT CHECKLIST:
Writing an Argument Essay

   ☐ Does your introduction present the issue you will discuss and clearly state your position? If necessary, revise to clarify your purpose.

   ☐ Is your topic debatable? Make sure you take a position on an issue that really has two sides.

   ☐ Does your thesis statement clearly express the stand you take on the issue? If necessary, revise to clarify your position.

   ☐ Are your readers likely to be hostile to, neutral toward, or in agreement with your position? Be sure you consider your audience's expectations when choosing the points you will make and deciding how you will present them.

   ☐ Is your essay an inductive argument or a deductive argument? If necessary, revise the structure of your argument so it conforms to the requirements of the option you have chosen.

   ☐ Have you addressed the major arguments against your position? Identify any additional opposing arguments, and refute them if you can.

   ☐ Do you have enough evidence to support your points? If not, add facts, examples, and the opinions of experts if necessary.

   ☐ Do all your points clearly support your position? If not, revise to eliminate any points that are not directly related to your argument.

   ☐ Do transitional words and phrases help readers follow the logic of your argument? Add transitions if necessary.

   ☐ Does your conclusion follow logically from the points you have made in your essay? If necessary, revise so your concluding paragraph summarizes and reinforces your main points.

   ☐ What problems did you experience in writing your essay? What would you do differently next time?

☑ REVIEW CHECKLIST:
Patterns of Essay Development

   ☐ Exemplification essays use specific examples to support a thesis. (See 14A.)

   ☐ Narrative essays tell a story by presenting a series of events in chronological order. (See 14B.)

(continued on the following page)

Teaching Tip
Give students an example of an essay that uses a combination of patterns. Have them work in groups to identify and label the patterns. In class discussion, compare the groups' responses.

(continued from the previous page)

- Descriptive essays use details to give readers a clear, vivid picture of a person, place, or object. (See 14C.)

- Process essays explain the steps in a procedure, telling how something is (or was) done. (See 14D.)

- Cause-and-effect essays identify causes or predict effects. (See 14E.)

- Comparison-and-contrast essays explain how two things are alike or how they are different. (See 14F.)

- Classification essays divide a whole into parts and sort various items into categories. (See 14G.)

- Definition essays use various patterns of development to develop an extended definition. (See 14H.)

- Argument essays take a stand on a debatable issue, using evidence to persuade readers to accept a position. (See 14I.)

UNIT FOUR

Writing Effective Sentences

Writing Simple Sentences

C H A P T E R

15

■ WRITING FIRST

Look at the picture above, and then write about a person with whom you would like to trade places. What is this person like? What appeals to you about his or her life?

A **sentence** is a group of words that expresses a complete thought. Every sentence includes both a <u>subject</u> and a <u>verb</u>.

A   Identifying Subjects

Every sentence includes a subject. The **subject** of a sentence tells who or what is being talked about in the sentence. Without a subject, a sentence is not complete.

<u>Derek Walcott</u> won the 1992 Nobel Prize in literature.

213

For information on subject-verb agreement with compound subjects, see 23A.

He was born in the Caribbean.

St. Lucia is an island in the Caribbean.

The subject of a sentence can be a noun or a pronoun. A **noun** names a person, place, or thing—*Derek Walcott, St. Lucia.* A **pronoun** takes the place of a noun—*I, you, he, she, it, we, they.*

The subject of a sentence can be *singular* or *plural.* A **singular subject** is one person, place, or thing (*Derek Walcott, St. Lucia, he*).

A **plural subject** is more than one person, place, or thing (*poems, people, they*).

Walcott's <u>poems</u> are studied in college courses.

A plural subject that joins two subjects with *and* is called a **compound subject**.

<u>St. Lucia and Trinidad</u> are Caribbean islands.

Teaching Tip
Tell students that if the subject ends with an *-s*, the verb usually does not. Write examples on the board.

FOCUS **Simple and Complete Subjects**

A sentence's **simple subject** is just a noun or a pronoun.

   poems   he

A sentence's **complete subject** is the simple subject along with all the words that describe it.

   Walcott's poems

A two-word name, such as *Derek Walcott,* is a simple subject.

ON THE WEB
For more practice, visit **Exercise Central** *at* <www.bedfordstmartins.com/ writingfirst>.

◆ PRACTICE 15-1

In the paragraph below, underline the complete subject of each sentence once. Then, place a check mark above the simple subject.

Example: The poet's <u>parents</u> were both teachers.

(1) <u>Derek Walcott</u> was born in 1930. (2) <u>His ancestors</u> came from Africa, the Netherlands, and England. (3) <u>Walcott's early years</u> were spent on the Caribbean island of St. Lucia. (4) <u>Writing</u> poetry occupied much of his time. (5) <u>His early poems</u> were published in Trinidad. (6) <u>He</u> later studied in Jamaica and in New York and founded the Trinidad Theatre Workshop. (7) <u>Walcott</u> eventually gained wide recognition as a poet. (8) <u>He</u> was a visiting lecturer at Harvard in 1981. (9) In 1990, <u>the</u>

● **Writing Tip**
Sometimes an *-ing* word can be a singular subject: *Reading is fundamental.*

ESL Tip
Refer students to 30A and 30B for more on using subjects correctly and to 30C for more on distinguishing singular and plural nouns.

renowned poet published *Omeros*. (10) This long poem about classical

Greek heroes is set in the West Indies. (11) In 1992, the sixty-two-year-

old Caribbean poet was honored with a Nobel Prize. (12) Walcott later

collaborated with songwriter Paul Simon on *The Capeman*, a Broadway

musical.

◆ **PRACTICE 15-2**

Add a simple subject to each of the following sentences.

Example: ___Pets___ can reduce stress, high blood pressure, and depression.

Answers may vary.

1. For one thing, ___pets___ allow us to express affection openly.

2. ___We___ can stroke, cuddle, and talk baby talk to a kitten or

puppy.

3. ___Pets___ also love us unconditionally, no matter what our faults.

4. Our ___animals___ do not care about our faults.

5. ___Social workers___ now take pets into nursing homes and hospitals.

6. For some patients, their only ___visitors___ are these animals.

7. These ___patients___ have better survival rates.

8. In addition, prison ___inmates___ sometimes train service dogs.

9. These ___dogs___ help disabled people.

10. Their ___trainers___ are making a positive contribution to society.

◆ **PRACTICE 15-3**

Underline the complete subject in each sentence. Then, write *S* above singular subjects and *P* above plural subjects. Remember, compound subjects are plural.

Example: An international space station is scheduled to be completed in 2004.

1. Sixteen nations are working together to build the station.

2. This million-pound satellite will contain six laboratories.

3. Living quarters will also be provided for seven people.

4. Scientists will use the laboratories to study how cells grow without

gravity.

5. They will also study the effects of reduced gravity on humans.

6. The station is being constructed by manned space flights from the sixteen nations.

7. Russia and the United States made the first trips in 1998.

8. Other flight crews have delivered supplies and parts for the station since then.

9. An international crew will live and work on the completed station.

10. The crew's return vehicle will be attached to the station to ensure their safe return to Earth.

■ **WRITING FIRST: Flashback**

Look back at your response to the Writing First exercise on page 213. Underline the complete subject of each of your sentences once. Then, place a check mark above the simple subject. Finally, list all the complete subjects on the lines below.

Answers will vary.

_____   _____

_____   _____

_____   _____

_____   _____

_____   _____

Now, write *S* beside each singular subject and *P* beside each plural subject. (Remember that a compound subject is plural.)

● **Writing Tip**
A preposition links its object (a noun or pronoun) to a verb, adjective, or another noun in the sentence. For more on prepositions, see 30K–M.

B | **Identifying Prepositional Phrases**

A **phrase** is a group of words that lacks a subject or a verb or both and therefore cannot stand alone as a sentence. A **prepositional phrase** consists of a **preposition** (a word such as *on, to, in,* or *with*) and its **object** (a noun or pronoun).

● **Writing Tip**
Prepositions are often combined with other words to form familiar expressions. (See 30L.)

Preposition	+	Object	=	Prepositional phrase
on		the stage		on the stage
to		Nia's house		to Nia's house
in		my new car		in my new car
with		them		with them

A prepositional phrase **modifies** (describes, or limits) another word or word group in the sentence.

The girl <u>with long red hair</u> was first in line. *(With long red hair modifies the noun* girl.*)*

Ken met his future wife <u>at Ted's house</u>. *(At Ted's house modifies the verb* met.*)*

Because the object of a preposition is a noun or a pronoun, it may appear to be the subject of a sentence. However, the object of a preposition can never be the subject of a sentence. To identify a sentence's true subject, cross out each prepositional phrase.

The <u>cost</u> ~~of the repairs~~ was astronomical.

~~At the end of the novel~~, ~~after an exciting chase~~, the <u>lovers</u> flee ~~to Mexico~~.

Remember that every prepositional phrase is introduced by a preposition.

Frequently Used Prepositions

about	behind	except	off	toward
above	below	for	on	under
across	beneath	from	onto	underneath
after	beside	in	out	until
against	between	inside	outside	up
along	beyond	into	over	upon
among	by	like	through	with
around	despite	near	throughout	within
at	during	of	to	without
before				

ESL Tip
Give examples of how prepositions show relationships between words. For instance, a rabbit can go *inside* a log, *behind* a log, *around* a log, *over* a log, and so forth. Have students give other examples.

ESL Tip
Consider giving students extra preposition exercises before the class gets too far into the chapter. Refer them to 30K.

◆ **PRACTICE 15-4**

Each of the following sentences includes at least one prepositional phrase. To identify each sentence's subject, begin by crossing out each prepositional phrase. Then, underline the simple subject of the sentence.

Example: ~~In twentieth-century presidential elections~~, third-party <u>candidates</u> attracted many voters.

(1) ~~With more than 27 percent~~ ~~of the vote,~~ <u>Theodore Roosevelt</u> was the strongest third-party presidential candidate ~~in history~~. (2) ~~In the 1912 race with Democrat Woodrow Wilson and Republican William H. Taft,~~ <u>Roosevelt</u> ran second ~~to Wilson~~. (3) ~~Until Roosevelt,~~ no third-party <u>candidate</u> had won a significant number ~~of votes~~. (4) ~~After 1912~~, however, some <u>candidates</u> ~~of other parties~~ made strong showings. (5) ~~For example,~~ <u>Robert M. LaFollette</u> ~~of the Progressive Party~~ won ~~about 16~~

ESL Tip
Nonnative speakers need to work extra hard on prepositions. Give them a few paragraphs from which you have deleted all prepositions, and have them insert appropriate words.

ESL Tip
Refer students to 30L for work on using prepositions in idiomatic expressions.

percent of the vote in the 1924 race. (6) In 1968, with more than 13 percent of the popular vote, American Independent Party candidate George C. Wallace placed third behind Republican Richard M. Nixon and Democrat Hubert H. Humphrey. (7) In 1980, John B. Anderson, an Independent, challenged Republican Ronald Reagan and Democrat Jimmy Carter and got 6.6 percent of the vote. (8) With nearly 19 percent of the popular vote, Independent Ross Perot ran a strong race against Democrat Bill Clinton and Republican George Bush in 1992. (9) In 2000, with the support of many environmentalists, Ralph Nader challenged Al Gore and George W. Bush for the presidency. (10) To this day, the two-party system of the United States has remained intact despite many challenges by third-party candidates.

■ WRITING FIRST: Flashback

Look back at your response to the Writing First exercise on page 213. Have you used any prepositional phrases? List them on the lines below.

Answers will vary.

_____

_____

_____

_____

C Identifying Verbs

In addition to its subject, every sentence also includes a verb. The **verb** tells what the subject does or connects the subject to words that describe or rename it. Without a verb, a sentence is not complete.

Action Verbs

An **action verb** tells what the subject does, did, or will do.

Nomar Garciaparra plays baseball.
Renee will drive to Tampa on Friday.

Amelia Earhart <u>flew</u> across the Atlantic.

Action verbs can also show mental and emotional actions.

Travis always <u>worries</u> about his job.

Sometimes, the subject of a sentence performs more than one action. In this case, the sentence includes two or more action verbs joined to form a **compound verb.**

He <u>hit</u> the ball, <u>threw</u> down his bat, and <u>ran</u> toward first base.

Linking Verbs

A **linking verb** does not show action. Instead, it connects the subject to a word or words that describe or rename it. The linking verb tells what the subject is (or what it was, will be, or seems to be).

A googolplex <u>is</u> an extremely large number.

Many linking verbs, like *is*, are forms of the verb *be*. Other linking verbs refer to the senses (*look, feel,* and so on).

The photocopy <u>looks</u> blurry.

Some students <u>feel</u> anxious about the future.

> **Teaching Tip**
> Have students memorize linking verbs.

> ● **Writing Tip**
> Some linking verbs, such as *look, smell, turn,* and *taste,* can also function as action verbs: *I will <u>look</u> for a clearer photocopy.*

Frequently Used Linking Verbs

act	feel	seem
appear	get	smell
be (am, is, are,	grow	sound
was, were)	look	taste
become	remain	turn

◆ PRACTICE 15-5

Underline the action verbs in the following sentences twice. Some sentences contain more than one action verb.

ON THE WEB
For more practice, visit Exercise Central *at* <*www.bedfordstmartins.com/ writingfirst*>.

1. Many critics <u>see</u> one romance novel as just like another.

2. The plot usually <u>involves</u> a beautiful young woman, or heroine, in some kind of danger.

3. A handsome stranger <u>offers</u> his help.

4. At first, she <u>distrusts</u> him.

5. Then, another man <u>enters</u> the story and <u>wins</u> the heroine's trust.

6. Readers, however, <u>see</u> this man as an evil villain.

7. Almost too late, the heroine too <u>realizes</u> the truth.

8. Luckily, the handsome hero <u>returns</u> and <u>saves</u> her from a nasty fate.

9. Many readers <u>enjoy</u> the predictable plots.

10. But critics <u>dislike</u> these books.

◆ PRACTICE 15-6

Underline the linking verbs in the following sentences twice. Some sentences contain more than one linking verb.

1. Urban legends <u>are</u> folk tales created in our own time to teach a lesson.

2. The most familiar urban legend <u>is</u> the story of Hookman.

3. According to this story, a young couple <u>is</u> alone in Lovers' Lane.

4. They <u>are</u> in a car in this secluded place, listening to a radio announcement.

5. An escaped murderer <u>is</u> nearby.

6. The murderer's left hand <u>is</u> a hook.

7. The young woman <u>becomes</u> hysterical.

8. Leaving Lovers' Lane, the car <u>seems</u> to scrape against something.

9. At home, they <u>are</u> stunned to see a hook hanging from the passenger door handle.

10. The purpose of this legend <u>is</u> to frighten young people into avoiding dangerous places.

◆ PRACTICE 15-7

Underline the verbs in each sentence twice. Remember that a verb can be an action verb or a linking verb.

Example: Some books <u>have</u> a great impact on their readers.

(1) Betty Smith <u>wrote</u> *A Tree Grows in Brooklyn*, a 1948 novel. (2) The novel <u>tells</u> the story of Francie Nolan. (3) Francie <u>is</u> very poor but <u>seems</u> determined to succeed. (4) She <u>loves</u> books and <u>is</u> an excellent student. (5) Francie <u>lives</u> with her parents and her younger brother, Neely. (6) She <u>dreams</u> of a better life for herself and her family. (7) Tragically, Francie's father <u>dies</u>. (8) Her mother <u>supports</u> her family and <u>does</u> her best for her children. (9) She <u>works</u> as a janitor in their apartment building. (10) Eventually, Francie <u>graduates</u> from high school, with a bright future ahead of her.

Helping Verbs

Many verbs consist of more than one word. The verb in the following sentence consists of two words.

Minh <u>must make</u> a decision about his future.

In this sentence, *make* is the **main verb**, and *must* is a **helping verb**.

FOCUS Helping Verbs

Helping verbs include forms of *be, have,* and *do* as well as the words *must, will, can, could, may, might, should,* and *would.* Some helping verbs, like forms of *be* and *have,* combine with main verbs to give information about when the action occurs. Forms of *do* combine with main verbs to form questions and negative statements. Still other helping verbs indicate willingness (*can*), possibility (*may*), necessity (*should*), obligation (*must*), and so on.

A sentence's **complete verb** is made up of a main verb plus any helping verbs that accompany it. In the following sentences, the complete verb is underlined twice, and the helping verbs are checkmarked.

Minh <u>should have gone</u> earlier. ✔ ✔

<u>Did</u> Minh <u>ask</u> the right questions? ✔

Minh <u>will work</u> hard. ✔

Minh <u>can</u> really <u>succeed</u>. ✔

● **Writing Tip**
Sometimes, other words can come between the parts of a complete verb.

FOCUS Helping Verbs with Participles

Present participles, such as *thinking,* and many irregular **past participles,** such as *gone,* cannot stand alone as main verbs in a sentence. They need a helping verb to make them complete.

INCORRECT   Minh going to the library.

CORRECT   Minh <u>is going</u> to the library.

INCORRECT   Minh gone to the library.

CORRECT   Minh <u>has gone</u> to the library.

For information on past participles, see Chapter 27.

◆ **PRACTICE 15-8**

The verbs in the sentences that follow consist of a main verb and one or more helping verbs. In each sentence, underline the complete verb twice, and put a check mark above the helping verb(s).

Example: The Salk polio vaccine ✔was given to more than a million schoolchildren in 1954.

(1) By the 1950s, parents ✔had become terrified of polio. (2) For years, it ✔had puzzled doctors and researchers. (3) Thousands had become ill each year in the United States alone. (4) Children ✔should ✔have ✔been playing happily. (5) Instead, they ✔would get very sick. (6) Polio ✔was sometimes called infantile paralysis. (7) In fact, it ✔did cause paralysis in children and in adults as well. (8) Some patients ✔could breathe only with the help of machines called iron lungs. (9) Others ✔would remain in wheelchairs for life. (10) By 1960, Jonas Salk's vaccine ✔had reduced the incidence of polio in the United States by more than 90 percent.

■ **WRITING FIRST: Flashback**

Look back at your response to the Writing First exercise on page 213. In each sentence, underline the complete verb twice, and put a check mark above each helping verb. Then, copy the helping verbs on the lines below.

Answers will vary. _____ _____ _____

_____ _____ _____ _____

■ **WRITING FIRST: Revising and Editing**

Look back at your response to the Writing First exercise on page 213. Circle every action verb. Then, try to replace some of them with different action verbs that express more precisely what the subject of each sentence is, was, or will be doing. For example, you might replace *makes* with *builds* or *creates*.

CHAPTER REVIEW

◆ EDITING PRACTICE

Read the following student passage. Underline the complete subject of each sentence once, and underline the complete verb of each sentence twice. If you have trouble locating the subject, try crossing out the prepositional phrases. The first sentence has been done for you.

Escape to Freedom

~~On April 14, 1979, at 10 p.m.~~, my family left Vietnam. My mother had hidden gold and jewelry ~~in water pipes~~. Now we could use these unconfiscated items. We could buy seats ~~on a fishing boat~~. Then we could escape ~~to freedom~~. The trip was extremely dangerous. Forty-two people drifted aimlessly ~~on the water~~. We drifted ~~for four days and five nights on the Pacific ocean~~. ~~At last, on the 18th of April~~, we saw land. We stopped ~~at Natuna Besar, Indonesia, for three days~~. Then, ~~on the 21st~~, we came ~~to Sedanau~~, another island ~~of Indonesia~~. ~~After a stay of one month~~, we traveled ~~to Tanjungpinang, Indonesia~~. We stayed there ~~for three and a half months~~. Life ~~in the refugee camp~~ was not luxurious. Our space was very limited. Food was scarce. Luckily, my father had once been a captain ~~in the army~~. As a result, our family was quickly resettled ~~to the United States~~.

Teaching Tip
Have students do this exercise collaboratively.

◆ COLLABORATIVE ACTIVITIES

1. Fold a sheet of paper in half vertically. Working in a group of three or four students, spend two minutes listing as many nouns as you can in the column to the left of the fold. When your time is up, exchange papers with another group of students. Limiting yourselves to five minutes, write an appropriate action verb beside each noun. Each noun will now be the subject of a short sentence.

2. Choose five short sentences from those you wrote for Collaborative Activity 1. Working in the same group, collaborate to create more fully developed sentences. First, expand each subject by adding words or prepositional phrases that give more information about the subject.

ESL Tip
Arrange groups so that non-native speakers are not isolated from native speakers.

(For example, you could expand *boat* to *the small, leaky boat with the red sail.*) Then, expand each sentence further, adding ideas after the verb. (For example, the sentence *The boat bounced* could become *The small, leaky boat with the red sail bounced helplessly on the water.*)

3. Collaborate in a group of three or four students to write one original sentence for each of the linking verbs listed on page 219. When you have finished, exchange papers with another group. Now, try to add words and phrases to the other group's sentences to make them more interesting.

☑ REVIEW CHECKLIST:
Writing Simple Sentences

- A sentence expresses a complete thought. The subject tells who or what is being talked about in the sentence. (See 15A.)

- Prepositions connect words and groups of words in a sentence. A prepositional phrase consists of a preposition and its object (a noun or pronoun). (See 15B.)

- The object of a preposition cannot be the subject of a sentence. (See 15B.)

- An action verb tells what the subject does, did, or will do. (See 15C.)

- A linking verb connects the subject to a word or words that describe or rename it. (See 15C.)

- Many verbs are made up of more than one word. The complete verb in a sentence includes the main verb plus any helping verbs. (See 15C.)

Writing Compound Sentences

■ WRITING FIRST

Look at the picture above. Imagine that you are the inventor of a familiar product—for example, Velcro, the zipper, or the rubber band—and that you are ready to introduce this product to the world. Begin by telling what this new invention is. Then, describe what it looks like, and give examples of its possible uses.

Word Power

innovation something newly introduced

functional designed for a particular need or activity

  A **Forming Compound Sentences with Coordinating Conjunctions**

A simple sentence includes a subject and a verb.

European <u>immigrants</u> <u>arrived</u> at Ellis Island.

Asian <u>immigrants</u> <u>arrived</u> at Angel Island.

225

● **Writing Tip**

The subject of a simple
sentence can be singular or
plural. (See 15A.)

Teaching Tip
To help students remember
the coordinating conjunc-
tions, use the mnemonic
FANBOYS: For, And, Nor,
But, Or, Yet, So.

ESL Tip
Refer students to 30C for a
review of singular and plural
nouns.

Teaching Tip
Remind students that when
a compound sentence is
formed with *nor,* the verb
comes before the subject in
the second part of the compound sentence.

A **compound sentence** is made up of two or more simple sentences.
One way to form a compound sentence is by joining two simple sentences
with a **coordinating conjunction** preceded by a comma.

European immigrants arrived at Ellis Island, <u>but</u> Asian immigrants
arrived at Angel Island.

Coordinating Conjunctions			
and	for	or	yet
but	nor	so	

Coordinating conjunctions join ideas of equal importance. They describe the relationship between two ideas, showing how and why the ideas
are connected. Different coordinating conjunctions have different meanings.

■ If you want to indicate addition, use *and.*

He acts like a child, <u>and</u> people think he is cute.

■ If you want to indicate contrast or contradiction, use *but* or *yet.*

He acts like a child, <u>but</u> he is an adult.
He acts like a child, <u>yet</u> he longs to be taken seriously.

■ If you want to indicate a cause-effect relationship, use *so* or *for.*

He acts like a child, <u>so</u> we treat him like one.
He acts like a child, <u>for</u> he craves attention.

■ If you want to present alternatives, use *or.*

He acts like a child, <u>or</u> he is ignored.

■ If you want to eliminate alternatives, use *nor.*

He does not act like a child, <u>nor</u> does he look like one.

Teaching Tip
Remind students that in a
compound sentence, there
is a complete sentence on
each side of the coordinating conjunction.

FOCUS **Punctuating with Coordinating Conjunctions**

When you use a coordinating conjunction to link two short sentences into a single compound sentence, always put a comma before
the coordinating conjunction.

We can stand in line all night, or we can go home now.

Remember, though, not to use a comma before a coordinating conjunction unless it links two *complete sentences.*

INCORRECT We can stand in line all night, or go home now.
CORRECT We can stand in line all night or go home now.

ON THE WEB
For more practice, visit
Exercise Central *at*
<www.bedfordstmartins.com/
writingfirst>.

◆ PRACTICE 16-1

Fill in the coordinating conjunction—*and, but, for, nor, or, so,* or *yet*—that most logically links the two parts of each compound sentence. Remember to insert a comma before each coordinating conjunction.

Example: Fairy tales have been told by many people around the world,___*but*___ the stories by two German brothers may be the most famous.

(1) Jakob and Wilhelm Grimm lived in the nineteenth century,___*and*___ they wrote many well-known fairy tales. (2) Most people think fondly of fairy tales,___*but/yet*___ the Brothers Grimm wrote many unpleasant and violent stories. (3) In their best-known works, children are abused,___*and*___ endings are not always happy. (4) Either innocent children are brutally punished for no reason,___*or*___ they are neglected. (5) For example, in "Hansel and Gretel," the stepmother mistreats the children,___*and*___ their father abandons them in the woods. (6) In this story, the events are horrifying,___*but/yet*___ the ending is still happy. (7) The children outwit the evil adults,___*so/and*___ they escape unharmed. (8) Apparently, they are not injured physically,___*nor*___ are they harmed emotionally. (9) Nevertheless, their story can hardly be called pleasant,___*for*___ it remains a story of child abuse and neglect.

◆ PRACTICE 16-2

Join each of the following pairs of simple sentences with a coordinating conjunction. Be sure to place a comma before the coordinating conjunction.

Example: A computer can make drafting essays easier*, and* It also lets you revise as often as possible.

1. Training a dog to heel is difficult*, for* Dogs naturally resist strict control.

2. A bodhran is an Irish drum*, and* It is played with a wooden stick.

3. Students should spend two hours of study time for each hour of class time*, or* They may not pass the course.

4. Years ago, students wrote their lessons on slates*, so* The teacher could correct each student's work.

5. Each state in the United States has two senators. *, but* The number of representatives depends on a state's population.

6. In 1973, only 2.5 percent of those in the U.S. military were women. *, but* By 1999, that percentage had increased to 14.1 percent.

7. A "small craft advisory" warns boaters of bad weather conditions. *, for* These conditions can be dangerous to small boats.

8. A digital video disc (DVD) looks like a compact disk. *, but* It can hold fifteen times as much information.

9. Hip-hop fashions include sneakers and baggy pants. *, and* These styles are very popular among today's young men.

10. The Mars spacecraft is in orbit around the Red Planet. *, and* It took the rocket six months to reach there.

◆ PRACTICE 16-3

Add coordinating conjunctions to combine simple sentences where necessary to relate one idea to another. Remember to put a comma before each coordinating conjunction you add.

Example: Years ago, few Americans lived to be one hundred. ~~Today,~~ *, but today,* there are over 32,000 centenarians.

Answers may vary.

(1) Diet, exercise, and family history may account for centenarians' long lives. *, but this* ~~(2) This~~ is not the whole story. (3) Recently, a study conducted in Georgia showed surprising common traits among centenarians. (4) They did not necessarily avoid tobacco and alcohol. *, nor* ~~(5) They~~ did ~~not~~ *they* eat low-fat diets. (6) In fact, they ate relatively large amounts of fat, cholesterol, and sugar. *, so diet* ~~(7) Diet~~ could not explain their long lives. (8) They did, however, share four key survival characteristics. (9) First, all of the centenarians were optimistic about life. *, and all* ~~(10) All~~ of them were positive thinkers. (11) They were also involved in religious life and had deep religious faith. (12) In addition, all the centenarians had continued to lead physically active lives. *, and they* ~~(13) They~~ remained mobile even as elderly people. (14) Finally, all were able to adapt to loss. (15) They had all experienced the deaths of friends, spouses, or children. *, but they* ~~(16) They~~ were able to get on with their lives.

◆ **PRACTICE 16-4**

Write another simple sentence to follow each of the sentences below. Then, connect the sentences with a coordinating conjunction and the correct punctuation.

Example: Many patients need organ transplants, *but there never*

seem to be enough available to meet the demand.

Answers will vary.

1. Smoking in bed is dangerous. _____

_____

2. Many cars are equipped with front and side air bags. _____

_____

3. Diamonds can cut glass. _____

_____

4. Kangaroos carry their young in pouches. _____

_____

5. Dancing is good exercise. _____

_____

6. Taking driving lessons reduces the possibility of accidents. _____

_____

7. Some businesses sponsor bowling leagues for their employees. _____

_____

8. Pretzels are a healthier snack than potato chips. _____

_____

9. Many so-called juices actually contain very little real fruit juice. _____

_____

10. Human beings tend to resist change. _____

_____

■ WRITING FIRST: Flashback

Look back at your response to the Writing First exercise on page 225. If you see any compound sentences, bracket them. If you see any pairs of simple sentences that could be combined, rewrite them on the lines provided on the next page, joining them with appropriate coordinating conjunctions to create compound sentences.

(continued on the following page)

(continued from the previous page)
Answers will vary.

1. _____

_____

2. _____

_____

3. _____

_____

Be sure each of your compound sentences includes a comma before the coordinating conjunction.

B Forming Compound Sentences with Semicolons

Another way to create a **compound sentence** is by joining two simple sentences with a *semicolon*.

The AIDS quilt contains thousands of panels; each panel is rectangular.

A semicolon generally connects simple sentences whose ideas are closely linked.

For information on avoiding sentence fragments, see Chapter 22.

FOCUS Using Semicolons to Join Sentences

Remember that a semicolon can join only two *complete sentences*. A semicolon cannot join a sentence and a fragment.

┌─────────────── FRAGMENT ───────────────┐
INCORRECT Because thousands are dying of AIDS; more research is clearly needed.

CORRECT Thousands are dying of AIDS; more research is clearly needed.

◆ PRACTICE 16-5

Combine each pair of simple sentences below by adding a semicolon in the appropriate place.

Example: People become famous for complicated reasons ; just being

the first to accomplish something is no guarantee.

1. Sometimes runners-up are better remembered than winners ; the triumphant are forgotten.

2. The race to reach the South Pole is a perfect example ; it illustrates my
point.

3. Robert Falcon Scott was a British naval officer ; Roald Amundsen was
a Norwegian explorer.

4. Scott's men used Siberian ponies to drag equipment to the Pole ; Amundsen's men used dogs.

5. Amundsen's men buried food all along the trail ; Scott's men left food in
only a few locations.

6. The Norwegian team skied to the Pole ; the British team tried to walk.

7. Amundsen's men made it to the Pole in December 1911 ; Scott's party
arrived in January 1912.

8. The Norwegians found their supplies on the way back ; the men arrived
back at their ship in good condition.

9. Scott's exhausted party could not get to their scarce provisions ; none of
the men survived the trek to the Pole.

10. Nevertheless, Scott and his men are remembered for trying to get to
the Pole ; the Norwegians—the "winners"—have been almost forgotten.

◆ PRACTICE 16-6

Each of the following simple sentences can be linked with a semicolon to
another simple sentence to form a compound sentence. In each case, add a
semicolon; then, complete the compound sentence with another sentence.

Example: My brother is addicted to fast food ; *he eats it every day.*

1. Fast-food restaurants are an American institution _____

Answers will vary. _____

2. Families eat at these restaurants _____

_____

3. Many teenagers work there _____

_____

4. McDonald's is known for its hamburgers _____

_____

Teaching Tip
Students may enjoy this
exercise more if they work
in pairs—and if they are encouraged to generate sen-
tences that are humorous
(and not necessarily factually accurate).

5. KFC is famous for its fried chicken _____

_____

6. Taco Bell serves Mexican-style food _____

_____

7. Pizza Hut specializes in pizza _____

_____

8. Many fast-food restaurants offer some low-fat menu items _____

_____

9. Some offer recyclable packaging _____

_____

10. Some even have playgrounds _____

_____

■ WRITING FIRST: Flashback

Look back at your response to the Writing First exercise on page
225. Do you see any pairs of simple sentences that you could connect with semicolons? If so, link each pair with a semicolon on the
following lines.

Answers will vary.

_____

_____

_____

C **Forming Compound Sentences
with Conjunctive Adverbs**

● **Writing Tip**

When a coordinating con-
junction links two sentences,
use a comma, not a semi-
colon, before the coordinating conjunction. (See 16A.)

Another way to combine two simple sentences into one **compound sentence** is with a **conjunctive adverb**. When you use a conjunctive adverb
to join two simple sentences, a semicolon always comes *before* the conjunctive adverb, and a comma always comes *after* it.

Some college students receive grants; <u>however</u>, others must take
out loans.

Teaching Tip
Have students memorize this
list of conjunctive adverbs.

Frequently Used Conjunctive Adverbs		
also	instead	still
besides	later	subsequently
consequently	meanwhile	then
eventually	moreover	therefore
finally	nevertheless	thus
furthermore	now	
however	otherwise	

Adding a conjunctive adverb makes the connection between ideas in a sentence clearer and more precise than it would be if the ideas were linked with just a semicolon. Different conjunctive adverbs convey different meanings.

- Some conjunctive adverbs signal addition (*also, besides, furthermore, moreover*).

    I have a lot on my mind; <u>also</u>, I have a lot of things to do.

- Some conjunctive adverbs make causal connections (*therefore, consequently, thus*).

    I have a lot on my mind; <u>therefore</u>, it is hard to concentrate.

- Some conjunctive adverbs indicate contradiction or contrast (*nevertheless, however, still*).

    I have a lot on my mind; <u>still</u>, I must try to relax.

- Some conjunctive adverbs present alternatives (*instead, otherwise*).

    I have a lot on my mind; <u>otherwise</u>, I could relax.
    I will try not to think; <u>instead</u>, I will relax.

- Some conjunctive adverbs indicate time sequence (*eventually, finally, later, meanwhile, now, subsequently, then*).

    I have a lot on my mind; <u>meanwhile</u>, I still have work to do.

FOCUS Transitional Expressions

Transitional expressions can also link two simple sentences into one compound sentence.

He had a miserable time at the party; <u>in addition</u>, he drank too much.

The transitional expression is preceded by a semicolon and followed by a comma.

● **Writing Tip**

Do not forget to place a semicolon before every conjunctive adverb or transitional expression that joins two sentences. If you leave out the semicolon, you create a run-on sentence. (See 21B.)

Frequently Used Transitional Expressions	
after all	in comparison
as a result	in contrast
at the same time	in fact
for example	in other words
for instance	of course
in addition	on the contrary

ON THE WEB

For more practice, visit
Exercise Central *at*
*<www.bedfordstmartins.com/
writingfirst>.*

◆ PRACTICE 16-7

Add semicolons and commas where required to set off conjunctive adverbs or transitional expressions that join two simple sentences.

Example: Ketchup is a popular condiment ; therefore , it is available in almost every restaurant.

(1) Andrew F. Smith, a food historian, wrote a book about the tomato ; subsequently , he wrote a book about ketchup. (2) The book, *Pure Ketchup*, was a big project ; in fact , Smith worked on it for five years. (3) The word *ketchup* may have come from a Chinese word ; however , Smith is not certain of the word's origins. (4) Ketchup has existed since ancient times ; in other words , it is a very old product. (5) Ketchup has changed a lot over the years ; for example , special dyes were developed in the nineteenth century to make it red. (6) Smith discusses many other changes ; for instance , preservative-free ketchup was invented in 1907. (7) Ketchup is now used by people in many cultures ; still , salsa is more popular than ketchup in the United States. (8) Today, designer ketchups are being developed ; meanwhile , Heinz has introduced green and purple ketchup in squeeze bottles. (9) Some of today's ketchups are chunky ; in addition , some ketchups are spicy. (10) Ketchup continues to evolve ; however , Smith is now working on a book about the history of popcorn.

◆ PRACTICE 16-8

Consulting the list of conjunctive adverbs on page 233 and the list of transitional expressions above, choose a word or expression that logically connects each pair of simple sentences on the next page into one compound sentence. Be sure to punctuate appropriately.

Example: Every year since 1927, *Time* has designated a Man of the

; however, the

Year. ~~The~~ Man of the Year has not always been a man.

Answers may vary.

(1) *Time* selects the Man of the Year to honor the person who has

; consequently, the

most influenced the previous year's events. ~~The~~ choice is often a promi-

nent politician. (2) In the 1920s and 1930s, world leaders were often

; for example,

chosen. Franklin Delano Roosevelt was chosen twice and Ethiopia's

Haile Selassie once. (3) During the war years, Hitler, Stalin, Churchill,

; in fact,

and Roosevelt were all chosen. Stalin was featured twice. (4) Occasion-

; for instance, in

ally, the Man of the Year was not an individual. ~~In~~ 1950, it was The

American Fighting Man. (5) In 1956, The Hungarian Freedom Fighter

; then, in

was Man of the Year. ~~In~~ 1966, *Time* editors chose The Young Generation.

; for example,

(6) Only a few individual women have been selected. Queen Elizabeth II

of England was featured in 1952 and Corazon Aquino, president of the

Philippines, in 1986. (7) In 1975, American Women were honored as a

; nevertheless, the

group. ~~The~~ Man of the Year has nearly always been male. (8) Very few

; still,

people of color have been designated Man of the Year. Martin Luther

King Jr. was honored in 1963. (9) The Man of the Year has almost always

; however, the

been one or more human beings. ~~The~~ Computer was selected in 1982

and Endangered Earth in 1988. (10) More recently, prominent politicians

; for example, in

have once again been chosen. ~~In~~ 2001, New York City mayor Rudy

Giuliani was *Time*'s Man of the Year (now called Person of the Year).

◆ PRACTICE 16-9

Add the suggested conjunctive adverb or transitional expression to each of
the following simple sentences. Then, add a new independent clause to
follow it. Be sure to punctuate correctly.

Example: (however) Commuting students frequently miss out on
the freedom of living on campus.

Students who commute to school frequently feel that they are missing

out on the freedom of living on campus; however, there are a lot of advan-

tages to being a commuter.

Answers will vary.

1. (in contrast) Living at home gives students access to free home-cooked

meals.

Living at home gives students access to free home-cooked meals; in contrast, dorm residents eat dining hall food.

2. (on the other hand) Commuters with cars have a wider choice of jobs.

Commuters with cars have a wider choice of jobs; on the other hand, students living on campus may have to take on-campus jobs.

3. (however) Commuters get to take part in family life.

Being at home means the commuters get to take part in family life; however, they also may miss out on social activities on campus.

4. (nonetheless) Commuters have a number of advantages over dorm residents.

Commuters have a number of advantages over dorm residents; nonetheless, residents may have a better college experience.

5. (in fact) At most colleges, commuters have access to social activities such as dances, clubs, and games.

At most colleges, commuters have access to social activities such as dances, clubs, and games; in fact, many campuses have their own commuter social groups.

6. (for instance) Unlike dorm students, most commuters have regular family responsibilities.

Unlike dorm students, most commuters have regular family responsibilities; for instance, commuters might have to help with cooking or cleaning.

7. (for example) Commuter students might have to help take care of younger or older family members.

Commuter students might have to help take care of younger or older family members; for example, the student might baby-sit for a younger brother or sister.

8. (consequently) Commuters might have to pay rent to live at home.

Commuters might have to pay rent to live at home; consequently, they really do need to have jobs.

9. (moreover) Commuters are always under the watchful eye of their parents.

Commuters are always under the watchful eye of their parents; moreover,

their parents are likely to be stricter than the dorm counselor.

10. (therefore) There are pros and cons to being a commuter.

There are pros and cons to being a commuter; therefore, commuters are

not necessarily at a disadvantage.

◆ PRACTICE 16-10

Using the specified topics and conjunctive adverbs or transitional expressions, create five compound sentences. Be sure to punctuate appropriately.

Example:
Topic: fad diets
Transitional expression: for example

People are always falling for fad diets; for example, some people eat only

pineapple to lose weight.

1. *Topic:* laws to protect people with disabilities
   Transitional expression: in addition

   Answers will vary.

Teaching Tip
Have students write these sentences on the board. Get at least two versions of each sentence.

2. *Topic:* single men and women as adoptive parents
   Conjunctive adverb: however

3. *Topic:* prayer in public schools
   Conjunctive adverb: therefore

4. *Topic:* high school proms
   Conjunctive adverb: also

5. *Topic:* course requirements at your school
   Conjunctive adverb: instead

■ WRITING FIRST: Flashback

Look back at your response to the Writing First exercise on page 225. Have you used any conjunctive adverbs or transitional expressions to link sentences? If so, check to make sure that you have punctuated them correctly. Then, check to see that you have used the word or expression that best shows the relationship between the ideas in the two sentences. Revise your work if necessary.

■ WRITING FIRST: Revising and Editing

Look back at your response to the Writing First exercise on page 225. Now, try to incorporate one of the new compound sentences you created in the Flashback exercises on pages 229 and 232. Then, check each compound sentence to make sure you have used the coordinating conjunction, conjunctive adverb, or transitional expression that best conveys your meaning and that you have punctuated these sentences correctly. When you have finished, look over a piece of writing you have done in response to another assignment, and try combining some simple sentences into compound sentences.

CHAPTER REVIEW

◆ EDITING PRACTICE

Read the following student essay. Then, create compound sentences by linking pairs of simple sentences where appropriate with a coordinating conjunction, a semicolon, or a semicolon followed by either a conjunctive adverb or a transitional expression. Remember to put commas before coordinating conjunctions and to use semicolons and commas correctly with conjunctive adverbs and transitional expressions. The first two sentences have been combined for you.
Answers may vary.

My Father's Life

My grandparents were born in Ukraine, ~~They~~ *, but they* raised my

father in western Pennsylvania. The ninth of their ten

children, he had a life I cannot begin to imagine. To me,

he is my big, strong, powerful Daddy*; however, he is also a* ~~In reality, he is a~~
child of poverty.

My grandfather worked for the American Car Foundry.
The family lived in a company house*, and they* ~~They~~ shopped at the
company store. In 1934, my grandfather was laid off*, so he* ~~He~~
went to work digging sewer lines for the government. At
that time, the family was on relief. Every week, they were
entitled to get food rations*, and my* ~~My~~ father would go to pick
up the food. They desperately needed the prunes, beans,
flour, margarine, and other things.

For years, my father wore his brothers' hand-me-down
clothes*; in addition, he* ~~He~~ wore thrift-shop shoes with cardboard over the
holes in the soles. He was often hungry*, so he* ~~He~~ would sometimes
sit by the side of the railroad tracks, waiting for the
engineer to throw him an orange. My father would do any
job to earn a quarter*; for example, once* ~~Once, for example,~~ he weeded a
mile-long row of tomato plants. For this work, he was paid
twenty-five cents and a pack of Necco wafers.

My father saved his pennies*; eventually,* ~~Eventually,~~ he was able
to buy a used bicycle for two dollars. He dropped out of
school at fourteen and got a job*, for the* ~~The~~ family badly needed
his income. He woke up every day at 4 a.m.*, and he* ~~He~~ rode his
bike to his job at a meatpacking plant. He worked for
fifty cents a day.

In 1943, at the age of seventeen, my father joined the
U.S. Navy*; thus, he* ~~He~~ discovered a new world. For the first time
in his life, he had enough to eat. He was always first in
line at the mess hall*; in fact, he* ~~He~~ went back for seconds and thirds
before anyone else. After the war ended in 1945, he was
discharged from the Navy. He went to work in a meat market
in New York City*; the* ~~The~~ only trade he knew was the meat
business. Three years later, he had saved enough to open
his own store, Pete's Quality Meats.

◆ COLLABORATIVE ACTIVITIES

1. Working in a small group, pair each of the simple sentences in the left-hand column that follows with a sentence in the right-hand column to create ten compound sentences. Use as many different coordinating conjunctions as you can to connect ideas. Be sure each coordinating conjunction you choose conveys a logical relationship between ideas, and remember to put a comma before each one. You may use some of the listed sentences more than once. *Note:* Many different combinations—some serious and factually accurate, some humorous—are possible.

Some dogs wear little sweaters.	Many are named Hamlet.
Pit bulls are raised to fight.	They live in groups.
Bonobos are pygmy chimpanzees.	One even sings Christmas carols.
Many people fear Dobermans.	They can wear bandanas.
Leopards have spots.	They can play Frisbee.
Dalmations can live in firehouses.	Many live in equatorial Zaire.
Horses can wear blankets.	Some people think they are gentle.
All mules are sterile.	They don't get cold in winter.
Great Danes are huge dogs.	They are half horse and half donkey.
Parrots can often speak.	They can be unpredictable.

2. Work in a group of three or four students to create a cast of five characters for a movie, a television pilot, or a music video. Working individually, write five descriptive short sentences—one about each character. Then, exchange papers with another student. Add a coordinating conjunction to each sentence on the list to create five new sentences.

Example

ORIGINAL SENTENCE   Mark is a handsome heartthrob.

NEW SENTENCE   Mark is a handsome heartthrob, but he has green dreadlocks.

Next, select the three characters who sound most interesting. Write additional descriptive sentences about those characters, using compound sentences whenever possible. Your new sentences can provide information about the characters' relationships with one another as well as about their personalities and physical traits.

✓ REVIEW CHECKLIST:
Writing Compound Sentences

- A compound sentence is made up of two simple sentences. (See 16A.)

- A coordinating conjunction—*and, but, for, nor, or, so,* or *yet*—can join two simple sentences into one compound sentence. A comma always comes before the coordinating conjunction. (See 16A.)

- A semicolon can join two simple sentences into one compound sentence. (See 16B.)

- A conjunctive adverb or transitional expression can also join two simple sentences into one compound sentence. When it joins two sentences, a conjunctive adverb or transitional expression is always preceded by a semicolon and followed by a comma. (See 16C.)

17

Writing Complex Sentences

PREVIEW

In this chapter, you will learn

■ to identify independent and dependent clauses (17A)

■ to use subordinating conjunctions to form complex sentences (17B)

■ to use relative pronouns to form complex sentences (17C)

Word Power

courtesy polite behavior

infringe (used with *on* or *upon*) to go beyond the limits of

offend to cause anger or resentment

■ WRITING FIRST

Look at the picture above. Then, describe something that you believe needs to be changed—for example, a rule, a law, a policy, a situation, or a custom. First, identify what you think needs to be changed; then, explain why you think a change is necessary.

A   Identifying Independent and Dependent Clauses

A **clause** is a group of words that contains a subject and a verb. An **independent clause** can stand alone as a sentence. In this case, it is a **simple sentence**.

> INDEPENDENT   The exhibit <u>was</u> controversial.
> CLAUSE

A **dependent clause** cannot stand alone as a sentence because it needs other words to complete its meaning.

INCORRECT   Because the exhibit was controversial.

What happened because the exhibit was controversial? To answer this question, you need to add an independent clause that completes the idea begun in the dependent clause. The result is a **complex sentence**, a sentence that consists of one independent clause along with one or more dependent clauses.

┌──────────── DEPENDENT CLAUSE ────────────┐ ┌────── INDEPENDENT CLAUSE ──────┐
Because the exhibit was controversial, many people came to see
└──────────┘
the paintings.

◆ PRACTICE 17-1

In the blank following each of the items below, indicate whether the group of words is an independent clause (*IC*) or a dependent clause (*DC*).

Example: Gymnastics became popular in the United States in the twentieth century. __IC__

1. Gymnastics exercises help develop all parts of the body. __IC__

2. The practice of gymnastics dates back to the athletes of ancient Greece. __IC__

3. Because a German named Frederick Jahn popularized gymnastics in the nineteenth century. __DC__

4. Although German immigrants to the United States engaged in gymnastics. __DC__

5. Gymnastics later became an event in the Olympic games. __IC__

6. Even though women's gymnastics once focused on physical grace rather than strength. __DC__

7. In the 1970s, women Olympic gymnasts began to dominate the games. __IC__

8. When Mary Lou Retton became the first American woman to win a gold medal for gymnastics in 1984. __DC__

9. Who was only sixteen years old at the time of her gold-medal win. __DC__

10. The first U.S. women's gymnastics team to win a gold medal competed in the 1996 games. __IC__

◆ PRACTICE 17-2

In the blank following each of the items below, indicate whether the group of words is an independent clause (*IC*) or a dependent clause (*DC*).

Example: When novelist Toni Morrison was born in Ohio in 1931.
_DC_

1. As a young reader, Toni Morrison admired the classic Russian novel-ists. _IC_

2. After she graduated from Howard University with a bachelor's degree in English. _DC_

3. Morrison based her novel *The Bluest Eye* on a childhood friend's prayers to God for blue eyes. _IC_

4. While she raised two sons as a single mother and worked as an editor at Random House. _DC_

5. As her reputation as a novelist grew with the publication of *Song of Solomon* and *Tar Baby*. _DC_

6. Her picture appeared on the cover of *Newsweek* in 1981. _IC_

7. Before her novel *Beloved* won the 1988 Pulitzer Prize for fiction. _DC_

8. *Beloved* was later made into a film starring Oprah Winfrey. _IC_

9. In 1993, Morrison became the first black woman to win the Nobel Prize in literature. _IC_

10. Who published the novel *Paradise* in 1998 to mixed reviews. _DC_

B   **Forming Complex Sentences with Subordinating Conjunctions**

Subordinating conjunctions—words like *although* and *because*—can be used to join two simple sentences (independent clauses) by making one sentence a dependent clause. The result is a **complex sentence** in which the subordinating conjunction indicates the relationship between the ideas in the two clauses it links.

TWO SENTENCES   He was stripped of his title for refusing to be inducted into the army. Many people consider Muhammad Ali a hero.

COMPLEX SENTENCE   <u>Although he was stripped of his title for refusing to be inducted into the army</u>, many people consider Muhammad Ali a hero.

Frequently Used Subordinating Conjunctions

after	even though	since	whenever
although	if	so that	where
as	if only	than	whereas
as if	in order that	that	wherever
as though	now that	though	whether
because	once	unless	while
before	provided that	until	
even if	rather than	when	

Teaching Tip
Have students create sentences that start with the subordinating conjunctions listed here.

Different subordinating conjunctions express different relationships between dependent and independent clauses.

Teaching Tip
Have students memorize the subordinating conjunctions and their relationships.

ESL Tip
Make sure students understand the subtly different meanings of different subordinating conjunctions.

Relationship between clauses	*Subordinating conjunction*	*Example*
Time	after, before, since, until, when, whenever, while	<u>When the whale surfaced</u>, Ahab threw his harpoon.
Reason or cause	as, because	Scientists scaled back the project <u>because the government cut funds</u>.
Result or effect	in order that, so that	<u>So that students' math scores will improve</u>, many schools have instituted special programs.
Condition	even if, if, unless	The rain forest could disappear <u>unless steps are taken immediately</u>.
Contrast	although, even though, though	<u>Although Thomas Edison had almost no formal education</u>, he was a productive inventor.
Location	where, wherever	Pittsburgh was built <u>where the Allegheny and Monongahela Rivers meet</u>.

● **Writing Tip**

A clause introduced by a
subordinating conjunction
does not express a complete
thought. Used by itself, it is
a sentence fragment. (See
22D.)

FOCUS Punctuating with Subordinating Conjunctions

Place a comma after the dependent clause when it comes *before* the
independent clause in the sentence. Do not use a comma when the
dependent clause comes *after* the independent idea in the sentence.

┌───────── DEPENDENT CLAUSE ─────────┐ ┌──── INDEPENDENT CLAUSE ────┐
Although she wore the scarlet letter, Hester carried herself
proudly.

┌───── INDEPENDENT CLAUSE ─────┐ ┌──── DEPENDENT CLAUSE ────┐
Hester carried herself proudly although she wore the scarlet
letter.

ON THE WEB

For more practice, visit
Exercise Central *at*
*<www.bedfordstmartins.com/
writingfirst>.*

◆ PRACTICE 17-3

Write an appropriate subordinating conjunction in each blank in the sentences below. Look at the list of subordinating conjunctions on page 245
to make sure you choose a conjunction that establishes a logical relationship between the two clauses it links. (The required punctuation has been
provided.)

Example: The World Wrestling Federation (WWF) is an empire
of live events, pay-per-view matches, magazines, and Web sites
_____*that*_____ presents the most famous wrestlers in the world.
Answers may vary.
(1) _____*When/As*_____ wrestlers enter the ring, they are accompanied
by bursts of flame, lightning, or the sound of a motorcycle engine.
(2) _____*While*_____ the fans roar in approval, Stone Cold Steve Austin may
throw a chair. (3) _____*Although*_____ Ron Van Damme (RVD) may manage to
do a full body slam on Chris Jericho, the match isn't over. (4) It doesn't
end _____*until*_____ the referee counts to three. (5) _____*Because*_____ Jericho
lifts one shoulder from the floor before the final count, the match must
go on. (6) _____*After*_____ a match is over, the action shifts to the locker
room. (7) _____*Even though*_____ they do not wrestle themselves, the wrestlers'
girlfriends play an important role in the WWF. (8) _____*Before*_____ the
match begins, they pump up their men by serving them cookies and

urging them to show no mercy in the ring. (9) These women go

_____*wherever*_____ they must to distract their man's opponents. (10) For most

WWF fans, the fun does not end _____*until*_____ the last match is finished.

◆ PRACTICE 17-4

Form one complex sentence by combining each of the following pairs of sentences. Use a subordinating conjunction from the list on page 245 to clarify the relationship between the dependent and independent clauses in each sentence. Make sure you include a comma where one is required.

> **Example:** Orville and Wilbur Wright built the first powered plane/
> *although they*
> ~~They~~ had no formal training as engineers.
> *Answers may vary.*

Although professional   *, in*
1. ~~Professional~~ midwives are used widely in Europe/ ~~In~~ the United States,

   they usually practice independently only in areas with few doctors.

When   *, a*
2. John Deere constructed his first steel plow in 1837/ ~~A~~ new era began in

   prairie agriculture.

3. Stephen Crane powerfully describes battles in *The Red Badge of*
   even though he
   Courage/ ~~He~~ never experienced a war.

After   *, thousands*
4. Elvis Presley died suddenly in 1977/ ~~Thousands~~ of his fans gathered in

   front of his mansion.

After   *, the*
5. Jonas Salk developed the first polio vaccine in the 1950s/ ~~The~~ inci-

   dence of polio began to decline rapidly in the United States.

When the   *, some*
6. ~~The~~ salaries of baseball players rose dramatically in the 1980s/ ~~Some~~

   sportswriters predicted a drop in attendance.

Before the   *,*
7. ~~The~~ Du Ponts arrived from France in 1800/ American gunpowder was

   inferior to the kind manufactured by the French.

After
8. Margaret Sanger opened her first birth-control clinic in America in
   , she
   1916/ ~~She~~ was arrested and sentenced to thirty days in jail.

Because
9. Thaddeus Stevens thought plantation land should be distributed to
   , he
   freed slaves/ ~~He~~ disagreed with Lincoln's peace terms for the South.

Even though
10. Steven Spielberg directed some of the most popular movies of all
    , he
    time/ ~~He~~ did not win an Academy Award until *Schindler's List.*

■ WRITING FIRST: Flashback

Look back at your response to the Writing First exercise on page 242. Identify two pairs of simple sentences that could be combined with subordinating conjunctions. On the lines below, combine each pair into a complex sentence by making one sentence a dependent clause. Check to make sure you have punctuated your new sentences correctly.

Answers will vary.

_____

_____

_____

_____

C   Forming Complex Sentences with Relative Pronouns

A **relative pronoun** (*who, that, which,* and so on) introduces a **dependent clause** that describes a noun or pronoun in the sentence.

> ● **Writing Tip**
>
> A clause introduced by a relative pronoun does not express a complete thought; it is therefore a fragment. (See 22D.)

Relative Pronouns			
that	which	whoever	whomever
what	who	whom	whose

> ● **Writing Tip**
>
> Remember, *who* refers to people, and *that* and *which* refer to things.

Relative pronouns can also join two simple sentences (independent clauses) to make a complex sentence. The relative pronoun shows the relationship between the ideas in the two sentences that it links.

TWO SENTENCES   Nadine Gordimer comes from South Africa. She won the Nobel Prize in literature in 1991.

COMPLEX SENTENCE   Nadine Gordimer, <u>who won the Nobel Prize in literature in 1991</u>, comes from South Africa.

TWO SENTENCES   Last week I had a job interview. It went very well.

COMPLEX SENTENCE   Last week I had a job interview <u>that went very well</u>.

TWO SENTENCES   Transistors have replaced vacuum tubes in radios and televisions. They were invented in 1948.

COMPLEX SENTENCE   Transistors, <u>which were invented in 1948</u>, have replaced vacuum tubes in radios and televisions.

> ● **Writing Tip**
>
> When you form a complex sentence, the relative pronoun substitutes for a noun or another pronoun in one of the original simple sentences.

ON THE WEB
For more practice, visit
Exercise Central *at*
*<www.bedfordstmartins.com/
writingfirst>*.

> **FOCUS** **Punctuating with Relative Pronouns**
>
> In general, commas are used to set off a dependent clause intro-
> duced by *which*. Commas are not used to set off a dependent clause
> introduced by *that*. Depending on its meaning in a sentence, a
> dependent clause introduced by *who* is sometimes but not always
> set off by commas.

◆ PRACTICE 17-5

Combine each of the following pairs of simple sentences into one complex
sentence, using the relative pronoun that follows each pair.

Example: The United States is frightening to many Japanese. It is
seen as a violent country. (which)

The United States, which is seen as a violent country, is frightening to

many Japanese.

1. This image is reinforced by a television show.
   It started several years ago. (that)

   This image is reinforced by a television show that started several years ago.

   _____

   _____

2. On Sunday nights, viewers watch Hyota overcome his latest disaster.
   He is a Japanese traveler trying to survive in America. (who)

   On Sunday nights, viewers watch Hyota, who is a Japanese traveler trying

   to survive in America, overcome his latest disaster.

   _____

> **Teaching Tip**
> Take this opportunity to
> explain the proper way of
> punctuating restrictive and
> nonrestrictive clauses. (See
> 31D.)

3. During one episode, Hyota was wandering through the streets, looking
   for someone to help him.
   The streets were full of people. (which)

   During one episode, Hyota was wandering through the streets, which

   were full of people, looking for someone to help him.

   _____

4. His questions were misunderstood.
   They were halfway between English and Japanese. (which)

His questions, which were halfway between English and Japanese, were

misunderstood.

5. This television program is very popular.
   It teaches American street expressions to Japanese viewers. (which)

   This television program, which teaches American street expressions to

   Japanese viewers, is very popular.

6. Most Japanese learn English in high school by reading formal passages from textbooks.
   The textbooks are designed to get them into universities. (that)

   Most Japanese learn English in high school by reading formal passages from

   textbooks that are designed to get them into universities.

7. The English they learn is of little use in the real world.
   It is not enough to protect them from street hustlers. (which)

   The English they learn, which is of little use in the real world, is not enough

   to protect them from street hustlers.

8. Some Japanese have been killed or injured in the United States.
   They could not understand spoken English. (who)

   Some Japanese who could not understand spoken English have been killed

   or injured in the United States.

9. For example, a sixteen-year-old Japanese exchange student was shot.
   He did not understand the command *freeze*. (who)

   For example, a sixteen-year-old Japanese exchange student who did not

   understand the command freeze was shot.

10. This case has led many Japanese to learn "usable English."
    It will help them when they travel to the United States. (that)

    This case has led many Japanese to learn "usable English" that will help

    them when they travel to the United States.

◆ **PRACTICE 17-6**

Combine each of the following pairs of simple sentences into one complex sentence, using a relative pronoun (*who, which,* or *that*).

> **Example:**   MTV made its cable debut in August 1981. It was the first television network devoted to popular music videos.

MTV, which was the first television network devoted to popular music

videos, made its cable debut In August 1981.

Answers will vary.

1. MTV's very first music video was performed by a group called the Buggles. It made the claim "Video Killed the Radio Star."

   MTV's very first music video, which was performed by a group called the

   Buggles, made the claim "Video Killed the Radio Star."

2. Most of MTV's early videos were fairly simple productions. They basically recorded the artists in live or studio performances.

   Most of MTV's early videos were fairly simple productions that basically

   recorded the artists in live or studio performances.

3. Recording executives soon realized the power of music videos in selling records.
   They had been suspicious of MTV at first.

   Recording executives, who had been suspicious of MTV at first, soon real-

   ized the power of music videos in selling records.

4. Music videos became highly elaborate productions. They featured multiple settings, special effects, and large casts of dancers.

   Music videos became highly elaborate productions that featured multiple

   settings, special effects, and large casts of dancers.

5. The Cars' "You Might Think" won best video at the first MTV music awards telecast.
   It aired in September 1984.

   The Cars' "You Might Think" won best video at the first MTV music awards

   telecast, which aired in September 1984.

6. The game show *Remote Control* debuted on MTV in 1987.
   It was a parody of *Jeopardy*.

   The game show Remote Control, which was a parody of Jeopardy, debuted

   on MTV in 1987.

   _____

7. The fashion program *House of Style* became popular in 1989 partly
   because of supermodel Cindy Crawford.
   She was its first host.

   The fashion program House of Style became popular in 1989 partly

   because of supermodel Cindy Crawford, who was its first host.

   _____

8. *The Real World* was an early reality-based series.
   It featured a group of young people living together in New York City.

   The Real World was an early reality-based series that featured a group of

   young people living together in New York City.

   _____

9. That same year, Arkansas governor Bill Clinton met with young voters
   on *Rock the Vote*.
   He would soon be elected president.

   That same year, Arkansas governor Bill Clinton, who would soon be elected

   president, met with young voters on Rock the Vote.

   _____

10. Today, MTV devotes less and less time to music videos.
    It produces many hours of original programming aimed at young people.

    Today, MTV, which devotes less and less time to music videos, produces

    many hours of original programming aimed at young people.

    _____

◆ PRACTICE 17-7

Fill in the blanks in the sentences that follow with a dependent clause that
begins with a relative pronoun (*who, which,* or *that*). The new dependent
clause should help complete the meaning of the original sentence.

Example: People _who are talking on cell phones_ may not be paying
close attention to their driving.
Answers will vary.

1. People _____

   should have their driver's licenses revoked.

2. A speeding car is like a weapon _____.

3. Teenagers _____

could be required to take driver's education first.

4. New drivers should be taught safety tips _____.

5. One activity _____

is eating while one is driving.

6. A driver _____

cannot possibly keep both hands on the steering wheel.

7. Putting on makeup while driving is another activity _____

_____.

8. To encourage safe driving, the police should be allowed to pull over

any driver _____.

9. For a first offense, a driver _____

could be given only a warning.

10. A second offense, however, would result in a fine _____

_____.

■ WRITING FIRST: Flashback

Look back at your response to the Writing First exercise on page 242. Identify two simple sentences that could be combined with a relative pronoun. (If you cannot find two appropriate sentences, write two new ones.) On the lines below, write the new complex sentence.

Answers will vary. _____

_____

_____

■ WRITING FIRST: Revising and Editing

Look back at your response to the Writing First exercise on page 242. Incorporating one of the new complex sentences you created

(continued on the following page)

> *(continued from the previous page)*
> in the Flashback exercises on pages 248 and 253, revise your work. Then, check to make sure there are no errors in your use of subordinating conjunctions and relative pronouns. When you have finished, look over a piece of writing you have done in response to another assignment, and try combining some simple sentences into complex sentences.

CHAPTER REVIEW

◆ EDITING PRACTICE

Read the following student essay. Then, revise it by combining pairs of simple sentences with subordinating conjunctions or relative pronouns that indicate the relationship between them. Be sure to punctuate correctly. The first sentence has been revised for you.
Answers may vary.

My Life in Haiti

My father and mother lived in Haiti / *although* I was born in the United States. My father and his brother opened a small business in Haiti / *when* I was a baby. *Because* I grew up in Haiti / I experienced the culture as a native, not a foreigner. My friends were all Haitian / *, who* ~~They~~ wanted only to play soccer. I tried to teach them baseball and football. Before I learned to speak English, I spoke only the Haitian Creole dialect. *When* I was a toddler / I went to New York to visit my grandmother. One day, *when* I was thirsty / I asked her in Creole for a glass of water. At the same time, I pointed to the refrigerator. My grandmother *, who spoke only English,* had no idea what I meant. ~~She spoke only English.~~ I finally had to point to a glass so she would know what I wanted.

In Haiti, I developed close relationships with the neighbors / *who* ~~They~~ lived on our street. *Because they* ~~They~~ never shut their doors / I was constantly walking in and out of their houses. Whenever I opened my mouth, one of them fed me some candy or a bowl of curried goat stew. Dina *, who* was an elderly Cuban

woman, ~~She~~ was like a grandmother to me. She encouraged me
because she
to eat, ~~She~~ thought I was too skinny. Lita, another neigh-

bor, was an excellent storyteller. She would tell my
until we
friends and me tales of voodoo, ~~We~~ were afraid to walk
Although her   *, we*
home. ~~Her~~ stories terrified us, ~~We~~ could not wait to hear

more.
                                        , who had been sick for a year,
    When I was twelve, my life in Haiti ended. My father
                                        Although my
died of cancer. ~~He had been sick for a year.~~ ~~My~~ mother and
                                    , she
I could have stayed in Haiti, ~~She~~ decided to return to her

parents in New York. She sold her share of the business to
            because we
my uncle, ~~We~~ needed the money. Sometimes, my mind wanders
                        Although my   ,
back to those days. ~~My~~ life in Haiti is over, I will never

forget the people I knew and loved there.

◆ COLLABORATIVE ACTIVITIES

1. Working in a group of four students, make a list of three or four of
   your favorite television shows. Divide into pairs, and with your partner, write two simple sentences describing each show. Next, use subordinating conjunctions or relative pronouns to combine each pair of
   sentences into one complex sentence. With your group, discuss how
   the ideas in each complex sentence are related, and make sure you
   have used the subordinating conjunction or relative pronoun that best
   conveys this relationship.

   EXAMPLE: *The Brady Bunch* portrays a 1970s family. It still appeals
               to many viewers.

               Although *The Brady Bunch* portrays a 1970s family, it
               still appeals to many viewers.

2. Imagine that you and the members of your group live in a neighborhood where workers are repairing underground power lines. As they
   work, the workers talk loudly and use foul language. Write a letter of
   complaint to the power company in which you explain that the workers' behavior is offensive to you and to your children. Tell the company
   that you want the offensive behavior to end. Write the first draft of
   your letter in simple sentences. After you have written this draft, work
   as a group to combine as many sentences as you can with subordinating conjunctions and relative pronouns.

3. Assume you are in a competition to determine which collaborative
   group in your class is best at writing complex sentences. Working in a
   group, prepare a letter to your instructor in which you present the
   strengths of your group. Be sure to use a subordinating conjunction or
   relative pronoun in each of the sentences in your letter. Finally, as a
   class, evaluate the letters from the groups and choose the letter that
   most successfully convinces you that its group is best.

☑ REVIEW CHECKLIST:

Writing Complex Sentences

- A clause is a group of words that contains a subject and a verb. An independent clause can stand alone as a sentence. A dependent clause cannot stand alone as a sentence because it needs other words to complete its meaning. (See 17A.)

- A complex sentence consists of one independent clause (simple sentence) combined with one or more dependent clauses. (See 17A.)

- When an independent clause is joined with a dependent clause, the result is a complex sentence. (See 17A.)

- Subordinating conjunctions—such as *although, after, when, while,* and *because*—can join two simple sentences into one complex sentence. (See 17B.)

- Always use a comma after a dependent clause when it comes before the independent clause in the sentence. Do not use a comma when the dependent clause follows the independent clause. (See 17B.)

- Relative pronouns—such as *who, which,* and *that*—can also join two simple sentences into one complex sentence. The relative pronoun shows the relationship between the ideas in the two sentences that it links. (See 17C.)

- When you link two simple sentences with a relative pronoun, use a comma before *which;* do not use a comma before *that. Who* is sometimes preceded by a comma.

Achieving Sentence Variety

PREVIEW

In this chapter, you will learn

- to vary sentence types (18A)

- to vary sentence openings (18B)

- to combine sentences (18C)

- to vary sentence length (18D)

■ WRITING FIRST

Plan a time capsule that your children will open when they are adults. What items would you include? How would you expect each item to communicate to your children what you and your world were like? Look at the picture above, and then explain your decisions.

Word Power

capsule a sealed container

memorabilia things worthy of remembering

nostalgia a longing for people or things that are no longer present

In Chapters 15 through 17, you learned to write simple, compound, and complex sentences. Now, you are ready to learn how to create more varied sentences. A passage of varied sentences flows more smoothly, is easier to read and understand, and is more interesting than one in which all the sentences are the same length and begin with the subject.

A Varying Sentence Types

Most English sentences are **statements**. Others are **questions** or **exclamations**. One way to vary your sentences is to use an occasional question or exclamation where it is appropriate.

In the following paragraph, a question and an exclamation add variety to the original.

Question

Exclamation

> In less than twenty years, the image of African Americans in television sitcoms seemed to change dramatically, reflecting the changing status of black men and women in American society. But had anything really changed? In *Beulah*, the 1950 sitcom that was the first to star an African-American woman, the title character was a maid. Her friends were portrayed as irresponsible and not very smart. *Amos 'n' Andy*, which also appeared in the 1950s, continued these negative stereotypes of black characters. In 1968, with the civil rights movement at its height, the NBC comedy hit *Julia* portrayed a black woman in a much more favorable light. A widowed nurse, raising a small boy on her own, Julia was a dedicated professional and a patient and devoted mother. The image of the African American was certainly more positive, but the character was no more balanced or three-dimensional than earlier black characters had been. Julia was not an object of ridicule; instead, she was a saint!

◆ PRACTICE 18-1

Revise the following passage by changing one of the statements into a question and one of the statements into an exclamation.

Example: Some people pursue two different careers at the same time. (statement)

Why do some people pursue two different careers at the same time? (question)

Answers will vary.

(1) Many working people have more than one job. (2) For example, a police officer might moonlight as a security guard, an actor might also work as a waiter, and an artist or writer might also teach. (3) These workers need their second jobs for survival. (4) In recent years, however, more and more successful professionals have decided to begin a second career without abandoning the first one. (5) Often, the second career seems to be very different from the first one. (6) For example, a teacher might also work as a professional model. (7) Sometimes, however, the two careers really do have something in common. (8) After all, both teaching and modeling involve performing for an audience. (9) Similarly,

a lawyer may be drawn to the ministry, another career that is dedicated
to justice. (10) ~~Many things motivate~~ *What motivates* people to combine two seemingly
different professions. (11) Those who do so say they do it not for the
money but for professional satisfaction. (12) Obviously, these workers
are very lucky people.

■ WRITING FIRST: Flashback

Look back at your response to the Writing First exercise on page
257. What questions does your writing answer? Write one or two
on the lines below.

Question 1: *Answers will vary.* _____

_____

Question 2: _____

_____

If you can, add one of these questions. (You may need to substitute
it for a sentence that is already there.)

If you think an exclamation would be an appropriate addition
to your writing, suggest one below.

Exclamation: _____

_____

Where could you add this exclamation?

B   Varying Sentence Openings

Varying the way you begin your sentences is another way of adding life to
your writing. If you always begin your sentences with the subject, your
writing is likely to seem dull and repetitive, as the writing in the paragraph
below does.

> Scientists have been observing a disturbing phenomenon. The pop-
> ulation of frogs, toads, and salamanders has been declining. This
> decline was first noticed in the mid-1980s. Some reports blamed chem-
> ical pollution. Some biologists began to suspect that a fungal disease
> was killing these amphibians. The most reasonable explanation seems
> to be that the amphibians' eggs are threatened by solar radiation. This
> radiation penetrates the thinned ozone layer, which used to shield
> them from the sun's rays.

Teaching Tip
Caution students against
using too many of one kind
of sentence opening. Starting every sentence with an
adverb can be just as dull as
always starting with the
subject.

■ **Computer Tip**
Use the Search or Find command to locate every use of
The, This, and *It* at the beginning of a sentence. Then,
revise as necessary to vary
sentence openings.

*For more on adverbs, see
Chapter 29.*

Beginning with Adverbs

Instead of opening every sentence with the subject, try beginning with one
or more **adverbs**, as the following paragraph illustrates.

> Scientists have been observing a disturbing phenomenon. Gradu-
> ally but steadily, the population of frogs, toads, and salamanders has
> been declining. This decline was first noticed in the mid-1980s. Some
> reports blamed chemical pollution. Some biologists began to suspect
> that a fungal disease was killing these amphibians. However, the most
> reasonable explanation seems to be that the amphibians' eggs are
> threatened by solar radiation. This radiation penetrates the thinned
> ozone layer, which used to shield them from the sun's rays.

Beginning with Prepositional Phrases

*For more on prepositions, see
15B.*

You can also begin some sentences with prepositional phrases. A **prepositional phrase** (such as *along the river* or *near the diner*) is made up of a
preposition and its object.

> In recent years, scientists have been observing a disturbing phe-
> nomenon. Gradually but steadily, the population of frogs, toads, and
> salamanders has been declining. This decline was first noticed in the
> mid-1980s. At first, some reports blamed chemical pollution. After a
> while, some biologists began to suspect that a fungal disease was
> killing these amphibians. However, the most reasonable explanation
> seems to be that the amphibians' eggs are threatened by solar radia-
> tion. This radiation penetrates the thinned ozone layer, which used to
> shield them from the sun's rays.

FOCUS Sentence Openings

Note that in addition to adding variety, adverbs and prepositional
phrases at the beginnings of sentences can also function as transitions, joining the sentences smoothly into a paragraph. (See 2D.)

◆ PRACTICE 18-2

Underline the adverb in each of the following sentences, and then rewrite
the sentence so that the adverb appears at the beginning. Be sure to punctuate correctly.

Example: Applicants often become nervous when being interviewed
for a job.

Often, applicants become nervous when being interviewed for a job.

ON THE WEB
For more practice, visit
Exercise Central *at*
<www.bedfordstmartins.com/
writingfirst>.

1. Job applicants <u>sometimes</u> feel tongue-tied when asked even simple

   questions.

   Sometimes, job applicants feel tongue-tied when asked even simple questions.

   _____

2. They may <u>occasionally</u> feel as though they are going to be ill.

   Occasionally, they may feel as though they are going to be ill.

   _____

3. There are, <u>however</u>, strategies that can control jitters during job inter-

   views.

   However, there are strategies that can control jitters during job inter-

   views.

4. Applicants should realize <u>first</u> that interviewers expect them to be a bit

   nervous.

   First, applicants should realize that interviewers expect them to be a bit

   nervous.

5. They should <u>then</u> understand that a simple mistake does not have to

   ruin the entire interview.

   Then, they should understand that a simple mistake does not have to

   ruin the entire interview.

6. It is <u>obviously</u> not a good idea to see a job interviewer as an enemy.

   Obviously, it is not a good idea to see a job interviewer as an enemy.

   _____

7. Experts <u>surprisingly</u> advise applicants to think of the interviewer as a

   close friend.

   Surprisingly, experts advise applicants to think of the interviewer as a

   close friend.

8. They suggest <u>also</u> that applicants use relaxation techniques before an

   interview.

   Also, they suggest that applicants use relaxation techniques before an

   interview.

9. Visualizing a calm and beautiful landscape can <u>usually</u> help one

   relax.

Usually, visualizing a calm and beautiful landscape can help one relax.

10. Job applicants must <u>ultimately</u> try to trust their own abilities during interviews.

Ultimately, job applicants must try to trust their own abilities during interviews.

◆ PRACTICE 18-3

In each of the following sentences, fill in the blank with an appropriate adverb. Be sure to punctuate correctly.

Example: _____*Slowly,*_____ the sun crept over the horizon.
Answers will vary.

1. _____ the speeding car appeared from out of nowhere.

2. _____ it crashed into the guard rail.

3. _____ the car jackknifed across the highway.

4. _____ drivers behind the crashed car slammed on their brakes.

5. _____ someone used a cell phone to call 911.

6. _____ a wailing siren could be heard.

7. _____ the ambulance arrived.

8. _____ emergency medical technicians went to work.

9. _____ a police officer was on hand to direct traffic.

10. _____ no one was badly hurt in the accident.

◆ PRACTICE 18-4

Underline the prepositional phrase in each of the following sentences, and then rewrite the sentence so that the prepositional phrase appears at the beginning. Be sure to punctuate correctly.

Example: Very few American women worked in factories <u>before the 1940s.</u>

Before the 1940s, very few American women worked in factories.

1. Many male factory workers became soldiers <u>during</u> World War II.

During World War II, many male factory workers became soldiers.

2. War-related industries faced a labor shortage <u>as a result</u>.

As a result, war-related industries faced a labor shortage.

3. The U.S. government encouraged women to take factory jobs <u>in the war's early years</u>.

In the war's early years, the U.S. government encouraged women to take factory jobs.

4. Women met this challenge <u>with great eagerness and patriotic pride</u>.

With great eagerness and patriotic pride, women met this challenge.

5. They entered the industrial workplace <u>in unprecedented numbers</u>.

In unprecedented numbers, they entered the industrial workplace.

6. Over six million women took factory jobs <u>between 1942 and 1945</u>.

Between 1942 and 1945, over six million women took factory jobs.

7. Productivity rose and quality improved <u>with their efforts</u>.

With their efforts, productivity rose and quality improved.

8. A new female image emerged <u>alongside this greater responsibility and independence</u>.

Alongside this greater responsibility and independence, a new female image emerged.

9. Many women felt comfortable wearing pants <u>for the first time</u>.

For the first time, many women felt comfortable wearing pants.

10. Most lost their factory jobs <u>after the war</u> and had to return to "women's work."

After the war, most lost their factory jobs and had to return to "women's work."

◆ PRACTICE 18-5

In each of the following sentences, fill in the blank with an appropriate prepositional phrase. Be sure to punctuate correctly.

Example: *By September,* most college students are back in school.
Answers will vary.

1. _____ the first year of college can be a difficult experience.

2. _____ students must make many adjustments.

3. _____ they face a new and unfamiliar environment.

4. _____ they must learn to work independently and budget their time.

5. _____ their classes may be large.

6. _____ they may feel lonely and even out of place.

7. _____ balancing job responsibilities with college can prove frustrating.

8. _____ being in college has become easier for many students.

9. _____ they have learned to be more comfortable in their new environment.

10. _____ they realize that the benefits of college are worth the challenges.

◆ **PRACTICE 18-6**

Several sentences in the following passage contain prepositional phrases and adverbs that could be moved to the beginnings of sentences. Revise the passage to vary the sentence openings by moving prepositional phrases to the beginnings of three sentences and moving adverbs to the beginnings of two other sentences. Be sure to place a comma after these prepositional phrases and adverbs.

Example: *Before the first day of school, some*
Some students already know how to succeed before the
first day of school.

(1) Why are some college students more successful than others?
(2) *Recently, a*
A study done at Harvard University recently provided some answers to this question and offered suggestions to students who want to get the most out of college. (3) According to the study, students should really get to know at least one professor each semester. (4) If they do this, they will have people to turn to for help when problems arise and will feel more connected to their school. (5) *After graduation, these*
These professors can also write letters of recommendation for them after graduation. (6) Students should also take small classes whenever possible and take interesting electives as well as required courses. (7) *In addition, the*
The study recommends in addition that students study in groups and that they take courses that require writing, preferably several short papers rather than one long one. (8) Another recommendation is that students take foreign language courses, which are

Throughout their college careers, students
usually small and often require group work. (9) ~~Students~~ should give
themselves a chance to become involved in outside activities ~~throughout~~
Finally, students
~~their college careers.~~ (10) ~~Students~~ must ~~finally~~ learn to manage their

time and to set aside large blocks of time to study.

◆ PRACTICE 18-7

Listed below are two adverbs and four prepositional phrases. In the passage that follows, add each of these words or phrases to the beginning of
a sentence in order to vary the sentence openings. Be sure your additions
connect ideas clearly and logically. Remember to add commas where they
are needed.

Occasionally	Sadly
For example	In fact
With their screams and chants	Of course

Sadly, pro
Example: ~~Pro~~ football players face great danger.

Answers may vary.
(1) Professional football is one of the most popular sports in the
Sadly,
country; it is also one of the most dangerous. (2) Bob Utley and Darryl

Stingley are now paraplegics because of injuries they suffered on the

field, and the disabled list increases each season.

(3) The league has established new rules to make the game safer, and
For example, a
some of these have cut down on serious injuries. (4) ~~A~~ player cannot

tackle a kicker after he has kicked the ball, and a player cannot tackle a

quarterback after he has thrown the ball or a runner after he has gone

out of bounds. (5) These precautions, however, do not always protect
Occasionally, players
players. (6) ~~Players~~ still tackle other players in violation of the rules

because they are angry and frustrated or even as a calculated strategy.
In fact, one
(7) ~~One~~ coach is rumored to have placed bounties on rival players. (8) A

team member collects by putting the opposing players out of commis-

sion for the entire game.
Of course, the
(9) ~~The~~ fans also share the blame for the violence of football.
With their screams and chants, they
(10) ~~They~~ encourage players to hit harder or play with more intensity.

(11) They believe their team should do anything to win. (12) The unfor-

tunate fact is that as football becomes more dangerous to players, it

becomes more popular with fans.

■ **WRITING FIRST Flashback**

Look back at your response to the Writing First exercise on page 257. Identify one sentence that you could revise by beginning it with an adverb and one that could open with a prepositional phrase. (Note that the adverb or prepositional phrase may already be somewhere in your sentence.) Write the revised sentences on the lines below.

1. _Answers will vary._____ , _____
   (Adverb)

   _____

2. _____ , _____
   (Prepositional phrase)

   _____

For information on forming compound sentences, see Chapter 16. For information on forming complex sentences, see Chapter 17.

C **Combining Sentences**

You can also create sentence variety by experimenting with different ways of combining sentences. You have already learned to combine simple sentences to create compound sentences (Chapter 16) and complex sentences (Chapter 17). Now, you will learn to combine sentences with *present participles, past participles, compounds,* or *appositives*. These different techniques will help you create varied, interesting sentences.

Using Present Participles

The **present participle** is the *-ing* form of a verb: *using, carrying.* You can use a present participle to combine two sentences.

TWO SENTENCES Duke Ellington composed more than a thousand songs. He worked hard to establish his reputation as a musician.

COMBINED <u>Composing</u> more than a thousand songs, Duke Ellington worked hard to establish his reputation as a musician. (present participle)

For more on present participles, see 25A.

When the sentences are combined, the present participle *(composing)* introduces a phrase that describes the sentence's subject *(Duke Ellington).*

Using Past Participles

Past participles of verbs are usually formed with *-ed (carried)* or *-d (used),* but there are also many irregular past participle forms *(known, written).*

For more on past participles, see 25B; for a list of irregular past participles, see 27B.

Two sentences can often be combined when one of them contains a past participle.

TWO SENTENCES   Nogales is located on the border between Arizona and Mexico. It is a bilingual city.

COMBINED   Located on the border between Arizona and Mexico, Nogales is a bilingual city. (past participle)

When the sentences are combined, the past participle *(located)* introduces a phrase that describes the sentence's subject *(Nogales)*.

● **Writing Tip**

Make sure that phrases introduced by present or past participles clearly refer to the words they describe. (See 25C and 25D.)

◆ PRACTICE 18-8

Use a present participle to combine each of the following pairs of sentences into a single sentence. Eliminate any unnecessary words, and use a comma to set off each phrase introduced by a present participle. When you are finished, underline the present participle in each new sentence.

ON THE WEB
For more practice, visit Exercise Central at <www.bedfordstmartins.com/writingfirst>.

Example: Moviegoers accepted Chaplin enthusiastically. They identified with his characters.

Accepting Chaplin enthusiastically, moviegoers identified with his characters.

or

Identifying with his characters, moviegoers accepted Chaplin enthusiastically.

Answers will vary.

Teaching Tip
In Practice 18-8, students may need to change a noun to a pronoun or vice versa when they combine sentences. Review the example sentences carefully.

1. Charlie Chaplin grew up in the slums of London. He began his acting career in vaudeville shows.

   Growing up in the slums of London, Charlie Chaplin began his acting career in vaudeville shows.

2. Chaplin arrived in Hollywood in 1910. He was soon discovered by film director Mack Sennett.

   Arriving in Hollywood in 1910, Chaplin was soon discovered by film director Mack Sennett.

3. Chaplin turned to writing and directing. He made his first famous film, *The Tramp,* in 1915.

   Turning to writing and directing, Chaplin made his first famous film, The Tramp, in 1915.

4. Chaplin wore baggy pants and a sad expression. He introduced his "little tramp" character.

   Wearing baggy pants and a sad expression, Chaplin introduced his "little tramp" character.

5. Chaplin continued to play the little tramp in other silent films. He starred in *The Kid* (1921) and *The Gold Rush* (1925).

Continuing to play the little tramp in other silent films, Chaplin starred in

The Kid (1921) and The Gold Rush (1925).

6. Chaplin moved from silent to talking movies. He made *City Lights* in 1931.

Moving from silent to talking movies, Chaplin made City Lights in 1931.

7. The little tramp charmed audiences in *City Lights*. He was last seen in *Modern Times* (1936).

Charming audiences in City Lights, the little tramp was last seen in Modern Times (1936).

8. Chaplin decided to make fun of Hitler. He directed and starred in *The Great Dictator* in 1940.

Deciding to make fun of Hitler, Chaplin directed and starred in The Great Dictator in 1940.

9. Chaplin departed from Hollywood in the 1950s. He settled in England.

Departing from Hollywood in the 1950s, Chaplin settled in England.

10. Charlie Chaplin died in 1977. He left behind many fans.

Leaving behind many fans, Charlie Chaplin died in 1977.

◆ PRACTICE 18-9

For each of the first five sentences that follow, fill in the blank with an appropriate present participle modifier. For each of the final five sentences, fill in the blank with an appropriate independent clause. Be sure to punctuate correctly.

Examples: *Selling candy door to door,* the team raised money for new uniforms.

Blasting its siren, *the fire truck raced through the busy streets.*
Answers will vary.

1. _____ the judge called for order in the courtroom.

2. _____ the miners found silver instead.

3. _____ migrating birds often

travel long distances in the early fall.

4. _____ fans waited patiently to buy tickets for the concert.

5. _____ the child seemed to be frightened.

6. Stepping up to home plate _____

_____

7. Traveling at high speeds _____

_____

8. Broiling in the ninety-degree weather _____

_____

9. Looking both ways first _____

_____

10. Talking to a group of news reporters _____

_____

◆ PRACTICE 18-10

Use a past participle to combine each of the following pairs of sentences into a single sentence. Eliminate any unnecessary words, and use a comma to set off each phrase introduced by a past participle. When you are finished, underline the past participle in each new sentence.

> **Teaching Tip**
> This exercise asks students to combine sentences; it does *not* say each revised sentence must *begin* with a participle. If this is what you want students to do, tell them so.

Example: Sacajawea was born in about 1787. She lived among her Shoshone tribespeople until the age of eleven.

Born in about 1787, Sacajawea lived among her Shoshone tribespeople until

the age of eleven.

Answers will vary.

1. She was captured as a young girl by a rival tribe. Sacajawea was later sold into slavery.

   Captured as a young girl by a rival tribe, Sacajawea was later sold into

   slavery.

   _____

2. She was saved by a French Canadian fur trader named Charbonneau. Sacajawea became his wife.

   Saved by a French Canadian fur trader named Charbonneau, Sacajawea

   became his wife.

   _____

3. The explorers Lewis and Clark hired Charbonneau in 1806. He brought his pregnant wife along on their westward expedition.

Hired by the explorers Lewis and Clark in 1806, Charbonneau brought his

pregnant wife along on their westward expedition.

4. Sacajawea was skilled in several native languages. She helped Lewis and Clark trade for horses and other goods.

Skilled in several native languages, Sacajawea helped Lewis and Clark

trade for horses and other goods.

5. The expedition was guided by Sacajawea's knowledge of the rugged terrain. It also benefited from her familiarity with native food plants.

Guided by Sacajawea's knowledge of the rugged terrain, the expedition

also benefited from her familiarity with native food plants.

6. Clark's journals were rescued by Sacajawea when the party's boat over-turned in whitewater. They would have been lost otherwise.

Rescued by Sacajawea when the party's boat overturned in whitewater,

Clark's journals would have been lost otherwise.

7. Lewis and Clark were protected by the presence of the Shoshone woman and her infant. They encountered little hostility from the tribes they met.

Protected by the presence of the Shoshone woman and her infant, Lewis

and Clark encountered little hostility from the tribes they met.

8. Clark was indebted to Sacajawea for the success of the journey. He wrote afterwards that she deserved much credit.

Indebted to Sacajawea for the success of the journey, Clark wrote after-

wards that she deserved much credit.

9. Sacajawea has been celebrated for many years as an American hero. She recently received an additional honor.

Celebrated for many years as an American hero, Sacajawea recently re-

ceived an additional honor.

10. The U.S. dollar coin now bears her likeness. It was minted in 2000.

Minted in 2000, the U.S. dollar coin now bears her likeness.

◆ PRACTICE 18-11

For each of the first five sentences that follow, fill in the blank with an appropriate past participle modifier. For each of the final five sentences, fill in the blank with an appropriate independent clause. Be sure to punctuate correctly.

Examples: *Buried away for many years,* the treasure was discovered by accident.

Advertised as children's books, *the Harry Potter stories also appeal to adults.*

Answers will vary.

1. _____ the child started crying when the storm began.

2. _____ the hikers rested wearily on the rocks at the top of the mountain.

3. _____ the small boat almost capsized.

4. _____ the balloons in the Macy's Thanksgiving Day parade soar above the crowds.

5. _____ family stories help families keep their traditions alive.

6. Annoyed by her parents _____

7. Lost in the woods for three days _____

8. Bored by the same old routine _____

9. Confronted with the evidence _____

10. Asked whether they supported the president _____

Using Compound Subjects or Compound Verbs

A **compound subject** consists of two nouns or pronouns, usually joined by *and*; a **compound verb** consists of two verbs, usually joined by *and*. You can use a compound subject or a compound verb to combine two sentences.

● **Writing Tip**

Remember that a compound subject joined by *and* takes a plural verb. (See 23A.)

TWO SENTENCES   Elijah McCoy was an African-American inventor. Garrett Morgan was also an African-American inventor.

COMBINED   <u>Elijah McCoy and Garrett Morgan</u> were African-American inventors. (compound subject)

TWO SENTENCES   Arundhati Roy's first novel, *The God of Small Things*, appeared in 1997. It won the Pulitzer Prize.

COMBINED   Arundhati Roy's first novel, *The God of Small Things*, <u>appeared</u> in 1997 <u>and won</u> the Pulitzer Prize.

ON THE WEB

For more practice, visit
Exercise Central *at*
<www.bedfordstmartins.com/
writingfirst>.

◆ **PRACTICE 18-12**

Creating a compound subject, combine each of the following pairs of sentences into a single sentence.

Example: The Magic Kingdom is a popular Florida theme park. Islands of Adventure is also a popular Florida theme park.

The Magic Kingdom and Islands of Adventure are popular Florida theme

parks.

1. American tourists flock to Orlando's theme parks. Foreign visitors also flock to Orlando's theme parks.

   American tourists and foreign visitors flock to Orlando's theme parks.

2. Dueling Dragons is a roller coaster at Islands of Adventure. The Incredible Hulk is also a roller coaster there.

   Dueling Dragons and the Incredible Hulk are roller coasters at Islands of

   Adventure.

3. At the Magic Kingdom, the roller coaster Space Mountain draws large crowds. The Pirates of the Caribbean ride draws large crowds as well.

   At the Magic Kingdom, the roller coaster Space Mountain and the Pirates

   of the Caribbean ride draw large crowds.

4. Costumed characters appear throughout the park. Colorful street performers also appear throughout the park.

   Costumed characters and colorful street performers appear throughout

   the park.

5. Children enjoy having their pictures taken with Mickey Mouse. Adults enjoy having their pictures taken with Mickey.

Children and adults enjoy having their pictures taken with Mickey Mouse.

_____

6. Typhoon Lagoon is a Disney water park. Blizzard Beach is another Disney water park.

Typhoon Lagoon and Blizzard Beach are Disney water parks.

_____

7. Three-dimensional films can surprise first-time theme park visitors. Simulated disaster rides can surprise first-time visitors as well.

Three-dimensional films and simulated disaster rides can surprise first-

time theme park visitors.

8. Of course, long waits in line can make a visit exhausting. Florida's hot weather can also make a visit exhausting.

Of course, long waits in line and Florida's hot weather can make a visit

exhausting.

9. Admission to the parks can be quite expensive. The food sold there can be quite expensive too.

Admission to the parks and the food sold there can be quite expensive.

_____

10. Still, the variety of rides makes the expense worthwhile for most visitors. The many entertaining shows also make the expense worthwhile.

Still, the variety of rides and the many entertaining shows make the ex-

pense worthwhile for most visitors.

◆ PRACTICE 18-13

Creating a compound verb, combine each of the following pairs of sentences into a single sentence.

Example: The inventor Thomas Edison left school at an early age. He first made his living selling newspapers.

The inventor Thomas Edison left school at an early age and first made his

living selling newspapers.

1. Despite his lack of formal education, Edison had a quick mind. He also showed a talent for problem solving.

Despite his lack of formal education, Edison had a quick mind and showed

a talent for problem solving.

2. His early work as a telegraph operator stimulated his interest in electricity. It also led him to experiment with inventions.

His early work as a telegraph operator stimulated his interest in electricity

and led him to experiment with inventions.

3. Edison patented the earliest phonograph in 1878. He created the first practical light bulb the following year.

Edison patented the earliest phonograph in 1878 and created the first

practical light bulb the following year.

4. His invention of a power distribution network allowed electricity to come into people's homes. This invention led to many conveniences.

His invention of a power distribution network allowed electricity to come

into people's homes and led to many conveniences.

5. Edison later developed an electric railroad. He also produced one of the first batteries to store long-term power.

Edison later developed an electric railroad and produced one of the first

batteries to store long-term power.

6. His early moving picture machine fascinated audiences. It became quite popular.

His early moving picture machine fascinated audiences and became quite

popular.

7. His early experiments with sound pictures were surprisingly successful. They would eventually lead to talking pictures.

His early experiments with sound pictures were surprisingly successful

and would eventually lead to talking pictures.

8. Edison held many patents. He made a fortune from his inventions.

Edison held many patents and made a fortune from his inventions.

9. Edison carried out much of his work in New Jersey. He had laboratories there in West Orange and Menlo Park.

Edison carried out much of his work in New Jersey and had laboratories

there in West Orange and Menlo Park.

10. A number of his enterprises were combined after his death. They were renamed the General Electric Company.

A number of his enterprises were combined after his death and were

renamed the General Electric Company.

◆ PRACTICE 18-14

Combine each of the following pairs of sentences into one sentence by creating a compound subject or a compound verb. Remember that a compound subject takes a plural verb.

● **Writing Tip**

Do not put a comma between the two parts of a compound subject or between the two parts of a compound verb. (See 31F.)

Example: The NCAA Presidents Commission wants to reform college athletic programs/ ~~It~~ recommends a number of measures for
and
doing so. (compound verb)

(1) These college presidents ^ want to improve the academic perfor-
and their supporters
mance of college athletes. ~~Their supporters also want to improve the academic performance of college athletes.~~ (2) Their first proposal raises the number of required core courses for entering freshmen/ ~~It~~ increases
and
the SAT scores necessary for admittance. (3) A second proposal requires athletes to earn a certain number of credits every year/ ~~It~~ mandates a
and
minimum grade point average for them. (4) Many athletic directors see the changes as unfair/ ~~They~~ are resisting them. (5) Many Big East coaches
and
believe standardized test scores are biased/ ~~They~~ want their use in
and
screening student athletes banned. (6) Some coaches ^ also fear that the
and other opponents of these requirements
new rules will force many athletes to choose easy majors. ~~Other opponents of these requirements fear the same thing.~~ (7) According to supporters, however, many athletes under the current system fail to advance academically/ ~~They~~ often finish their eligibility fifty or more hours short
and
of graduation. (8) The new rules, they say, give student athletes a fair chance/ ~~They~~ also keep them on the graduation track. (9) In the support-
and
ers' view, poor supervision by athletic directors ^ is to be blamed for the
and lack of support for academic excellence are
poor performance of student athletes. ~~Lack of support for academic excellence is also to blame.~~

Teaching Tip

Show students that combining two sentences into one with a compound subject often results in a more concise sentence. Refer students to 20B.

Using Appositives

An **appositive** is a word or word group that identifies or renames a noun or pronoun. Using an appositive is often a good way to combine two sentences about the same subject.

● **Writing Tip**

When you combine sentences with an appositive, set off the appositive with commas. (See 31C.)

TWO SENTENCES   C. J. Walker was the first American woman to become a self-made millionaire. She marketed a line of hair-care products for black women.

COMBINED   C. J. Walker, <u>the first American woman to become a self-made millionaire</u>, marketed a line of hair-care products for black women. (appositive)

Notice that in addition to appearing in the middle of a sentence, an appositive can also come at the beginning or at the end of a sentence.

<u>The first American woman to become a self-made millionaire</u>, C. J. Walker marketed a line of hair-care products for black women.

Several books have been written about C. J. Walker, <u>the first American woman to become a self-made millionaire</u>.

◆ PRACTICE 18-15

ON THE WEB
For more practice, visit
Exercise Central *at*
<www.bedfordstmartins.com/
writingfirst>.

Use appositives to combine each of the following pairs of sentences into one sentence. Note that the appositive may appear at the beginning, in the middle, or at the end of the sentence. Be sure to use commas appropriately.

Example: Lorraine Hansberry's *A Raisin in the Sun*, ~~was~~ one of the

first American plays to focus on the experiences of African-Americans,

~~It~~ was produced on Broadway in 1959.

Answers will vary.

A playwright who wrote the prize-winning A Raisin in the Sun,

(1) Lorraine Hansberry was born in Chicago in 1930. ~~She was a~~

~~playwright who wrote the prize-winning *A Raisin in the Sun*.~~ (2) Hansberry's father, ~~was~~ a successful businessman, ~~He~~ moved the family from

the south side of Chicago to a predominately white neighborhood when

Hansberry was eight. (3) Hostile neighbors there were responsible for

throwing a brick through a window of their house, ~~This was~~ an act

Hansberry never forgot. (4) Such experiences inspired *A Raisin in the*

Sun, ~~It is~~ the story of a family's struggle to escape a cramped apartment

in a poor Chicago neighborhood. (5) Lena Younger, ~~is~~ the mother of the

family, ~~She~~ is about to receive a ten-thousand-dollar insurance payment

following her husband's death. (6) Her son wants to use the money to

                                    something

invest in a liquor store, ~~This is~~ ~~an enterprise~~ Lena finds unacceptable.

(7) Her dream for the family, ~~is~~ a house with a yard her grandson can

play in, ~~This dream~~ leads her to purchase a home in a white neighbor-

hood. (8) Her plans are almost shattered when Walter invests the rest
of the insurance money in a scheme to obtain a liquor license illegally.
~~This is~~ a deal that quickly goes bad. (9) One of their new white neighbors has offered the Younger family a bribe not to move into the
neighborhood. It is a deal Walter now decides to accept. (10) Lena is
a woman who knows her son's heart. She makes Walter realize that to
accept this money and give up their dream would be a betrayal of his
father's memory.

■ WRITING FIRST: Flashback

Look back at your response to the Writing First exercise on page
257. Underline two or three pairs of sentences that you think could
be combined. On the lines below, combine each pair of sentences
into a single sentence, using one of the methods discussed in 18C.
Use a different method for each pair of sentences.

1. _Answers will vary._ _____

_____

2. _____

_____

3. _____

_____

D   Varying Sentence Length

A paragraph of short, choppy sentences—or a paragraph of long, ram-
bling sentences—can be very monotonous. By mixing long and short sentences, perhaps combining some simple sentences to create compound
and complex sentences, you can create a more interesting paragraph.

In the following paragraph, the sentences are all quite short, and the
result is a dull passage.

> The world's first drive-in movie theater opened on June 6, 1933, in
> Camden, New Jersey. Automobiles became more popular. Drive-ins did
> too. By the 1950s, there were more than four thousand drive-ins in the
> United States. Over the years, the high cost of land led to the decline

■ Computer Tip

Some word-processing pro-
grams can tell you how long
your average sentence is
and how many words are in
your shortest and longest
sentences. Use this feature
to help you vary sentence
length.

of drive-ins. So did the rising popularity of television. Now, the drive-in movie theater has been replaced by the multiplex. There are no drive-ins at all in Alaska. There are none in Rhode Island or Delaware, either. New Jersey's last drive-in closed in 1991.

The revised paragraph that appears below is more interesting because it mixes long and short sentences.

The world's first drive-in movie theater opened on June 6, 1933, in Camden, New Jersey. As automobiles became more popular, drive-ins did too, and by the 1950s, there were more than four thousand drive-ins in the United States. Today, there are fewer than a thousand. Over the years, the high cost of land, along with the rising popularity of television, led to a decline in the number of drive-ins. Now, the drive-in movie theater has been replaced by the multiplex and the VCR. There are no drive-ins at all in Alaska, Rhode Island, or Delaware, and New Jersey's last drive-in closed in 1991.

To increase sentence variety, the writer combined some of the original paragraph's short sentences, creating longer simple, compound, and complex sentences. He also added a new short sentence ("Today, there are fewer than a thousand") for emphasis after a long one.

● **Writing Tip**

For information on creating compound and complex sentences, see Chapters 16 and 17.

ON THE WEB

For more practice, visit Exercise Central *at* <www.bedfordstmartins.com/ writingfirst>.

◆ **PRACTICE 18-16**

The following passage contains a series of short, choppy sentences that can be combined. Revise it so that it mixes long and short sentences. Be sure to use commas and other punctuation appropriately.

Example: Kente cloth has special significance for many African Americans/ ~~Many~~ *, but many* other people do not understand this significance.

Answers will vary.

(1) Kente cloth is made in western Africa/ ~~(2) It is~~ *and* produced primarily by the Ashanti people. (3) It has been worn for hundreds of years by African royalty/ ~~(4) They~~ *, who* consider it a sign of power and status. (5) Many African Americans wear kente cloth/ ~~(6) They~~ *because they* see it as a link to their heritage. (7) Each pattern on the cloth has a name/ ~~(8) Each~~ *, and each* color has a special significance. (9) For example, red and yellow suggest a long and healthy life/ ~~(10) Green~~ *while green* and white suggest a good harvest. (11) *Although* African women may wear kente cloth as a dress or head wrap/ ~~(12)~~ African-American women, like men, usually wear strips of cloth around their shoulders. (13) Men and women of African descent wear kente cloth as a sign of racial pride/ ~~(14) It~~ *; in fact, it* often decorates college students' gowns at graduation.

■ WRITING FIRST: Flashback

Look back at your response to the Writing First exercise on page
257. Count the number of words in each sentence, and write the
results on the following lines.
Answers will vary.

Sentence 1 _____   Sentence 6 _____

Sentence 2 _____   Sentence 7 _____

Sentence 3 _____   Sentence 8 _____

Sentence 4 _____   Sentence 9 _____

Sentence 5 _____   Sentence 10 _____

Now, write a new short sentence to follow your longest sentence.

New sentence: _____

_____

_____

■ WRITING FIRST: Revising and Editing

Look back at your response to the Writing First exercise on page
257. Using any strategies from this chapter that seem appropriate,
revise your writing so that your sentences are varied, interesting,
and smoothly connected. (You may want to incorporate sentences
you generated in the Flashback exercises on pages 259, 266, 277,
and above.) When you are finished, revise the sentences in an assignment you have completed for another course.

CHAPTER REVIEW

◆ **EDITING PRACTICE**

The following student essay lacks sentence variety. All of its sentences are
statements beginning with the subject, and it contains a number of short,
choppy sentences. Using the strategies discussed in this chapter, revise
the essay to achieve greater sentence variety. The first sentence has been
edited for you.

Teaching Tip
Have students work as a
group on the sentences in
this paragraph. Ask them to
use certain types of beginnings, specifying how many
participles, compounds, appositives, and so on they
should use.

Answers will vary.

A Wholesome Vegetarian Diet

Increasingly,
~~Y~~oung people who care about animal rights are ~~increas-~~
~~ingly~~ turning to a strict vegetarian diet. *Called vegans,* ~~S~~uch strict

vegetarians ~~are called vegans. They~~ avoid eating all animal

products including eggs, cow's milk, and dairy cheese.
However,
~~A~~nimal products do provide some essential nutrients~~,~~ ~~how-~~
and
~~ever. They~~ cannot be dropped from one's diet without proper

substitutes. *Therefore,* ~~V~~egans must~~,~~ ~~therefore,~~ be careful to substi-

tute non-animal foods that provide the nutrition they need.
How can they be sure to do this?
~~They can be sure to do this in a variety of ways.~~
For a start,
~~T~~hey can ~~for a start~~ learn how to get enough protein.

Tofu ~~is~~ a versatile soy bean product~~,~~ ~~It~~ contains high

levels of protein. It is widely available in its natural
, and
state~~,~~ ~~It~~ is also found in prepared foods such as veggie
Naturally,
burgers and soy dogs. ~~N~~ot everyone finds tofu appetizing~~,~~
and legumes (peas and beans) are good sources
~~naturally.~~ Peanut butter ~~is a good source~~ of protein for

non-tofu eaters. ~~Legumes (peas and beans) are also a good~~
Snacking
~~source of protein. Vegans snack~~ on foods like sunflower
, vegans
seeds~~,~~ ~~They~~ can get protein from between-meal treats as

well.

Calcium and iron are also essential to health. ~~Soy~~
Made *, soy milk*
~~milk is made~~ from non-dairy products~~,~~ ~~It~~ is an excellent
and dried figs
source of calcium. Fortified orange juice provides high

levels of calcium as well. ~~Dried figs provide high levels~~
Often,
~~of calcium too.~~ ~~C~~alcium-rich broccoli, collard greens, and

kale are ~~often~~ dietary staples for green vegetable lovers.

Vegans who want a good source of iron may start the day

with Grape Nuts~~,~~ ~~Grape Nuts is~~ a breakfast cereal with a
In fact,
particularly high bran content. ~~A~~ny kind of bran flakes~~,~~ ~~in~~

~~fact,~~ can add iron to one's diet.

Beginning any kind of new diet requires people to ad-
Eventually,
just their eating habits carefully. ~~V~~egans ~~eventually~~ find

they can fulfill their daily nutritional requirements with

relative ease.

◆ **COLLABORATIVE ACTIVITIES**

Read the following list of sentences.

Many well-known African-American writers left the United States in the years following World War II.

Many went to Paris.

Richard Wright was a novelist.

He wrote *Native Son* and *Black Boy*.

He wrote *Uncle Tom's Children*.

He left the United States for Paris in 1947.

James Baldwin wrote *Another Country, The Fire Next Time,* and *Giovanni's Room.*

He also wrote essays.

He came to Paris in 1948.

Chester Himes was a detective story writer.

He arrived in Paris in 1953.

William Gardner Smith was a novelist and journalist.

He also left the United States for Paris.

These expatriates found Paris more hospitable than America.

They also found it less racist.

1. Working in a small group, add to the list one related sentence that is a question or an exclamation. Then, begin one or more of the sentences on the list with an appropriate adverb or prepositional phrase.
2. Continuing to work in your group, combine all the sentences on the list to create a varied and interesting paragraph. Use the strategies illustrated in 18C as a guide.
3. When your group's revisions are complete, trade paragraphs with another group and further edit the other group's paragraph to improve sentence variety.

✔ REVIEW CHECKLIST:
Achieving Sentence Variety

☐ Vary sentence types, using an occasional question or exclamation. (See 18A.)

☐ Vary sentence openings. (See 18B.)

☐ Combine sentences. (See 18C.)

☐ Vary sentence length. (See 18D.)

Using Parallelism

Word Power

enlighten to give insight to; to educate

enrich to make fuller or more rewarding

inspire to stimulate to action; to motivate

● **Writing Tip**

The more complicated your ideas, the more you need parallelism. By repeating certain grammatical structures, you identify comparable or equivalent ideas and indicate the relationships among them.

▼ **Student Voices**

When I write a list of points, reasons, examples, or arguments, I have to remind myself to use parallel structure.
Michelle Cooper

■ WRITING FIRST

Look at the picture above, and then discuss three positive things about your school, neighborhood, or workplace. Support your statements with specific examples.

A Recognizing Parallel Structure

Parallelism is the use of the same grammatical constructions to present comparable or equivalent ideas. For example, nouns are used with nouns, verbs with verbs, adjectives with adjectives, phrases with phrases, and clauses with clauses.

Parallel
Casey is a <u>snowboarder</u>, not a <u>skier</u>. (two nouns)
We saw the ducks <u>fly</u>, <u>swim</u>, and <u>fish</u>. (three verbs)

The road of life is <u>long</u>, <u>bumpy</u>, and <u>steep</u>. (three adjectives)

<u>Making the team</u> was one thing; <u>staying on it</u> was another. (two phrases)

My, what big eyes you have, grandma! My, what big ears you have! My, what big teeth you have! (three independent clauses)

Faulty parallelism occurs when different grammatical constructions are used to present comparable or equivalent ideas. For example, notice how the sentences that follow fail to convey the links among related ideas.

Not Parallel

Casey is a snowboarder, but skiing is not something that interests him.

We saw the ducks fly, and some swam, and others were fishing.

The road of life is long, has a lot of bumps, and climbs steeply.

Making the team was one thing, but she was worried about staying on the team.

My, what big eyes you have, Grandma! And you do have big ears. Your teeth are also quite large.

To correct faulty parallelism, reword the comparable ideas in your sentences so that they are expressed in matching grammatical constructions.

We saw the ducks fly, ~~and some swam, and others were~~ _{swim, and} fish~~ing~~.

ON THE WEB
For more practice, visit **Exercise Central** *at* <www.bedfordstmartins.com/writingfirst>.

◆ **PRACTICE 19-1**

In the following sentences, decide whether the underlined words are parallel. If so, write *P* in the blank. If not, rewrite the sentences so that the ideas they express are presented in parallel terms.

Examples: As a shopper, I <u>insist on quality</u>, <u>expect good service</u>, and <u>seek out value</u>. __P__

For me, <u>getting an A on a math test</u> is harder than <u>~~when I swim~~ ten miles</u>. ___ *swimming*

1. People today are <u>working more</u> and <u>playing less</u>. __P__

2. Some smokers say that they smoke cigarettes to help <u>wake themselves up</u>, <u>give themselves a break</u>, and <u>~~also so that they can~~ keep themselves going</u>. ___

3. They also admit that cigarettes are <u>expensive</u>, <u>smelly</u>, and <u>~~have dangers~~</u>. ___ *dangerous.*

4. Surfing the Internet can be <u>addictive</u> and <u>time-consuming</u>. __P__

Teaching Tip, ESL Tip, Teaching Tip sidebars present.

5. <u>Being happy in life</u> is more important to me than ~~that I make~~ a lot of money. ___

                     making

6. The team <u>lost the game</u> even though the quarterback <u>played his best</u>.

   P

7. Judges must <u>care about justice</u>, <u>uphold the laws</u>, and ~~they should~~ treat <u>defendants fairly</u>. ___

8. <u>According to the newspaper, the economy is getting stronger.</u> <u>According to my wallet, the economy is getting weaker.</u> ___ *P*

9. <u>Love is blind</u>, but ~~the feeling of~~ <u>hate is blinder</u>. ___

10. To succeed, <u>set realistic goals</u>, <u>work toward them diligently</u>, and ~~you must also~~ <u>believe in yourself</u>. ___.

■ WRITING FIRST: Flashback

Look back at your response to the Writing First exercise on page 282, and underline the parallel words, phrases, and clauses. Revise, if necessary, to make sure that comparable ideas are presented in parallel terms.

B   Using Parallel Structure

● **Writing Tip**

Many everyday writing tasks require parallelism. For example, items listed in a résumé should be in parallel form.

Parallel structure is especially important for emphasizing the relationships in *paired items, comparisons,* and *items in a series.*

Paired Items

Use parallel structure when you connect ideas with a coordinating conjunction—*and, but, for, nor, or, so,* and *yet.*

> George believes in <u>doing a good job</u> *and* <u>minding his own business</u>.
> You can <u>pay me now</u> *or* <u>pay me later</u>.

Also use parallel structure for paired items joined by correlative conjunctions, such as *both . . . and, not only . . . but also, either . . . or, neither . . . nor,* and *rather . . . than.*

> Jan is *both* <u>artistically talented</u> *and* <u>mechanically inclined</u>.

The group's new recording *not only* has a dance beat *but also* has thought-provoking lyrics.

I'd *rather* eat one worm by itself *than* eat twenty with ice cream.

Comparisons Formed with *Than* or *As*

Use parallel structure for comparisons formed with *than* or *as*.

> Working hard is more important than being lucky.
> She cares about her patients as much as she cares about her family.

Items in a Series

Use parallel structure for items in a series—words, phrases, or clauses.

> Every Wednesday I have English, math, and psychology.

> Increased demand, high factory output, and a strong dollar help the economy.

> She is a champion because she stays in excellent physical condition, puts in long hours of practice, and has an intense desire to win.

◆ PRACTICE 19-2

Fill in the blanks in the following sentences with parallel words, phrases, or clauses of your own that make sense in context.

> **Example:** A good teacher ___knows the subject___ and
>
> ___respects the students.___
> *Answers will vary.*

1. Before a test, I am both _____ and _____.

2. My ideal mate is _____, _____, and _____.

3. Next semester I will either _____

   or _____.

4. I define *success* more as _____

   than as _____.

5. Rich people _____, but poor people _____

   _____.

6. I have noticed that some _____,

   while other _____.

7. To advance in a job, you must _____, _____, and

   _____.

For information on punctuating items in a series, see 31A.

● **Writing Tip**
Elements in an outline should be presented in parallel terms. See Appendix B, Section 8, for an example of an outline.

● **Writing Tip**
Items listed in a bulleted or numbered list should be parallel.

Teaching Tip
Practice 19-2 works well as a test and is quick and easy to grade. You may want to save this exercise for the end of the chapter.

ON THE WEB
For more practice, visit Exercise Central *at* <www.bedfordstmartins.com/writingfirst>.

8. Three reasons to go to college are _____, _____,

and _____.

9. _____ is more important to me than _____

_____.

10. I enjoy _____ more than _____.

◆ PRACTICE 19-3

Rewrite the following sentences so that the ideas are presented in parallel
terms. Add punctuation as needed.

Example: California's San Gabriel Valley is close to mountains, and
beaches and deserts are nearby.

California's San Gabriel Valley is close to mountains, beaches, and

deserts.

1. Pasadena and Claremont are major cities in the valley. So is Pomona.

   Pasadena, Claremont, and Pomona are major cities in the valley.

2. Pasadena offers the famous Rose Bowl stadium, and the Norton
   Simon Museum and the historic Wrigley house are also there.

   Pasadena offers the famous Rose Bowl stadium, the Norton Simon

   Museum, and the historic Wrigley house.

3. Watching the big Tournament of Roses Parade is more exciting than it
   is to view the Macy's Thanksgiving parade.

   Watching the big Tournament of Roses Parade is more exciting than viewing

   the Macy's Thanksgiving parade.

4. You can watch from the crowded parade route. The comfort of your
   living room is also a possibility.

   You can watch from the crowded parade route or from the comfort of your

   living room.

5. Judges rate the rose-covered floats on their originality, what artistic
   merit they have, and the overall impact they make.

   Judges rate the rose-covered floats on their originality, artistic merit, and

   overall impact.

6. Some people enjoy going to the parade more than when they go to the
   Rose Bowl game.

Some people enjoy going to the parade more than they enjoy going to the

Rose Bowl game.

7. The Rose Bowl game is not only America's oldest collegiate championship but also the bowl game that is the country's most popular.

The Rose Bowl game is not only America's oldest collegiate championship

but also the country's most popular bowl game.

8. Held every fall in Pomona, the Los Angeles County Fair offers carnival rides, popular performers, and there are agricultural shows included.

Held every fall in Pomona, the Los Angeles County Fair offers carnival rides,

popular performers, and agricultural shows.

9. Visitors come to play challenging skill games, and they also can enjoy various ethnic foods.

Visitors come to play challenging skill games and enjoy various ethnic foods.

10. The starting gate was introduced at the valley's Santa Anita Race Track, and so was electrical timing, as well as the photo finish.

The starting gate, electrical timing, and the photo finish were introduced at

the valley's Santa Anita Race Track.

■ WRITING FIRST: Flashback

Look back at your response to the Writing First exercise on page 282. On the lines below, write three new sentences that you could add to your response, and then revise them as follows. (1) In one sentence, use a coordinating conjunction such as *and* or *but;* (2) in another sentence, create a comparison using *than* or *as;* (3) in a third sentence, present items in a series. When you have finished, check to make sure that you have used parallel structure in each sentence and that you have punctuated correctly.

1. *Answers will vary.*

(continued on the following page)

(continued from the previous page)

2. _____

_____

_____

_____

3. _____

_____

_____

_____

■ WRITING FIRST: Revising and Editing

Look back at your response to the Writing First exercise on page 282, and try to add one or more of the sentences you generated in the Flashback exercise above. Then, revise your work, correcting faulty parallelism and adding parallel constructions where necessary to emphasize a relationship or increase clarity. When you are finished, do the same for another assignment you are currently working on.

CHAPTER REVIEW

◆ EDITING PRACTICE

Read the following student essay, into which examples of faulty parallelism have been introduced. Identify the sentences you think need to be corrected, and make the changes required to achieve parallelism. Be sure to supply all words necessary for clarity, grammar, and sense, adding punctuation as needed. The first sentence has been edited for you.
Answers will vary.

Questionable Heroes

   Heroes are people who are looked up to for their out-
                                    admirable
standing achievements, and their personal qualities ~~are also~~
                            ^   .
~~admired.~~ Earlier generations looked up to heroes who played
                                              ^
a part in their country's history, who contributed some-

thing to society, and ~~they also liked people~~ who showed

moral or intellectual superiority. These heroes included

the colonial Americans who established this country~~/~~ ,the ~~The~~

abolitionists who brought an end to slavery, and the sol-

diers who ~~because they~~ served their country in time of war~~/~~ .

~~were also included.~~ Most young people today, however, do

not understand the real definition of a hero. They find

their heroes not in books or in history~~/~~ but in television ~~is~~ .

~~the place they look.~~ Not only do they admire rock perform-

ers, but also they admire athletes and movie stars ~~are admired by them.~~

The heroes of today are recognized not for their hon-

esty or leadership~~/~~ but ~~they are liked~~ for the entertain-

ment they provide. How can big-name celebrities like Arnold

Schwarzenegger, Madonna, and Michael Jordan compare to gen-

uine heroes like George Washington, Thomas Jefferson, or

Martin Luther King Jr.? The answer is that they do not.

Washington helped the thirteen colonies gain their indepen-

dence from Great Britain, and Jefferson drafted the Declaration of Indepen-

dence ~~was drafted by Jefferson.~~ In addition, Martin Luther

King Jr. risked his life to achieve equal rights. By con-

trast, the people who are on the covers of magazines today

are honored only because of their looks or their ability to ~~they can~~ toss

a football. Sadly, many of today's heroes are admired not

because of anything they have actually done~~/~~ but ~~people~~

~~admire them~~ because of the image they project.

Fictional characters have always served as role models

for children. Early American heroes like Johnny Appleseed

and Molly Pitcher were brave and generous. ~~also acted generously.~~

Compare these figures to Bart Simpson, a cartoon character

who has brought the concept of heroism to a new low. His

crude behavior, his lack of interest in school, and his ~~the~~

~~fact that his~~ questionable values make his attraction a

mystery. Sold-out Halloween masks of Simpson, however, are

proof of his great popularity.

```
     Clearly, the stature of heroes has diminished over
time. The forgotten heroes of the past who represented
honesty, loyalty, and leadership have been replaced by in-
dividuals who are sarcastic, cynical, and juvenile. Heroes
like George Washington, Thomas Jefferson, and Martin Luther
King Jr. stand much higher than the slick media creations
of today.
```

◆ COLLABORATIVE ACTIVITIES

1. Working in a group, list three or four qualities that you associate with each word in the following pairs.

   Brothers/sisters
   Teachers/students
   Parents/children
   City/country
   Baseball/football
   The Internet/television
   Work/play

2. Write a compound sentence comparing each of the above pairs of words. Use a coordinating conjunction to join the clauses, and make sure each sentence uses clear parallel structure, mentions both words, and includes the qualities you listed for the words in Collaborative Activity 1.

3. Choose the three best sentences your group has written for Collaborative Activity 2. Assign one student from each group to write these sentences on the board so the entire class can read them. The class can then decide which sentences use parallelism most effectively.

✔ REVIEW CHECKLIST:
Using Parallelism

- Use matching grammatical constructions to present comparable or equivalent ideas. (See 19A.)

- Use parallel constructions with paired items. (See 19B.)

- Use parallel constructions in comparisons formed with *than* or *as*. (See 19B.)

- Use parallel constructions for items in a series. (See 19B.)

Using Words Effectively

PREVIEW

In this chapter, you will learn

- to use specific words (20A)

- to use concise language (20B)

- to avoid clichés (20C)

- to use similes and metaphors (20D)

- to avoid sexist language (20E)

■ WRITING FIRST

Look at the picture above, and then describe your dream house. What would it look like? What items would it contain? Be as specific as possible.

Word Power

appealing   attractive or interesting

ideal   a model of perfection; the best of its kind

practical   useful

A   Using Specific Words

To write well, you need to use specific words that convey your ideas with precision and clarity.

Specific words refer to particular people, places, things, ideas, or qualities; **general** words refer to entire classes or groups. Statements that contain specific words are generally more vivid than ones that contain only generalities. All of the following sentences are grammatically correct, but they are not specific.

▼ Student Voices
I try to find synonyms for words I keep repeating. Sometimes, I use a thesaurus.
    Jessica Zimmermann

Sentences with General Words

While walking in the woods, I saw an <u>animal</u>.

<u>Someone</u> decided to run for Congress.

<u>Weapons</u> are responsible for many murders.

Denise bought new <u>clothes</u>.

I really enjoyed my <u>meal</u>.

Darrell had always wanted a <u>classic car</u>.

Specific words make the following revised sentences clearer and more precise.

Sentences with Specific Words

While walking in the woods, I saw a <u>baby skunk</u>.

<u>Rebecca</u> decided to run for Congress.

<u>Saturday night specials</u> are responsible for many murders.

Denise bought a new <u>blue vest</u>.

I really enjoyed my <u>pepperoni pizza</u>.

Darrell had always wanted a <u>black 1957 Chevy convertible</u>.

FOCUS **Using Specific Words**

One way to strengthen your writing is to avoid **utility words**—general words like *good, nice,* or *great* that some writers use instead of
taking the time to think of more specific words. For example, when
you say the ocean looked *pretty*, do you really mean that it *sparkled,
glistened, rippled, foamed, surged,* or *billowed?*

ON THE WEB
For more practice, visit
Exercise Central *at
<www.bedfordstmartins.com/
writingfirst>.*

◆ PRACTICE 20-1

In the following passage, the writer describes an old store in the town of
Nameless, Tennessee. Underline the specific words in the passage that help
you experience the scene the writer describes. The first sentence has been
done for you.

(1) The old store, lighted only by <u>three fifty-watt bulbs</u>, smelled of
<u>coal oil</u> and <u>baking bread</u>. (2) In the <u>middle of the</u> <u>rectangular room</u>,
where the <u>oak floor</u> sagged a little, stood an <u>iron stove</u>. (3) To the right
was a <u>wooden table</u> with an <u>unfinished game of checkers</u> and a stool
made from an <u>apple-tree stump</u>. (4) On shelves around the walls sat
<u>earthen jugs</u> with <u>corncob stoppers</u>, a few <u>canned goods</u>, and some of
the <u>two thousand old clocks and clockworks</u> Thurmond Watts owned.
(5) Only one was ticking; the others he just looked at.

William Least Heat-Moon, *Blue Highways*

◆ **PRACTICE 20-2**

In the blank beside each of the five general words below, write a more specific word. Then, use the more specific word in a sentence of your own.

   Example: talked ___*chattered*___

   All through dinner, my six-year-old chattered excitedly about his first day

   of school.

   Answers will vary.

1. car _____

   _____

   _____

2. walk _____

   _____

   _____

3. big _____

   _____

   _____

4. animal _____

   _____

   _____

5. clothing _____

   _____

   _____

◆ **PRACTICE 20-3**

The following letter of application for a job uses very general words.
Choose a job that you might want to apply for. As you rewrite the paragraph on a separate page, substitute specific language for the general language of the original, and add details where necessary. Start by making
the first sentence, which identifies the job, more specific: for example, "I
would like to apply for the dental technician position you advertised in
today's *Post*." Go on to include specific information about your background and qualifications, expanding the original paragraph into a three-
paragraph letter.

Teaching Tip
Use this opportunity to
teach students how to write
a job application letter and
résumé, even if that is not
part of the course requirements. Make sure they un-
derstand the importance of
using specific language in
describing their goals and
experience.

   I would like to apply for the position you advertised in today's
paper. I graduated from high school and am currently attending college. I have taken several courses that have prepared me to fulfill the
duties the position requires. I also have several personal qualities that

I think you would find important in a person holding this position. In addition, I have had certain experiences that qualify me for such a job. I would appreciate the opportunity to meet with you to discuss your needs as an employer. Thank you.

■ WRITING FIRST: Flashback

Look back at your response to the Writing First exercise on page 291. Find several general words, and write those words on the lines below. For each word, substitute another word that is more specific.

General words   *Specific alternatives*

Answers will vary.

B   Using Concise Language

● Writing Tip

A short sentence is not necessarily a concise sentence. A sentence is concise when it contains only the words it needs to convey its ideas.

Concise writing comes right to the point and says what it has to say in as few words as possible. Too often, however, writers use empty phrases that add nothing to a sentence's meaning. A good way to test a sentence for nonessential words is to see if crossing out the words changes its meaning.

~~It is a fact that~~ the United States was not prepared to fight World War II.

If the sentence's meaning does not change, you can assume the sentence is better off without the extra words.

WORDY   Due to the fact that I was tired, I missed my first class.

CONCISE   Because I was tired, I missed my first class.

WORDY   In order to follow the plot, you must make an outline.

CONCISE   To follow the plot, you must make an outline.

● Writing Tip

Avoid flowery language and complicated sentences. Good writing is clear and concise.

FOCUS   Using Concise Language

The following phrases add nothing to a sentence. You can usually delete or condense them with no loss of meaning.

(continued on the following page)

(continued from the previous page)	
Wordy	*Concise*
It is clear that	(delete)
It is a fact that	(delete)
The reason is that	Because
It is my opinion that	I think/I believe
Due to the fact that	Because
Despite the fact that	Although
At the present time	Today/Currently
At that time	Then
In most cases	Usually
In order to	To
In the final analysis	Finally
Subsequent to	After

Repetition also adds words to your writing. Although repetition can be used effectively—for example, to emphasize important ideas—unnecessary repetition should be eliminated. Notice how easily these sentences can be edited to eliminate unnecessary repetition.

WORDY   My instructor told me the book was <u>old-fashioned and outdated</u>. (An old-fashioned book *is* outdated.)

CONCISE   My instructor told me the book was ~~old-fashioned and~~ outdated.

WORDY   The <u>terrible tragedy</u> of the fire could have been avoided. (A tragedy is *always* terrible.)

CONCISE   The ~~terrible~~ tragedy of the fire could have been avoided.

◆ PRACTICE 20-4

To make the following sentences more concise, eliminate any unnecessary repetition, and delete or condense wordy expressions.

Example: ~~It is a fact that many~~ *Many* grown-up children have trouble getting their parents/ ~~their mother and father/~~ to treat them as adults.

Answers may vary.
(1) Adult children can become frustrated ~~due to the fact that~~ *because* their parents seem to treat them as if they were not capable of making their own decisions ~~by themselves.~~ (2) For example, some parents constantly criticize ~~all the time~~ and offer ~~unwanted~~ advice that their children do not want to hear. (3) When this happens, the children may begin to whine childishly ~~and in a juvenile manner~~ or even throw a temper tantrum *although*

~~despite the fact that~~ such behavior only reinforces their parents' attitude.
(4) *Usually,* ~~In most cases,~~ there are better ways to improve one's parents' behavior ~~for the better.~~ (5) *To* ~~In order to~~ get parents to stop being critical, an adult child might turn the tables and encourage his or her parents to ~~have a discussion and~~ talk about their own childhoods. (6) The child can then point out any similarities between the parents' behavior ~~then~~ in the past and his or her behavior ~~now~~ in the present. (7) *Adult* ~~Another thing adult~~ children might also ~~do is to~~ explain that while they value their parents' opinion, they are still going to make their own decisions ~~for themselves.~~ (8) Finally, an adult child should not sit by idly ~~doing nothing~~ when family stories are being told ~~or related.~~ (9) *Although* ~~Despite the fact that~~ parents may have been telling these stories the same way for ~~years and~~ years, the child may have a very different ~~or contradictory~~ perspective on the event. (10) Expressing ~~and talking about~~ this different perspective can help an adult child define his or her position in the family in a new way ~~that is different from the old way.~~

■ WRITING FIRST: Flashback

Look back at your response to the Writing First exercise on page 291. Identify a sentence that contains unnecessary repetition. Rewrite the sentence on the lines below, editing it so it is more concise.

Answers will vary.

C   Avoiding Clichés

Teaching Tip
Ask students for other examples of overused expressions. Write these on the board, and have students think of more original or more direct ways of expressing these ideas.

One way of making your writing more effective is to avoid **clichés**, expressions that have been used so often they have lost their impact. Writers tend to plug in such ready-made phrases—for example, "easier said than done," "last but not least," and "work like a dog"—without giving them much thought, but these worn-out expressions deaden writing and do little to create interest.

When you identify a cliché in your writing, replace it with a direct statement—or, if possible, substitute a fresher expression.

CLICHÉ   When school was over, she felt <u>free as a bird</u>.

REVISED When school was over, she felt free.

CLICHÉ   These days, you have to be <u>sick as a dog</u> before you are admitted to a hospital.

REVISED These days, you have to be seriously ill before you are admitted to a hospital.

Computer Tip

Many grammar-checking programs flag clichés and wordy constructions. Remember, however, that although a grammar checker may highlight trouble spots, you, not the computer, must decide whether (and how) to revise.

◆ **PRACTICE 20-5**

Cross out any clichés in the following sentences, and either substitute a fresher expression or restate the idea in more direct language.

ON THE WEB
For more practice, visit Exercise Central *at* <www.bedfordstmartins.com/ writingfirst>.

                                                        free of financial worries
Example: Lottery winners often think they will be ~~on easy street~~ for
                                                                ^
the rest of their lives.
Answers will vary.

(1) Many people think that a million-dollar lottery jackpot allows the
                        long hours   *a comfortable life.*
winner to stop working ~~like a dog~~ and start living ~~high on the hog.~~ (2) ~~All~~
                              ^   *In fact,*   ^
~~things considered, however,~~ the reality for lottery winners is quite different
                          ^   *win big prizes*
(3) For one thing, lottery winners who ~~hit the jackpot~~ do not receive their
                                              ^
winnings all at once; instead, payments—for example, $50,000—are usually

spread out over twenty years. (4) Of that $50,000 a year, close to $20,000
                                    winner
goes to taxes and anything else the ~~lucky stiff~~ owes the government, such
                                          ^   *who ask for money,*
as student loans. (5) Next come relatives and friends ~~with their hands~~
                      with difficult choices to make.   ^
~~out,~~ leaving winners ~~between a rock and a hard place.~~ (6) They can either
give   ^   *lose the friendship of*
~~cough up~~ gifts and loans or ~~wave bye-bye to~~ many of their loved ones.
^   *Even worse,*   ^
(7) ~~Adding insult to injury,~~ many lottery winners have lost their jobs
      ^
because employers thought that once they were "millionaires," they no

longer needed to draw a salary. (8) Many lottery winners wind up ~~way~~
              serious   *Faced with financial difficulties,*
~~over their heads~~ in debt within a few years. (9) ~~In their hour of need,~~ many
                ^   ^
would like to sell their future payments to companies that offer lump-sum
                                              almost impossible,
payments of forty to forty-five cents on the dollar. (10) This is ~~easier said~~
                                                                ^
than done, however, because most state lotteries do not allow winners to

sell their winnings.

Teaching Tip
Have students keep a file of overused expressions and add to it any such expressions they encounter in their reading (or in their own writing). They can refer to this as they revise their own work.

■ **WRITING FIRST: Flashback**

Look back at your response to the Writing First exercise on page 291. If you have used any clichés, list them below. Then, either re-place each cliché with a more direct statement, or think of a more original way of expressing the idea.

Cliché   *Revised*

Answers will vary.

_____   _____

_____   _____

_____   _____

D   **Using Similes and Metaphors**

A **simile** is a comparison of two unlike things that uses *like* or *as*.

His arm hung at his side <u>like</u> a broken branch.

He was <u>as</u> content <u>as</u> a cat napping on a windowsill.

A **metaphor** is a comparison of two unlike things that does *not* use *like* or *as*.

Invaders from another world, the dandelions conquered my garden.

He was a beast of burden, hauling cement from the mixer to the building site.

The force of similes and metaphors comes from the surprise of see-ing two seemingly unlike things being compared and, as a result, seeing a hidden or unnoticed similarity between them. Used in moderation, similes and metaphors can make your writing more lively and more interesting.

◆ **PRACTICE 20-6**

Use your imagination to complete each of the following by creating three appropriate similes.

Example: A boring class is like *toast without jam.*

a straitjacket.

a bedtime story.

Answers will vary.

1. A good friend is like _____

    _____

    _____

2. A thunderstorm is like _____

    _____

    _____

3. Falling in love is like _____

    _____

    _____

◆ PRACTICE 20-7

Think of a person you know well. Using that person as your subject, fill in each of the following blanks to create metaphors. Try to complete each metaphor with more than a single word, as in the example.

Example: If ___*my baby sister*___ were an animal, _*she*_ would be

a curious little kitten.

Answers will vary.

1. If _____ were an animal, ____ would be _____

_____

2. If _____ were a food, ____ would be _____

_____

3. If _____were a means of transportation, ____ would be

_____

4. If _____ were a natural phenomenon, ____ would be _____

_____

5. If _____ were a toy, ____ would be _____

_____

■ WRITING FIRST: Flashback

Look back at your response to the Writing First exercise on page 291. Find two sentences that could be enriched with a simile or a

(continued on the following page)

(continued from the previous page)

metaphor. On the lines below, rewrite these two sentences, adding a simile to one sentence and a metaphor to the other.

1. *Answers will vary.* _____

   _____

2. _____

   _____

E   Avoiding Sexist Language

Sexist language refers to men and women in derogatory or insulting terms. Sexist language is not just words like *hunk, bimbo,* or *babe,* which many people find objectionable. It can also be words or phrases that unnecessarily call attention to gender or that suggest a job or profession is exclusively male or female when it actually is not.

You can avoid sexist usage by being sensitive and using a little common sense. There is always an acceptable nonsexist alternative for a sexist term.

● **Writing Tip**

It is also considered sexist to give information about a woman—for example, her marital status or how she dresses—that you would not offer about a man.

● **Writing Tip**

In addition to avoiding sexist language, you should also avoid potentially offensive references to a person's age, physical condition, or sexual orientation.

For a discussion of subjects like everyone *(indefinite pronoun antecedents), see 28E.*

Sexist	*Nonsexist*
man, mankind	humanity, humankind, human race
businessman	executive, business person
fireman, policeman, mailman	fire fighter, police officer, letter carrier
male nurse, woman engineer	nurse, engineer
congressman	member of Congress, representative
stewardess, steward	flight attendant
man and wife	man and woman, husband and wife
manmade	synthetic
chairman	chair, chairperson
anchorwoman, anchorman	anchor

■ **Computer Tip**

Use the Find or Search feature of your word processor to check uses of *he.* If you have used *he* to refer to a subject that could be of either gender, revise to correct the problem.

FOCUS   **Avoiding Sexist Language**

Do not use *he* when your subject could be either male or female.

Everyone should complete <u>his</u> assignment by next week.

You can correct this problem in three ways.

(continued on the following page)

(continued from the previous page)

■ Use *he or she* or *his or her*.

Everyone should complete <u>his or her</u> assignment by next week.

■ Use plural forms.

Students should complete <u>their</u> assignment by next week.

■ Eliminate the pronoun.

Everyone should complete <u>the</u> assignment by next week.

◆ PRACTICE 20-8

Edit the following sentences to eliminate sexist language.

Answers will vary.

1. Many people today would like to see more ~~policemen~~ *police officers* patrolling the streets.

2. A doctor should be honest with his *or her (or omit "his")* patients.

3. The attorneys representing the plaintiff are Geraldo Diaz and ~~Mrs.~~ Barbara Wilkerson.

4. Chris Fox is the ~~female~~ mayor of Port London, Maine.

5. Travel to other planets will be a significant step for ~~man.~~ *humanity.*

ON THE WEB

For more practice, visit **Exercise Central** *at* <www.bedfordstmartins.com/writingfirst>.

■ WRITING FIRST: Flashback

Look back at your response to the Writing First exercise on page 291. Have you used any words or phrases that unnecessarily call attention to gender? Have you used *he* when your subject could be either male or female? Rewrite on the lines below any sentences in which these problems occur. Then, cross out the sexist language and substitute acceptable nonsexist alternatives.

_____

_____

_____

_____

■ WRITING FIRST: Revising and Editing

Look back at your response to the Writing First exercise on page 291. Revise the paragraph, making sure your language is as specific as possible, and avoid using clichés or sexist expressions. Be sure to incorporate the revisions you made in this chapter's Flashback exercises. When you have finished, revise another writing assignment you are currently working on.

CHAPTER REVIEW

◆ EDITING PRACTICE

Read the following student essay carefully, and then revise it, making sure your revision is as concise as possible and uses specific words and no sexist language or clichés. If you can, add an occasional simile or metaphor to add interest. Finally, underline any expressions that seem particularly fresh and original. The first sentence has been edited for you.
Answers will vary.

A Day at the Pool

bright
It all begins on a ~~nice~~ summer day as we carry

our neatly packed pool equipment from the car and head to

the pool. We walk across the bumpy, gravel-covered parking

bright red
lot with our arms piled high with a ~~pretty~~ beach bag, a
green-and-white   *pink and green*
~~gaily striped~~ beach chair, ~~colored~~ beach towels, and an
orange   *with a picture of a lion on it.*   *blue metal doors*
~~interesting~~ drinking cup. We make it through the ~~entrance~~
women's
and walk into the ~~ladies'~~ locker room. The walls are lined
dented metal
with lockers, and past the lockers is a metal door held

open by a wooden wedge. Walking through the doorway, we

proceed to our usual spot in the shaded grass area. This

is where we spend our day socializing with other "pool

guys.
princesses" and checking out the ~~hunks.~~

As I sit, I hear the sounds of children crying and

laughing and of parents yelling at them. Suddenly, the

noises cease at the sound of a loud, high-pitched whistle.

All eyes are on the ~~female~~ lifeguard. She is dressed in a
black one-piece *white* *a pair of sea horses*
~~nice~~ bathing suit covered by a *white* tank top with ~~an unusual~~

~~design~~ on the front. She is wearing black Ray-Ban sun-

glasses, and she holds a silver whistle in her mouth. She
regally
sits on her high wooden platform and raises her hand,

pointing her finger at the accused. Then, as quickly as the

silence began, it ceases.
Because
~~Due to the fact~~ I am hungry, I go to the snack bar.
buttery
I am enticed by the scent of freshly popped popcorn, the
pungent
~~tantalizing~~ aroma of spicy fries, and the equally tempting

smell of hamburgers. The choice is difficult. I finally
cold and sweet
decide on a bright banana-yellow popsicle. It tastes ~~good~~
quenches *When* *away from the counter, I*
and ~~takes care of~~ my thirst. I turn ~~and~~ come face to face
sunburned.
with a small child. His cheeks are ~~red from overexposure to~~

~~the burning rays of the sun.~~ His nose is a white painted
because
triangle, and his eyes are invisible ~~due to the fact that~~
plastic
he is wearing ~~funny~~ Superman sunglasses. Slithering around

him, I head back to the safety of my towel.

Reaching my chair, I look down to see a strange tod-
quietly on it.
dler sitting ~~as quiet as a mouse.~~ He seems to have claimed

my seat as his own. He looks up and smiles as drool slides

out of the corner of his mouth. As he rises and waddles

off, his wet diaper sags around his knees. When I look

down, I discover that he has left his mark on my chair. At

this point, I decide it is time to go home.

We gather our belongings and head for the car. Again

we pass through the metal door, down the hallway of

lockers, out the exit to the parking lot, and across the

gravel parking lot to our car. After we load our trunk, we
as
get into the car only to find that the air is ~~so~~ hot and
as pancake syrup.
thick. As I sit in the hot car, I wonder whether it makes

sense to go through all this trouble just to spend a

couple of hours at the pool.

◆ **COLLABORATIVE ACTIVITIES**

1. Photocopy two or three paragraphs of description from a romance novel, a western novel, or a mystery novel, and bring your paragraphs to class. Working in a group, choose one paragraph that seems to need clearer, more specific language.

2. As a group, revise the paragraph you chose for Collaborative Activity 1, making it as clear and specific as possible and eliminating any clichés or sexist language.

3. Exchange your revised paragraph from Collaborative Activity 2 with the paragraph revised by another group, and check the other group's work. Make any additional changes you think your paragraph needs.

☑ REVIEW CHECKLIST:
Using Words Effectively

☐ Use specific words that convey your ideas precisely and clearly. (See 20A.)

☐ Use concise language that comes right to the point and says what it has to say in the fewest possible words. (See 20B.)

☐ Avoid clichés (overused expressions). (See 20C.)

☐ Whenever possible, use similes and metaphors to make your writing more lively and more interesting. (See 20D.)

☐ Avoid sexist language. (See 20E.)

UNIT FIVE

Solving Common Sentence Problems

Run-Ons and Commas Splices

■ WRITING FIRST

Why do you think so many American children are physically out of shape? What do you think can be done about this problem? Look at the picture above, and then write down your thoughts on this issue.

Word Power

lethargic sluggishly indifferent

obese extremely overweight

sedentary accustomed to sitting or to engaging in little exercise

A Recognizing Run-Ons and Comma Splices

A **run-on** is an error that occurs when two sentences (independent clauses) are joined without punctuation.

RUN-ON   More and more students are earning high school equivalency diplomas the value of these diplomas is currently under debate.

Teaching Tip
Virtually all students sometimes write run-ons and comma splices. Plan on having students do a lot of exercises in class and for homework.

307

A **comma splice** is an error that occurs when two sentences are joined with just a comma.

COMMA SPLICE More and more students are earning high school equivalency diplomas, the value of these diplomas is currently under debate.

◆ **PRACTICE 21-1**

Some of the sentences in the following passage are correct, but others are run-ons or comma splices. In the answer space after each sentence, write *C* if the sentence is correct, *RO* if it is a run-on, and *CS* if it is a comma splice.

Example: "Race movies" had all-black casts, they were intended for African-American audiences. _CS_

(1) In 1919, African-American director Oscar Micheaux filmed *Within Our Gates* this movie examined black life in Chicago. _RO_ (2) The film included scenes of violence, it even depicted two lynchings. _CS_ (3) It also treated interracial relationships white censors banned it. _RO_ (4) Race riots had occurred in Chicago that year, the censors feared violence. _CS_ (5) Micheaux appealed to the board they agreed to the film's release in Chicago. _RO_ (6) The movie was shown, twelve hundred feet of film were omitted. _CS_ (7) Micheaux later made many low-budget movies, but few survive today. _C_ (8) Some are musicals others are melodramas. _RO_ (9) Few are socially conscious films like *Within Our Gates*. _C_ (10) One, *Body and Soul*, was Paul Robeson's first film. _C_ (11) Micheaux died in 1951. _C_ (12) In 1990, an uncut version of *Within Our Gates* was discovered in Madrid, it was shown in Chicago for the first time in 1992. _CS_

■ WRITING FIRST: Flashback

Look back at your response to the Writing First exercise on page 307. Do you see any run-ons or comma splices? If so, put brackets around them.

B   Correcting Run-Ons and Comma Splices

You can correct a run-on or comma splice in five different ways.

1. Create two separate sentences.

INCORRECT   Muslims fast during daylight for a period of thirty days this period is called Ramadan. (run-on)

INCORRECT   Muslims fast during daylight for a period of thirty days, this period is called Ramadan. (comma splice)

CORRECT   Muslims fast during daylight for a period of thirty days. This period is called Ramadan. (two separate sentences)

2. Use a coordinating conjunction.

If you want to indicate a particular relationship between ideas—for example, cause and effect or contrast—you can connect two independent clauses with a coordinating conjunction (*and, but, or, nor, for, so,* or *yet*) that makes this relationship clear. Always place a comma before the coordinating conjunction.

INCORRECT   The Emancipation Proclamation freed U.S. slaves in 1863 slaves in Texas were not officially freed until June 19, 1865 ("Juneteenth"). (run-on)

INCORRECT   The Emancipation Proclamation freed U.S. slaves in 1863, slaves in Texas were not officially freed until June 19, 1865 ("Juneteenth"). (comma splice)

CORRECT   The Emancipation Proclamation freed U.S. slaves in 1863, but slaves in Texas were not officially freed until June 19, 1865 ("Juneteenth"). (clauses connected with a comma followed by a coordinating conjunction)

3. Use a semicolon.

If you want to indicate a particularly close connection—or a strong contrast—between two ideas, use a semicolon.

INCORRECT   The swastika was an ancient symbol of good luck it was also the official emblem of the Nazi Party. (run-on)

INCORRECT   The swastika was an ancient symbol of good luck, it was also the official emblem of the Nazi Party. (comma splice)

CORRECT   The swastika was an ancient symbol of good luck; it was also the official emblem of the Nazi Party. (clauses connected with a semicolon)

4. Use a semicolon followed by a conjunctive adverb or transitional expression.

To clarify a specific relationship between two closely related ideas, add a conjunctive adverb or transitional expression after the semicolon.

INCORRECT   *Its* is a possessive pronoun *it's* is a contraction. (run-on)

INCORRECT   *Its* is a possessive pronoun, *it's* is a contraction. (comma splice)

CORRECT   *Its* is a possessive pronoun; however, *it's* is a contraction. (clauses connected with a semicolon followed by a conjunctive adverb)

▼ **Student Voices**

My high school teachers said I wrote run-ons, so I started writing really short sentences. Now my sentences are too choppy. I need to find another way to revise.

Richard Greene

For more on connecting ideas with a coordinating conjunction, see 16A.

Teaching Tip

To help students remember the coordinating conjunctions, use the mnemonic *FANBOYS:* For, And, Nor, But, Or, Yet, So.

For more on connecting ideas with a semicolon, see 16B.

Teaching Tip

Review the use of semicolons, referring students to 16B. Explain that if a period will not work where the semicolon is, then the semicolon is probably incorrect.

● **Writing Tip**

Conjunctive adverbs include words such as *however* and *therefore;* transitional expressions include *in fact, as a result,* and *for example.* (See 16C.)

> **FOCUS** Run-Ons and Comma Splices with Conjunctive Adverbs or Transitional Expressions
>
> Run-ons and comma splices often occur when you use a conjunctive adverb or transitional expression to join two independent clauses *without also using a semicolon.*
>
> INCORRECT Some students have microwaves and refrigerators in their dorm rooms as a result, electrical circuits are overloaded. (run-on)
>
> INCORRECT Some students have microwaves and refrigerators in their dorm rooms, as a result, electrical circuits are overloaded. (comma splice)
>
> To correct this kind of run-on or comma splice, simply add the missing semicolon.
>
> CORRECT Some students have microwaves and refrigerators in their dorm rooms; as a result, electrical circuits are overloaded.

For more on connecting ideas with a subordinating conjunction or relative pronoun, see Chapter 17.

5. Use a subordinating conjunction or relative pronoun. When one idea is dependent on another, you can turn the dependent idea into a dependent clause by adding a subordinating conjunction (such as *when, although,* or *because*) or a relative pronoun (such as *who, which,* or *that*).

INCORRECT Horace Mann was the first president of Antioch College he encouraged the development of students' social consciences. (run-on)

INCORRECT Horace Mann was the first president of Antioch College, he encouraged the development of students' social consciences. (comma splice)

CORRECT When Horace Mann was the first president of Antioch College, he encouraged the development of students' social consciences. (clauses connected by a subordinating conjunction)

CORRECT Horace Mann, who was the first president of Antioch College, encouraged the development of students' social consciences. (clauses connected by a relative pronoun)

> ● **Writing Tip**
>
> When you use a relative pronoun to correct a run-on or comma splice, the relative pronoun takes the place of another pronoun in the sentence.

◆ PRACTICE 21-2

ON THE WEB
For more practice, visit **Exercise Central** *at* *<www.bedfordstmartins.com/ writingfirst>.*

Correct each of the run-ons and comma splices on the next page in one of the following four ways: by creating two separate sentences, by using a coordinating conjunction, by using a semicolon, or by using a semicolon followed by a conjunctive adverb or transitional expression. Be sure punctuation is correct. Remember to put a semicolon before, and a comma after, each conjunctive adverb or transitional expression.

Example: Some people believe chronic sex offenders should be given therapy; however, others believe they should be jailed indefinitely.

Answers may vary.

1. Nursing offers job security and high pay; therefore, many people are choosing nursing as a career.

2. Anne Boleyn was the second wife of Henry VIII, and her daughter was Elizabeth I.

3. The Democratic Republic of the Congo was previously known as Zaire; before that, it was the Belgian Congo.

4. Housewife Jean Nidetch started Weight Watchers in 1961. She sold the company for $100 million in 1978.

5. Millions of Jews were killed during the Holocaust; in addition, Catholics, Gypsies, homosexuals, and other "undesirables" were killed.

6. Sojourner Truth was born a slave, but she eventually became a leading abolitionist and feminist.

7. Japanese athletes play various positions on American baseball teams; however, until recently all the Japanese players were pitchers.

8. Oliver Wendell Holmes Jr. was a Supreme Court Justice; his father was a physician and writer.

9. Père Noel is the French name for Santa Claus; he is also known as Father Christmas and St. Nicholas.

10. Latin is one classical language; Greek is another.

◆ PRACTICE 21-3

Consulting the list of subordinating conjunctions on page 245 and the list of relative pronouns on page 248, correct the following run-ons and comma splices. Be sure to add correct punctuation where necessary.

Examples: Harlem was a rural area until the nineteenth century, when improved transportation linked it to lower Manhattan.

The community, which was soon home to people escaping the crowds of New York City, it became a fashionable suburb.

Answers may vary.

(1) Harlem, which was populated mostly by European immigrants at the turn of the last century, it saw an influx of African Americans beginning

in 1910. (2) *As this* ~~This~~ migration from the South continued for several decades, Harlem became one of the largest African-American communities in the United States. (3) Many African-American artists and writers created a settlement in Harlem during the 1920s, *which* ~~this~~ led to a flowering of African-American art. (4) This "Harlem Renaissance" was an important era in American literary history *although* it is not even mentioned in some textbooks. (5) *When scholars* ~~Scholars~~ of the era recognize the great works of the Harlem Renaissance, they point to the writers Langston Hughes and Countee Cullen and the artists Henry Tanner and Sargent Johnson. (6) Zora Neale Hurston*, who* moved to Harlem from her native Florida in 1925, ~~she~~ began work there on a book of African-American folklore. (7) *Because* Harlem was an exciting place in the 1920s, people from all over the city went there to listen to jazz and to dance. (8) The white playwright Eugene O'Neill went to Harlem to audition actors for his play *The Emperor Jones*, *which* ~~it~~ made an international star of the great Paul Robeson. (9) *While contemporary* ~~Contemporary~~ African-American artists know about the Harlem Renaissance, it is still not familiar to many others. (10) *When the* ~~The~~ Great Depression occurred in the 1930s, it led to the end of the Harlem Renaissance.

◆ PRACTICE 21-4

Correct each run-on and comma splice in the following passage in the way that best indicates the relationship between ideas. Be sure you use appropriate punctuation.

Example: Coney Island was once a bustling seaside resort, *but* it declined considerably over the recent years.

Answers may vary.
In the late nineteenth century, Coney Island was famous; in fact, it was legendary. Every summer, it was crowded, *and* people mailed hundreds of thousands of postcards from the resort on some days. Coney Island*, which* was considered exotic and exciting, ~~it~~ even had a hotel shaped like an elephant. *Although some* ~~Some~~ people saw Coney Island as seedy, others thought it was a wonderful, magical place. It had beaches, hotels, racetracks, and a stadium; however, by the turn of the century, it was best known for three

amusement parks. These parks were Luna Park, Steeplechase, and

Dreamland. ~~Gaslight~~ *Even though gaslight* was still the norm in New York, a million electric

lights lit Luna Park. *While* Steeplechase offered many rides, its main attraction

was a two-mile ride on mechanical horses. At Dreamland, people could

see a submarine*;* in addition, they could travel through an Eskimo village

or visit Lilliputia, with its three hundred midgets. Today, the old Coney

Island no longer exists. Fire destroyed Dreamland in 1911, *and* Luna Park

burned down in 1946. In 1964, Steeplechase closed. The once-grand

Coney Island is gone*. Still,* ~~still~~ its beach and its boardwalk endure. Its famous

roller coaster, the Cyclone, still exists, *and* its giant Ferris wheel, the Wonder

Wheel, keeps on turning. Now, a ballpark has been built for a new minor

league baseball team*. The* ~~the~~ new team is called the Brooklyn Cyclones.

■ WRITING FIRST: Flashback

For each run-on or comma splice you identified in the Flashback
exercise on page 308, write two possible corrected versions here.

Answers will vary.

_____

_____

_____

_____

_____

■ WRITING FIRST: Revising and Editing

Look back at your responses to the Writing First exercise on page
307 and the Flashback exercises on page 308 and above. For each
run-on and comma splice you found, choose the revision that best
conveys your meaning, and revise your Writing First exercise accordingly. If you do not find any run-ons or comma splices in your
own writing, work with a classmate to correct his or her writing, or
edit the work you did for another assignment.

CHAPTER REVIEW

◆ EDITING PRACTICE

Read the following student essay, into which sentence errors have been introduced. Then, revise it by eliminating run-ons and comma splices and carefully correcting them to indicate the relationships between ideas. Be sure punctuation is correct. The first error has been corrected for you.

Answers may vary.

Blood Sports

Since the time of ancient Rome, citizens have rushed to the stadium to see battles. *While* Christians fought lions in ancient times, athletes now fight each other. ~~Society~~ *Although society* may have evolved morally to some degree, I believe only our laws keep us from behaving like the ancient Romans.

I played "barbaric" sports for ten years. My parents*, who* encouraged my athletic career*,* ~~they~~ got me started in sports early on. Between the ages of ten and seventeen, I was very active in martial arts, *and* for four years, I played high school football. As a young child, I competed in karate tournaments*, where* I was injured frequently. I broke my nose three times*;* I also broke my hand twice and my foot once. As a competitor, I enjoyed the thrill of battle*;* however*,* I feared serious injury. Eventually, I gave up karate*;* instead*,* I concentrated on football.

Extreme force was very important in high school football. I played defense, *and* I often hurt my opponents. Once, *when* I hit a quarterback in his hip with my helmet*,* the blow knocked him to the ground. ~~They~~ *When they* carried him off the field, my team's fans went berserk. For weeks, people congratulated me*;* still*,* I felt uncomfortable. I now understand that playing sports requires a great deal of physical aggressiveness and pain. I accept this as part of the game*,* I just don't want to play anymore.

◆ COLLABORATIVE ACTIVITIES

1. Find an interesting paragraph from a newspaper or magazine article. Working in a small group, recopy it onto a separate sheet of paper, creating run-ons and comma splices. Exchange exercises with another group.

2. Work in a small group to correct each run-on and comma splice in an exercise prepared by another group of students. When you have finished, return the exercise to the group that created it.

3. Continuing to work with members of your group, evaluate the other group's work on your exercise, comparing it to the original newspaper or magazine paragraph. Pay particular attention to punctuation. Where the students' version differs from the original, decide whether their version is incorrect or whether it represents an acceptable (or even superior) alternative to the original.

☑ REVIEW CHECKLIST:
Run-Ons and Comma Splices

- A run-on is an error that occurs when two sentences are joined without punctuation. (See 21A.)

- A comma splice is an error that occurs when two sentences are joined with just a comma. (See 21A.)

- Correct a run-on or comma splice by creating two separate sentences, by using a coordinating conjunction, by using a semicolon, by using a semicolon followed by a conjunctive adverb or transitional expression, or by connecting clauses with a subordinating conjunction or relative pronoun. (See 21B.)

Sentence Fragments

Word Power

unique unlike any other

transform to change completely

empower to give strength or power to

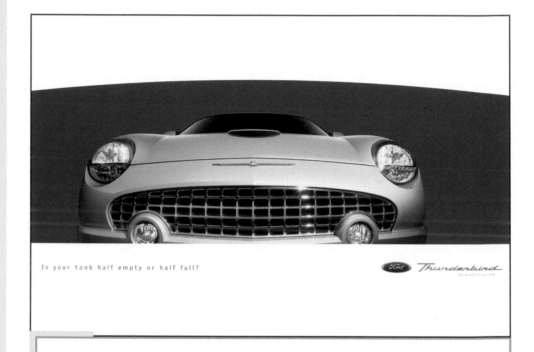

Is your tank half empty or half full?

Ford *Thunderbird*

■ WRITING FIRST

Look at the advertisement above, and then write several lines of copy for a magazine ad for your favorite beverage, footwear, or health or beauty product.

A   Recognizing Sentence Fragments

A **sentence fragment** is an incomplete sentence. Every sentence must include at least one subject and one verb, and every sentence must express a complete thought. If a group of words does not do *all* these things, it is a fragment and not a sentence—even if it begins with a capital letter and ends with a period.

> SENTENCE   The <u>actors</u> in the play *Into the Woods* <u>were</u> ethnically diverse. (includes both a subject and a verb and expresses a complete thought)

Because a sentence must have both a subject and a verb and express a complete thought, the following groups of words are not complete sentences but fragments.

FRAGMENT   The actors in the play *Into the Woods*. (What point is
(NO VERB)   being made about the actors?)

FRAGMENT   Were ethnically diverse. (What was ethnically diverse?)
(NO SUBJECT)

● **Writing Tip**

You may see sentence fragments used in advertisements and other informal writing (*A full head of hair in just 30 minutes!*), but fragments are not acceptable in college writing.

FOCUS **Identifying Sentence Fragments**

Sentence fragments almost always appear in paragraphs and longer passages, right beside complete sentences.

┌─ COMPLETE SENTENCE ─┐ ┌─── FRAGMENT ───┐
Celia took two electives. Physics 320 and Spanish 101.

The fragment above does not have a verb. The complete sentence that precedes it, however, has both a subject (*Celia*) and a verb (*took*).

Often, as in this case, you can correct a sentence fragment by attaching it to an adjacent sentence that supplies the missing words.

Celia took two electives, Physics 320 and Spanish 101.

▼ **Student Voices**

Thinking of a sentence fragment as a piece of a sentence helps me remember that the fragment needs to be attached to a whole sentence.

Keith Jackson

Teaching Tip
Consider giving students a pretest to see how much time you need to spend on fragments and to determine the types of problems your students have.

◆ **PRACTICE 22-1**

Each of the following items is a fragment. On the line following each fragment, indicate what is missing and what needs to be changed to make it a complete sentence. There are four possible ways to correct these sentence fragments: (1) add a subject; (2) add a verb; (3) add a subject and a verb; or (if the fragment has a subject and a verb) (4) revise to express a complete thought.

ON THE WEB
For more practice, visit Exercise Central *at* <www.bedfordstmartins.com/writingfirst>.

Example: At the beginning of the test. *add a subject and a verb*

1. The students in the classroom. *add a verb*

2. Before the teacher handed out the answer sheets. *revise to express a complete thought*

3. With a number-two pencil. *add a subject and a verb*

4. Opened their test booklets. *add a subject*

5. After twenty-five minutes. *add a subject and a verb*

6. Began the second part of the test. *add a subject*

7. The last set of questions. *add a verb*

8. When the teacher called "Time." *revise to express a complete thought*

9. Breathed a sigh of relief. _add a subject_ _____

10. Quickly out into the hallway. _add a subject and a verb_ _____

ESL Tip
Nonnative speakers may not
have any more trouble with
fragments than other stu-
dents. If they are not having
problems in this area, work
with them on problem areas
such as count and noncount
nouns (discussed in 30E).

◆ **PRACTICE 22-2**

In the following passage, some of the numbered groups of words are missing a subject, a verb, or both. Identify each fragment by labeling it *F*. Then,
attach each fragment to a nearby word group to create a complete new
sentence. Finally, rewrite the entire passage, using complete sentences, on
the lines provided.

Example: Martha Grimes, Ruth Rendell, and Deborah Crombie

write detective novels. _____ Set in England. _F_

Martha Grimes, Ruth Rendell, and Deborah Crombie write detective novels

set in England.

(1) Sara Paretsky writes detective novels. _____ (2) Such as *Burn*

Marks and *Guardian Angel*. _F_ (3) These novels are about V. I. War-

shawski. _____ (4) A private detective. _F_ (5) V. I. lives and works in

Chicago. _____ (6) The Windy City. _F_ (7) Every day as a detective.

_F_ (8) V. I. takes risks. _____ (9) V. I. is tough. _____ (10) She is also a

woman. _____

Rewrite:

Sara Paretsky writes detective novels, such as Burn Marks and Guardian Angel.

These novels are about V. I. Warshawski, a private detective. V. I. lives and works

in Chicago, the Windy City. Every day as a detective, V. I. takes risks. V. I. is

tough. She is also a woman.

■ **WRITING FIRST: Flashback**

Look back at your response to the Writing First exercise on page
316. Do all your sentences seem complete? If you think any are not
complete, copy them here.

Answers will vary.

_____

_____

_____

B   Correcting Phrase Fragments

Every sentence must include a subject and a verb. A **phrase** is a group of words that is missing a subject or a verb or both. When you punctuate a phrase as if it is a sentence, you create a fragment.

Two kinds of phrases that are often written as sentence fragments are *appositives* and *prepositional phrases*.

Appositive Fragments

An **appositive** is a phrase that identifies or renames a noun or a pronoun. An appositive cannot stand alone as a sentence. To correct an appositive fragment, add the words needed to make it a complete sentence: the nouns or pronouns that the appositive identifies. (You will often find these words in an adjacent sentence.)

For more on appositives, see 18C. For information on punctuating appositives, see 31C.

APPOSITIVE
┌── FRAG ──┐

INCORRECT   He decorated the room in his favorite colors. Brown and
black.

CORRECT   He decorated the room in his favorite colors, brown and
black.

Sometimes an expression like *such as, for example,* or *for instance* introduces an appositive. Even if an appositive is introduced by one of these expressions, it is still a fragment.

APPOSITIVE
┌── FRAG ──┐

INCORRECT   A good diet should include high-fiber foods. Such as
leafy vegetables, fruits, beans, and whole-grain bread.

CORRECT   A good diet should include high-fiber foods, such as leafy
vegetables, fruits, beans, and whole-grain bread.

Prepositional Phrase Fragments

A **prepositional phrase** consists of a preposition and its object. A prepositional phrase cannot stand alone as a sentence. To correct a prepositional phrase fragment, add the words needed to make it a complete sentence. (You will often find these words in an adjacent sentence.)

For more on prepositional phrases, see 15B.

PREPOSITIONAL PHRASE
┌──── FRAG ────┐

INCORRECT   She promised to stand by him. In sickness and in health.

CORRECT   She promised to stand by him in sickness and in health.

◆ PRACTICE 22-3

Each of the following items includes an appositive fragment. In each case, revise to correct the appositive fragment.

ON THE WEB
For more practice, visit
Exercise Central *at*
<www.bedfordstmartins.com/ writingfirst>.

Example: The Pledge of Allegiance was written in 1892 by Francis Bellamy. A Baptist minister.

The Pledge of Allegiance was written in 1892 by Francis Bellamy, a Baptist

minister.

1. Most scholars agree that the U.S. flag was designed by Francis Hopkinson. A New Jersey delegate to the Continental Congress.

    Most scholars agree that the U.S. flag was designed by Francis Hopkinson,

    a New Jersey delegate to the Continental Congress.

2. For the new flag, the Continental Congress required certain design features. Such as the original thirteen stars and thirteen stripes.

    For the new flag, the Continental Congress required certain design fea-

    tures, such as the original thirteen stars and thirteen stripes.

3. The first flag may have been sewn by Betsy Ross. A Philadelphia seamstress.

    The first flag may have been sewn by Betsy Ross, a Philadelphia seam-

    stress.

4. The United States has adopted a number of other patriotic symbols. Such as the Pledge of Allegiance and the National Anthem.

    The United States has adopted a number of other patriotic symbols,

    such as the Pledge of Allegiance and the National Anthem.

5. The Pledge of Allegiance was first recited during a ceremony in 1892. The four-hundredth anniversary of Columbus's arrival in the New World.

    The Pledge of Allegiance was first recited during a ceremony in 1892, the

    four-hundredth anniversary of Columbus's arrival in the New World.

6. Congress officially recognized the Pledge in 1942. The first year the United States participated in World War II.

    Congress officially recognized the Pledge in 1942, the first year the United

    States participated in World War II.

7. In 1814, Francis Scott Key composed "The Star-Spangled Banner" during a fierce naval battle. An attack by a British warship on Fort McHenry in Baltimore's harbor.

    In 1814, Francis Scott Key composed "The Star-Spangled Banner" during

    a fierce naval battle, an attack by a British warship on Fort McHenry in

    Baltimore's harbor.

8. Key's lyrics were later set to the tune of a popular drinking song. "To Anacreon in Heaven."

Key's lyrics were later set to the tune of a popular drinking song, "To

Anacreon in Heaven."

9. When "The Star-Spangled Banner" was proposed as the National Anthem in 1929, some people argued for other songs. Such as "America" or "America the Beautiful."

When "The Star-Spangled Banner" was proposed as the National Anthem

in 1929, some people argued for other songs, such as "America" or

"America the Beautiful."

10. The fact that "The Star-Spangled Banner" is difficult to sing was their main objection. An objection many might still agree with today.

The fact that "The Star-Spangled Banner" is difficult to sing was their

main objection, an objection many might still agree with today.

◆ PRACTICE 22-4

Each of the following items includes a prepositional phrase fragment. In each case, revise to correct the prepositional phrase fragment.

Example: The order of one's birth in a family has a strong influence. On one's personality.

The order of one's birth in a family has a strong influence on one's person-

ality.

1. First-born children are reliable, serious, and goal-oriented. In most cases.

First-born children are reliable, serious, and goal-oriented in most cases.

2. First-borns often display distinct leadership qualities. As children and later as adults.

First-borns often display distinct leadership qualities as children and

later as adults.

3. Only children have personality characteristics like those of first-borns. In larger families.

Only children have personality characteristics like those of first-borns in

larger families.

4. In addition to many business leaders. More than half of the U.S. presidents have been first-born or only children.

In addition to many business leaders, more than half of the U.S. presi-

dents have been first-born or only children.

5. Second-born children may compete with their older sibling but more often pursue different interests. In terms of academics and other activities.

   Second-born children may compete with their older sibling but more often

   pursue different interests in terms of academics and other activities.

6. If the first-born child is a good student, for example, the second-born child might pursue sports or music. As a way to stand out.

   If the first-born child is a good student, for example, the second-born

   child might pursue sports or music as a way to stand out.

7. In large families, middle-born children often form close personal relationships. Among themselves or with friends outside of the family.

   In large families, middle-born children often form close personal relation-

   ships among themselves or with friends outside of the family.

8. The youngest child in a family is always seeking ways to get attention. From the older members of the family.

   The youngest child in a family is always seeking ways to get attention

   from the older members of the family.

9. Youngest children can be charming and funny but sometimes manipulative. In their relationships with other family members.

   Youngest children can be charming and funny but sometimes manipula-

   tive in their relationships with other family members.

10. As adults, they are likely to be impulsive and to take a while to settle down. Into careers and marriages.

    As adults, they are likely to be impulsive and to take a while to settle

    down into careers and marriages.

◆ PRACTICE 22-5

Each of the following items is a phrase fragment, not a sentence, because it lacks a subject or a verb or both. Correct each fragment by adding any words needed to turn the fragment into a complete sentence.

Example: During World War I. *A flu epidemic killed millions of people*

during World War I.

Answers will vary.

1. The best player on the Yankees. _____

   _____

2. From a developing nation in Africa. _____

   _____

3. Such as tulips or roses. _____

_____

4. Behind door number 3. _____

_____

5. The worst week of my life. _____

_____

6. With a new car in the driveway. _____

_____

7. A very small animal. _____

_____

8. For a long time. _____

_____

9. Turkey, stuffing, potatoes, and cranberry sauce. _____

_____

10. In less than a year. _____

_____

11. A difficult career decision. _____

_____

12. From one end of the neighborhood to the other. _____

_____

13. An amazing money-back guarantee. _____

_____

14. Along the path to the beach. _____

_____

15. King of the beasts. _____

_____

■ WRITING FIRST: Flashback

Look back at your response to the Writing First exercise on page
316. Are any phrases incorrectly punctuated as sentences? On the

(continued on the following page)

(continued from the previous page)
lines below, correct each fragment you find by adding any words necessary to create complete sentences. (Hint: You may find these words in a sentence that comes before or after the fragment.)

Answers will vary.

_____

_____

_____

_____

C Correcting Incomplete Verbs

Writing Tip

Helping verbs include forms of *be, have,* and *do.* (See 15C.)

Every sentence must include a **complete verb**. Present participles and past participles are not complete verbs. They need helping verbs to complete them.

A **present participle**, such as *looking,* is not a complete verb because it cannot stand alone in a sentence without a **helping verb** (*is looking, was looking, were looking,* and so on). When you use a present participle without a helping verb, you create a fragment.

FRAGMENT   The twins always looking for trouble.

To correct the fragment, add a helping verb.

CORRECT   The twins <u>are</u> always looking for trouble.

For a list of irregular past participles, see 27B.

An irregular **past participle**, such as *hidden,* is not a complete verb because it cannot stand alone in a sentence without a helping verb (*is hidden, was hidden, has hidden,* and so on). When you use one of these past participles without a helping verb, you create a fragment.

FRAGMENT   The letter hidden behind the sofa pillow.

To correct the fragment, add a helping verb.

CORRECT   The letter <u>was</u> hidden behind the sofa pillow.

Writing Tip

Be careful not to create dangling modifiers with participles. (See 25C.)

FOCUS Correcting Participle Fragments

Sometimes you need to add a subject as well as a helping verb to correct a participle fragment. In most cases, you will find the missing subject and verb in an adjacent sentence.

(continued on the following page)

(continued from the previous page)

INCORRECT The twins spent most of the day outside. <u>Looking for trouble</u>.

CORRECT The twins spent most of the day outside, looking for trouble.

INCORRECT We finally found the letter. <u>Hidden behind the sofa pillow</u>.

CORRECT We finally found the letter, hidden behind the sofa pillow.

An **infinitive**, which consists of *to* plus the base form of the verb (*to be, to go, to write*), is not a complete verb. An infinitive phrase (*to be free, to go home, to write a novel*) cannot stand alone as a sentence because it does not include a subject or a complete verb.

INCORRECT Eric considered dropping out of school. <u>To start his own business</u>.

To correct an infinitive phrase fragment, you can add the words necessary to complete the sentence.

CORRECT Eric considered dropping out of school. He thought he might like to start his own business.

Often, however, the easiest way to correct an infinitive phrase fragment is to attach it to an adjacent sentence.

CORRECT Eric considered dropping out of school to start his own business.

◆ PRACTICE 22-6

Each of the following items is a fragment because it does not have a complete verb. Correct each fragment by adding a helping verb.

Example: The sun setting behind the clouds. *The sun was setting behind the clouds.*

Answers will vary.

1. The family been worried about money for a long time. _____

_____

2. The Huangs trying to decide where to live. _____

_____

3. Both Luz and Kate chosen to receive a fellowship. _____

_____

4. Janis always complaining about the lab manual. _____

_____

5. Asbestos fallen from the heating ducts. _____

_____

6. Many recent graduates wondering which job to take. _____

_____

7. Amanda deciding whether or not to get a new cell phone. _____

_____

8. Romeo and Juliet forbidden to see each other. _____

_____

9. Most people minding their own business. _____

_____

10. Margaret forgotten the name of the reference book she needed. _____

_____

◆ **PRACTICE 22-7**

Each of the following items is a fragment because it is missing a subject
and its verb is not complete. Correct each fragment by attaching it to a
new sentence that contains a subject and a complete verb.

    Example: Running for his life.

         Running for his life, he dashed out the door.

    Answers will vary.

1. Speeding down the freeway. _____

2. Taken to the cleaner's. _____

3. To major in biology. _____

4. Becoming a better athlete. _____

5. Enlisting in the air force. _____

6. To write a play about the Chinese-American experience. _____

_____

7. Been out of town for three weeks. _____

8. Really feeling optimistic about the future. _____

9. To play the lead in the musical. _____

10. Just written a fifteen-page research paper. _____

11. To get away with murder. _____

12. Trying hard to be helpful. _____

13. Gone on a long journey. _____

14. To graduate with honors. _____

15. Reading *Sports Illustrated* and eating an apple. _____

◆ PRACTICE 22-8

Each of the following items includes a participle fragment. In each case, correct the participle fragment by attaching it to the adjacent sentence.

Example: Today, animated films are quite popular. Appealing to children and adults alike.

Today, animated films are quite popular, appealing to children and adults

alike.

1. Prior to the 1990s, most animated films were hand-drawn. Requiring painstaking skill.

   Prior to the 1990s, most animated films were hand-drawn, requiring

   painstaking skill.

2. In recent years, this process has been changed. Replaced by computerized graphics.

   In recent years, this process has been changed, replaced by computer-

   ized graphics.

3. Some people object to computer animation. Criticizing it as too mechanical.

   Some people object to computer animation, criticizing it as too mechani-

   cal.

4. Still, computer animation has gained a wide audience. Impressed by its range of visual possibilities.

   Still, computer animation has gained a wide audience, impressed by its

   range of visual possibilities.

5. The first full-length animated film was Walt Disney's *Snow White and the Seven Dwarfs*. Released originally in 1937.

   The first full-length animated film was Walt Disney's Snow White and the

   Seven Dwarfs, released originally in 1937.

6. For decades after that, the Disney studios provided the very best in an-imated storytelling. Focusing on fairy tales and classics of children's literature.

For decades after that, the Disney studios provided the very best in

animated storytelling, focusing on fairy tales and classics of children's

literature.

7. Disney's conventional animation reached its peak with *Beauty and the Beast.* Considered by many the equivalent of a great live-action feature.

Disney's conventional animation reached its peak with Beauty and the

Beast, considered by many the equivalent of a great live-action feature.

8. Disney then ventured into the area of digital animation. Creating the highly successful *Toy Story* series.

Disney then ventured into the area of digital animation, creating the

highly successful Toy Story series.

9. DreamWorks studios has become Disney's main competitor. Producing such hits as *Antz* and *Shrek.*

DreamWorks studios has become Disney's main competitor, producing

such hits as Antz and Shrek.

10. We can only guess at the possibilities for future animation. Influenced by continuing technological innovation.

We can only guess at the possibilities for future animation, influenced by

continuing technological innovation.

◆ PRACTICE 22-9

Each of the following items includes an infinitive phrase fragment. Cor-rect the first five by adding the words necessary to make the the infinitive fragment a complete sentence.

Example: Most milk we drink today is pasteurized. To destroy disease-causing organisms.

Most milk we drink today is pasteurized. This process is used to destroy

disease-causing organisms.

Correct the final five by attaching the infinitive fragment to the adjacent sentence.

Example: Many wetlands have been destroyed. To create new hous-ing developments.

Many wetlands have been destroyed to create new housing developments.

Answers may vary.

1. Emergency medical technicians receive intensive training. To prepare them for saving lives.

   Emergency medical technicians receive intensive training. This training is

   meant to prepare them for saving lives.

2. Many states have adopted standardized testing of students. To rank local school districts.

   Many states have adopted standardized testing of students. They use

   these tests to rank local school districts.

3. Retailers often locate frequently purchased items at the back of their stores. To increase customer traffic.

   Retailers often locate frequently purchased items at the back of their

   stores. They do this to increase customer traffic.

4. The handshake originated as an act between suspicious strangers. To show that they were unarmed.

   The handshake originated as an act between suspicious strangers. They

   shook hands to show that they were unarmed.

5. Japan's Tokyo Zoo is closed for two months each year. To give the animals a vacation from visitors.

   Japan's Tokyo Zoo is closed for two months each year. This is done to

   give the animals a vacation from visitors.

6. Chimpanzees have been observed picking the leaves off twigs. To create a tool for scooping honey.

   Chimpanzees have been observed picking the leaves off twigs to create a

   tool for scooping honey.

7. More and more, people rely on e-mail. To keep them in touch with family and friends.

   More and more, people rely on e-mail to keep them in touch with family

   and friends.

8. Some student writers are taught the technique of freewriting. To help them overcome writer's block.

   Some student writers are taught the technique of freewriting to help

   them overcome writer's block.

9. Early telephone users said "Ahoy" instead of "Hello." To greet incoming callers.

   Early telephone users said "Ahoy" instead of "Hello" to greet incoming

   callers.

10. The public bus system is being expanded. To provide service for more commuters.

The public bus system is being expanded to provide service for more

commuters.

■ WRITING FIRST: Flashback

Look back at your response to the Writing First exercise on page 316. Underline any present or past participles or infinitives. Are the sentences in which they appear complete? Correct each fragment you find by adding the words necessary to complete them. Write your corrected sentences on the lines below.

_____

_____

_____

_____

_____

Teaching Tip
Review the use of commas in complex sentences (Chapter 17). To help students remember to use a comma when a dependent clause comes at the beginning of a sentence (but not when it comes at the end), tell them the comma is there to say, "Hey, I know I'm a fragment, but the rest of my sentence is coming."

D ▏ **Correcting Dependent Clause Fragments**

Every sentence must express a complete thought. A **dependent clause** is a group of words that includes a subject and a verb but does not express a complete thought. Therefore, it cannot stand alone as a sentence. To correct a dependent clause fragment, you must complete the thought. The following dependent clause is punctuated as if it were a sentence.

After Simon won the lottery.

This sentence fragment includes both a subject (*Simon*) and a complete verb (*won*), but it does not express a complete thought. What happened after Simon won the lottery? To turn this fragment into a sentence, you need to complete the thought.

After Simon won the lottery, <u>he quit his night job</u>.

Dependent Clauses Introduced by Subordinating Conjunctions

Some dependent clauses are introduced by **subordinating conjunctions**.

FRAGMENT <u>Although</u> Marisol had always dreamed of coming to America.

This sentence fragment includes a subject *(Marisol)* and a complete verb *(had dreamed)*, but it is not a sentence; it is a dependent clause introduced by the subordinating conjunction *although*.

One way to correct this fragment is to add an **independent clause** (a complete sentence) to complete the idea and finish the sentence.

> SENTENCE Although Marisol had always dreamed of coming to America, she did not have enough money for the trip until 1985.

Another way to correct the fragment is to delete the subordinating conjunction *although*, the word that makes the idea incomplete.

> SENTENCE Marisol had always dreamed of coming to America.

● **Writing Tip**

Subordinating conjunctions include *although, because, even, if,* and *though*. (See 17B.)

Dependent Clauses Introduced by Relative Pronouns

Other dependent clauses are introduced by **relative pronouns** (*who, which, that,* and so on).

> FRAGMENT Novelist Richard Wright, <u>who</u> came to Paris in 1947.
>
> FRAGMENT A quinceañera, <u>which</u> celebrates a Latina's fifteenth birthday.
>
> FRAGMENT A key World War II battle <u>that</u> was fought on the Pacific island of Guadalcanal.

For more on relative pronouns, see 17C.

Each of the above sentence fragments includes a subject *(Richard Wright, quinceañera, battle)* and a complete verb *(came, celebrates, was fought)*. However, they are not sentences because they do not express complete thoughts. In each case, a relative pronoun creates a dependent clause.

One way to correct each fragment is to add the words needed to complete the idea.

> SENTENCE Novelist Richard Wright, who came to Paris in 1947, spent the rest of his life there.
>
> SENTENCE A quinceañera, which celebrates a Latina's fifteenth birthday, signifies her entrance into womanhood.
>
> SENTENCE A key World War II battle that was fought on the Pacific island of Guadalcanal took place in 1943.

Another way to correct the fragments is to delete the relative pronouns that make the ideas incomplete.

> SENTENCE Novelist Richard Wright came to Paris in 1947.
>
> SENTENCE A quinceañera celebrates a Latina's fifteenth birthday.
>
> SENTENCE A key World War II battle was fought on the Pacific island of Guadalcanal.

◆ PRACTICE 22-10

Correct each of these dependent clause fragments in two ways. First, make the fragment a complete sentence by adding a group of words that completes the idea. Second, delete the subordinating conjunction or relative pronoun that makes the idea incomplete.

ON THE WEB
For more practice, visit Exercise Central *at* <www.bedfordstmartins.com/writingfirst>.

Example: Before it became a state.

   Revised: *Before it became a state, West Virginia was part*
   of Virginia.

   Revised: *It became a state.*

1. Because many homeless people are mentally ill.

   Revised: *Answers will vary.*

   _____

   Revised: *Many homeless people are mentally ill.*

   _____

2. The film that frightened me.

   Revised: *Answers will vary.*

   _____

   Revised: *The film frightened me.*

   _____

3. Although people disagree about the effects of violent video games.

   Revised: *Answers will vary.*

   _____

   Revised: *People disagree about the effects of violent video games.*

   _____

4. People who drink and drive.

   Revised: *Answers will vary.*

   _____

   Revised: *People drink and drive.*

   _____

5. As competition for athletic scholarships increased.

   Revised: *Answers will vary.*

   _____

   Revised: *Competition for athletic scholarships increased.*

   _____

6. Whenever a new semester begins.

Revised: *Answers will vary.*

Revised: *A new semester begins.*

7. Pizza, which is high in fat.

Revised: *Answers will vary.*

Revised: *Pizza is high in fat.*

8. Animals that are used in medical research.

Revised: *Answers will vary.*

Revised: *Animals are used in medical research.*

9. Unless something is likely to change.

Revised: *Answers will vary.*

Revised: *Something is likely to change.*

10. Although it is a very controversial issue.

Revised: *Answers will vary.*

Revised: *It is a very controversial issue.*

◆ PRACTICE 22-11

All of the following are fragments. Turn each fragment into a complete sentence, and write the revised sentence on the line below the fragment. Whenever possible, try creating two different revisions.

Example: Waiting in the dugout.

Revised: *Waiting in the dugout, the players chewed tobacco.*

Revised: *The players were waiting in the dugout.*

Answers will vary.

1. Because three-year-olds are still very attached to their parents.

Revised: _____

_____

Revised: _____

_____

2. Going around in circles.

Revised: _____

_____

Revised: _____

_____

3. To win the prize for the most unusual costume.

Revised: _____

_____

Revised: _____

_____

4. Students who thought they could not afford to go to college.

Revised: _____

_____

Revised: _____

_____

5. On an important secret mission.

Revised: _____

_____

Revised: _____

_____

6. Although many instructors see cheating as a serious problem.

Revised: _____

_____

Revised: _____

_____

7. Hoping to get another helping of chocolate fudge cake.

Revised: _____

_____

Revised: _____

_____

8. The rule that I always felt was the most unfair.

Revised: _____

_____

Revised: _____

_____

9. A really exceptional worker.

Revised: _____

_____

Revised: _____

_____

10. Finished in record time.

Revised: _____

_____

Revised: _____

_____

■ WRITING FIRST: Flashback

Look back at your response to the Writing First exercise on page
316. Underline every subordinating conjunction you find (first,
consult the list on page 245), and underline *which, that,* and *who*
wherever you find them. Do any of these words create a dependent
clause that is punctuated as if it is a sentence? On the lines below,
correct each fragment you find either by crossing out the subordinating conjunction or relative pronoun or by attaching the fragment to another word group to create a complete sentence.

(continued on the following page)

(continued from the previous page)

Answers will vary.

_____

_____

_____

_____

_____

_____

■ WRITING FIRST: Revising and Editing

Look back at your response to the Writing First exercise on page 316. Incorporating corrections from all the Flashback exercises in this chapter, revise your work. Then, check one more time to make sure every sentence is complete. If you do not find any fragments, work with a classmate to correct his or her writing, or edit the work you did in response to another assignment.

CHAPTER REVIEW

◆ EDITING PRACTICE

Read the following student essay, into which incomplete sentences have been introduced. Underline each fragment. Then, correct it by adding the words necessary to complete it or attaching it to an adjacent sentence that completes the idea. The first fragment has been underlined and corrected for you.

My First Job

Like many other teenagers, I got my first job when I was in high school. I worked as a salesperson, ~~In~~ *in* a retail clothing chain. At first, I was really excited. *I learned* ~~Learning~~ about pricing procedures, ~~arranging~~ *arranged* displays, and ~~getting~~ *got* to see all the new styles. I also got to use my employee discount, ~~A~~ *a* benefit that saved me a lot of money.

were
People always coming into the store, asking for help
      ^
in finding things. They would have requests like "Could you

tell me where to find a blue and purple lambswool sweater?"

and "You're about the same size as my niece. Could you try

this on for me?" Sometimes, the customers were annoying.
                                              when
Still, I felt useful and important/ ~~When~~ I was able to
                                 ^
help them.

    The job had its bad side, though. I always seemed to
              , constantly
be running/ ~~Constantly~~ straightening the same racks over
          ^
          I was also
and over. ~~Also~~ rearranging displays several times every
         ^
night. When the store was busy, it was very hectic. Not

all the customers were patient or polite. Some lost their
          because
tempers/ ~~Because~~ they could not find a particular size or
        ^
color. Then, they took out their anger on me. On slow
                                       ,
nights, when the store was almost empty/ I was restless and
                                       ^
                                                   at
bored. Eventually, I found a more stimulating position/ ~~At~~
                                                       ^
a preschool for developmentally delayed children.

◆ COLLABORATIVE ACTIVITIES

1. Exchange workbooks with another student, and read each other's responses to the Writing First exercise on page 316. On a separate sheet
   of paper, list five fragments that describe the product your partner has
   written about. When your own workbook is returned to you, revise
   each fragment written by your partner, creating a complete sentence
   for each one. Finally, add one of these new sentences to your own Writing First exercise.
2. Working in a group of three or four students, add different subordinating conjunctions to sentences *a* through *d* on the next page to create several different fragments. (See 17B for a list of subordinating
   conjunctions.) Turn each of the resulting fragments into a complete
   sentence by adding a word group that completes the idea.

Example

SENTENCE	FRAGMENT	NEW SENTENCE
I left the party.	As I left the party	As I left the party, I fell.
	After I left the party	After I left the party, the fun stopped.
	Until I left the party	Until I left the party, I had no idea it was so late.

SENTENCES

   a. My mind wanders.

   b. She caught the ball.

   c. He made a wish.

   d. Disaster struck.

3. Working in a group of three or four students, build as many sentences as you can from the fragments listed below, each of which is introduced by a past or present participle. Use your imagination to create as many creative, comical, or even silly sentences as you can.

Example

FRAGMENT   Known for his incredible memory

SENTENCES   Zack, known for his incredible memory, has somehow managed to forget everything he learned about chemistry.

            Known for his incredible memory, Monty the Magnificent mesmerized audiences.

FRAGMENTS

   a. wandering in the desert

   b. stranded in the jungle

   c. looking for his ideal mate

   d. always using as much ketchup as possible

   e. folded, stapled, and mutilated

☑ REVIEW CHECKLIST:

Sentence Fragments

▪ A sentence fragment is an incomplete sentence. Every sentence must include a subject and a verb and express a complete thought. (See 22A.)

▪ Phrases cannot stand alone as sentences. (See 22B.)

▪ Every sentence must include a complete verb. (See 22C.)

▪ Dependent clauses cannot stand alone as sentences. (See 22D.)

Subject-Verb Agreement

■ WRITING FIRST

Look at the painting above. Then, using present tense verbs, describe what you think the artist is trying to convey. For example, what might this woman be thinking?

A Understanding Subject-Verb Agreement

A sentence's subject (a noun or pronoun) and its verb must **agree** in number. Singular subjects must have singular verbs, and plural subjects must have plural verbs.

>   s   v
> The museum <u>opens</u> at ten o'clock. (singular noun subject *museum* takes singular verb *opens*)

>   s   v
> The museums <u>open</u> at ten o'clock. (plural noun subject *museums* takes plural verb *open*)

Word Power

composition the arrangement of parts to make a whole

interact to act on one another

realistic presented or depicted as something really is

339

For more on identifying plural noun and pronoun subjects, see 28B and 28C.

● Writing Tip

Subject-verb agreement presents special problems with the irregular verb *be*. (See 23B.)

Teaching Tip

Write a sentence with correct subject-verb agreement on the board—for example, *The supervisor wants to hear from you.* Point out that usually an *s* follows either the subject or the verb, but not both. (Consider giving an example of an exception to this rule—for example, *Gladys wants to hear from you.*)

Teaching Tip

Tell students that the rules that govern compound subjects and *or* also govern compound subjects and *neither . . . nor.*

Teaching Tip

Tell students that an *s* following a verb usually means the verb is singular. For example, in the sentence *He plays golf,* because *he* refers to just one person, the verb needs an *s*. (Be sure to point out the exception that occurs with *I* and *you*.)

$\overset{s}{\text{She}}$ always $\overset{v}{\underline{\text{watches}}}$ the eleven o'clock news. (singular pronoun subject *she* takes singular verb *watches*)

$\overset{s}{\text{They}}$ always $\overset{v}{\underline{\text{watch}}}$ the eleven o'clock news. (plural pronoun subject *they* takes plural verb *watch*)

Most subject-verb agreement problems occur in the present tense, where third-person singular subjects require special verb forms. Regular verbs form the third-person singular by adding *-s* or *-es* to the base form (the form of the verb used with *I*).

Subject-Verb Agreement with Regular Verbs

	Singular	**Plural**
First person	I play	Molly and I/we play
Second person	you play	you play
Third person	he/she/it plays	they play
	the man plays	the men play
	Molly plays	Molly and Sam play

In verb tenses other than the present, the same form of the regular verb is used with every subject: *I played, he played, they played; I will play, she will play, they will play.*

FOCUS **Subject-Verb Agreement with Compound Subjects**

The subject of a sentence is not always a single word. It can also be a **compound subject**, consisting of two or more words. Special rules govern subject-verb agreement with compound subjects.

■ When the parts of a compound subject are connected by *and*, the compound subject takes a plural verb.

$\underline{\overset{s}{\text{John and Marsha}}}$ $\overset{v}{\underline{\text{share}}}$ an office.

■ If both parts of a compound subject connected by *or* are singular, the compound subject takes a singular verb.

$\underline{\overset{s}{\text{John or Marsha}}}$ $\overset{v}{\underline{\text{locks}}}$ up at the end of the day.

■ If both parts of a compound subject connected by *or* are plural, the compound subject takes a plural verb.

$\underline{\overset{s}{\text{Buses or trains}}}$ $\overset{v}{\underline{\text{take}}}$ you to the center of the city.

(continued on the following page)

(continued from the previous page)

■ If one part of a compound subject connected by *or* is singular and the other part is plural, the verb agrees with the word that is closer to it.

s   v

The mayor or the council members meet with community groups.

s   v

The council members or the mayor meets with community groups.

◆ PRACTICE 23-1

Underline the correct form of the verb in each of the following sentences. Make sure the verb agrees with its subject.

ON THE WEB
For more practice, visit Exercise Central *at* <www.bedfordstmartins.com/ writingfirst>.

Example: Radio stations (broadcast/broadcasts) many kinds of music.

(1) Most music fans (know/knows) about salsa, a popular style of Latin music. (2) However, they probably (need/needs) a little education when it comes to ranchera, a blend of traditional forms of regional Mexican music. (3) These forms (include/includes) mariachi music as well as rural-influenced ballads and waltz-like tunes. (4) The ranchera style (appeal/appeals) particularly to a wide number of Americans of Mexican descent. (5) Its performers (sell/sells) millions of records a year, and they often (top/tops) Billboard's Latin charts. (6) In fact, regional Mexican recordings (outsell/outsells) any other form of Latin music in the United States. (7) This popularity (surprise/surprises) many people because the mainstream music industry (give/gives) most of its attention to Latin pop stars who sing in English. (8) Older ranchera lovers (tend/tends) to be first-generation, working-class immigrants, but more and more young listeners (seem/seems) drawn to ranchera because of their pride in their Mexican heritage. (9) When one Los Angeles nightclub (host/hosts) a ranchera night, it (draw/draws) a large crowd of English-speaking fans in their twenties. (10) Clearly, ranchera stars (deserve/ deserves) more attention from the music industry.

◆ **PRACTICE 23-2**

Fill in the blank with the correct present tense form of the verb.

> **Example:** Every day, she ___*visits*___ the computer lab in the basement of Reinhold Hall. (visit)

(1) I ___*write*___ with a computer. (write) (2) It ___*makes*___ my work easier. (make) (3) Our instructors ___*supervise*___ our work. (supervise) (4) They ___*collect*___ our computer disks. (collect) (5) Each week, Ms. Keane and Mr. Marlowe ___*give*___ back the disks. (give) (6) The disks ___*contain*___ our instructors' comments. (contain) (7) I ___*put*___ my disk into the computer (put) and ___*read*___ Mr. Marlowe's comments as I revise. (read) (8) We ___*like*___ this technique for marking papers. (like) (9) One student says he ___*hates*___ the computer, however. (hate) (10) The screen ___*gives*___ him headaches. (give)

◆ **PRACTICE 23-3**

Underline the correct form of the verb in each of the following sentences. Make sure that the verb agrees with its compound subject.

> **Example:** Gloves or a scarf (make/<u>makes</u>) a good wintertime gift.

1. Cars and trucks (<u>fill</u>/fills) the municipal parking lot each day.

2. Grapes or an apple (provide/<u>provides</u>) a nutritious addition to a lunch box.

3. A security officer and a video monitoring system (<u>survey</u>/surveys) the bank's lobby during business hours.

4. A vegetable dish or french fries (<u>come</u>/comes) with the entrée.

5. A pianist or a guitarist (play/<u>plays</u>) at the club every weekend.

6. Nurses or nurse practitioners (<u>offer</u>/offers) round-the-clock patient care.

7. According to the old saying, fish and houseguests (<u>smell</u>/smells) after three days.

8. Flowers or a get-well balloon (cheer/<u>cheers</u>) people up when they are ill.

9. The restaurant owner or her daughter always (greet/<u>greets</u>) customers at the door.

10. A sliding glass door or French windows (<u>allow</u>/allows) the greatest

amount of light into a room.

■ **WRITING FIRST: Flashback**

Look back at your response to the Writing First exercise on page 339. Choose two sentences that contain present tense verbs, and rewrite them on the lines below. Underline the subject of each sentence once and the verb twice. If the subject and verb of each sentence do not agree, correct them here.

_____

_____

_____

_____

_____

Teaching Tip
Before students do this Flashback exercise, review the difference between simple and complete subjects. Tell students that in this Flashback, they are being asked to underline the *simple* subject of each of the two sentences.

B   **Avoiding Agreement Problems with *Be, Have,* and *Do***

The irregular verbs *be, have,* and *do* often present problems with subject-verb agreement in the present tense. Memorizing their forms is the only sure way to avoid such problems.

Teaching Tip
You may need to remind students that standard written English does not use *be* as a helping verb; for example, *He be trying to get my attention* is incorrect.

For more on regular and irregular verbs, see 26A and 26B.

Subject-Verb Agreement with Be

	Singular	**Plural**
First person	I am	we are
Second person	you are	you are
Third person	he/she/it is	they are
	Tran is	Tran and Ryan are
	the boy is	the boys are

Subject-Verb Agreement with Have

	Singular	**Plural**
First person	I have	we have
Second person	you have	you have
Third person	he/she/it has	they have
	Shana has	Shana and Robert have
	the student has	the students have

Teaching Tip
The dialect-related use of *be* and *have* is a sensitive issue for some students. You may want to address it outside of class.

Subject-Verb Agreement with Do		
	Singular	**Plural**
First person	I do	we do
Second person	you do	you do
Third person	he/she/it does	they do
	Ken does	Ken and Mia do
	the book does	the books do

◆ PRACTICE 23-4

Fill in the blank with the correct present tense form of the verb *be, have,* or *do*.

Example: Sometimes, people __*do*__ damage without really meaning to. (do)

(1) Biologists __*have*__ serious worries about the damage that exotic animals can cause when they move into places where native species have developed few defenses against them. (have) (2) The English sparrow __*is*__ one example. (be) (3) It __*has*__ a role in the decline in the number of bluebirds. (have) (4) On the Galapagos Islands, cats __*are*__ another example. (be) (5) Introduced by early explorers, they currently __*do*__ much damage to the eggs of the giant tortoises that live on the islands. (do) (6) Scientists today __*are*__ worried about a new problem. (be) (7) This __*is*__ a situation caused by fish and wildlife agencies that deliberately introduce exotic fish into lakes and streams. (be) (8) They __*do*__ this to please those who enjoy fishing. (do) (9) Although popular with people who fish, this policy __*has*__ major drawbacks. (have) (10) It __*has*__ one drawback in particular: many species of fish have been pushed close to extinction. (have)

■ WRITING FIRST: Flashback

Look back at your response to the Writing First exercise on page 339. Have you used a form of *be, have,* or *do* in any of your sentences? If so, write these sentences on the lines that follow. Have

(continued on the following page)

(continued from the previous page)
you used the correct forms of *be, have,* and *do?* Correct any agreement errors here.

Answers will vary.

C Avoiding Agreement Problems When a Prepositional Phrase Comes between the Subject and the Verb

Sometimes, a subject-verb agreement problem occurs when a prepositional phrase (a phrase that begins with *of, in, between,* and so on) comes between the subject and the verb. In such cases, the object of the preposition appears to be the subject of the sentence when really it is not. This error can lead to an incorrect verb choice, as in the three incorrect sentences below.

For more on prepositional phrases, see 15B. For a list of prepositions, see 30L.

● **Writing Tip**

Keep in mind that a prepositional phrase cannot contain the subject of a sentence.

INCORRECT High levels of mercury occurs in some fish.

CORRECT High <u>levels</u> of mercury <u>occur</u> in some fish.
                s   v

INCORRECT Water in the fuel lines cause an engine to stall.

CORRECT <u>Water</u> in the fuel lines <u>causes</u> an engine to stall.
             s   v

INCORRECT Food between the teeth result in decay.

CORRECT <u>Food</u> between the teeth <u>results</u> in decay.
         s   v

By crossing out the prepositional phrase, you can easily see if there are any agreement errors.

High levels ~~of mercury~~ occur in some fish.

Water ~~in the fuel lines~~ causes an engine to stall.

Food ~~between the teeth~~ results in decay.

FOCUS Words That Come between Subject and Verb

Prepositional phrases introduced by *in addition to, along with, together with, as well as, except,* and *including* can be especially

(continued on the following page)

● **Writing Tip**

An agreement error can also occur when any long group of words comes between the subject and the verb. To check for agreement, find the subject and the verb, and then cross out the words between them.

ON THE WEB

For more practice, visit Exercise Central at <www.bedfordstmartins.com/ writingfirst>.

(continued from the previous page)

confusing. A noun or pronoun that follows such a phrase is an object of the preposition; therefore, it cannot be the subject of the sentence.

St. Thomas, ~~along with St. Croix and St. John~~, is part of the United States Virgin Islands.

◆ **PRACTICE 23-5**

In each of the following sentences, cross out the prepositional phrase that separates the subject and the verb. Then, underline the subject of the sentence once and the verb that agrees with the subject twice.

Example: The food ~~on the carpet~~ (suggest/<u>suggests</u>) that Hiro and Mika had a party.

1. The cupids ~~in the painting~~ (<u>symbolize</u>/symbolizes) lost innocence.

2. Fans ~~at a concert~~ (<u>get</u>/gets) angry if the band is late.

3. The appliances ~~in the kitchen~~ (<u>make</u>/makes) strange noises.

4. The United States, ~~along with Germany and Japan~~, (produce/<u>produces</u>) most of the world's cars.

5. A good set ~~of skis and poles~~ (cost/<u>costs</u>) a lot.

6. Unfortunately, one ~~out of ten men~~ (<u>gets</u>/get) prostate cancer.

7. Workers ~~in the city~~ (pays/<u>pay</u>) a high wage tax.

8. Each summer, fires ~~from lightning~~ (cause/<u>causes</u>) hundreds of millions of dollars in property damage.

9. Volunteers, ~~including people like my father~~, (help/<u>helps</u>) paramedics in my community.

10. A doctor, ~~together with two nurses~~, (staff/<u>staffs</u>) the clinic at the health center.

■ WRITING FIRST: Flashback

Look back at your response to the Writing First exercise on page 339. Can you find any sentences in which a prepositional phrase

(continued on the following page)

(continued from the previous page)
comes between the subject and the verb? Write each subject and verb on the lines below.

Subject

Answers will vary.

_____

_____

_____

Verb

_____

_____

_____

_____

Now, correct any errors in subject-verb agreement.

D **Avoiding Agreement Problems with Indefinite Pronouns as Subjects**

An **indefinite pronoun** is a pronoun that does not refer to a particular person, place, or idea. When an indefinite pronoun is the subject of a sentence, the verb must agree with it. Most indefinite pronouns, such as *no one* and *everyone*, are singular and take a singular verb.

● **Writing Tip**
Many indefinite pronouns end in *-one*, *-body*, or *-thing*. These words are almost always singular.

    s   v
No one likes getting up early.

    s   v
Everyone likes to sleep late.

    s   v
Somebody likes beets.

For information on pronoun-antecedent agreement with indefinite pronouns, see 28E.

Singular Indefinite Pronouns

another	either	neither	one
anybody	everybody	nobody	somebody
anyone	everyone	no one	someone
anything	everything	nothing	something
each	much		

Teaching Tip
Establish the fact that *everybody* and other words in the list are singular. Point out that words such as *anybody*, *somebody*, and *someone* end with a clear reference to a single person (*-body*, *-one*).

A few indefinite pronouns are plural (*both, many, several, few, others*) and take a plural verb.

    s   v
Many were left homeless by the storm.

FOCUS Indefinite Pronouns as Subjects

If a prepositional phrase comes between the indefinite pronoun and the verb, cross out the prepositional phrase to help you identify the sentence's subject.

s   v
Each <s>of the boys</s> has a bike.

s   v
Many <s>of the boys</s> have bikes.

ON THE WEB
For more practice, visit Exercise Central *at* <www.bedfordstmartins.com/ writingfirst>.

◆ PRACTICE 23-6

Circle the correct verb in each sentence.

Example: Each of the three streams in our area (**is**/are) polluted.

1. One of the streams no longer (have/**has**) any fish.

2. Another (contain, **contains**) a lot of algae.

3. Everybody (want/**wants**) to improve the situation.

4. No one (are/**is**) willing to do anything.

5. Somebody always (take/**takes**) control.

6. Everyone (know/**knows**) that pollution is difficult to control.

7. Neither of the candidates (seem/**seems**) willing to act.

8. Whenever anyone (ask/**asks**) them for suggestions, neither (have, **has**) any.

9. According to the candidates, everything (**is**/are) being done that can be done.

10. One of my friends (say/**says**) that she will not vote for either candidate.

■ WRITING FIRST: Flashback

Look back at your response to the Writing First exercise on page 339. Do any of the sentences contain indefinite pronouns that act as subjects? Do the verbs in these sentences agree with the indefinite pronoun subjects? If you find any that do not, rewrite the correct form of the verb below.

(continued on the following page)

(continued from the previous page)

Indefinite pronoun subject	Verb
Answers will vary.	

E Avoiding Agreement Problems
When the Verb Comes before the Subject

A verb always agrees with its subject, even if the verb comes *before* the subject. In questions, for example, word order is reversed, with the verb coming before the subject or with the subject coming between two parts of the verb.

>   V   S
> Where is the telephone booth?

> V   S   V
> Are you going to the party?

If you have trouble identifying the subject of a question, answer the question.

>   V   S
> Where is the telephone booth?

>   S   V
> The telephone booth is outside.

ESL Tip
Point out to students that questions violate conventional English word order. Write a series of statements on the board, and have students change them into questions.

FOCUS *There Is* and *There Are*

In a sentence that begins with *there is* or *there are,* the subject comes after the form of the verb *be.* (*There* can never be the subject.)

>   V   S
> There are nine justices on the Supreme Court.

>   V   S
> There is one chief justice on the Court.

ON THE WEB
For more practice, visit
Exercise Central *at*
<www.bedfordstmartins.com/
writingfirst>.

◆ **PRACTICE 23-7**

Underline the subject of each sentence, and circle the correct form of the verb.

> **Example:** Who (is/are) the writer who won the 1992 Nobel Prize in literature?

1. Where (is/are) the Bering Straits?

2. Why (do/does) the compound change color after being exposed to light?

3. (Is/Are) the twins identical or fraternal?

4. How (do/does) Congress override a presidential veto?

5. What (have/has) this got to do with me?

6. There (is/are) ten computers in the writing center.

7. There (is/are) more than nine million people living in Mexico City.

8. There (is/are) several reference books in this library that can help you with your research.

9. There (is/are) four reasons that we should save the spotted owl from extinction.

10. There (is/are) more than one way to answer the question.

■ WRITING FIRST: Flashback

Look back at your response to the Writing First exercise on page 339. Do you have any sentences in which the verb comes before the subject? If so, write those sentences on the lines below. If the subject and verb of any sentence do not agree, correct the sentence here.

_____

_____

_____

_____

F **Avoiding Agreement Problems with Dependent Clauses**

For more on who, which, that,
and other relative pronouns,
see 17C.

The verb in a dependent clause introduced by the relative pronoun *who,* *which,* or *that* must agree with the word to which the relative pronoun refers. The relative pronouns are singular when they refer to a singular word and plural when they refer to a plural word.

The author, who writes about Chinese immigrants, spoke at our college. (The verb *writes* is singular because the relative pronoun *who* refers to *author.*)

This course, which has a waiting list, is open only to juniors and seniors. (The verb *has* is singular because the relative pronoun *which* refers to *course,* which is singular.)

Computers that have flat-screen monitors are expensive. (The verb *have* is plural because the relative pronoun *that* refers to *computers,* which is plural.)

● **Writing Tip**
The verb in the dependent clause (introduced by the relative pronoun) must agree with the word to which the relative pronoun refers.

◆ PRACTICE 23-8

Draw an arrow from *who, which,* or *that* to the word that it refers to. Then, circle the correct form of the verb.

Example: Edgar Allan Poe, who (tell/**tells**) tales of horror, was born in 1809.

ON THE WEB
For more practice, visit Exercise Central *at* <www.bedfordstmartins.com/ writingfirst>.

(1) Poe's "The Fall of the House of Usher" is a story that (have/**has**) entertained many readers. (2) The story, which (contain/**contains**) the poem "The Haunted Palace," was published in 1839. (3) The narrator, who (have/**has**) not seen Roderick Usher for many years, is summoned to the House of Usher. (4) The decaying mansion, which (**is**/are) dark and dreary, stands at the edge of a swamp. (5) Roderick's twin sister, Madeline, who (live/**lives**) in the house, is very ill. (6) At one point in the story, Roderick's sister, who (**is**/are) in a trance, is thought to be dead. (7) Roderick buries her in the family vault that (**is**/are) under the house. (8) Later, Madeline, who (**is**/are) dressed in her shroud, walks into the room. (9) Roderick, who (**is**/are) terrified, falls down dead. (10) Running outside, the narrator sees the house, which (have/**has**) split apart, sink into the swamp.

■ WRITING FIRST: Flashback

Look back at your response to the Writing First exercise on page 339. Can you find any sentences that include the relative pronoun *who, which,* or *that?* Write any such sentences on the lines below.

(continued on the following page)

(continued from the previous page)

Check to make sure you have used a singular verb when *who,* *which,* or *that* refers to a singular word, and a plural verb when the reference is to a plural word. Make any corrections here.

_____

_____

_____

_____

_____

■ WRITING FIRST: Revising and Editing

Look back at your response to the Writing First exercise on page 339. Incorporating changes and corrections from this chapter's Flashback exercises, revise your work, making sure all your verbs agree with their subjects. When you have finished, rewrite the entire paragraph on a separate sheet of paper, changing all the singular subjects to plural subjects and the plural subjects to singular ones. (For example, *picture* would become *pictures,* and *he* or *she* would become *they.*) Then, change the verbs so they agree with their new subjects.

CHAPTER REVIEW

◆ EDITING PRACTICE

Read the following student essay, into which errors of subject-verb agreement have been introduced. Decide whether each of the underlined verbs agrees with its subject. If it does not, cross out the verb and write in the correct form. If it does, write *C* above the verb. The first sentence has been done for you.

Watching Movies

I <u>believe</u> [*C*] that to be appreciated fully, movies ~~has~~ [*have*]
to be seen in a theater on a big screen. There ~~is~~ [*are*] many
reasons why I and other movie-goers ~~feels~~ [*feel*] this way. In

many cases, a blockbuster movie's sound or its other

special effects ~~requires~~ *require* a theater screening if the movie
C

is to achieve its full impact for viewers. Even movies that
~~have~~

~~has~~ no special effects ~~benefits~~ *benefit* from being seen on a large
C

screen. There *is* something about sitting with other people

in a darkened theater that audiences ~~responds~~ *respond* to in a

special way.

I ~~has~~ *have* a good friend who ~~disagree~~ *disagrees* with me. He, along

with others, ~~argue~~ *argues* that the price of movies ~~are~~ *is* too high.

Too often, people in the audience ~~makes~~ *make* noise and *have*
C

conversations during the screening. Even worse, my friend

~~say~~ *says*, viewers *feel* that it ~~be~~ *is* acceptable to go in and out
C

of the theater whenever they ~~chooses~~ *choose*. These distractions

~~makes~~ *make* it hard to concentrate on the movie. Movie fans like

my friend who *do* not appreciate such interruptions ~~prefers~~ *prefer*
C

to wait until a film ~~come~~ *comes* out on video. Then they *are*
C

able to watch it in private, and there ~~are~~ *is* nobody to

disturb them.

It is true that members of a theater audience ~~does~~ *do*

sometimes cause disruptions. I, however, *see* these as minor

disturbances that ~~has~~ *have* little effect on my enjoyment of a

movie. The spectacle of big-screen movies ~~fascinate~~ *fascinates* me so

that I hardly ~~notices~~ *notice* what is going on around me. Anyone

who ~~think~~ *thinks* watching videos on television is better than see-

ing movies in theaters cannot truly love the art of film.

◆ COLLABORATIVE ACTIVITIES

1. Working in a group of four students, list ten nouns (five singular and five plural) — people, places, or things — on the left-hand side of a sheet of paper. Beside each noun, write the present tense form of a verb that could logically go with the noun. Exchange papers with another group, and check to see that singular nouns have singular verbs and plural nouns have plural verbs.

2. Working with your group, expand each noun-and-verb combination you listed in Collaborative Activity 1 into a complete sentence. Next, write a sentence that could logically follow each of these sentences, using a pronoun as the subject of the new sentence. Make sure the

pronoun you choose refers to the noun in the previous sentence, as in the example *Alan watches three movies a week. He is addicted to films.* Check to be certain the subjects in your sentences agree with the verbs.

3. Exchange the final version of your edited Writing First exercise with another student in your group. Answer the following questions about each sentence in your partner's exercise.

- Does the sentence contain a prepositional phrase that comes between the subject and the verb?
- Does the sentence contain an indefinite pronoun used as a subject?
- Does the verb come before the subject?
- Does the sentence include a dependent clause introduced by a relative pronoun (*who, which,* or *that*)?

As you answer these questions, check to make sure all the verbs agree with their subjects. When your own exercise is returned to you, make any necessary corrections.

☑ REVIEW CHECKLIST:
Subject-Verb Agreement

- Singular subjects (nouns and pronouns) take singular verbs, and plural subjects take plural verbs. Special rules govern subject-verb agreement with compound subjects. (See 23A.)

- The irregular verbs *be, have,* and *do* often present problems with subject-verb agreement in the present tense. (See 23B.)

- Prepositional phrases that come between the subject and the verb do not affect subject-verb agreement. (See 23C.)

- Most indefinite pronouns, such as *no one* and *everyone,* are singular and take a singular verb when they serve as the subject of a sentence. A few are plural and take plural verbs. (See 23D.)

- A sentence's subject and verb must always agree, even if the verb comes before the subject. (See 23E.)

- The verb in a dependent clause introduced by the relative pronouns *who, which,* or *that* must agree with the word to which the relative pronoun refers. The relative pronouns are singular when they refer to a singular word and plural when they refer to a plural word. (See 23F.)

Illogical Shifts

PREVIEW

In this chapter, you will learn

- ■ to avoid illogical shifts in tense (24A)

- ■ to avoid illogical shifts in person (24B)

- ■ to avoid illogical shifts in number (24C)

- ■ to avoid illogical shifts in voice (24D)

■ WRITING FIRST

Look at the picture above, and write about what parents can do to help their children succeed in life. How can parents motivate their children to set appropriate goals and work to achieve them?

Word Power

aspire to strive toward a goal

encourage to inspire with hope or confidence

nurture to nourish; to educate or train

A **shift** occurs anytime a writer changes *tense, person, number,* or *voice*. As you write and revise, be sure that any shifts you make are logical. An **illogical shift** occurs when a writer changes tense, person, number, or voice for no good reason.

A   Avoiding Illogical Shifts in Tense

An **illogical shift in tense** occurs when a writer shifts from one tense to another for no apparent reason.

● **Writing Tip**

Tense is the form a verb takes to show when an action took place or a situation occurred. For more on tense, see Chapters 26 and 27.

ON THE WEB

For more practice, visit Exercise Central *at* *<www.bedfordstmartins.com/ writingfirst>.*

Teaching Tip

Tell students that a shift in tense is sometimes necessary: *Last year I was an English major, but now I am a finance major.*

Teaching Tip

Have students assign a year to each verb. (They should assign the current year to events occurring "now.") For instance, in the first example sentence, both actions occur in the same year (in the past), so both should use the past tense. In the second example sentence, the second action occurs a year later and, in fact, "now," so it requires the present tense. Students enjoy this activity, and it helps them remember to watch for unwarranted tense shifts.

ILLOGICAL SHIFT IN TENSE | The dog <u>walked</u> to the fireplace. Then, he <u>circles</u> twice and <u>lies</u> down in front of the fire. (past to present)

REVISED | The dog <u>walked</u> to the fireplace. Then, he <u>circled</u> twice and <u>lay</u> down in front of the fire. (consistent past)

REVISED | The dog <u>walks</u> to the fireplace. Then, he <u>circles</u> twice and <u>lies</u> down in front of the fire. (consistent present)

◆ **PRACTICE 24-1**

Edit the following sentences for illogical shifts in tense. If a sentence is correct, write *C* in the blank.

Examples

She was surprised when she ~~receives~~ the news. _____ (illogical shift)
(received)

Last year, she was a captain on the force. Now, she is chief of police.
__*C*__ (logical shift)

(1) When Beverly Harvard became the chief of the Atlanta police force, she ~~is~~ the first African-American woman ever to hold that title in a major US city. _____ (was) (2) She started on the police force when she was twenty-two, at a time when mostly white men ~~work~~ as Atlanta police officers. _____ (worked) (3) Now, more than half the department is African-American, and women ~~made~~ up about a quarter of the force. _____ (make) (4) Harvard first thought about joining the force because her husband and a male friend said they ~~do~~ not believe women ~~are~~ capable of doing police work. _____ (did) (were) (5) Her husband even ~~agrees~~ to pay her $100 if she made it onto the force. _____ (agreed) (6) She accepted the challenge, and today she looks back on her first years of training with amazement at how little she knew then. __*C*__ (7) In fact, when she entered the police academy, she did not really plan to be a police officer; she just ~~wants~~ to prove her husband wrong and to win the $100 bet. _____ (wanted) (8) One thing that helped her to advance was her administrative ability; another ~~is~~ her talent for effective management. _____ (was) (9) When her promotion was announced, some veteran officers ~~criticize~~ her appointment as police chief, but most younger officers praised the choice. _____ (criticized) (10) Eventually, most members of the force

came to appreciate her accessibility and ~~are~~ *were* happy about her willingness

to listen to new ideas and approaches. _____

■ WRITING FIRST: Flashback

Look back at your response to the Writing First exercise on page 355. Check each sentence to make sure you have no illogical shifts from one tense to another. If you find an incorrect sentence, rewrite it below, correcting any illogical shifts in tense.

Answers will vary.

_____

_____

_____

_____

B   Avoiding Illogical Shifts in Person

Person is the form a pronoun takes to indicate who is speaking, spoken about, or spoken to.

Person

	Singular	**Plural**
First person	I	we
Second person	you	you
Third person	he, she, it	they

An **illogical shift in person** occurs when a writer shifts from one person to another for no apparent reason. Most errors occur in the second and third person.

ILLOGICAL SHIFT   The <u>hikers</u> were told that <u>you</u> had to stay on the trail. (third to second person)

REVISED   The <u>hikers</u> were told that <u>they</u> had to stay on the trail. (consistent use of third person)

ILLOGICAL SHIFT   <u>Anyone</u> can learn to cook if <u>you</u> practice. (third to second person)

REVISED   <u>You</u> can learn to cook if <u>you</u> practice. (consistent use of second person)

REVISED   <u>Anyone</u> can learn to cook if <u>he or she</u> practices. (consistent use of third person)

Teaching Tip
Point out that the first sentence is illogical because it begins by talking about hikers but then suddenly switches to talking about *you.*

● **Writing Tip**
Be careful not to use the pronoun *he* to refer to an indefinite pronoun antecedent, such as *anyone,* that could be either masculine or feminine. (See 28E.)

*For more on subject-verb
agreement, see Chapter 23.*

● **Writing Tip**

Be careful not to use *he* to
refer to a noun that could be
either masculine or femi-
nine. (See 20E.)

ON THE WEB
For more practice, visit
Exercise Central *at
<www.bedfordstmartins.com/
writingfirst>.*

◆ **PRACTICE 24-2**

The following sentences contain illogical shifts between the second person
and the third person. Edit each sentence so that it uses third-person pronouns consistently. Be sure to change the verb if necessary to make it agree
with the new subject.

Example: Before a person finds a job in the fashion industry, ~~you~~
he or she has
~~have~~ to have some experience.

(1) Young people who want a career in the fashion industry do not
they
always realize how hard ~~you~~ will have to work. (2) They think that work-
they
ing in the world of fashion will be glamorous and that ~~you~~ will quickly
he or she is,
make a fortune. (3) In reality, no matter how talented ~~you are~~, a recent
college graduate entering the industry is paid only about $22,000 a year.
(4) The manufacturers and retailers who employ new graduates expect
them   *they*
~~you~~ to work for three years or more at this salary before ~~you~~ are pro-
he or she is
moted. (5) A young designer may receive a big raise if ~~you are~~ very talented, but this is unusual. (6) New employees have to pay their dues, and
they   *their*
~~you~~ soon realize that most of ~~your~~ duties are tedious. (7) Employees may be
they color
excited to land a job as an assistant designer but then find that ~~you color~~
in designs that have already been drawn. (8) Other beginners in fashion
they   *their*
houses discover that ~~you~~ spend most of ~~your~~ time sewing or typing up
orders. (9) If a person is serious about working in the fashion industry, ~~you~~
he or she has
~~have~~ to be realistic. (10) For most newcomers to the industry, the ability
they   *their*
to do what ~~you~~ are told to do is more important than ~~your~~ artistic talent
or fashion sense.

■ WRITING FIRST: Flashback

Look back at your response to the Writing First exercise on page
355. Check each sentence to make sure there are no illogical shifts
in person. If you find an incorrect sentence, rewrite it on the lines
below, correcting any illogical shifts in person.

(continued on the following page)

(continued from the previous page)

Answers will vary.

_____

_____

_____

_____

C   Avoiding Illogical Shifts in Number

Number is the form a noun, pronoun, or verb takes to indicate whether it is singular (one) or plural (more than one).

Number

Singular	**Plural**
I	we
he, she	they
Fred	Fred and Ethel
man	men
an encyclopedia	encyclopedias
his, her	their
am, is, was	are, were

An **illogical shift in number** occurs when a writer shifts from singular to plural (or the other way around) for no apparent reason.

ILLOGICAL SHIFT IN NUMBER   Each <u>visitor</u> to the museum must check <u>their</u> cameras at the entrance. (singular to plural)

REVISED   Each <u>visitor</u> to the museum must check <u>his or her</u> camera at the entrance. (consistent singular)

REVISED   <u>Visitors</u> to the museum must check <u>their</u> cameras at the entrance. (consistent plural)

◆ PRACTICE 24-3

Edit the following sentences for illogical shifts from singular to plural. You can either change the singular element to the plural or change the plural element to the singular. Be sure to change the verb so it agrees with the new subject. If the sentence is correct, write *C* in the blank.

Examples:

Each attorney first makes ~~their~~ *his or her* opening speech. _____

~~A good juror~~ *Good jurors* takes their time in making their decision. _____

● **Writing Tip**

A pronoun must agree in number with the word it refers to (its antecedent). (See 28D.) A verb must agree in number with its subject. (See 23A.)

ON THE WEB
For more practice, visit **Exercise Central** *at* <www.bedfordstmartins.com/ writingfirst>.

Answers may vary.

(1) According to recent studies, a juror may have ~~their~~ *his or her* mind made up before the trial even begins. _____ (2) As attorneys offer their opening arguments, a juror may immediately decide whether ~~they think~~ *he or she thinks* the defendant is innocent or guilty. _____ (3) This unfounded conclusion often depends on which attorney makes ~~their~~ *his or her* initial description of the case the most dramatic. _____ (4) During the trial, that juror will pay attention only to evidence that corresponds to the decision ~~they have~~ *he or she has* already made. _____ (5) A ~~juror~~ *Jurors* with poor decision-making skills ~~is~~ *are* also not likely to listen to challenges to their opinions when the full jury comes together to deliberate. _____ (6) No matter how wrong they are, such a ~~juror argues~~ *jurors argue* their positions strongly and ~~urges~~ *urge* the strictest sentencing or the highest damage payments. _____ (7) These jurors believe their responsibility is to argue for their version of the truth rather than to weigh all the evidence and alternative possibilities. _*C*_ (8) Such a ~~juror~~ *jurors* will even make up their own evidence to support their case. _____ (9) For example, one juror argued that a man being tried for murder was acting in ~~their~~ *his* own defense because the victim was probably carrying a knife, but no knife was mentioned during the trial. _____ (10) Studies suggest that a ~~person~~ *people* who ~~jumps~~ *jump* to conclusions on a jury probably will not take their time when making other important decisions in life. _____

■ **WRITING FIRST: Flashback**

Look back at your response to the Writing First exercise on page 355. Find all the sentences in which you use the pronoun *they* or *their*. Check every sentence to make sure each of these pronouns refers to a plural noun or pronoun. If you find an incorrect sentence, rewrite it on the lines below, correcting any illogical shifts in number.

Answers will vary.

_____

_____

_____

_____

D Avoiding Illogical Shifts in Voice

When the subject of a sentence *performs* the action, the sentence is in the **active voice**. When the subject of a sentence *receives* the action, the sentence is in the **passive voice**.

ACTIVE VOICE   Nat Turner <u>organized</u> a slave rebellion in August 1831. (Subject *Nat Turner* performs the action.)

PASSIVE VOICE   A slave <u>rebellion</u> <u>was organized</u> by Nat Turner in 1831. (Subject *rebellion* receives the action.)

An **illogical shift in voice** occurs when a writer shifts from active to passive voice or from passive to active voice for no apparent reason.

ILLOGICAL SHIFT IN VOICE   J. D. Salinger <u>wrote</u> *The Catcher in the Rye,* and *Franny and Zooey* <u>was</u> also <u>written</u> by him. (active to passive)

REVISED   J. D. Salinger <u>wrote</u> *The Catcher in the Rye,* and he also <u>wrote</u> *Franny and Zooey.* (consistent voice)

ILLOGICAL SHIFT IN VOICE   Radium <u>was discovered</u> by Marie Curie, and Watson and Crick <u>described</u> the structure of DNA. (passive to active)

REVISED   Marie Curie <u>discovered</u> radium, and Watson and Crick <u>described</u> the structure of DNA. (consistent voice)

FOCUS Correcting Illogical Shifts in Voice

The active voice is stronger and more direct than the passive voice. For this reason, you should usually use the active voice in your college writing. To change a sentence from the passive to the active voice, determine who or what performs the action, and make this noun the subject of a new active voice sentence.

PASSIVE VOICE   The campus escort service <u>is used</u> by some of my friends. (*Some of my friends* performs the action.)

ACTIVE VOICE   Some of my friends <u>use</u> the campus escort service.

Use the passive voice in your college writing only when the action being performed is more important than the person performing it. To change a sentence from the active to the passive voice, determine who or what receives the action, and make this noun the subject of a new passive voice sentence.

ACTIVE VOICE   I <u>completed</u> the report on schedule. (*Report* receives the action.)

PASSIVE VOICE   The report <u>was completed</u> on schedule.

Teaching Tip

Tell students that to convert passive voice to active voice, they should ask themselves, "By whom was the action done?" and make the answer the subject of the sentence.

■ Computer Tip

To see if your writing overuses the passive voice, use the Search or Find command to look for *is, are, was,* and *were,* which often appear as part of passive voice verbs.

ON THE WEB
For more practice, visit
Exercise Central *at*
<www.bedfordstmartins.com/
writingfirst>.

◆ **PRACTICE 24-4**

The following sentences contain illogical shifts in voice. Revise each sentence by changing the underlined passive voice verb to the active voice.

Example
Several researchers are interested in leadership qualities, and a study of decision making <u>was conducted</u> by them recently.

Several researchers are interested in leadership qualities, *and they recently conducted a study of decision making.*

1. A local university funded the study, and the research team <u>was led</u> by Dr. Alicia Flynn.

   A local university funded the study, *and Dr. Alicia Flynn led the research team.*

ESL Tip
Have students label passive and active verbs before they make their corrections.

2. The researchers developed a series of questions about decision making, and then a hundred subjects <u>were interviewed</u> by them.

   The researchers developed a series of questions about decision making, *and then they interviewed a hundred subjects.*

3. Instinct alone <u>was relied on</u> by two-thirds of the subjects and only one-third used logical analysis.

   Two-thirds of the subjects relied on instinct alone and only one-third used logical analysis.

4. After the researchers completed the study, a report <u>was written</u> about their findings.

   After the researchers completed the study, *they wrote a report about their findings.*

5. The report <u>was read</u> by many experts, and most of them found the results surprising.

   Many experts read the report , and most of them found the results surprising.

■ WRITING FIRST: Flashback

Look back at your response to the Writing First exercise on page 355. Check each sentence to make sure there are no illogical shifts

(continued on the following page)

(continued from the previous page)

in voice. If you find an incorrect sentence, rewrite it on the lines below, correcting any illogical shifts in voice.

Answers will vary.

_____

_____

_____

_____

_____

■ WRITING FIRST: Revising and Editing

Look back at your response to the Writing First exercise on page 355. Revise any illogical shifts in tense, person, number, or voice by incorporating the changes and corrections you made in this chapter's Flashback exercises. When you have finished, do the same for another assignment you are currently working on.

CHAPTER REVIEW

◆ EDITING PRACTICE

Read the following student essay, into which illogical shifts in tense, person, number, and voice have been introduced. Edit the passage to eliminate the unnecessary shifts, making sure subjects and verbs agree. The first sentence has been edited for you.

Answers may vary.

The Mixing of Cultures

Because the United States is the melting pot of the
                    draws
world, it ~~drew~~ thousands of immigrants from Europe, Asia,

and Africa. Many of them come to the United States because
        want
they ~~wanted~~ to become Americans. At the same time, they

also want to preserve parts of their original cultures.

This conflict confuses many immigrants. Some immigrants
                                            they
think that in order to become American, ~~you~~ have to give

up ~~your~~ *their* ethnic identity. Others, however, realize that it is possible to become an American without losing ~~your~~ *their* ethnic identity. To me, in fact, this is the strength of the United States: as a Filipino American, I am able to be both Filipino and American. I know of no other country in the world where this ~~was~~ *is* true.

Many Filipino Americans are able to maintain their Filipino culture in the United States. For example, they decorate their houses to remind themselves of traditional houses in the Philippines. Filipinos also try to preserve their native language. Although ~~every Filipino speaks~~ *all Filipinos speak* English, Tagalog ~~is also spoken by them~~ *they also speak*--usually at home. On holidays, Filipinos observe the traditions of the Philippines. They sing Filipino folk songs, do traditional dances, and cook Filipino foods. ~~Everyone tries~~ *They all try* to visit their relatives in the Philippines as often as they can. In this way, a Filipino child can often experience ~~their~~ *his or her* ethnic culture firsthand.

A Filipino family that wants to hold on to ~~their~~ *its* ethnic background can enjoy life in America. Here, cultures mix and enrich one another. Each culture has something to offer America--~~their~~ *its* food, language, and traditions. At the same time, America ~~had~~ *has* something to offer each culture--economic opportunity, education, and freedom.

◆ COLLABORATIVE ACTIVITIES

1. On a separate sheet of paper, write five sentences that include shifts from present to past tense, some logical and some illogical. Exchange papers with another person in your group, and revise any incorrect sentences.

2. As a group, compose a test made up of five sentences containing illogical shifts in tense, person, number, and voice. Exchange tests with another group in the class. After you have taken their test, compare your answers with theirs.

3. As a group, choose five words from the list on the next page, and use each as the subject of a sentence. Make sure each sentence includes a pronoun that refers to the subject.

Example: Doctors must know their patients.

doctors	anything	a parent	everybody
someone	raccoons	anyone	a woman
workers	no one	children	everyone
something	a book	anybody	people

Make sure the sentences you have written do not include any illogical shifts in person or number.

☑ REVIEW CHECKLIST:
Illogical Shifts

- An illogical shift in tense occurs when a writer shifts from one tense to another for no apparent reason. (See 24A.)

- An illogical shift in person occurs when a writer shifts from one tense to another for no apparent reason. (See 24B.)

- An illogical shift in number occurs when a writer shifts from singular to plural (or the other way around) for no apparent reason. (See 24C.)

- An illogical shift in voice occurs when a writer shifts from active to passive or from passive to active for no apparent reason. (See 24D.)

Dangling and Misplaced Modifiers

■ WRITING FIRST

Look at the picture above, and then explain the process that is taking place.

A **modifier** is a word or word group that functions as an adjective or an adverb. Thus, a modifier describes or limits other words in a sentence. In order to avoid confusion, a modifier should be placed as close as possible to the word or words it modifies—ideally, directly before or directly after them. Many word groups that act as modifiers are introduced by present or past participles.

A   Identifying Present Participle Modifiers

A **present participle modifier** consists of the present participle form of the verb (the *-ing* form) along with the words it introduces. A present participle modifier provides information about a noun or pronoun that appears right before or right after it in the sentence.

PRESENT PARTICIPLE MODIFIER

Running through the streets, Archimedes could not wait to tell people what he had discovered.

PRESENT PARTICIPLE MODIFIER

Steve Jobs, using his garage as a workshop, invented the personal computer.

For more on present participles, see 18C.

FOCUS **Punctuating Sentences with Present Participle Modifiers**

Use commas to set off a present participle modifier from the rest of the sentence.

PRESENT PARTICIPLE MODIFIER

Remembering his working-class roots, Paul McCartney returned to Liverpool to give a concert.

PRESENT PARTICIPLE MODIFIER

Paul McCartney, remembering his working-class roots, returned to Liverpool to give a concert.

Teaching Tip
Review the formation of past participles, referring students to 27A and 27B.

◆ **PRACTICE 25-1**

Underline the present participle modifier in each of the following sentences. Draw an arrow from the modifier to the word or word group it modifies.

Example: Seeking social acceptance, some college students join fraternities or sororities.

(1) Tracing their origins to the late 1700s, social organizations for college students have a long history on many campuses. (2) Naming themselves with two or three Greek letters, these organizations are now generally called fraternities or sororities. (3) The earliest fraternities, focusing on academics, were essentially honor societies. (4) Recognizing scholarship in various fields, they provided an intellectual gathering place. (5) Evolving out of these, modern fraternities and sororities now are mainly social clubs. (6) Providing a variety of activities, many clubs encourage members to perform community service and raise money for

Teaching Tip
Remind students that they should avoid using the same opening strategy for every sentence. Refer them to 18B.

worthwhile causes. (7) Reflecting members' interests, fraternities and sororities also sponsor parties and opportunities for members to network with former graduates. (8) Potential members, wanting to get into such clubs, subject themselves to a period of hazing. (9) Taking various forms, such hazing may involve serious humiliation and even dangerous stunts. (10) Responding to abusive and violent hazing, many colleges have limited the fraternities and sororities allowed on campus.

■ WRITING FIRST: Flashback

Look back at your response to the Writing First exercise on page 366. Find any sentences that contain present participle modifiers, and write them on the lines below. (If you cannot find any, write two new sentences.) Check to make sure you have punctuated your sentences correctly.

Answers will vary.

_____

_____

_____

B Identifying Past Participle Modifiers

● **Writing Tip**

Not all past participles end in -*d* or -*ed*. Irregular verbs have irregular past participle forms—*known, cut,* and *written,* for example. (See 18C and 27B.)

A **past participle modifier** consists of the past participle form of the verb (usually ending in -*d* or -*ed*) along with the words it introduces. A past participle modifier provides information about a noun or a pronoun that is located next to it in the sentence.

PAST PARTICIPLE MODIFIER

Rejected by Hamlet, Ophelia goes mad and drowns herself.

PAST PARTICIPLE MODIFIER

Hamlet, written by William Shakespeare, is a tragedy.

FOCUS Punctuating Sentences with Past Participle Modifiers

Use commas to set off a past participle modifier from the rest of the sentence.

(continued on the following page)

For more on irregular past participles, see 27B.

(continued from the previous page)

PAST PARTICIPLE MODIFIER

Terrorized by bandits, the villagers decided to fight back.

PAST PARTICIPLE MODIFIER

The villagers, terrorized by bandits, decided to fight back.

◆ PRACTICE 25-2

Underline the past participle modifier in each of the following sentences.
Draw an arrow from each past participle modifier to the word or word
group it modifies.

> **Example:** Seized by the F.B.I., a fossilized *Tyrannosaurus rex* caused
> a great deal of controversy.

(1) The best-preserved fossil ever found, it was claimed by a South
Dakota dealer. (2) Uncovered several years ago, the fossil was found on
government land. (3) The fossil hunters, excited by the find, paid the
Indian owner of the land $5,000. (4) Known as "Sue," the fossil was
stored at a private museum in Hill City, South Dakota. (5) Supported by
previous rulings, a judge ordered the fossil turned over to the government. (6) Accompanied by federal agents, local law enforcement officials
impounded the fossil. (7) Questioned by the press, some fossil hunters
praised the verdict. (8) Others said that commercial dealers, hindered
by the verdict, would stop collecting fossils. (9) Shocked by the ruling,
the dealer appealed. (10) Believed to be the first legal civil action
involving a *Tyrannosaurus rex,* the case was settled in favor of the
dealer.

Teaching Tip
Have students write Practice
25-2 on the board so that
other students can check
their own work and ask
questions. Let students explain why they wrote what
they wrote.

■ WRITING FIRST: Flashback

Look back at your response to the Writing First exercise on page
366. Identify any sentences that contain past participle modifiers,
and write them on the lines below. (If you cannot find any, write
two new sentences.) Check to make sure you have punctuated your
sentences correctly.

(continued on the following page)

> *(continued from the previous page)*
>
> *Answers will vary.*
> _____
>
> _____
>
> _____
>
> _____

C Correcting Dangling Modifiers

● **Writing Tip**

Often a dangling modifier comes at the beginning of a sentence.

A **dangling modifier** "dangles" when it cannot logically describe any word or word group in the sentence.

Using my computer, the report was finished in two days.

In the sentence above, the present participle modifier *Using my computer* appears to refer to *the report*, but this makes no sense. (How can the report use a computer?) The word to which the modifier should logically refer is not included in the sentence. To correct this sentence, you need to supply the missing word.

Using my computer, I finished the report in two days.

Teaching Tip

Spend extra time explaining why these examples are incorrect. This concept is difficult for many students to grasp.

As in the example above, the easiest way to correct a dangling modifier is to supply a word or word group to which the dangling modifier can logically refer.

INCORRECT Moving the microscope's mirror, the light can be directed onto the slide. (Did the light move the mirror?)

CORRECT Moving the microscope's mirror, you can direct the light onto the slide.

INCORRECT Paid in advance, the furniture was delivered. (Was the furniture paid in advance?)

CORRECT Paid in advance, the movers delivered the furniture.

◆ PRACTICE 25-3

ON THE WEB
For more practice, visit
Exercise Central *at*
<www.bedfordstmartins.com/writingfirst>.

Rewrite the following sentences, which contain dangling modifiers, so that each modifier refers to a word or word group it can logically modify.

Example: Waiting inside, my bus passed by.

Waiting inside, I missed my bus.

Answers will vary.

1. Paid by the school, the books were sorted in the library.

_____

_____

2. Pushing on the brakes, my car would not stop for the red light.

_____

_____

3. Short of money, the trip was canceled.

_____

_____

4. Working overtime, his salary almost doubled.

_____

_____

5. Angered by the noise, the concert was called off.

_____

_____

6. Using the proper formula, the problem was easily solved.

_____

_____

7. Tired and hungry, the assignment was finished by midnight.

_____

_____

8. Sitting in the park, the pigeons were fed.

_____

_____

9. Staying in bed on Sunday, the newspaper was read from beginning to end.

_____

_____

10. Driving for a long time, my leg began to hurt.

_____

_____

◆ **PRACTICE 25-4**

Complete the following sentences by supplying words to which the modifiers can logically refer.

Example: Dancing with the man of her dreams, *she decided that it was time to wake up.*

Answers will vary.

1. Tired of studying, _____

_____

2. Sleeping late this morning, _____

_____

3. Seeing a strange light in the sky, _____

_____

4. Warned about driving in the snow, _____

_____

5. Alerted by a sound from outside, _____

_____

6. Sent to fight in a foreign land, _____

_____

7. Jumping over the rail and grabbing the chandelier, _____

_____

8. Told by her instructor to study more, _____

_____

9. Wanting desperately to go to the concert, _____

_____

10. Distrusting the advice he got from his friends, _____

_____

■ WRITING FIRST: Flashback

Look back at your response to the Writing First exercise on page 366. Do any of your sentences contain dangling modifiers? On the lines below, rewrite any sentence that contains a dangling modifier,

(continued on the following page)

(continued from the previous page)
and correct it by supplying a word or word group to which the
modifier can logically refer.

Answers will vary.

1. _____

_____

_____

2. _____

_____

_____

D   Correcting Misplaced Modifiers

A **misplaced modifier** is a modifier (often introduced by a present or
past participle) that has no clear relationship to the word it modifies
because it is too far from it. As a result, it appears to modify the
wrong word. Frequently, the result is confusing, illogical, or even silly. To
correct this problem, you need to place the modifier as close as possible
to the word or words it modifies—usually directly before or directly
after it.

Teaching Tip
To help students understand
the difference between a
dangling modifier and a misplaced modifier, point out
that in a misplaced modifier,
the word it modifies actually
appears in the sentence.

INCORRECT   Sarah fed the dog <u>wearing her pajamas</u>. (Was the dog
wearing Sarah's pajamas?)

CORRECT   <u>Wearing her pajamas</u>, Sarah fed the dog.

INCORRECT   <u>Dressed in a raincoat and boots</u>, I thought my son was
prepared for the storm. (Who was dressed in a raincoat
and boots?)

CORRECT   I thought my son, <u>dressed in a raincoat and boots</u>, was
prepared for the storm.

Not all misplaced modifiers are participles. Prepositional phrases,
too, can modify other words in the sentence, and they must be placed carefully.

*For more on prepositional
phrases, see 15B.*

INCORRECT   At the wedding, she danced with the groom <u>in a
beautiful white gown</u>. (Was the groom wearing a white
gown?)

CORRECT   At the wedding, she danced <u>in a beautiful white gown</u>
with the groom.

Teaching Tip
Ask students to explain the
meaning of each sentence.

ESL Tip
Nonnative speakers may
have an especially hard time
with the placement of limiting modifiers. Consider giving these students additional
practice exercises.

ON THE WEB
For more practice, visit
Exercise Central *at*
<www.bedfordstmartins.com/
writingfirst>.

Teaching Tip
Respond to each sentence
humorously where possible;
for example, "My pizzas
prefer to sit."

FOCUS Misplaced Modifiers

Be especially careful when placing **limiting modifiers** such as
almost, even, hardly, just, nearly, only, and *simply.* Notice how the
meaning of the following sentences changes when the modifier *only*
is placed in different positions.

<u>Only</u> David could go to the movies yesterday.

David could <u>only</u> go to the movies yesterday.

David could go <u>only</u> to the movies yesterday.

David could go to the movies <u>only</u> yesterday.

◆ **PRACTICE 25-5**

Rewrite the following sentences, which contain misplaced modifiers, so
that each modifier clearly refers to the word it logically modifies.

Example: Mark ate a pizza standing in front of the refrigerator.

Standing in front of the refrigerator, Mark ate a pizza.

1. The cat broke the vase frightened by a noise.

   Frightened by a noise, the cat broke the vase.

2. Running across my bathroom ceiling, I saw two large, hairy bugs.

   I saw two large, hairy bugs running across my bathroom ceiling.

3. Lori looked at the man sitting in the chair with red hair.

   Lori looked at the man with red hair sitting in the chair.

4. *Titanic* is a film about a love affair directed by James Cameron.

   Titanic is a film directed by James Cameron about a love affair.

5. With their deadly venom, people are sometimes killed by snakes.

   People are sometimes killed by snakes with their deadly venom.

6. *Pudd'nhead Wilson* is a book about an exchange of identities by Mark Twain.

   Pudd'nhead Wilson by Mark Twain is a book about an exchange of identities.

   _____

7. I ran outside and saw eight tiny reindeer in my bathrobe.

   I ran outside in my bathrobe and saw eight tiny reindeer.

   _____

8. Barking all night, I listened to my neighbor's dog.

   I listened to my neighbor's dog barking all night.

   _____

9. The exterminator sprayed the insect wearing a mask.

   Wearing a mask, the exterminator sprayed the insect.

   _____

10. With a mysterious smile, Leonardo da Vinci painted the *Mona Lisa*.

    Leonardo da Vinci painted the Mona Lisa with a mysterious smile.

    _____

■ WRITING FIRST: Flashback

Look back at your response to the Writing First exercise on page 366. Do any sentences contain misplaced modifiers? On the lines below, rewrite any such sentences by placing the modifiers as close as possible to a word or word group they can logically modify.

1. *Answers will vary.* _____

   _____

2. _____

   _____

■ WRITING FIRST: Revising and Editing

Look back at your response to the Writing First exercise on page 366. Then, add two sentences, one with a present participle modifier and one with a past participle modifier. If you like, you

(continued on the following page)

> *(continued from the previous page)*
> can use the sentences you generated in the Flashback exercises on pages 368 and 369. Finally, check your work for any dangling or misplaced modifiers.

CHAPTER REVIEW

◆ EDITING PRACTICE

Read the following student essay, into which modification errors have been introduced. Rewrite sentences to correct dangling and misplaced modifiers. In some cases, you may have to supply a word or word group to which the modifier can logically refer. The first incorrect sentence has been corrected for you.
Answers may vary.

The ABCs of My Education

Born in New York City, *I spent* my early years ~~were spent~~ in the South Bronx. My parents worked hard but made just enough money to get by. Raised in this environment, *I saw* ~~there was~~ violence everywhere. I watched my friends get involved with gangs and drugs and ruin their lives. Concerned about me, *one of my parents* ~~I~~ walked *me* to school every day ~~with one of my parents.~~ *Believing that school was a safe place for me,* ~~They~~ took a lot of time out of their lives to see that I got an education, ~~believing that school was a safe place for me.~~ Getting older, ~~school was the place where~~ I stayed longer and longer *at school*. After a while, I started getting good grades, and my guidance counselor *, seeing my potential,* recommended me to the A Better Chance (A.B.C.) program, ~~seeing my potential.~~

The A.B.C. program is nationally acclaimed. Participating in the program, ~~the classes help~~ children with limited opportunities *take extra classes to* receive better academic support. *Based on my record,* I was able to go to Strath Haven High School in Pennsylvania, ~~based on my record.~~ Arriving at my new school, *I found* it ~~was~~ difficult ~~for me~~ to adjust. My teachers encouraged every student *in the program* to aim for college ~~in the program~~, and I was no exception. With the help of my teachers, my friends, and especially my parents, I began to excel. Graduating in the

top 20 percent of my class, *I felt* my dreams had come true.

The A.B.C. program helped me realize the importance of
a good education. I hope to return to the South Bronx, *Finished with my schooling,*
~~finished with my schooling,~~ to become a teacher. Teaching
in the Bronx, my students ~~will be shown~~ *I will show* the value of education. I will also tell them that they themselves can ~~only~~ *only*
choose to make something positive of their lives.

◆ COLLABORATIVE ACTIVITIES

1. Working in a group of five or six students, make a list of five present participle modifiers and five past participle modifiers. Exchange your list with another group, and complete one another's sentences.

   Examples:
   Typing as fast as he could, _____

   Typing as fast as he could, <u>John could not wait to finish writing his screenplay</u>, *The Tomato That Ate Cleveland*.

2. Working in a team of three students, compete with other teams to compose sentences that contain outrageous and confusing dangling or misplaced modifiers. As a class, correct the sentences. Then, vote on which group developed the most challenging sentences.

3. In a group of four or five students, find examples of confusing dangling and misplaced modifiers in magazines and newspapers. Rewrite the sentences, making sure each modifier is placed as close as possible to the word or word group it describes.

☑ REVIEW CHECKLIST:
Dangling and Misplaced Modifiers

   ▫ A present participle modifier consists of the present participle (the *-ing* form of the verb) along with the words it introduces. (See 25A.)

   ▫ A past participle modifier consists of the past participle form of the verb (usually ending in *-d* or *-ed*) along with the words it introduces. (See 25B.)

   ▫ Correct a dangling modifier by supplying a word or word group to which the dangling modifier can logically refer. (See 25C.)

   ▫ Correct a misplaced modifier by placing the modifier as close as possible to the word or word group it modifies. (See 25D.)

UNIT SIX

Understanding Basic Grammar

Verbs: Past Tense

Obituaries

June 23, 1988   *The St. James Times*

Edward J. DeRoo dies—writer, scholar, naturalist

Edward John DeRoo

Author and professor emeritus Edward John DeRoo of Head of the Harbor, Saint James, died of heart failure Monday, June 20, at University Hospital at Stony Brook. He was 65. Dr. DeRoo was a professor of communications at Nassau Community College until he retired two years ago following open heart surgery.

During his 23 years at the college, he taught TV and film production, mass media, and interpersonal communications, and was recipient of a state university fellowship grant for filmmaking.

He wrote five novels, which were published in the United States and England. They included *The Fires of Youth, The Young Wolves,* and *The Little Caesars.* In the 1960s he was also the weekly drama columnist for the *Long Island Post* and *The West Side News.*

Before coming to Long Island, he had taught at the University of New Mexico, Texas at El Paso, and the University of Southern California. While in California in the 1950s he had his own TV program, *The Halls of Science,* for five years, and also several small roles as an actor in Hollywood films.

In the late 1940s he had been a playwright, director, and actor with The Cleveland Playhouse. Four of his comedies saw local productions by the Salisbury Players in libraries in Nassau.

His degrees include a doctorate in education from Columbia, a master of fine arts from the Yale Drama School, master of arts from the University of Denver and bachelor of arts from the University of Rochester. He was a World War II veteran.

Since retirement he had returned to writing and was active in the Smithtown Writers Guild and Suffolk County's Taproots writing group. One of his short stories was recently purchased by the PEN syndicate affiliated with the National Endowment for the Arts. He was a Friend of the Arts at the State University at Stony Brook, and for many years was a linesman with the National Lawn Tennis Umpires Association. Under the auspices of the National Wildlife Federation, Dr. DeRoo and his wife created a certified wildlife habitat at their Head of the Harbor home.

Dr. DeRoo leaves his wife R. Deborah DeRoo, a son, Adrian of Riverdale, a daughter, Deborah of Montreal, and a stepdaughter, Andrea Kovacs of Manhattan.

Services were held at the St. James Funeral Home on Wednesday, June 22.

■ WRITING FIRST

Look at the newspaper obituary that is reproduced above, and then write your own obituary. (Refer to yourself by name or by *he* or *she.*) As you write, assume that you have led a long life and have achieved almost everything you hoped you would, and be sure to include the accomplishments for which you would most like to be remembered. Remember to use transitional words and phrases that clearly show the relationship of one event in your life to another.

Word Power

accomplishment something completed successfully; an achievement

longevity long life

objective a goal

● **Writing Tip**

Not all verbs ending in *-ed*
or *-d* are in the past tense.
Some are past participles.
(See 27A.)

ESL Tip

Verb tense is frequently a
challenge for nonnative
speakers. Check everything
they write, and have them
write often.

● **Writing Tip**

All regular verbs use the
same form for singular and
plural in the past tense: *I
cheered. They cheered.*

ON THE WEB

For more practice, visit
Exercise Central *at*
*<www.bedfordstmartins.com/
writingfirst>.*

A Understanding Regular Verbs in the Past Tense

Tense is the form a verb takes to show when an action or situation took
place. The **past tense** is the form a verb takes to show that an action
occurred in the past. **Regular verbs** form the past tense by adding either
-ed or *-d* to the **base form** of the verb (the present tense form of the verb
that is used with the pronoun *I*).

FOCUS **Regular Verbs in the Past Tense**

- Most regular verbs form the past tense by adding *-ed* to the base
  form of the verb.

  I <u>registered</u> for classes yesterday.

  Juan <u>walked</u> to the concert.

- Regular verbs that end in *-e* form the past tense by adding *-d*.

  Walt Disney <u>produced</u> short cartoons in 1928.

  Tisha <u>liked</u> to read romance novels.

- Regular verbs that end in *-y* form the past tense by changing the
  y to *i* and adding *-ed*.

  tr<u>y</u>   tr<u>ied</u>

  appl<u>y</u>   appl<u>ied</u>

◆ PRACTICE 26-1

Change the verbs in the following sentences to the past tense. Cross out the
present tense form of each underlined verb, and write the past tense form
above it.

> **Example:**   My grandparents ~~live~~ *lived* in a small town.

(1) My grandparents ~~own~~ *owned* a combination magazine stand and candy
store in downtown Madison. (2) They ~~stock~~ *stocked* about three hundred different magazines that ~~range~~ *ranged* in subject matter from health and fitness to
guns and ammo to angels and flying saucers. (3) Customers sometimes
~~browse~~ *browsed* for an hour or more. (4) As they ~~look~~ *looked* through the magazines,
they often ~~munch~~ *munched* on candy bars or ~~try~~ *tried* a soda. (5) When the candy bar
or soda ~~turns~~ *turned* out to be a customer's only purchase, my grandfather
~~wants~~ *wanted* to throw out the "library patron." (6) My grandmother, however,

recognized
~~recognizes~~ the importance of customer satisfaction. (7) She always
insisted
^
~~insists~~ that my grandfather be more patient. (8) My grandfather some-
^   *refused*
times ~~refuses~~ to listen to her. (9) He never actually ~~kicks~~ out a customer.
^   *kicked*
stormed
(10) Sometimes, though, he noisily ~~storms~~ out of the store, leaving my
^
grandmother to deal with the startled customer.

■ WRITING FIRST: Flashback

Look back at your response to the Writing First exercise on page
381. Underline the past tense verbs that end in *-ed* and *-d*. Then,
write them on the lines below.

Answers will vary. _____ _____ _____

_____ _____ _____

_____ _____ _____

_____

Teaching Tip
This Flashback works well
as a proofreading exercise. If
students have omitted necessary endings, they usually
recognize their errors.

B   Understanding Irregular Verbs in the Past Tense

Unlike regular verbs, whose past tense forms end in *-ed* or *-d*, **irregular
verbs** have irregular forms in the past tense. In fact, their past tense forms
may look very different from their present tense forms.

The following chart lists the base form and past tense form of many of
the most commonly used irregular verbs.

▼ **Student Voices**
*My spell checker doesn't
pick up verb tenses used
incorrectly, so I still have to
proofread.*
Doreen Queenan

■ **Computer Tip**
Use the Search or Find command to locate the irregular
verbs that give you the most
trouble.

ESL Tip
Ask students to give ex-
amples of irregular verbs
in their native languages.

Irregular Verbs in the Past Tense

Base Form	Past	Base Form	Past
awake	awoke	catch	caught
be	was, were	choose	chose
beat	beat	come	came
become	became	cost	cost
begin	began	cut	cut
bet	bet	dive	dove (dived)
bite	bit	do	did
blow	blew	draw	drew
break	broke	drink	drank
bring	brought	drive	drove
build	built	eat	ate
buy	bought	fall	fell

(continued on the following page)

ESL Tip
Irregular past tense verb
forms are challenging for
native speakers, but even
more so for nonnative ones.
Have students write sen-
tences using some of the
verbs in the chart.

(continued from the previous page)

Base Form	Past	Base Form	Past
feed	fed	rise	rose
feel	felt	run	ran
fight	fought	say	said
find	found	see	saw
fly	flew	sell	sold
forgive	forgave	send	sent
freeze	froze	set	set
get	got	shake	shook
give	gave	shine	shone (shined)
go (goes)	went	sing	sang
grow	grew	sit	sat
have	had	sleep	slept
hear	heard	speak	spoke
hide	hid	spend	spent
hold	held	spring	sprang
hurt	hurt	stand	stood
keep	kept	steal	stole
know	knew	stick	stuck
lay (to place)	laid	sting	stung
lead	led	swear	swore
leave	left	swim	swam
let	let	take	took
lie (to recline)	lay	teach	taught
light	lit	tear	tore
lose	lost	tell	told
make	made	think	thought
meet	met	throw	threw
pay	paid	understand	understood
quit	quit	wake	woke
read	read	wear	wore
ride	rode	win	won
ring	rang	write	wrote

ON THE WEB
For more practice, visit
Exercise Central *at*
*<www.bedfordstmartins.com/
writingfirst>.*

◆ PRACTICE 26-2

In the following sentences, fill in the correct past tense form of the irregular verb in parentheses. Use the chart that begins on the preceding page to help you find the correct irregular verb form. If you do not find a verb on the chart, look it up in the dictionary.

Example: They _____*said*_____ (say) it couldn't be done.

(1) At the world championship games played in Tokyo in 1991, long-jumper Mike Powell _____*broke*_____ (break) the longest-standing record in track and field. (2) His leap of twenty-nine feet, four and one-half inches _____*brought*_____ (bring) him worldwide attention. (3) He also _____*beat*_____

(beat) his great rival, Olympic gold-medalist Carl Lewis. (4) The next year, competing against Lewis in the 1992 Olympics, Powell _____swore_____ (swear) to himself that he would take the gold. (5) Lewis, however, _____let_____ (let) it be known that he _____felt_____ (feel) he could overtake Powell's record during the games. (6) Lewis _____made_____ (make) a valiant attempt, but he still _____fell_____ (fall) short of Powell's record. (7) Even so, Lewis's winning jump _____kept_____ (keep) Powell from achieving a gold medal; he _____took_____ (take) home a silver medal instead. (8) At the Atlanta Olympics in 1996, things _____went_____ (go) even worse for Powell. (9) He _____hurt_____ (hurt) his groin and in his final jump _____lost_____ (lose) his balance and ended up flat on his face. (10) Again, Carl Lewis _____won_____ (win) the gold medal, his fourth in the long-jump. (11) Mike Powell _____left_____ (leave) the Atlanta Olympics without a single medal; still, he _____came_____ (come) away with his world record intact. (12) In fact, as of 2001, Mike Powell still _____held_____ (hold) the world record for the longest jump.

■ WRITING FIRST: Flashback

Look back at your response to the Writing First exercise on page 381. Circle each irregular past tense verb you find. Then, write each one in the column on the left. In the column on the right, write the verb's base form. (If necessary, consult the list of irregular verbs on pages 383–384 or a dictionary.)

Past Tense	Base Form
Answers will vary.	

● **Writing Tip**

Be is the only verb in English with more than one past tense form. For detailed information about subject-verb agreement with *be*, see 23B.

Teaching Tip

Challenge students to identify another verb as irregular as *be*. Explain that *be* is the most irregular verb in the English language.

ON THE WEB

For more practice, visit **Exercise Central** *at <www.bedfordstmartins.com/writingfirst>.*

ESL Tip

Point out that the verb *be* is irregular in many languages. Ask students to tell the class how *be* is conjugated in their native language.

C   **Problem Verbs in the Past Tense: *Be***

The irregular verb *be* can be especially troublesome because it has two different past tense forms—*was* and *were*.

Carlo <u>was</u> interested in becoming a city planner. (singular)

They <u>were</u> happy to help out at the school. (plural)

Past Tense Forms of the Verb Be

	Singular	**Plural**
First person	I <u>was</u> tired.	We <u>were</u> tired.
Second person	You <u>were</u> tired.	You <u>were</u> tired.
Third person	He <u>was</u> tired.	
	She <u>was</u> tired.	They <u>were</u> tired.
	It <u>was</u> tired.	
	The man <u>was</u> tired.	Frank and Billy <u>were</u> tired.

◆ **PRACTICE 26-3**

Edit the following passage for errors in the use of the verb *be*. Cross out any underlined verbs that are incorrect, and write the correct forms above them. If a verb form is correct, label it *C*.

    Example: Until recently, there <u>was</u> *[were]* no well-known Korean-American comics.

(1) Korean-American comic Margaret Cho <u>was</u> *[C]* one of the first people of Asian descent to achieve success in stand-up comedy. (2) She <u>were</u> *[was]* only sixteen when she began to perform her act. (3) Her parents <u>was</u> *[were]* quite conservative, and they <u>were</u> *[C]* opposed to her career choice. (4) Cho <u>was</u> *[C]* not to be stopped, though. (5) Even when an agent refused to sign her as a client because he said no Asians <u>was</u> *[were]* going to make it in stand-up comedy, Cho did not back down. (6) She <u>were</u> *[was]* an immediate hit on college campuses, where her comic routines <u>was</u> *[were]* very popular. (7) Variety show hosts <u>were</u> *[C]* quick to book her, and she <u>was</u> *[C]* soon cast in her own television series, *All-American Girl*. (8) The program <u>were</u> *[was]* cancelled after only one season, but Cho's fans <u>was</u> *[were]* still eager to see her. (9) Her one-woman show, called "I'm the One That I Want," <u>were</u> *[was]* a sell-out all over the country, and it won numerous awards. (10) A filmed version of this

performance <u>was</u> also released. (11) "Notorious C.H.O.," her most recent

show, <u>were</u> similarly successful, and it ended with a sold-out show at

C (above "was")

was (above "were")

Carnegie Hall in New York City.

■ WRITING FIRST: Flashback

Look back at your response to the Writing First exercise on page 381. Find all the sentences in which you use the past tense of *be*. Copy two or three of these sentences on the lines below, and underline each subject of the verb *be*. Make sure you have used the correct form of the verb in each case.

1. *Answers will vary.* _____

_____

2. _____

_____

3. _____

_____

Teaching Tip
Use this exercise, along with the list of irregular past forms on pages 383–384, as a review.

D Problem Verbs in the Past Tense: *Can/Could* and *Will/Would*

The helping verbs *can/could* and *will/would* present problems because their past tense forms are sometimes confused with their present tense forms.

For more on helping verbs, see 15C.

Can/Could

Can, a present tense verb, means "is able to" or "are able to."

First-year students <u>can</u> apply for financial aid.

Could, the past tense of *can*, means "was able to" or "were able to."

Escape artist Harry Houdini claimed that he <u>could</u> escape from any prison.

Will/Would

Will, a present tense verb, talks about the future from a point in the present.

A solar eclipse <u>will</u> occur in ten months.

Would, the past tense of *will,* talks about the future from a point in the past.

I told him yesterday that I <u>would</u> think about it.

FOCUS **Will and Would**

Note that *will* is used with *can,* and *would* is used with *could.*

I <u>will</u> feed the cats if I <u>can</u> find their food.
I <u>would</u> feed the cats if I <u>could</u> find their food.

◆ **PRACTICE 26-4**

ON THE WEB
For more practice, visit
Exercise Central *at*
*<www.bedfordstmartins.com/
writingfirst>.*

Circle the appropriate helping verb from the choices in parentheses.

Example: Years ago, travel took so long that my grandfather (will/
(would)) rarely drive more than ten miles from home.

(1) Twenty years ago, it (can/(could)) take hours to travel across the state. (2) With the new highway, the trip now ((can)/could) take as little as an hour. (3) As people make the drive, they ((will)/would) be surprised. (4) Before I made the trip, I (will/(would)) not have believed the difference. (5) On the old highway, I (can/(could)) get stuck behind a truck on those winding, two-lane roads. (6) With the new highway, I ((can)/could) zip along on four lanes in each direction. (7) Because they were so low, those old roads (will/(would)) often be flooded. (8) The new highway ((will)/ would) never flood because it is elevated. (9) If they (can/(could)) go back to the old ways, some people would do so. (10) However, I ((will)/would) always try to adapt to progress and to change if I can.

■ WRITING FIRST: Flashback

Look back at your response to the Writing First exercise on page 381. On the following lines, add a few sentences that describe what you would have accomplished if you had had the chance. Be sure to use *could* and *would* in your sentences.

(continued on the following page)

(continued from the previous page)

Answers will vary.

_____

_____

_____

_____

_____

_____

_____

■ WRITING FIRST: Revising and Editing

Look back at your response to the Writing First exercise on page 381. Make sure you have used the correct past tense form for each of your verbs. If you have not, cross out the incorrect form, and write the proper past tense form of the verb above the line.

CHAPTER REVIEW

◆ EDITING PRACTICE

Read the following student essay, into which errors in past tense verb forms have been introduced. Decide whether each of the underlined past tense verbs is correct. If the verb is correct, write *C* above it. If it is not, cross out the verb, and write in the correct past tense form. The first sentence has been corrected for you. (If necessary, consult the list of irregular verbs on pages 383–384.)

Teaching Tip
This Editing Practice can be used as a sentence-combining exercise. Start by pointing out how many of the sentences currently have subject-verb beginnings.

Healing

The window seat ~~were~~ *was* our favorite place to sit. I piled comfortable pillows on the ledge and ~~spended~~ *spent* several minutes rearranging them. My friend and I ~~lied~~ *lay* on our backs and propped our feet on the wall. We <u>sat</u> *C* with our arms around our legs and ~~thinked~~ *thought* about the mysteries of life. We also stared at the people on the street below and

Teaching Tip
Refer students to 34E for more on using *lie* and *lay*.

wondered ~~wonder~~ who they *were* ~~was~~ and where they *were* ~~was~~ going. We imagined that they *could* ~~can~~ be millionaires, foreign spies, or ruthless drug smugglers. We believed that everyone except us *led* ~~leaded~~ wonderful and exciting lives.

I *C* heard a voice call my name. Reluctantly, I *stood* ~~standed~~ up, tearing myself away from my imaginary world. My dearest and oldest friend--my teddy bear--and I reentered the real world. I grabbed Teddy and *brought* ~~brung~~ him close to my chest. Together we *went* ~~go~~ into the cold sitting room, where twelve other girls *sat* ~~sit~~ around a table eating breakfast. None of them looked happy. In the unit for eating disorders, meals *were* ~~was~~ always tense. Nobody *wanted* ~~wants~~ to eat, but the nurses watched us until we *ate* ~~eated~~ every crumb. I *C* set Teddy on the chair beside me and stared gloomily at the food on our plate. I closed my eyes and *took* ~~taked~~ the first bite. I *felt* ~~feeled~~ the calories adding inches of ugly fat. Each swallow *was* ~~were~~ like a nail being ripped from my finger. At last, it *C* was over. I had survived breakfast.

Days passed slowly; each passing minute *C* was a triumph. I learned how to eat properly. I learned about other people's problems. I also learned that people loved me. Eventually, even Teddy stopped feeling sorry for me. I *began* ~~begun~~ to smile--and laugh. Sometimes, I even considered myself happy. My doctors challenged me--and, surprisingly, I *rose* ~~rised~~ to the occasion.

◆ COLLABORATIVE ACTIVITIES

1. Working in a group of three or four students, choose a famous living figure—an actor, a sports star, or a musician, for example—and brainstorm together to list details about this person's life. Then, working on your own, use the details to write a profile of the famous person.

2. Working in a group, list several contemporary problems that you think will be solved within ten or fifteen years. Each member of the group should then select a problem from the list and write a paragraph or two describing how the problem could be solved. As a group, arrange the paragraphs so that they form the body of an essay. Develop a thesis statement, write an introduction and a conclusion, and then revise the body paragraphs of the essay.

3. Form a group with three other students. What national or world events do you remember most vividly? Take ten minutes to list news events that you think have defined the last five years. On your own, write a short essay in which you discuss the significance of the three or four events that the members of your group agree were the most important.

✔ REVIEW CHECKLIST:
Verbs: Past Tense

■ The past tense is the form a verb takes to show that an action has occurred in the past. (See 26A.)

■ Regular verbs form the past tense by adding either *-ed* or *-d* to the present tense form of the verb. (See 26A.)

■ Irregular verbs have irregular forms in the past tense. (See 26B.)

■ *Be* has two different forms in the past tense—*was* and *were*. (See 26C.)

■ *Could* is the past tense of *can*. *Would* is the past tense of *will*. (See 26D.)

Teaching Tip
Have students write a paragraph using a certain number of past tense verbs from the list on pages 383–384.

Verbs: Past Participles

PREVIEW

In this chapter, you will learn

- to identify regular past participles (27A)

- to identify irregular past participles (27B)

- to use the present perfect tense (27C)

- to use the past perfect tense (27D)

- to use past participles as adjectives (27E)

Word Power

benefit something that promotes well-being

diversion something that distracts or relaxes the mind

■ WRITING FIRST

Look at the picture above. Then, write about an activity—a hobby or a sport, for example—that you have been involved in for a relatively long time. Begin by identifying the activity and stating why it has been important to you. Then, describe the activity, paying particular attention to what you have gained from it over the years.

A ▌ Identifying Regular Past Participles

Every verb has a past participle form. The **past participle** form of a regular verb is identical to its past tense form. Both are formed by adding *-d* or *-ed* to the **base form** of the verb (the present tense form of the verb used with *I*).

PAST TENSE
He <u>earned</u>.

PAST PARTICIPLE
He has <u>earned</u>.

Together with a **helping verb** (a form of the verb *have*), past participles form the present perfect and past perfect tenses.

                      HELPING VERB   PAST PARTICIPLE

PRESENT PERFECT   The government <u>has changed</u> its policy on illegal
TENSE   immigration.

                  HELPING VERB   PAST PARTICIPLE

PAST PERFECT   I <u>had finished</u> studying for the test by Tuesday.
TENSE

> ● **Writing Tip**
>
> Note that the helping verb changes its form to agree with the subject, but the past participle always has the same form: *I <u>have</u> earned*/*She <u>has</u> earned*.

For more on the present perfect and past perfect tenses, see 27C and 27D.

◆ **PRACTICE 27-1**

Fill in the correct past participle form of each verb in parentheses.

Example: Coffee prices have _____*dropped*_____ (drop) recently.

(1) Americans have _____*started*_____ (start) a coffee craze in the last fifteen years. (2) Since the early 1980s, more than ten thousand coffee bars have _____*opened*_____ (open) in the United States. (3) Many of these bars have _____*appeared*_____ (appear) in metropolitan areas. (4) However, they have _____*sprouted*_____ (sprout) in suburban malls and small college towns, too. (5) One chain alone has _____*expanded*_____ (expand) to more than four hundred outlets. (6) Americans have always _____*enjoyed*_____ (enjoy) coffee. (7) In fact, Americans have traditionally _____*consumed*_____ (consume) one-third of the world's yearly coffee production. (8) One survey has _____*estimated*_____ (estimate) that Americans drink 130 million cups a day. (9) Tastes have _____*changed*_____ (change), though. (10) Today's market has _____*broadened*_____ (broaden) to include cappuccino and latte.

ON THE WEB
For more practice, visit **Exercise Central** *at <www.bedfordstmartins.com/ writingfirst>.*

■ WRITING FIRST: Flashback

Look back at your response to the Writing First exercise on page 392. Identify each helping verb (a form of the verb *have*) that is followed by a regular past participle (ending in *-ed* or *-d*). Write both the helping verb and the past participle on the following lines.

(continued on the following page)

(continued from the previous page)

Helping Verb   Regular Past Participle

Answers will vary.

_____   _____

_____   _____

_____   _____

_____   _____

B Identifying Irregular Past Participles

Irregular verbs nearly always have irregular past participles. They do not
form the past participle by adding *-ed* or *-d* to the base form of the verb.

Base Form	Past Tense	Past Participle
choose	chose	chosen
buy	bought	bought
ride	rode	ridden

The following chart lists the base form, the past tense form, and the
past participle of the most commonly used irregular verbs.

Irregular Past Participles

Base Form	Past Tense	Past Participle
awake	awoke	awoken
be (am, are)	was (were)	been
beat	beat	beaten
become	became	become
begin	began	begun
bet	bet	bet
bite	bit	bitten
blow	blew	blown
break	broke	broken
bring	brought	brought
build	built	built
buy	bought	bought
catch	caught	caught
choose	chose	chosen
come	came	come
cost	cost	cost
cut	cut	cut

(continued on the following page)

(continued from the previous page)

Base Form	Past Tense	Past Participle
dive	dove, dived	dived
do	did	done
draw	drew	drawn
drink	drank	drunk
drive	drove	driven
eat	ate	eaten
fall	fell	fallen
feed	fed	fed
feel	felt	felt
fight	fought	fought
find	found	found
fly	flew	flown
forgive	forgave	forgiven
freeze	froze	frozen
get	got	got, gotten
give	gave	given
go	went	gone
grow	grew	grown
have	had	had
hear	heard	heard
hide	hid	hidden
hold	held	held
hurt	hurt	hurt
keep	kept	kept
know	knew	known
lay (to place)	laid	laid
lead	led	led
leave	left	left
let	let	let
lie (to recline)	lay	lain
light	lit	lit
lose	lost	lost
make	made	made
meet	met	met
pay	paid	paid
quit	quit	quit
read	read	read
ride	rode	ridden
ring	rang	rung
rise	rose	risen
run	ran	run
say	said	said
see	saw	seen
sell	sold	sold

(continued on the following page)

(continued from the previous page)

Base Form	Past Tense	Past Participle
send	sent	sent
set	set	set
shake	shook	shaken
shine	shone, shined	shone, shined
sing	sang	sung
sit	sat	sat
sleep	slept	slept
speak	spoke	spoken
spend	spent	spent
spring	sprang	sprung
stand	stood	stood
steal	stole	stolen
stick	stuck	stuck
sting	stung	stung
swear	swore	sworn
swim	swam	swum
take	took	taken
teach	taught	taught
tear	tore	torn
tell	told	told
think	thought	thought
throw	threw	thrown
understand	understood	understood
wake	woke, waked	woken, waked
wear	wore	worn
win	won	won
write	wrote	written

◆ **PRACTICE 27-2**

Fill in the correct past participle of the verb in parentheses. Refer to the chart above as needed. If you cannot find a particular verb on the chart, look it up in the dictionary.

Example: The network has _____*won*_____ (win) a loyal audience.

(1) Nick at Nite has _____*found*_____ (find) a receptive audience for old television programs. (2) The cable network Nickelodeon, which broadcasts children's programs during the day, has _____*caught*_____ (catch) on with adults at night. (3) It has _____*drawn*_____ (draw) viewers away from current network sitcoms to ones from the 1980s and earlier. (4) Many viewers have _____*known*_____ (know) and loved these

■ **Computer Tip**

For additional practice, use the Find or Search command to find all uses of *have, has,* and *had* in a piece of your own writing. See if the correct past participle form follows each helping verb.

ON THE WEB

For more practice, visit
Exercise Central *at*
<*www.bedfordstmartins.com/
writingfirst*>.

shows since they were children. (5) They feel this affection even if

they have not _____ *seen* _____ (see) the shows for years. (6) They have

_____ *run* _____ (run) the candy-making machine with Lucy, _____ *seen* _____

(see) Archie Bunker yell at his son-in-law, and _____ *kept* _____ (keep)

up with the antics of the Brady children. (7) As they have _____ *gotten* _____

(get) older, viewers have _____ *grown* _____ (grow) nostalgic for these

familiar characters. (8) Young viewers have _____ *had* _____ (have) a

chance to discover them for the first time. (9) Both older and younger

viewers have _____ *begun* _____ (begin) to appreciate the shows for their

old-fashioned humor. (10) Nick has also _____ *made* _____ (make) a

name for itself with its clever commercials and station breaks, which

imitate 1950s style.

◆ PRACTICE 27-3

Edit the following passage for errors in irregular past participles. Cross
out any underlined past participles that are incorrect, and write in the correct form above them. If the verb form is correct, label it *C*.

> **Example:** In recent years, some people have ~~standed~~ *stood* up against
> overseas sweatshops.

ESL Tip
After students have com-
pleted Practice 27-3, give
them a correct version of the
exercise. Have them copy
the correct paragraph and
then compare it with their
own version.

(1) The problem of U.S. manufacturers using overseas sweatshops

has ~~became~~ *become* controversial over the last few decades. (2) Manufacturers

have ~~sended~~ *sent* their goods to developing countries where employees work

under terrible conditions for very low wages. (3) Some companies, such

as Nike, have ~~came~~ *come* under fire for such practices, and celebrities who

lend their names to lines of clothing manufactured in sweatshops have

~~finded~~ *found* themselves severely criticized. (4) Many people have ~~went~~ *gone* as far

as to boycott products manufactured in overseas sweatshops. (5) Re-

cently, colleges have taken *C* heat for using overseas sweatshops that have

~~maked~~ *made* clothing and other items featuring school names. (6) Student pro-

testors have ~~sprang~~ *sprung* into action upon learning that their colleges have

~~selled~~ *sold* goods manufactured in overseas sweatshops. (7) They have ~~spoke~~ *spoken*

out against such practices, and schools have had *C* to respond. (8) While

Teaching Tip
Point out that words (such
as *not, also, even, always,
never,* and *hardly*) can come
between the helping verb
and the past participle.

manufacturers may have ~~losed~~ *lost* money by increasing wages for overseas

workers, they have ~~understanded~~ *understood* that this is the right thing to do.

(9) They have <u>made</u> *C* a promise to their customers that they will not

employ sweatshop labor. (10) Still, customers have not always ~~forgave~~ *forgiven*

the manufacturers' history of such practices.

■ WRITING FIRST: Flashback

Look back at your response to the Writing First exercise on page
392, and identify each form of the helping verb *have* that is
followed by an irregular past participle. Then, write both the helping verb and the irregular past participle below.

Helping Verb	*Irregular Past Participle*
Answers will vary.	

C Using the Present Perfect Tense

The past participle can be used to form different verb tenses. For example,
the past participle can be combined with the present tense forms of *have*
to form the **present perfect tense**.

The Present Perfect Tense
(have *or* has + *past participle*)

Singular	**Plural**
I <u>have gained.</u>	We <u>have gained.</u>
You <u>have gained.</u>	You <u>have gained.</u>
He <u>has gained.</u>	They <u>have gained.</u>
She <u>has gained.</u>	
It <u>has gained.</u>	

As you have already learned, the past tense is used to indicate an action that began and ended in the past. The present perfect tense has different uses.

Use the present perfect tense to indicate an action that began in the past and continues into the present.

PRESENT PERFECT   The <u>nurse</u> <u>has worked</u> at the Welsh Mountain clinic for two years. (The working began in the past and continues into the present.)

Also use the present perfect tense to indicate that an action has just occurred.

PRESENT PERFECT   I <u>have</u> just <u>eaten</u>. (The eating has just occurred.)

● **Writing Tip**
The words *just, now, already,* and *recently* show that an action has just occurred.

◆ PRACTICE 27-4

Circle the appropriate verb tense (past tense or present perfect) from the choices in parentheses.

ON THE WEB
For more practice, visit Exercise Central *at* <www.bedfordstmartins.com/ writingfirst>.

Example: My new kitten (began/(has begun)) to dominate the household already.

(1) I (was/(have been)) a cat addict all my life. (2) I ((got)/have gotten) my first cat when I was seven years old. (3) I ((named)/have named) him Tweetie after the little bird in the cartoons. (4) Since then, I (owned/(have owned)) many more felines. (5) At one point, I ((had)/have had) five cats at once. (6) Last year, one ((died)/has died). (7) My sister ((adopted)/has adopted) another when she got married. (8) Since then, I (took/(have taken)) care of the other three cats. (9) Through the years, my cats (gave/(have given)) me much pleasure but also a lot of aggravation. (10) Anyone who (raised/(has raised)) cats will understand what I mean.

◆ PRACTICE 27-5

Fill in the appropriate verb tense (past tense or present perfect) of the verb in parentheses.

Example: In 2000, many polls ___*predicted*___ (predict) the presidential election results inaccurately.

(1) Newspapers and magazines in America ___*have presented*___ (present) the results of public opinion polls since the mid-1900s. (2) Until the

early twentieth century, these polls _____*were*_____ (be) unscientific and their results far from accurate. (3) In the 1930s, however, George Horace Gallup _____*developed*_____ (develop) original techniques for polling. (4) Over the last sixty years, these methods _____*have achieved*_____ (achieve) considerable success in predicting elections. (5) Since its development, the Gallup poll _____*has become*_____ (become) the best known of all public opinion polls. (6) Such polls _____*have occupied*_____ (occupy) a larger and larger place in our public lives. (7) In recent years, however, some critics _____*have begun*_____ (begin) to argue against the extensive use of polls to measure public opinion.

■ **WRITING FIRST: Flashback**

Look back at your response to the Writing First exercise on page 392. Choose three sentences with past tense verbs, and rewrite them below, changing past tense to present perfect tense. How does your revision change the meaning of each sentence?

1. _*Answers will vary.*_____

_____

_____

2. _____

_____

_____

3. _____

_____

_____

D   Using the Past Perfect Tense

The past participle can also be used to form the **past perfect tense**, which consists of the past tense of *have* plus the past participle.

The Past Perfect Tense
(had + past participle)

Singular	**Plural**
I had returned.	We had returned.
You had returned.	You had returned.
He had returned.	They had returned.
She had returned.	
It had returned.	

Use the past perfect tense to show that an action occurred before another past action.

PAST PERFECT TENSE   PAST TENSE

Chief Sitting Bull <u>had fought</u> many battles before he <u>defeated</u> General Custer.

This sentence identifies two actions that happened in the past—the fighting done by Sitting Bull, and his defeat of Custer. The verb in the first part of the sentence (*had fought*) is in the past perfect tense. The verb in the second part of the sentence (*defeated*) is in the past tense. The use of the past perfect tense indicates that Sitting Bull's battles took place *before* he defeated Custer.

◆ PRACTICE 27-6

Circle the appropriate verb tense (present perfect or past perfect) from the choices in parentheses.

ON THE WEB
For more practice, visit Exercise Central *at* <www.bedfordstmartins.com/ writingfirst>.

Example: Although the children (have eaten/(had eaten)) dinner, they still had room for ice cream.

1. Ren wondered where he (has left/(had left)) his keys.

2. He now believes he ((has lost)/had lost) them.

3. The receptionist told the interviewer that the applicant (has arrived/ (had arrived)).

4. The interviewer says that she ((has waited)/had waited) for an hour.

5. The jury decided that the defendant (has lied/(had lied)) on the witness stand.

6. The jury members are still deliberating although they ((have been)/had been) in the jury room for three days.

7. By the time I reached the restaurant, I (have decided/~~had decided~~) to order a pepperoni pizza.

8. By the time my pizza is ready, I usually (~~have finished~~/had finished) my pinball game.

9. The movie (has been/~~had been~~) on only ten minutes when I turned it off.

10. This movie is excellent; I (~~have seen~~/had seen) it at least five times.

■ **WRITING FIRST: Flashback**

Look back at your response to the Flashback on page 400. Rewrite your three present perfect tense sentences on the following lines, this time changing them to the past perfect tense. How do your revisions change the meaning of each sentence?

1. _Answers will vary._ _____

_____

_____

2. _____

_____

_____

3. _____

_____

● **Writing Tip**

A linking verb—such as *seemed* or *looked*—connects a subject to the word that describes it. (See 15C.)

● **Writing Tip**

The **passive voice** is formed with the past participle and a form of the verb *to be: The article was written by my instructor.* Use the passive voice only when an action is more important than the person performing it. In all other cases, use the active voice: *My instructor wrote the article.* For more on changing a sentence from passive to active voice, see 24D.

E | **Using Past Participles as Adjectives**

In addition to functioning as a verb, the past participle can function as an adjective after a **linking verb**, as it does in the following sentences, where the past participle describes the subject.

Jason seemed <u>surprised</u>.

He looked <u>shocked</u>.

The past participle can also function as an adjective before a noun.

I cleaned up the <u>broken</u> glass.

The <u>exhausted</u> runner finally crossed the finish line.

◆ PRACTICE 27-7

Edit the following passage for errors in past participle forms used as adjectives. Cross out any underlined participles that are incorrect, and write the correct form above them. If the participle form is correct, label it *C*.

> *C*
> **Example:** College students are often <u>strapped</u> for cash.

(1) College students are often *surprised* <u>surprise</u> when they find *preapproved* <u>preapprove</u> applications for credit cards turning up in their mail. (2) Credit-card companies also recruit *C* <u>targeted</u> students through booths that are *located* <u>locate</u> near student unions and libraries. (3) The booths are *designed* <u>design</u> to attract new customers with offers of *inscribed* <u>inscribe</u> coffee mugs and tote bags. (4) Why have companies gone to all this effort to attract *C* <u>qualified</u> students?

(5) Most older Americans already have at least five credit cards that are *stuffed* <u>stuff</u> in their billfolds. (6) Banks and credit-card companies see younger college students as their major *C* <u>untapped</u> market. (7) According to experts, students are also a good credit risk because *concerned* <u>concern</u> parents may bail them out when they are not able to pay a bill. (8) Finally, people tend to feel *tied* <u>tie</u> to their first credit card. (9) Companies want to be the first card that is *acquired* <u>acquire</u> by a customer. (10) For this reason, it is a *C* <u>known</u> fact that credit-card companies target *uninformed* <u>uninform</u> college students.

Teaching Tip
Students often omit *-ed* endings in past participles because they do not pronounce them. Remind them that regular past participle forms end in *-d* or *-ed*.

Teaching Tip
Refer students to 29A for more on the use of adjectives as modifiers.

■ WRITING FIRST: Flashback

Look back at your response to the Writing First exercise on page 392. Choose three nouns you used in your writing, and list them in the right-hand column below. Then, think of a past participle that can modify each noun, and write the modifier in the left-hand column.

Past Participle   *Noun*

1. ___*Answers will vary.*___   _____

2. _____   _____

3. _____   _____

(continued on the following page)

(continued from the previous page)

Now, use each of these nouns and its past participle modifier in an original sentence.

1. *Answers will vary.* _____

_____

2. _____

_____

3. _____

_____

■ WRITING FIRST: Revising and Editing

Look back at your response to the Writing First exercise on page 392. Do you need to revise any sentences to add the correct present perfect and past perfect tense verb forms? If so, cross out the incorrect verb forms, and write your corrections above them. When you have finished, check the past participles and perfect tenses in another writing assignment on which you are currently working.

CHAPTER REVIEW

◆ **EDITING PRACTICE**

Read the following student essay, into which errors in the use of past participles and the perfect tenses have been introduced. Decide whether each of the underlined verbs or participles is correct. If it is correct, write *C* above it. If it is not, write in the correct verb form. The first error has been corrected for you.

Drug Testing in High Schools

In recent years, some high schools in the United
            begun
States have ~~began~~ to test their students for illegal drug
                                            taken
use. For a decade or more, student athletes have ~~took~~ drug
tests in order to participate in sporting events. In some
schools, however, the number of students now being tested

grown
has ~~growed~~ to include anyone who participates in extracur-

ricular activities, such as drama, choir, or band. Some
　　　　　　　　C　　*felt*
schools have even ~~feel~~ the need to test their entire stu-
　　　　　　　　　used
dent bodies. They have ~~use~~ such tests to suspend students
　　　　　tested
who have ~~test~~ positive as well as any student who has
　C　　　　　　　　　　　　　*caused*
refused to take the test. This practice has ~~cause~~ concern

on the part of some students, parents, and proponents of
　　　　　　　　　　　　　　led
civil liberties and has ~~lead~~ to significant controversy.

　　People who protest such universal student drug test-
　　　　fought　　　　　　　　　　　　　*argued*
ing have ~~fighted~~ the issue in court. They have ~~argue~~ that
　　　　　　　　　　　　　　　　done
testing all students, even those who have ~~did~~ nothing to
　　　　　　　　　　　　　　chosen
indicate drug use and who have ~~chose~~ not to participate in
　　　　　　　　　　　　　　　　　　　C
after-school activities, is unfair. The courts have tended
　　　　　　　　　　　　　　　　　set
to agree. In the case of a Texas school that had ~~setted~~ up

a policy of testing all students for drug use, a federal
　　　　　　　　　　　　had
judge decided the school ~~has~~ violated students' right to
　　　　　　made
privacy. Courts have ~~make~~ similar decisions in other cases.
　　　　　　　　　　　　　　expressed
Some school administrators have ~~express~~ disappointment with
　　　　　　　　　　　　sent
these legal decisions. They have ~~sended~~ out the message

that drug testing at school is an effective deterrent to

drug use among teenagers. In addition, many parents have
said
~~sayed~~ that they want their children to be tested for drugs
　　　　　　　　　　　　　　　　　　　C
at school. In general, however, students have been less

supportive of school drug testing. This issue will probably

continue to provoke debate for years to come.

◆ COLLABORATIVE ACTIVITIES

1. Exchange Writing First exercises with another student. Read each
   other's work, making sure that present perfect and past perfect tenses
   are used correctly.

2. Assume that you are a restaurant employee who has been nominated
   for the prestigious Employee of the Year Award. To win this award
   (along with a thousand-dollar prize), you have to explain in writing
   what you have done during the past year to deserve this honor. Write
   a letter to your supervisor and the awards committee. When you have
   finished, trade papers with another student, and edit his or her letter.

Teaching Tip
Collaborative Activity 2
works well for getting students involved in a classroom discussion.

Read all the letters to the class, and have the class decide which is the most convincing.

☑ REVIEW CHECKLIST:
Verbs: Past Participles

- The past participle of regular verbs is formed by adding -*ed* or -*d* to the base form. (See 27A.)

- Irregular verbs usually have irregular past participles. (See 27B.)

- The past participle can be used to form different verb tenses. For example, the past participle can be combined with the present tense forms of *have* to form the present perfect tense. It shows a continuing action, usually one that began in the past and continues into the present. (See 27C.)

- The past participle is also used to form the past perfect tense, which consists of the past tense of *have* plus the past participle. It describes an action that occurred before another past tense action. (See 27D.)

- The past participle can function as an adjective. (See 27E.)

Nouns and Pronouns

PREVIEW

In this chapter, you will learn

- to identify nouns (28A)

- to form plural nouns (28B)

- to identify pronouns (28C)

- to understand pronoun-antecedent agreement (28D)

- to solve special problems with pronoun-antecedent agreement (28E)

- to understand pronoun case (28F)

- to solve special problems with pronoun case (28G)

- to identify reflexive and intensive pronouns (28H)

■ WRITING FIRST

Look at the picture above, and then explain why you like a particular musician or group, television show, or movie. Assume your readers are not familiar with your subject.

A Identifying Nouns

A **noun** is a word that names a person *(singer, Jennifer Lopez)*, an animal *(dolphin, Flipper)*, a place *(downtown, Houston)*, an object *(game, Scrabble)*, or an idea *(happiness, Darwinism)*.

A **singular noun** names one thing. A **plural noun** names more than one thing.

407

28 B

For information on capitalizing proper nouns, see 33A.

FOCUS **Common and Proper Nouns**

Most nouns, called **common nouns**, begin with lowercase letters.

character   holiday

Some nouns, called **proper nouns**, name particular people, animals, places, objects, or events. A proper noun always begins with a capital letter.

Homer Simpson   Labor Day

B **Forming Plural Nouns**

Most nouns add *-s* to form plurals. Other nouns, whose singular forms end in *-s, -ss, -sh, -ch, -x,* or *-z,* add *-es* to form plurals. Some nouns that end in *-s* or *-z* double the *s* or *z* before adding *-es.*

Singular	Plural
street	streets
gas	gases
class	classes
bush	bushes
church	churches
fox	foxes
quiz	quizzes

ESL Tip

Briefly review subject-verb agreement. Remind students that if the subject ends in *-s,* the verb usually does not. Refer students to Chapter 23.

Irregular Noun Plurals

Some nouns form plurals in unusual ways.

■ Nouns whose plural forms are the same as their singular forms

Singular	Plural
a deer	a few deer
this species	these species
a television series	two television series

■ Nouns ending in *-f* or *-fe*

Singular	Plural
each half	both halves
my life	our lives
a lone thief	a gang of thieves

ESL Tip

Tell students that they can sometimes figure out whether a word is singular or plural by the word that introduces it. For example, *each* always introduces a singular noun, and *many* always introduces a plural noun. Refer students to 30E.

(continued on the following page)

(continued from the previous page)

Singular	Plural
one loaf	two loaves
the third shelf	several shelves

Familiar exceptions: roof (plural *roofs*), proof (plural *proofs*), belief (plural *beliefs*)

■ Nouns ending in *-y*

Singular	Plural
another baby	more babies
every worry	many worries

Note that when a vowel (*a, e, i, o, u*) comes before the *y*, the noun has a regular plural form: monkey (plural *monkeys*), day (plural *days*).

■ Hyphenated compound nouns

Singular	Plural
Lucia's sister-in-law	Lucia's two favorite sisters-in-law
a mother-to-be	twin mothers-to-be
the first runner-up	all the runners-up

■ Miscellaneous irregular plurals

Singular	Plural
that child	all children
a good man	a few good men
the woman	lots of women
my left foot	both feet
a wisdom tooth	my two front teeth
this bacterium	some bacteria

◆ PRACTICE 28-1

Next to each of the following singular nouns, write the plural form of the noun. Then, circle the plural forms of irregular nouns.

Examples: bottle ___*bottles*___   child ___(*children*)___

1. headache ___*headaches*___

2. life ___(*lives*)___

3. foot ___(*feet*)___

4. chain ___*chains*___

5. deer ___(*deer*)___

6. honey ___*honeys*___

7. bride-to-be ___(*brides-to-be*)___

8. woman ___(*women*)___

9. loaf ___(*loaves*)___

10. kiss ___*kisses*___

11. beach ___*beaches*___

12. duty ___(*duties*)___

● **Writing Tip**

When a noun has an irregular plural, the dictionary lists its plural form.

13. son-in-law _____ (sons-in-law)

14. species _____ (species)

15. wife _____ (wives)

16. city _____ (cities)

17. elf _____ (elves)

18. tooth _____ (teeth)

19. catalog _____ catalogs

20. patty _____ (patties)

◆ PRACTICE 28-2

Proofread the underlined nouns in the following paragraph, checking for correct singular or plural forms. If a correction needs to be made, cross out the noun and write the correct form above it. If the noun is correct, write *C* above it.

     Example: Many ~~studys~~ *studies* prove this.

     (1) I recently talked to some unmarried ~~friend~~ *friends* about what they look for in a person of the opposite sex. (2) Most of the ~~woman~~ *women* said that their ~~standardes~~ *standards* were the same whether they just wanted to date a ~~men~~ *man* for fun or to consider him as a potential mate. (3) Both just-for-fun dates and potential ~~husband-to-bes~~ *husbands-to-be* were considered real ~~catchs~~ *catches* if they had decent jobs, if they were considerate and honest, and if they had good ~~sensess~~ *senses* of humor. (4) My male buddies *C*, however, had different ~~ideaes~~ *ideas*. (5) They wanted dates *C* to be good-looking, to have outgoing ~~personalitys,~~ *personalities,* and to have independent ~~lifes~~ *lives* of their own. (6) Potential ~~wifes,~~ *wives,* on the other hand, should not be too attractive to other ~~mens,~~ *men,* should be homebodies, and should see themselves not as independent but as ~~halfes~~ *halves* of a whole. (7) Sometimes I think the two ~~sexs~~ *sexes* are different ~~specieses.~~ *species.*

Teaching Tip
The content of Practice 28-2 can stimulate lively class discussion. If this is the case, you might decide to teach John Gray's "Men Are from Mars, Women Are from Venus" at this point. (See 36F.)

Teaching Tip
Review the use of comparison and contrast as a strategy for paragraph development. Refer students to Chapter 8.

■ WRITING FIRST: Flashback

Look back at your response to the Writing First exercise on page 407. Circle each noun. Write any plural nouns on the lines below, and circle any irregular plurals.

Answers will vary. _____ _____ _____

_____ _____ _____ _____

C Identifying Pronouns

A **pronoun** is a word that refers to or takes the place of a noun or another pronoun.

For lists of pronouns, see 28E, 28F, and 28H.

> Michelle was really excited. She had finally found a job that made her happy. (*She* refers to *Michelle; her* refers to *she.*)

Without pronouns, your sentences would be tedious because you would have to repeat the same nouns over and over again.

> Michelle was really excited. Michelle had finally found a job that made Michelle happy.

Pronouns, like nouns, can be singular or plural. The pronouns *I, he, she,* and *it* are always singular and take the place of singular nouns or pronouns.

> Geoff left his jacket at work, so he went back to get it before it could be stolen. (*He* refers to *Geoff; it* refers to *it.*)

The pronouns *we* and *they* are always plural and take the place of plural nouns or pronouns.

> Jessie and Dan got up early, but they still missed their train. (*They* refers to *Jessie and Dan; their* refers to *they.*)

The pronoun *you* can be either singular or plural.

> When the volunteers met the mayor, they said, "We really admire you." The mayor replied, "I admire you, too."

◆ PRACTICE 28-3

In the following sentences, fill in each blank with an appropriate pronoun.

Example: <u>I</u> like to be direct with my friends.

(1) <u>I</u> pride myself on always being honest. (2) My father used to tell me that honesty is the best policy, and <u>he</u> was right. (3) Sometimes my honesty hurts my friends' feelings, and <u>they</u> tell me that <u>I</u> am being rude to them. (4) <u>I</u> answer them by saying that <u>we</u> all need to hear the honest truth about ourselves sometimes. (5) My friend Linda understands my point, and <u>she</u> is always eager to let me hear the honest truth about myself whenever <u>I</u> have made a comment about her. (6) She tells me, "If <u>you</u> are going to dish <u>it</u> out, then <u>you</u> had better learn to take <u>it</u> yourself." (7) It's true that if her comment is really strong, <u>it</u> can upset me for a day or two. (8) But then <u>I</u>

● **Writing Tip**
Too many pronouns can make a paragraph monotonous, especially when pronouns begin several sentences in a row. Vary your sentence openings. (See 18B.)

remember that it's only Linda's opinion, and _she_ is never right about anything.

■ WRITING FIRST: Flashback

Look back at your response to the Writing First exercise on page 407. In the column on the left, list all the pronouns (*I, he, she, it, we, you, they*) you used. In the column on the right, list the noun or pronoun each pronoun replaces.

Pronoun	*Noun*
Answers will vary.	

D   **Understanding Pronoun-Antecedent Agreement**

The word that a pronoun refers to is called the pronoun's **antecedent**. In the following sentence, the noun *leaf* is the antecedent of the pronoun *it*.

The leaf turned yellow, but i̲t̲ did not fall.

A pronoun must always agree in **number** with its antecedent. If an antecedent is singular, as it is in the sentence above, the pronoun must be singular. If the antecedent is plural, as it is in the sentence below, the pronoun must also be plural.

The leaves turned yellow, but t̲h̲e̲y̲ did not fall.

Pronouns must also agree with their antecedents in **gender**. If an antecedent is feminine, the pronoun that refers to it must also be feminine.

Melissa passed h̲e̲r̲ driver's exam with flying colors.

If an antecedent is masculine, the pronoun that refers to it must be masculine.

Matt wondered what courses he should take.

If an antecedent is neuter (that is, neither masculine nor feminine), the pronoun that refers to it must also be neuter.

Lee's car broke down, but she refused to fix it again.

FOCUS **Vague Pronoun References**

A pronoun should always refer to a specific antecedent.

VAGUE   On the evening news, they said a baseball strike was inevitable.

REVISED   On the evening news, the sportscaster said a baseball strike was inevitable.

◆ **PRACTICE 28-4**

In the following sentences, circle the antecedent of each underlined pronoun. Then, draw an arrow from the pronoun to the antecedent.

Example: College students today often fear they will be the victims of crime on campus.

(1) Few campuses are as safe as they should be, experts say. (2) However, crime on most campuses is probably no worse that it is in any other community. (3) Still, students have a right to know how safe their campuses are. (4) My friend Joyce never sets foot on campus without her can of Mace. (5) Joyce believes she must be prepared for the worst. (6) Her boyfriend attended a self-defense program that he said was very helpful. (7) My friends do not let fear of crime keep them from enjoying the college experience. (8) We know that our school is doing all it can to provide a safe environment.

ON THE WEB
For more practice, visit
Exercise Central *at*
*<www.bedfordstmartins.com/
writingfirst>.*

PRACTICE 28-5

Fill in each blank in the following passage with an appropriate pronoun.

Example: Multiplexes are springing up everywhere; sometimes

they are replacing drive-ins.

(1) Drive-in movie theaters used to be common in the United States, but now _they_ are fairly rare. (2) In 1958, there were more than four thousand drive-ins across the country, but _they_ have been reduced to fewer than nine hundred today. (3) One of the most amazing is the Thunderbird Drive-In in Ft. Lauderdale, Florida; _it_ has twelve different screens. (4) Owner Preston Henn says _it_ is the largest drive-in theater in the world. (5) _He_ opened the theater with only one screen in 1963. (6) _He_ also opened a flea market on the property. (7) _It_ is now one of the largest flea markets in the state, with over two thousand vendors. (8) The vendors think _they_ are getting a good deal, and so do moviegoers.

■ WRITING FIRST: Flashback

Look back at your response to the Writing First exercise on page 407. Underline each pronoun in your paragraph, circle its antecedent, and draw an arrow from each pronoun to its antecedent. Do all your pronouns agree with their antecedents? If not, correct your pronouns.

| E | **Solving Special Problems with Pronoun-Antecedent Agreement** |

Certain situations present special problems with pronoun-antecedent agreement.

Compound Antecedents

A **compound antecedent** consists of two or more words connected by *and* or *or*. Compound antecedents connected by *and* are plural, and they are used with plural pronouns.

> During World War II, Belgium and France tried to protect their borders.

For information on subject-verb agreement with compound subjects, see 23A.

Compound antecedents connected by *or* may take a singular or a plural pronoun. When both elements of a compound antecedent connected by *or* are singular, use a singular pronoun to refer to the compound antecedent.

Either a dog or a cat must have put its paw in the frosting.

When both elements are plural, use a plural pronoun.

Are dogs or cats more loyal to their owners?

When one element of a compound antecedent connected by *or* is singular and one is plural, use the pronoun that agrees with the word closer to it.

Is it possible that European nations or Russia may send its [not *their*] troops?

Is it possible that Russia or European nations may send their [not *its*] troops?

◆ PRACTICE 28-6

In each of the following sentences, underline the compound antecedent and circle the connecting word *(and* or *or)*. Then, circle the appropriate pronoun in parentheses.

Example: Groucho and Harpo were younger than (his/their) brother Chico.

1. Larry and Curly were younger than (his/their) partner Moe.

2. Either Chip or Dale has a stripe down (his/their) back.

3. Most critics believe Laurel and Hardy did (his/their) best work in silent comedies.

4. Lucy and Ethel never seem to learn (her/their) lesson.

5. Either *MASH* or *The Fugitive* had the highest ratings for any television show in (its/their) final episode.

6. Was it Francis Ford Coppola or Martin Scorcese who achieved the triumph of (his/their) career with *The Godfather?*

7. Either film or videotapes lose (its/their) clarity over time.

8. Either Tower or Blockbuster is having (its/their) grand opening today.

9. The popcorn and soft drinks here are expensive for (its/their) size.

10. Do comedies or dramas have a greater impact on (its/their) audiences?

Indefinite Pronoun Antecedents

Some pronouns are called **indefinite pronouns** because they do not refer to any particular person or thing.

Most indefinite pronouns are singular.

28 E

● **Writing Tip**

Some indefinite pronouns
(such as *all, any, more, most,
none,* and *some*) can be either singular or plural. (*All*
is quiet. *All* were qualified.)

*For information on subject-
verb agreement with indefinite
pronouns, see 23D.*

ESL Tip

Remind students that singular indefinite pronouns do
not have plural forms.

Singular Indefinite Pronouns

another	everybody	no one
anybody	everyone	nothing
anyone	everything	one
anything	much	somebody
each	neither	someone
either	nobody	something

When an indefinite pronoun antecedent is singular, use a singular pronoun to refer to it.

> Everything was in <u>its</u> place. (*Everything* is singular, so it is used
> with the singular pronoun *its*.)

Some indefinite pronouns are plural.

Plural Indefinite Pronouns

both

few

many

others

several

When an indefinite pronoun antecedent is plural, use a plural pronoun to
refer to it.

> They all wanted to graduate early, but few received <u>their</u> diplomas
> in January. (*Few* is plural, so it is used with the plural pronoun
> *their*.)

▼ **Student Voices**
*It's hard to remember not to
write things like "Everyone
finished their homework."*
Michael McManus

FOCUS *His or Her* **with Singular Indefinite Pronouns**

Even though the indefinite pronouns *anybody, anyone, everybody,
everyone, somebody, someone,* and so on are singular, many people
use plural pronouns to refer to them.

> <u>Everyone</u> must hand in <u>their</u> completed work before 2 P.M.

This usage is widely accepted in spoken English. Nevertheless, indefinite pronouns like *everyone* are singular, and written English
requires a singular pronoun.

Although using the singular pronoun *his* to refer to *everyone* is
technically correct, doing so assumes that *everyone* refers to an individual who is male. Using *his or her* allows for the possibility that
the indefinite pronoun may refer to either a male or a female.

(continued on the following page)

(continued from the previous page)

Everyone must hand in his or her completed work before
2 P.M.

When used repeatedly, however, *he or she, him or her,* and *his or her* can create wordy or awkward sentences. Whenever possible, use plural forms.

All students must hand in their completed work before 2 P.M.

FOCUS   **Indefinite Pronouns with *Of***

Some singular indefinite pronouns may be used in phrases with *of* —*each of, either of, neither of,* or *one of,* for example. Even in such phrases, these indefinite pronoun antecedents are always singular and take singular pronouns.

Each of the routes has its [not *their*] own special challenges.

◆ PRACTICE 28-7

In the following sentences, first circle the indefinite pronoun. Then, circle the pronoun in parentheses that refers to the indefinite pronoun antecedent.

Example: (Each) of the artists will have ((his or her)/their) own exhibit.

1. (Either) of those paintings will be sold with ((its)/their) frame.

2. (Each) of the artist's brushes has ((its)/their) own use.

3. (Everything) in the room made ((its)/their) contribution to the whole design.

4. (Everyone) must remember to take ((his or her)/their) paint box.

5. (Neither) of my sisters wanted ((her)/their) picture displayed.

6. (Many) of the men brought (his/(their)) children to the exhibit.

7. (Several) of the colors must be mixed with (its/(their)) contrasting colors.

8. When (someone) compliments your work, be sure to tell ((him or her)/them) that it's for sale.

9. (Anyone) can improve ((his or her)/their) skills as an artist.

10. (Both) of these workrooms have (its/(their)) own advantages.

◆ **PRACTICE 28-8**

Edit the following sentences for errors in pronoun-antecedent agreement.
In some sentences, substitute *his or her* for *their* when the antecedent is
singular. In other sentences, replace the antecedent with a plural word.

Examples:

his or her
Everyone will be responsible for ~~their~~ own transportation.

All
~~Each of~~ the children took their books out of their backpacks.

Answers may vary.   *his or her*
1. Everyone has the right to ~~their~~ own opinion.

All students
2. ~~Everyone~~ can eat their lunch in the cafeteria.

his or her
3. Somebody forgot ~~their~~ backpack.

All
4. ~~Each of~~ the patients had their own rooms, with their own televisions

and their own private baths.

his or her
5. Someone in the store has left ~~their~~ car's lights on.

its
6. Simone keeps everything in her kitchen in ~~their~~ own little container.

his or her
7. Each of the applicants must have ~~their~~ driver's license.

8. Anybody who has ever juggled a job and children knows how valuable
his or her
~~their~~ free time can be.

its
9. Either of the coffeemakers comes with ~~their~~ own filter.

Most people wait
10. ~~Almost everyone waits~~ until the last minute to file their income tax

returns.

Collective Noun Antecedents

Collective nouns are words (like *band* and *team*) that name a group of
people or things but are singular. Because they are singular, collective
noun antecedents are used with singular pronouns.

The band played on, but <u>it</u> never played our song.

Frequently Used Collective Nouns			
army	club	gang	mob
association	committee	government	posse
band	company	group	team
class	family	jury	union

◆ PRACTICE 28-9

Circle the collective noun antecedent in the following sentences. Then, circle the correct pronoun in parentheses.

Example: The (jury) returned with ((its)/their) verdict.

1. The (company) provides ((its)/their) employees with very generous benefits.

2. Each (study group) is supposed to hand in ((its)/their) joint project by the end of the week.

3. Any (government) should be concerned for the welfare of ((its)/their) citizens.

4. The (Black Students Union) is sponsoring a party to celebrate ((its)/their) fifteenth anniversary.

5. Every (family) has ((its)/their) share of troubles.

6. An (army) is only as strong as the loyalty of ((its)/their) soldiers.

7. Even the best (team) has ((its)/their) off days.

8. The (orchestra) has just signed a contract to make ((its)/their) first record.

9. The (gang) is known for ((its)/their) violent initiation rites.

10. I wouldn't join any (club) that would have me as one of ((its)/their) members.

◆ PRACTICE 28-10

Edit the following passage for correct pronoun-antecedent agreement. First, identify the antecedent of each underlined pronoun. Then, cross out any pronoun that does not agree with its antecedent, and write the correct form above it. If the pronoun is correct, write *C* above it.

Example: Diversity is an important goal for the American corporation and ~~their~~ *its* workers.

(1) Diversity has come to corporate America. (2) Today, the average
company counts among ~~their~~ *its* employees many more women and members of minority groups than at any other time in our history. (3) The
U.S. government has established laws to protect *its* citizens from discrimination in employment. (4) Anyone who can prove discrimination
can usually see ~~their~~ *his or her* company fined. (5) For this reason, a corporation
and ~~their~~ *its* board will usually set diversity as one of ~~its~~ *their* goals. (6) Having a

> ● **Writing Tip**
>
> Note that some antecedents will be compounds, some will be indefinite pronouns, and some will be collective nouns.

diverse work force, however, does not mean that an organization has

truly met the needs of <u>its</u> employees. (7) While a Hispanic employee or

his or her

a female employee may now find that ~~their~~ opportunities are greater,

issues remain to be resolved. (8) Employees and management must first

their

understand ~~its~~ common goals. (9) Only then will a company be able to

implement the kinds of policies that will make it possible for each of

its

~~their~~ employees to work at <u>his or her</u> best. (10) For example, a vice presi-

his or her

dent or a mail-room clerk may need to take time off to see ~~their~~ family

through a crisis. (11) Company policy should allow such leave time to

his or her

anyone in the company, regardless of ~~their~~ position. In a truly diverse

work force, all workers must be treated fairly.

■ WRITING FIRST: Flashback

Look back at your response to the Writing First exercise on page 407.
Does your paragraph contain any antecedents that are compounds,
indefinite pronouns, or collective nouns? If so, list them below.

Compounds	*Indefinite Pronouns*	*Collective Nouns*
Answers will vary.		

Have you used the correct pronoun to refer to each of these antecedents? If not, correct your pronouns.

F | **Understanding Pronoun Case**

A **personal pronoun** refers to a particular person or thing. Personal pronouns change form according to the way they function in a sentence. Personal pronouns can be *subjective, objective,* or *possessive.*

When a pronoun functions as a sentence's subject, it is in the **subjective case**.

Finally, <u>she</u> realized that dreams could come true.

Personal Pronouns

Subjective Case	Objective Case	Possessive Case
I	me	my, mine
he	him	his
she	her	her, hers
it	it	its
we	us	our, ours
you	you	your, yours
they	them	their, theirs
who	whom	whose
whoever	whomever	

When a pronoun functions as an object, it is in the **objective case**.

If Joanna hurries, she can stop <u>him</u>. (The pronoun *him* is the direct object of the verb *can stop*.)

Professor Miller sent <u>us</u> information about his research. (The pronoun *us* is the indirect object of the verb *sent*.)

Marc threw the ball to <u>them</u>. (The pronoun *them* is the object of the preposition *to*.)

FOCUS **Objects**

A **direct object** is a noun or pronoun that receives the action of the verb.

DIRECT OBJECT
What did I send yesterday? I sent a <u>fax</u> yesterday.

DIRECT OBJECT
Whom will I call today? I'll call <u>him</u> today.

An **indirect object** is the noun or pronoun that tells to whom or for whom the verb's action was done.

INDIRECT OBJECT
To whom did I send a fax? I sent <u>Adam</u> a fax.

INDIRECT OBJECT
To whom did I give money? I gave <u>her</u> money.

A word or word group introduced by a preposition is called the **object of the preposition**. (See 15B.)

OBJECT OF PREPOSITION
From what did she run? She ran from the <u>fire</u>.

OBJECT OF PREPOSITION
For whom did Kelly work? Kelly worked for <u>them</u>.

When a pronoun shows ownership, it is in the **possessive case**.

> Hieu took his lunch to the meeting. (The pronoun *his* indicates that the lunch belongs to Hieu.)

> Debbie and Kim decided to take their lunches, too. (The pronoun *their* indicates that the lunches belong to Debbie and Kim.)

Teaching Tip
You may tell your students, if necessary, that they may consult the chart on page 421.

◆ PRACTICE 28-11

In the following passage, fill in the blank after each pronoun to indicate whether the pronoun is subjective (*S*), objective (*O*), or possessive (*P*).

Example: We _S_ voted for her _O_ in the election.

(1) I _S_ was never much interested in politics until last year when my _P_ older sister, Nadia, decided to run for a seat on the school board. (2) Nadia's decision surprised me _O_ because she _S_ had never shown much interest in politics either. (3) However, public education had become important to her _O_ because her _P_ son was in his _P_ second year of school. (4) Other family members supported Nadia's decision when they _S_ realized its _P_ importance to our _P_ community. (5) We _S_ all said to Nadia, "You _S_ go for your _P_ dream," and all of us _O_ were eager to join the campaign. (6) Nadia's opponent was a man who _S_ had served on the school board for two terms. (7) When Nadia challenged him _O_ to a debate, he _S_ declined, saying that my _P_ sister was no real competition. (8) After that, many people switched their _P_ support to Nadia because it _S_ seemed to them _O_ that whoever _S_ chose to run for election should be prepared to debate. (9) People whose _P_ minds were changed by this event were crucial to the outcome of the vote. (10) It was Nadia for whom _O_ the majority voted, and the victory was hers _P_.

■ WRITING FIRST: Flashback

Look back at your response to the Writing First exercise on page 407. On the following lines, list all the personal pronouns you have used, classifying them as subjective, objective, or possessive.

(continued on the following page)

(continued from the previous page)

Subjective	Objective	Possessive
_____	_____	_____
_____	_____	_____
_____	_____	_____

Have you used correct pronoun case in every sentence? Make any necessary corrections.

G   Solving Special Problems with Pronoun Case

Three special situations can cause problems when you are trying to determine which pronoun case to use. One problem occurs with pronouns *in compounds,* another occurs with pronouns *in comparisons,* and the third occurs with the pronouns *who* and *whom.*

Pronouns in Compounds

Sometimes a pronoun is linked to a noun or to another pronoun with *and* or *or* to form a **compound**.

> The teacher and I met for an hour.
>
> She and I had a good meeting.

To determine whether to use the subjective or objective case for a pronoun in a compound, follow the same rules that apply for a pronoun that is not part of a compound.

If the compound in which the pronoun appears is the sentence's subject, use the subjective case.

> Toby and I [not *me*] like jazz.
>
> He and I [not *me*] went to the movies.

If the compound in which the pronoun appears is the object of the verb or the object of a preposition, use the objective case.

> The school sent my father and me [not *I*] the financial aid forms.
>
> This fight is between her and me [not *I*].

● Writing Tip

The first-person pronoun always comes last in constructions like *Toby and I* and *My father and me.*

FOCUS   Choosing Pronouns in Compounds

To determine which pronoun case to use in a compound that joins a noun and a pronoun, rewrite the sentence with just the pronoun.

(continued on the following page)

Teaching Tip

Explain that the objective case is used with the contraction *let's: Let's you and me* [not *I*] *go swimming.* Remind students that *let's* includes the objective case pronoun *us.*

28 G

Teaching Tip
You may want to have students do Practice 28-12 (p. 425) before moving on to the next section.

> *(continued from the previous page)*
> Toby and [*I* or *me?*] like jazz.
>
> <u>I</u> like jazz. (not *Me like jazz*)
>
> Toby and <u>I</u> like jazz.

Pronouns in Comparisons

Writing Tip
To decide whether to use the subjective or objective form of a pronoun, add in brackets the words needed to complete the comparison.

Sometimes a pronoun appears after the word *than* or *as* in a **comparison**.

> John is luckier <u>than</u> <u>I</u>.
> The inheritance changed Raymond as much <u>as her</u>.

If the pronoun is a subject, use the subjective case.

> John is luckier <u>than I</u> [am].

If the pronoun is an object, use the objective case.

> The inheritance changed Raymond as much <u>as</u> [it changed] <u>her</u>.

FOCUS **Choosing Pronouns in Comparisons**

Sometimes the pronoun you use can change your sentence's meaning. For example, if you say, "I like Cheerios more than he," you mean that you like Cheerios more than the other person likes them.

> I like Cheerios more than he [does].

If, however, you say, "I like Cheerios more than him," you mean that you like Cheerios more than you like the other person.

> I like Cheerios more than [I like] him.

Teaching Tip
You may want to have students do Practice 28-13 (p. 425) before moving on to the next section.

The Pronouns *Who* and *Whom, Whoever* and *Whomever*

Writing Tip
In conversation, people often use *who* for both subjective case (*Who wrote that song?*) and objective case (*Who are you going with?*). In writing, always use *whom* for the objective case: *With whom are you going?*

To determine whether to use *who* or *whom* (or *whoever* or *whomever*), you need to know how the pronoun functions within the clause in which it appears.

When the pronoun is the subject of the clause, use *who* or *whoever*.

> I wonder <u>who</u> wrote that song. (*Who* is the subject of the clause *who wrote that song.*)

> I will vote for <u>whoever</u> supports the youth center. (*Whoever* is the subject of the clause *whoever supports the youth center.*)

When the pronoun is the object, use *whom* or *whomever.*

<u>Whom</u> do the police suspect? *(Whom is the direct object of the verb suspect.)*

I wonder <u>whom</u> the song is about. *(Whom is the object of the preposition about in the clause whom the song is about.)*

Vote for <u>whomever</u> you prefer. *(Whomever is the object of the verb prefer in the clause whomever you prefer.)*

FOCUS *Who* and *Whom*

To determine whether to use *who* or *whom,* try substituting another pronoun for *who* or *whom* in the clause. If you can substitute *he* or *she,* use *who;* if you can substitute *him* or *her,* use *whom.*

[<u>Who</u>/Whom] wrote a love song? <u>He</u> wrote a love song.

[Who/<u>Whom</u>] was the song about? The song was about <u>her.</u>

The same test will work for *whoever* and *whomever.*

◆ **PRACTICE 28-12**

In the following sentences, check the underlined pronouns, which are part of compound constructions, for correct subjective or objective case. If a correction needs to be made, cross out the pronoun and write the correct form above it. If the pronoun is correct, write *C* above it.

ON THE WEB
For more practice, visit
Exercise Central *at*
*<www.bedfordstmartins.com/
writingfirst>.*

                                                            C
Example: The reward was divided between my friend and <u>me</u>.

                                                        me
(1) The deejay at the wedding reception asked Dionne and <s>I</s> to do an

        She   *C*
encore. (2) <s>Her</s> and <u>I</u> enjoy singing together. (3) The first time we sang,

                        him   *She*   *I*
we really played up to <s>he</s> and the crowd. (4) <s>Her</s> and <s>me</s> talked with him

for a few minutes about what we should sing for the encore. (5) Dionne

        I   *C*
and <u>me</u> couldn't agree. (6) Dionne and <u>I</u> always have trouble deciding on

                                                    C   *me*
a song. (7) Finally, the deejay made the decision for <u>her</u> and <s>I</s>. (8) After

C   *C*   *They*
<u>she</u> and <u>I</u> finished, the guests went wild. (9) <s>Them</s> and the servers started

                                                        me
chanting, "More, more, more." (10) It was too much for Dionne and <s>I</s> to

believe.

◆ **PRACTICE 28-13**

Each of the following sentences includes a comparison with a pronoun following *than* or *as*. Write in each blank the correct form (subjective or objective) of the pronouns in parentheses. In brackets, add the word or words needed to complete the comparison.

Example: He's a better poker player than ___I [am]___ (I/me).

1. Denzel Washington is a better actor than ___she [is]___ (she/her).

2. They are such a mismatched couple. Most people like her much more than _[they like] him_ (he/him).

3. No one enjoys shopping more than ___she [does]___ (she/her).

4. My brother and our Aunt Cecile were very close. Her death affected him more than _[it affected] me_ (I/me).

5. Could any two people have a better relationship than ___we [have]___ (we/us)?

6. I'll admit my roommate drives better than ___I [drive]___ (I/me).

7. We at Steer Hut serve juicier steaks than _they [serve]_ (they/them).

8. Even if you are as old as ___I [am]___ (I/me), you're not as smart.

9. That jacket fits you better than _[it fits] me_ (I/me).

10. The Trumps may be richer than ___we [are]___ (we/us), but I'll bet they don't have as much fun.

◆ **PRACTICE 28-14**

Circle the correct form of *who* or *whom* (or *whoever* or *whomever*) in parentheses in each sentence.

Example: With (who/**whom**) did Rob collaborate?

1. The defense team learned (**who**/whom) was going to testify for the prosecution.

2. (Who/**Whom**) does she think she can find to be a witness?

3. I think the runner (**who**/whom) crosses the finish line first will be the winner.

4. They will argue their case to (**whoever**/whomever) will listen.

5. It will take time to decide (**who**/whom) the record holder is.

6. Take these forms to the clerk (who/whom) is at the front desk.

7. We will have to penalize (whoever/whomever) misses the first training session.

8. (Who/Whom) did Kobe take to the prom?

9. We saw the man (who/whom) fired the shots.

10. To (who/whom) am I speaking?

■ WRITING FIRST: Flashback

Look back at your response to the Writing First exercise on page 407. Can you find any sentences that contain a pronoun used in a compound or a comparison? If so, write the sentences here, making sure to use the appropriate pronoun case.

Answers will vary.

_____

_____

Circle any uses of *who* and *whom*. Have you used these pronouns correctly?

H Identifying Reflexive and Intensive Pronouns

Two special kinds of pronouns, *reflexive pronouns* and *intensive pronouns*, also always agree with their antecedents in person and number. Although the functions of the two kinds of pronouns are different, their forms are identical.

Reflexive and Intensive Pronouns

Singular Forms

Antecedent	*Reflexive or Intensive Pronoun*
I	myself
you	yourself
he	himself
she	herself
it	itself

Plural Forms

Antecedent	*Reflexive or Intensive Pronoun*
we	ourselves
you	yourselves
they	themselves

Reflexive Pronouns

Reflexive pronouns always end in *-self* (singular) or *-selves* (plural).
They indicate that people or things did something to themselves or for
themselves.

> Rosanna lost herself in the novel.

> You need to watch yourself when you mix those solutions.

> Mehul and Paul made themselves cold drinks.

Intensive Pronouns

Intensive pronouns also end in *-self* or *-selves*. However, they always appear directly after their antecedents, and they are used for emphasis.

> I myself have had some experience in sales and marketing.

> The victim himself collected the reward.

> They themselves were uncertain of the significance of their findings.

◆ PRACTICE 28-15

ON THE WEB
For more practice, visit
Exercise Central *at
<www.bedfordstmartins.com/
writingfirst>.*

Fill in the correct reflexive or intensive pronoun in each of the following
sentences.

Example: Sometimes I find _____myself_____ daydreaming in class.

1. The leaders gave _____themselves_____ more credit than they deserved.

2. That woman takes _____herself_____ too seriously.

3. The president _____himself_____ visited the AIDS patients.

4. I don't see _____myself_____ as a particularly funny person.

5. Have you _____yourself_____ ever actually seen an extraterrestrial?

6. We Americans pride_____ourselves_____ on our tolerance of diversity,
   but we can still be narrow-minded.

7. The bird settled _____itself_____ on my window ledge.

8. You should all give _____yourselves_____ a big pat on the back for a job
   well done.

9. Dorothy and the others hardly recognized _____themselves_____ after their
   makeovers.

10. I _____myself_____ am opposed to the legislation, but I know that
    others support it.

■ WRITING FIRST: Flashback

Look back at your response to the Writing First exercise on page 407. Have you used any reflexive or intensive pronouns? If so, list them here.

Reflexive pronouns: _____

Intensive pronouns: _____

If not, write two new sentences, one using a reflexive pronoun and one using an intensive pronoun.

■ WRITING FIRST: Revising and Editing

Look back at your response to the Writing First exercise on page 407. Change every singular noun to a plural noun and every plural noun to a singular noun. Then, edit your pronouns so singular pronouns refer to singular nouns and plural pronouns refer to plural nouns. You might also do this exercise with a piece of writing you did for another class.

CHAPTER REVIEW

◆ **EDITING PRACTICE**

Read the following student essay, into which noun and pronoun errors have been introduced. Check for errors in plural noun forms, pronoun case, and pronoun-antecedent agreement. Make any editing changes you think are necessary. The first sentence has been edited for you.

```
                    Going beyond Books
                        activities
        Extracurricular  activitys  can  be  just  as  important  for
                       s        ^
a  college  student  as  their  coursework.  Two  students  I
                    ^
myself  have  met  illustrate  the  truth  of  this  statement.  For
both
each  of  them,  their  extracurricular  activities  made  a  real
^
difference.
```

Julia joined our school's rifle team. As the only female on the team, she had some problems at first. Eventually, though, her teammates saw that she could shoot as well as ~~them,~~ *they,* and she began to feel comfortable with the group and ~~their~~ *its* routine. In her first year, her team won the state Junior Varsity championship, and judges ranked ~~them~~ *it* third in the region. In her second year, ~~her~~ *she* and the team placed sixth in the championship match. Julia found she enjoyed these triumphs. Like her teammates, she enjoyed rifle shooting because the sport requires precision and concentration as well as intense competition. It also gave ~~she~~ *her* and her teammates an occasional escape from ~~her~~ *their* studies. Most important, Julia had the opportunity to visit other campuses when she competed in away matches and to meet other competitors, some of ~~who~~ *whom* were also ~~woman.~~ *women.* For Julia, intercollegiate competition offered a lot of benefits.

Chris, a chemistry major, received similar benefits from his participation in the student chapter of the American Chemical Society (ACS). By the time he was a sophomore, he was president of our school's chapter. Serving in this office taught him how to handle leadership and responsibility. The organization's goal was to educate ~~their~~ *its* members about chemistry through seminars and visits to industry sites. ~~They~~ *It* also encouraged members to attend social functions with other chemistry majors and faculty. Chris was active in organizing all these events. Through the school's ACS chapter, ~~a student~~ *students* like Chris could increase their knowledge of chemistry beyond what their textbooks offered.

Many students believe courses are what school is all about, but Julia and Chris would disagree. For students like ~~they,~~ *them,* time spent on extracurricular activities can be as valuable as time spent in a classroom or library. Studying and extracurricular activities are two ~~halfs~~ *halves* of a whole educational experience.

◆ COLLABORATIVE ACTIVITIES

1. Working in a group, fill in the following chart, writing one noun on each line. If the noun is a proper noun, be sure to capitalize it.

Cars	Trees	Foods	Famous Couples	Cities
Answers will vary.				

Now, using as many of the nouns listed above as you can, write a one-paragraph news article that describes an imaginary event. Exchange your work with another group, and check the other group's article to be sure the correct pronoun form refers to each noun. Return the articles to their original groups for editing.

2. Working in a group, write a silly story that uses each of these nouns at least once: *Martians, eggplant, MTV, toupee, kangaroo, Iceland, bat, herd,* and *kayak.* Then, exchange stories with another group. After you have read the other group's story, edit it so that it includes all of the following pronouns: *it, its, itself, they, their, them, themselves.* Return the edited story to its authors. Finally, reread your group's story, and check to make sure pronoun-antecedent agreement is clear and correct.

✔ REVIEW CHECKLIST:
Nouns and Pronouns

- A noun is a word that names something. A singular noun names one thing; a plural noun names more than one thing. (See 28A.)

- Most nouns add -*s* to form plurals. Some nouns have irregular plural forms. (See 28B.)

- A pronoun is a word that takes the place of a noun or another pronoun. (See 28C.)

- The word a pronoun refers to is called the pronoun's antecedent. A pronoun and its antecedent must always agree in number and gender. (See 28D.)

(continued on the following page)

(continued from the previous page)

- Compound antecedents connected by *and* are plural and are used with plural pronouns. Compound antecedents connected by *or* may take singular or plural pronouns. (See 28E.)

- Most indefinite pronoun antecedents are singular and are used with singular pronouns; some are plural and are used with plural antecedents. (See 28E.)

- Collective noun antecedents are singular and must be used with singular pronouns. (See 28E.)

- Personal pronouns can be in the subjective, objective, or possessive case. (See 28F.)

- Pronouns present special problems when they are used in compounds and comparisons. The pronouns *who* and *whom* and *whoever* and *whomever* also cause problems. (See 28G.)

- Reflexive and intensive pronouns must agree with their antecedents in person and number. (See 28H.)

Adjectives and Adverbs

PREVIEW

In this chapter, you will learn

■ to understand the difference between adjectives and adverbs (29A)

■ to identify demonstrative adjectives (29A)

■ to form comparatives and superlatives of adjectives and adverbs (29B)

■ WRITING FIRST

What are the advantages and disadvantages of being educated at home by parents or other relatives instead of at school by professional teachers? Look at the picture above, and then discuss your opinions on this topic.

Word Power

tutor   a private instructor

extracurricular   outside the regular course of study

socialize   to make fit for companionship with others

cohort   a group united by common experiences

A   Identifying Adjectives and Adverbs

Adjectives and adverbs are words that modify—that is, describe or limit—other words. They help make sentences more specific and more interesting.

An **adjective** answers the question *What kind? Which one?* or *How many?* Adjectives modify nouns or pronouns.

433

● **Writing Tip**

Some adjectives, such as *Turkish,* are capitalized because they are formed from proper nouns. Proper nouns name particular people, places, and things. For more on proper nouns, see 28A.

The Turkish city of Istanbul spans two continents. *(Turkish modifies the noun city,* and *two* modifies the noun *continents.)*

It is fascinating because of its location and history. *(Fascinating modifies the pronoun it.)*

FOCUS **Demonstrative Adjectives**

Demonstrative adjectives—*this, that, these,* and *those*—do not describe other words. They simply identify particular nouns.

This and *that* identify singular nouns and pronouns.

> This encyclopedia is much more thorough and up-to-date than that one.

These and *those* identify plural nouns.

> These words and phrases are French, but those expressions are Creole.

An **adverb** answers the question *How? Why? When? Where?* or *To what extent?* Adverbs modify verbs, adjectives, or other adverbs.

Traffic moved steadily. *(Steadily* modifies the verb *moved.)*

Still, we were quite impatient. *(Quite* modifies the adjective *impatient.)*

Very slowly, we inched into the center lane. *(Very* modifies the adverb *slowly.)*

FOCUS **Distinguishing Adjectives from Adverbs**

Many adverbs are formed when *-ly* is added to an adjective form.

Adjective	*Adverb*
slow	slowly
nice	nicely
quick	quickly
real	really

(continued on the following page)

● **Writing Tip**

Some adjectives—*lovely, friendly,* and *lively,* for example—end in *-ly.* Do not mistake these words for adverbs.

(continued from the previous page)

ADJECTIVE Let me give you one quick reminder. (*Quick* modifies the noun *reminder.*)

ADVERB He quickly changed the subject. (*Quickly* modifies the verb *changed.*)

ADJECTIVE Tell me your real name. (*Real* modifies the noun *name.*)

ADVERB It was really rude of her to ignore me. (*Really* modifies the adjective *rude.*)

◆ PRACTICE 29-1

In the following sentences, circle the correct form (adjective or adverb) from the choices in parentheses.

ON THE WEB
For more practice, visit Exercise Central *at* <www.bedfordstmartins.com/ writingfirst>.

Example: Women who are (serious/seriously) walkers or runners need to wear athletic shoes that fit.

(1) Doctors have found that many athletic shoes are (poor/poorly) designed for women. (2) Women's athletic shoes are (actual/actually) just smaller versions of men's shoes. (3) Consequently, they cannot provide a (true/truly) comfortable fit. (4) Studies have shown that to get a shoe that fits (comfortable/comfortably) in the heel, most women must buy one that is too (tight/tightly) for the front of the foot. (5) This can have a (real/really) negative impact on athletic performance. (6) It can also cause (serious/seriously) pain and even physical deformity. (7) Some athletic shoe manufacturers have begun to market athletic shoes that are designed (specific/specifically) for women. (8) Experts say that women must become informed consumers and choose (careful/carefully) when they shop for athletic shoes. (9) One (important/importantly) piece of advice is to shop for shoes (immediate/immediately) after exercising or at the end of a work day, when the foot is at its largest. (10) Experts advise that athletic shoes should feel (comfortable/comfortably) from the moment they are tried on—or else be returned to the box.

Teaching Tip
Explain that a linking verb such as *feel* is followed by an adjective, not an adverb. Refer students to 15C.

FOCUS *Good* and *Well*

Be careful not to confuse *good* and *well*. Unlike regular adjectives, whose adverb form adds *-ly*, the adjective *good* is irregular. Its adverb form is *well*.

ADJECTIVE   Fred Astaire was a <u>good</u> dancer. (*Good* modifies the noun *dancer*.)

ADVERB   He danced especially <u>well</u> with Ginger Rogers. (*Well* modifies the verb *danced*.)

Always use *well* when you are describing a person's health.

He really didn't feel <u>well</u> [not *good*] after eating an entire pizza.

◆ PRACTICE 29-2

Circle the correct form (*good* or *well*) in the sentences below.

> **Example:** Eating (good/*well*) is part of (*good*/well) living.

(1) A particular food can sometimes be (*good*/well) for you in ways you might not expect. (2) For example, if you are feeling down and just not doing (good/*well*) emotionally, you might need a carbohydrate pick-me-up. (3) Some doctors recommend pasta, rice cakes, or pretzels as (*good*/well) sources of carbohydrates. (4) If you need to perform (good/*well*) mentally—on a test, for example—protein-rich foods may be helpful. (5) Three to four ounces of fish or chicken can be especially (*good*/well) for helping you remain alert. (6) Carbohydrates can be eaten with the protein, but you would do (good/*well*) to avoid overeating, which can make you drowsy. (7) Most people know that caffeine works (good/*well*) to help overcome drowsiness. (8) Caffeine can also be a (*good*/well) stimulant for helping one stay alert. (9) High-fat foods are also useful because they encourage the brain to produce endorphins, the same substances that make us feel so (*good*/well) when we are with someone we love. (10) However, the greatest amount of endorphins is produced in people who exercise regularly and eat (good/*well*).

■ **WRITING FIRST: Flashback**

Look back at your response to the Writing First exercise on page 433. Underline each adjective and adverb, and draw an arrow from each to the word it describes or identifies. Do all adjectives modify nouns or pronouns? Do all adverbs modify verbs, adjectives, or other adverbs? Have you used *good* and *well* correctly? On the lines below, revise any sentences that use adjectives or adverbs incorrectly.

Answers will vary.

<hr>

B   Understanding Comparatives and Superlatives

Sometimes an adjective or adverb describes something by comparing it to something else. The **comparative** form of an adjective or adverb compares two people or things. Adjectives and adverbs form the comparative with *-er* or *more*. The **superlative** form of an adjective or adverb compares more than two things. Adjectives and adverbs form the superlative with *-est* or *most*.

ADJECTIVES	This film is <u>dull</u> and <u>predictable</u>.
COMPARATIVE	The film I saw last week was even <u>duller</u> and <u>more predictable</u> than this one.
SUPERLATIVE	The film I saw last night was the <u>dullest</u> and <u>most predictable</u> one I've ever seen.
ADVERB	For a beginner, Jane did needlepoint <u>skillfully</u>.
COMPARATIVE	After she had watched the demonstration, Jane did needlepoint <u>more skillfully</u> than Rosie.
SUPERLATIVE	Of the twelve beginners, Jane did needlepoint the <u>most skillfully</u>.

● **Writing Tip**

Some adverbs—such as *very, somewhat, quite, extremely,* and *rather*—do not have comparative or superlative forms.

● **Writing Tip**

Demonstrative adjectives (*this, that, these,* and *those*) do not have comparative or superlative forms.

● **Writing Tip**

The adjective *unique* means "the only one." For this reason, it has no comparative or superlative form (*more unique* and *most unique* are incorrect).

Forming Comparatives and Superlatives

Adjectives

■ One-syllable adjectives generally form the comparative with *-er* and the superlative with *-est*.

great   greater   greatest

(continued on the following page)

(continued from the previous page)

■ Adjectives with two or more syllables form the comparative with *more* and the superlative with *most*.

> wonderful   more wonderful   most wonderful

> Exception: Two-syllable adjectives ending in *-y* add *-er* or *-est* after changing the *y* to an *i*.

> funny   funnier   funniest

Adverbs

■ All adverbs ending in *-ly* form the comparative with *more* and the superlative with *most*.

> efficiently   more efficiently   most efficiently

■ Some other adverbs form the comparative with *-er* and the superlative with *-est*.

> soon   sooner   soonest

FOCUS **Special Problems with Comparatives and Superlatives**

■ Never use both *-er* and *more* to form the comparative or both *-est* and *most* to form the superlative.

> Nothing could have been <u>more awful</u>. (not *more awfuller*)

> Space Mountain is the <u>most frightening</u> (not *most frighteningest*) ride at Disney World.

■ Never use the superlative when you are comparing only two things.

> This is the <u>more serious</u> (not *most serious*) of the two problems.

■ Never use the comparative when you are comparing more than two things.

> This is the <u>worst</u> (not *worse*) day of my life.

ON THE WEB

For more practice, visit
Exercise Central *at*
*<www.bedfordstmartins.com/
writingfirst>.*

Teaching Tip
Tell students that when they form comparatives, they should have only one ending with an *r* sound (not *more greater* or *more better*, for example).

◆ **PRACTICE 29-3**

Fill in the correct comparative form of the word supplied in parentheses.

Example: Children tend to be _____*noisier*_____ (noisy) than adults.

1. Traffic always moves ___*more slowly*___ (slow) during rush hour than late at night.

2. The weather report says temperatures will be ___*colder*___ (cold) tomorrow.

3. Some elderly people are ___*healthier*___ (healthy) than younger people.

4. It has been proven that pigs are ___*more intelligent*___ (intelligent) than dogs.

5. When someone asks you to repeat yourself, you usually answer ___*more loudly*___ (loud).

6. The ___*taller*___ (tall) the building, the more damage the earthquake caused.

7. They want to teach their son to be ___*more respectful*___ (respectful) of women than many young men are.

8. Las Vegas is ___*more famous*___ (famous) for its casinos than for its natural resources.

9. The WaterDrop is ___*wilder*___ (wild) than any other ride in the park.

10. You must move ___*more quickly*___ (quick) if you expect to catch the ball.

◆ **PRACTICE 29-4**

Fill in the correct superlative form of the word supplied in parentheses.

Example: Consumers now pay the ___*highest*___ (high) surcharge ever when they buy tickets for arena events.

(1) Ticketmaster is the ___*largest*___ (large) seller of sports and entertainment tickets in the country. (2) The company was the ___*earliest*___ (early) to sell concert and sporting event tickets both by phone and through retail outlets. (3) It has also been the ___*most successful*___ (successful) at making deals to keep rival ticket agencies from carrying tickets for large arenas and stadiums. (4) Its markup on tickets adds at least 20 percent to the cost of each ticket sold and is

by far the _____*greatest*_____ (great) in the business. (5) Because Ticket-master is the _____*most powerful*_____ (powerful) ticket outlet in the country, however, fans have no choice but to pay the price. (6) Critics have argued that Ticketmaster's control of the market is the _____*strongest*_____ (strong) monopoly in the country. (7) In 1994, the rock group Pearl Jam launched the _____*most serious*_____ (serious) offensive to date against the ticket giant. (8) Wanting its fans to be able to buy the _____*cheapest*_____ (cheap) tickets possible, Pearl Jam proposed to lower its own profits as well as Ticketmaster's for its 1994 summer tour. Ticketmaster refused. (9) Still one of the _____*most popular*_____ (popular) groups in the country, Pearl Jam has tried to use arenas that are not controlled by Ticketmaster for its more recent tours. (10) Ticketmaster's president argues that it has suc-ceeded not because of unfairness but because it has worked the _____*hardest*_____ (hard) and is the _____*most aggressive*_____ (aggressive) com-pany in the business.

FOCUS *Good/Well and Bad/Badly*

Most adjectives and adverbs form the comparative with *-er* or *more* and the superlative with *-est* or *most*. The adjectives *good* and *bad* and their adverb forms *well* and *badly* are exceptions.

Adjective	Comparative Form	Superlative Form
good	better	best
bad	worse	worst

Adverb	Comparative Form	Superlative Form
well	better	best
badly	worse	worst

◆ PRACTICE 29-5

Fill in the correct comparative or superlative form of *good, well, bad,* or *badly.*

Example: She is at her _____*best*_____ (good) when she is under pressure.

1. Today in track practice, Luisa performed _____*better*_____ (well) than she has in weeks.

2. In fact, she ran her _____*best*_____ (good) time ever in the fifty meter.

3. When things are bad, we wonder whether they will get _____*better*_____ (good) or _____*worse*_____ (bad).

4. I've had some bad meals before, but this is the _____*worst*_____ (bad).

5. The world always looks _____*better*_____ (good) when you're in love than when you're not.

6. Athletes generally play their _____*worst*_____ (badly) when their concentration is poorest.

7. The Sport Shop's prices may be good, but Athletic Attic's are the _____*best*_____ (good) in town.

8. There are _____*better*_____ (good) ways to solve conflicts than by fighting.

9. People seem to hear _____*better*_____ (well) when they agree with what you're saying than when they don't agree with you.

10. Of all the children, Manda took the _____*best*_____ (good) care of her toys.

■ **WRITING FIRST: Flashback**

Look back at your response to the Writing First exercise on page 433. Copy the adjectives and adverbs from your paragraph in the column on the left. Then, write the comparative and superlative forms for each adjective or adverb in the other columns.

Adjective or Adverb	*Comparative Form*	*Superlative Form*
Answers will vary.		

Teaching Tip
Remind students that absolute adjectives such as *perfect, unique, dead, impossible,* and *infinite* do not have comparative or superlative forms.

■ WRITING FIRST: Revising and Editing

Look back at your response to the Writing First exercise on page 433. Have you used adjectives and adverbs that effectively communicate the situation you describe? Have you used enough adjectives and adverbs to explain your ideas to readers? Add or substitute modifying words as needed to make your writing more precise and more interesting. Delete any unnecessary adjectives and adverbs.

CHAPTER REVIEW

◆ EDITING PRACTICE

Read the following student essay, into which errors in the use of adjectives and adverbs have been introduced. Make any changes necessary to correct adjectives incorrectly used for adverbs and adverbs incorrectly used for adjectives. Also correct any errors in the use of comparatives and superlatives and in the use of demonstrative adjectives. If you like, you may add adjectives and adverbs that you feel would make the writer's ideas clearer or more specific. The first sentence has been edited for you.
Answers may vary.

Starting Over

A wedding can be the ~~joyfullest~~ *most joyful* occasion in two

people's lives, the beginning of a couple's ~~most~~ happiest

years. For some unlucky women, however, a wedding can be

the ~~worse~~ *worst* thing that ever happens; it is the beginning not

of their happiness but of their battered lives. As I went

through the joyful day of my wedding, I wanted ~~bad~~ *badly* to find

happiness for the rest of my life, but what I hoped and

wished for did not come true.

I was married in the savannah belt of the Sudan in

the eastern part of Africa, where I grew up. I was barely

twenty-two years old. The first two years of my marriage

progressed ~~peaceful~~ *peacefully*, but problems started as soon as our

first child was born.

Many American women say, "If my husband gave me just

one beating, that would be it. I'd leave." But ~~those~~ *this modern* atti-

tude does not work in cultures where tradition has over-
shadowed women's rights and divorce is not accepted. All
women can do is accept their *sad* ̶s̶a̶d̶l̶y̶ fate. Battered women
give many reasons for staying in their *abusive* marriages, but fear
is the *most common* ̶c̶o̶m̶m̶o̶n̶e̶s̶t̶. Fear immobilizes these women, ruling
their decisions, their actions, and their very lives. This
is how it was for me.

Of course, I was *really* ̶r̶e̶a̶l̶ afraid whenever my husband hit
me. I would run to my mother's house and cry, but she
would always talk me into going back and being more
patient ̶p̶a̶t̶i̶e̶n̶t̶l̶y̶ with my husband. Our tradition discourages
divorce, and wife-beating is taken for granted. The
situation is really quite ironic: Islam, the religion I
practice, sets harsh punishments for abusive husbands, but
tradition has so overpowered religion that the laws do not
really work very *well* ̶g̶o̶o̶d̶.

One night, after nine years of torture, I asked myself
whether life had treated me *fairly* ̶f̶a̶i̶r̶. True, I had a high
school diploma and two of the *most beautiful* ̶b̶e̶a̶u̶t̶i̶f̶u̶l̶l̶e̶s̶t̶ children in the
world, but all this was not enough. I realized that to
stand up to the husband who treated me so *badly* ̶b̶a̶d̶, I would
have to achieve a ̶m̶o̶r̶e̶ better education than he had. That
night, I decided to get a college education in the United
States. My husband *strongly* opposed my decision, but with the support of my father and mother, I was able to begin to
change my life.

This period has been *really* ̶r̶e̶a̶l̶ difficult for me. I miss my
children every day. But I hope that one day I will be able
to fight our traditions intellectually and with dignity so
that my little daughters will remember even when I am gone
that their mother fought back and won.

◆ COLLABORATIVE ACTIVITIES

1. Working in a small group, write a plot summary for an imaginary film.
   Begin with one of the following three sentences.

29 B

■ Dirk and Clive were sworn enemies, but that night on Boulder Ridge they vowed to work together just this once, for the good of their country.

■ Genevieve entered the room in a cloud of perfume, and when she spoke, her voice was like velvet.

■ The desert sun beat down on her head, but Susanna was determined to protect what was hers, no matter what the cost.

2. Trade summaries with another group. Add as many adjectives and adverbs as you can to the other group's summary. Make sure each modifier is appropriate.

3. Reread your group's plot summary and edit it carefully, paying special attention to the way adjectives and adverbs are used.

☑ REVIEW CHECKLIST:
Adjectives and Adverbs

☐ Adjectives modify nouns or pronouns. (See 29A.)

☐ Demonstrative adjectives—*this, that, these,* and *those*—identify particular nouns. (See 29A.)

☐ Adverbs modify verbs, adjectives, or other adverbs. (See 29A.)

☐ To compare two people or things, use the comparative form of an adjective or adverb. To compare more than two people or things, use the superlative form of an adjective or adverb. Adjectives and adverbs form the comparative with *-er* or *more* and the superlative with *-est* or *most*. (See 29B.)

☐ The adjectives *good* and *bad* and their adverb forms *well* and *badly* have irregular comparative and superlative forms. (See 29B.)

Grammar and Usage Issues for ESL Writers

PREVIEW

In this chapter, you will learn

■ to include subjects in sentences (30A)
■ to avoid special problems with subjects (30B)
■ to identify plural nouns (30C)
■ to understand count and noncount nouns (30D)
■ to use determiners with count and noncount nouns (30E)
■ to understand articles (30F)
■ to form negative statements and questions (30G)
■ to indicate verb tense (30H)
■ to recognize stative verbs (30I)
■ to place modifiers in order (30J)
■ to choose correct prepositions (30K)
■ to use prepositions in familiar expressions (30L)
■ to use prepositions in two-word verbs (30M)

■ WRITING FIRST

Look at the painting above, and then explain how you and your family celebrate a holiday that is important to you.

Learning English as a second language involves more than just learning grammar. In fact, if you have been studying English as a second language, you may know as much about English grammar as many native speakers do—or even more. However, you will still need to learn the conventions and rules that are second nature to most (though by no means all) native speakers. This chapter covers the grammar and usage issues that give non-native speakers the most trouble.

Word Power

ritual a procedure that is followed faithfully

tradition the passing down of parts of a culture from generation to generation

A   Including Subjects in Sentences

English requires that every sentence state its subject. In fact, every dependent clause must also have a subject.

INCORRECT   Elvis Presley was only 42 years old when died.

CORRECT   Elvis Presley was only 42 years old when <u>he</u> died.

English even requires a false or "dummy" subject to fill the subject position in sentences like the following one.

<u>It</u> is hot in this room.

It is not correct to write just *Hot in this room* or *Is hot in this room.*

◆ **PRACTICE 30-1**

ON THE WEB

For more practice, visit
Exercise Central *at*
<www.bedfordstmartins.com/
writingfirst>.

Each of the following sentences is missing the subject of a dependent or an independent clause. On the lines after each sentence, rewrite it, adding an appropriate subject. Then, underline the subject you have added.

Example: Reality TV programs are very popular, but critics say are going too far.

Reality TV programs are very popular, but critics say <u>they</u> are going too far.

_____

1. When the first season of the reality show *Survivor* aired, was an immediate hit.

   When the first season of the reality show Survivor aired, <u>it</u> was an imme-

   diate hit.

2. At first, media experts thought was strange that a show like *Survivor* would be so successful.

   At first, media experts thought <u>it</u> was strange that a show like Survivor

   would be so successful.

3. For a while, *Survivor* became a cultural phenomenon—probably because was seldom in bad taste.

   For a while, Survivor became a cultural phenomenon—probably because <u>it</u>

   was seldom in bad taste.

4. Millions of Americans planned their evening so that could be sure not to miss the next episode.

   Millions of Americans planned their evening so that <u>they</u> could be sure

   not to miss the next episode.

5. Was surprising to see the controversial shows that suddenly appeared on the air.

   <u>It</u> was surprising to see the controversial shows that suddenly appeared

   on the air.

6. Many people refused to watch shows that felt were "morally corrupt."

   Many people refused to watch shows that they felt were "morally

   corrupt."

7. A recent poll asked viewers: "Do enjoy reality TV, or has it gone too far?"

   A recent poll asked viewers: "Do you enjoy reality TV, or has it gone too

   far?"

8. Most viewers thought that reality TV had gone too far even though enjoyed *Survivor* and similar shows.

   Most viewers thought that reality TV had gone too far even though they

   enjoyed Survivor and similar shows.

9. Turns out that reality TV is nothing new.

   It turns out that reality TV is nothing new.

10. In 1973, the documentary *An American Family* showed members of the Loud family as went about their daily lives.

    In 1973, the documentary An American Family showed members of the

    Loud family as they went about their daily lives.

B Avoiding Special Problems with Subjects

Some languages commonly begin a sentence with a word or phrase that has no grammatical link to the sentence but that states clearly what the sentence is about. If you speak such a language, you might write a sentence like this one.

> INCORRECT Career plan I am studying to be a computer scientist.

A sentence like this cannot occur in English. The phrase *career plan* cannot be a subject because the sentence already includes one: the pronoun *I*, which agrees with the verb *am studying*. In addition, *career plan* is not connected to the rest of the sentence in any other way. One way to revise this sentence is to rewrite it so that *career plan* is the subject.

> CORRECT My career plan is to be a computer scientist.

Another way to revise the sentence is to make *career plan* the object of a preposition.

> CORRECT In terms of my career plan, I am studying to be a computer scientist.

● Writing Tip
Special dictionaries help nonnative speakers answer usage questions. Your college librarian or English instructor can help you find a dictionary that meets your needs.

For more on subjects, see 15A.

Standard English also does not permit a two-part subject in which the second part is a pronoun referring to the same person or thing as the first part.

INCORRECT   The Caspian Sea it is the largest lake in the world.

CORRECT   The Caspian Sea is the largest lake in the world.

When the real subject follows the verb, and the normal subject position before the verb is empty, it must be filled by a "dummy" subject, such as *there*.

INCORRECT   Are many rivers in my country.

CORRECT   <u>There</u> are many rivers in my country.

ON THE WEB

For more practice, visit
Exercise Central *at*
*<www.bedfordstmartins.com/
writingfirst>.*

◆ PRACTICE 30-2

The following sentences contain problems with subjects. Rewrite each sentence correctly on the lines provided. (Some of the sentences can be corrected in more than one way.)

Example: My opinion the birth of the United States is an interesting subject.

In my opinion, the birth of the United States is an interesting subject.

Answers will vary.

1. By the 1700s, were thirteen British colonies in North America.

   By the 1700s, there were thirteen British colonies in North America.

2. On July 4, 1776, the colonies they declared their independence from England.

   On July 4, 1776, the colonies declared their independence from England.

3. The Revolutionary War it went on for eight years.

   The Revolutionary War went on for eight years.

4. Was a bit of confusion over how to set up a government.

   There was a bit of confusion over how to set up a government.

5. The first Congress the colonies sent representatives to Philadelphia in 1787.

   For the first Congress, the colonies sent representatives to Philadelphia

   in 1787.

6. These men they are called "the founding fathers."

These men are called "the founding fathers."

7. One of their goals they wanted to protect the rights of individuals.

One of their goals was to protect the rights of individuals.

8. The Constitution it is the formal statement of the U.S. system of government.

The Constitution is the formal statement of the U.S. system of

government.

9. The effectiveness of the Constitution the Constitution works because it was written to allow additions or amendments.

The Constitution works because it was written to allow additions or

amendments.

10. Today, are twenty-six amendments to the U.S. Constitution.

Today, there are twenty-six amendments to the U.S. Constitution.

■ WRITING FIRST: Flashback

Look back at your response to the Writing First exercise on page 445. Does every sentence state its subject? Underline the subject of each sentence. If a sentence does not have a subject, add one. If any sentence has a two-part subject, cross out the extra words.

C   Identifying Plural Nouns

In English, most nouns add -s to form plurals. Every time you use a noun, ask yourself whether you are talking about one item or more than one, and choose a singular or plural form accordingly. Consider this sentence.

CORRECT   The books in both branches of the library are deteriorating.

The three nouns in this sentence are underlined: one is singular (*library*), and the other two are plural (*books, branches*). You might think that the word *both* is enough to indicate that *branch* is plural, and that it is obvious that there would have to be more than one book in any branch of a

For more on singular and plural nouns, see 28A and 28B.

ON THE WEB
For more practice, visit
Exercise Central *at*
*<www.bedfordstmartins.com/
writingfirst>.*

Teaching Tip
Before students do this exercise, direct them to 28B, which deals with irregular noun plurals.

library. But even if a sentence includes information that tells you that a noun is plural, you must always use a form that shows explicitly that a noun is plural.

◆ PRACTICE 30-3

Underline the plural nouns in the following sentences. (Not all the sentences contain plural nouns.)

Example: The shark is one of the earth's most feared <u>animals</u>.

1. There are about 360 <u>species</u> of <u>sharks</u>.

2. These <u>fish</u> live in <u>oceans</u> and <u>seas</u> throughout the world but are most commonly found in warm water.

3. <u>Sharks</u> vary greatly in size and behavior.

4. Whale <u>sharks</u> are the largest, growing up to 40 <u>feet</u> long and weighing over 15 <u>tons</u>.

5. The smallest shark measures as little as half a foot and weighs less than an ounce.

6. Some <u>sharks</u> live in the deepest <u>areas</u> of the ocean, while other <u>sharks</u> stay near the water's surface.

7. Although all <u>sharks</u> are <u>meat-eaters</u>, only a few <u>species</u> are a danger to <u>people</u>.

8. Most <u>sharks</u> eat live <u>fish</u>, including their fellow <u>sharks</u>.

9. Since the <u>1950s</u>, <u>sharks</u> have been used more and more in scientific research.

10. Few <u>sharks</u> have ever been found with cancer, and <u>scientists</u> hope to find out what protects these <u>creatures</u> from this disease.

■ WRITING FIRST: Flashback

Look back at your response to the Writing First exercise on page 445. List all the plural nouns on the lines below.

Answers will vary. _____ _____ _____ _____

_____ _____ _____ _____

Does each plural noun have a form that shows the noun is plural? Correct any errors you find.

D Understanding Count and Noncount Nouns

A **count noun** names one particular thing or a group of particular things: *a teacher, a panther, a bed, an ocean, a cloud; two teachers, many panthers, three beds, two oceans, several clouds.* A **noncount noun**, however, names things that cannot be counted: *gold, cream, sand, blood, smoke.*

Count nouns usually have a singular form and a plural form: *cloud, clouds.* Noncount nouns usually have only a singular form: *smoke.* Note how the nouns *cloud* and *smoke* differ in the way they are used in sentences.

CORRECT The sky is full of clouds.

CORRECT The sky is full of smoke.

INCORRECT The sky is full of smokes.

CORRECT I see ten clouds.

INCORRECT I see ten smokes.

Often, the same idea can be represented with either a count noun or a noncount noun.

Count	Noncount
people (plural of *person*)	humanity [*not* humanities]
tables, chairs, beds	furniture [*not* furnitures]
letters	mail [*not* mails]
tools	equipment [*not* equipments]
facts	information [*not* informations]

Some words can be either count or noncount, depending on the meaning intended.

COUNT He had many interesting <u>experiences</u> at his first job.

NONCOUNT It is often difficult to get a job if you do not have <u>experience</u>.

FOCUS **Count and Noncount Nouns**

Here are some general guidelines for using count and noncount nouns.

■ Use a count noun to refer to a living animal, but use a noncount noun to refer to the food that comes from that animal.

COUNT There are three live <u>lobsters</u> in the tank.

NONCOUNT This restaurant specializes in <u>lobster</u>.

■ If you use a noncount noun for a substance or class of things that can come in different varieties, you can often make that noun plural if you want to talk about those varieties.

(continued on the following page)

● **Writing Tip**
Sometimes a noncount noun such as *smoke* appears to have a plural form (*smokes*). Although such forms end in *-s,* they are verbs and not plural nouns: *He <u>smokes</u> two cigars a day.*

▼ **Student Voices**
The hardest thing about the English language is all the rules.

George Lin

(continued from the previous page)

NONCOUNT   <u>Cheese</u> is a rich source of calcium.

COUNT   Many different <u>cheeses</u> come from Italy.

■ If you want to shift attention from a concept in general to specific examples of it, you can often use a noncount noun as a count noun.

NONCOUNT   You have a great deal of <u>talent</u>.

COUNT   My <u>talents</u> do not include singing.

ON THE WEB

For more practice, visit
Exercise Central *at*
<www.bedfordstmartins.com/ writingfirst>.

◆ PRACTICE 30-4

In each of the following sentences, identify the underlined word as a count or noncount noun. If it is a noncount noun, circle the *N* following the sentence, but do not write in the blank. If it is a count noun, circle the *C*, and then write the plural form of the noun in the blank.

Examples: Psychologists, sociologists, and anthropologists work in

the field of behavioral <u>science</u>.   Ⓝ   C _____

They all have the same <u>goal</u>: to understand human behavior.   N   Ⓒ

_____*goals*_____

1. Each type of scientist has a different <u>approach</u> to solving a problem.

   N   Ⓒ   ____*approaches*____

2. An <u>example</u> is the problem of homeless people on our cities' streets.

   N   Ⓒ   ____*examples*____

3. Sociologists concentrate on the social causes of <u>homelessness</u>.   Ⓝ   C

   _____

4. They might study how <u>unemployment</u> contributes to a rise in the number of homeless people.   Ⓝ   C   _____

5. A <u>shortage</u> of inexpensive housing can also cause someone to lose his or her home.   N   Ⓒ   ____*shortages*____

6. A sociologist's next question could be: How does <u>society</u> deal with homeless people?   Ⓝ   C   _____

7. Psychologists, on the other hand, are interested in the <u>individual</u>.

   N   Ⓒ   ____*individuals*____

8. Their focus would be on how a homeless <u>person</u> feels and thinks.

N Ⓒ _____ *people*

9. Anthropologists are interested in studying culture, a society's <u>system</u> of

beliefs and its ways of doing things.   N Ⓒ _____ *systems*

10. An anthropologist might focus on how the <u>homeless</u> find food and

shelter and on how they raise their children.   Ⓝ C _____

E   Using Determiners with Count and Noncount Nouns

Determiners are adjectives that *identify* rather than describe the nouns
they modify. Determiners may also *quantify* nouns (that is, indicate an
amount or a number).

Determiners include the following words.

- Articles: *a, an, the*
- Demonstrative pronouns: *this, these, that, those*
- Possessive pronouns: *my, our, your, his, her, its, their*
- Possessive nouns: *Sheila's, my friend's,* and so on
- *Whose, which, what*
- *All, both, each, every, some, any, either, no, neither, many, most, much, a
  few, a little, few, little, several, enough*
- All numerals: *one, two,* and so on

When a determiner is accompanied by one or more other adjectives,
the determiner always comes first. For example, in the phrase *my expensive new digital watch, my* is a determiner; you cannot put *expensive, new,
digital,* or any other adjective before *my.*

A singular count noun must be accompanied by a determiner—for example, *my watch* or *the new digital watch,* not just *watch* or *new digital
watch.* Noncount nouns and plural count nouns, however, sometimes have
determiners but sometimes do not. *This honey is sweet* and *Honey is sweet*
are both acceptable, as are *These berries are juicy* and *Berries are juicy.* (In
each case, the meaning is different.) You cannot say *Berry is juicy,* however; say instead *This berry is juicy, Every berry is juicy,* or *A berry is juicy.*

FOCUS   **Determiners**

Some determiners can be used only with certain types of nouns.

- *This* and *that* can be used only with singular nouns (count or
  noncount): *this berry, that honey.*

(continued on the following page)

(continued from the previous page)

- *These, those, a few, few, many, both,* and *several* can only be used with plural count nouns: *these berries, those apples, a few ideas, few people, many students, both sides, several directions.*
- *Much* and *a little* can be used only with noncount nouns: *much affection, a little honey.*
- *Some* and *enough* can be used only with noncount or plural count nouns: *some honey, some berries, enough trouble, enough problems.*
- *A, an, every,* and *each* can be used only with singular count nouns: *a berry, an elephant, every possibility, each citizen.*

ON THE WEB
For more practice, visit
Exercise Central *at*
<www.bedfordstmartins.com/ writingfirst>.

◆ PRACTICE 30-5

In each of the following sentences, circle the more appropriate choice from each pair of words or phrases in parentheses.

Examples:
Volcanoes are among the most destructive of (all/every) natural forces on earth.

People have always been fascinated and terrified by (this/these) force of nature.

1. Not (all/every) volcano is considered a danger.

2. In (major some/some major) volcanic eruptions, huge clouds rise over the mountain.

3. (A few violent/Violent a few) eruptions are so dramatic that they blow the mountain apart.

4. (Most/Much) volcanic eruptions cannot be predicted.

5. Since the 1400s, almost 200,000 people have lost (his/their) lives in volcanic eruptions.

6. When a volcano erupts, (little/a little) can be done to prevent property damage.

7. (Many/Much) lives can be saved, however, if people in the area are evacuated in time.

8. Unfortunately, when people realize an eruption is about to take place, there rarely is (every/enough) time to escape.

9. Volcanoes can be dangerous, but they also produce (a little/some) benefits.

10. For example, (**a few**/a little) countries around the world use geothermal energy—from underground steam in volcanic areas—to produce electric power.

■ WRITING FIRST: Flashback

Look back at your response to the Writing First exercise on page 445. List all the count nouns in the column on the left and all the noncount nouns in the column on the right.

Count nouns	Noncount nouns
Answers will vary.	

Have you used count and noncount nouns correctly? Correct any errors you find.

F   Understanding Articles

The definite article *the* and the indefinite articles *a* and *an* are determiners that tell readers whether the noun that follows is one they can identify (*the book*) or one they cannot yet identify (*a book*).

Definite Articles

When the definite article *the* is used with a noun, the writer is saying to readers, "You can identify which particular thing or things I have in mind. The information you need to make that identification is available to you. Either you have it already, or I am about to supply it to you."

Readers can find the necessary information in the following ways.

■ By looking at other information in the sentence.

> Meet me at <u>the</u> corner of Main Street and Lafayette Road.

In this example, *the* is used with the noun *corner* because other words in the sentence tell readers which particular corner the writer has in mind: the one located at Main and Lafayette.

■ By looking at information in other sentences.

ESL Tip
Article use gives most non-native speakers trouble. Go over 30F in class, encouraging students to give as many additional examples as they can.

Aisha ordered a slice of pie and a cup of coffee. The pie was delicious. She asked for a second slice.

Here, *the* is used before the word *pie* in the second sentence to indicate that it is the same pie identified in the first sentence. Notice, however, that the noun *slice* in the third sentence is preceded by an indefinite article (*a*) because it is not the same slice referred to in the first sentence.

■ By drawing on general knowledge.

The earth revolves around the sun.

Here, *the* is used with the nouns *earth* and *sun* because readers are expected to know which particular things the writer is referring to.

*For information on the su-
perlative forms of adjectives
and adverbs, see 29B.*

FOCUS **Definite Articles**

Always use *the* (rather than *a* or *an*) in the following situations.

■ Before the word *same: the same day*
■ Before the superlative form of an adjective: *the youngest son*
■ Before a number indicating order or sequence: *the third time*

Indefinite Articles

When an indefinite article is used with a noun, the writer is saying to readers, "I don't expect you to have enough information right now to identify a particular thing that I have in mind. I do expect you to recognize that I'm referring to only one item."

Consider the following sentences.

We need a table for our computer.

I have a folding table; maybe you can use that.

In the first sentence, the writer is referring to a hypothetical table, not an actual one. Because the table is indefinite to the writer, it is clearly indefinite to the reader, so *a* is used, not *the*. The second sentence refers to an actual table, but because the writer does not expect the reader to be able to identify the table specifically, it is also used with *a* rather than *the*.

FOCUS **Indefinite Articles**

Unlike the definite article, the indefinite articles *a* and *an* occur only with singular count nouns. *A* is used when the next sound is a consonant, and *an* is used when the next sound is a vowel. In choosing *a* or *an*, pay attention to sounds rather than to spelling: *a house, a year, a union*, but *an hour, an uncle.*

Teaching Tip
Refer students to the Focus
box on page 521 for a review
of vowels and consonants.

No Article

Only noncount and plural count nouns can stand without articles: *butter, chocolate, cookies, strawberries* (but *a cookie* or *the strawberry*).

Nouns without articles can be used to make generalizations.

For more on count and non-count nouns, see 30D.

> <u>Infants</u> need <u>affection</u> as well as <u>food</u>.

Here, the absence of articles before the nouns *infants, affection,* and *food* indicates that the statement is not about particular infants, affection, or food but about infants, affection, and food in general. Remember not to use *the* in such sentences; in English, a sentence like *The infants need affection as well as food* can only refer to particular, identifiable infants, not to infants in general.

Articles with Proper Nouns

Proper nouns can be divided into two classes: names that take *the* and names that take no article.

For more on proper nouns, see 28A and 33A.

- Names of people usually take no article unless they are used in the plural to refer to members of a family, in which case they take *the: Napoleon, Mahatma Gandhi,* but *the Parkers.*
- Names of places that are plural in form usually take *the: the Andes, the United States.*
- The names of most places on land (cities, states, provinces, and countries) take no article: *Salt Lake City, Mississippi, Alberta, Japan.* The names of most bodies of water (rivers, seas, and oceans, although not lakes or bays) take *the: the Mississippi, the Mediterranean, the Pacific,* but *Lake Erie* and *San Francisco Bay.*
- Names of streets take no article: *Main Street.* Names of highways take *the: the Belt Parkway.*

Teaching Tip

Remind students that plurals of proper nouns (such as *the Parkers*) do not include apostrophes unless they are possessive.

◆ PRACTICE 30-6

In the following passage, decide whether each blank needs a definite article (*the*), an indefinite article (*a* or *an*), or no article. If a definite or indefinite article is needed, write it in the space provided. If no article is needed, leave the space blank.

ON THE WEB

For more practice, visit Exercise Central at <www.bedfordstmartins.com/ writingfirst>.

Example: Vicente Fox was born on _____ July 2, 1942, in *the* Mexican capital of Mexico City.

(1) Vicente was *the* second of nine children born to José Luis Fox, *a* wealthy farmer, and Mercedes Quesada. (2) When Vicente was only four days old, *the* Fox family went to live in San Francisco del Rincón, in *the* state of Guanajuato. (3) Vicente Fox studied _____ business administration at the Universidad Iberoamericana in Mexico City. (4) He then traveled to *the* United States, where he received *a* degree in

management at _____ Harvard University. (5) When he returned to Mexico, he went to work for Coca-Cola, and over _the_ next fifteen years, he climbed _the_ corporate ladder and became _the_ company's youngest manager and eventually Coca-Cola's president for Mexico and _____ Latin America. (6) Fox entered _____ politics by joining _the_ National Action Party during _the_ 1980s. (7) In 1988, he was elected to _____ Congress. (8) _A_ few years later, in 1991, he ran for _the_ post of governor of Guanajuato but lost. (9) Four years later, he won by _a_ landslide. (10) In 1999, Fox took _a_ leave of absence as governor to run in _the_ presidential elections. (11) In one interview during his campaign, he said he wanted to rebuild Mexico into _a_ country "where _____ security and _____ justice prevail, where no one is above _the_ law." (12) After promoting himself as _a_ "down-to-earth man of _the_ people," on July 2, 2000, Vicente Fox became _the_ first opposition candidate to reach _the_ presidency of _the_ Republic of Mexico.

■ WRITING FIRST: Flashback

Look back at your response to the Writing First exercise on page 445. Circle each definite article (*the*) and indefinite article (*a* or *an*) you have used. Have you used articles correctly? Correct any errors you find.

| **G** | **Forming Negative Statements and Questions** |

Negative Statements

For more on helping verbs, see 15C.

To form a negative statement, add the word *not* directly after the first helping verb of the complete verb.

> Global warming has been getting worse.
> Global warming has **not** been getting worse.

When there is no helping verb, a form of the verb *do* must be inserted before *not*.

Automobile traffic contributes to pollution.

Automobile traffic <u>does not</u> contribute to pollution.

Remember that when *do* is used as a helping verb, the form of *do* used must match the tense and number of the original main verb. Note that in the negative statement above, the main verb loses its tense and appears in the base form (*contribute*, not *contributes*).

For information on subject-verb agreement with the verb do, see 23B.

Questions

To form a question, move the helping verb that follows the subject to the position directly before the subject.

The governor <u>is</u> trying to compromise.

<u>Is</u> the governor trying to compromise?

The governor <u>is</u> working on the budget.

<u>Is</u> the governor working on the budget?

The same rule stated above applies even when the verb is in the past or future tense.

The governor <u>was</u> trying to lower state taxes.

<u>Was</u> the governor trying to lower state taxes?

The governor <u>will</u> try to get re-elected.

<u>Will</u> the governor try to get re-elected?

When the verb does not include a helping verb, you must supply a form of *do*. To form a question, put *do* directly before the subject.

The governor <u>works</u> hard.

<u>Does</u> the governor <u>work</u> hard?

The governor <u>improved</u> life in his state.

<u>Did</u> the governor <u>improve</u> life in his state?

Note: The helping verb never comes before the subject in a question that begins with a subject like *who* or *which*.

<u>Who</u> is talking to the governor?

<u>Which</u> bills have been vetoed by the governor?

> **ESL Tip**
>
> If a statement includes more than one helping verb, move only the *first* helping verb when you form a question: *The governor <u>will be</u> working on the budget;* <u>Will</u> *the governor <u>be</u> working on the budget?*

◆ PRACTICE 30-7

Rewrite each of the following sentences in two ways: first, turn the sentence into a question; then, rewrite the original sentence as a negative statement.

Example: Her newest album is selling as well as her first one.

Question: <u>Is her newest album selling as well as her first one?</u>

Negative statement: <u>Her newest album is not selling as well as her first one.</u>

ON THE WEB
For more practice, visit Exercise Central *at* <www.bedfordstmartins.com/ writingfirst>.

1. Converting metric measurements to English measurements is difficult.

   Question: *Is converting metric measurements to English measurements difficult?*

   Negative statement: *Converting metric measurements to English measurements is not difficult.*

2. The early frost damaged many crops.

   Question: *Did the early frost damage many crops?*

   Negative statement: *The early frost did not damage many crops.*

3. That family was very influential in the early 1900s.

   Question: *Was that family very influential in the early 1900s?*

   Negative statement: *That family was not very influential in the early 1900s.*

4. Most stores in downtown areas open on Sundays.

   Question: *Do most stores in downtown areas open on Sundays?*

   Negative statement: *Most stores in downtown areas do not open on Sundays.*

5. The winner of the presidential election has always been the candidate who got the most votes.

   Question: *Has the winner of the presidential election always been the candidate who got the most votes?*

   Negative statement: *The winner of the presidential election has not always been the candidate who got the most votes.*

6. Many great artists attain recognition and success during their life-times.

   Question: *Do many great artists attain recognition and success during their lifetimes?*

   Negative statement: *Many great artists do not attain recognition and success during their lifetimes.*

7. The prosecutor can verify the accuracy of the witness's story.

Question: *Can the prosecutor verify the accuracy of the witness's story?*

Negative statement: *The prosecutor cannot verify the accuracy of the witness's story.*

8. The next Olympic Games will be held in the United States.

Question: *Will the next Olympic Games be held in the United States?*

Negative statement: *The next Olympic Games will not be held in the United States.*

9. Customs officers at the border have been requiring motorists to show proof of citizenship.

Question: *Have customs officers at the border been requiring motorists to show proof of citizenship?*

Negative statement: *Customs officers at the border have not been requiring motorists to show proof of citizenship.*

10. The policy of segregation of blacks and whites in the American South ended with the Civil War.

Question: *Did the policy of segregation of blacks and whites in the American South end with the Civil War?*

Negative statement: *The policy of segregation of blacks and whites in the American South did not end with the Civil War.*

■ WRITING FIRST: Flashback

Look back at your response to the Writing First exercise on page 445. Do you see any negative statements? If so, check to make sure you have formed them correctly. Then, on the lines below, write a question that you could add to your Writing First exercise.

Question: *Answers will vary.*

Check carefully to make sure you have formed the question correctly.

*For more on verb tense, see
Chapters 26 and 27.*

H   Indicating Verb Tense

In English, a verb's form must always indicate when an action took place (for instance, in the past or in the present). Use the appropriate tense of the verb, even if the time is obvious or if the sentence includes other indications of time (such as *two years ago* or *at present*).

CORRECT   Albert Einstein <u>emigrated</u> from Germany in 1933.

INCORRECT   Albert Einstein <u>emigrate</u> from Germany in 1933.

■ WRITING FIRST: Flashback

Look back at your response to the Writing First exercise on page 445. Are all your verbs in the present tense? Correct any errors you find.

I   Recognizing Stative Verbs

Stative verbs usually tell us that someone or something is in a state that will not change, at least for a while.

Hiro <u>knows</u> American history very well.

The **present progressive** tense consists of the present tense of *be* plus the present participle (*I am going*). The **past progressive** tense consists of the past tense of *be* plus the present participle (*I was going*). Most English verbs show action, and these action verbs can be used in the progressive tenses. Stative verbs, however, are rarely used in the progressive tenses.

INCORRECT   Hiro <u>is knowing</u> American history very well.

FOCUS   Stative Verbs

Verbs that are stative often refer to mental states like *know, understand, think, believe, want, like, love,* and *hate*. Other stative verbs include *be, have, need, own, belong, weigh, cost,* and *mean*. Certain verbs of sense perception, like *see* and *hear,* are also stative even though they can refer to momentary events rather than unchanging states.

Many verbs have more than one meaning, and some of these verbs are active with one meaning but stative with another. An example is the verb *weigh*.

ACTIVE   The butcher <u>weighs</u> the meat.

STATIVE   The meat <u>weighs</u> three pounds.

In the first sentence above, the verb *weigh* means "to put on a scale"; it is active, not stative. In the second sentence, however, the same verb means "to have weight," so it is stative, not active. It would be unacceptable to say, "The meat is weighing three pounds," but "The butcher is weighing the meat" would be correct.

ON THE WEB
For more practice, visit Exercise Central *at* <www.bedfordstmartins.com/ writingfirst>.

◆ **PRACTICE 30-8**

In each of the following sentences, circle the verb or verbs. Then, correct any problems with stative verbs by crossing out the incorrect verb tense and writing the correct verb tense above the line. If the verb is correct, write *C* above it.

Example: Many people ~~are thinking~~ *think* that the typical American does not follow *C* a healthy diet.

1. Unfortunately, this view ~~is being~~ *is* close to the truth.

2. A diet that ~~is including~~ *includes* high levels of sugar, salt, fat, and cholesterol ~~is often causing~~ *often causes* serious health problems.

3. We ~~are knowing~~ *know* that nutrition is an important part of health.

4. Busy families ~~are wanting~~ *want* food that is inexpensive and easy to prepare.

5. Many convenience foods, frozen or canned, ~~are having~~ *have* very little food value.

6. Too many Americans ~~are weighing~~ *weigh* much more than they should.

7. Some people's eating habits are changing, *C* however, and more and more Americans are becoming *C* more concerned about nutrition.

8. Some experts believe *C* that Americans are trying *C* to eat better.

9. Unfortunately, a recent survey ~~was showing~~ *showed* that too many Americans are *C* still couch potatoes.

10. Health experts ~~are agreeing~~ *agree* that Americans of all ages ~~are needing~~ *need* to get more exercise.

■ **WRITING FIRST: Flashback**

Look back at your response to the Writing First exercise on page 445. Can you identify any stative verbs? If so, list them here.

Stative verbs: *Answers will vary.* _____ _____

_____ _____ _____

Check carefully to be sure you have not used any of these verbs in a progressive tense. Correct any errors you find.

J Placing Modifiers in Order

Adjectives and other modifiers that come before a noun usually follow a set order.

Required Order

For more on determiners, see 30E.

■ Determiners always come first in a series of modifiers: *these fragile glasses*. The determiners *all* or *both* always precede any other determiners: *all these glasses*.
■ If one of the modifiers is a noun, the modifier must come directly before the noun it modifies: *these wine glasses*.
■ Descriptive adjectives are placed between the determiners and the noun modifiers: *these fragile wine glasses*. If there are two or more of these adjectives, the following order is preferred.

Preferred Order

■ Adjectives that show the writer's attitude generally precede adjectives that merely describe: *these lovely fragile wine glasses*.
■ Adjectives that indicate size generally come early: *these lovely large fragile wine glasses*.

◆ PRACTICE 30-9

ON THE WEB
For more practice, visit
Exercise Central *at*
*<www.bedfordstmartins.com/
writingfirst>.*

Arrange each group of adjectives in the correct order, and rewrite the complete phrase in the blank.

Example: (annual, impressive, the, publisher's) report

the publisher's impressive annual report

1. (brand-new, a, apartment, high-rise) building

   a brand-new high-rise apartment building

2. (gifted, twenty-five-year-old, Venezuelan, this) author

   this gifted twenty-five-year-old Venezuelan author

3. (successful, short-story, numerous) collections

   numerous successful short-story collections

4. (her, all, intriguing, suspense) novels

   all her intriguing suspense novels

5. (publisher's, best-selling, the, three) works

   the publisher's three best-selling works

6. (main, story's, two, this) characters

   this story's two main characters

7. (young, a, strong-willed) woman

   a strong-willed young woman

8. (middle-aged, attractive, the, British) poet

   the attractive middle-aged British poet

9. (exquisite, wedding, an, white) gown

   an exquisite white wedding gown

10. (elaborate, wedding, an, million-dollar) reception

    an elaborate million-dollar wedding reception

■ WRITING FIRST: Flashback

Look back at your response to the Writing First exercise on page 445. Have you used several modifiers before a single noun? If so, list here all the modifiers and the noun that follows them.

Modifiers: _*Answers will vary.*_ _____ Noun: _____

Modifiers: _____ _____ _____ Noun: _____

Have you arranged the modifiers in the correct order? Make any necessary corrections.

K Choosing Correct Prepositions

A **preposition** links a noun (or a word or word group that functions as a noun) to a verb, an adjective, or another noun in the sentence. Thus, prepositions show the precise relationships between words—for example, whether a book is *on, near,* or *under* a table.

I thought I had left the book <u>on</u> the table or somewhere <u>near</u> the table, but I found it <u>under</u> the table.

The prepositions *at, in,* and *on* sometimes cause problems for non-native speakers of English. For example, to identify the location of a place or an event, you can use *at, in,* or *on.*

■ The preposition *at* specifies an exact point in space or time.

The museum is <u>at</u> 1000 Fifth Avenue. Let's meet there <u>at</u> 10:00 tomorrow morning.

■ Expanses of space or time are treated as containers and therefore require *in.*

Jean-Pierre went to school <u>in</u> the 1970s.

■ *On* must be used in two cases: with names of streets (but not with exact addresses), and with days of the week or month.

We will move into our new office <u>on</u> 18th Street either <u>on</u> Monday or <u>on</u> March 12.

L Using Prepositions in Familiar Expressions

Many familiar expressions end with prepositions. Learning to write clearly and *idiomatically*—in keeping with the conventions of written English—means learning which preposition is used in such expressions. Even native speakers of English sometimes have trouble choosing the correct preposition.

The sentences that follow illustrate idiomatic use of prepositions in various expressions. Note that sometimes different prepositions are used with the same word. For example, both *on* and *for* can be used with *wait* to form two different expressions with two different meanings (*He waited on their table; She waited for the bus*). Which preposition you choose depends on your meaning. (In the list that follows, pairs of similar expressions that end with different prepositions are bracketed.)

Expression with Preposition	Sample Sentence
acquainted with	During orientation, the university offers workshops to make sure that students are <u>acquainted with</u> its rules and regulations.
addicted to	I think Abby is becoming <u>addicted to</u> pretzels.

agree on (a plan or objective)	It is vital that all members of the school board <u>agree on</u> goals for the coming year.
agree to (a proposal)	Striking workers finally <u>agreed to</u> the terms of management's offer.
angry about or at (a situation)	Taxpayers are understandably <u>angry about</u> (or <u>at</u>) the deterioration of city recreation facilities.
angry with (a person)	When the mayor refused to hire more police officers, his constituents became <u>angry with</u> him.
approve of	Amy's adviser <u>approved of</u> her decision to study in Guatemala.
bored with	Salah got <u>bored with</u> economics, so he changed his major to psychology.
capable of	Hannah is a good talker, but she is not <u>capable of</u> acting as her own lawyer.
consist of	The deluxe fruit basket <u>consisted of</u> five pathetic pears, two tiny apples, a few limp bunches of grapes, and one lonely kiwi.
contrast with	Coach Headley's relaxed style <u>contrasts</u> sharply <u>with</u> the previous coach's more formal approach.
convenient for	The proposed location of the new day-care center is <u>convenient for</u> many families.
deal with	Many parents and educators believe it is possible to <u>deal with</u> the special needs of autistic children in a regular classroom.
depend on	Children <u>depend on</u> their parents for emotional as well as financial support.
differ from (something else)	A capitalist system <u>differs from</u> a socialist system in its view of private ownership.
differ with (someone else)	When Miles realized that he <u>differed with</u> his boss on most important issues, he handed in his resignation.
emigrate from	My grandfather and his brother <u>emigrated from</u> the part of Russia that is now Ukraine.
grateful for (a favor)	If you can arrange an interview next week, I will be very <u>grateful for</u> your time and trouble.
grateful to (someone)	Jerry Garcia was always <u>grateful to</u> his loyal fans.
immigrate to	Many Cubans want to leave their country and <u>immigrate to</u> the United States.
impatient with	Keshia often gets <u>impatient with</u> her four younger brothers.
interested in	Tomiko had always been <u>interested in</u> computers, so no one was surprised when she became a Web designer.
interfere with	College athletes often find that their dedication to sports <u>interferes with</u> their schoolwork.

M Using Prepositions in Two-Word Verbs

Some verbs consist of two words, a verb and a preposition. If the preposition introduces a prepositional phrase, the preposition always comes right after the verb. In the following sentence, *over* introduces the prepositional phrase *over the manual;* therefore, *over* must come right after the verb *(go).*

> CORRECT   Please <u>go over</u> the manual carefully.

> INCORRECT   Please <u>go</u> the manual <u>over</u> carefully.

In other two-word verbs, words that look like prepositions do not always function as prepositions. For example, in the sentence below, the second word of the verb *(up)* does not introduce a prepositional phrase; instead, it combines with the first word of the verb to form a two-word verb with its own meaning. Verbs like these are also not usually separated.

> CORRECT   The student <u>spoke up</u> without hesitation.

> INCORRECT   The student <u>spoke</u> without hesitation <u>up</u>.

Some Common Inseparable Two-Word Verbs

come across	grow up
get along	run into
go over	stay away
give in	speak up

In some cases, however, a two-word verb may be split. For example, some two-word verbs, called **transitive verbs**, express an action toward an object. When the object of a transitive verb is a noun, the second word of the verb can come either before or after the object. In the sentence below, *turn off* is a transitive verb. Because the object of the verb *turn off* is a noun *(printer),* the second word of the verb can come either before or after the verb's object.

> CORRECT   Please <u>turn off</u> the printer.

> CORRECT   Please <u>turn</u> the printer <u>off</u>.

When the object of a transitive verb is a pronoun, however, these two-word verbs *must* be split, and the pronoun must come between the two parts.

> CORRECT   Please <u>turn</u> it <u>off</u>.

> INCORRECT   Please <u>turn off</u> it.

Some Common Separable Two-Word Verbs

ask out	call up	fill out	hang up
bring up	drop off	give away	let out

(continued on the following page)

(continued from the previous page)

make up	put on	think over	turn off
put away	shut off	throw away	try out
put back	take down	turn down	wake up

Remember, when the object of the verb is a pronoun, these two-word verbs must be split and the pronoun must come between the two parts (e.g., *take (it) down, put (it) on, let (it) out,* and *make (it) up*).

◆ PRACTICE 30-11

In each of the following sentences, look closely at the two-word verb, and decide whether the preposition is correctly placed in the sentence. If it is, write *C* in the blank after the sentence. If the preposition needs to be moved, edit the sentence.

ON THE WEB
For more practice, visit **Exercise Central** *at* <www.bedfordstmartins.com/ writingfirst>.

Example: How many timid students sit in the back of the classroom
and hope that the professor will not call them ~~on~~? *on ?* _____

1. Some people who have dreams of going to college have to set ~~aside~~ *them aside*
them for a variety of reasons. _____

2. Many colleges and universities recognize the difficulty some people
face and have found a way to deal ~~it with.~~ *with it.* _____

3. Students are no longer obligated to put in hours and hours sitting in
classrooms. _*C*_

4. Thanks to the Internet and other technology, the education system has
developed "distance education" and is constantly working ~~it on~~ *on it* in
order to improve it. _____

5. "Distance learning" takes place when a teacher and student are separated by physical distance, and technology hooks ~~up them.~~ *them up.* _____

6. A distance-education program involves several people, and any program's success depends ~~their efforts on.~~ *on their efforts.* _____

7. Several technological options are available—including telephone,
video, and computer—but distance educators should remember that
different students have different needs and that it is important to focus
on those needs. _*C*_

8. Although some online courses are free, most students must pay for them. _____ *C*

9. Teachers can distribute assignments, and students can hand ~~in them~~ by fax or e-mail. _____
   (above: *them in*)

10. If the subject of distance learning interests you, you can look ~~it into~~ at <www.askjeeves.com>. _____
    (above: *into it*)

■ WRITING FIRST: Flashback

Look back at your response to the Writing First exercise on page 445. Have you used any two-word verbs? If so, list them here.

_____

_____

Have you placed the preposition correctly in each case? Make any necessary corrections.

■ WRITING FIRST: Revising and Editing

Look back at your response to the Writing First exercise on page 445. Then, review all your Flashback exercises, and be sure you have made all necessary corrections in grammar and usage. When you have finished, add any additional transitional words and phrases you need to make the celebration you have described clear to your readers.

CHAPTER REVIEW

◆ EDITING PRACTICE

Read the following student essay, which contains errors in the use of subjects, articles and determiners, stative verbs, and idiomatic expressions. Check each underlined word or phrase. If it is not used correctly, cross it out and write the correct word or phrase above the line. If the underlined word or phrase is correct, write *C* above it. The title of the essay has been edited for you.

How to Succeed ~~on~~ *in* Multinational Business

Success in multinational business often depends ~~in~~ *on* people's ability to understand other countries' cultures. Understanding how cultures differ ~~with~~ *from* our own is not, however, ~~an~~ *the* only key to ~~multinational these~~ *these multinational* enterprises. ~~Is~~ *It is* also crucial that people doing business internationally ~~they~~ learn to adapt to ~~this~~ *these* cultures. One cause of the *C* problems that can arise is ethnocentrism. ~~The ethno-centrism~~ *Ethnocentrism* is the belief that one's own culture's way of doing something is ~~a~~ *the* best way. When a company uses the same methods overseas that it uses ~~in~~ *at* home, does not adapt a product to fit the cultural needs of another country, and sends representatives without international ~~experiences,~~ *experience,* ~~could~~ *there could* be problems.

To avoid ~~the~~ ethnocentrism, a company wanting to sell its product internationally ~~it~~ should do ~~a few~~ *some* market research. For example, if ~~an~~ *C* American company goes into a new market and looks ~~it at~~ *at it* without considering language, religion, values, customs, and other ~~element,~~ *elements,* the results can often be disastrous.

~~A~~ *C* knowledge of the local language is important for an international businessperson for ~~a little~~ *a few* reasons. If the person ~~he or she~~ knows the language, ~~is~~ *it is* possible to communicate directly, without an interpreter. In addition, people are usually more comfortable when they ~~meet~~ *C* with people who speak their language. Most important, it is easier for a person who ~~is knowing~~ *knows* the local language to become better acquainted ~~to~~ *with* the culture.

An understanding of ~~other~~ *C* countries' customs and manners is also crucial to an international business's success--and the same is true for individual businesspeople. Although businesspeople often call one another by their first names in ~~United States,~~ *the United States,* addressing someone by his or her first name can be extremely offensive in some cultures.

Although arriving on time for a business appointment is

normal practice in ~~much~~ *many* places, ~~the~~ punctuality is consid-

ered less important in other ~~country~~ *countries*. Even the type of

clothing that people wear can determine whether or not *they*

will establish a ~~business healthy~~ *healthy business* relationship with someone

from ~~the~~ *a* culture different from their own.
the

   As ~~a~~ *the* world becomes smaller, the marketplace is becom- *C*

ing global. In ~~those~~ *that* setting, individuals from numerous

cultures will come together. Not only the individuals but

also the multinational companies within today's global

market must show the highest ~~respects~~ *respect* for other cultures.

◆ COLLABORATIVE ACTIVITIES

Teaching Tip
Collaborative Activity 1 is an
effective review; it can also
be fun, especially if students
use lots of modifying words.

1. Working in a small group, make a list of ten prepositional phrases that include the prepositions *above, around, at, between, from, in, on, over, under,* and *with*. Use specific nouns as objects of these prepositions, and use as many modifying words as you wish. (Try, for example, to write something like *above their hideous wedding portrait*, not just *above the picture*.)

2. Exchange lists with another group. Still working collaboratively, compose a list of ten sentences, each including one of the other group's ten prepositional phrases. Give your list of ten sentences to another group.

3. Working with this new list of ten sentences, substitute a different prepositional phrase for each one that appears in a sentence. Make sure each sentence still makes sense.

☑ REVIEW CHECKLIST:
Grammar and Usage Issues for ESL Writers

▪ In almost all cases, English sentences must state their subjects. (See 30A and 30B.)

▪ In English, most nouns add *-s* to form plurals. Always use a form that indicates that a noun is plural. (See 30C.)

▪ English nouns may be count nouns or noncount nouns. A count noun names one particular thing or a group of particular things (*a teacher, oceans*). A noncount noun names something that cannot be counted (*gold, sand*). (See 30D.)

(continued on the following page)

(continued from the previous page)

- Determiners are adjectives that identify rather than describe the nouns they modify. Determiners may also indicate amount or number. (See 30E.)

- The definite article *the* and the indefinite articles *a* and *an* are determiners that indicate whether the noun that follows is one readers can identify (*the book*) or one they cannot yet identify (*a book*). (See 30F.)

- To form a negative statement, add the word *not* directly after the first helping verb of the complete verb. To form a question, move the helping verb that follows the subject to the position directly before the subject. (See 30G.)

- A verb's form must indicate when an action took place. (See 30H.)

- Stative verbs indicate that someone or something is in a state that will not change, at least for a while. Stative verbs are rarely used in the progressive tenses. (See 30I.)

- Adjectives and other modifiers that come before a noun usually follow a set order. (See 30J.)

- The prepositions *at, in,* and *on* sometimes cause problems for nonnative speakers of English. (See 30K.)

- Many familiar expressions end with prepositions. (See 30L.)

- When the preposition in a two-word verb introduces a prepositional phrase, the preposition comes right after the verb. In some cases, however, a two-word verb may be split. (See 30M.)

UNIT SEVEN

Understanding Punctuation, Mechanics, and Spelling

Using Commas

PREVIEW

In this chapter, you will learn

■ to use commas in a series (31A)

■ to use commas to set off introductory phrases, conjunctive adverbs, and transitional expressions (31B)

■ to use commas with appositives (31C)

■ to use commas to set off nonrestrictive clauses (31D)

■ to use commas in dates and addresses (31E)

■ to avoid unnecessary commas (31F)

■ WRITING FIRST

Look at the picture above, and then describe an ideal public housing complex for low-income families. Where should it be located? What kinds of buildings should be constructed? What facilities and services should be offered to residents?

Word Power

subsidized assisted or supported financially

low-density sparsely settled; not crowded

A **comma** is a punctuation mark that separates words or groups of words within sentences. Thus, commas keep ideas distinct from one another. In earlier chapters, you learned to use a comma between two independent clauses linked by a coordinating conjunction (16A) and to use a comma after a dependent clause that comes before an independent clause (17B). Commas have several other uses, as you will learn in this chapter.

A   Using Commas in a Series

Use commas to separate all elements in a **series** of three or more words or
word groups.

Leyla, Zack, and Kathleen campaigned for Representative Fattah.

Leyla, Zack, or Kathleen will be elected president of Students for
Fattah.

Leyla made phone calls, licked envelopes, and ran errands for the
campaign.

Leyla is president, Zack is vice-president, and Kathleen is treasurer.

FOCUS   Using Commas in a Series

Newspapers and magazines usually omit the comma before the
coordinating conjunction in a series. However, your writing will be
clearer if you use a comma before the coordinating conjunction.

Leyla, Zack, and Kathleen worked on the campaign.

Exception: Do not use *any* commas if all the items in a series are
separated by coordinating conjunctions.

Leyla or Zack or Kathleen will be elected president of Students for Fattah.

◆ PRACTICE 31-1

Edit the following sentences for the use of commas in a series. If the sentence is correct, write *C* in the blank.

Examples

Costa Rica produces bananas, cocoa, and sugar cane. __*C*__

The pool rules state that there is no running, or jumping, or diving.

_____

1. A talented musician, he plays guitar, bass, and drums. _____

2. The organization's goals are feeding the hungry, housing the homeless,

   and helping the unemployed find work. _____

3. *The Price Is Right, Let's Make a Deal,* and *Jeopardy!* are three of the

   longest-running game shows in television history. __*C*__

4. In native Hawaiian culture, yellow was the color worn by the royalty, red was worn by priests, and a mixture of the two colors was worn by others of high rank. _____

5. The remarkable diary kept by young Anne Frank while her family hid from the Nazis is insightful, touching, and sometimes humorous. _____

6. A standard bookcase is sixty inches tall, forty-eight inches wide, and twelve inches deep. _____

7. Most coffins manufactured in the United States are lined with bronze, ~~or~~ copper, or lead. _____

8. Young, handsome, and sensitive, Leonardo DiCaprio was the 1990s answer to the 1950s actor James Dean. _____

9. California's capital is Sacramento, its largest city is Los Angeles, and its oldest settlement is San Diego. _____

10. Watching television, playing video games, and riding his bicycle are the average ten-year-old boy's favorite pastimes. _C_

■ **WRITING FIRST: Flashback**

Look back at your response to the Writing First exercise on page 479. If you have included a series of three or more words or word groups in any of your sentences, copy it here. Did you use commas correctly to separate elements in the series? If not, correct your punctuation. If no sentence includes a series, write a new sentence that does on the lines below.

Answers will vary.

_____

_____

B | **Using Commas to Set Off Introductory Phrases, Conjunctive Adverbs, and Transitional Expressions**

Use a comma to set off an introductory phrase from the rest of the sentence.

<u>In the event of a fire</u>, proceed to the nearest exit.

For lists of frequently used conjunctive adverbs and transitional expressions, see 16C.

● **Writing Tip**

A conjunctive adverb or
transitional expression that
joins two complete sen-
tences requires a semicolon
and a comma: *Thoreau spent
only one night in jail; however, he spent more than two
years at Walden Pond.*

Walking home, Nelida decided to change her major.

To keep fit, people should try to exercise regularly.

Also use commas to set off conjunctive adverbs or transitional expressions whether they appear at the beginning, in the middle, or at the end of
a sentence.

In fact, Thoreau spent only one night in jail.

He was, of course, bailed out by a friend.

He did spend more than two years at Walden Pond, however.

FOCUS **Using Commas in Direct Address**

Always use commas to set off the name of someone whom you are
addressing (speaking to) directly, whether the name appears at the
beginning, in the middle, or at the end of a sentence.

Molly, come here and look at this.

Come here, Molly, and look at this.

Come here and look at this, Molly.

ON THE WEB
For more practice, visit
Exercise Central *at
<www.bedfordstmartins.com/
writingfirst>.*

Teaching Tip
Review the use of commas
in introductory phrases, asking students to read sen-
tences aloud so they can
hear where the natural
pauses occur.

◆ **PRACTICE 31-2**

Edit the following sentences for the use of commas with introductory
phrases. If the sentence is correct, write *C* in the blank.

Examples

From professional athletes to teenagers, people have begun to find
alternatives to steroids.

Regulated by the Drug Enforcement Administration, steroids are a
controlled substance and can be legally obtained only with a prescription. __C__

(1) In recent years, many Olympic athletes have been disqualified because they tested positive for banned drugs. ____ (2) To the surprise of
many fans, these drugs are not always steroids. ____ (3) For example,
some athletes have been accused of taking a drug called clenabutal,
which is meant for animals. __C__ (4) In addition to clenabutal, the poi-

son strychnine has also been detected. ____ (5) Banned by the rules of the Olympics, these drugs still appeal to athletes because they supposedly enhance performance. ____ (6) Because of the laws prohibiting steroids, many athletes have turned to these and other unregulated substances. ____ (7) Often called dietary supplements, these alternative chemicals are supposed to enhance athletic performance in the same way steroids supposedly do. ____ (8) According to the *Journal of the American Medical Association*, these dietary supplements do no such thing. ____ (9) Instead of enhancing performance, they often cause considerable damage to the body. ____ (10) Over the course of the last few years, investigators have collected more than three thousand samples of such products sold on the black market. ____

◆ PRACTICE 31-3

Edit the following sentences for the use of commas with conjunctive adverbs and transitional expressions. If the sentence is correct, write *C* in the blank.

Example: Some holidays, of course, are fairly new.

(1) For example, the African-American celebration of Kwanzaa is less than forty years old. ____ (2) This holiday to remind us of important African traditions has, however, attracted many celebrants over its short life. ____ (3) By the way, the word *Kwanzaa* means "first fruits" in Swahili. ____ (4) In other words, Kwanzaa stands for renewal. __C__ (5) This can, in fact, be demonstrated in some of the seven principles of Kwanzaa. ____ (6) Kwanzaa is, after all, celebrated over seven days to focus on each of these seven principles. ____ (7) The focus, first of all, is on unity *(umoja)*. ____ (8) Also, Kwanzaa focuses on personal self-determination *(kujichagulia)*. ____ (9) In addition, Kwanzaa celebrations emphasize three kinds of community responsibility *(ujima, ujamaa,* and *nia)*. ____ (10) The other principles of Kwanzaa are creativity *(kuumba)* and, finally, faith *(imani)*. ____

■ WRITING FIRST: Flashback

Look back at your response to the Writing First exercise on page 479. Underline any introductory phrases, conjunctive adverbs, or transitional expressions. Have you set off each of these with commas where appropriate? Revise any incorrect sentences here, adding commas where needed.

Answers will vary.

_____

_____

_____

_____

C Using Commas with Appositives

Use commas to set off an **appositive**—a word or word group that identifies or renames a noun or pronoun.

> I have visited only one country, <u>Canada</u>, outside the United States.
>
> Carlos Santana, <u>leader of the group Santana</u>, played at Woodstock in 1969.

FOCUS Using Commas with Appositives

Most appositives are set off by commas, whether they fall at the beginning, in the middle, or at the end of a sentence.

> <u>A dreamer</u>, he spent his life thinking about what he could not have.
>
> He always wanted to build a house, <u>a big white one</u>, overlooking the ocean.
>
> He finally built his dream house, <u>a log cabin</u>.

ON THE WEB

For more practice, visit Exercise Central *at* <www.bedfordstmartins.com/ writingfirst>.

◆ PRACTICE 31-4

Edit the following sentences for the correct use of commas to set off appositives. If the sentence is correct, write *C* in the blank.

Examples

The Buccaneers have not joined the Cheese League, the group of NFL teams that holds summer training in Wisconsin. ——

William Filene, the Boston merchant who founded Filene's department store, invented the concept of the "bargain basement." ——

1. Traditional Chinese medicine is based on meridians, channels of energy believed to run in regular patterns through the body. ——

2. Acupuncture, the insertion of thin needles at precise points in the body, stimulates these meridians. ——

3. Herbal medicine, the basis of many Chinese healing techniques, requires twelve years of study. ——

4. Gary Larson, creator of the popular *Far Side* cartoons, ended the series in 1995. ——

5. A musician at heart, Larson said he wanted to spend more time practicing the guitar. _C_

6. *Far Side* calendars and other product tie-ins earned Larson over $500 million, a lot of money for guitar lessons. ——

7. Nigeria, the most populous country in Africa, is also one of the fastest-growing nations in the world. ——

8. On the southwest coast of Nigeria lies Lagos, a major port. ——

9. The Yoruban people, the Nigerian settlers of Lagos, are unusual in Africa because they tend to form large urban communities. ——

10. A predominantly Christian people, the Yoruba have incorporated many native religious rituals into their practice of Christianity. ——

■ WRITING FIRST: Flashback

Look back at your response to the Writing First exercise on page 479. Have you used any appositives? Underline each one. Have you set off appositives with commas? Revise any incorrect sentences on the lines that follow.

(continued on the following page)

(continued from the previous page)

Answers will vary.

D   **Using Commas to Set Off Nonrestrictive Clauses**

Use commas to set off **nonrestrictive clauses**, clauses that are not essential to a sentence's meaning. Do not use commas to set off **restrictive
clauses**.

A **restrictive** clause contains essential information; therefore, it is *not*
set off from the rest of the sentence by commas.

> Many rock stars <u>who recorded hits in the 1950s</u> made little money
> from their songs.

In the sentence above, the clause *who recorded hits in the 1950s* supplies
specific information that is essential to the idea the sentence is communicating: it tells readers which group of rock stars made little money. Without the clause, the sentence does not communicate the same idea because
it does not tell which rock stars made little money.

> Many rock stars made little money from their songs.

FOCUS   *Who, Which,* and *That*

■ *Who* can introduce either a restrictive or a nonrestrictive clause.

     RESTRICTIVE   Many parents <u>who work</u> feel a lot of stress.
                 (no commas)

     NONRESTRICTIVE   Both of my parents, <u>who have always wanted
                 the best for their children</u>, have worked two
                 jobs for years. (clause set off by commas)

■ *Which* always introduces a nonrestrictive clause.

     The job, <u>which had excellent benefits</u>, did not pay well.
     (clause set off by commas)

■ *That* always introduces a restrictive clause.

     He accepted the job <u>that had the best benefits</u>. (no commas)

A **nonrestrictive** clause does *not* contain essential information; therefore, a nonrestrictive clause *is* set off from the rest of the sentence by commas.

> Telephone calling-card fraud, <u>which cost consumers and phone companies four billion dollars last year</u>, is increasing.

Here, the underlined clause provides extra information to help readers understand the sentence, but the sentence communicates the same idea without this information.

> Telephone calling-card fraud is increasing.

◆ PRACTICE 31-5

Edit the following sentences so that commas set off all nonrestrictive clauses. (Remember, commas are *not* used to set off restrictive clauses.) If a sentence is correct, write C in the blank.

ON THE WEB
For more practice, visit Exercise Central *at* <www.bedfordstmartins.com/writingfirst>.

Teaching Tip
Have students do Practice 31-5 in groups. (Fewer papers allow you more time for careful grading.) Students can also form groups to look over the graded assignment.

Example: An Alaska museum exhibition that celebrates the Alaska highway has rescued the story of its construction. __*C*__

(1) During the 1940s, a group of African-American soldiers who defied the forces of nature and human prejudice were shipped to Alaska. __*C*__ (2) They built the Alaska highway, which stretches twelve hundred miles across Alaska. ____ (3) The African-American troops who worked on the highway have received little attention in most historical accounts. __*C*__ (4) The highway, which cut through some of the roughest terrain in the world, was begun in 1942. ____ (5) The Japanese had just landed in the Aleutian Islands, which lay west of the tip of the Alaska Peninsula. ____ (6) Military officials, who oversaw the project, doubted the ability of the African-American troops. ____ (7) As a result, they made them work under conditions, that made construction difficult. ____ (8) The African-American troops who worked on the road proved their commanders wrong by finishing the highway months ahead of schedule. __*C*__ (9) In one case, white engineers, who surveyed a river, said it would take two weeks to bridge. ____ (10) To the engineers' surprise, the African-American soldiers who worked on the project beat the estimate by half a day. __*C*__ (11) A military report that was issued in 1945 praised them.

_C_ (12) It said the goals that the black regiments achieved would be remembered through the ages. _C_

■ WRITING FIRST: Flashback

Look back at your response to the Writing First exercise on page 479. Make sure you have included commas to set off nonrestrictive clauses and have *not* set off restrictive elements with commas.

E   Using Commas in Dates and Addresses

Dates

Use commas in dates to separate the day of the week from the month and the day of the month from the year.

> The first Cinco de Mayo we celebrated in the United States was Tuesday, May 5, 1998.

When a date that includes commas does not fall at the end of a sentence, place a comma after the date.

> Tuesday, May 5, 1998, was the first Cinco de Mayo we celebrated in the United States.

Addresses

Use commas in addresses to separate the street address from the city and the city from the state or country.

> The office of the famous fictional detective Sherlock Holmes was located at 221b Baker Street, London, England.

When an address that includes commas does not fall at the end of a sentence, place a comma after the state or country.

> The office at 221b Baker Street, London, England, belonged to the famous fictional detective Sherlock Holmes.

◆ PRACTICE 31-6

Edit the following sentences for the correct use of commas in dates and addresses. Add any missing commas, and cross out any unnecessary commas. If the sentence is correct, write *C* in the blank.

Examples:

June 3, 1968, is the day my parents were married. _____

Their wedding took place in Santiago, Chile. _____

1. The American Declaration of Independence was approved on July 4, 1776. _____

2. The Pelican Man's Bird Sanctuary is located at 1705 Ken Thompson Parkway, Sarasota, Florida. _____

3. At 175 Carlton Avenue, Brooklyn, New York, is the house where Richard Wright began writing *Native Son*. _____

4. I found this information in the February 12, 1994, issue of the *New York Times*. _____

5. The Mexican hero Father Miguel Hidalgo y Costilla was shot by a firing squad on June 30, 1811. __*C*__

6. The Palacio de Gobierno at Plaza de Armas, Guadalajara, Mexico, houses a mural of the famous revolutionary. _____

7. The Pueblo Grande Museum is located at 1469 East Washington Street, Phoenix, Arizona. _____

8. Brigham Young led the first settlers into the valley that is now Salt Lake City, Utah, in July, 1847. _____

9. St. Louis, Missouri, was the birthplace of writer Maya Angelou, but she spent most of her childhood in Stamps, Arkansas. _____

10. Some records list the actress's birthday as May 19, 1928, while others indicate she was born on May 20, 1924. _____

F Avoiding Unnecessary Commas

In addition to knowing where commas are required, it is also important to know when *not* to use commas.

Do not use a comma before the first item in a series.

INCORRECT   *Duck Soup* starred, Groucho, Chico, and Harpo Marx.

CORRECT   *Duck Soup* starred Groucho, Chico, and Harpo Marx.

● **Writing Tip**

Use a comma between all items in a series. (See 31A.)

Do not use a comma after the last item in a series.

INCORRECT   Groucho, Chico, and Harpo Marx, starred in *Duck Soup*.

CORRECT   Groucho, Chico, and Harpo Marx starred in *Duck Soup*.

Do not use a comma between a subject and a verb.

INCORRECT   Students and their teachers, should try to respect one another.

CORRECT   Students and their teachers should try to respect one another.

Do not use a comma before the coordinating conjunction that separates the two parts of a compound verb.

INCORRECT   The transit workers voted to strike, and walked off the job.

CORRECT   The transit workers voted to strike and walked off the job.

Do not use a comma before the coordinating conjunction that separates the two parts of a compound subject.

INCORRECT   The transit workers, and the sanitation workers voted to strike.

CORRECT   The transit workers and the sanitation workers voted to strike.

Do not use a comma to set off a restrictive clause.

INCORRECT   People, who live in glass houses, should not throw stones.

CORRECT   People who live in glass houses should not throw stones.

Finally, do not use a comma before a dependent clause that follows an independent clause.

INCORRECT   He was exhausted, because he had driven all night.

CORRECT   He was exhausted because he had driven all night.

◆ PRACTICE 31-7

Some of the following sentences contain unnecessary commas. Edit to correct for unnecessary commas. If the sentence is correct, write C in the blank following it.

Example: Both the Dominican Republic/ and the republic of Haiti

occupy the West Indian island of Hispaniola. _____

1. The capital of the Dominican Republic/ is Santo Domingo. _____

2. The country's tropical climate, generous rainfall, and fertile soil/ make

the Dominican Republic suitable for many kinds of crops. _____

3. Chief among these are/ sugarcane, coffee, cocoa, and rice. _____

● Writing Tip

Use a comma before a coordinating conjunction that links independent clauses in a compound sentence: *The transit workers voted to strike, and they walked off the job.*

Teaching Tip

Remind students that not every *and* and *but* is preceded by a comma.

● Writing Tip

Use commas to set off a nonrestrictive clause. (See 31D.)

● Writing Tip

Use a comma after a dependent clause that comes before an independent clause: *Because he had driven all night, he was exhausted.*

4. Mining is also important to the country's economy/ because the land is rich in many ores. _____

5. Spanish is the official language of the Dominican Republic, and Roman Catholicism is the state religion. __*C*__

6. In recent years, resort areas have opened/ and brought many tourists to the country. _____

7. Tourists who visit the Dominican Republic/ remark on its tropical beauty. _____

8. Military attacks from abroad/ and internal political unrest have marked much of the Dominican Republic's history. _____

9. Because the republic's economy has not always been strong, many Dominicans have immigrated to the United States. __*C*__

10. Most Dominican immigrants maintain close ties to their home country/ and return often to visit. _____

■ WRITING FIRST: Flashback

Look back at your response to the Writing First exercise on page 479. Check your work carefully to make sure you have not used commas in any of the situations listed in 31F. Make any necessary corrections.

■ WRITING FIRST: Revising and Editing

Look back at your response to the Writing First exercise on page 479. Then, make the following additions.

1. Add a sentence that includes a series of three or more words or word groups.
2. Add introductory phrases to two of your sentences.
3. Add an appositive to one of your sentences.
4. Add a conjunctive adverb or transitional expression to one of your sentences.
5. Add a nonrestrictive clause to one of your sentences.

When you have made all the additions, reread your work to check your use of commas in the new material.

■ **Computer Tip**

Use the Find or Search command to highlight all the commas in your writing. Check to see if you have used the commas correctly.

CHAPTER REVIEW

◆ EDITING PRACTICE

Read the following student essay, from which some commas have been intentionally deleted. Add commas where necessary between items in a series and with introductory phrases, conjunctive adverbs or transitional expressions, appositives, and nonrestrictive clauses. Cross out any unnecessary commas. The first sentence has been edited for you.

Brave Orchid

One of the most important characters in The Woman Warrior, Maxine Hong Kingston's autobiographical work, is Brave Orchid, Kingston's mother. Brave Orchid, a complex character, is an imaginative storyteller, who tells vivid tales of China. A quiet woman, she still impresses her school classmates with her intelligence. She is also a traditional woman. However, she will stop at nothing to make her family exactly what she wants it to be. Brave Orchid strongly believes in herself; even so, she sees herself as a failure.

In her native China, Brave Orchid trains to be a midwife. The other women in her class envy her independence, brilliance, and courage. One day, Brave Orchid proves her courageousness by confronting the Fox Spirit, and telling him he will not win. First of all, she tells him she can endure any pain that he inflicts on her. Next, she gathers together the women in the dormitory to burn the ghost away. After this event, the other women admire her even more.

Working hard, Brave Orchid becomes a midwife in China. After coming to America, however, she cannot work as a midwife. Instead, she works in a Chinese laundry, and picks tomatoes. None of her classmates in China could have imagined this outcome. During her later years in America, Brave Orchid becomes a woman, who is overbearing and domineering. We see another side of her at this point in the book. She bosses her children around, she tries to ruin her sister's life and she criticizes everyone and everything around her. Her daughter, a straight-A student is the object of her worst criticism.

Brave Orchid's intentions are good. Nevertheless she devotes her energy to the wrong things. She wants the people around her to be as strong as she is. Because she bullies them however she eventually loses them. In addition she is too busy noticing her daughter's faults to see all her accomplishments. Brave Orchid an independent woman and a brilliant student never reaches her goals. She is hard on the people around her because she is disappointed in herself.

◆ COLLABORATIVE ACTIVITIES

1. Bring a homemaking, sports, or fashion magazine to class. Working in a small group, look at the people pictured in the ads. In what roles are men most often depicted? In what roles are women most often presented? Identify the three or four most common roles for each sex, and give each kind of character a descriptive name—*jock* or *mother,* for example.

2. Working on your own, choose one type of character from the list your group made in the preceding activity. Then, write a paragraph in which you describe this character's typical appearance and habits. Refer to the appropriate magazine pictures to support your characterization.

3. Collaborating with other members of your group, write two paragraphs, one discussing how men are portrayed in ads and one discussing how women are portrayed.

4. Circle every comma in the paragraph you wrote for Collaborative Activity 2. Work with your group to explain why each comma is used. If no one in your group can justify a particular comma's use, cross it out.

☑ REVIEW CHECKLIST:
Using Commas

- Use commas to separate all elements in a series of three or more words or word groups. (See 31A.)

(continued on the following page)

(continued from the previous page)

- Use commas to set off introductory phrases, conjunctive adverbs, and transitional expressions from the rest of the sentence. (See 31B.)

- Use commas to set off appositives from the rest of the sentence. (See 31C.)

- Use commas to set off nonrestrictive clauses. (See 31D.)

- Use commas to separate parts of dates and addresses. (See 31E.)

- Avoid unnecessary commas. (See 31F.)

Using Apostrophes

PREVIEW

In this chapter, you will learn

■ to use apostrophes to form contractions (32A)

■ to use apostrophes to form possessives (32B)

■ to revise incorrect use of apostrophes (32C)

■ WRITING FIRST

Certain household tasks have traditionally been considered "men's work," and others have been viewed as "women's work." Although the family, like the workplace, has changed considerably in recent years, some habits and behavior patterns have remained the same. Look at the picture above, and then discuss the tasks that are considered "men's work" and "women's work" in your current household (or in the household in which you grew up). Be sure to give examples of the responsibilities of different people in your household.

Word Power

gender sexual identity (male or female)

stereotype (n) a conventional, usually oversimplified, opinion or belief; (v) to develop a fixed opinion

An **apostrophe** is a punctuation mark that is used in two situations: to form a contraction, and to form the possessive of a noun or an indefinite pronoun.

● **Writing Tip**

Even though contractions
are used in speech and informal writing, they are not
acceptable in most business
or college writing situations.

Teaching Tip

Remind students that this
list does not include every
contraction. For example,
other personal pronouns (*he,
she, they*) can also be combined with forms of *be* and
have. (Students will need
to know this to do Practice
32-1.)

ON THE WEB

For more practice, visit
Exercise Central *at*
<*www.bedfordstmartins.com/
writingfirst*>.

ESL Tip

Nonnative speakers often
misplace or omit apostro-
phes in contractions. Spend
extra time checking these
students' work.

A **Using Apostrophes to Form Contractions**

A **contraction** is a word that uses an apostrophe to combine two words.
The apostrophe takes the place of the omitted letters.

> I didn't (*did not*) realize how late it was.

> It's (*it is*) not right for cheaters to go unpunished.

Frequently Used Contractions

I + am = I'm	are + not = aren't
we + are = we're	can + not = can't
you + are = you're	do + not = don't
it + is = it's	will + not = won't
I + have = I've	should + not = shouldn't
I + will = I'll	let + us = let's
there + is = there's	that + is = that's
is + not = isn't	who + is = who's

◆ **PRACTICE 32-1**

In the following sentences, add apostrophes to contractions if needed. If
the sentence is correct, write *C* in the blank.

> **Example:** If you ~~dont~~ *don't* eat healthy foods, you ~~are'nt~~ *aren't* going to feel your
>
> best. _____

(1) ~~Were~~ *We're* all trying hard to watch our diets, but ~~its~~ *it's* not easy. _____
(2) Have you ever noticed how ~~wer'e~~ *we're* bombarded by images of high-
calorie, high-fat foods? _____ (3) Maybe we ~~shouldnt~~ *shouldn't* be so tempted, but
it's hard to resist the lure of the fast-food chains and their commercials.
_____ (4) Of course, the actual sandwich ~~doesnt~~ *doesn't* look much like the one
on television, but that ~~isnt~~ *isn't* the point. _____ (5) When ~~wer'e~~ *we're* away from
home and hungry, ~~its~~ *it's* the picture of that burger that pops into our minds.
_____ (6) ~~Well~~ *We'll* be likely to rush to a fast-food place for lunch instead of
looking for a meal ~~thats~~ *that's* healthier. _____ (7) It ~~should'nt~~ *shouldn't* be so hard to
find a fast, healthy meal. _____ (8) For example, a grilled chicken sand-
wich doesn't have nearly as much fat or as many calories as a burger
has. _C_ (9) ~~Its~~ *It's* still not the perfect meal for a dieter, but it ~~isnt~~ *isn't* too bad.
_____ (10) When we ~~dont~~ *don't* have many options, ~~wev'e~~ *we've* got to make the best
of the situation. _____

■ **WRITING FIRST: Flashback**

Look back at your response to the Writing First exercise on page 495, and underline any contractions. Have you used apostrophes correctly to replace the missing letters? Recopy all the contractions correctly on the lines below. Then, rewrite the contractions as two separate words.

Answers will vary.

Contractions   **Separate Words**

_____   _____   _____

_____   _____   _____

_____   _____   _____

B   Using Apostrophes to Form Possessives

Possessive forms indicate ownership. Nouns and indefinite pronouns do not have special possessive forms. Instead, they use apostrophes to indicate ownership.

● **Writing Tip**

Possessive pronouns have special forms, such as *its* and *his*, and these forms never include apostrophes. For information on possessive pronouns, see 28F.

Singular Nouns and Indefinite Pronouns

To form the possessive of singular nouns (including names) and indefinite pronouns, add an apostrophe plus an -*s*.

> Cesar Chavez's goal *(the goal of Cesar Chavez)* was justice for American farm workers.

> The strike's outcome *(the outcome of the strike)* was uncertain.

> Whether it would succeed was anyone's guess *(the guess of anyone)*.

For more on indefinite pronouns, see 23D and 28E.

FOCUS   Singular Nouns Ending in -*s*

Even if a singular noun already ends in -*s*, add an apostrophe plus an -*s* to form the possessive.

> The class's next assignment was a research paper.

> Dr. Ramos's patients are participating in a double-blind study.

▼ **Student Voices**

I never know where to put the apostrophe to form the possessive of a word that ends in -s.

Krishna Mahajan

● **Writing Tip**

Most nouns form the plural
by adding -s. For a list of
frequently used irregular
noun plurals, see 28B.

ON THE WEB
For more practice, visit
Exercise Central *at*
<www.bedfordstmartins.com/
writingfirst>.

Plural Nouns

To form the possessive of plural nouns ending in -s (including names), add just an apostrophe (not an apostrophe plus -s).

> The two <u>drugs'</u> side effects *(the side effects of the two drugs)* were quite different.
> The <u>Johnsons'</u> front door *(the front door of the Johnsons)* is red.

Some irregular noun plurals do not end in -s. If a plural noun does not end in -s, add an apostrophe plus an s to form the possessive.

> The <u>men's</u> room is right next to the <u>women's</u> room.

◆ PRACTICE 32-2

Rewrite the following phrases, changing the noun or indefinite pronoun that follows *of* to the possessive form. Be sure to distinguish between singular and plural nouns.

Examples:

the mayor of the city _*the city's mayor*_

the uniforms of the players _*the players' uniforms*_

1. the video of the singer _*the singer's video*_

2. the scores of the students _*the students' scores*_

3. the first novel of the writer _*the writer's first novel*_

4. the office of the boss _*the boss's office*_

5. the union of the players _*the players' union*_

6. the specialty of the restaurant _*the restaurant's specialty*_

7. the bedroom of the children _*the children's bedroom*_

8. the high cost of the tickets _*the tickets' high cost*_

9. the dreams of everyone _*everyone's dreams*_

10. the owner of the dogs _*the dogs' owner*_

■ WRITING FIRST: Flashback

Look back at your response to the Writing First exercise on page 495. Circle any possessive forms of nouns or indefinite pronouns. Have you used apostrophes correctly to form these possessives? If not, rewrite them correctly in the appropriate columns on the next page.

(continued on the following page)

(continued from the previous page)

Singular Nouns	Indefinite Pronouns	Plural Nouns
Answers will vary.		
_____	_____	_____
_____	_____	_____

C Revising Incorrect Use of Apostrophes

Be careful not to confuse a plural noun *(boys)* with the singular possessive form of the noun *(boy's)*. Never use an apostrophe with a plural noun unless the noun is possessive.

> Termites can be dangerous <u>pests</u> [not *pest's*].
>
> The <u>Velezes</u> [not *Velez's*] live on Maple Drive.

Also, be careful not to use apostrophes with possessive pronouns that end in *-s: theirs* (not *their's*), *hers* (not *her's*), *its* (not *it's*), *ours* (not *our's*), and *yours* (not *your's*).

> ### FOCUS Possessive Pronouns
>
> Be especially careful not to confuse possessive pronouns with sound-alike contractions. Possessive pronouns never include apostrophes.
>
> | Possessive Pronoun | Contraction |
> |---|---|
> | The dog bit <u>its</u> master. | <u>It's</u> *(it is)* time for breakfast. |
> | The choice is <u>theirs</u>. | <u>There's</u> *(there is)* no place like home. |
> | <u>Whose</u> house is this? | <u>Who's</u> *(who is)* on first? |
> | Is this <u>your</u> house? | <u>You're</u> *(you are)* late again. |

■ **Computer Tip**

Your computer's spell checker will not tell you when you have used a contraction for a possessive form—*it's* for *its*, for example. If you are not sure you have used the correct form, consult a dictionary.

◆ PRACTICE 32-3

Check the underlined words in the following sentences for correct use of apostrophes. If a correction needs to be made, cross out the word, and write the correct version above it. If the noun or pronoun is correct, write *C* above it.

ON THE WEB

For more practice, visit Exercise Central *at* <www.bedfordstmartins.com/ writingfirst>.

> **Example:** The <u>president's</u> ^C views were presented after several other
>
> <del>speaker's</del> *speakers* first presented <del>their's</del> *theirs.*

Teaching Tip
Even strong writers often
have trouble distinguishing
plural nouns from singular
possessive forms and using
apostrophes correctly with
possessive pronouns. You
may want to review 32C and
Practice 32-3 in class.

1. ~~Parent's~~ *Parents* should realize that when it comes to disciplining children, the responsibility is ~~their's~~ *theirs.*

2. It's *C* also important that parents offer praise for a child's *C* good behavior.

3. In ~~it's~~ *its* first few ~~week's~~ *weeks* of life, a child is already developing a personality.

4. His and ~~her's~~ *hers* towels used to be popular with ~~couple's~~ *couples,* but it's *C* not so common to see them today.

5. All the ~~Ryan's~~ *Ryans* spent four ~~year's~~ *years* in college and then went on to graduate school.

6. From the radio came the lyrics "You're *C* the one ~~who's~~ *whose* love I've been waiting for."

7. If you expect to miss any ~~classes'~~ *classes,* you will have to make arrangements with someone who's *C* willing to tell you ~~you're~~ *your* assignment.

8. No other school's *C* cheerleading squad ever tried as many tricky stunts as ~~our's~~ *ours* did.

9. Surprise ~~test's~~ *tests* are a regular feature of my economics teacher's *C* class.

10. Jazz's *C* influence on many mainstream ~~musician's~~ *musicians* is one of the book's *C* main ~~subject's.~~ *subjects.*

■ WRITING FIRST: Flashback

Look back at your response to the Writing First exercise on page 495. Circle each plural noun. Then, circle each possessive pronoun that ends in -*s*. Have you incorrectly used an apostrophe with any of the circled words? If so, revise your work.

■ WRITING FIRST: Revising and Editing

Look back at your response to the Writing First exercise on page 495. Because this is an informal exercise, contractions are acceptable; in fact, they may be preferable because they give your writing a conversational tone. Edit your writing so that you have used contractions in all possible situations.

(continued on the following page)

> *(continued from the previous page)*
>   Now, add two sentences—one that includes a singular posses-
> sive noun and one that includes a plural possessive noun. Make
> sure these two new sentences fit smoothly into your writing and
> that they, too, use contractions wherever possible.

CHAPTER REVIEW

◆ EDITING PRACTICE

Read the following student essay, into which errors in the use of apostrophes have been introduced. Edit it to eliminate errors by crossing out incorrect words and writing corrections above them. (Note that this is an
informal response paper, so contractions are acceptable.) The first sentence has been edited for you.

*For more on informal response
writing, see 35E.*

                        The Women of Messina
                   Shakespeare's
        In William ~~Shakespeares'~~ play <u>Much Ado about Nothing</u>,

the women of Messina, whether they are seen as love objects
     shrews,   *woman's*
or ~~shrew's,~~ have very few options. A ~~womans~~ role is to

please a man. She can try to resist, but she will probably
                        play's
wind up giving in. The ~~plays~~ two women, Hero and Beatrice,
                                          Hero's
are very different. Hero is the obedient one. ~~Heros'~~
                                                  man's
cousin, Beatrice, tries to challenge the rules of the ~~mans~~

world in which she lives. However, in a place like Messina,

even women like Beatrice find it hard to get the respect
                theirs.
that should be ~~their's.~~
                                                     She's
        Right from the start, we are drawn to Beatrice. ~~Shes~~
                                        situations,
funny, she has a clever comment for most ~~situation's,~~ and
                                   people's
she always speaks her mind about other ~~peoples~~ behavior.

Unlike Hero, she tries to stand up to the men in her life,
                        Benedick's
as we see in her and ~~Benedicks~~ conversations. But even

though Beatrice's intelligence is obvious, she often mocks
        It's
herself. ~~Its~~ obvious that she doesn't have much self-
                        isn't
esteem. In fact, Beatrice ~~is'nt~~ the strong woman she seems

to be.

Ultimately, Beatrice does get her man, and she will be happy--but at what cost? ~~Benedicks'~~ *Benedick's* last words to her are "Peace! I will stop your mouth." Then, he kisses her. The kiss is a symbolic end to their bickering. It is also the mark of ~~Beatrices'~~ *Beatrice's* defeat. She has lost. Benedick has shut her up. Now, she will be Benedick's wife and do what he wants her to do. Granted, she will have more say in her marriage than Hero will have in ~~her's,~~ *hers,* but she is still defeated. Even Beatrice, the most rebellious of ~~Messinas~~ *Messina's* women, finds it impossible to achieve anything of importance in ~~Messinas'~~ *Messina's* male-dominated society.

◆ COLLABORATIVE ACTIVITIES

1. Working in a group of four and building on your individual responses to the Writing First exercise at the beginning of the chapter, consider which specific occupational and professional roles are still associated largely with men and which are associated primarily with women. Make two lists, heading one "women's jobs" and one "men's jobs."

2. Now, work in pairs, with one pair of students in each group concentrating on men and the other pair on women. Write a paragraph that attempts to justify why the particular jobs you listed should or should not be restricted to one gender. In your discussion, list the various qualities men or women possess that qualify (or disqualify) them for particular jobs. Use possessive forms whenever possible—for example, *women's energy* (not *women have energy*).

3. Bring to class a book, magazine, or newspaper whose style is informal—for example, a romance novel, *TV Guide,* your school newspaper, or even a comic book. Working in a group, circle every contraction you can find on one page of each publication, and substitute for each contraction the words it combines. Are your substitutions an improvement? (You may want to read a few paragraphs aloud before you reach a conclusion.)

☑ REVIEW CHECKLIST:
Using Apostrophes

- Use apostrophes to form contractions. (See 32A.)

- Use an apostrophe plus an -*s* to form the possessive of singular nouns and indefinite pronouns, even when a noun ends in -*s*. (See 32B.)

(continued on the following page)

(continued from the previous page)

■ Use an apostrophe alone to form the possessive of plural nouns ending in *-s,* including names. If a plural noun does not end in *-s,* add an apostrophe plus an *s.* (See 32B.)

■ Do not use apostrophes with plural nouns unless they are possessive. Do not use apostrophes with possessive pronouns. (See 32C.)

Understanding Mechanics

PREVIEW

In this chapter, you will learn

- to capitalize proper nouns (33A)

- to punctuate direct quotations (33B)

- to set off titles of books, stories, and other works (33C)

- to use minor punctuation marks (33D)

Word Power

compelling forceful

empathize to identify with

plot a series of events in a narrative or drama

■ WRITING FIRST

Look at the picture above, and then describe a memorable scene from your favorite movie. Begin by giving the film's title and listing the names of the major stars and the characters they play. Then, tell what happens in the scene, quoting a few lines of dialogue if possible.

A Capitalizing Proper Nouns

A **proper noun** names a particular person, animal, place, object, or idea. Proper nouns are always capitalized. The list that follows explains and illustrates specific rules for capitalizing proper nouns and also includes some important exceptions to those rules.

1. Always capitalize names of races, ethnic groups, tribes, nationalities, languages, and religions.

   The census data revealed a diverse community of Caucasians, African Americans, and Asian Americans, with a few Latino and Navajo residents. Native languages include English, Korean, and Spanish. Most people identified themselves as Catholic, Protestant, or Muslim.

2. Capitalize names of specific people and the titles that accompany them. In general, do not capitalize titles used without a name.

   In 1994, President Nelson Mandela was elected to lead South Africa.

   The newly elected fraternity president addressed the crowd.

3. Capitalize names of specific family members and their titles. Do not capitalize words that identify family relationships, including those introduced by possessive pronouns.

   The twins, Aunt Edna and Aunt Evelyn, are Dad's sisters.

   My aunts, my father's sisters, are twins.

Teaching Tip

Explain that titles such as those in item 3 are capitalized because they are used as names.

4. Capitalize names of specific countries, cities, towns, bodies of water, streets, and so forth. Do not capitalize words that do not name particular places.

   The Seine runs through Paris, France.

   The river runs through the city.

5. Capitalize names of specific geographical regions. Do not capitalize such words when they specify direction.

   William Faulkner's novels are set in the American South.

   Turn right at the golf course, and go south for about a mile.

6. Capitalize names of specific buildings and monuments. Do not capitalize general references to buildings and monuments.

   He drove past the Liberty Bell and looked for a parking space near City Hall.

   He drove past the monument and looked for a parking space near the building.

7. Capitalize names of specific groups, clubs, teams, and associations. Do not capitalize general references to such groups.

   The Teamsters Union represents workers who were at the stadium for the Republican Party convention, the Rolling Stones concert, and the Phillies-Astros game.

   The union represents workers who were at the stadium for the political party's convention, the rock group's concert, and the baseball teams' game.

8. Capitalize names of specific historical periods, events, and documents. Do not capitalize nonspecific references to periods, events, or documents.

The Emancipation Proclamation was signed during the Civil War, not during Reconstruction.

The document was signed during the war, not during the postwar period.

9. Capitalize names of businesses, government agencies, schools, and other institutions. Do not capitalize nonspecific references to such institutions.

The Department of Education and Apple Computer have launched a partnership project with Central High School.

A government agency and a computer company have launched a partnership project with a high school.

10. Capitalize brand names. Do not capitalize general references to kinds of products.

While Jeff waited for his turn at the Xerox machine, he drank a can of Coke.

While Jeff waited for his turn at the copier, he drank a can of soda.

11. Capitalize titles of specific academic courses. Do not capitalize names of general academic subject areas, except for proper nouns—for example, a language or a country.

Are Introduction to American Government and Biology 200 closed yet?

Are the introductory American government course and the biology course closed yet?

12. Capitalize days of the week, months of the year, and holidays. Do not capitalize the names of seasons.

The Jewish holiday of Passover usually falls in April.

The Jewish holiday of Passover falls in the spring.

Writing Tip

Trade names that have become part of the language—*nylon* and *aspirin*, for example—are no longer capitalized.

ON THE WEB

For more practice, visit
Exercise Central *at*
<www.bedfordstmartins.com/
writingfirst>.

Teaching Tip

Have students do Practice 33-1 in pairs.

◆ **PRACTICE 33-1**

Edit the following sentences, capitalizing letters or changing capitals to lowercase where necessary.

Example: The third largest City in the united states is chicago, illinois.

(1) Located in the midwest on lake Michigan, chicago is an important port city, a rail and highway hub, and the site of o'hare international airport, the Nation's busiest. (2) The financial center of the city is Lasalle

street, and the lakefront is home to Grant park, where there are many Museums and monuments. (3) To the North of the city, soldier field is home to the chicago bears, the city's football team, and wrigley field is home to the chicago cubs, an american league Baseball Team. (4) In the mid-1600s, the site of what is now Chicago was visited by father jacques marquette, a catholic missionary to the ottawa and huron tribes, who were native to the area. (5) By the 1700s, the city was a trading post run by john kinzie. (6) The city grew rapidly in the 1800s, and immigrants included germans, irish, italians, poles, greeks, and chinese, along with african americans who migrated from the south. (7) In 1871, much of the city was destroyed in one of the worst fires in united states history; the fire started when, according to legend, mrs. O'Leary's Cow kicked over a burning lantern. (8) Today, Chicago's skyline is marked by many Skyscrapers, built by businesses like the john hancock company, sears, and amoco. (9) I know Chicago well because my Mother grew up there and my aunt jean and uncle amos still live there. (10) I also got information from the Chicago Chamber of Commerce when I wrote a paper for introductory research writing, a course I took at Graystone high school.

■ WRITING FIRST: Flashback

Look back at your response to the Writing First exercise on page 504. Underline every proper noun. Does each proper noun begin with a capital letter? On the lines below, correct any that do not.

Answers will vary. _____ _____

_____ _____ _____

B **Punctuating Direct Quotations**

A **direct quotation** reproduces the *exact* words of a speaker or writer. Direct quotations are always placed within quotation marks.

Lauren said, "My brother and Tina have gotten engaged."

A famous advertiser wrote, "Don't sell the steak; sell the sizzle."

When a quotation is a complete sentence, it begins with a capital letter. When a quotation falls at the end of a sentence, as in the two examples above, the period is placed inside the quotation marks. If the quotation is a question or exclamation, the question mark or exclamation point is also placed inside the quotation marks.

> The instructor asked, "Has anyone read *Sula*?"

> Officer Warren shouted, "Hold it right there!"

If the quotation itself is not a question or an exclamation, the question mark or exclamation point goes *outside* the quotation marks.

> Did Joe really say, "I quit"?

> I can't believe he really said, "I quit"!

FOCUS Indirect Quotations

Be careful not to confuse direct and indirect quotations. A direct quotation reproduces someone's *exact* words, but an **indirect quotation** simply summarizes what was said or written.
Indirect quotations are not placed within quotation marks.

DIRECT QUOTATION Martin Luther King Jr. said, "I have a dream."

INDIRECT QUOTATION Martin Luther King Jr. said that he had a dream.

FOCUS Identifying Tags

A direct quotation is usually accompanied by an **identifying tag**, a phrase that names the person or work being quoted.

Identifying Tag at the Beginning

When the identifying tag comes *before* the quotation, it is followed by a comma.

> Alexandre Dumas wrote, "Nothing succeeds like success."

Identifying Tag at the End

When the identifying tag comes at the *end* of the sentence, it is followed by a period. A comma (or, sometimes, a question mark or exclamation point) inside the closing quotation marks separates the quotation from the identifying tag.

(continued on the following page)

(continued from the previous page)

"Life is like a box of chocolates," stated Forrest Gump.

"Is that so?" his friends wondered.

Identifying Tag in the Middle

When the identifying tag comes in the *middle* of the quoted sentence, it is followed by a comma. The first part of the quotation is also followed by a comma, placed inside the quotation marks. Because the part of the quotation that follows the tag is not a new sentence, it does not begin with a capital letter.

"This is my life," Bette insisted, "and I'll live it as I please."

Identifying Tag between Two Sentences

When the identifying tag comes between two quoted sentences, it is followed by a period, and the second quoted sentence begins with a capital letter.

"Producer Berry Gordy is an important figure in the history of music," Tony explained. "He was the creative force behind Motown records."

◆ **PRACTICE 33-2**

In the following sentences containing direct quotations, first underline the identifying tag. Then, punctuate the quotation correctly, adding capital letters as necessary.

ON THE WEB
For more practice, visit **Exercise Central** *at* <www.bedfordstmartins.com/ writingfirst>.

Example: Why" Darryl asked "are teachers so strict about deadlines?"

1. We who are about to die salute you said the gladiators to the emperor.

2. When we turned on the television, the newscaster was saying ladies and gentlemen, we have a new president-elect.

3. The bigger they are said boxer John L. Sullivan the harder they fall.

4. Do you take Michael to be your lawfully wedded husband asked the minister.

5. Lisa Marie replied I do.

6. If you believe the *National Enquirer* my friend always says then you'll believe anything.

7. When asked for the jury's verdict, the foreman replied we find the defendant not guilty.

Teaching Tip
Have students write sentences from Practice 33-2 on the board. Review fragments, which can be caused by incorrect punctuation of tags. (Refer students to Chapter 22.)

8. I had felt for a long time that if I was ever told to get up so a white person could sit Rosa Parks recalled I would refuse to do so.

9. Yabba dabba doo Fred exclaimed this brontoburger looks great.

10. Where's my money Addie Pray asked you give me my money.

◆ PRACTICE 33-3

These quotations are followed in parentheses by the names of the people who wrote or spoke them. On the blank lines, write a sentence that includes the quotation and places the identifying tag in the position that the directions specify. Be sure to punctuate and capitalize correctly.

> **Example:** Nothing endures but change. (written by the Greek philosopher Heraclitus)
>
> Identifying tag in the middle _"Nothing endures," wrote the Greek philosopher Heraclitus, "but change."_

1. One is not born a woman; one becomes one. (written by essayist Simone de Beauvoir)

   Identifying tag at the beginning _Essayist Simone de Beauvoir wrote, "One is not born a woman; one becomes one."_

2. I want a kinder, gentler nation. (spoken by former president George Bush)

   Identifying tag at the end _"I want a kinder, gentler nation," said former president George Bush._

3. Tribe follows tribe, and nation follows nation. (spoken by Suquamish Chief Seattle in 1854)

   Identifying tag in the middle _"Tribe follows tribe," said Suquamish Chief Seattle in 1854, "and nation follows nation."_

4. When I'm good, I'm very good. When I'm bad, I'm better. (spoken by actress Mae West in the classic film *I'm No Angel*)

   Identifying tag in the middle _"When I'm good, I'm very good," said actress Mae West in the classic film I'm No Angel. "When I'm bad, I'm better."_

5. The rich rob the poor, and the poor rob one another. (spoken by abolitionist Sojourner Truth)

   Identifying tag at the beginning _Abolitionist Sojourner Truth said, "The rich rob the poor, and the poor rob one another."_

6. Heaven is like an egg, and the earth is like the yolk of the egg. (written by Chinese philosopher Chang Heng)

Identifying tag in the middle *"Heaven is like an egg," wrote the Chinese philosopher Chang Heng, "and the earth is like the yolk of the egg."*

7. When I found I had crossed that line, I looked at my hands to see if I was the same person. (spoken by former slave Harriet Tubman)

Identifying tag at the beginning *Former slave Harriet Tubman said, "When I found I had crossed that line, I looked at my hands to see if I was the same person."*

8. If a man hasn't discovered something he will die for, then he isn't fit to live. (spoken by Martin Luther King Jr.)

Identifying tag at the end *"If a man hasn't discovered something he will die for, then he isn't fit to live," said Martin Luther King Jr.*

9. No man chooses evil because it is evil. He only mistakes it for happiness. (written in 1790 by Mary Wollstonecraft)

Identifying tag in the middle *"No man chooses evil because it is evil," wrote Mary Wollstonecraft in 1790. "He only mistakes it for happiness."*

10. Marriage is an evil, but a necessary evil. (written by the ancient Greek poet Menander)

Identifying tag at the beginning *The ancient Greek poet Menander wrote, "Marriage is an evil, but a necessary evil."*

■ WRITING FIRST: Flashback

Look back at your response to the Writing First exercise on page 504. Make sure you have enclosed any direct quotations in quotation marks, placed other punctuation correctly, and that you have capitalized where necessary. Revise any incorrectly punctuated quotations on the following lines.

Answers will vary.

C   **Setting Off Titles of Books, Stories, and Other Works**

Some titles are typed in *italics* (or underlined to indicate italics). Others are enclosed in quotation marks. The following box shows how to set off different kinds of titles.

Teaching Tip
Remind students that they should underline to indicate italics in handwritten passages. MLA style recommends underlining in typed passages as well, but you may prefer that students use italics.

Italicized Titles	Titles in Quotation Marks
Books: *How the García Girls Lost Their Accents* Newspapers: the *Miami Herald* Magazines: *People* Long poems: *John Brown's Body* Plays: *Death of a Salesman* Films: *The Rocky Horror Picture Show* Television or radio series: *Star Trek: The Next Generation*	Book chapters: "Understand-ing Mechanics" Short stories: "The Tell-Tale Heart" Essays and articles: "The Suspected Shopper" Short poems: "Richard Cory" Songs: "America the Beautiful" Individual episodes of televi-sion or radio series: "The Montgomery Bus Boycott," an episode of the PBS series *Eyes on the Prize*

FOCUS Capital Letters in Titles

The first letters of all important words in a title are capitalized. Do not capitalize an article (*a, an, the*), a preposition (*to, of, around,* and so on), or a coordinating conjunction (*and, but,* and so on) unless it is the first or last word of the title or subtitle (*On the Road;* "To an Athlete Dying Young"; *No Way Out; And Quiet Flows the Don*).

◆ **PRACTICE 33-4**

Edit the following sentences, capitalizing letters as necessary in titles.

Example: Eudora Welty's "a worn path" is a very moving short story.

1. Directed by the wacky Ed Wood, the 1959 movie *plan nine from outer space* has been called the worst picture of all time.

2. Gary Larson's cartoon collections include the books *in search of the far side, it came from the far side,* and *valley of the far side.*

3. En Vogue's first hit album, *born to sing,* included the songs "you don't have to worry," "time goes on," and "just can't stay away."

4. Everyone should read Martin Luther King Jr.'s "i have a dream" and "letter from birmingham jail."

5. NBC has had hits with shows like *the weakest link, friends,* and *law and order.*

◆ **PRACTICE 33-5**

In the following sentences, underline or insert quotation marks around titles. (Remember that titles of books and other long works are underlined, and titles of stories, essays, and other shorter works are enclosed in quotation marks.)

> **Example:**   An article in the <u>New York Times</u> called "It's Not Easy Being Green" is a profile of former Chicago Bulls player Dennis Rodman, who once had green hair.

1. Sui Sin Far's short story ["]The Wisdom of the New,["] from her book <u>Mrs. Spring Fragrance</u>, is about the clash between Chinese and American cultures in the early twentieth century.

2. Major league baseball games traditionally open with fans singing ["]The Star-Spangled Banner.["]

3. Interesting information about fighting skin cancer can be found in the article ["]Putting Sunscreens to the Test,["] which appeared in the magazine <u>Consumer Reports</u>.

4. One of the best-known poems of the twentieth century is Robert Frost's ["]The Road Not Taken.["]

5. Ang Lee has directed several well-received films, including <u>Crouching Tiger, Hidden Dragon</u>.

6. It is surprising how many people enjoy reruns of the 1960s television series <u>Bewitched</u> and <u>I Dream of Jeannie</u>.

7. The title of Lorraine Hansberry's play <u>A Raisin in the Sun</u> comes from Langston Hughes's poem ["]Harlem.["]

8. In his autobiography, <u>Breaking the Surface</u>, Olympic diving champion Greg Louganis wrote about his struggle with AIDS.

■ WRITING FIRST: Flashback

Look back at your response to the Writing First exercise on page 504. Circle the film's title. Have you underlined it? Are capital letters used where necessary? Make any corrections on the lines below.

Answers will vary.

*For information on sentence
types, see 18A.*

D | Using Minor Punctuation Marks

A statement ends with a **period**, a question ends with a **question mark**, and an exclamation ends with an **exclamation point**. Other important punctuation marks are the **comma** (Chapter 31), the **apostrophe** (Chapter 32), and the **semicolon** (16B). Three additional punctuation marks— *colons, dashes,* and *parentheses*—are used to set off material from the rest of the sentence.

The Colon

Use a **colon** to introduce a quotation.

> Our family motto is a simple one: "Accept no substitutes."

Use a colon to introduce an explanation, a clarification, or an example.

> Only one thing kept him from climbing Mt. Everest: fear of heights.

Also use a colon to introduce a list.

> I left my job for four reasons: boring work, poor working conditions, low pay, and a terrible supervisor.

The Dash

Use **dashes** to emphasize information by setting it off from the rest of the sentence.

> I parked my car—a red Firebird—in a towaway zone.

Parentheses

Use **parentheses** to present material that is not an essential part of the sentence.

> The weather in Portland (a city in Oregon) was overcast.

● **Writing Tip**

When a colon introduces a quotation, example, or list, it must follow a complete sentence.

● **Writing Tip**

All items in a list should be parallel. (See Chapter 19.)

● **Writing Tip**

Dashes give writing an informal tone; use them sparingly in college and professional writing.

◆ PRACTICE 33-6

Add colons, dashes, and parentheses to the following sentences where necessary.

> **Example:** New Orleans (population 465,000) is the largest city in Louisiana.
>
> *Answers will vary.*

1. New Orleans has two nicknames: the "Crescent City" and the "City that Care Forgot."

2. The oldest part of the city—known as the French Quarter—dates to the early 1700s.

ON THE WEB
For more practice, visit
Exercise Central *at*
*<www.bedfordstmartins.com/
writingfirst>.*

3. The French Quarter is famous for several attractions its unique build-

ings, its fine food, its street musicians, and its wild nightlife.

4. Jackson Square called Place d'Armes by the original French settlers

lies at the heart of the French Quarter.

5. The square a gathering place for artists and other merchants centers

on a monument to Andrew Jackson.

6. Located next to Jackson Square is a famous coffee house the Café du

Monde.

7. Its popular beignets pronounced ben-*yeas* are deep-fried pastries

covered with sugar.

8. Visitors to New Orleans can try many traditional foods crayfish,

gumbos, blackened fish, and "dirty" rice.

9. New Orleans visitors people from all over the world particularly enjoy

the laid-back atmosphere of the city.

10. This atmosphere is summed up in the city's unofficial motto "Let the

good times roll."

■ WRITING FIRST: Flashback

Look back at your response to the Writing First exercise on page
504. Do you see places where you might add a quotation, an example, or a list that could be introduced by a colon? Write your
possible additions here.

Quotation _____

Example _____

List _____

■ WRITING FIRST: Revising and Editing

Look back at your response to the Writing First exercise on page
504. If you have quoted specific lines of dialogue from the film, try
varying the placement of the identifying tags you have used. If you
did not include quotations, try adding one or two. Then, add the

(continued on the following page)

(continued from the previous page)
quotation, example, or list from the Flashback on page 515 to your Writing First exercise, introducing it with a colon. Finally, edit for proper use of capital letters, quotation marks, and underlining.

CHAPTER REVIEW

◆ EDITING PRACTICE

Read the following student essay, into which errors in capitalization and punctuation and in the use of direct quotations and titles have been introduced. Edit the passage to correct any such errors. The first sentence has been edited for you.

The World of Gary Soto

My favorite Author is Gary Soto, a mexican-american poet and fiction writer whose first book of poetry, The Elements of San Joaquin, was published in 1977. Soto was born in 1952 in fresno, california, and grew up in a large spanish-speaking family. His Father he died when Soto was five worked in a factory, and his Mother picked grapes and other crops in the farms of the san joaquin valley. Much of Soto's writing is influenced by childhood memories. "These are the pictures I take with me when I write" he once said. "they stir the past, the memories that are so vivid."

Soto attended fresno city college and later studied at the university of California at fresno, where he originally majored in Geology. There, according to Soto: "One day I came across a book of poetry on a shelf in the college library. I read it, liked it, and began to write poems of my own"

One of Soto's best poems is Oranges from his 1985 book, Black Hair. In this poem, he describes the events of a cold december afternoon when a boy takes his Girlfriend into a drugstore to buy her a treat. She wants a chocolate that costs a Dime, but he only has a Nickel. He gives the Saleslady the coin plus an orange he has in his pocket, and, knowing what is going on, she lets him pay for the candy this way. In another poem, "How Things Work," Soto also writes about money. This poem is about how People are connected by one important thing the money they spend.

This theme of money is picked up again in the Title of one of Soto's books of stories, Nickel And Dime. The first story is called "We Ain't Asking Much" and is about Roberto, who loses his job, cannot pay his rent, and ends up on the Street, trying to sell Christmas ornaments made of twigs to rich people. Silver, a Character in another story, has something in common with Soto he is a poet but he also has trouble making enough money to live on. It is interesting that Silver lives in Oakland near San Francisco, where Soto himself lives.

Does Soto write from Personal Experience? He says that this is only partly true "Although the experiences in my stories, poems, and novels may seem autobiographical, much of what I write is the stuff of imagination."

◆ COLLABORATIVE ACTIVITIES

1. Imagine that you and the other members of your group are the nominations committee for this year's Emmy, Oscar, or Grammy Awards. Work together to compile a list of categories and several nominees for each category.

   Trade lists with another group. From each category, select the individual artist or work you believe deserves to win the award. Write a sentence about each winner, explaining why each is the best in its category.

   When you have finished, exchange papers with another group. Check one another's papers for correct use of capitals, quotation marks, and underlining.

2. Using a separate sheet of paper, work in groups to list as many items in each of the following five categories as you can: planets, islands, musicians or bands, automobile models, sports teams. Be sure all your items are proper nouns.

On the lines below, write five original sentences using one proper noun from each category in each sentence.

■ *Answers will vary.*

■ _____

■ _____

■ _____

■ _____

Teaching Tip

Encourage students to write
at least five or six sentences
of dialogue.

3. Working in pairs, write a conversation between two characters, real or fictional, who have very different positions on a particular issue. Place all direct quotations within quotation marks, and include identifying tags that clearly indicate which character is speaking. (Begin a new paragraph each time a new person speaks.)

Exchange your conversations with another pair of students, and check their work to see that all directly quoted speech is set within quotation marks and that capital letters and all other punctuation are used correctly.

☑ REVIEW CHECKLIST:
Understanding Mechanics

☐ Capitalize proper nouns. (See 33A.)

☐ Always place direct quotations within quotation marks. (See 33B.)

☐ In titles, capitalize all important words, as well as the first and the last words. Use italics or quotation marks to set off titles. (See 33C.)

☐ Use colons, dashes, and parentheses to set off material from the rest of the sentence. (See 33D.)

Understanding Spelling

PREVIEW

In this chapter, you will learn

■ to become a better speller (34A)

■ to know when to use *ie* and *ei* (34B)

■ to understand prefixes (34C)

■ to understand suffixes (34D)

■ to identify commonly confused words (34E)

■ WRITING FIRST

Look at the picture above. Then, write about whether or not you think elementary school students should be required to wear uniforms.

Word Power
conducive to leading to; contributing to

economical thrifty

individuality the quality of being distinct from others

A Becoming a Better Speller

Improving your spelling may take time, but the following steps can make this task a lot easier.

● **Writing Tip**
The best place to check spelling is a good college dictionary. It will also tell you how to pronounce a word and which syllables to stress.

1. *Use a dictionary.* As you proofread your papers, circle words whose spellings you are unsure of. After you have finished your draft, look up these words in the dictionary to make sure they are spelled correctly.

2. *Use a spell checker.* When you write on a computer, use your spell checker. It will correct most misspelled words and also identify many typos, such as transposed or omitted letters.

519

3. *Proofread carefully.* Even if you have used a spell checker, always proofread your papers for spelling before you hand them in.

4. *Keep a personal spelling list.* Write down all the words you misspell. If
you keep a writing journal, set aside a few pages in the back for your
personal spelling list. Whenever your instructor hands back one of
your papers, look for misspelled words—usually circled and marked
sp. Add these to your personal spelling list.

5. *Look for patterns in your misspelling.* Do you consistently misspell
words with *ei* combinations? Do you have trouble forming plurals?
Once you figure out which errors you make most frequently, you can
take steps to eliminate them.

6. *Learn the basic spelling rules.* Memorize the spelling rules in this chapter, especially those that apply to areas in which you are weak. Remember that each rule can help you spell many words correctly.

7. *Review the list of commonly confused words on pages 527 to 535.* If you
have problems with any of these word pairs, add them to your personal
spelling list.

8. *Make flash cards.* If you consistently have trouble with spelling, put individual words on 3 × 5 cards. You can use them to test yourself
periodically.

9. *Use memory cues.* Memory cues help you remember how to spell certain words. For example, remembering that *definite* contains the word
finite will help you remember that *definite* is spelled with an *i,* not an *a.*

10. *Learn to spell some of the most frequently misspelled words.* Identify
those on the list below that give you trouble, and add them to your personal spelling list.

Frequently Misspelled Words

across	disappoint	loneliness	reference
all right	early	medicine	restaurant
a lot	embarrass	minute	roommate
already	entrance	necessary	secretary
argument	environment	noticeable	sentence
beautiful	everything	occasion	separate
becoming	exercise	occur	speech
beginning	experience	occurred	studying
believe	finally	occurrences	surprise
benefit	forty	occurring	tomato
calendar	fulfill	occurs	tomatoes
cannot	generally	personnel	truly
careful	government	possible	until
careless	grammar	potato	usually
cemetery	harass	potatoes	Wednesday
certain	height	prejudice	weird
conscience	holiday	prescription	window
definite	integration	privilege	withhold
definitely	intelligence	probably	woman
dependent	interest	professor	women
describe	interfere	receive	writing
develop	judgment	recognize	written

Because English pronunciation is not always a reliable guide for spelling, most people find it useful to memorize some spelling rules.

FOCUS **Vowels and Consonants**

Knowing which letters are vowels and which are consonants will help you understand the spelling rules presented in this chapter.

> *Vowels: a, e, i, o, u*
>
> *Consonants: b, c, d, f, g, h, j, k, l, m, n, p, q, r, s, t, v, w, x, z*

The letter *y* may be considered either a vowel or a consonant, depending on how it is pronounced. In *young, y* acts as a consonant because it has the sound of *y;* in *truly,* it acts as a vowel because it has the sound of *ee.*

B   **Deciding between *ie* and *ei***

Memorize this rule: *i* comes before *e* except after *c,* or when the *ei* sound is pronounced *ay* (as in *neighbor*).

i before *e*	except after *c*	or when *ei* is pronounced *ay*
achieve	ceiling	eight
believe	conceive	freight
friend	deceive	neighbor
		weigh

FOCUS **Exceptions to the "*i before e*" Rule**

There are some exceptions to the "*i before e*" rule. The exceptions follow no pattern, so you must memorize them.

ancient	either	leisure	seize
caffeine	foreign	neither	species
conscience	height	science	weird

ON THE WEB

For more practice, visit
Exercise Central *at*
<www.bedfordstmartins.com/
writingfirst>.

◆ **PRACTICE 34-1**

Proofread the underlined words in the following sentences for correct spelling. If a correction needs to be made, cross out the incorrect word, and write the correct spelling above it. If the word is spelled correctly, write *C* above it.

Example: It was a *C* relief to ~~recieve~~ *receive* the good news.

1. Be sure to ~~wiegh~~ *weigh* the pros and cons before making important deci-

   sions, particularly those involving *C* friends.

2. When your *C* beliefs are tested, you may be able to ~~acheive~~ *achieve* a better

   understanding of yourself.

3. In our *C* society, many people ~~decieve~~ *deceive* themselves into ~~beleiving~~ *believing* that they

   are better than everyone else.

4. ~~Cheifly~~ *Chiefly* because they have been lucky, they have reached a certain

   C height in the world.

5. They think that the blood running through *C* their ~~viens~~ *veins* makes them

   belong to a higher *C* species than the average person.

6. In fact, they are probably ~~niether~~ *neither* smarter nor more talented than oth-

   ers, but they are certainly *C* deficient in humility.

7. ~~Thier~~ *Their* *C* impatient attitude can cause others a lot of ~~greif~~ *grief.*

8. I have always ~~percieved~~ *perceived* myself as thoughtful of others, and my

   C conscience leads me to treat everyone with respect.

9. There are a ~~vareity~~ *variety* of ways to learn a ~~foriegn~~ *foreign* language.

10. *Dark City* is a really *C* weird movie, even for *C* science fiction.

■ WRITING FIRST

Look back at your response to the Writing First exercise on page 519. Underline any words that have *ie* or *ei* combinations, and check a dictionary to make sure they are spelled correctly. Correct any spelling errors on the lines below.

Answers will vary.

C   Understanding Prefixes

A **prefix** is a group of letters added at the beginning of a word that changes the word's meaning. Adding a prefix to a word never affects the spelling of the original word.

dis + service = disservice   pre + heat = preheat
un + able = unable   un + natural = unnatural
co + operate = cooperate   over + rate = overrate

◆ PRACTICE 34-2

Write in the blank the new word that results when the specified prefix is added to each of the following words.

ON THE WEB
For more practice, visit
Exercise Central *at*
<www.bedfordstmartins.com/ writingfirst>.

Example: dis + respect = ___*disrespect*___

1. un + happy = ___*unhappy*___

2. tele + vision = ___*television*___

3. pre + existing = ___*preexisting*___

4. dis + satisfied = ___*dissatisfied*___

5. un + necessary = ___*unnecessary*___

6. non + negotiable = ___*nonnegotiable*___

7. im + patient = ___*impatient*___

8. out + think = ___*outthink*___

9. over + react = ___*overreact*___

10. dis + solve = ___*dissolve*___

■ WRITING FIRST: Flashback

Look back at your response to the Writing First exercise on page 519. Underline words that have prefixes, and check a dictionary to make sure each word is spelled correctly. Correct any spelling errors on the lines below.

Answers will vary. _____   _____

_____   _____

D   Understanding Suffixes

A **suffix** is a group of letters attached to the end of a word that changes the word's meaning or its part of speech. Adding a suffix to a word can change the spelling of the original word.

Words Ending in Silent *e*

If a word ends with a silent (unpronounced) *e*, drop the *e* if the suffix begins with a vowel.

DROP THE *E*

hope + <u>ing</u> = hoping   dance + <u>er</u> = dancer

continue + <u>ous</u> = continuous   insure + <u>able</u> = insurable

EXCEPTIONS

change + able = changeable   courage + ous = courageous

notice + able = noticeable   replace + able = replaceable

Keep the *e* if the suffix begins with a consonant.

KEEP THE *E*

hope + <u>ful</u> = hopeful   bore + <u>dom</u> = boredom

excite + <u>ment</u> = excitement   same + <u>ness</u> = sameness

EXCEPTIONS

argue + ment = argument   true + ly = truly

judge + ment = judgment   nine + th = ninth

◆ **PRACTICE 34-3**

ON THE WEB
For more practice, visit
Exercise Central *at*
<*www.bedfordstmartins.com/*
writingfirst>.

Write in the blank the new word that results from adding the specified suffix to each of the following words.

Examples:

insure + ance = _____insurance_____

love + ly = _____lovely_____

1. lone + ly = _lonely_

2. use + ful = _useful_

3. revise + ing = _revising_

4. base + ment = _basement_

5. desire + able = _desirable_

6. true + ly = _truly_

7. microscope + ic = _microscopic_

8. prepare + ation = _preparation_

9. nine + th = _ninth_

10. indicate + ion = _indication_

11. effective + ness = _effectiveness_

12. arrange + ment = _arrangement_

13. fortune + ate = _fortunate_

14. taste + ful = _tasteful_

15. argue + ment = _argument_

16. disable + ed = _disabled_

17. advertise + ment = _advertisement_

18. notice + able = _noticeable_

19. care + less = _careless_

20. judge + ment = _judgment_

Words Ending in -y

When you add a suffix to a word that ends in *y,* change the *-y* to an *i* if the letter before the *y* is a consonant.

CHANGE Y TO *I*

beauty + ful = beaut̲iful   busy + ly = bus̲ily

try + ed = tr̲ied   friendly + er = friendl̲ier

EXCEPTIONS

■   Keep the *y* if the suffix starts with an *i.*

cry + ̲ing = crying   baby + ̲ish = babyish

■   Keep the *y* when you add a suffix to some one-syllable words.

shy + er = shyer   dry + ness = dryness

Keep the *y* if the letter before the *y* is a vowel.

KEEP THE Y

ann̲oy + ance = ann̲oyance   enj̲oy + ment = enj̲oyment

pl̲ay + ful = pl̲ayful   displ̲ay + ed = displ̲ayed

EXCEPTIONS

day + ly = daily   say + ed = said

gay + ly = gaily   pay + ed = paid

◆ PRACTICE 34-4

Write in the blank the new word that results from adding the specified suffix to each of the following words.

Examples:

study + ed = _____*studied*_____

employ + ment = _____*employment*_____

1. happy + ness = *happiness*   9. forty + ish = *fortyish*

2. convey + or = *conveyor*   10. day + ly = *daily*

3. deny + ing = *denying*   11. cry + ed = *cried*

4. carry + ed = *carried*   12. delay + ed = *delayed*

5. ready + ness = *readiness*   13. busy + ness = *business*

6. annoy + ing = *annoying*   14. lonely + ness = *loneliness*

7. destroy + er = *destroyer*   15. spy + ing = *spying*

8. twenty + eth = *twentieth*   16. prepay + ed = *prepaid*

17. lively + hood = _livelihood_   19. joy + ful = _joyful_

18. ally + ance = _alliance_   20. marry + ing = _marrying_

Doubling the Final Consonant

For more information on vowels and consonants, see the Focus box in 34A.

When you add a suffix that begins with a vowel—for example, *-ed*, *-er*, or *-ing*—double the final consonant in the original word if (1) the last three letters of the word have a consonant-vowel-consonant pattern (cvc), *and* (2) the word has one syllable, or the last syllable is stressed.

FINAL CONSONANT DOUBLED

cut	+	ing	=	cutting (cvc—one syllable)
bat	+	er	=	batter (cvc—one syllable)
pet	+	ed	=	petted (cvc—one syllable)
commit	+	ed	=	committed (cvc—stress is on last syllable)
occur	+	ing	=	occurring (cvc—stress is on last syllable)

FINAL CONSONANT NOT DOUBLED

answer	+	ed	=	answered (cvc—stress is not on last syllable)
happen	+	ing	=	happening (cvc—stress is not on last syllable)
act	+	ing	=	acting (no cvc)

▼ **Student Voices**
I always misspell words with consecutive letter pairs, like committee.
Nicholas Kinlaw

Teaching Tip
As a homework assignment, have students think of other examples to add to the suffix charts on pages 524, 525, and 526.

◆ PRACTICE 34-5

Write in the blank the new word that results from adding the specified suffix to each of the following words.

Examples:

rot + ing = _rotting_

narrow + er = _narrower_

1. hope + ed = _hoped_   11. appeal + ing = _appealing_

2. shop + er = _shopper_   12. resist + ed = _resisted_

3. rest + ing = _resting_   13. refer + ing = _referring_

4. combat + ed = _combatted_   14. skip + er = _skipper_

5. reveal + ing = _revealing_   15. omit + ed = _omitted_

6. open + er = _opener_   16. want + ing = _wanting_

7. unzip + ed = _unzipped_   17. fat + er = _fatter_

8. trap + ed = _trapped_   18. fast + er = _faster_

9. cram + ing = _cramming_   19. repel + ed = _repelled_

10. star + ing = _starring_   20. repeal + ed = _repealed_

┌───┐
■ WRITING FIRST: Flashback

Look back at your response to the Writing First exercise on page 519. Underline words that have suffixes, and check a dictionary to make sure each word is spelled correctly. Correct any spelling errors on the lines below.

Answers will vary.

_____   _____

_____   _____
└───┘

E   Learning Commonly Confused Words

Accept/Except   *Accept* means "to receive something." *Except* means "with the exception of" or "to leave out or exclude."

"I <u>accept</u> your challenge," said Alexander Hamilton to Aaron Burr.

Everyone <u>except</u> Darryl visited the museum.

Affect/Effect   *Affect* is a verb meaning "to influence." *Effect* is a noun meaning "result" and sometimes a verb meaning "to bring about."

Carmen's job could <u>affect</u> her grades.

Overexposure to sun can have a long-term <u>effect</u> on skin.

Commissioner Williams tried to <u>effect</u> changes in police procedure.

All ready/Already   *All ready* means "completely prepared." *Already* means "previously, before."

Serge was <u>all ready</u> to take the history test.

Gina had <u>already</u> been to Italy.

Brake/Break   *Brake* is a noun that means "a device to slow or stop a vehicle." *Break* is a verb meaning "to smash" or "to detach" and sometimes a noun meaning either "a gap" or "an interruption" or "a stroke of luck."

Peter got into an accident because his foot slipped off the <u>brake</u>.

Babe Ruth thought no one would ever <u>break</u> his home run record.

The baseball game was postponed until there was a <u>break</u> in the bad weather.

Buy/By   *Buy* means "to purchase." *By* is a preposition meaning "close to" or "next to" or "by means of."

The Stamp Act forced colonists to <u>buy</u> stamps for many public documents.

He drove <u>by</u> but did not stop.

■ Computer Tip

Delete commonly confused words from your computer's spell checker so they will always be flagged as possible errors.

Teaching Tip

Teach students how to use mnemonic devices to remember spellings. (For example, *their* refers to ownership, and so does *heir*; *there* refers to location, and so does *here*.)

ON THE WEB
For more practice, visit
Exercise Central *at*
<www.bedfordstmartins.com/
writingfirst>.

He stayed <u>by</u> her side all the way to the hospital.

Malcolm X wanted "freedom <u>by</u> any means necessary."

◆ **PRACTICE 34-6**

Proofread the underlined words in the following sentences for correct spelling. If a correction needs to be made, cross out the incorrect word, and write the correct spelling above it. If the word is spelled correctly, write *C* above it.

    Example: We must ~~except~~ *accept* the fact that the human heart can <u>break</u>. *C*

1. The ~~affects~~ *effects* of several new AIDS drugs have ~~all ready~~ *already* been reported.

2. *Consumer Reports* gave high ratings to the ~~breaks~~ *brakes* on all the new cars tested ~~accept~~ *except* one.

3. Advertisements urge us to ~~by~~ *buy* a new product even if we <u>already</u> *C* own a comparable item.

4. If you ~~except~~ *accept* the charges for a collect telephone call through the ITC network, you will probably have to ~~brake~~ *break* your piggy bank to pay their bill.

5. Cigarette smoking <u>affects</u> *C* the lungs <u>by</u> *C* creating deposits of tar that inhibit breathing.

6. The show was ~~already~~ *all ready* to begin <u>except</u> *C* that the star had not arrived.

7. People who live ~~buy~~ *by* the landfill have complained for years about its ~~affects~~ *effects* on the neighborhood.

8. The physical therapy program has ~~all ready~~ *already* ~~excepted~~ *accepted* 20 percent more applicants than it admitted last year.

9. Even a hairline <u>break</u> *C* in a bone can strongly ~~effect~~ *affect* an athlete's performance.

10. When they ~~by~~ *buy* their textbooks, most students <u>accept</u> *C* the fact that they will lose money if they resell them.

Conscience/Conscious *Conscience* is a noun that refers to the part of the mind that urges a person to choose right over wrong. *Conscious* is an adjective that means "aware" or "deliberate."

    After he cheated at cards, his <u>conscience</u> started to bother him.

    As she walked through the woods, she became <u>conscious</u> of the hum of insects.

    Elliott made a <u>conscious</u> decision to stop smoking.

Everyday/Every day   *Everyday* is a single word that means "ordinary" or "common." *Every day* is two words that mean "occurring daily."

> *I Love Lucy* was a successful comedy show because it appealed to everyday people.

> Every day, Lucy and Ethel would find a new way to get into trouble.

Fine/Find   *Fine* means "superior quality" or "a sum of money paid as a penalty." *Find* means "to locate."

> He sang a fine solo at church last Sunday.

> Demi had to pay a fine for speeding.

> Some people still use a willow rod to find water.

Hear/Here   *Hear* means "to perceive sound by ear." *Here* means "at or in this place."

> I moved to the front so I could hear the speaker.

> My great-grandfather came here in 1883.

Its/It's   *Its* is the possessive form of *it*. *It's* is the contraction of *it is* or *it has*.

> The airline canceled its flights because of the snow.

> It's twelve o'clock, and we are late.

> Ever since it's been in the accident, the car has rattled.

◆ **PRACTICE 34-7**

Proofread the underlined words in the following sentences for correct spelling. If a correction needs to be made, cross out the incorrect word, and write the correct spelling above it. If the word is spelled correctly, write *C* above it.

> **Example:**   ~~It's~~ [C] often difficult for celebrities to adjust to ~~every day~~ [everyday] life.

1. ~~Hear~~ [Here] at Simonson's Fashions, we try to make our customers feel that ~~everyday~~ [every day] is a sale day.

2. The minister was a ~~find~~ [fine] person, and ~~its~~ [it's] a shame that he died so young.

3. That inner voice you hear [C] is your ~~conscious~~ [conscience] telling you how you should behave.

4. In the ~~every day~~ [everyday] world of work and school, it can be hard to ~~fine~~ [find] the time to relax and appreciate life.

5. By the time I became ~~conscience~~ [conscious] of the leaking pipe, ~~it's~~ [its] damage had run to more than a hundred dollars.

6. The judge slapped the major corporation with a thousand-dollar fine [C] for ~~everyday~~ [every day] that it was not in compliance with the county's safety codes.

> **Teaching Tip**
> Students often use *it's* instead of *its*. Read aloud a sentence containing this error, replacing the contraction with the two words it stands for (for example, *The book fell off of it is shelf*). The error should be immediately apparent.

7. When immigrants first arrive ~~hear~~ *here* in the United States, they may find *C*
that ~~its~~ *it's* difficult to adjust to their new home.

8. In ~~every day~~ *everyday* decision making, let your conscience *C* be your guide when
it comes to moral issues.

9. Even though they ~~here~~ *hear* over and over about the dangers of drinking
and driving, young people always think, "It's *C* not going to happen to
us."

10. The college is holding ~~it's~~ *its* fourth annual contest to ~~fine~~ *find* the most popular teacher on campus.

Know/Knew/New/No *Know* means "to have an understanding of" or "to
have fixed in the mind." *Knew* is the past tense form of the verb *know*. *New*
means "recent or never used." *No* means "not any," "not at all," or "not
one."

I know there will be a lunar eclipse tonight.

He knew how to install a new light switch.

You have no right to say that.

Lie/Lay *Lie* means "to rest or recline." The past tense of *lie* is *lay*. *Lay*
means "to put or place something down." The past tense of *lay* is *laid*.

Every Sunday I lie in bed until noon.

They lay on the grass until it began to rain, and then they went
home.

Tammy told Carl to lay his cards on the table.

Brooke and Cassia finally laid down their hockey sticks.

Loose/Lose *Loose* means "not fixed or rigid" or "not attached securely."
Lose means "to mislay" or "to misplace."

In the 1940s, many women wore loose-fitting pants.

I don't gamble because I hate to lose.

Mine/Mind *Mine* is a possessive pronoun that indicates ownership. *Mind*
can be a noun meaning "human consciousness" or "intelligence" or a verb
meaning "to obey" or "to attend to."

That red mountain bike is mine.

A mind is a terrible thing to waste.

"Mind your manners when you visit your grandmother," Dad said.

Passed/Past *Passed* is the past tense of the verb *pass*. It means "moved
by" or "succeeded in." *Past* is a noun meaning "earlier than the present
time."

The car that passed me must have been doing more than eighty
miles an hour.

David finally <u>passed</u> his driving test.

The novel was set in the <u>past</u>.

Peace/Piece   *Peace* means "the absence of war" or "calm." *Piece* means "a part of something."

The British prime minister thought he had achieved <u>peace</u> with honor.

My <u>peace</u> of mind was destroyed when the flying saucer landed.

"Have a <u>piece</u> of cake," said Marie.

◆ PRACTICE 34-8

Proofread the underlined words in the following sentences for correct spelling. If a correction needs to be made, cross out the incorrect word, and write the correct spelling above it. If the word is spelled correctly, write *C* above it.

Example: I thought I would ~~<u>loose</u>~~ *lose* my <u>mind</u>. *C*

1. In the ~~<u>passed,</u>~~ *past,* many people ~~<u>new</u>~~ *knew* their neighbors well.

2. Today, however, we often ~~<u>loose</u>~~ *lose* touch with our neighbors or do not <u>know</u> *C* them at all.

3. In a search for inner ~~<u>piece</u>~~ *peace* and serenity, we may use relaxation techniques to get in touch with our unconscious <u>minds</u>. *C*

4. We may want to ~~<u>loose</u>~~ *lose* ourselves in a place where <u>no</u> *C* other person can reach us.

5. She <u>lay</u> *C* in bed reading for an hour and then ~~<u>lay</u>~~ *laid* the book on the table.

6. I don't <u>mind</u> *C* if I ~~<u>loose</u>~~ *lose* occasionally; ~~<u>know</u>~~ *no* person can be a winner every time.

7. Once they have ~~<u>past</u>~~ *passed* a test, some students put everything they have learned for it out of their <u>minds</u>. *C*

8. In the <u>past</u>, *C* dress codes in schools were not nearly as ~~<u>lose</u>~~ *loose* as they are today, and most parents ~~<u>lay</u>~~ *laid* down the law about curfews.

9. A musician may ~~<u>no</u>~~ *know* a <u>piece</u> *C* of music by heart and still not ~~<u>mine</u>~~ *mind* listening to it over and over again.

10. You may ~~<u>loose</u>~~ *lose* your way if you wander ~~<u>passed</u>~~ *past* the warning signs.

Plain/Plane   *Plain* means "simple, not elaborate." *Plane* is the shortened form of *airplane*.

Sometimes the Amish are referred to as the <u>plain</u> people.

Chuck Yeager was the first person to fly a <u>plane</u> faster than the speed of sound.

Principal/Principle *Principal* means "first" or "highest" or "the head of a school." *Principle* means "a law or basic assumption."

She had the <u>principal</u> role in the movie.

I'll never forget the day the <u>principal</u> called me into his office.

It was against his <u>principles</u> to lie.

Quiet/Quit/Quite *Quiet* means "free of noise" or "still." *Quit* means "to leave a job" or "to give up." *Quite* means "actually" or "very."

Jane looked forward to the <u>quiet</u> evenings at the lake.

Sammy <u>quit</u> his job and followed the girls into the parking lot.

"You haven't <u>quite</u> got the hang of it yet," she said.

After practicing all summer, Tamika got <u>quite</u> good at handball.

Raise/Rise *Raise* means "to elevate" or "to increase in size, quantity, or worth." The past tense of *raise* is *raised*. *Rise* means "to stand up" or "to move from a lower position to a higher position." The past tense of *rise* is *rose*.

Carlos <u>raises</u> his hand whenever the teacher asks for volunteers.

They finally <u>raised</u> the money for the down payment.

The crowd <u>rises</u> every time their team scores a touchdown.

Sarah <u>rose</u> before dawn so she could see the eclipse.

Right/Write *Right* means "correct" or "the opposite of left." *Write* means "to form letters with a writing instrument."

If you turn <u>right</u> at the corner, you will be going in the <u>right</u> direction.

All students are required to <u>write</u> three short papers.

Sit/Set *Sit* means "to assume a sitting position." The past tense of *sit* is *sat*. *Set* means "to put down or place" or "to adjust something to a desired position." The past tense of *set* is *set*.

I usually <u>sit</u> in the front row at the movies.

They <u>sat</u> at the clinic waiting for their names to be called.

Elizabeth <u>set</u> the mail on the kitchen table and left for work.

Every semester I <u>set</u> goals for myself.

Suppose/Supposed *Suppose* means "to consider" or "to assume." *Supposed* is both the past tense and the past participle of *suppose*. *Supposed* also means "expected" or "required." (Note that when *supposed* has this meaning, it is followed by *to*.)

<u>Suppose</u> researchers were to find a cure for AIDS.

We <u>supposed</u> the movie would be over by ten o'clock.

You were <u>supposed</u> to finish a draft of the report by today.

● **Writing Tip**

Be careful not to drop the *d* of *supposed* before *to: He is* <u>supposed</u> *to study*, not *He is* <u>suppose</u> *to study*.

◆ **PRACTICE 34-9**

Proofread the underlined words in the following sentences for correct spelling. If a correction needs to be made, cross out the incorrect word, and write the correct spelling above it. If the word is spelled correctly, write *C* above it.

                            C   *supposed*

Example: A principal is ~~suppose~~ to care about his or her students' welfare.

                           plane   *quite*

1. Last week I flew in a ~~plain~~ that made ~~quit~~ a rough landing.

          right   *principles*

2. It is not ~~write~~ to expect everyone to agree with your personal ~~principals~~

    of morality in every case.

                                  supposed   *quiet*

3. In earlier times, children were always ~~suppose~~ to be ~~quite~~ and not

    speak when their elders were talking.

                          C   *C*

4. My favorite teacher never <u>raised</u> his voice in anger, and this <u>set</u> a good

    example for students.

                                      principal

5. Surveys have shown that many college students' ~~principle~~ goal in life

                 C

    is to become <u>quite</u> wealthy.

    C   *right*

6. <u>Suppose</u> for a moment that the defense is ~~write~~ and the district attor-

    ney is wrong.

                 plain   *quite*

7. The book had a ~~plane~~ cover, but it was ~~quiet~~ sensational.

                   C   *set*

8. All test-takers are <u>supposed</u> to <u>sit</u> their books on the table at the front

    of the room.

                                 C

9. Even the strictest high school <u>principals</u> cannot always keep students

  quiet

   ~~quite~~ and orderly in the hallways.

                               plane   *sit*

10. Some passengers insist when they fly on a ~~plain~~ that they have to ~~set~~

                  C

    on the <u>right</u> side of the aisle, while others insist on sitting on the left.

Their/There/They're   *Their* is the possessive form of the pronoun *they.* *There* means "at or in that place." *There* is also used in the phrases *there is* and *there are.* *They're* is the contraction of "they are."

    Jane Addams wanted poor people to improve <u>their</u> living conditions.

    I put the book over <u>there</u>.

    <u>There</u> are three reasons I will not eat meat.

    <u>They're</u> the best volunteer firefighters I've ever seen.

Then/Than   *Then* means "at that time" or "next in time." *Than* is used to introduce the second element in a comparison.

● **Writing Tip**

Do not use the informal spelling *thru* for *through*.

He was young and naive <u>then</u>.

I went to the job interview and <u>then</u> stopped off for a chocolate shake.

My dog is smarter <u>than</u> your dog.

Threw/Through   *Threw* is the past tense of *throw*. *Through* means "in one side and out the opposite side" or "finished."

Satchel Paige <u>threw</u> a baseball more than ninety-five miles an hour.

It takes almost thirty minutes to go <u>through</u> the tunnel.

"I'm <u>through</u>," said Clark Kent, storming out of Perry White's office.

To/Too/Two   *To* means "in the direction of." *Too* means "also" or "more than enough." *Two* denotes the numeral 2.

During spring break, I am going <u>to</u> Disney World.

My roommates are coming <u>too</u>.

The microwave popcorn is <u>too</u> hot to eat.

"If we get rid of the Tin Man and the Cowardly Lion, the <u>two</u> of us can go to Oz," said the Scarecrow to Dorothy.

Use/Used   *Use* means "to put into service" or "to consume." *Used* is both the past tense and past participle of *use*. *Used* also means "accustomed." (Note that when *used* has this meaning, it is followed by *to*.)

I <u>use</u> a soft cloth to clean my glasses.

"Hey! Who <u>used</u> all the hot water?" he yelled from the shower.

Mary had <u>used</u> all the firewood during the storm.

After two years in Alaska, they got <u>used</u> to the short winter days.

◆ PRACTICE 34-10

Proofread the underlined words in the following sentences for correct spelling. If a correction needs to be made, cross out the incorrect word, and write the correct spelling above it. If the word is spelled correctly, write *C* above it.

Example: Most chemicals are not dangerous when ~~their~~ *they're* <u>used</u> *C* properly.

1. ~~Their~~ *There* is more <u>than</u> *C* one way to get ahead in this world.

2. Critics charge that in preventing crime our country's criminal justice system often does ~~two~~ *too* little ~~to~~ *too* late.

3. An appeals judge ~~through~~ *threw* out the evidence that the jury had <u>used</u> *C*.

4. When they think of ~~there~~ *their* past, people often wonder whether they were better off earlier ~~then~~ *than* they are now.

5. Eighty percent of the students who responded ~~too~~ *to* the survey said that ~~their~~ *they're* in favor of a moment of silence, but they aren't in favor of school prayer.

6. It *used* ~~use~~ to take more *than* ~~then~~ thirty hours to drive from New York to

Miami.

7. Before the interstate highway was opened, drivers had to maneuver

their *C* cars *through* ~~threw~~ many small towns.

8. Fewer people *used* ~~use~~ to make the trip in the past because it was just *too* ~~to~~

much trouble then *C*.

9. When the president threw *C* out the first ball of the baseball season this

afternoon, he *used* ~~use~~ his left hand.

10. When *two* too people are in love, *they're* ~~their~~ often unable to see any fault in each

other.

Weather/Whether   *Weather* refers to the state of the atmosphere with respect to temperature, humidity, precipitation, and so on. *Whether* is used
to introduce alternative possibilities.

The *Farmer's Almanac* says that the weather this winter will be
severe.

Whether or not this prediction will be correct is anyone's guess.

Where/Were/We're   *Where* means "at or in what place." *Were* is the past
tense of *are*. *We're* is the contraction of "we are."

Where are you going, and where have you been?

Charlic Chaplin and Mary Pickford were popular stars of silent
movies.

We're doing our back-to-school shopping early this year.

Whose/Who's   *Whose* is the possessive form of *who*. *Who's* is the contraction of either "who is" or "who has."

My roommate asked, "Whose book is this?"

"Who's there?" squealed the second little pig as he leaned against
the door.

Who's left a yellow 1957 Chevrolet blocking the driveway?

Your/You're   *Your* is the possessive form of *you*. *You're* is the contraction
of "you are."

"You should have worn your running shoes," said the hare as he
passed the tortoise.

"You're too kind," said the tortoise sarcastically.

◆ **PRACTICE 34-11**

Proofread the underlined words in the following sentences for correct
spelling. If a correction needs to be made, cross out the incorrect word,
and write the correct spelling above it. If the word is spelled correctly,
write *C* above it.

Example: As citizens, ~~were~~ *we're* all concerned with where *C* our country is going.

1. Authorities are attempting to discover ~~who's~~ *whose* fingerprints ~~were~~ *C* left at the scene of the crime.

2. Cancer does not care ~~weather~~ *whether* ~~your~~ *you're* rich or poor, young or old, black or white; it can strike anyone.

3. Santa Fe, ~~were~~ *where* I lived for many years, has better weather *C* than New Jersey has.

4. Whenever we listen to politicians debate, ~~were~~ *we're* likely to be wondering ~~whose~~ *who's* telling the truth.

5. You should take your *C* time before deciding ~~weather~~ *whether* to focus your *C* energy on school or on work.

6. The people ~~who's~~ *whose* lives influenced me the most ~~were~~ *C* my grandmother and grandfather.

7. You cannot just sit around wondering ~~whose~~ *who's* going to make ~~you're~~ *your* dreams come true.

8. Even when the weather *C* report advises us that it's going to be sunny, ~~were~~ *we're* always careful to carry an umbrella.

9. By the time ~~your~~ *you're* in high school, people expect you to have decided ~~were~~ *where* you want to be ten years from now.

10. Only someone ~~who's~~ *C* experienced combat understands the difficulty of deciding ~~weather~~ *whether* to face the enemy or retreat.

■ WRITING FIRST: Flashback

Look back at your response to the Writing First exercise on page 519. Identify any words that appear on the lists of commonly confused words (pages 527–535), and check to make sure you have spelled them correctly. Correct any misspelled words, and then write them here.

Answers will vary.

_____   _____

_____   _____

■ WRITING FIRST: Revising and Editing

Type your response to the Writing First exercise on page 519 if you
have not already done so. Now, run a spell check. Did the computer
pick up all the errors? Which did it identify? Which did it miss?
Correct the spelling errors the computer identified as well as the
ones that you found while proofreading. (You can also check
spelling in this way in a longer writing assignment you are currently working on.)

CHAPTER REVIEW

◆ EDITING PRACTICE

Read the following student essay, into which spelling errors have been introduced. Identify the words you think are misspelled; then, look them up
in a dictionary. Finally, cross out each incorrectly spelled word, and write
the correct spelling above the line. The first sentence has been edited for
you.

Fudging

The origin of the word fudge is ~~unnown~~. *unknown.* ~~It's~~ *Its* meaning

seems to have been adopted from many ~~diffrent~~ *different* sources. At

present, it has ~~too~~ *two* meanings. The first is "a rich candy

made of sugar, butter, milk, and chocolate." The second--

and more ~~intresting~~ *interesting*--definition is "to fake or falsify."

~~Everone~~ *Everyone* can remember fudging on an essay test during

his or her academic career. A good ~~freind~~ *friend* of mine, for

example, could not answer a question on a history test

because he did not know all the causes of World War II.

What did he do? He made some causes up and got a B. Some

people, like my friend, have had great ~~sucess~~ *success* and become

expert fudgers. Those students who were able to get away

with fudging in high school continue to fudge in college

and beyond. Many politicians, for example, feel ~~comfortible~~ *comfortable*

fudging ~~there~~ *their* ~~campain~~ *campaign* speeches to attract voters. They

promise to fight corruption, find homes for the homeless,

and put an end to crime. Of course, these are empty
promises. How are voters ~~suppose~~ to judge a ~~canidate~~ if he
                          ^supposed   ^candidate
or she does not tell them the truth?

Fudging takes place not only in politics but also in
                                      ^science,
many other professions. In ~~sceince,~~ people fudge to save
time and money. Many products on the market are the result
        ^scientific
of ~~sceintific~~ fudging. Some researchers manufacture data
        ^their
so that ~~there~~ research projects can be finished quickly and
cheaply. For example, in the 1980s, a firm fudged data to
                      ^Administration   ^its
get the Food and Drug ~~Aministration~~ to approve one of ~~it's~~
                            ^lose ^weight.
products: a pill to help people ~~loose~~ ~~wieght.~~ When con-
                                                  ^pulled
sumers complained they were getting sick, the FDA ~~puled~~ the
                      ^whether
pill off the market. Of course, ~~weather~~ or not the researcher
                                                    ^already
was fired makes no difference. The damage was ~~all ready~~
done.

◆ COLLABORATIVE ACTIVITIES

1. Working in pairs, compare responses to the Writing First exercise on
   page 537. How many misspelled words did both you and your partner
   find? How many errors did you and your partner have in common?

2. Are there any patterns of misspelling in your Writing First exercises?
   What types of spelling errors seem most common?

3. Collaborate with your partner to make a spelling list for the two of you,
   and then work with other groups to create a spelling list for the whole
   class. When you have finished, determine which types of errors are
   most common.

☑ REVIEW CHECKLIST:
Understanding Spelling

☐ Follow the steps to becoming a better speller. (See 34A.)

☐ *I* comes before *e*, except after *c* or in any *ay* sound, as in *neighbor.* (See 34B.)

☐ Adding a prefix to a word never affects the word's spelling. (See 34C.)

☐ Adding a suffix to a word may change the word's spelling. (See 34D.)

(continued on the following page)

(continued from the previous page)

■ When a word ends with silent *e,* drop the *e* if the suffix begins with a vowel. Keep the *e* if the suffix begins with a consonant. (See 34D.)

■ When you add a suffix to a word that ends with a *y,* change the *y* to an *i* if the letter before the *y* is a consonant. Keep the *y* if the letter before the *y* is a vowel. (See 34D.)

■ When you add a suffix that begins in a vowel, double the final consonant in the original word if (1) the last three letters of the word have a consonant-vowel-consonant pattern (cvc), and (2) the word has one syllable, or the last syllable is stressed. (See 34D.)

■ Memorize the most commonly confused words. (See 34E.)

UNIT EIGHT

Reading Essays

Reading for College

PREVIEW

In this chapter, you will learn

■ how to preview a reading selection (35A)

■ how to highlight a reading selection (35B)

■ how to annotate a reading selection (35C)

■ how to outline a reading selection (35D)

■ how to write a response paragraph (35E)

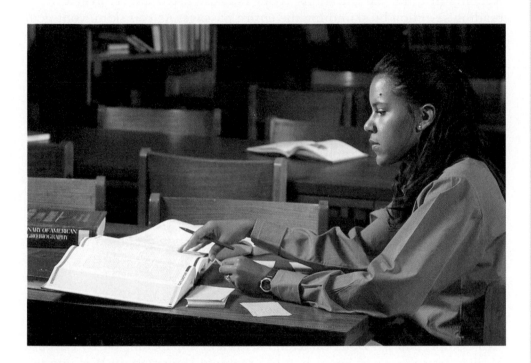

Reading is essential to all your college courses. To get the most out of your reading, you should approach the books and articles you read in a practical way, always asking yourself what they can offer you. You should also approach assigned readings critically, just as you approach your own writing when you reread and revise.

Reading critically does not mean finding fault with every point and challenging or arguing with every idea, but it does mean wondering, commenting, questioning, and judging. Most of all, it means being an active rather than a passive reader. Being an **active reader** means participating in the reading process: approaching a reading assignment with a clear understanding of your purpose, previewing a selection, highlighting and annotating it, and perhaps outlining it—all *before* you begin to respond in writing to what you have read.

In order to gain an understanding of your purpose for reading, you should start by answering some questions.

Questions about Purpose

■ Why are you reading?
■ Will you be expected to discuss the reading selection in class or in a conference with your instructor?

■ Will you have to write about what you are reading? If so, will you be expected to respond informally (for example, in a journal entry) or more formally (for example, in an essay)?

■ Will you be tested on the material?

Once you understand your purpose, you are ready to begin reading.

A Previewing a Reading Selection

Keeping in mind the Questions about Purpose listed above, **preview** the reading selection by skimming the entire passage. As you skim, your goal is to get a sense of the writer's main idea and key supporting points. You do this by looking for various **visual signals**.

Using Visual Signals to Preview a Reading Selection

■ Look at the title.
■ Look at the opening and closing paragraphs.
■ Look at each paragraph's topic sentence.
■ Look at section headings.
■ Look at *italicized* and **boldfaced** words.
■ Look at numbered lists.
■ Look at bulleted lists (like this one).
■ Look at illustrations (graphs, charts, tables, photographs, and so on).
■ Look at any boxed information.
■ Look at any information that appears in color.

◆ PRACTICE 35-1

"No Comprendo" ("I Don't Understand") is a newspaper article by Barbara Mujica, a professor of Spanish at Georgetown University in Washington, D.C. In this article, Mujica argues against bilingual education.

In preparation for class discussion and for other activities that will be assigned later in this chapter, preview the article. As you read, try to identify the writer's main idea and key supporting points, and then write them on the lines that follow the article on page 546.

No Comprendo

Last spring, my niece phoned me in tears. She was graduating   1
from high school and had to make a decision. An outstanding soccer
player, she was offered athletic scholarships by several colleges. So
why was she crying?

My niece came to the United States from South America as a child.   2
Although she had received good grades in her schools in Miami, she
spoke English with a heavy accent, and her comprehension and writing skills were deficient. She was afraid that once she left the Miami

environment, she would feel uncomfortable and, worse still, have difficulty keeping up with class work.

Programs that keep foreign-born children in Spanish-language classrooms for years are only part of the problem. During a visit to my niece's former school, I observed that all business, not just teaching, was conducted in Spanish. In the office, secretaries spoke to the administrators and the children in Spanish. Announcements over the public-address system were made in an English so fractured that it was almost incomprehensible.   3

I asked my niece's mother why, after years in public schools, her daughter had poor English skills. "It's the whole environment," she replied. "All kinds of services are available in Spanish or Spanglish.[1] Sports and after-school activities are conducted in Spanglish. That's what the kids hear on the radio and in the street."   4

Until recently, immigrants made learning English a priority. But even when they didn't learn English themselves, their children grew up speaking it. Thousands of first-generation Americans still strive to learn English, but others face reduced educational and career opportunities because they have not mastered this basic skill they need to get ahead.   5

According to the 1990 census, 40 percent of the Hispanics born in the United States do not graduate from high school, and the Department of Education says that a lack of proficiency in English is an important factor in the drop-out rate.   6

People and agencies that favor providing services only in foreign languages want to help people who do not speak English, but they may be doing these people a disservice by condemning them to a linguistic ghetto from which they cannot easily escape.   7

And my niece? She turned down all of her scholarship opportunities, deciding instead to attend a small college in Miami, where she will never have to put her English to the test.   8

---

1. A mixture of Spanish and English.

Author's main idea

Because Hispanics are not being encouraged to learn English, their opportunities are limited.

Key supporting points

1. *Author's niece is afraid to accept a scholarship away from Miami.*

2. *Students are not required to use English.*

3. *Many services are provided in Spanish.*

4. *40% of Hispanics do not graduate from high school.*

B Highlighting a Reading Selection

After you have previewed a reading selection, read through it carefully, highlighting as you read. **Highlighting** a selection involves using a combination of underlining and symbols to identify key ideas. This active reading strategy will help you to understand the writer's ideas and make connections among these ideas when you reread. Your highlighting should be selective. Remember, you will eventually be rereading every highlighted word, phrase, and sentence—so highlight only the most important, most useful information.

The most effective highlighting uses different symbols to indicate different things. When you reread—for example, when you are preparing to take an exam or write a paper—these symbols will convey specific information to you. The number and kinds of highlighting symbols you use are up to you. All that matters is that your symbols are clear and easy to remember.

> ### Using Highlighting Symbols
>
> ■ <u>Underline</u> key ideas—for example, topic sentences.
> ■ Box or circle words or phrases you want to remember.
> ■ Place a check mark (✔) or star (✳) next to an important idea.
> ■ Place a double check mark (✔✔) or double star (✳✳) next to an especially significant idea.
> ■ Draw lines or arrows to connect related ideas.
> ■ Put a question mark (?) beside a word or idea that you need to look up.
> ■ Number the writer's key supporting points or examples.

Here is how a student highlighted an excerpt from a newspaper column, "Barbie at Thirty-Five" by Anna Quindlen.

Consider the recent study at the University of Arizona investigating the <u>attitudes of white and black teenage girls toward body image</u>. The ✳

attitudes of the white girls were a nightmare. Ninety percent expressed

✔ dissatisfaction with their own bodies, and many said they saw dieting

as a kind of all-purpose panacea. "I think the reason I would diet

would be to gain self-confidence," said one. "I'd feel like it was a way

of getting control," said another. And they were curiously united in

their description of the perfect girl. She's 5 feet 7 inches, weighs just

over 100 pounds, has long legs and flowing hair. The researchers con-

cluded, "The ideal girl was a living manifestation of the Barbie doll."

While white girls described an impossible ideal, black teenagers

talked about appearance in terms of style, attitude, pride, and person-

ality. White respondents talked "thin," black ones "shapely." Seventy

percent of the black teenagers said they were satisfied with their ✔

weight, and there was little emphasis on dieting. "We're all brought up

and taught to be realistic about life," said one, "and we don't look at

things the way you want them to be. You look at them the way they

are."

The student who highlighted this passage was preparing to write an
essay about eating disorders. She began by underlining and starring
Quindlen's main idea. She then boxed the names of the two key groups the
passage compares—*white girls* and *black teenagers*—and underlined two
phrases that illustrate how the attitudes of the two groups differ (*dissatisfaction with their own bodies* and *satisfied with their weight*). Check marks
in the margin remind the student of the importance of these two phrases,
and arrows connect each phrase to the appropriate group of girls.

The student also circled three related terms that characterize white
girls' attitudes—*perfect girl, Barbie doll,* and *impossible ideal*—drawing
lines to connect them to one another. Finally, she circled the unfamiliar
word *panacea* and put a question mark above it to remind herself to look
the word up in a dictionary.

◆ PRACTICE 35-2

Review the highlighted passage above by Anna Quindlen. How would your
own highlighting of this passage be similar to or different from the sample student highlighting?

◆ PRACTICE 35-3

Reread "No Comprendo" (pages 544–545). As you reread, highlight the
article by underlining and starring main ideas, boxing and circling key
words, checkmarking important points, and, if you wish, drawing lines

and arrows to connect related ideas. Be sure to circle each unfamiliar word and to put a question mark in the margin beside it.

C   Annotating a Reading Selection

As you highlight, you should also *annotate* what you are reading. **Annotating** a passage involves making notes—of questions, reactions, reminders, ideas for writing or discussion—in the margins or between the lines. Keeping this kind of informal record of ideas as they occur to you can help prepare you for class discussion and provide a useful source of material for writing.

As you read a passage, asking yourself the following questions will help you make useful annotations.

> *Questions for Reading Critically*
>
> ■ What is the writer saying? What do you think the writer is suggesting or implying? What makes you think so?
> ■ What is the writer's purpose—his or her reason for writing?
> ■ What kind of audience is the writer addressing?
> ■ Is the writer responding to another writer's ideas?
> ■ What is the writer's main idea?
> ■ How does the writer support his or her points? Does the writer use facts? Opinions? Both?
> ■ What kind of supporting details and examples does the writer use?
> ■ Does the writer include enough supporting details and examples?
> ■ What pattern of development does the writer use to arrange his or her ideas? Is this pattern the best choice?
> ■ Does the writer seem well informed? Reasonable? Fair?
> ■ Do you understand the writer's vocabulary?
> ■ Do you understand the writer's ideas?
> ■ Do you agree with the points the writer is making?
> ■ How are the ideas presented in this reading selection like (or unlike) those presented in other selections you have read?

The following passage reproduces the student's highlighting from pages 546–547 and also illustrates her annotations.

Consider the recent study at the University of Arizona investigating the attitudes of white and black teenage girls toward body image. The � attitudes of the white girls were a nightmare. Ninety percent expressed ✓ dissatisfaction with their own bodies, and many said they saw dieting

= *cure-all*   as a kind of all-purpose panacea. "I think the reason I would diet would be to gain self-confidence," said one. "I'd feel like it was a way of getting control," said another. And they were curiously united in their description of the (perfect girl.) She's 5 feet 7 inches, weighs just over 100 pounds, has long legs and flowing hair. The researchers concluded, "The ideal girl was a living manifestation of the (Barbie doll.)"

While white girls described an (impossible ideal,) black teenagers talked about appearance in terms of style, attitude, pride, and personality. White respondents talked "thin," black ones "shapely." Seventy percent of the black teenagers said they were <u>satisfied with their weight</u>, and there was little emphasis on dieting. "We're all brought up and taught to be realistic about life," said one, "and we don't look at things the way you want them to be. You look at them the way they are." *vs. Barbie doll (=unrealistic)*   *overgeneralization?*

Need for control, perfection. Why? Media? Parents?

Barbie doll = plastic, unreal, superficial

✔ *"Thin" vs. "shapely"*

Only 30% dissatisfied — vs. 90% of white girls

With her annotations, this student recorded the meaning of the word *panacea*, put the Barbie doll reference and the contrasting statistics into her own words, and recorded questions she intended to explore further.

◆ **PRACTICE 35-4**

Reread "No Comprendo" (pages 544–545). As you reread, refer to the Questions for Reading Critically (page 548), and use them to help you annotate the article by writing down your own thoughts and questions in the margins. Note where you agree or disagree with the writer, and briefly explain why. Quickly summarize any points you think are particularly important. Take time to look up any unfamiliar words you have circled and write brief definitions. Think of these annotations as your preparation for discussing the article in class and eventually writing about it.

◆ **PRACTICE 35-5**

Trade workbooks with another student, and read over his or her highlighting and annotating of "No Comprendo." How are your written responses similar to the other student's? How are they different? Do your classmate's responses help you see anything new about the article?

D   **Outlining a Reading Selection**

Outlining is another technique you can use to help you understand a passage you are reading. Unlike a **formal outline**, which follows strict conventions, an **informal outline** enables you to record and arrange a passage's

● **Writing Tip**

Formal outlines can help you keep track of ideas in long essays or research papers. See 12E and Appendix B, section 8, for examples of formal outlines.

ideas quickly and easily. After you have finished an informal outline of a reading selection, you should be able to see the writer's emphasis (which ideas are more important than others) as well as how the ideas are related.

FOCUS Making an Informal Outline

1. Write or type the selection's main idea across the top of a sheet of paper. (This will remind you of the writer's focus and help keep your outline on track.)
2. At the left margin, write down the most important idea of the first body paragraph or first part of the selection.
3. Indent the next line a few spaces, and list the examples or details that support this idea.
4. As ideas become more specific, indent further. (Ideas that have the same degree of importance are indented the same distance from the left margin.)
5. Repeat the process with each body paragraph or part of the selection.

Computer Tip

Use your computer's Tab key to help you set up your outline.

The student who highlighted and annotated the passage from Anna Quindlen's "Barbie at Thirty-Five" (pages 548–549) made the following informal outline to help her understand the ideas in the passage.

```
Main idea: Black and white teenage girls have very dif-
ferent attitudes about their body images.


White girls dissatisfied
     90% dissatisfied with appearance
     Dieting=cure-all
         —self-confidence
         —control
     Ideal=unrealistic
         —tall and thin
         —Barbie doll
Black girls satisfied
     70% satisfied with weight
     Dieting not important
     Ideal=realistic
         —shapely
         —not thin
```

◆ **PRACTICE 35-6**

Working on your own or in a small group, make an informal outline of "No Comprendo" (pages 544–545). Refer to your highlighting and annotations as you construct your outline. When you have finished, check to make certain your outline indicates the writer's emphasis and the relationships among her ideas.

E Writing a Response Paragraph

Once you have highlighted and annotated a reading selection, you are ready to write about it—perhaps in a **response paragraph** in which you record your informal reactions to the writer's ideas.

Because a response paragraph is informal, no special guidelines or rules govern its format or structure. As in any paragraph, however, you should include a topic sentence, write in complete sentences, and link sentences with appropriate transitions. Informal style and personal opinions are acceptable.

The student who highlighted, annotated, and outlined the Quindlen passage wrote this response paragraph.

For more on writing a paragraph, see Chapters 1 and 2.

> Why are white and black girls' body images so different? Why do black girls think it's okay to be "shapely" while white girls are obsessed with being thin? Maybe it's because music videos and movies and fashion magazines show so many more white models, all half-starved, with perfect hair and legs. Or maybe white girls get different messages from their parents or the people they date. Do white and black girls' attitudes about their bodies stay the same when they get older? And what about <u>male</u> teenagers' self-images? Do white and black <u>guys</u> have different body images too?

> **Teaching Tip**
> Remind students that contractions are acceptable here only because this is an informal paragraph.

The process of writing this paragraph was very helpful to the student. The questions she asked raised a number of interesting ideas that she could explore in class discussion or in a longer, more formal, and more fully developed piece of writing.

◆ PRACTICE 35-7

On a separate sheet of paper, write an informal response paragraph expressing your reactions to "No Comprendo" (pages 544–545) and the issue of bilingual education.

☑ REVIEW CHECKLIST:
Reading for College

- Preview the reading selection. (See 35A.)
- Highlight the reading selection. (See 35B.)
- Annotate the reading selection. (See 35C.)
- Outline the reading selection. (See 35D.)
- Write a response paragraph. (See 35E.)

Readings for Writers

See Chapters 3–11 for information on using various patterns for developing paragraphs; see Chapter 14 for information on writing essays that use these patterns of development.

The following nineteen essays by professional writers offer interesting material to read, react to, think critically about, discuss, and write about. In addition, these essays illustrate some of the ways you can organize ideas in your own writing.

The essays in this chapter use the nine patterns of development you learned about in Units 1 to 3 of this book: exemplification, narration, description, process, cause and effect, comparison and contrast, classification, definition, and argument. These patterns are not your only options for arranging ideas in essays; in fact, many essays combine several patterns of development. Still, understanding how each of these nine patterns works will help you choose the most effective organization strategy when you are writing for a particular purpose and audience.

In this chapter, two essays by professional writers illustrate each pattern of development. (For argument, three model essays are included.) Each essay is preceded by a short introduction that tells you something about the writer and suggests what to look for as you read. Following each selection are four sets of questions. Questions that you can work on in collaboration with other students are marked with an asterisk (*).

For more on highlighting and annotating, see Chapter 35.

- **Reacting to the Reading** questions suggest guidelines for highlighting and annotating the essay.
- **Reacting to Words** questions focus on the writer's word choice.
- **Reacting to Ideas** questions encourage you to respond critically to the writer's ideas and perhaps to consider his or her audience or purpose.
- **Reacting to the Pattern** questions ask you to consider how ideas are arranged within the essay and how they are connected to one another.

Each section ends with **Writing Practice** suggestions that give you opportunities to explore in writing ideas related to the section's readings.

A   Exemplification

For more on how to write an exemplification essay, see 14A.

An **exemplification** essay uses one or more specific examples to support a thesis statement. The two selections that follow, "Don't Call Me a Hot Tamale" by Judith Ortiz Cofer and "The Suspected Shopper" by Ellen

Goodman, are exemplification essays. The first uses a series of short examples to support a thesis; the second uses a single extended example.

DON'T CALL ME A HOT TAMALE

Judith Ortiz Cofer

Award-winning poet, novelist, and essayist Judith Ortiz Cofer often writes about her experiences as a Latina—a Hispanic woman—living in a non-Hispanic culture. In "Don't Call Me a Hot Tamale" (1993), she discusses how being Puerto Rican has affected her in the world beyond Puerto Rico. Note that all her examples illustrate the stereotypes she encounters not simply in reaction to her heritage but also in reaction to her gender.

Teaching Tip
Remind students to familiarize themselves with the end-of-essay questions before they read the essay.

1   On a bus to London from Oxford University, where I was earning some graduate credits one summer, a young man, obviously fresh from a pub, approached my seat. With both hands over his heart, he went down on his knees in the aisle and broke into an Irish tenor's rendition of "Maria" from *West Side Story*. I was not amused. "Maria" had followed me to London, reminding me of a prime fact of my life: You can leave the island of Puerto Rico, master the English language, and travel as far as you can, but if you're a Latina, especially one who so clearly belongs to Rita Moreno's[1] gene pool, the island travels with you.

ESL Tip
In choosing essays to assign, consider the nonnative students in your class. For example, assigning an essay by a Latino writer might help engage students whose first language is Spanish.

2   Growing up in New Jersey and wanting most of all to belong, I lived in two completely different worlds. My parents designed our life as a microcosm of their *casas* on the island—we spoke in Spanish, ate Puerto Rican food bought at the *bodega*, and practiced strict Catholicism complete with Sunday mass in Spanish.

3   I was kept under tight surveillance by my parents, since my virtue and modesty were, by their cultural equation, the same as their honor. As teenagers, my friends and I were lectured constantly on how to behave as proper *señoritas*. But it was a conflicting message we received, since our Puerto Rican mothers also encouraged us to look and act like women by dressing us in clothes our Anglo schoolmates and their mothers found too "mature" and flashy. I often felt humiliated when I appeared at an American friend's birthday party wearing a dress more suitable for a semiformal. At Puerto Rican festivities, neither the music nor the colors we wore could be too loud.

4   I remember Career Day in high school, when our teachers told us to come dressed as if for a job interview. That morning, I agonized in front of my closet, trying to figure out what a "career girl" would wear, because the only model I had was Marlo Thomas[2] on TV. To me and my Puerto Rican girlfriends, dressing up meant wearing our mother's ornate jewelry and clothing.

5   At school that day, the teachers assailed us for wearing "everything at once"—meaning too much jewelry and too many accessories. And it was

---

1. A Puerto Rican actress, dancer, and singer. She is well known for her role in the movie musical *West Side Story*, a version of Shakespeare's *Romeo and Juliet* featuring Anglos and Puerto Ricans in New York City.
2. Star of a 1966–71 television comedy about a young woman living on her own in New York City.

painfully obvious that the other students in their tailored skirts and silk blouses thought we were hopeless and vulgar. The way they looked at us was a taste of the cultural clash that awaited us in the real world, where prospective employers and men on the street would often misinterpret our tight skirts and bright colors as a come-on.

It is custom, not chromosomes, that leads us to choose scarlet over pale pink. Our mothers had grown up on a tropical island where the natural environment was a riot of primary colors, where showing your skin was one way to keep cool as well as to look sexy. On the island, women felt freer to dress and move provocatively since they were protected by the traditions and laws of a Spanish/Catholic system of morality and machismo, the main rule of which was: *You may look at my sister, but if you touch her I will kill you.* The extended family and church structure provided them with a circle of safety on the island; if a man "wronged" a girl, everyone would close in to save her family honor. 6

Off-island, signals often get mixed. When a Puerto Rican girl who is dressed in her idea of what is attractive meets a man from the mainstream culture who has been trained to react to certain types of clothing as a sexual signal, a clash is likely to take place. She is seen as a Hot Tamale, a sexual firebrand. I learned this lesson at my first formal dance when my date leaned over and painfully planted a sloppy, overeager kiss on my mouth. When I didn't respond with sufficient passion, he said in a resentful tone: "I thought you Latin girls were supposed to mature early." It was only the first time I would feel like a fruit or vegetable—I was supposed to *ripen*, not just grow into womanhood like other girls. 7

These stereotypes, though rarer, still surface in my life. I recently stayed at a classy metropolitan hotel. After having dinner with a friend, I was returning to my room when a middle-aged man in a tuxedo stepped directly into my path. With his champagne glass extended toward me, he exclaimed, "Evita!"[3] 8

Blocking my way, he bellowed the song "Don't Cry for Me, Argentina." Playing to the gathering crowd, he began to sing loudly a ditty to the tune of "La Bamba"[4]—except the lyrics were about a girl named Maria whose exploits all rhymed with her name and gonorrhea. 9

I knew that this same man—probably a corporate executive, even worldly by most standards—would never have regaled a white woman with a dirty song in public. But to him, I was just a character in his universe of "others," all cartoons. 10

Still, I am one of the lucky ones. There are thousands of Latinas without the privilege of the education that my parents gave me. For them every day is a struggle against the misconceptions perpetuated by the myth of the Latina as whore, domestic worker or criminal. 11

Rather than fight these pervasive stereotypes, I try to replace them with a more interesting set of realities. I travel around the U.S. reading from my books of poetry and my novel. With the stories I tell, the dreams and fears I examine in my work, I try to get my audience past the particulars of my skin color, my accent or my clothes. 12

---

3. Eva Perón, wife of Juan Perón, president of Argentina in the 1940s and 1950s. She is the subject of the musical *Evita*.
4. A song with Spanish lyrics popular in the late 1950s.

I once wrote a poem in which I called Latinas "God's brown daugh- 13
ters." It is really a prayer, of sorts, for communication and respect. In it,
Latin women pray "in Spanish to an Anglo God/with a Jewish heritage,"
and they are "fervently hoping/that if not omnipotent,/at least He be
bilingual."

Reacting to the Reading

1. Preview the essay. As you read it more carefully, highlight and annotate
   as needed to help you understand the writer's ideas.
2. Underline the essay's thesis statement. In the margins of the essay,
   number the examples Cofer uses to support this thesis.

Reacting to Words

*1. Define these words: *tamale* (title), *rendition* (paragraph 1), *microcosm*
   (2), *ornate* (4), *assailed* (5), *riot* (6), *machismo* (6), *firebrand* (7), *regaled*
   (10), *perpetuated* (11), *pervasive* (12), *omnipotent* (13). Can you suggest
   a synonym for each word that will work in the essay?
2. What does the phrase *hot tamale* suggest to you? What do you think
   Cofer intends it to suggest? Can you think of a word or phrase that
   might be more effective?

Teaching Tip
Students may need help
defining words. With nonnative students, consider going
over the definitions in class
before assigning the reading.

Reacting to Ideas

*1. Cofer states her thesis in paragraph 1: "You can leave the island of
   Puerto Rico, master the English language, and travel as far as you can,
   but if you're a Latina, . . . the island travels with you." Restate this
   thesis in your own words. Do you think this statement applies only to
   Latinas or to other ethnic groups as well? Explain.
2. How, according to Cofer, are the signals sent by dress and appearance
   interpreted differently in Puerto Rico and "off-island" (paragraph 7)?
   How does this difference create problems for Cofer? Do you think
   there is anything she can do to avoid these problems?

Teaching Tip
Remind students to answer
all questions in complete
sentences.

Reacting to the Pattern

1. What examples does Cofer use to support her thesis? Do you think she
   uses enough examples to convince readers that her thesis is reasonable?
2. Cofer begins her essay with an example. Do you think this is an effective opening strategy? Why or why not? How else might Cofer have
   begun her essay?
3. All of Cofer's examples are personal experiences. Are they as convincing as statistics or examples from current news articles would be? Are
   they *more* convincing? Explain.

Writing Practice

1. What kinds of examples can you think of to counteract the stereotype
   of the Latina as "whore, domestic worker or criminal" (paragraph 11)?
   Write a letter to a television network in which you propose the addition of several different Latina characters to actual programs in which
   they might appear.

2. What do you think Cofer can do to avoid being stereotyped? Write an essay that gives examples of specific things she might do to change the way others see her. In your thesis, state why she should (or should not) make changes.

3. Do you think others stereotype you because of your heritage—or because of your age, your gender, your dress, or where you live? Discuss some specific instances of such stereotyping.

THE SUSPECTED SHOPPER

Ellen Goodman

Journalist Ellen Goodman wrote "The Suspected Shopper" for her syndicated newspaper column. Note that although Goodman develops a single extended example of a "suspected shopper"—herself—throughout her essay, she supports her thesis with specific examples of incidents in which she was suspected. As you read, consider whether the essay (written in 1981) is still relevant to readers today—or whether it is perhaps even more relevant.

1   It is Saturday, Shopping Saturday, as it's called by the merchants who spread their wares like plush welcome mats across the pages of my newspaper.

2   But the real market I discover is a different, less eager place than the one I read about. On this Shopping Saturday I don't find welcomes, I find warnings and wariness.

3   At the first store, a bold sign of the times confronts me: SHOPLIFTERS WILL BE PROSECUTED TO THE FULL EXTENT OF THE LAW.

4   At the second store, instead of a greeter, I find a doorkeeper. It is his job, his duty, to bar my entrance. To pass, I must give up the shopping bag on my arm. I check it in and check it out.

5   At the third store, I venture as far as the dressing room. Here I meet another worker paid to protect the merchandise rather than to sell it. The guard of this dressing room counts the number of items I carry in and will count the number of items I carry out.

6   In the mirror, a long, white, plastic security tag juts out from the blouse tucked into the skirt. I try futilely to pat it down along my left hip, try futilely to zip the skirt.

7   Finally, during these strange gyrations, a thought seeps through years of dulled consciousness, layers of denial. Something has happened to the relationship between shops and shoppers. I no longer feel like a woman in search of a shirt. I feel like an enemy at Checkpoint Charlie.[1]

8   I finally, belatedly, realize that I am treated less like a customer these days and more like a criminal. And I hate it. This change happened gradually, and understandably. Security rose in tandem with theft. The defenses of the shopkeepers went up, step by step, with the offenses of the thieves.

9   But now as the weapons escalate, it's the average consumer, the innocent bystander, who is hit by friendly fire.

10 I don't remember the first time an errant security tag buzzed at the doorway, the first time I saw a camera eye in a dress department. I accepted it as part of the price of living in a tight honesty market.

1. A military security checkpoint.

In the supermarket, they began to insist on a mug shot before they 11
would cash my check. I tried not to take it personally. At the drugstore, the
cashier began to staple my bags closed. And I tried not to take it personally.

Now, these experiences have accumulated until I feel routinely treated 12
like a suspect. At the jewelry store, the door is unlocked only for those who
pass judgment. In the junior department, the suede pants are permanently
attached to the hangers. In the gift shop, the cases are only opened with
a key.

I am not surprised anymore, but I am finally aware of just how 13
unpleasant it is to be dealt with as guilty until we prove our innocence.
Anyplace we are not known, we are not trusted. The old slogan, "Let the
Consumer Beware," has been replaced with a new slogan: "Beware of the
Consumer."

It is no fun to be Belgium[2] in the war between sales and security. Thiev- 14
ery has changed the atmosphere of the marketplace. Merchant distrust has
spread through the ventilation system of a whole business, a whole city,
and it infects all of us.

At the cashier counter today, with my shirt in hand, I the Accused stand 15
quietly while the saleswoman takes my credit card. I watch her round up
the usual suspicions. In front of my face, without a hint of embarrassment,
she checks my charge number against the list of stolen credit vehicles.
While I stand there, she calls the clearinghouse of bad debtors.

Having passed both tests, I am instructed to add my name, address, 16
serial number to the bottom of the charge. She checks one signature
against another, the picture against the person. Only then does she release
the shirt into my custody.

And so this Shopping Saturday I take home six ounces of silk and a 17
load of resentment.

Reacting to the Reading

1. Preview the essay. As you read it more carefully, highlight and annotate
   as needed to help you understand the writer's ideas.
2. Reread the essay, and review your highlighting and annotations. In the
   margins of the essay, supplement Goodman's examples with one or two
   examples from your personal experience (or from the experiences of
   your friends) that support her thesis.

Reacting to Words

*1. Define these words: *futilely* (paragraph 6), *gyrations* (7), *belatedly* (8),
   tandem (8), *errant* (10). Can you suggest a synonym for each word that
   will work in the essay?
2. What is Goodman's purpose in choosing words like *enemy* (paragraph
   7) and *mug shot* (11)? How do they help to support her thesis? Can you
   find additional words or expressions that serve the same purpose?

Reacting to Ideas

*1. Goodman, a middle-class white woman, uses *we* in the sentence
   "Anyplace we are not known, we are not trusted" (paragraph 13). Who

2. Country located between France and Germany, which were enemies in several wars.

is this *we?* Do you think Goodman is really part of the group with which she identifies?

2. In paragraph 8, Goodman says the change in attitude she observes is understandable. Do you think she is right?

3. Do you think shoplifting is more or less of a problem today than it was in 1981 when Goodman wrote her essay? What makes you think so?

Reacting to the Pattern

1. In paragraph 8, Goodman states her thesis: "I finally, belatedly, realize that I am treated less like a customer these days and more like a criminal." However, she introduces a number of her examples even before she states this thesis. Why do you think she does this?

2. List the specific examples of times when Goodman was "treated less like a customer . . . and more like a criminal" (paragraph 8).

3. How does Goodman arrange the specific examples that support her thesis? Is each discussed in an individual paragraph, or are examples grouped together?

Writing Practice

1. Why do you think people shoplift? Write an exemplification essay in which you discuss a different reason in each body paragraph.

2. Have you ever been torn between giving in to peer pressure and maintaining your own sense of right and wrong? Develop an extended example that illustrates what it was like to be caught in the middle and explains how you resolved the problem.

3. What do you think merchants can do to reduce shoplifting without making shoppers feel like criminals? Using exemplification to organize your ideas, write a letter to a store where you are a regular customer.

B   Narration

For more on how to write a narrative essay, see 14B.

A **narrative** essay tells a story by presenting a series of events in chronological order. In the first of the two essays that follow, "The Sanctuary of School," Lynda Barry tells a story about home and family. In the second, "Thirty-Eight Who Saw Murder Didn't Call the Police," Martin Gansberg reports the story of a tragic murder.

THE SANCTUARY OF SCHOOL

Lynda Barry

In her cartoon strip "Ernie Pook's Comeek," which appears in a number of newspapers and magazines, Lynda Barry looks at the world through the eyes of children. Her characters remind adult readers of the complicated world of young people and of the clarity with which they see social situations. In "The Sanctuary of School," Barry tells a story from her own childhood. As you read this essay, note how Barry relates her personal experience to a broader issue.

1   I was 7 years old the first time I snuck out of the house in the dark. It was winter and my parents had been fighting all night. They were short on money and long on relatives who kept "temporarily" moving into our house because they had nowhere else to go.

2   My brother and I were used to giving up our bedroom. We slept on the couch, something we actually liked because it put us that much closer to the light of our lives, our television.

3   At night when everyone was asleep, we lay on our pillows watching it with the sound off. We watched Steve Allen's mouth moving. We watched Johnny Carson's mouth moving.[1] We watched movies filled with gangsters shooting machine guns into packed rooms, dying soldiers hurling a last grenade and beautiful women crying at windows. Then the sign-off finally came and we tried to sleep.

4   The morning I snuck out, I woke up filled with a panic about needing to get to school. The sun wasn't quite up yet but my anxiety was so fierce that I just got dressed, walked quietly across the kitchen and let myself out the back door.

5   It was quiet outside. Stars were still out. Nothing moved and no one was in the street. It was as if someone had turned the sound off on the world.

6   I walked the alley, breaking thin ice over the puddles with my shoes. I didn't know why I was walking to school in the dark. I didn't think about it. All I knew was a feeling of panic, like the panic that strikes kids when they realize they are lost.

7   That feeling eased the moment I turned the corner and saw the dark outline of my school at the top of the hill. My school was made up of about 15 nondescript portable classrooms set down on a fenced concrete lot in a rundown Seattle neighborhood, but it had the most beautiful view of the Cascade Mountains. You could see them from anywhere on the playfield and you could see them from the windows of my classroom—Room 2.

8   I walked over to the monkey bars and hooked my arms around the cold metal. I stood for a long time just looking across Rainier Valley. The sky was beginning to whiten and I could hear a few birds.

9   In a perfect world my absence at home would not have gone unnoticed. I would have had two parents in a panic to locate me, instead of two parents in a panic to locate an answer to the hard question of survival during a deep financial and emotional crisis.

10   But in an overcrowded and unhappy home, it's incredibly easy for any child to slip away. The high levels of frustration, depression and anger in my house made my brother and me invisible. We were children with the sound turned off. And for us, as for the steadily increasing number of neglected children in this country, the only place where we could count on being noticed was at school.

11   "Hey there, young lady. Did you forget to go home last night?" It was Mr. Gunderson, our janitor, whom we all loved. He was nice and he was funny and he was old with white hair, thick glasses and an unbelievable number of keys. I could hear them jingling as he walked across the playfield. I felt incredibly happy to see him.

---

1. Steve Allen and Johnny Carson were late-night television hosts.

He let me push his wheeled garbage can between the different portables as he unlocked each room. He let me turn on the lights and raise the window shades and I saw my school slowly come to life. I saw Mrs. Holman, our school secretary, walk into the office without her orange lipstick on yet. She waved. 12

I saw the fifth-grade teacher Mr. Cunningham, walking under the breezeway eating a hard roll. He waved. 13

And I saw my teacher, Mrs. Claire LeSane, walking toward us in a red coat and calling my name in a very happy and surprised way, and suddenly my throat got tight and my eyes stung and I ran toward her crying. It was something that surprised us both. 14

It's only thinking about it now, 28 years later, that I realize I was crying from relief. I was with my teacher, and in a while I was going to sit at my desk, with my crayons and pencils and books and classmates all around me, and for the next six hours I was going to enjoy a thoroughly secure, warm and stable world. It was a world I absolutely relied on. Without it, I don't know where I would have gone that morning. 15

Mrs. LeSane asked me what was wrong and when I said "Nothing," she seemingly left it at that. But she asked me if I would carry her purse for her, an honor above all honors, and she asked if I wanted to come into Room 2 early and paint. 16

She believed in the natural healing power of painting and drawing for troubled children. In the back of her room there was always a drawing table and an easel with plenty of supplies, and sometimes during the day she would come up to you for what seemed like no good reason and quietly ask if you wanted to go to the back table and "make some pictures for Mrs. LeSane." We all had a chance at it—to sit apart from the class for a while to paint, draw and silently work out impossible problems on 11 × 17 sheets of newsprint. 17

Drawing came to mean everything to me. At the back table in Room 2, I learned to build myself a life preserver that I could carry into my home. 18

We all know that a good education system saves lives, but the people of this country are still told that cutting the budget for public schools is necessary, that poor salaries for teachers are all we can manage and that art, music and all creative activities must be the first to go when times are lean. 19

Before- and after-school programs are cut and we are told that public schools are not made for baby-sitting children. If parents are neglectful temporarily or permanently, for whatever reason, it's certainly sad, but their unlucky children must fend for themselves. Or slip through the cracks. Or wander in a dark night alone. 20

We are told in a thousand ways that not only are public schools not important, but that the children who attend them, the children who need them most, are not important either. We leave them to learn from the blind eye of a television, or to the mercy of "a thousand points of light"[2] that can be as far away as stars. 21

I was lucky. I had Mrs. LeSane. I had Mr. Gunderson. I had an abundance of art supplies. And I had a particular brand of neglect in my home that allowed me to slip away and get to them. But what about the rest of the kids who weren't as lucky? What happened to them? 22

---

2. Phrase used by former president George Bush to promote volunteerism rather than government programs.

By the time the bell rang that morning I had finished my drawing and 23
Mrs. LeSane pinned it up on the special bulletin board she reserved for
drawings from the back table. It was the same picture I always drew—a
sun in the corner of a blue sky over a nice house with flowers all around it.

Mrs. LeSane asked us to please stand, face the flag, place our right 24
hands over our hearts and say the Pledge of Allegiance. Children across the
country do it faithfully. I wonder now when the country will face its children and say a pledge right back.

Reacting to the Reading

1. Preview the essay. As you read it more carefully, highlight and annotate
   as needed to help you understand the writer's ideas.
2. Underline passages that describe Barry's home life in negative terms
   and her school life in positive terms. What specific features of the two
   places are contrasted?

Reacting to Words

*1. Define these words: *nondescript* (paragraph 7), *fend* (20). Can you suggest a synonym for each word that will work in the essay?
2. Look up the word *sanctuary* in a dictionary. Which of the listed definitions do you think comes closest to Barry's meaning?

Teaching Tip
Students may need help
defining words. With nonnative students, consider going
over the definitions in class
before assigning the reading.

Reacting to Ideas

1. In paragraph 10, Barry characterizes herself and her brother as "children with the sound turned off." What do you think she means?
2. List the ways in which Barry's home and school worlds are different.
*3. What is the main point of Barry's essay—the idea that she wants to
   convince readers to accept? Is this idea actually stated in her essay? If
   so, where? If not, do you think it should be?

Teaching Tip
Remind students to answer
all questions in complete
sentences.

Reacting to the Pattern

1. Paragraphs 9–10 and 19–22 interrupt Barry's story. What purpose do
   these paragraphs serve? Do you think the essay would be more effective if paragraphs 9 and 10 came earlier? If paragraphs 19–22 came
   after paragraph 24? Explain.
2. What transitional words and phrases does Barry use to move readers
   from one event to the next? Do you think her essay needs more transitions? If so, where should they be added?

Writing Practice

1. Did you see elementary school as a sanctuary or as something quite
   different? Write a narrative essay that conveys to readers what school
   meant to you when you were a child.
2. In addition to school, television was a sanctuary for Barry and her
   brother. Did television watching (or some other activity) serve this
   function for you when you were younger? Is there some activity that
   fills this role now? In a narrative essay, tell about your own "sanctuary."
3. What role does college play in your life? Write an article for your
   school newspaper in which you use narration to illustrate what school
   means to you now that you are an adult.

THIRTY-EIGHT WHO SAW MURDER
DIDN'T CALL THE POLICE

Martin Gansberg

This newspaper story uses objective language to tell about an incident that occurred in New York City in 1964. As Gansberg reconstructs a crime two weeks after it happened, he gives readers a detailed picture of the sequence of events that led up to a young woman's murder—in full view of thirty-eight of her "respectable, law-abiding" neighbors. As you read, consider how you might have acted if you had been a witness to this tragedy.

1 For more than half an hour 38 respectable, law-abiding citizens in Queens watched a killer stalk and stab a woman in three separate attacks in Kew Gardens.

2 Twice their chatter and the sudden glow of their bedroom lights interrupted him and frightened him off. Each time he returned, sought her out, and stabbed her again. Not one person telephoned the police during the assault; one witness called after the woman was dead.

3 That was two weeks ago today.

4 Still shocked is Assistant Chief Inspector Frederick M. Lussen, in charge of the borough's detectives and a veteran of 25 years of homicide investigations. He can give a matter-of-fact recitation on many murders. But the Kew Gardens slaying baffles him—not because it is a murder, but because the "good people" failed to call the police.

5 "As we have reconstructed the crime," he said, "the assailant had three chances to kill this woman during a 35-minute period. He returned twice to complete the job. If we had been called when he first attacked, the woman might not be dead now."

6 This is what the police say happened beginning at 3:20 a.m. in the staid, middle-class, tree-lined Austin Street area:

7 Twenty-eight-year-old Catherine Genovese, who was called Kitty by almost everyone in the neighborhood, was returning home from her job as manager of a bar in Hollis. She parked her red Fiat in a lot adjacent to the Kew Gardens Long Island Rail Road Station, facing Mowbray Place. Like many residents of the neighborhood, she had parked there day after day since her arrival from Connecticut a year ago, although the railroad frowns on the practice.

8 She turned off the lights of her car, locked the door, and started to walk the 100 feet to the entrance of her apartment at 82-70 Austin Street, which is in a Tudor building, with stores on the first floor and apartments on the second.

9 The entrance to the apartment is in the rear of the building because the front is rented to retail stores. At night the quiet neighborhood is shrouded in the slumbering darkness that marks most residential areas.

10 Miss Genovese noticed a man at the far end of the lot, near a seven-story apartment house at 82-40 Austin Street. She halted. Then, nervously, she headed up Austin Street toward Lefferts Boulevard, where there is a call box to the 102nd Police Precinct in nearby Richmond Hill.

11 She got as far as a street light in front of a bookstore before the man grabbed her. She screamed. Lights went on in the 10-story apartment house at 82-67 Austin Street, which faces the bookstore. Windows slid open and voices punctuated the early-morning stillness.

Miss Genovese screamed: "Oh, my God, he stabbed me! Please help   12
me! Please help me!"

From one of the upper windows in the apartment house, a man called   13
down: "Let that girl alone!"

The assailant looked up at him, shrugged, and walked down Austin   14
Street toward a white sedan parked a short distance away. Miss Genovese
struggled to her feet.

Lights went out. The killer returned to Miss Genovese, now trying to   15
make her way around the side of the building by the parking lot to get to
her apartment. The assailant stabbed her again.

"I'm dying!" she shrieked. "I'm dying!"   16

Windows were opened again, and lights went on in many apartments.   17
The assailant got into his car and drove away. Miss Genovese staggered to
her feet. A city bus, O-10, the Lefferts Boulevard line to Kennedy International Airport, passed. It was 3:35 a.m.

The assailant returned. By then, Miss Genovese had crawled to the   18
back of the building, where the freshly painted brown doors to the apartment house held out hope for safety. The killer tried the first door;
she wasn't there. At the second door, 82-62 Austin Street, he saw her
slumped on the floor at the foot of the stairs. He stabbed her a third time
—fatally.

It was 3:50 by the time the police received their first call, from a man   19
who was a neighbor of Miss Genovese. In two minutes they were at the
scene. The neighbor, a 70-year-old woman, and another woman were the
only persons on the street. Nobody else came forward.

The man explained that he had called the police after much delibera-   20
tion. He had phoned a friend in Nassau County for advice and then he had
crossed the roof of the building to the apartment of the elderly woman to
get her to make the call.

"I didn't want to get involved," he sheepishly told police.   21

Six days later, the police arrested Winston Moseley, a 29-year-old busi-   22
ness machine operator, and charged him with homicide. Moseley had
no previous record. He is married, has two children and owns a home at
133-19 Sutter Avenue, South Ozone Park, Queens. On Wednesday, a court
committed him to Kings County Hospital for psychiatric observation.

When questioned by the police, Moseley also said that he had slain   23
Mrs. Annie May Johnson, 24, of 146-12 133d Avenue, Jamaica, on Feb. 29
and Barbara Kralik, 15, of 174-17 140th Avenue, Springfield Gardens, last
July. In the Kralik case, the police are holding Alvin L. Mitchell, who is said
to have confessed to that slaying.

The police stressed how simple it would have been to have gotten in   24
touch with them. "A phone call," said one of the detectives, "would have
done it." The police may be reached by dialing "O" for operator or SPring
7-3100.

Today witnesses from the neighborhood, which is made up of one-   25
family homes in the $35,000 to $60,000 range with the exception of the
two apartment houses near the railroad station, find it difficult to explain
why they didn't call the police.

A housewife, knowingly if quite casually, said, "We thought it was a   26
lovers' quarrel." A husband and wife both said, "Frankly, we were afraid."
They seemed aware of the fact that events might have been different. A
distraught woman, wiping her hands in her apron, said, "I didn't want my
husband to get involved."

One couple, now willing to talk about that night, said they heard the 27 first screams. The husband looked thoughtfully at the bookstore where the killer first grabbed Miss Genovese.

"We went to the window to see what was happening," he said, "but the 28 light from our bedroom made it difficult to see the street." The wife, still apprehensive, added: "I put out the light and we were able to see better."

Asked why they hadn't called the police, she shrugged and replied: "I 29 don't know."

A man peeked out from a slight opening in the doorway to his apart- 30 ment and rattled off an account of the killer's second attack. Why hadn't he called the police at the time? "I was tired," he said without emotion. "I went back to bed."

It was 4:25 a.m. when the ambulance arrived to take the body of Miss 31 Genovese. It drove off. "Then," a solemn police detective said, "the people came out."

Reacting to the Reading

1. Preview the essay. As you read it more carefully, highlight and annotate as needed to help you understand the writer's ideas.
2. Place a check mark beside each passage of dialogue Gansberg uses. Then, add brief marginal annotations next to three of these passages.

Reacting to Words

*1. Define these words: *staid* (paragraph 6), *shrouded* (9). Can you suggest a synonym for each word that will work in the essay?
2. What is Gansberg's purpose in using terms like *respectable* (paragraph 1), *law-abiding* (1), and *good people* (4)? What is your reaction to these words?

Reacting to Ideas

1. What reasons do the witnesses give for not coming to Kitty Genovese's aid? Why do *you* think no one helped her? Do you think the witnesses should be held accountable for their lack of action?
*2. Suppose Genovese's attack were to occur today. How do you think her neighbors would react? What might be different about the situation?

Reacting to the Pattern

1. What other patterns could Gansberg have used to develop his essay? For instance, could he have used comparison and contrast? Exemplification? Given the alternatives, do you think narration is the best choice? Why or why not?
*2. Gansberg uses many transitional words and phrases, including references to specific times, to move readers from one event to the next. List as many of these transitions as you can. Do you think more transitions should be added?

Writing Practice

1. Write a narrative essay about a time when you were a witness who chose not to become involved in events you were observing.

2. Find a brief newspaper article that tells a story about a similar incident in which bystanders witnessed a crime. Expand the article into a longer essay, inventing characters, dialogue, and additional details.

3. Retell Kitty Genovese's story—but this time, have a witness come to her rescue.

C Description

A **descriptive** essay tells what something looks, sounds, smells, tastes, or feels like. It uses details to give readers a clear, vivid picture of a person, place, or object. In "Summer Picnic Fish Fry," Maya Angelou describes a community picnic. In "Guavas," Esmeralda Santiago describes a fruit.

For more on how to write a descriptive essay, see 14C.

SUMMER PICNIC FISH FRY

Maya Angelou

Maya Angelou is a poet, historian, actress, playwright, civil rights activist, producer, and director. At the request of President Clinton, she wrote and delivered a poem at his 1993 inauguration. "Summer Picnic Fish Fry," from her autobiographical *I Know Why the Caged Bird Sings* (1969), presents a vivid picture of a specific time (the 1930s) and place (the rural Arkansas town of Stamps). As you read, notice how Angelou, from her place on the grass, takes in the entire picnic, one scene at a time.

> "Acka Backa, Sody Cracka
> Acka Backa, Boo
> Acka Backa, Sody Cracka
> I'm in love with you."

The sounds of tag beat through the trees while the top branches waved in contrapuntal rhythms. I lay on a moment of green grass and telescoped the children's game to my vision. The girls ran about wild, now here, now there, never here, never was, they seemed to have no more direction than a splattered egg. But it was a shared if seldom voiced knowledge that all movements fitted, and worked according to a larger plan. I raised a platform for my mind's eye and marveled down on the outcome of "Acka Backa." The gay picnic dresses dashed, stopped and darted like beautiful dragonflies over a dark pool. The boys, black whips in the sunlight, popped behind the trees where their girls had fled, half hidden and throbbing in the shadows.

The summer picnic fish fry in the clearing by the pond was the biggest outdoor event of the year. Everyone was there. All churches were represented, as well as the social groups (Elks, Eastern Star, Masons, Knights of Columbus, Daughters of Pythias), professional people (Negro teachers from Lafayette county) and all the excited children.

Musicians brought cigar-box guitars, harmonicas, juice harps, combs   3
wrapped in tissue paper and even bathtub basses.

The amount and variety of foods would have found approval on the   4
menu of a Roman epicure. Pans of fried chicken, covered with dishtowels,
sat under benches next to a mountain of potato salad crammed with hard-
boiled eggs. Whole rust-red sticks of bologna were clothed in cheese-cloth.
Homemade pickles and chow-chow, and baked country hams, aromatic
with cloves and pineapples, vied for prominence. Our steady customers
had ordered cold watermelons, so Bailey[1] and I chugged the striped-green
fruit into the Coca-Cola box and filled all the tubs with ice as well as the
big black wash pot that Momma used to boil her laundry. Now they too lay
sweating in the happy afternoon air.

The summer picnic gave ladies a chance to show off their baking   5
hands. On the barbecue pit, chickens and spareribs sputtered in their own
fat and a sauce whose recipe was guarded in the family like a scandalous
affair. However, in the ecumenical light of the summer picnic every true
baking artist could reveal her prize to the delight and criticism of the town.
Orange sponge cakes and dark brown mounds dripping Hershey's chocolate stood layer to layer with ice-white coconuts and light brown caramels.
Pound cakes sagged with their buttery weight and small children could no
more resist licking the icings than their mothers could avoid slapping the
sticky fingers.

Proven fishermen and weekend amateurs sat on the trunks of trees at   6
the pond. They pulled the struggling bass and the silver perch from the
swift water. A rotating crew of young girls scaled and cleaned the catch
and busy women in starched aprons salted and rolled the fish in corn
meal, then dropped them in Dutch ovens trembling with boiling fat.

On one corner of the clearing a gospel group was rehearsing. Their   7
harmony, packed as tight as sardines, floated over the music of the county
singers and melted into the songs of the small children's ring games.

"Boys, don'chew let that ball fall on none of my cakes, you do and it'll   8
be me on you."

"Yes, ma'am," and nothing changed. The boys continued hitting the   9
tennis ball with pailings snatched from a fence and running holes in the
ground, colliding with everyone.

Reacting to the Reading

1. Preview the essay. As you read it more carefully, highlight and annotate
   as needed to help you understand the writer's ideas.
2. Circle all the words in the essay that designate colors. In the margin,
   write a brief note explaining what these words and phrases add to the
   essay.

Reacting to Words

*1. Define these words: *contrapuntal* (paragraph 1), *epicure* (4), *aromatic*
    (4), *vied* (4), *ecumenical* (5), *colliding* (9). Can you suggest a synonym
    for each word that will work in the essay?
2. Find several examples of vivid action verbs (for example, *sagged* in
   paragraph 5). What does each verb mean? What does it suggest?

---

1. The author's brother.

*3. Angelou uses some unusual **metaphors** (for example, "boys, black whips in the sunlight" in paragraph 1) and **similes** (for example, "harmony, packed as tight as sardines" in paragraph 7). Find as many similes and metaphors as you can. Which ones are most effective? Why?

For more on metaphors and similes, see 20D.

Reacting to Ideas

1. What do you think Angelou means in paragraph 1 when she says that she "raised a platform for [her] mind's eye"?
2. What is it about the picnic that makes it so memorable to Angelou and the other townspeople?

> **Teaching Tip**
> Remind students to answer all questions in complete sentences.

Reacting to the Pattern

*1. In paragraph 2, Angelou says, "The summer picnic fish fry in the clearing by the pond was the biggest outdoor event of the year. Everyone was there." How do these statements establish her essay's dominant impression? What mood does Angelou want her details to convey?
2. Angelou, seated on the grass, begins her description with the sights and sounds of children playing tag and ends with her observation of another children's game. What does she see in between these two scenes? Trace her observations as she moves her gaze around the picnic.
3. Is this essay primarily subjective or objective description? Explain.

Writing Practice

1. Describe a large outdoor family or community event that you have attended. Be sure to include concrete, sensory details about the setting, food, guests, and activities, and make your description as visual and vivid as possible.
2. Describe a scene at which you, like Angelou, were an observer rather than a participant. Begin by describing the location from which you viewed the scene.

GUAVAS

Esmeralda Santiago

Writer Esmeralda Santiago grew up in Puerto Rico as the eldest of eleven children raised by a single mother. The family moved to New York when she was thirteen years old. She has written a childhood memoir, *When I Was Puerto Rican* (1993), and its sequel, *Almost a Woman* (1998), describing the family's move to Brooklyn. After graduating from the High School of the Performing Arts in Manhattan, Santiago spent eight years studying part-time at community colleges before being accepted on full scholarship to Harvard University. In recent years, Santiago has also founded a film and production company, helped found a shelter for battered women, and most recently worked as an editor. As you read this selection, take note of which of the five senses Santiago uses to describe the experience of eating a guava.

Barco que no anda, no llega a puerto.

A ship that doesn't sail, never reaches port.

1   There are guavas at the Shop & Save. I pick one the size of a tennis ball and finger the prickly stem end. It feels familiarly bumpy and firm. The guava is not quite ripe; the skin is still a dark green. I smell it and imagine a pale pink center, the seeds tightly embedded in the flesh.

2   A ripe guava is yellow, although some varieties have a pink tinge. The skin is thick, firm, and sweet. Its heart is bright pink and almost solid with seeds. The most delicious part of the guava surrounds the tiny seeds. If you don't know how to eat a guava, the seeds end up in the crevices between your teeth.

3   When you bite into a ripe guava, your teeth must grip the bumpy surface and sink into the thick edible skin without hitting the center. It takes experience to do this, as it's quite tricky to determine how far beyond the skin the seeds begin.

4   Some years, when the rains have been plentiful and the nights cool, you can bite into a guava and not find many seeds. The guava bushes grow close to the ground, their branches laden with green then yellow fruit that seem to ripen overnight. These guavas are large and juicy, almost seedless, their roundness enticing you to have one more, just one more, because next year the rains may not come.

5   As children, we didn't always wait for the fruit to ripen. We raided the bushes as soon as the guavas were large enough to bend the branch.

6   A green guava is sour and hard. You bite into it at its widest point, because it's easier to grasp with your teeth. You hear the skin, meat, and seeds crunching inside your head, while the inside of your mouth explodes in little spurts of sour.

7   You grimace, your eyes water, and your cheeks disappear as your lips purse into a tight O. But you have another and then another, enjoying the crunchy sounds, the acid taste, the gritty texture of the unripe center. At night, your mother makes you drink castor oil, which she says tastes better than a green guava. That's when you know for sure that you're a child and she has stopped being one.

8   I had my last guava the day we left Puerto Rico. It was large and juicy, almost red in the center, and so fragrant that I didn't want to eat it because I would lose the smell. All the way to the airport I scratched at it with my teeth, making little dents in the skin, chewing small pieces with my front teeth, so that I could feel the texture against my tongue, the tiny pink pellets of sweet.

9   Today, I stand before a stack of dark green guavas, each perfectly round and hard, each $1.59. The one in my hand is tempting. It smells faintly of late summer afternoons and hopscotch under the mango tree. But this is autumn in New York, and I'm no longer a child.

10   The guava joins its sisters under the harsh fluorescent lights of the exotic fruit display. I push my cart away, toward the apples and pears of my adulthood, their nearly seedless ripeness predictable and bittersweet.

Reacting to the Reading

1. Preview the essay. As you read it more carefully, highlight and annotate as needed to help you understand the writer's ideas.

2. Circle all the words in the essay that convey information about guavas' physical appearance (how they look).

Reacting to Words

*1. Define these words: *guava* (title), *edible* (paragraph 3), *laden* (4), *enticing* (4), *spurts* (6), *grimace* (7), *pellets* (8). Can you suggest a synonym for each word that will work in the essay?

*2. Write an alternate one-word title for this selection.

Teaching Tip
Students may need help defining words. With nonnative students, consider going over the definitions in class before assigning the reading.

Reacting to Ideas

1. How is the fruit in the Shop & Save different from the fruit of Santiago's childhood?

*2. Is this essay just about guavas, or is it really about something else? Explain.

Teaching Tip
Remind students to answer all questions in complete sentences.

Reacting to the Pattern

1. Santiago begins and ends her essay at the Shop & Save, but her imagination takes her somewhere else. Where? What sends her thoughts away from the supermarket?

2. Santiago describes several kinds of guavas. How are they different?

*3 In addition to describing how guavas look, Santiago also describes their smell, taste, and feel. Where does she use language that conveys how guavas taste? How they smell? How they feel?

4. If Santiago had written a purely objective description, what would she have left out? What might she have added?

Writing Practice

1. Write a subjective description of a food you loved when you were a child. Try to describe the smell, taste, and feel of the food as well as its appearance.

2. Write an essay about a friend or family member with whom you associate a particular food or meal. Include descriptions of that person engaged in eating or in preparing food.

3. How have your tastes in food changed since you were a child? Trace the development of your food preferences, beginning as far back as you can remember. Be sure to describe the foods that defined each stage of your life.

D	**Process**

A **process** essay explains the steps in a procedure, telling how something is (or was) done. In "Slice of Life," Russell Baker gives a set of instructions for carving a turkey. In "Indelible Marks," Joyce Howe explains the routine of her family's laundry business.

For more on how to write a process essay, see 14D.

SLICE OF LIFE

Russell Baker

Pulitzer Prize–winning columnist and author Russell Baker is known for his keen political insight and sharp social commentary. He is also known for being funny. The source of much of Baker's humor is his deadpan approach, in which he pretends to be completely serious. In the following essay, note how he uses this approach to turn what seems to be a straightforward set of instructions into a humorous discussion of a holiday ritual.

Teaching Tip
Remind students to familiarize themselves with the end-of-essay questions before they read the essay.

How to carve a turkey: 1

Assemble the following tools—carving knife, stone for sharpening 2
carving knife, hot water, soap, wash cloth, two bath towels, barbells, meat cleaver. If the house lacks a meat cleaver, an ax may be substituted. If it is, add bandages, sutures, and iodine to above list.

Begin by moving the turkey from the roasting pan to a suitable carv- 3
ing area. This is done by inserting the carving knife into the posterior stuffed area of the turkey and the knife-sharpening stone into the stuffed area under the neck.

Thus skewered, the turkey may be lifted out of the hot grease with rel- 4
ative safety. Should the turkey drop to the floor, however, remove the knife and stone, roll the turkey gingerly into the two bath towels, wrap them several times around it and lift the encased fowl to the carving place.

You are now ready to begin carving. Sharpen the knife on the stone 5
and insert it where the thigh joins the torso. If you do this correctly, which is improbable, the knife will almost immediately encounter a barrier of bone and gristle. This may very well be the joint. It could, however, be your thumb. If not, execute a vigorous sawing motion until satisfied that the knife has been defeated. Withdraw the knife and ask someone nearby, in as testy a manner as possible, why the knives at your house are not kept in better carving condition.

Exercise the biceps and forearms by lifting barbells until they are 6
strong enough for you to tackle the leg joint with bare hands. Wrapping one hand firmly around the thigh, seize the turkey's torso in the other hand and scream. Run cold water over hands to relieve pain of burns.

Now, take a bath towel in each hand and repeat the above maneu- 7
ver. The entire leg should snap away from the chassis with a distinct crack, and the rest of the turkey, obedient to Newton's law[1] about equal and opposite reactions, should roll in the opposite direction, which means that if you are carving at the table the turkey will probably come to rest in someone's lap.

Get the turkey out of the lap with as little fuss as possible, and con- 8
centrate on the leg. Use the meat cleaver to sever the sinewy leather which binds the thigh to the drumstick.

If using the alternate, ax method, this operation should be performed 9
on a cement walk outside the house in order to preserve the table.

Repeat the above operation on the turkey's uncarved side. You now 10
have two thighs and two drumsticks. Using the wash cloth, soap and hot

---

1. Sir Isaac Newton, seventeenth-century physicist and mathematician known for formulating the laws of gravity and light and for inventing calculus.

water, bathe thoroughly and, if possible, go to a movie. Otherwise, look each person in the eye and say, "I don't suppose anyone wants white meat."

If compelled to carve the breast anyhow, sharpen the knife on the stone again with sufficient awkwardness to tip over the gravy bowl on the person who started the stampede for white meat. 11

While everyone is rushing about to mop the gravy off her slacks, hack at the turkey breast until it starts crumbling off the carcass in ugly chunks. 12

The alternative method for carving white meat is to visit around the neighborhood until you find someone who has a good carving knife and borrow it, if you find one, which is unlikely. 13

This method enables you to watch the football game on neighbors' television sets and also creates the possibility that somebody back at your table will grow tired of waiting and do the carving herself. 14

In this case, upon returning home, cast a pained stare upon the mound of chopped white meat that has been hacked out by the family carving knife and refuse to do any more carving that day. No one who cares about the artistry of carving can be expected to work upon the mutilations of amateurs, and it would be a betrayal of the carver's art to do so. 15

Reacting to the Reading

1. Preview the essay. As you read it more carefully, highlight and annotate as needed to help you understand the writer's ideas.
2. Underline or star the cautions and warnings Baker provides for readers.

Reacting to Words

*1. Define these words: *sutures* (paragraph 2), *gingerly* (4), *encased* (4), *torso* (5), *execute* (5), *testy* (5), *chassis* (7). Can you suggest a synonym for each word that will work in the essay?
2. In paragraph 14, Baker uses *herself* to refer to *somebody*. What is your reaction to this pronoun use? What other options did Baker have? Why do you think he chose to use *herself*?

Reacting to Ideas

1. This process is not intended to be taken seriously or followed exactly. How can you tell?
*2. List the steps in Baker's process of carving a turkey. Then, cross out all nonessential or humorous material. Are the instructions that remain logically ordered? Clear? Accurate?

Reacting to the Pattern

1. What stylistic signals tell you that this essay is a set of instructions and not an explanation of a process?
*2. Do you think the phrase "How to carve a turkey" is an adequate introduction for this essay? What other kind of introduction might Baker have written?
3. Review the various cautions and warnings that you identified in Reacting to the Reading question 2. Are they all necessary? Explain.

> **Teaching Tip**
> Students may need help defining words. With nonnative students, consider going over the definitions in class before assigning the reading.

> **Teaching Tip**
> You may want to refer students to 28E for further explanation of these options.

> **Teaching Tip**
> Remind students to answer all questions in complete sentences.

36 D

Writing Practice

1. Write a new introductory paragraph for this essay. Then, turn Baker's instructions into a straightforward process explanation, deleting any material you consider irrelevant to your purpose. Be sure to include all necessary articles (*a, an, the*) and transitions.

2. List the steps in a recipe for preparing one of your favorite dishes. Then, expand your recipe into an essay, adding transitions and cautions and reminders. Finally, add opening and closing paragraphs that describe the finished product and tell readers why the dish is worth preparing.

3. Write an essay that explains to your fellow students how you juggle the demands of family, work, and school in a typical day. Organize your essay either as a process explanation or as a set of instructions.

INDELIBLE MARKS

Joyce Howe

Joyce Howe grew up in Queens, New York, in a neighborhood where everyone knew her father as "the man who ran the Chinese laundry." As his daughter, she had mixed feelings about his occupation and felt ashamed that she lived with her parents and sisters behind the store and helped in the laundry business. In this passage from a 1983 essay, she explains the process by which laundry was sorted, washed, dried, starched, ironed, folded, and wrapped. As you read, try to get a sense of what the process meant to Howe.

In Queens, on the block where we moved, my father was known as the man who ran the Chinese laundry, like Ernie who ran the deli, Benny the upholsterer, and the butcher a few doors down. To all of his customers he was Joe. And they—middle-aged housewives, young bachelors and students, mainly white—were known to him by a first name or by the unique indelible "mark" on their collars and hems. (This "mark," consisting of one or more characters, was written on each item for the duration of a customer's patronage; if he switched laundries, the new establishment usually did not bother changing it.) With all of them, as tickets, laundry bills, and change passed from hand to hand over the wide counter, my father exchanged comments: "Too much of this rain, huh?", "Yeah, the Mets looked lousy last night," or "How's the wife and the kids?"

Saturday was his busiest day. It was not only the day more customers came in and out, but it was also one of the three days on which the long and tedious job of laundry-sorting was done. The entire floor of the store became a dumping ground for soiled clothes. My father divided the laundry into piles: 10 to 15 sheets and pillowcases were bundled up into one sheet and the ticket stubs of the customers whose laundry made up the bundle were then stapled together and put aside for later identification. "Wet items," such as towels, underwear, and socks, were separated into two categories—light and dark; shirts were separated into four categories—colored, white, starch, and no starch. Each pile of "wet items" and shirts was then placed in a laundry bag with its respective tag.

1

2

The bags and bundles were picked up Sunday morning by the truck drivers, who had names like Rocky and Louie, from the wholesale laundry or "wet wash" contracted by my father. ("Hand laundry" has been a misnomer since the late 1930s and '40s, when a whole new industry of Chinese-operated wholesale laundries and pressing concerns sprang up and contracted to do the actual washing and pressing for laundrymen.) Every Sunday, we were awakened from our sleep by the sound of the drivers' keys turning in the front door's locks.

When the "wet wash" drivers returned Monday with the previous day's load, the sheets and pillowcases, or "flat pieces," were wrapped in a heavy brown paper which my mother later would use for tablecloths. The shirts returned in the same bags they went out in. My father pulled out the bag of shirts to be starched and hand-ironed, leaving the rest for the shirt-press truck to pick up that night. On Tuesday night, they returned—clean, pressed, folded—in large square cardboard boxes, each shirt ringed in its own pale blue paper band.

For a short time, we had our own automatic dryer to take care of the damp "wet items" when they returned. After it broke down, irreparably, the dryer retired, and was left to hold stacks of comic books and board games. My sisters and I took turns making pilgrimages to the local laundromat, our metal shopping cart bent from the weight of the load. We wheeled those three blocks three times a week. On my turn, I always hoped that no one I knew would see me as I struggled with two hands to keep laundry and cart intact when maneuvering the high curbs. Even then, the irony of going from the laundry to the laundromat was not lost.

Of course, there were days when the system was off, when the shirt press might return its load late, or when my father didn't feel well enough to wrap every package. On those days, we were all expected to help. We made sure that the promise my father had made to customers on Saturday that their shirts would be ready by Wednesday was kept. Behind the tan curtain drawn across our plate-glass window every evening at seven and the door's pulled venetian blind, we settled into a tableau. My family formed a late-night assembly line, each member taking his place amid the shelves, boxes, white cones of string, rolls of wrapping paper, and the familiar fragrance of newly laundered cloth.

Reacting to the Reading

1. Preview the essay. As you read it more carefully, highlight and annotate as needed to help you understand the writer's ideas.

2. In the margins of the essay, number the steps in the process that is presented in paragraphs 2 through 6.

Reacting to Words

*1. Define these words: *indelible* (paragraph 1), *duration* (1), *patronage* (1), *tedious* (2), *irreparably* (5), *pilgrimages* (5), *tableau* (6). Can you suggest a synonym for each word that will work in the essay?

2. Howe's father makes a "unique indelible 'mark'" (paragraph 1) on the collars of each customer's shirts. Where else does he make an indelible mark?

Reacting to Ideas

1. What does Howe achieve by describing this process?
2. Do you think Howe's memories of her childhood as the laundryman's daughter are largely positive or negative? Support your position with specific examples.

Reacting to the Pattern

1. Is this essay a set of instructions or an explanation of how a process is performed? How can you tell?
*2. Using the numbers you wrote in the margins for Reacting to the Reading question 2 as a guide, list the individual steps in the process Howe describes. Does the process vary at all, or is it always the same?

Writing Practice

1. Write a process essay explaining the daily routine you follow in a job you hold (or held). Include a thesis statement that tells readers how you feel about the job.
2. Write a process essay in which you tell how to perform a particular task at a job—for example, how to keep a potential customer on the phone during a sales call, how to clean a deep-fat fryer, or how to set up the housekeeping corner at a day-care center.
3. Write a process essay in which you take readers through the stages of a successful job search. In your conclusion, identify the job you found.

E   Cause and Effect

For more on how to write a cause-and-effect essay, see 14E.

A **cause-and-effect** essay identifies causes or predicts effects; sometimes it does both. In "The 'Black Table' Is Still There," Lawrence Otis Graham focuses on a troubling situation from his junior high school days. In "Who Killed the Bog Men of Denmark? And Why?," Maurice Shadbolt unravels a two-thousand-year-old mystery.

THE "BLACK TABLE" IS STILL THERE

Lawrence Otis Graham

A corporate lawyer and best-selling author, Graham is best known for "Invisible Man," an article he wrote about the racism he encountered while working as a busboy at an exclusive country club during a leave from his job as a lawyer. In the following 1991 essay, Graham reflects on the "black table," a situation that has continued in the school cafeteria since his junior high days. As you read, note how his conclusions about what motivates people to sit where they sit have changed over the years.

Teaching Tip
Remind students to familiarize themselves with the end-
of-essay questions before
they read the essay.

During a recent visit to my old junior high school in Westchester   1
County, I came upon something that I never expected to see again, something that was a source of fear and dread for three hours each school
morning of my early adolescence: the all-black lunch table in the cafeteria
of my predominantly white suburban junior high school.

As I look back on 27 years of often being the first and only black per-   2
son integrating such activities and institutions as the college newspaper,
the high school tennis team, summer music camps, our all-white suburban neighborhood, my eating club at Princeton or my private social club
at Harvard Law School, the one scenario that puzzled me the most then
and now is the all-black lunch table.

Why was it there? Why did the black kids separate themselves? What   3
did the table say about the integration that was supposedly going on in
home rooms and gym classes? What did it say about the black kids? The
white kids? What did it say about me when I refused to sit there, day after
day, for three years?

Each afternoon, at 12:03 p.m., after the fourth period ended, I found   4
myself among 600 12-, 13- and 14-year-olds who marched into the
brightly-lit cafeteria and dashed for a seat at one of the 27 blue formica
lunch tables.

No matter who I walked in with—usually a white friend—no matter   5
what mood I was in, there was one thing that was certain: I would not sit
at the black table.

I would never consider sitting at the black table.   6

What was wrong with me? What was I afraid of?   7

I would like to think that my decision was a heroic one, made in order   8
to express my solidarity with the theories of integration that my community was espousing. But I was just 12 at the time, and there was nothing
heroic in my actions.

I avoided the black table for a very simple reason: I was afraid that by   9
sitting at the black table I'd lose all my white friends. I thought that by sitting there I'd be making a racist, anti-white statement.

Is that what the all-black table means? Is it a rejection of white people?   10
I no longer think so.

At the time, I was angry that there was a black lunch table. I believed   11
that the black kids were the reason why other kids didn't mix more. I
was ready to believe that their self-segregation was the cause of white
bigotry.

Ironically, I even believed this after my best friend (who was white)   12
told me I probably shouldn't come to his bar mitzvah because I'd be the
only black and people would feel uncomfortable. I even believed this
after my Saturday afternoon visit, at age 10, to a private country club
pool prompted incensed white parents to pull their kids from the pool in
terror.

In the face of this blatantly racist (anti-black) behavior, I still somehow   13
managed to blame only the black kids for being the barrier to integration
in my school and my little world. What was I thinking?

I realize now how wrong I was. During that same time, there were at   14
least two tables of athletes, an Italian table, a Jewish girls' table, a Jewish
boys' table (where I usually sat), a table of kids who were into heavy metal
music and smoking pot, a table of middle class Irish kids. Weren't these
tables just as segregationist as the black table? At the time, no one thought

so. At the time, no one even acknowledged the segregated nature of these other tables.

Maybe it's the color difference that makes all-black tables or all-black groups attract the scrutiny and wrath of so many people. It scares and angers people; it exasperates. It did those things to me, and I'm black. 15

As an integrating black person, I know that my decision *not* to join the black lunch table attracted its own kind of scrutiny and wrath from my classmates. At the same time that I heard angry words like "Oreo" and "white boy" being hurled at me from the black table, I was also dodging impatient questions from white classmates: "Why do all those black kids sit together?" or "Why don't you ever sit with the other blacks?" 16

The black lunch table, like those other segregated tables, is a comment on the superficial inroads that integration has made in society. Perhaps I should be happy that even this is a long way from where we started. Yet, I can't get over the fact that the 27th table in my junior high school cafeteria is still known as the "black table"—14 years after my adolescence. 17

Reacting to the Reading

1. Preview the essay. As you read it more carefully, highlight and annotate as needed to help you understand the writer's ideas.

2. Graham asks a number of questions in this essay—for example, in paragraph 3 and in paragraph 7. In marginal annotations, answer two or three of these questions.

Reacting to Words

*1. Define these words: *scenario* (paragraph 2), *espousing* (8), *bar mitzvah* (12), *incensed* (12), *blatantly* (13), *scrutiny* (15), *wrath* (15), *inroads* (17). Can you suggest a synonym for each word that will work in the essay?

2. What images does the phrase *black table* bring to mind? Does it have positive or negative connotations to you? Can you think of another term Graham might use to identify the black table?

Reacting to Ideas

*1. Why didn't Graham sit at the black table? Do you understand the forces that motivated him? Do you think he should have sat with the other African-American students?

2. When he was in junior high school, who did Graham think was at fault for the existence of the black table? Who does he now think was at fault? Do you agree with him?

3. In paragraph 14, Graham considers other lunch tables and asks, "Weren't these tables just as segregationist as the black table?" Answer his question.

Reacting to the Pattern

1. Is Graham's essay primarily about causes or about effects? Explain your answer.

*2. Graham focuses largely on his own experiences and actions. Where, if anywhere, does he consider other forces that could have created seg-

36 E 577

Shadbolt • Who
Killed the Bog Men
of Denmark? And Why?

regated lunch tables? Do you think he should have considered other causes? For example, should he have discussed the school administration's role? Housing patterns in his community? Explain your position.

Writing Practice

1. Graham's essay, written in 1991, describes his adolescence fourteen years earlier (1977). Try to recall the lunch tables in the cafeteria of your own junior high school or middle school. Were they segregated as they were in Graham's school? What factors do you believe led students to sit where they did? Write a cause-and-effect essay that discusses the possible causes of the seating patterns you remember.

2. What do you see as the *effects* of segregated lunch tables? Do you think they are necessarily a bad thing, or do they have advantages? Write a cause-and-effect essay that explores the possible results of such seating patterns.

3. What kinds of self-segregation (by race, gender, class, and so on) do you observe in your school, workplace, or community? In an essay, discuss both causes and effects.

WHO KILLED THE BOG MEN OF DENMARK? AND WHY?

Maurice Shadbolt

Maurice Shadbolt has published memoirs, short stories, plays, and historical novels, many of which center on family history and the local culture of his native New Zealand. His nearly fifty-year career as a writer began in 1959 with the publication of *The New Zealanders*, a collection of short stories, shortly after which he emigrated to Europe. His most recent books include *Selected Stories* (1998) and *From the Edge of the Sky* (1999), a memoir. In the following essay, note how Shadbolt works backward from the finding of the bog men to the cause of their deaths as discovered by the Højgaard brothers.

> **Teaching Tip**
> Remind students to familiarize themselves with the end-of-essay questions before they read the essay.

Every year in the Danish town of Silkeborg, thousands of visitors file past the face of a murder victim. No one will ever know his name. It is enough to know that 2000 years ago he was as human as ourselves. That face has moved men and women to poetry, and to tears.

Last summer I journeyed to the lake-girt Danish town and, peering at that face behind glass in a modest museum, I felt awe—for his every wrinkle and whisker tell a vivid and terrible tale from Denmark's distant past. The rope which choked off the man's breath is still around his neck. Yet it is a perplexingly peaceful face, inscrutable, one to haunt the imagination.

This strangest of ancient murder mysteries began . . . on May 8, 1950, when two brothers, Emil and Viggo Højgaard, were digging peat in Tollund Fen, near Silkeborg. Their spring sowing finished, the brothers were storing up the umber-brown peat for their kitchen range, and for warmth in the winter to come. It was a peaceful task on a sunny morning. Snipe called from the aspens and firs fringing the dank bowl of the fen, where only heather and coarse grass grew. Then, at a depth of nine feet, their spades suddenly struck something.

They were gazing, with fright and fascination, at a face underfoot. The   4
corpse was naked but for a skin cap, resting on its side as if asleep, arms
and legs bent. The face was gentle, with eyes closed and lips lightly pursed.
There was stubble on the chin. The bewildered brothers called the Silkeborg police.

Quick to the scene, the police did not recognize the man as anyone   5
listed missing. Shrewdly guessing the brothers might have blundered into
a black hole in Europe's past, the police called in archeologists.

Enter Prof. Peter Glob, a distinguished scholar from nearby Aarhus   6
University, who carefully dislodged a lump of peat from beside the dead
man's head. A rope made of two twisted hide thongs encircled his neck. He
had been strangled or hanged. But when, and by whom? Glob ordered a
box to be built about the corpse and the peat in which it lay, so nothing
might be disturbed.

Next day, the box, weighing nearly a ton, was manhandled out of the   7
bog onto a horse-drawn cart, on its way for examination at Copenhagen's
National Museum. One of Glob's helpers collapsed and died with the huge
effort. It seemed a dark omen, as if some old god were claiming a modern
man in place of a man from the past.

Bog bodies were nothing new—since records have been kept, Den-   8
mark's bogs have surrendered no fewer than 400—and the preservative
qualities of the humic acid in peat have long been known. But not until the
19th century did scientists and historians begin to glimpse the finds and
understand that the bodies belonged to remote, murky recesses of European prehistory. None survived long: the corpses were either buried again
or crumbled quickly with exposure to light and air.

When peat-digging was revived during and after World War II, bodies   9
were unearthed in abundance—first in 1942 at Store Arden, then in 1946,
1947 and 1948 at Borre Fen. Artifacts found beside them positively identified them as people of Denmark's Early Iron Age, from 400 B.C. to A.D. 400.
None, then, was less than 1500 years old, and some were probably much
older. The first of the Borre Fen finds—a full-grown male—was to prove
especially significant: Borre Fen man, too, had died violently, with a noose
about his neck, strangled or hanged. And his last meal had consisted of
grain.

Peter Glob, alongside his artist father (a portraitist and distinguished   10
amateur archeologist), had been digging into Denmark's dim past since he
was a mere eight years old. For him, the Tollund man, who had by far the
best-preserved head to survive from antiquity, was a supreme challenge.
Since 1936, Glob had been living imaginatively with the pagan hunters
and farmers of 2000 years ago, fossicking[1] among their corroded artifacts,
foraging among the foundations of their simple villages; he knew their
habits, the rhythms of their lives. Suddenly, here was a man of that very
time. "Majesty and gentleness," he recalls, "seemed to stamp his features
as they did when he was alive." What was this enigmatic face trying to tell
him?

Glob was intrigued by the fact that so many of the people found in   11
bogs had died violently: strangled or hanged, throats slit, heads battered.
Perhaps they had been travelers set upon by brigands, or executed criminals. But there might be a different explanation. These murder victims all
belonged to the Danish Iron Age. If they were to be explained away as vic-

1. (Australian and New Zealand English) Searching for by picking through or rummaging.

36 E   579

Shadbolt • Who
Killed the Bog Men
of Denmark? And Why?

tims of robber bands, there should be a much greater spread in time—into other ages. Nor would executed criminals all have had so many common traits.

Glob considered the body with care. X rays of Tollund man's vertebrae, taken to determine whether he had been strangled or hanged, produced inconclusive results. The condition of the wisdom teeth suggested a man well over 20 years old. An autopsy revealed that the heart, lungs and liver were well preserved; most important, the alimentary canal was undisturbed, containing the dead man's last meal—a 2000-year-old gruel of hand-milled grains and seeds: barley, linseed, flaxseed, knotgrass, among others. Knowledge of prehistoric agriculture made it possible to determine that the man had lived in the first 200 years A.D. The mixture of grains and seeds suggested a meal prepared in winter or early spring.

Since Iron Age men were not vegetarians, why were there no traces of meat? Glob also marveled that the man's hands and feet were soft; he appeared to have done little or no heavy labor in his lifetime. Possibly, then, he was high-ranking in Iron Age society.

Then, on April 26, 1952, peat-digging villagers from Grauballe, 11 miles east of Tollund, turned up a second spectacularly well-preserved body, and again Glob was fast to the scene. Unmistakably another murder victim, this discovery was, unlike Tollund man, far from serene. The man's throat had been slashed savagely from ear to ear. His face was twisted with terror, and his lips were parted with a centuries-silenced cry of pain.

Glob swiftly removed the body—still imbedded in a great block of peat—for preservation and study. Carbon-dating of body tissue proved Grauballe man to be about 1650 years old, a contemporary of Constantine the Great. Grauballe man was in extraordinary condition: his fingerprints and footprints came up clearly. Tallish and dark-haired, Grauballe man, like Tollund man, had never done any heavy manual work. He had been slain in his late 30s. Another similarity came to light when Grauballe man's last meal was analyzed: it had been eaten immediately before death and like Tollund man's, like Borre Fen man's too, it was a gruel of grains and seeds, a meal of winter, or early spring. All three had perished in a similar season.

Who had killed these men of the bogs? Why in winter, or early spring? Why should they—apparently—have led privileged lives? And why the same kind of meals before their sudden ends?

The bodies had told Glob all they could. Now he turned to one of his favorite sources—the Roman historian Tacitus. Nearly 2000 years ago Tacitus recorded the oral traditions of Germanic tribes who inhabited northwest Europe. Tacitus' account of these wild, brave and generous blue-eyed people often shed light into dark corners of Denmark's past. Glob found these lines: "At a time laid down in the distant past, all peoples that are related by blood meet in a sacred wood. Here they celebrate their barbarous rites with a human sacrifice."

Elsewhere, Tacitus wrote: "These people are distinguished by a common worship of Nerthus, or Mother Earth. They believe that she interests herself in human affairs." Tacitus confirmed early spring as a time among the Germanic tribes for offerings and human sacrifice. They were asking the goddess to hasten the coming of spring, and the summer harvest. Men chosen for sacrifice might well have been given a symbolic meal, made up of plant seeds, before being consecrated through death to the goddess—thus explaining the absence of meat. The sacrificial men, with their delicate features, neat hands and feet, might have been persons of high rank chosen by lot for sacrifice, or priests, ritually married to Nerthus.

Tacitus supplied another essential clue: the symbol of Nerthus, he recorded, was a twisted metal "torque," or neck ring, worn by the living to honor the goddess. The leather nooses about the necks of Tollund man and the body from Borre Fen and some earlier bodies were replicas of those neck rings. Glob concluded that it was Nerthus—Mother Earth herself— who had preserved her victims perfectly in her peaty bosom long after those who had fed them into the bogs were dust.   19

Peter Glob was satisfied. He had found the killer and identified the victims. The centuries-old mystery of Denmark's bog bodies was no more.   20

Reacting to the Reading

1. Preview the essay. As you read it more carefully, highlight and annotate as needed to help you understand the writer's ideas.

2. Circle all the adjectives used to describe the bog man found by the Højgaard brothers.

Reacting to Words

*1. Define these words: *bog* (title), *perplexingly* (paragraph 2), *sowing* (3), *peat* (3), *fen* (3), *manhandled* (7), *murky* (8), *antiquity* (10), *pagan* (10), *brigands* (11). Can you suggest a synonym for each word that will work in the essay?

2. Review the adjectives used to describe the man discovered by the Højgaards. How do these words shape your reaction to him?

Reacting to Ideas

*1. Why do you think the face of the anonymous man found in the bog "has moved men and women to poetry, and to tears" (paragraph 1)?

2. Why does Shadbolt give readers so much information about Peter Glob and his role in the investigation? How would the essay be different without this information?

*3. Why do you suppose the "strangest of ancient murder mysteries" (paragraph 3) might still be of interest to modern readers?

Reacting to the Pattern

*1. Identify at least one *result* (or *effect*) of each of the following: the Højgaard brothers find a body; the box containing the body is moved; peat digging is revived after World War II.

*2. Identify at least one *cause* of each of the following: the man's hands and feet are soft; his last meal was grain; he died a violent death; he has a rope around his neck.

3. Is this essay's emphasis on causes, on effects, or on both causes and effects? Explain.

Writing Practice

1. Write a biography of the man the Højgaard brothers found, including an explanation of why he died. You may give the man a name and invent people and events.

Teaching Tip
Students may need help defining words. With nonnative students, consider going over the definitions in class before assigning the reading.

Teaching Tip
Remind students to answer all questions in complete sentences.

2. Write an article for the Silkeborg daily newspaper in which you discuss the effect on the townspeople of the discovery of the bog man.

3. Write an essay that solves a "mystery" in your own life. For example, explain the causes of a friend's surprising actions or the reasons why your family settled where it did years (or generations) ago.

F   Comparison and Contrast

A **comparison-and-contrast** essay explains how two things are alike or how they are different; sometimes it discusses both similarities and differences. In "Words and People," linguist Richard Lederer compares the two items in his essay's title. In "Men Are from Mars, Women Are from Venus," John Gray compares men and women.

For more on how to write a comparison-and-contrast essay, see 14F.

> **Teaching Tip**
> Before beginning this section, review the difference between point-by-point and subject-by-subject comparison. Refer students to 14F.

> **Teaching Tip**
> Remind students to familiarize themselves with the end-of-essay questions before they read the essay.

WORDS AND PEOPLE

Richard Lederer

After a twenty-seven-year teaching career, Richard Lederer earned a Ph.D. in English and Linguistics and began writing books and articles on the popular use and abuse of the English language. His books include *Anguished English* (1989), *Fractured English* (1996), and *The Miracle of Language* (1999); his weekly column, "Looking at Language," appears in newspapers and magazines across the country. He cohosts the National Public Radio show "A Way with Words," an on-air forum about issues of language ranging from pronunciation to puns. In the following essay, note all the different ways Lederer compares words with people.

1   Has it ever struck you how human words are?

2   Like people, words are born, grow up, get married, have children, and even die. They may be very old, like *man* and *wife* and *home*. They may be very young, like *veggies* and *househusband*. They may be newly born and struggling to live, as *netiquette*, *gangsta rap*, and *political correctness*. Or they may repose in the tomb of history, as *leechcraft*, the Anglo-Saxon word for the practice of medicine, and *murfles*, a long-defunct word for freckles or pimples.

3   Our lives are filled with people and words, and in both cases we are bound to be impressed with their vast numbers and infinite variety. Some words, like *OK*, are famous all over the world. Others, like *foozle* (a bungling golf stroke) and *groak* (to stare at other people's food, hoping that they will offer you some), are scarcely known, even at home.

4   There are some words that we will probably never meet, such as *schizocarps* (pinwheels that grow on maple trees) and *vomer* (the slender bone separating the nostrils), and others that are with us every day of our lives, such as *I, the, and, to,* and *of,* the five most frequently used English words.

5   As with people, words have all sorts of shapes, sizes, backgrounds, and personalities. They may be very large, like *pneumonoultramicroscopicsilicovolcaniosis*, a forty-one-letter *hippopotomonstrosesquipedalian* word for black lung disease. They may be very small, like *a* and *I*.

Some words are multinational in their heritage, as *remacadamize*, which is Latin, Celtic, Hebrew, and Greek in parentage. Some come of Old English stock, as *sun* and *moon* and *grass* and *goodness*. Some have a distinctly continental flavor—*kindergarten, lingerie, spaghetti*. Others are unmistakably American—*stunt* and *baseball*.

Words, like people, go up and down in the world. Some are born into low station and come up in life. With the passing of time, they may acquire *prestige* (which used to mean "trickery") and *glamour* (which began life as a synonym for "grammar"). Others slide downhill in reputation, such as *homely* (which originally meant "homelike, good around the home"), *awful* ("awe-inspiring"), and *idiot* ("one who did not hold public office").

Words like *remunerative, encomium,* and *perspicacious* are so dignified that they can intimidate us, whereas others, like *booze, burp,* and *blubber,* are markedly inelegant in character. Some words, such as *ecdysiast,* H. L. Mencken's Greek-derived name for a stripteaser, love to put on fancy airs; others, like *vidiot* and *palimony,* are winkingly playful. Certain words strike us as beautiful, like *luminous* and *gossamer,* others as rather ugly—*guzzle* and *scrod;* some as quiet—*dawn* and *dusk,* others as noisy—*thunder* and *crash.*

That words and people so resemble each other should come as no surprise. Words and people were created at the same time. Before language found a home in the mouths of humans, it was not fully language; before we possessed language, we were not fully human. Not only do we have language. We *are* language.

Reacting to the Reading

1. Preview the essay. As you read it more carefully, highlight and annotate as needed to help you understand the writer's ideas.

2. Number the similarities between words and people that Lederer identifies. (Note that in some paragraphs, he discusses more than one similarity.)

Reacting to Words

*1. Define these words: *repose* (paragraph 2), *defunct* (2), *multinational* (6), *stock* (6), *station* (7), *markedly* (8). Can you suggest a synonym for each word that will work in the essay?

2. Choose five unfamiliar words from those that Lederer uses as examples, and look them up in a dictionary. Then, use each word in a sentence.

*3. Give several additional examples for each kind of word Lederer discusses.

Reacting to Ideas

1. In your own words, list all the similarities Lederer identifies between words and people. Try to use complete sentences—for example, "Both words and people can be either famous or unknown."

2. Although Lederer is comparing words and people, all his examples are words. Why do you suppose he does not give examples of people to illustrate his parallels? Do you think he *should* have supplied examples of people? Explain.

Teaching Tip

Students may need help defining words. With nonnative students, consider going over the definitions in class before assigning the reading.

Teaching Tip

Remind students to answer all questions in complete sentences.

*3. Supply an example of a person that corresponds to each kind of word Lederer discusses.

Reacting to the Pattern

1. Is Lederer's opening strategy of beginning his essay with a question effective? Why or why not? How might the opening paragraph be expanded?

2. Is this a subject-by-subject or a point-by-point comparison? Explain.

*3. Can you think of any similarities between words and people that Lederer does not list? Give examples of both words and people to make the similarities clear.

For more on point-by-point and subject-by-subject comparison, see 14F.

Writing Practice

1. Choose one paragraph of Lederer's essay, and expand it into an essay. Use his topic sentence as your thesis statement, and add examples to support it. (If Lederer does not include a clear topic sentence, write a new one.)

2. Find an unfamiliar word in the dictionary, and use its definition to help you write the word's biography, tracing the story of its different usages. Then, compare the word to a person you know—or to a famous person.

MEN ARE FROM MARS, WOMEN ARE FROM VENUS

John Gray

Marriage counselor, seminar leader, and author John Gray has written a number of books that examine relationships between men and women. His best-known book, *Men Are from Mars, Women Are from Venus* (1992), uses a two-planet model to show how, in his view, men and women are at times so different that they might as well come from different planets. In the following excerpt from this book, Gray contrasts the different communication styles that he believes are characteristic of men and women. As you read, consider whether Gray's comparison oversimplifies the gender differences he discusses.

Teaching Tip
Remind students to familiarize themselves with the end-of-essay questions before they read the essay.

The most frequently expressed complaint women have about men is that men don't listen. Either a man completely ignores [a woman] when she speaks to him, or he listens for a few beats, assesses what is bothering her, and then proudly puts on his Mr. Fix-It cap and offers her a solution to make her feel better. He is confused when she doesn't appreciate this gesture of love. No matter how many times she tells him that he's not listening, he doesn't get it and keeps doing the same thing. She wants empathy, but he thinks she wants solutions.

The most frequently expressed complaint men have about women is that women are always trying to change them. When a woman loves a man she feels responsible to assist him in growing and tries to help him improve the way he does things. She forms a home-improvement committee, and he becomes her primary focus. No matter how much he resists her help, she persists—waiting for any opportunity to help him or tell him what to do. She thinks she's nurturing him, while he feels he's being controlled. Instead, he wants her acceptance.

These two problems can finally be solved by first understanding why 3
men offer solutions and why women seek to improve. Let's pretend to go back in time, where by observing life on Mars and Venus—before the planets discovered one another or came to Earth—we can gain some insights into men and women.

Martians value power, competency, efficiency, and achievement. They 4
are always doing things to prove themselves and develop their power and skills. Their sense of self is defined through their ability to achieve results. They experience fulfillment primarily through success and accomplishment.

Everything on Mars is a reflection of these values. Even their dress is 5
designed to reflect their skills and competence. Police officers, soldiers, businessmen, scientists, cab drivers, technicians, and chefs all wear uniforms or at least hats to reflect their competence and power.

They don't read magazines like *Psychology Today, Self,* or *People.* They 6
are more concerned with outdoor activities, like hunting, fishing, and racing cars. They are interested in the news, weather, and sports and couldn't care less about romance novels and self-help books.

They are more interested in "objects" and "things" rather than people 7
and feelings. Even today on Earth, while women fantasize about romance, men fantasize about powerful cars, faster computers, gadgets, gizmos, and new more powerful technology. Men are preoccupied with the "things" that can help them express power by creating results and achieving their goals.

Achieving goals is very important to a Martian because it is a way for 8
him to prove his competence and thus feel good about himself. And for him to feel good about himself he must achieve these goals by himself. Someone else can't achieve them for him. Martians pride themselves in doing things all by themselves. Autonomy is a symbol of efficiency, power, and competence.

Understanding this Martian characteristic can help women under- 9
stand why men resist so much being corrected or being told what to do. To offer a man unsolicited advice is to presume that he doesn't know what to do or that he can't do it on his own. Men are very touchy about this, because the issue of competence is so very important to them.

Because he is handling his problems on his own, a Martian rarely talks 10
about his problems unless he needs expert advice. He reasons: "Why involve someone else when I can do it by myself?" He keeps his problems to himself unless he requires help from another to find a solution. Asking for help when you can do it yourself is perceived as a sign of weakness.

However, if he truly does need help, then it is a sign of wisdom to get it. 11
In this case, he will find someone he respects and then talk about his problem. Talking about a problem on Mars is an invitation for advice. Another Martian feels honored by the opportunity. Automatically he puts on his Mr. Fix-It hat, listens for a while, and then offers some jewels of advice.

This Martian custom is one of the reasons men instinctively offer solu- 12
tions when women talk about problems. When a woman innocently shares upset feelings or explores out loud the problems of her day, a man mistakenly assumes she is looking for some expert advice. He puts on his Mr. Fix-It hat and begins giving advice; this is his way of showing love and of trying to help.

He wants to help her feel better by solving her problems. He wants to   13
be useful to her. He feels he can be valued and thus worthy of her love
when his abilities are used to solve her problems.

Once he has offered a solution, however, and she continues to be upset   14
it becomes increasingly difficult for him to listen because his solution is
being rejected and he feels increasingly useless.

He has no idea that by just listening with empathy and interest he can   15
be supportive. He does not know that on Venus talking about problems is
not an invitation to offer a solution.

Venusians have different values. They value love, communication,   16
beauty, and relationships. They spend a lot of time supporting, helping,
and nurturing one another. Their sense of self is defined through their feelings and the quality of their relationships. They experience fulfillment
through sharing and relating.

Everything on Venus reflects these values. Rather than building high-   17
ways and tall buildings, the Venusians are more concerned with living together in harmony, community, and loving cooperation. Relationships are
more important than work and technology. In most ways their world is the
opposite of Mars.

They do not wear uniforms like the Martians (to reveal their compe-   18
tence). On the contrary, they enjoy wearing a different outfit every day,
according to how they are feeling. Personal expression, especially of their
feelings, is very important. They may even change outfits several times a
day as their mood changes.

Communication is of primary importance. To share their personal feel-   19
ings is much more important than achieving goals and success. Talking
and relating to one another is a source of tremendous fulfillment.

This is hard for a man to comprehend. He can come close to under-   20
standing a woman's experience of sharing and relating by comparing it to
the satisfaction he feels when he wins a race, achieves a goal, or solves a
problem.

Instead of being goal oriented, women are relationship oriented; they   21
are more concerned with expressing their goodness, love, and caring. Two
Martians go to lunch to discuss a project or business goal; they have a
problem to solve. In addition, Martians view going to a restaurant as an
efficient way to approach food: no shopping, no cooking, and no washing
dishes. For Venusians, going to lunch is an opportunity to nurture a relationship, for both giving support to and receiving support from a friend.
Women's restaurant talk can be very open and intimate, almost like the
dialogue that occurs between therapist and patient.

On Venus, everyone studies psychology and has at least a master's   22
degree in counseling. They are very involved in personal growth, spiritual-
ity, and everything that can nurture life, healing, and growth. Venus is covered with parks, organic gardens, shopping centers, and restaurants.

Venusians are very intuitive. They have developed this ability through   23
centuries of anticipating the needs of others. They pride themselves in
being considerate of the needs and feelings of others. A sign of great love
is to offer help and assistance to another Venusian without being asked.

Because proving one's competence is not as important to a Venusian,   24
offering help is not offensive, and needing help is not a sign of weakness.
A man, however, may feel offended because when a woman offers advice
he doesn't feel she trusts his ability to do it himself.

A woman has no conception of this male sensitivity because for her it 25 is another feather in her hat if someone offers to help her. It makes her feel loved and cherished. But offering help to a man can make him feel incompetent, weak, and even unloved.

On Venus it is a sign of caring to give advice and suggestions. Venu- 26 sians firmly believe that when something is working it can always work better. Their nature is to want to improve things. When they care about someone, they freely point out what can be improved and suggest how to do it. Offering advice and constructive criticism is an act of love.

Mars is very different. Martians are more solution oriented. If some- 27 thing is working, their motto is don't change it. Their instinct is to leave it alone if it is working. "Don't fix it unless it is broken" is a common expression.

When a woman tries to improve a man, he feels she is trying to fix him. 28 He receives the message that he is broken. She doesn't realize her caring attempts to help him may humiliate him. She mistakenly thinks she is just helping him to grow.

Reacting to the Reading

1. Preview the essay. As you read it more carefully, highlight and annotate as needed to help you understand the writer's ideas.
2. In marginal annotations, number the specific characteristics of men and women that Gray identifies. Then, make an outline for a point-by-point comparison.

Reacting to Words

*1. Define these words: *empathy* (paragraph 1), *nurturing* (2), *autonomy* (8), *unsolicited* (9). Can you suggest a synonym for each word that will work in the essay?
2. Do you think referring to men as Martians and women as Venusians is an effective strategy? What other contrasting labels might work?

Reacting to Ideas

*1. Do you think Gray is serious? What makes you think so?
*2. Do you think Gray's specific observations about men and women are accurate? Is he stereotyping men and women? Explain.
*3. Do you agree with Gray's general point that men and women seem to be from two different planets? Why or why not?

Reacting to the Pattern

1. This essay is a subject-by-subject comparison. How does Gray signal the movement from the first subject to the second subject? Why do you suppose he chose to write a subject-by-subject rather than a point-by-point comparison?
*2. If you were going to add a more fully developed conclusion to sum up this selection's points, what closing strategy would you use? Do you think the selection needs such a conclusion?

Writing Practice

1. Are young (or adolescent) boys and girls also from two different planets? Take a position on this issue, and support it in a subject-by-subject comparison. In your thesis statement, try to account for the differences you identify between boys and girls.

2. Identify one general area in which you believe men's and women's attitudes, behavior, or expectations are very different—for example, dating, careers, eating habits, sports, housekeeping, or driving. Write a comparison-and-contrast essay (serious or humorous) that explores the differences you identify.

3. Are men and women portrayed differently in television dramas (including soap operas) and comedies? Choose a program that has several well-developed male and female characters, and contrast the men and the women in terms of their actions and their conversations.

G Classification

A **classification** essay divides a whole into parts and sorts various items into categories. Jo-Ellan Dimitrius and Mark Mazzarella's "Liars" considers four different kinds of liars. Scott Russell Sanders's "The Men We Carry in Our Minds" classifies the working men he has known.

For more on how to write a classification essay, see 14G.

LIARS

Jo-Ellan Dimitrius and Mark Mazzarella

Los Angeles lawyer Jo-Ellan Dimitrius is a jury-consultant who worked on some of the best-known criminal trials of the 1980s and 1990s, including the Rodney King, O. J. Simpson, and Reginald Denny cases. In the last fifteen years, Dimitrius has worked in civil and criminal trials to assist lawyers in selecting juries and evaluating witnesses by predicting human behavior. Mark Mazzarella is a practicing trial lawyer in San Diego, California, who writes about the formation and management of impressions in juries. He and Jo-Ellan Dimitrius have cowritten *Put Your Best Foot Forward* (2000) and *Reading People* (1998). As you read, think about how Dimitrius and Mazzarella's classification of liars could be useful beyond the courtroom.

> **Teaching Tip**
> Remind students to familiarize themselves with the end-of-essay questions before they read the essay.

If people were all honest with one another, reading them would be a lot easier. The problem is that people lie. I'm not talking about those who are wrong but sincerely believe they are correct, or about the delusional few who genuinely can't tell fact from fantasy. Rather, I'm referring to the one characteristic that is probably the most important in any relationship: truthfulness. And if we assume it's there when it's not—watch out! 1

Much of the information we gather about someone comes directly from the horse's mouth. If he is lying, the information is wrong, and we're likely to misjudge him. That's why it's so crucial to identify liars as soon as 2 possible, and, if you have reason to doubt a person's honesty, to continue to test it until you're entirely at ease with your conclusion.

I have found that most liars fall into one of four basic categories: the occasional liar, the frequent liar, the habitual liar, and the professional liar.

The Occasional Liar

The occasional liar, like most of us, will lie now and then to avoid an unpleasant situation or because he doesn't want to admit doing something wrong or embarrassing. Also like most of us, he does not like to lie and feels very uncomfortable when he does. Because he's uncomfortable, he'll usually reveal his lie through his appearance, body language, and voice. The stress lying causes him will leak out through such things as poor eye contact, fidgeting, or a change in the tone, volume, or patterns of his speech.

The occasional liar often gives his lie some thought, so it may be logical and consistent with the rest of his story. Because it's well thought out, you probably won't be able to spot the lie by its content or context, or by information from third-party sources. In fact, the occasional liar will seldom lie about something that could be easily verified. Consequently, when dealing with an occasional liar, you need to focus on the various visual and oral clues he exhibits.

The Frequent Liar

The frequent liar recognizes what she's doing but doesn't mind it as much as the occasional liar does, so she lies more regularly. Practice makes perfect: the frequent liar is much less likely to reveal her lie through her appearance, body language, and voice. Also, since it doesn't bother her as much to lie, the typical stress-related symptoms won't be as obvious. Any clues in her appearance, voice, and body language might be rather subtle. Often a better way to detect a frequent liar is to focus on the internal consistency and logic of her statements. Since the frequent liar lies more often, and tends to think her lies through less carefully than the occasional liar, she can get sloppy.

The Habitual Liar

The habitual liar lies so frequently that he has lost sight of what he is doing much of the time. In most cases, if he actually thought about it, he would realize he was lying. But he doesn't much care whether what he's saying is true or false. He simply says whatever comes to mind. Because he doesn't care that he's lying, the habitual liar will give very few, if any, physical or vocal clues that he's being dishonest. But because he gives so little thought to his lies and they come so thick and fast, the habitual liar doesn't bother to keep track of them. As a result they are often inconsistent and obvious. So while it's hard to detect the physical and vocal clues in a habitual liar, it's easier to spot his inconsistencies. Listen carefully and ask yourself whether the liar is contradicting himself and whether what he's saying makes sense. Asking a third party about the liar's stories will also help you confirm your suspicions.

The habitual liar is fairly uncommon, so most of us are temporarily taken in when we encounter one. An acquaintance of mine told me she worked with a woman for several months before her suspicions that the co-worker was a habitual liar were confirmed by an obvious and quite ridiculous lie. The liar, a brown-eyed brunette, came to work one day sporting blue contact lenses of an almost alien hue. When my friend commented on her lenses, the liar said, "These aren't contacts. They're my real eye color. It's just that I've always worn brown contact lenses before."

More than once, a client has told me that his adversary lies all the time 9 and will undoubtedly lie on the witness stand. I counsel my client not to worry: the habitual liar is the easiest target in a lawsuit. In real life, she can run from one person to another, from one situation to the next, lying as she goes, and no one compares notes. There are no court reporters or transcripts of testimony; no one reveals what every witness has said to every other witness, and nobody pores over everything the liar has written on the subject to see whether it's all consistent. But in litigation, that is exactly what happens—and suddenly the habitual liar is exposed. It's very rewarding to see.

The Professional Liar

The professional liar is the hardest to identify. He doesn't lie indiscrimi- 10 nately, like the habitual liar. He lies for a purpose. For example, a mechanic who routinely cons motorists about their "faulty" transmissions will have his diagnosis carefully prepared. A real estate salesman who doesn't want to acknowledge a leaky roof will respond quickly to an inquiry about the stains on the ceiling with a rehearsed, very spontaneous sounding statement: "That was old damage from a water leak in the attic. All it needs is a little touch-up paint."

The professional liar has thought the lie through and knows exactly 11 what he's going to say, how it will fly, and whether the customer can easily verify it. Such a well-practiced lie will not be revealed by the liar's voice, body language, or appearance. The lie will be consistent, both internally and logically. The only sure way to detect it is to check the liar's statements against entirely independent sources. Have the roof inspected. Get a second opinion from another mechanic. Take nothing for granted.

Before you make a definitive call about someone who is truly impor- 12 tant to you, always ask yourself whether the information you have about him is reliable. Is he being truthful? If your goal is to accurately evaluate someone, you can't afford to skip this step.

Reacting to the Reading

1. Preview the essay. As you read it more carefully, highlight and annotate as needed to help you understand the writer's ideas.
2. In the margins of the essay, write a one-sentence definition of each of the four categories of liar the writers discuss. Be sure to use your own words for the definitions.

Reacting to Words

*1. Define these words: *delusional* (paragraph 1), *crucial* (2), *context* (5), *verified* (5), *adversary* (9), *pores* (9), *litigation* (9). Can you suggest a synonym for each word that will work in the essay?
2. When referring to the different types of liars, the writers alternate the pronouns *he* and *she*. Why do you think they do this? Do you find it confusing? What other alternatives do they have?

> **Teaching Tip**
> Students may need help defining words. With nonnative students, consider going over the definitions in class before assigning the reading.

Reacting to Ideas

1. According to the authors, why is it so important to identify liars?
*2. Which kind of liar do you see as most dangerous? Why?
*3. Do you think a lie is ever acceptable? Explain.

Reacting to the Pattern

1. What determines the order in which the four kinds of liars are presented? Does this arrangement make sense to you?
2. The writers devote considerably more space to the "habitual liar" and the "professional liar" than to the other two kinds. What material do they include for these two categories and not for the other two? Why do you think they do this?

Writing Practice

1. Write an essay about the different kinds of lies told by "occasional liars." Be sure to include at least three different categories.
2. Using "Liars" as a model, write a classification essay that discusses three or four categories of cheaters. Give each category a name.
3. Write a classification essay about different kinds of heroes. In setting up your categories, consider what motivates people to perform heroic acts.

THE MEN WE CARRY IN OUR MINDS

Scott Russell Sanders

Scott Russell Sanders is a professor of English and an essayist. His essays are personal reflections that include social commentary and philosophical reflection and are often set in the Midwest, where he was born and raised. In "The Men We Carry in Our Minds," Sanders reflects on the working lives of the men he knew when he was a boy and classifies them according to their work. His essay discusses not only his boyhood impressions of the work these men did but also the direction his own professional life has taken. As you read, notice how Sanders moves from classifying men's work to comparing men's lives to women's lives.

The first men, besides my father, I remember seeing were black convicts and white guards, in the cottonfield across the road from our farm on the outskirts of Memphis. I must have been three or four. The prisoners wore dingy gray-and-black zebra suits, heavy as canvas, sodden with sweat. Hatless, stooped, they chopped weeds in the fierce heat, row after row, breathing the acrid dust of boll-weevil poison. The overseers wore dazzling white shirts and broad shadowy hats. The oiled barrels of their shotguns flashed in the sunlight. Their faces in memory are utterly blank. Of course those men, white and black, have become for me an emblem of racial hatred. But they have also come to stand for the twin poles of my early vision of manhood—the brute toiling animal and the boss. 1

When I was a boy, the men I knew labored with their bodies. They were marginal farmers, just scraping by, or welders, steelworkers, carpenters; 2

they swept floors, dug ditches, mined coal, or drove trucks, their forearms ropy with muscle; they trained horses, stoked furnaces, built tires, stood on assembly lines wrestling parts onto cars and refrigerators. They got up before light, worked all day long whatever the weather, and when they came home at night they looked as though somebody had been whipping them. In the evenings and on weekends they worked on their own places, tilling gardens that were lumpy with clay, fixing broken-down cars, hammering on houses that were always too drafty, too leaky, too small.

The bodies of the men I knew were twisted and maimed in ways visible and invisible. The nails of their hands were black and split, the hands tattooed with scars. Some had lost fingers. Heavy lifting had given many of them finicky backs and guts weak from hernias. Racing against conveyor belts had given them ulcers. Their ankles and knees ached from years of standing on concrete. Anyone who had worked for long around machines was hard of hearing. They squinted, and the skin of their faces was creased like the leather of old work gloves. There were times, studying them, when I dreaded growing up. Most of them coughed, from dust or cigarettes, and most of them drank cheap wine or whiskey, so their eyes looked bloodshot and bruised. The fathers of my friends always seemed older than the mothers. Men wore out sooner. Only women lived into old age.

As a boy I also knew another sort of men, who did not sweat and break down like mules. They were soldiers, and so far as I could tell they scarcely worked at all. During my early school years we lived on a military base, an arsenal in Ohio, and every day I saw GIs in the guardshacks, on the stoops of barracks, at the wheels of olive drab Chevrolets. The chief fact of their lives was boredom. Long after I left the Arsenal I came to recognize the sour smell the soldiers gave off as that of souls in limbo. They were all waiting—for wars, for transfers, for leaves, for promotions, for the end of their hitch—like so many braves waiting for the hunt to begin. Unlike the warriors of older tribes, however, they would have no say about when the battle would start or how it would be waged. Their waiting was broken only when they practiced for war. They fired guns at targets, drove tanks across the churned-up fields of the military reservation, set off bombs in the wrecks of old fighter planes. I knew this was all play. But I also felt certain that when the hour for killing arrived, they would kill. When the real shooting started, many of them would die. This was what soldiers were *for*, just as a hammer was for driving nails.

Warriors and toilers: those seemed, in my boyhood vision, to be the chief destinies for men. They weren't the only destinies, as I learned from having a few male teachers, from reading books, and from watching television. But the men on television—the politicians, the astronauts, the generals, the savvy lawyers, the philosophical doctors, the bosses who gave orders to both soldiers and laborers—seemed as removed and unreal to me as the figures in tapestries. I could no more imagine growing up to become one of these cool, potent creatures than I could imagine becoming a prince.

A nearer and more hopeful example was that of my father, who had escaped from a red-dirt farm to a tire factory, and from the assembly line to the front office. Eventually he dressed in a white shirt and tie. He carried himself as if he had been born to work with his mind. But his body, remembering the earlier years of slogging work, began to give out on him in his fifties, and it quit on him entirely before he turned sixty-five. Even such a partial escape from man's fate as he had accomplished did not seem possible for most of the boys I knew. They joined the Army, stood in line for jobs in the smoky plants, helped build highways. They were bound to work as their fathers had worked, killing themselves or preparing to kill others.

A scholarship enabled me not only to attend college, a rare enough feat in my circle, but even to study in a university meant for the children of the rich. Here I met for the first time young men who had assumed from birth that they would lead lives of comfort and power. And for the first time I met women who told me that men were guilty of having kept all the joys and privileges of the earth for themselves. I was baffled. What privileges? What joys? I thought about the maimed, dismal lives of most of the men back home. What had they stolen from their wives and daughters? The right to go five days a week, twelve months a year, for thirty or forty years to a steel mill or a coal mine? The right to drop bombs and die in war? The right to feel every leak in the roof, every gap in the fence, every cough in the engine, as a wound they must mend? The right to feel, when the lay-off comes or the plant shuts down, not only afraid but ashamed? [7]

I was slow to understand the deep grievances of women. This was because, as a boy, I had envied them. Before college, the only people I had ever known who were interested in art or music or literature, the only ones who read books, the only ones who ever seemed to enjoy a sense of ease and grace were the mothers and daughters. Like the menfolk, they fretted about money, they scrimped and made-do. But, when the pay stopped coming in, they were not the ones who had failed. Nor did they have to go to war, and that seemed to me a blessed fact. By comparison with the narrow, ironclad days of fathers, there was an expansiveness, I thought, in the days of mothers. They went to see neighbors, to shop in town, to run errands at school, at the library, at church. No doubt, had I looked harder at their lives, I would have envied them less. It was not my fate to become a woman, so it was easier for me to see the graces. Few of them held jobs outside the home, and those who did filled thankless roles as clerks and waitresses. I didn't see, then, what a prison a house could be, since houses seemed to me brighter, handsomer places than any factory. I did not realize—because such things were never spoken of—how often women suffered from men's bullying. I did learn about the wretchedness of abandoned wives, single mothers, widows; but I also learned about the wretchedness of lone men. Even then I could see how exhausting it was for a mother to cater all day to the needs of young children. But if I had been asked, as a boy, to choose between tending a baby and tending a machine, I think I would have chosen the baby. (Having now tended both, I know I would choose the baby.) [8]

So I was baffled when the women at college accused me and my sex of having cornered the world's pleasures. I think something like my bafflement has been felt by other boys (and by girls as well) who grew up in dirt-poor farm country, in mining country, in black ghettos, in Hispanic barrios, in the shadows of factories, in Third World nations—any place where the fate of men is as grim and bleak as the fate of women. Toilers and warriors. I realize now how ancient these identities are, how deep the tug they exert on men, the undertow of a thousand generations. The miseries I saw, as a boy, in the lives of nearly all men I continue to see in the lives of many—the body-breaking toil, the tedium, the call to be tough, the humiliating powerlessness, the battle for a living and for territory. [9]

When the women I met at college thought about the joys and privileges   10
of men, they did not carry in their minds the sort of men I had known in
my childhood. They thought of their fathers, who were bankers, physicians, architects, stockbrokers, the big wheels of the big cities. These
fathers rode the train to work or drove cars that cost more than any of my
childhood houses. They were attended from morning to night by female
helpers, wives and nurses and secretaries. They were never laid off, never
short of cash at month's end, never lined up for welfare. These fathers
made decisions that mattered. They ran the world.

The daughters of such men wanted to share in this power, this glory.   11
So did I. They yearned for a say over their future, for jobs worthy of their
abilities, for the right to live at peace, unmolested, whole. Yes, I thought,
yes yes. The difference between me and these daughters was that they saw
me, because of my sex, as destined from birth to become like their fathers,
and therefore as an enemy to their desires. But I knew better. I wasn't an
enemy, in fact or in feeling. I was an ally. If I had known, then, how to tell
them so, would they have believed me? Would they now?

Reacting to the Reading

1. Preview the essay. As you read it more carefully, highlight and annotate
   as needed to help you understand the writer's ideas.
2. In the margins of the essay, name and number the categories Sanders
   identifies. If he does not name a particular category, supply a suitable
   name.

Reacting to Words

*1. Define these words: *sodden* (paragraph 1), *acrid* (1), *overseers* (1), *tilling* (2), *finicky* (3), *toilers* (5), *savvy* (5), *expansiveness* (8), *undertow*
   (9), *yearned* (11). Can you suggest a synonym for each word that will
   work in the essay?
2. Suggest two or three alternative names for the categories *warriors* and
   toilers (paragraph 5). Do you think any of your suggestions are better
   than Sanders's choices?

> **Teaching Tip**
> Students may need help
> defining words. With nonna-
> tive students, consider going
> over the definitions in class
> before assigning the reading.

Reacting to Ideas

1. When Sanders was young, what did he see as his destiny? How did he
   escape his fate? How else might he have escaped?
2. What were the grievances of the women Sanders met at college? Why
   did Sanders have trouble understanding these grievances?
*3. Who do you believe has an easier life—men or women? Explain.

> **Teaching Tip**
> Remind students to answer
> all questions in complete
> sentences.

Reacting to the Pattern

1. What two types of men did Sanders know when he was young? How
   are they different? What do they have in common?
2. What kinds of men discussed in the essay do not fit into the two categories Sanders identifies in paragraphs 2–4? Why don't they fit?
*3. Sanders does not categorize the women he discusses. Can you think of
   a few categories into which these women could fit?

Writing Practice

1. Write a classification essay in which you identify and discuss three or four categories of workers (females as well as males) you observed in your community when you were growing up. In your thesis statement, draw a conclusion about the relative status and rewards of these workers' jobs.

2. Consider your own work history as well as your future career. Write a classification essay in which you discuss your experience in several different categories of employment in the past, present, and future. Give each category a descriptive title, and include a thesis statement that sums up your progress.

3. Categorize the workers in your current place of employment or on your college campus.

| **H** | **Definition** |

For more on how to write a definition essay, see 14H.

A **definition** essay presents an extended definition, using other patterns of development to move beyond a simple dictionary definition. In "The Wife-Beater," Gayle Rosenwald Smith defines an item of clothing. In "Dyslexia," Eileen Simpson defines a reading disorder.

THE WIFE-BEATER

Gayle Rosenwald Smith

Philadelphia lawyer Gayle Rosenwald Smith, who specializes in family law, has coauthored *What Every Woman Should Know about Divorce and Custody* (1998). Her articles have been published in newspapers such as the *Chicago Tribune* and the *Philadelphia Inquirer.* As you read, think about the connotations of violence and masculinity in Smith's definition of a "wife-beater."

1   Everybody wears them. The Gap sells them. Fashion designers Dolce and Gabbana have lavished them with jewels. Their previous greatest resurgence occurred in the 1950s, when Marlon Brando's Stanley Kowalski wore one in Tennessee Williams' *A Streetcar Named Desire.* They are all the rage.

2   What are they called?

3   The name is the issue. For they are known as "wife-beaters."

4   A Web search shows that kids nationwide are wearing the skinny-ribbed white T-shirts that can be worn alone or under another shirt. Women have adopted them with the same gusto as men. A search of boutiques shows that these wearers include professionals who wear them, adorned with designer accessories, under their pricey suits. They are available in all colors, sizes and price ranges.

5   Wearers under 25 do not seem to be disturbed by the name. But I sure am.

It's an odd name for an undershirt. And even though the ugly stereo-   6
types behind the name are both obvious and toxic, it appears to be cool to
say the name without fear of (or without caring about) hurting anyone.

That the name is fueled by stereotype is now an academically estab-   7
lished fact, although various sources disagree on exactly when shirt and
name came together. The *Oxford Dictionary* defines the term *wife-beater* as:

"1. A man who physically abuses his wife and

2. Tank-style underwear shirts. Origin: based on the stereotype that
physically abusive husbands wear that particular type of shirt."

The *World Book Dictionary* locates the origin of the term *wife-beater* in   8
the 1970s, from the stereotype of the Midwestern male wearing an undershirt while beating his wife. The shirts are said to have been popular in the
1980s at all types of sporting events, especially ones at which one sits in
the sun and develops "wife-beater marks." The undershirts also attained
popularity at wet T-shirt contests, in which the wet, ribbed tees accentu-
ated contestants' breasts.

In an article in the style section of the New York Times, Jesse Sheid-   9
lower, principal editor of the *Oxford English Dictionary*'s American office,
says the association of the undershirt and the term *wife-beater* arose in
1997 from varied sources, including gay and gang subcultures and rap
music.

In the article, some sources argued that the reference in the term was   10
not to spousal abuse per se but to popular-culture figures such as Ralph
Cramden and Tony Soprano. And what about Archie Bunker?

It's not just the name that worries me. Fashion headlines reveal that we   11
want to overthrow '90s grunge and return to shoulder pads and hardware-
studded suits. Am I reading too much into a fashion statement that the
return is also to male dominance where physical abuse is acceptable as a
means of control?

There has to be a better term. After all, it's a pretty rare piece of cloth-   12
ing that can make both men and women look sexier. You'd expect a term
connoting flattery—not violence.

Wearers under 25 may not want to hear this, but here it is. More   13
than 4 million women are victims of severe assaults by boyfriends and
husbands each year. By conservative estimate, family violence occurs in
2 million families each year in the United States. Average age of the bat-
terer: 31.

Possibly the last statistic is telling. Maybe youth today would rather   14
ignore the overtones of the term *wife-beater*. It is also true, however, that
the children of abusers often learn the behavior from their elders.

Therein lies perhaps the worst difficulty: that this name for this shirt   15
teaches the wrong thing about men. Some articles quote women who felt
the shirts looked great, especially on guys with great bodies. One woman
stated that it even made guys look "manly."

So *manly* equals *violent*? Not by me, and I hope not by anyone on any   16
side of age 25.

Reacting to the Reading

1. Preview the essay. As you read it more carefully, highlight and annotate
   as needed to help you understand the writer's ideas.

2. Smith's essay opens with the sentence, "Everybody wears them." Underline this sentence (if you have not already done so). Then, place a

check mark beside each sentence in the essay that supports this opening statement.

Reacting to Words

*1. Define these words: *lavished* (paragraph 1), *resurgence* (1), *gusto* (4), *toxic* (6), *connoting* (12). Can you suggest a synonym for each word that will work in the essay?

2. Smith uses informal words and expressions—*kids* (4), *pricey* (4), and *Not by me* (16)—as well as contractions, in her essay. Do you think this informal style undercuts her serious message? Explain.

Reacting to Ideas

*1. Beyond simply defining the term *wife-beater*, what is Smith's purpose for writing this essay? How can you tell?

2. What does Smith actually propose or recommend to her readers? For example, does she think people should stop wearing "wife-beater" T-shirts?

*3. In paragraph 11, Smith asks, "Am I reading too much into a fashion statement . . . ?" Answer her question.

Reacting to the Pattern

*1. Where in her essay does Smith develop her definition with examples? Where does she use description? Can you identify any other patterns of development?

2. Where does Smith present a formal (dictionary) definition of *wife-beater*? Where does she give information about the term's origin? Why does she include these two sections?

Writing Practice

1. Define another article of clothing that, like the "wife-beater" T-shirt, has taken on some special significance. (For example, you could write about baggy jeans or baseball caps.) Focus on the garment and its wearers (not on its name), discussing the impression the article of clothing makes and the associations it has for its wearers and for others. You can use description, exemplification, or classification to develop your essay.

2. Think of an item or activity that has a name with a negative, even offensive, connotation—for example, the name *bobos* for generic-brand sneakers. Define the item, developing your definition with description and examples, and try in your definition to persuade people why they should stop using the negative term.

DYSLEXIA

Eileen Simpson

In *Reversals: A Personal Account of Victory over Dyslexia* (1979), psychotherapist and author Eileen Simpson tells the story of her own struggle with dyslexia. In her account, she describes how she was able to overcome dyslexia only when she understood what it was and how it made reading difficult. As you read the following excerpt from *Reversals*, watch for the various ways in which Simpson develops her definition, and note especially her use of exemplification.

Dyslexia (from the Greek, *dys,* faulty, + *lexis,* speech, cognate with the Latin *legere,* to read), developmental or specific dyslexia as it's technically called, the disorder I suffered from, is the inability of otherwise normal children to read. Children whose intelligence is below average, whose vision or hearing is defective, who have not had proper schooling, or who are too emotionally disturbed or brain-damaged to profit from it belong in other diagnostic categories. They, too, may be unable to learn to read, but they cannot properly be called dyslexics.

For more than seventy years the essential nature of the affliction has been hotly disputed by psychologists, neurologists, and educators. It is generally agreed, however, that it is the result of a neurophysiological flaw in the brain's ability to process language. It is probably inherited, although some experts are reluctant to say this because they fear people will equate "inherited" with "untreatable." Treatable it certainly is: not a disease to be cured, but a malfunction that requires retraining.

Reading is the most complex skill a child entering school is asked to develop. What makes it complex, in part, is that letters are less constant than objects. A car seen from a distance, close to, from above, or below, or in a mirror still looks like a car even though the optical image changes. The letters of the alphabet are more whimsical. Take the letter *b.* Turned upside down it becomes a *p.* Looked at in a mirror, it becomes a *d.* Capitalized, it becomes something quite different, a *B.* The *M* upside down is a *W.* The *E* flipped over becomes Ǝ. This reversed *E* is familiar to mothers of normal children who have just begun to go to school. The earliest examples of art work they bring home often have I LOVƎ YOU written on them.

Dyslexics differ from other children in that they read, spell, and write letters upside down and turned around far more frequently and for a much longer time. In what seems like a capricious manner, they also add letters, syllables, and words, or, just as capriciously, delete them. With palindromic words (was-saw, on-no), it is the order of the letters rather than the orientation they change. The new word makes sense, but not the sense intended. Then there are other words where the changed order—"sorty" for story—does not make sense at all.

The inability to recognize that g, *g,* and G are the same letter, the inability to maintain the orientation of the letters, to retain the order in which they appear, and to follow a line of text without jumping above or below it—all the results of the flaw—can make of an orderly page of words a dish of alphabet soup.

Also essential for reading is the ability to store words in memory and to retrieve them. This very particular kind of memory dyslexics lack. So, too, do they lack the ability to hear what the eye sees, and to see what they hear. If the eye sees "off," the ear must hear "off" and not "of," or "for." If the ear hears "saw," the eye must see that it looks like "saw" on the page and not "was." Lacking these skills, a sentence or paragraph becomes a coded message to which the dyslexic can't find the key.

It is only a slight exaggeration to say that those who learned to read without difficulty can best understand the labor reading is for a dyslexic by turning a page of text upside down and trying to decipher it.

While the literature is replete with illustrations of the way these chil- 8
dren write and spell, there are surprisingly few examples of how they read.
One, used for propaganda purposes to alert the public to the vulnerability
of dyslexics in a literate society, is a sign warning that behind it are guard
dogs trained to kill. The dyslexic reads:

> Wurring
> Guard God
> Patoly

for

> Warning
> Guard Dog
> Patrol

and, of course, remains ignorant of the danger.

Looking for a more commonplace example, and hoping to recapture 9
the way I must have read in fourth grade, I recently observed dyslexic
children at the Educational Therapy Clinic in Princeton, through the
courtesy of Elizabeth Travers, the director. The first child I saw, eight-
year-old Anna (whose red hair and brown eyes reminded me of myself at
that age), had just come to the Clinic and was learning the alphabet.
Given the story of "Little Red Riding Hood," which is at the second grade
level, she began confidently enough, repeating the title from memory,
then came to a dead stop. With much coaxing throughout, she read as
follows:

> Grandma you a top. Grandma [looks over at picture of Red Riding
> Hood]. Red Riding Hood [long pause, presses index finger into the
> paper. Looks at me for help. I urge: Go ahead] the a [puts head
> close to the page, nose almost touching] on Grandma

for

> Once upon a time there was a little girl who had a red coat with a
> red hood. Etc.

"Grandma" was obviously a memory from having heard the story read 10
aloud. Had I needed a reminder of how maddening my silences must have
been to Miss Henderson, and how much patience is required to teach
these children, Anna, who took almost ten minutes to read these few lines,
furnished it. The main difference between Anna and me at that age is that
Anna clearly felt no need to invent. She was perplexed, but not anxious,
and seemed to have infinite tolerance for her long silences.

Toby, a nine-year-old boy with superior intelligence, had a year of 11
tutoring behind him and could have managed "Little Red Riding Hood"
with ease. His text was taken from the *Reader's Digest's Reading Skill
Builder,* Grade IV. He read:

> A kangaroo likes as if he had but truck together warm. His saw
> neck and head do not . . . [Here Toby sighed with fatigue] seem to

feel happy back. They and tried and so every a tiger Moses and shoots from lonesome day and shouts and long shore animals. And each farm play with five friends . . .

He broke off with the complaint, "This is too hard. Do I have to read   12
any more?"

His text was: 13

A kangaroo looks as if he had been put together wrong. His small neck and head do not seem to fit with his heavy back legs and thick tail. Soft eyes, a twinkly little nose and short front legs seem strange on such a large strong animal. And each front paw has five fingers, like a man's hand.

An English expert gives the following bizarre example of an adult   14
dyslexic's performance:

An the bee-what in the tel mother of the biothodoodoo to the majoram or that emidrate eni eni Krastrei, mestriet to Ketra lotombreidi to ra from treido as that.

His text, taken from a college catalogue the examiner happened to   15
have close at hand, was:

It shall be in the power of the college to examine or not every licentiate, previous to his admission to the fellowship, as they shall think fit.

That evening when I read aloud to Auntie for the first time, I probably   16
began as Toby did, my memory of the classroom lesson keeping me close to the text. When memory ran out, and Auntie did not correct my errors, I began to invent. When she still didn't stop me, I may well have begun to improvise in the manner of this patient—anything to keep going and keep up the myth that I was reading—until Auntie brought the "gibberish" to a halt.

Reacting to the Reading

1. Preview the essay. As you read it more carefully, highlight and annotate as needed to help you understand the writer's ideas.
2. Underline the definition of *dyslexia* in the essay; in a marginal annotation, paraphrase the definition.

Reacting to Words

*1. Define these words: *process* (paragraph 2), *whimsical* (3), *capricious* (4), *orientation* (5), *replete* (8), *commonplace* (9), *perplexed* (10), *gibberish* (16). Can you suggest a synonym for each word that will work in the essay?
2. Can you think of a synonym or near-synonym for *dyslexia?* If not, try to coin a suitable word to describe the disorder.

Teaching Tip
Students may need help defining words. With nonnative students, consider going over the definitions in class before assigning the reading.

Reacting to Ideas

1. What is dyslexia? How are children with dyslexia different from their peers?

2. What central point or idea do you think Simpson wishes to communicate to her readers? Does she ever actually state this idea? If so, where? If not, do you think she should?

*3. If you were dyslexic, how would your life be different?

Reacting to the Pattern

1. Simpson develops her definition of dyslexia with examples. Identify some of these examples. Do you find the material drawn from her own childhood struggle with dyslexia more or less effective than the examples of cases she observes as an adult? Explain.

*2. What other patterns does Simpson use to develop her definition?

Writing Practice

1. Choose a problem—physical, economic, or behavioral—that handicaps you as a student. Identify the problem, define it, and give examples to expand your definition.

2. Consider the tasks you do each day at home, at school, and at work. How would you manage these tasks differently if you were dyslexic? Write an essay in which you define *dyslexia* in terms of the things you, as a dyslexic adult, would not be able to do.

I   Argument

For more on how to write an argument essay, see 14I.

An **argument** essay takes a stand on one side of a debatable issue, using facts, examples, and expert opinion to persuade readers to accept a position. The writers of the three essays that follow—Alan M. Dershowitz in "Why Fear National ID Cards?", Charles Krauthammer in "The New Prohibitionism," and Martin Luther King Jr. in "I Have a Dream"—attempt to convince readers to accept their positions—or at least to acknowledge that they are reasonable.

WHY FEAR NATIONAL ID CARDS?

Alan M. Dershowitz

Alan M. Dershowitz is a Harvard Law School professor, columnist, and lawyer whose clients have included Klaus von Bulow, O. J. Simpson, Mia Farrow, and Mike Tyson. Dershowitz is the author of *The Best Defense* (1983), *The Abuse Excuse* (1995), *The Advocate's Devil* (1999), and *Supreme Injustice: How the High Court Hijacked Election 2000* (2001), among many others. His articles appear regularly in the *New York Times Magazine*, *The Nation*, the *Washington Post*, *Harper's*, the *Los Angeles Times*, and numerous law reviews. As you read, consider

how Dershowitz acknowledges opposing viewpoints while still successfully arguing his case.

1   At many bridges and tunnels across the country, drivers avoid long
delays at the toll booths with an unobtrusive device that fits on a car's
dashboard. Instead of fumbling for change, they drive right through; the
device sends a radio signal that records their passage. They are billed later.
It's a tradeoff between privacy and convenience: the toll-takers know more
about you—when you entered and left Manhattan, for instance—but you
save time and money.

2   An optional national identity card could be used in a similar way, offering a similar kind of tradeoff: a little less anonymity for a lot more
security. Anyone who had the card could be allowed to pass through air-
ports or building security more expeditiously, and anyone who opted out
could be examined much more closely.

3   As a civil libertarian, I am instinctively skeptical of such tradeoffs. But
I support a national identity card with a chip that can match the holder's
fingerprint. It could be an effective tool for preventing terrorism, reducing
the need for other law-enforcement mechanisms—especially racial and
ethnic profiling—that pose even greater dangers to civil liberties.

4   I can hear the objections: What about the specter of Big Brother? What
about fears of identity cards leading to more intrusive measures? (The
National Rifle Association, for example, worries that a government that
registered people might also decide to register guns.) What about fears
that such cards would lead to increased deportation of illegal immigrants?

5   First, we already require photo ID's for many activities, including flying, driving, drinking, and check-cashing. And fingerprints differ from
photographs only in that they are harder to fake. The vast majority of
Americans routinely carry photo ID's in their wallets and pocketbooks.
These ID's are issued by state motor vehicle bureaus and other public and
private entities. A national card would be uniform and difficult to forge or
alter. It would reduce the likelihood that someone could, intentionally or
not, get lost in the cracks of multiple bureaucracies.

6   The fear of an intrusive government can be addressed by setting criteria for any official who demands to see the card. Even without a national
card, people are always being asked to show identification. The existence
of a national card need not change the rules about when ID can properly
be demanded. It is true that the card would facilitate the deportation of
illegal immigrants. But President Bush has proposed giving legal status to
many of the illegal immigrants now in this country. And legal immigrants
would actually benefit from a national ID card that could demonstrate
their status to government officials.

7   Finally, there is the question of the right to anonymity. I don't believe
we can afford to recognize such a right in this age of terrorism. No such
right is hinted at in the Constitution. And though the Supreme Court has
identified a right to privacy, privacy and anonymity are not the same.
American taxpayers, voters and drivers long ago gave up any right of
anonymity without loss of our right to engage in lawful conduct within
zones of privacy. Rights are a function of experience, and our recent experiences teach that it is far too easy to be anonymous—even to create a
false identity—in this large and decentralized country. A national ID card
would not prevent all threats of terrorism, but it would make it more

difficult for potential terrorists to hide in open view, as many of the Sept. 11 hijackers apparently managed to do.

A national ID card could actually enhance civil liberties by reducing the need for racial and ethnic stereotyping. There would be no excuse for hassling someone merely because he belongs to a particular racial or ethnic group if he presented a card that matched his print and that permitted his name to be checked instantly against the kind of computerized criminal-history retrieval systems that are already in use. (If there is too much personal information in the system, or if the information is being used improperly, that is a separate issue. The only information the card need contain is name, address, photo and print.)

8

From a civil liberties perspective, I prefer a system that takes a little bit of freedom from all to one that takes a great deal of freedom and dignity from the few—especially since those few are usually from a racially or ethnically disfavored group. A national ID card would be much more effective in preventing terrorism than profiling millions of men simply because of their appearance.

9

Reacting to the Reading

1. Preview the essay. As you read it more carefully, highlight and annotate as needed to help you understand the writer's ideas.
2. Underline Dershowitz's thesis statement. In the margin, rewrite it in your own words.

Reacting to Words

*1. Define these words: *unobtrusive* (paragraph 1), *anonymity* (2), *expeditiously* (2), *opted* (2), *skeptical* (3), *specter* (4), *intrusive* (4). Can you suggest a synonym for each word that will work in the essay?
2. In paragraph 3, Dershowitz identifies himself as a civil libertarian. What is a civil libertarian? Why do you think Dershowitz feels the need to identify himself in this manner?

Teaching Tip
Students may need help defining words. With nonnative students, consider going over the definitions in class before assigning the reading.

Reacting to Ideas

*1. Do you agree with Dershowitz that trading "a little less anonymity for a lot more security" (paragraph 2) is a good idea? Why or why not?
2. Dershowitz believes that a system of national ID cards would reduce the threat of terrorism. Why does he think so?
3. Dershowitz believes that a system of national ID cards would "enhance civil liberties by reducing the need for racial and ethnic stereotyping" (paragraph 8). How does he explain this?

Teaching Tip
Remind students to answer all questions in complete sentences.

Reacting to the Pattern

*1. Dershowitz opens his essay with a discussion alluding to the EZ Pass system for collecting highway tolls. Why does he begin in this way? Is this an effective opening strategy?
2. According to Dershowitz, what are the advantages of national identity cards?
*3. What opposing arguments does Dershowitz present? How does he refute (that is, argue against) them? Is his refutation of these arguments convincing?

Writing Practice

1. Reread paragraphs 4 through 7, and make a list of the objections Dershowitz identifies. Then, write a letter to your congressional representative in which you argue *against* instituting a system of national identity cards.

2. In recent years, many African Americans have been victims of unwarranted police stops for "driving while black"; in the wake of the September 11, 2001, terrorist attacks, some Arab Americans have faced a similar problem, which has been called "flying while brown." In both cases, the issue at hand is racial and ethnic stereotyping that inconveniences—and might even endanger—innocent people. Write an essay in support of national identity cards, focusing on their possible role in eliminating this kind of stereotyping. Use examples from your own experience if possible.

THE NEW PROHIBITIONISM

Charles Krauthammer

Charles Krauthammer is the author of a Pulitzer Prize–winning column for the *Washington Post* and a frequent contributor to various magazines. His work often discusses current political and social issues. In the following column, Krauthammer constructs an argument about the antismoking movement. Krauthammer's medical training (he was a practicing psychiatrist) and experience as a political and social commentator are evident in the way he develops his argument. As you read, note the ways in which he builds support for his thesis.

> **Teaching Tip**
> Remind students to familiarize themselves with the end-of-essay questions before they read the essay.

The oddest thing about the current national crusade against tobacco is not its frenzy—our culture lives from one frenzy to the next—but its selectivity. Of course tobacco is a great national killer. It deserves all the pummeling it gets. But alcohol is a great national killer too, and it has enjoyed an amazingly free ride amid the fury of the New Prohibitionism. 1

Joe Camel[1] has been banished forever, but those beloved Budweiser frogs—succeeded by even cuter Budweiser lizards—keep marching along, right into the consciousness of every TV-watching kid in the country. 2

For 26 years[2] television has been free of cigarette ads. Why? Because TV persuades as nothing else, and we don't want young people—inveterate TV watchers—persuaded. Yet television is bursting with exhortations to drink. TV sports in particular, a staple of adolescents, is one long hymn to the glories of beer. 3

And the sports-worshipping years are precisely the time that kids learn to drink. The median age at which they start drinking is just over 13. A 1990 survey found that 56% of students in Grades 5 through 12 say alcohol advertising encourages them to drink. Surprise! 4

---

1. Retired cartoon image used to advertise Camel cigarettes; withdrawn by industry following complaints that it was aimed at underage smokers.

2. Cigarette commercials were banned from television in 1971; Krauthammer is writing in 1997.

Am I for Prohibition? No. But I am for a little perspective. We tend to think of the turn-of-the-century temperance movement as little blue-haired ladies trying to prevent people from having a good time on Saturday night. In fact, the temperance movement was part of a much larger progressive movement seeking to improve the appalling conditions of the urban working class. These were greatly exacerbated by rampant alcoholism that contributed to extraordinary levels of spousal and child abuse, abandonment and destitution. 5

Alcohol is still a cause of staggering devastation. It kills 100,000 Americans a year—not only from disease but also from accidents. In 1996, 41% of all U.S. traffic fatalities were alcohol related. It causes huge economic losses and untold suffering. Why, then, do the Bud frogs get to play the Super Bowl while Joe Camel goes the way of the Marlboro Man?[3] 6

The most plausible answer is that tobacco is worse because it kills more people. Indeed it does. But 100,000 people a year is still a fair carnage. Moreover, the really compelling comparison is this: alcohol is far more deadly than tobacco *to innocent bystanders*. In a free society, should we not consider behavior that injures others more worthy of regulation than behavior that merely injures oneself? The primary motive for gun control, after all, is concern about homicide, not suicide. 7

The antitobacco folk, aware of this bedrock belief, try to play up the harm smokers cause others. Thus the attorneys general seeking billions of dollars in damages from the tobacco companies are claiming that taxpayers have been unfairly made to pay for the treatment of smoking-related illnesses. 8

A clever ploy. But the hardheaded truth is that premature death from smoking, which generally affects people in their late-middle and early retirement years, is an economic boon to society. The money saved on pensions and on the truly expensive health care that comes with old age—something these smokers never achieve—surely balances, if it does not exceed, the cost of treating tobacco-related diseases. 9

The alternative and more dramatic antitobacco tactic is to portray smoking as an assault on nonsmokers via secondhand smoke. Now, secondhand smoke is certainly a nuisance. But the claim that it is a killer is highly dubious. "The statistical evidence," reported the nonpartisan Congressional Research Service in 1994, "does not appear to support a conclusion that there are substantive health effects of passive smoking." 10

Unlike secondhand smoke, secondhand booze is a world-class killer. Drunk driving alone kills 17,000 people a year. And alcohol's influence extends far beyond driving: it contributes to everything from bar fights to domestic violence. One study found that 44% of assailants in cases of marital abuse had been drinking. Another study found that 60% of wife batterers had been under the influence. Whatever claims you make against tobacco, you'd have quite a time looking for cases of the nicotine-crazed turning on their wives with a butcher knife. 11

Moreover, look at the *kinds* of people alcohol kills. Drunk drivers kill toddlers. They kill teens. They kill whole families. Tobacco does not kill toddlers and teens. Tobacco strikes late. It kills, but at a very long remove in time. Its victims generally have already had their chance at life. Tobacco merely shortens life; alcohol can deprive people of it. 12

---

3. Image of a rugged cowboy, used to advertise Marlboro cigarettes.

Still undecided which of the two poisons is more deserving of social 13
disapprobation? Here's the ultimate test. Ask yourself this: If you knew
your child was going to become addicted to either alcohol or tobacco,
which would you choose?

Reacting to the Reading

1. Preview the essay. As you read it more carefully, highlight and annotate
   as needed to help you understand the writer's ideas.
2. Underline the transitional words and phrases that signal the movement from one part of the argument to another or that connect specific
   points to other points or to the thesis statement.

Reacting to Words

*1. Define these words: *prohibitionism* (title), *selectivity* (paragraph 1),
   pummeling (1), *inveterate* (3), *median* (4), *temperance* (5), *devastation*
   (6), *plausible* (7), *boon* (9), *dubious* (10), *disapprobation* (13). Can you
   suggest a synonym for each word that will work in the essay?
2. Krauthammer uses the word *kill* in many of the sentences of paragraph 12. Why does he do this? Would the paragraph be more effective
   if he used a different word in some sentences?

> **Teaching Tip**
> Students may need help
> defining words. With nonna-
> tive students, consider going
> over the definitions in class
> before assigning the reading.

Reacting to Ideas

*1. Do you agree with Krauthammer when he says, "TV persuades as noth-
   ing else" (paragraph 3)? Do you believe that television advertising
   images like the Budweiser frogs can encourage children to drink?
2. How convincing is Krauthammer's argument that premature death
   from smoking "is an economic boon to society" (paragraph 9)? Can
   you think of another argument that might be more effective?
3. Krauthammer argues against the current "national crusade against
   tobacco" (paragraph 1) by maintaining that alcohol is far more deadly
   than tobacco. Does this line of reasoning make sense? Does the fact
   that alcohol may be more dangerous than tobacco eliminate the need
   for legislation against tobacco?

> **Teaching Tip**
> Remind students to answer
> all questions in complete
> sentences.

Reacting to the Pattern

*1. Throughout his essay, Krauthammer asks a series of questions. What
   function do these questions serve? Is this technique effective?
2. Krauthammer supports his position by contrasting alcohol and
   tobacco. What points does he make about each? What other points
   could he have made?
3. Krauthammer concludes by asking readers whether they would rather
   have their children addicted to tobacco or to alcohol. What is his purpose in doing so? Is this a reasonable question?

Writing Practice

1. Do you think government prohibition of smoking would work? Write
   an essay in which you argue for or against the banning of all tobacco
   products. Be sure to consider the problems that such a policy would
   create.

*2. Can you think of a product—firearms or over-the-counter medications, for example—whose sale should be controlled more strictly than it is now? Write an essay in which you present an argument for controlling this product's sale, discussing the problems that this product causes and suggesting ways that controls could improve the situation. Make sure your essay has a clearly stated thesis.

3. Instead of banning tobacco products, what can local and state governments do to discourage people from smoking? Write an essay in which you argue for a particular course of action—for example, charging smokers higher health-insurance premiums.

I HAVE A DREAM

Martin Luther King Jr.

On August 28, 1963, Martin Luther King Jr. delivered the following speech on the steps in front of the Lincoln Memorial in Washington, D.C. King used the occasion of this speech—the March on Washington, in which more than two hundred thousand people participated— to reinforce his ideas about racial equality and nonviolent protest. The speech itself is a deductive argument that makes a compelling case for racial justice in the United States. As you read, notice King's effective use of repetition.

Five score years ago, a great American, in whose symbolic shadow we stand, signed the Emancipation Proclamation. This momentous decree came as a great beacon light of hope to millions of Negro slaves who had been seared in the flames of withering injustice. It came as a joyous daybreak to end the long night of captivity. 1

But one hundred years later, we must face the tragic fact that the Negro is still not free. One hundred years later, the life of the Negro is still sadly crippled by the manacles of segregation and the chains of discrimination. One hundred years later, the Negro lives on a lonely island of poverty in the midst of a vast ocean of material prosperity. One hundred years later, the Negro is still languishing in the corners of American society and finds himself an exile in his own land. So we have come here today to dramatize an appalling condition. 2

In a sense we have come to our nation's capital to cash a check. When the architects of our republic wrote the magnificent words of the Constitution and the Declaration of Independence, they were signing a promissory note to which every American was to fall heir. This note was a promise that all men—yes, black men as well as white men—would be guaranteed the unalienable rights of life, liberty, and the pursuit of happiness. 3

It is obvious today that America has defaulted on this promissory note insofar as her citizens of color are concerned. Instead of honoring this sacred obligation, America has given the Negro people a bad check, a check which has come back marked "insufficient funds." But we refuse to believe that there are insufficient funds in the great vaults of opportunity of this nation. So we have come to cash this check—a check that will give us upon demand the riches of freedom and the security of justice. We have also come to this hallowed spot to remind America of the fierce urgency of *now*. This is no time to engage in the luxury of cooling off or to take the 4 tranquilizing drugs of gradualism. *Now* is the time to make real the promises of Democracy. *Now* is the time to rise from the dark and desolate valley of segregation to the sunlit path of racial justice. *Now* is the time to open the doors of opportunity to all of God's children. *Now* is the time to lift our nation from the quicksands of racial injustice to the solid rock of brotherhood.

It would be fatal for the nation to overlook the urgency of the moment and to underestimate the determination of the Negro. This sweltering summer of the Negro's legitimate discontent will not pass until there is an invigorating autumn of freedom and equality; 1963 is not an end, but a beginning. Those who hope that the Negro needed to blow off steam and will now be content will have a rude awakening if the nation returns to business as usual. There will be neither rest nor tranquility in America until the Negro is granted his citizenship rights. The whirlwinds of revolt will continue to shake the foundations of our nation until the bright day of justice emerges. 5

But there is something that I must say to my people who stand on the warm threshold which leads into the palace of justice. In the process of gaining our rightful place we must not be guilty of wrongful deeds. Let us not seek to satisfy our thirst for freedom by drinking from the cup of bitterness and hatred. We must forever conduct our struggle on the high plane of dignity and discipline. We must not allow our creative protest to degenerate into physical violence. Again and again we must rise to the majestic heights of meeting physical force with soul force. The marvelous new militancy which has engulfed the Negro community must not lead us to a distrust of all white people, for many of our white brothers, as evidenced by their presence here today, have come to realize that their destiny is tied up with our destiny and their freedom is inextricably bound to our freedom. We cannot walk alone. 6

And as we walk, we must make the pledge that we shall march ahead. We cannot turn back. There are those who are asking the devotees of civil rights, "When will you be satisfied?" We can never be satisfied as long as the Negro is the victim of the unspeakable horrors of police brutality. We can never be satisfied as long as our bodies, heavy with the fatigue of travel, cannot gain lodging in the motels of the highways and the hotels of the cities. We cannot be satisfied as long as the Negro's basic mobility is from a smaller ghetto to a larger one. We can never be satisfied as long as a Negro in Mississippi cannot vote and a Negro in New York believes he has nothing for which to vote. No, no, we are not satisfied, and we will not be satisfied until justice rolls down like waters and righteousness like a mighty stream. 7

I am not unmindful that some of you have come here out of great trials and tribulations. Some of you have come fresh from narrow jail cells. Some of you have come from areas where your quest for freedom left you battered by the storms of persecution and staggered by the winds of police brutality. You have been the veterans of creative suffering. Continue to work with the faith that unearned suffering is redemptive. 8

Go back to Mississippi, go back to Alabama, go back to South Carolina, go back to Georgia, go back to Louisiana, go back to the slums and ghettos of our northern cities, knowing that somehow this situation can and will be changed. Let us not wallow in the valley of despair. 9

I say to you today, my friends, that in spite of the difficulties and frustrations of the moment I still have a dream. It is a dream deeply rooted in the American dream. 10

I have a dream that one day this nation will rise up and live out the true   11
meaning of its creed: "We hold these truths to be self-evident, that all men
are created equal."

I have a dream that one day on the red hills of Georgia the sons of   12
former slaves and the sons of former slaveowners will be able to sit down
together at the table of brotherhood.

I have a dream that one day even the state of Mississippi, a desert state   13
sweltering with the heat of injustice and oppression, will be transformed
into an oasis of freedom and justice.

I have a dream that my four little children will one day live in a nation   14
where they will not be judged by the color of their skin but by the content
of their character.

I have a dream today.   15

I have a dream that one day the state of Alabama, whose governor's lips   16
are presently dripping with the words of interposition and nullification,
will be transformed into a situation where little black boys and black girls
will be able to join hands with little white boys and white girls and walk
together as sisters and brothers.

I have a dream today.   17

I have a dream that one day every valley shall be exalted, every hill and   18
mountain shall be made low, the rough places will be made plain, and the
crooked places will be made straight, and the glory of the Lord shall be
revealed, and all flesh shall see it together.

This is our hope. This is the faith with which I return to the South.   19
With this faith we will be able to hew out of the mountain of despair a
stone of hope. With this faith we will be able to transform the jangling
discords of our nation into a beautiful symphony of brotherhood. With
this faith we will be able to work together, to pray together, to struggle
together, to go to jail together, to stand up for freedom together, knowing
that we will be free one day.

This will be the day when all of God's children will be able to sing with   20
new meaning

> My country, 'tis of thee,
> Sweet land of liberty,
>   Of thee I sing:
> Land where my fathers died,
> Land of the pilgrim's pride,
> From every mountainside,
>   Let freedom ring.

So let freedom ring from the prodigious hilltops of New Hampshire.   21
Let freedom ring from the mighty mountains of New York. Let freedom
ring from the heightening Alleghenies of Pennsylvania. Let freedom ring
from the snowcapped Rockies of Colorado. Let freedom ring from the curvaceous peaks of California.

But not only that. Let freedom ring from Stone Mountain of Georgia.   22
Let freedom ring from Lookout Mountain of Tennessee. Let freedom ring
from every hill and molehill of Mississippi. From every mountainside, let
freedom ring.

When we let freedom ring, when we let it ring from every village and   23
every hamlet, from every state and every city, we will be able to speed up
that day when all of God's children, black men and white men, Jews and
Gentiles, Protestants and Catholics, will be able to join hands and sing in

the words of the old Negro spiritual, "Free at last! Free at last! Thank God almighty, we are free at last!"

Reacting to the Reading

1. Preview the essay. As you read it more carefully, highlight and annotate as needed to help you understand the writer's ideas.
2. Highlight the passage in which King outlines his dream for the United States. In a marginal annotation, explain what he means when he says his dream is "deeply rooted in the American dream" (paragraph 10).

Reacting to Words

*1. Define these words: *score* (paragraph 1), *beacon* (1), *withering* (1), *languishing* (2), *appalling* (2), *promissory* (3), *unalienable* (3), *hallowed* (4), *gradualism* (4), *invigorating* (5), *inextricably* (6), *redemptive* (8), *wallow* (9), *prodigious* (21), *curvaceous* (21). Can you suggest a synonym for each word that will work in the essay?

2. King uses a number of words again and again in his speech. Identify some of these words. Why do you think he repeats them? Would the speech have been more (or less) effective without this repetition?

> **Teaching Tip**
> Students may need help defining words. With nonnative students, consider going over the definitions in class before assigning the reading.

Reacting to Ideas

1. In paragraph 3, King says that he and the other marchers have come to Washington "to cash a check." How does this image convey what he and the other protesters want to achieve? Can you think of another image that might also work here?
2. In this speech, King addresses the marchers who have come to Washington. Whom else do you think he is addressing?
3. Do you think the current racial climate in the United States still warrants King's criticism? Are we any closer today than we were in 1963 to realizing his dream?

> **Teaching Tip**
> Remind students to answer all questions in complete sentences.

Reacting to the Pattern

*1. King uses a deductive argument to present his ideas about racial justice. Do you think an inductive argument would have been more effective?

2. King's argument reaches its conclusion in paragraph 4. What does he do in the rest of his speech?
3. Why do you think King chose to include only a few specific examples to illustrate his points? Should he have provided more evidence?

For more on deductive arguments, see 14I.

Writing Practice

1. In paragraph 4, King says, "America has defaulted on this promissory note. . . ." Can you think of some person or organization that has defaulted on its promissory note to you? Write an argument essay in which you make your case. If you wish, you may use King's image of a bad check.
2. Write an essay in which you argue that if King were alive today, he would (or would not) think his dream of racial justice had been realized.
3. Choose an issue you feel strongly about. Write a letter to the editor of your local paper in which you take a strong stand on this issue.

Strategies for College Success

Learning the time-tested strategies discussed in this appendix can help to make your life as a college student more productive and less stressful.

1 Learning Orientation Strategies

Some strategies come in handy even before school begins, as you orient yourself to life as a college student. In fact, you may already have discovered some of them.

- Make sure you have a college catalog, a photo ID, a student handbook, a parking permit, and any other items that entering students at your school are expected to have.
- Read your school's orientation materials (distributed as handouts or posted on the school Web site) very carefully. These materials will help you to familiarize yourself with campus buildings and offices, course offerings, faculty members, extracurricular activities, and so on.
- Be sure you know your academic adviser's name (and how to spell it), e-mail address, office location, and office hours. Copy this information into your personal address book.
- Get a copy of the library's orientation materials. These will tell you about the library's hours and services and explain procedures such as how to use the online catalog.
- Be sure you know where things are—not just how to find the library and the parking lot, but also where you can do photocopying or buy a newspaper. You might as well learn to find your way around before things get too hectic.

2 Learning First-Week Strategies

College can seem like a confusing place at first, but from your first day as a college student, there are steps you can take to help you get your bearings.

1. *Make yourself at home*. Find places on campus where you can get something to eat or drink, and find a good place to study or relax before or between classes. As you explore the campus, try to locate all the things you need to feel comfortable—for example, pay phones, ATMs, and rest rooms.

2. *Know where you are going and when you need to be there*. Check the building and room number for each of your classes and the days and hours the class meets. Copy this information onto the front cover of the appropriate notebook. Pay particular attention to classes with irregular schedules (for example, a class that meets from 9 a.m. to 10 a.m. on Tuesdays but from 11 a.m. to 12 noon on Thursdays).

3. *Get to know your fellow students*. Get the name, phone number, and e-mail address of two students in each of your classes. If you miss class, you will need to get in touch with someone to find out what material you missed.

4. *Familiarize yourself with each course's syllabus*. At the first meeting of every course, your instructor will hand out a **syllabus**, an outline or summary of course requirements, policies, and procedures. (The syllabus may also be posted on the course's Web page.) A syllabus gives you three kinds of useful information.

   ■ Practical information, such as the instructor's office number and e-mail address and what books and supplies to buy
   ■ Information that can help you plan a study schedule—for example, when assignments are due and when exams are scheduled
   ■ Information about the instructor's policies on absences, grading, class participation, and so on

   Read each syllabus carefully, ask questions about anything you do not understand, refer to all your course syllabi regularly—and do not lose them.

5. *Buy books and supplies*. When you buy your books and supplies, be sure to keep the receipts, and do not write your name in your books until you are certain that you are not going to drop a course. (If you write in a book, you will not be able to return it.) If your roster of courses is not definite, wait a few days to buy your texts. You should, however, buy some items right away: a separate notebook and folder for each course you are taking, a college dictionary, and a pocket organizer (see A7). In addition to the books and other items required for a particular course (for example, a lab notebook, a programmable

▼ **Student Voices**
I check out each of my classes before I buy my books, to make sure I want to stay in the class.
        Kristin Barnett

▼ **Student Voices**
I like using an online dictionary because I don't have to leave the computer to find out what a word means.
        Amit Parmar

FOCUS **Using a Dictionary**

Even though your computer has a spell checker, you still need to buy a dictionary. A college dictionary tells you not only how to spell words but also what words mean and how to use them.

calculator, art supplies), you should buy pens and pencils in different colors, blank computer disks, paper clips or a stapler, Post-it notes, highlighter pens, and so on. (Remember to buy a backpack or bookbag in which to keep all these items!)

6. *Set up your notebooks*. Establish a separate notebook (or a separate section of a divided notebook) for each of your classes. Copy your instructor's name, e-mail address, phone number, and office hours and location into the inside front cover of the notebook; write your own name, address, and phone number on the outside.

3 Learning Day-to-Day Strategies

As you get busier and busier, you may find that it is hard to keep everything under control. Here are some strategies to help you as you move through the semester.

1. *Find a place to study*. As a college student, you will need your own private place to work and study. Even if it is just a desk in one corner of your dorm room (or, if you are living at home, in one corner of your bedroom or at the back of your basement or garage), you will need a place that is yours alone, a place that will be undisturbed when you leave it. (The kitchen table, which you share with roommates or family members, will not work.) This space should include everything you will need to make your work easier—quiet, good lighting, a comfortable chair, a clean work surface, storage for supplies, and so on.

2. *Set up a bookshelf*. Keep your textbooks, dictionary, calculator, supplies, and everything else you use regularly for your coursework in one place—ideally, in your own work space. That way, when you need something, you will know exactly where it is.

3. *Set up a study schedule*. Identify thirty- to forty-five-minute blocks of free time before, between, and after classes. Set this time aside for review. Remember, studying should be part of your regular routine, not something you do only the night before an exam.

4. *Establish priorities*. It is very important to understand what your priorities are. Before you can establish priorities, however, you have to know which assignments are due first, which ones can be done in

FOCUS Skills Check

Do not wait until you have a paper to write to discover that your computer skills need improvement. Be sure your basic word-processing skills are at the level you need for your work. If you need help, get it right away.

steps, and which tasks or steps will be most time consuming. Then, you must decide which tasks are most pressing. For example, studying for a test to be given the next day is more pressing than reviewing notes for a test scheduled for the following week. Finally, you have to decide which tasks are more important than others. For example, studying for a midterm is more important than studying for a quiz, and the midterm for a course you are in danger of failing is more important than the midterm for a course in which you are doing well. Remember, you cannot do everything at once; you need to know what must be done immediately and what can wait.

5. *Check your mail*. Check your campus mailbox or e-mail account regularly—if possible, several times a day. If you miss a message, you may miss important information about changes in assignments, canceled classes, or rescheduled quizzes.

6. *Schedule conferences*. Try to meet with each of your instructors during the semester even if you are not required to do so. You might schedule one conference during the second or third week of school and another a week or two before a major exam or paper is due. Your instructors will appreciate and respect your initiative.

7. ***Become familiar with the student services available on your campus***. College is hard work, and you cannot do everything on your own. There is nothing shameful about getting help from your school's writing lab or tutoring center or from the center for disabled students (which serves students with learning disabilities as well as physical challenges), the office of international students, or the counseling center, as well as from your adviser or course instructors. Think of yourself as a consumer. You are paying for your education, and you are entitled to—and should take advantage of—all the available services you need.

FOCUS **Asking for Help**

Despite all your careful planning, you may still run into trouble. For example, you may miss an exam and have to make it up; you may miss several days of classes in a row and fall behind in your work; you may have trouble understanding the material in one of your courses; or a family member may get sick. Do not wait until you are overwhelmed to ask for help. If you have an ongoing personal problem or a family emergency, let your instructors know immediately.

---

4   **Learning Note-Taking Strategies**

Learning to take notes in a college class takes practice, but taking good notes is essential for success in college. Here are some basic guidelines that will help you develop and improve your note-taking skills.

During Class

1. *Come to class*. If you miss class, you miss notes—so come to class, and come on time. In class, sit where you can see the board or screen and hear the instructor. Do not feel you have to keep sitting in the same place in each class every day; change your seat until you find a spot that is comfortable for you.

2. *Date your notes*. Begin each class by writing the date at the top of the page. Instructors frequently identify material that will be on a test by dates. If you do not date your notes, you may not know what to study.

3. *Know what to write down*. You cannot possibly write down everything an instructor says. If you try, you will miss a lot of important information. Listen carefully *before* you write, and listen for cues to what is important. For example, sometimes the instructor will tell you that something is important, or that a particular piece of information will be on a test. If the instructor emphasizes an idea or underlines it on the board, you should do the same in your notes. Of course, if you have done the assigned reading before class, you will recognize important topics and know to take especially careful notes when these topics are introduced in class.

4. *Include examples*. Try to write down an example for each general concept introduced in class—something that will help you remember what the instructor was talking about. (If you do not have time to include examples as you take notes during class, add them when you review your notes.) For instance, if your world history instructor is explaining *nationalism*, you should write down not only a definition but also an example, such as "Germany in 1848."

5. *Write legibly, and use helpful signals*. Use dark (blue or black) ink for your note-taking, but keep a red or green pen handy to highlight important information, jot down announcements (such as a change in a test date), note gaps in your notes, or question confusing points. Do not take notes in pencil, which is hard to read and not as permanent as ink.

6. *Ask questions*. If you do not hear (or do not understand) something your instructor said, or if you need an example to help you understand something, *ask!* But do not immediately turn to another student for clarification. Instead, wait to see if the instructor explains further, or if he or she pauses to ask if anyone has a question. If you are not comfortable asking a question during class, make a note of the question and ask the instructor—or send an e-mail—after class.

After Class

1. *Review your notes*. After every class, try to spend ten or fifteen minutes rereading your notes, filling in gaps and examples while the material is still fresh in your mind.

2. *Recopy information*. When you have a break between classes, or when you get home, recopy important pieces of information from your notes.

- Copy announcements (such as quiz dates) onto your calendar.
- Copy reminders (for example, a note to schedule a conference before your next paper is due) into your organizer.
- Copy questions you have to ask the instructor onto the top of the next blank page in your class notebook.

For information on calendars and organizers, see A7.

Before the Next Class

1. *Reread your notes*. Leave time to skim the previous class's notes once more just before each class. This strategy will get you oriented for the class to come and will remind you of anything that needs clarification or further explanation.

2. *Ask for help*. Call a classmate if you need to fill in missing information; if you still need help, see the instructor during his or her office hours, or come to class early so you can ask your question before class begins.

▼ **Student Voices**
After each class, I give the day's notes a title so I can remember the topic of each class. This helps me find the information when I study.
                              Lisa Liebman

---

5 Learning Homework Strategies

Doing homework is an important part of your education. Homework gives you a chance to practice your skills and measure your progress. If you are having trouble with the homework, chances are you are having trouble with the course. Ask the instructor or teaching assistant for help *now;* do not wait until the day before the exam. Here are some tips for getting the most out of your homework.

1. *Write down the assignment*. Do not expect to remember an assignment; copy it down. If you are not sure exactly what you are supposed to do, check with your instructor or another student.

2. *Do your homework, and do it on time*. Teachers assign homework to reinforce classwork, and they expect homework to be done on a regular basis. It is easy to fall behind in college, but trying to do three—or five—nights' worth of homework in one night is not a good idea. If you do several assignments at once, you not only overload yourself, you also miss important day-to-day connections with classwork.

3. *Be an active reader*. Get into the habit of highlighting your textbooks and other material as you read.

4. *Join study groups*. A study group of three or four students can be a valuable support system for homework as well as for exams. If your schedule permits, do some homework assignments—or at least review your homework—with other students on a regular basis. In addition to learning information, you will learn different strategies for doing assignments.

Teaching Tip
Help students establish study groups for your class. Use a sign-up sheet or some other device to help students take the initiative. (They may prefer to form groups without your direct involvement.)

For information on specific reading strategies, see Chapter 35.

A 6

6   Learning Exam-Taking Strategies

Preparation for an exam should begin well before the exam is announced. In a sense, you begin this preparation on the first day of class.

Before the Exam

1. *Attend every class*. Regular attendance in class—where you can listen, ask questions, and take notes—is the best possible preparation for exams. If you do have to miss a class, arrange to copy (and read) another student's notes *before the next class* so you will be able to follow the discussion.

2. *Keep up with the reading*. Read every assignment, and read it before the class in which it will be discussed. If you do not, you may have trouble understanding what is going on in class.

3. *Take careful notes*. Take careful, thorough notes, but be selective. If you can, compare your notes on a regular basis with those of other students in the class; working together, you can fill in gaps or correct errors. Establishing a buddy system will also force you to review your notes regularly instead of just on the night before the exam.

4. *Study on your own*. When an exam is announced, adjust your study schedule—and your priorities—so you have time to review everything. (This is especially important if you have more than one exam in a short period of time.) Over a period of several days, review all your material (class notes, readings, and so on), and then review it again. Make a note of anything you do not understand, and keep track of topics you need to review. Try to predict the most likely questions, and—if you have time—practice answering them.

5. *Study with a group*. If you can set up a study group, you should certainly do so. Studying with others can help you understand the material better. However, do not come to group sessions unprepared and expect to get everything from the other students. You must first study on your own.

6. *Make an appointment with your instructor*. Set up an appointment with the instructor or with the course's teaching assistant a few days before the exam. Bring to this conference any specific questions you have about course content and about the format of the upcoming exam. (Be sure to review all your study material before the conference.)

7. *Review the material one last time*. The night before the exam is not the time to begin your studying; it is the time to review. When you have finished your review, get a good night's sleep.

Teaching Tip

If you give exams in your course, be sure to give students specific information about the kinds of questions you will be asking. You might even consider giving a practice exam.

During the Exam

By the time you walk into the exam room, you will already have done all you could to get ready for the test. Your goal now is to keep the momentum going and not do anything to undermine all your hard work.

FOCUS Writing Essay Exams

If you are asked to write an essay on an exam, remember that what you are really being asked to do is write a **thesis-and-support essay**. Chapter 12 of this text tells you how to do this.

1. ***Read through the entire exam***. Be sure you understand how much time you have, how many points each question is worth, and exactly what each question is asking you to do. Many exam questions call for just a short answer—*yes* or *no, true* or *false*. Others ask you to fill in a blank with a few words, and still others require you to select the best answer from among several choices. If you are not absolutely certain what kind of answer a particular question calls for, ask the instructor or the proctor *before* you begin to write. (Remember, on some tests there is no penalty for guessing, but on other tests it is best to answer only those questions you have time to read and consider carefully.)

2. ***Budget your time***. Once you understand how much each section of the exam and each question are worth, plan your time and set your priorities, devoting the most time to the most important questions. If you know you tend to rush through exams, or if you find you often run out of time before you get to the end of a test, you might try putting a mark on your paper when about one-third of the allotted time has passed (for a one-hour exam, put a mark on your paper after twenty minutes) to make sure you are pacing yourself appropriately.

3. ***Reread each question***. Carefully reread each question *before* you start to answer it. Underline the **key words**—the words that give specific information about how to approach the question and how to phrase your answer.

   Remember, even if everything you write is correct, your response is not acceptable if you do not answer the question. If a question asks you to *compare* two novels, writing a *summary* of one of them will not be acceptable.

FOCUS Key Words

Here are some helpful key words to look for on exams.

analyze	explain	suggest results, ef-
argue	give examples	fects, outcomes
compare	identify	summarize
contrast	illustrate	support
define	recount	take a stand
demonstrate	suggest causes, ori-	trace
describe	gins, contributing	
evaluate	factors	

A 7

*For more on brainstorming,
see 1C and 12C.*

*For more on topic sentences,
see 2A and 2C.*

ESL Tip
Brainstorming may be an
unfamiliar concept to nonnative speakers. Make sure
all students understand this
term.

4. ***Brainstorm to help yourself recall the material***. If you are writing a
   paragraph or an essay, look frequently at the question as you brainstorm. (You can write your brainstorming notes on the inside cover of
   the exam book.) Quickly write down all the relevant points you can
   think of—what the textbook had to say, your instructor's comments,
   and so on. The more you can think of now, the more you will have to
   choose from when you write your answer.

5. ***Write down the main idea***. Looking closely at the way the question is
   worded and at your brainstorming notes, write a sentence that states
   the main idea of your answer. If you are writing a paragraph, this sentence will be your topic sentence; if you are writing an essay, it will be
   your thesis statement.

6. ***List your main points***. You do not want to waste your limited (and
   valuable) time writing a detailed outline, but an informal outline that
   lists just your key points is worth the little time it takes. An informal
   outline will help you plan a clear direction for your paragraph or essay.

7. ***Draft your answer***. You will spend most of your time actually writing
   the answers to the questions on the exam. Follow your outline, keep track
   of time, and consult your brainstorming notes when you need to—but
   stay focused on your writing.

8. ***Reread, revise, and edit***. When you have finished drafting your answer, reread it carefully to make sure it says everything you want it to
   say—and that it answers the question.

7 Learning Time-Management Strategies

Learning to manage your time is very important for success in college.
Here are some strategies you can adopt to make this task easier.

1. ***Use an organizer***. Whether you prefer a print organizer or an electronic one, you should certainly use one—and use it *consistently*. If
   you are most comfortable with paper and pencil, purchase a "week-on-
   two-pages" academic year organizer (one that begins in September,
   not January); the "week-on-two-pages" format (see pp. 619–620) gives
   you more writing room for Monday through Friday than for the weekend, and it also lets you view an entire week at once.

   Carry your organizer with you at all times. At the beginning of the
   semester, copy down key pieces of information from your course syllabi—for example, the date of every quiz and exam and the due date
   of every paper. As the semester progresses, continue to write in assignments and deadlines. Also, enter information such as days when a
   class will be canceled or will meet in the computer lab or in the library,
   reminders to bring a particular book or piece of equipment to class,
   and appointments with instructors or other college personnel. You can
   also jot down reminders and schedule appointments that are not related to school—for example, changes in your work hours, a dentist
   appointment, or lunch with a friend. (In addition to writing notes on
   the pages for each date, some students like to keep a separate month-

by-month "to do" list. Crossing out completed items can give you a feeling of accomplishment—and make the road ahead look shorter.)

The first sample organizer below shows how you can use an organizer to keep track of deadlines, appointments, and reminders. The second sample organizer (p. 620) includes not only this information but also a study schedule, with notes about particular tasks to be done each day.

2. *Use a calendar*. Buy a large calendar, and post it where you will see it every morning—on your desk, in your car, or on the refrigerator. At the beginning of the semester, fill in important dates such as school holidays, work commitments, exam dates, and due dates for papers and projects. When you return from school each day, update the calendar with any new information you have entered into your organizer.

3. *Plan ahead*. If you think you will need help from a writing lab tutor to revise a paper that is due in two weeks, do not wait until day thirteen to make an appointment; all the time slots may be filled by then. To be safe, make an appointment for help about a week in advance.

4. *Learn to enjoy downtime*. One final—and very important—point to remember is that you are entitled to "waste" a little time. When you have a free minute, take time for yourself—and do not feel guilty about it.

> ▼ **Student Voices**
> *I keep my calendar right next to the hook where I hang my keys and my ID. This forces me to check my calendar every day before I leave home.*
> Jen Borowski

September 2003

15 Monday

Buy note cards for speech

Call Writing Center for appt Fri. PM

16 Tuesday

Work 12–3

17 Wednesday

Speech 10 AM

6 PM— Meet w/soc. study group

September 2003

Thursday **18**

Soc. exam!

Work 3–5

Friday **19**

Lab quiz

4 PM— writing center

Saturday **20**

Sunday **21**

		September				
S	M	T	W	T	F	S
	1	2	3	4	5	6
7	8	9	10	11	12	13
14	15	16	17	18	19	20
21	22	23	24	25	26	27
28	29	30				

Sample Organizer Page: Deadlines, Appointments, and Reminders Only

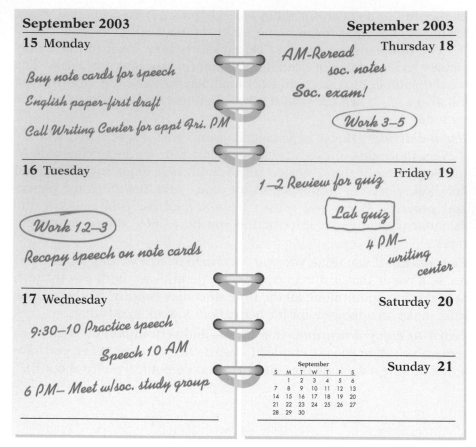

Sample Organizer Page: Deadlines, Appointments, Reminders, and Study Schedule

8 Learning Internet Strategies

The **Internet** is a network of millions of computers at colleges and universities, government agencies, research institutions, businesses, and libraries all over the world. The Internet can give you access to a world of information—information that can help you in school and in your everyday life. Here are some of the things you can do on the Internet.

- Send and receive messages via e-mail
- Send and receive text files (for example, assignments), graphics, sound, animation, film clips, and live video
- Read articles and other documents about practically any subject, from asteroids to engineering to Zen Buddhism
- Send messages to electronic "bulletin boards" set up for your classes or for other groups, and read messages sent by others

When people refer to the Internet, they often mean the **World Wide Web**. The Web, which forms an important part of the Internet, is a collection of millions of documents on every imaginable topic. The Web relies on **hypertext links**—specially highlighted words and phrases. By clicking your computer's mouse on these links, you can move easily from one part of a document to another, or from one **Web site** (collection of documents) to another.

For example, a Web article discussing immigration might have the word *Cuban* highlighted in a different color from the rest of the text. Clicking on this word might take you to a discussion of Cuban immigration. This discussion, in turn, might include links to articles, bulletin board postings, or other material about Cuban history, Cuban politics, Fidel Castro, Cuban cultural life in the United States, and so on.

Finding Information on the Internet

To use the Internet, you need an Internet **browser**, a tool that enables you to display Web pages. The most popular browsers are Netscape Navigator and Microsoft Internet Explorer. Most new computers come with one of these browsers already installed.

Before you can access the Internet, you have to be **online**—that is, connected to an **Internet service provider (ISP)**. Many colleges and universities provide Internet access free of charge to students. In addition, companies such as America Online provide access for a monthly fee. Once you are online, you need to connect to a **search engine**, a program that helps you find information by sorting through the millions of documents that are available on the Internet. Among the most popular search engines are AltaVista <www.altavista.com>, Infoseek <www.infoseek.com>, and Yahoo <www.yahoo.com>.

There are three ways to use a search engine to find information.

1. *You can enter a Web site's URL.* All search engines have a box in which you can enter a Web site's electronic address, or **URL**. When you click on the URL or hit your computer's Enter or Return key, the search engine connects you to the Web site. For example, to find information about family members who entered the United States through Ellis Island, you would enter this URL: *www.ellisislandrecords.com.*

2. *You can do a keyword search.* All search engines let you do a **keyword search**: you type a term into a box, and the search engine looks for documents that contain the term, listing all the **hits** (documents containing one or both of these words) that it found. If you type in a broad term like *civil war,* you might get hundreds of thousands of hits—more than you could possibly consider. If this occurs, do not give up. Narrow your search by using a more specific term—*the Battle of Gettysburg,* for example. You can focus your search even further by putting quotation marks around the term (*"Battle of Gettysburg"*). When you do this, the search engine will search only for documents that contain this phrase.

3. *You can do a subject search.* Some search engines, such as Yahoo, let you do a **subject search**. First, you choose a broad subject from a list of subjects: The Humanities, The Arts, Entertainment, Business, and so on. Each of these general subjects leads you to more specific subjects, until eventually you get to the subtopic that you want. For example, you could start your search on Yahoo with the general topic Entertainment. Clicking on this topic would lead you to *Movies* and then to *Movie Reviews.* Finally, you would get to a list of movie reviews that might link to a review of the specific movie you are interested in.

Teaching Tip
At the start of the semester, assess your students' levels of computer and Internet expertise.

Computer Tip
To practice finding and evaluating information on the Internet, try using one of the search engines listed in this section to locate a Web site that focuses on a topic you know a lot about. Evaluate the site using the guidelines listed on pages 622–623.

Computer Tip
It is a good idea to **bookmark** useful sites by selecting the Bookmark or Favorites option at the top of your browser screen. Once you bookmark a site, you can easily return to it whenever you want.

FOCUS   Accessing Web Sites: Troubleshooting

Sometimes your computer will tell you that a site you want to visit is unavailable or does not exist. When this occurs, consider the following possibilities before moving on to another site.

■ *Check to make sure the URL is correct.* To reach a site, you have to type its URL accurately. Do not add spaces between items in the address or put a period at the end. Any error will send you to the wrong site—or to no site at all.

■ *Check to make sure you are connected to the Internet.* To reach a site, you have to be connected to the Internet. If you are not properly connected, your computer will indicate this.

■ *Check to make sure your computer is connected to your phone line.* A loose connection or an unplugged phone jack will make it impossible for you to access the Internet. If your computer is not connected to a phone line, it will indicate that it is not receiving a dial tone.

■ *Check to make sure the site still exists.* Web sites, especially those maintained by individuals, frequently disappear because people either cannot afford to maintain a site or lose interest in doing so. If you entered a URL correctly, your computer is functioning properly, and you still cannot access a site, chances are that the site no longer exists.

■ *Try revisiting the site later.* Sometimes Web sites experience technical problems that prevent them from being accessed. Your computer will tell you if a site is temporarily unreachable.

Evaluating Web Sites

Not every Web site is a valuable source of information. In fact, anyone can put information on the Internet. For this reason, it is a good idea to approach Web sites with skepticism. In a sense, Web sites are like strangers knocking at your door: before you let them in, you need to be sure they are honest and trustworthy. To determine whether information you find on the Internet is believable and useful, you must evaluate the Web site where you found the information.

FOCUS   Evaluating Web Sites

To decide whether to use information from a particular Web site, try to answer the following questions:

(continued on the following page)

(continued from the previous page)

■ *Is the site reliable?* Never rely on information by an unidentified author; always try to determine the author of material on a Web site. Also, try to determine the author's qualifications. For example, say you are looking at a site that discusses Labrador retrievers. Is the author a breeder? A veterinarian? Someone who has had a Lab as a pet? The first two authors would probably be authorities on the subject; the third author might not be.

■ *Does the site have a hidden purpose?* When you evaluate a Web site, be sure to consider its purpose. For example, a site discussing the health benefits of herbal medicine would have one purpose if it were sponsored by a university and another if it were sponsored by a company selling herbal remedies. Researchers who post information on a university site are trying to inform others about their findings. Retailers, however, put information online to sell a product; therefore, they sometimes make exaggerated claims about its usefulness.

■ *Is the site up-to-date?* If a site has not been recently updated, you should question the information it contains. A discussion of foot-and-mouth disease in England, for example, would be out of date if it were written before the widespread outbreak in 2001. You would have to continue your search until you found a more current discussion.

■ *Is the information on the site trustworthy?* A site should include evidence to support what it says. If it does not, consider the information to be unsupported personal opinion. Points should be supported with facts, examples, statistics, and expert opinions—not rumors or third-hand opinions.

■ *Does the site contain needlessly elaborate graphics?* With Web sites, substance counts more than style. When you come across a site that has slick visuals—animation, bright colors, and lots of pictures—don't be misled. Make sure that these graphic elements do not mask weak logic or uninformed opinion.

■ **Computer Tip**

A Web site's URL can give you information about the site's purpose. For example, the suffix *.edu* indicates that the site is sponsored by an educational institution; *.gov* indicates a government agency; *.org* indicates a nonprofit organization; and *.com* indicates a business.

Teaching Tip

To give your students practice evaluating Web sites, divide them into groups of three or four, and ask them to access two or three of the Web sites listed on pages 624–626. Have them choose one site, evaluate it according to the guidelines listed here, and then present their findings to the class.

Using the Internet to Locate Information for Assignments

You can use the Internet to find information about the subjects you are studying. For example, if in your communication class you were discussing early television sitcoms, you could go to the Internet and find Web sites devoted to this subject. You could also find specific sites for shows such as *I Love Lucy, The Honeymooners,* and *The Brady Bunch.* The following sites can help you access information that will be useful for many of your courses.

Academic Subjects on the Web

The Humanities

Art history

Art History Resources on the Web

<http://witcombe.sbc.edu/ARTHLinks.html>

Film

The Internet Movie Database

<http://www.imdb.com>

History

HyperHistory Online

<http://www.hyperhistory.com/online_n2/History_n2/a.html>

Literature

The On-Line Books Page

<http://digital.library.upenn.edu/books>

Philosophy

Stanford Encyclopedia of Philosophy

<http://plato.stanford.edu>

The Natural Sciences

Biology

Biodiversity and Biological Collections Web Server

<http://biodiversity.uno.edu>

Chemistry

WWW Chemistry Resources

<http://www.chem.ucla.edu/chempointers.html>

Engineering

The Engineer's Reference

<http://www.eng-sol.com>

Mathematics

Math.com

<http://www.math.com>

Physics

Web Links: Physics around the World

<http://physicsweb.org/resources>

The Social Sciences

Education

Education World®

<http://www.education-world.com>

Political science

Political Resources on the Net

<http://www.politicalresources.net>

Psychology

PsychCrawler

<http://www.psychcrawler.com>

Sociology and social work

Social Work and Social Services Web Sites

<http://gwbweb.wustl.edu/websites.html>

FOCUS **Avoiding Plagiarism**

When you transfer information from Web sites into your notes, you may be tempted to "cut and paste" text without noting where the text came from. If you then copy this text into a draft of your paper, you are committing plagiarism—and plagiarism is the theft of ideas.

(continued on the following page)

(continued from the previous page)

Every college has rules that students must follow when using words, ideas, and visuals from books, articles, and Internet sources. Consult your school's Web site or student handbook for information on the appropriate use of such information.

Using the Internet to Improve Your Writing

The Internet has many Web sites that can help you with your writing. Sites like the following ones include links to other useful sites.

Writing Help on the Web

The *Writing First* site
<http://www.bedfordstmartins.com/writingfirst>

Help with the writing process
Principles of Composition
<http://webster.commnet.edu/grammar/composition/composition.htm>

The UVic Writer's Guide
<http://web.uvic.ca/wguide>

Help finding something to say
Paradigm Online Writing Assistant: Choosing a Subject
<http://www.powa.org/whtfrms.htm>

Help writing paragraphs
Purposes of Paragraphs
<http://www.fas.harvard.edu/~wricntr/para.html>

Writing Paragraphs
<http://www.uottawa.ca/academic/arts/writcent/hypergrammar/paragrph.html>

Advice on revision
Paradigm: Global and Local Perspectives
<http://www.powa.org/revifrms.htm>

Tips on grammar
The Online English Grammar
<http://www.edunet.com/english/grammar>

Guide to Grammar and Writing
<http://webster.commnet.edu/grammar/index.htm>

Tips on proofreading
Tips for Effective Proofreading
<http://www.ualr.edu/~owl/tipsforproofreading.htm>

Proofreading
<http://www.bgsu.edu/departments/writing-lab/goproofreading.html>

Online writing centers
LEO: Literacy Education Online
<http://leo.stcloudstate.edu>

Online Writing Lab
<http://owl.english.purdue.edu>

A 8

Using the Internet to Locate Everyday Information

The Internet can make your daily life easier. For example, you can use the Internet to access news and weather reports, download voter registration forms, get travel information, find directions, obtain consumer information, locate people, find movie reviews—or even find a job. The following sites are just a sample of the many resources available on the Internet.

Everyday Information on the Web

The Bible
The Unbound Bible
<http://www.unboundbible.org>

Book reviews
The New York Times *on the Web: Books*
<http://www.nytimes.com/books>

Calendars
Calendar Zone
<http://www.calendarzone.com>

Census data
U.S. Census Bureau Newsletter: Census and You
<http://www.census.gov/prod/www/abs/cen-you.html>

City and county data
U.S. Census Bureau: County and City Data Book
<http://www.census.gov/statab/www/ccdb.html>

Computers
Free On-Line Dictionary of Computing
<http://foldoc.doc.ic.ac.uk/foldoc/index.html>

Dictionaries
yourDictionary.com™
<http://www.yourdictionary.com>

Employment
America's Job Bank
<http://www.ajb.dni.us>

Encyclopedias
Britannica.com®
<http://www.britannica.com>

Genealogy
Lineages
<http://www.lineages.com>

Insurance company ratings
A. M. Best Insurance Information
<http://ambest.com/insurance>

Law and legal information
American Law Sources On-line
<http://lawsource.com/also>

Maps and directions
MapBlast!
<http://www.mapblast.com/myblast/index.mb>

Movie reviews
The Internet Movie Database
<http://www.imdb.com>

Newspapers
Newspapers.Com
<http://www.newspapers.com>

Telephone directories
AnyWho
<http://www.tollfree.att.net>

Switchboard.com
<http://www.switchboard.com>

Weather forecasts and information
National Weather Service Home Page
<http://www.nws.noaa.gov>

Writing a Research Paper

When you write a research paper, you find material—from books, articles, television programs, the Internet, and other sources—to support your ideas. You will have an easier time writing a research paper if you follow these steps.

1. Choose a topic.
2. Look for sources.
3. Zero in on your topic.
4. Do research.
5. Take notes.
6. Watch out for plagiarism.
7. Draft a thesis statement.
8. Make an outline.
9. Write your paper.
10. Document your sources.

Teaching Tip
Although in a developmental writing class you probably will not need to spend a lot of time on research, keep in mind that students do need to know the basics of research for other courses, often before they complete freshman composition.

1 Choosing a Topic

The first step in writing a research paper is finding a topic to write about. Before you choose a topic, ask yourself the following questions.

■ What is your page limit?
■ When is your paper due?
■ How many sources are you expected to use?
■ What kind of sources are you expected to use?

Teaching Tip
Encourage students to choose a research topic they know something about.

The answers to these questions will help you tell if your topic is too broad or too narrow.

When Allison Rogers, a student in a composition course, was asked to write a three- to five-page research paper that was due in five weeks, she decided that she wanted to write about the violence she saw in society. She knew, however, that the general topic "violence" would be too broad for her paper. After considering a number of possible topics, Allison decided to write about the effect of violent movies on behavior. In her film class, she had just seen the movie *Natural Born Killers* and was shocked by its graphic violence. She remembered hearing that the movie had caused a great deal of controversy and that two teenagers who committed murder had actually used it as a defense in their trial. This is what led Allison to wonder about the link between film violence and behavior. She thought this topic would work well because she could discuss it in the required number of pages and because she would be able to finish her paper within the five-week time limit.

Teaching Tip
If your college library offers tours, encourage students to go on one to familiarize themselves with the library's resources.

2 Looking for Sources

To get an overview of your topic and to see whether you will be able to find enough material, quickly survey the resources of your library. (First, arrange a meeting with your college librarian, who can answer questions, give suggestions, and point you toward helpful resources.)

Begin by searching your library's catalog by subject to see what books it lists on your topic. For example, under the general subject of *violence*, Allison saw the related headings *movie violence* and *media violence*. Under each of these headings, she found a variety of books and government studies on the topic.

In addition to books, you can look for articles. To do this, consult an index such as *Readers' Guide to Periodical Literature*, which lists articles in newspapers and magazines, or *InfoTrac*, a computer database that contains the texts of many articles. (Your librarian can show you how to use these resources.) A quick look at *Readers' Guide* showed Allison that many articles had been written about violence in the media.

For information about using the Internet for research, see Appendix A, section 8.

The Internet can also help you get an overview of your topic. Begin by carrying out an Internet search with a **search engine**, a program that helps you find information available on the Internet. (The most popular search engines are Yahoo, Infoseek, and AltaVista.) When Allison entered the key words *movie violence* and *Natural Born Killers*, she found many articles that related to her topic. (Ask your librarian to demonstrate effective searching techniques.)

3 Zeroing In on Your Topic

As you skim the library's resources, the subject headings as well as the titles of books and articles should help you zero in on your topic. For example, Allison discovered that several of the books and a number of the articles she located focused on the effect of media violence on society. A few focused specifically on children, examining the effect of violent movies and television on their behavior. Because she was an early childhood education major, Allison decided to concentrate on the effect of media violence on children. Following her instructor's guidelines, she knew the purpose of her paper would be either to *present information* about media violence and children or *make a point* about it. She could present information by discussing some of the current research into the relationship between media violence and violent behavior in children, or she could make the point that media violence can have a negative effect on the behavior of children.

4   Doing Research

Once you have zeroed in on your topic, you need to gather information. Go back to the library and check out any books you think will be useful. Photocopy relevant magazine articles, and make copies of material stored on microfilm or microfiche. If you use a computer database such as *Info-Trac*, print out the full text of any articles you plan to use. In addition, browse the World Wide Web for possible sources. Remember, the quality and reliability of material found on the Web can vary, so use only information from reliable sources—a Web site sponsored by a well-known national publication or organization, for example.

When Allison searched the Web using the key term *media violence*, she found the Web site produced by ERIC Counseling and Student Services Clearinghouse. This site contained "Children and Television Violence," an article posted by the American Psychological Association, a nationally recognized and reliable professional organization.

● **Writing Tip**
Do not forget to record the page numbers of all material you copy.

● **Writing Tip**
Record full publication information (including page numbers) for all material you photocopy or download; you will need this information when you document your sources.

● **Writing Tip**
If you are not sure whether a source is reliable, check with your instructor or college librarian.

5   Taking Notes

Once you have gathered the material you will need, read it carefully, recording any information you think you can use in your paper. As you take notes, keep your topic in mind; this will help you decide what material is useful. Record your notes on three-by-five-inch cards, on separate sheets of paper, or in a computer file you have created for this purpose.

Paraphrasing

When you use information from a source in your writing, you do not always *quote* the exact words of your source. More often, you *paraphrase* or *summarize* a source, putting its ideas into your own words.

When you **paraphrase**, you present the ideas of a source in your own words, following the order and emphasis of the original. You paraphrase when you want to make a discussion easier to understand while still conveying a clear sense of the original. Here is a passage from the article "Children and Television Violence," followed by Allison's paraphrase.

Original

> Children often behave differently after they've been watching violent programs on television. In one study done at Pennsylvania State University, about 100 preschool children were observed both before and after watching television; some watched cartoons that had many aggressive and violent acts; others watched shows that did not have any kind of violence. The researchers noticed real differences between the children who watched the violent shows and those who watched nonviolent ones.

Teaching Tip
Remind students that they
should read a passage several times and then put it
away before trying to paraphrase it. Looking at the material as they write almost
always results in plagiarism.

Paraphrase

> At Pennsylvania State University, researchers did a
> study. They divided 100 young children into two groups.
> One group watched television programs that contained a
> lot of violence. The other group watched programs that
> contained very little violence. Researchers found that
> the two groups of children behaved very differently.

Summarizing

When you write a **summary**, you also put the ideas of a source into your own words. Unlike a paraphrase, however, a summary condenses a passage, giving only the general idea of the original. Here is Allison's summary of the original passage on page 629.

● **Writing Tip**

In a paraphrase or a sum-
mary, you present only the
source's ideas, not your own
ideas or opinions about the
source.

Summary

> According to a study conducted at Pennsylvania State
> University, young children who watched violent televi-
> sion shows behaved differently from those who watched
> nonviolent shows.

Quoting

When you **quote**, you use the exact words of a source, enclosing them in quotation marks. Because too many quotations can distract readers, quote only when an author's words are memorable or when you want to give readers the flavor of the original source.

> According to the article "Children and Television Vio-
> lence," "Children often behave differently after they've
> been watching violent programs on television."

Integrating Sources

To show readers why you are using a source and to integrate source material smoothly into your essay, introduce paraphrases, summaries, and quotations with a phrase that identifies the source or its author. You can position this identifying phrase at various places in a sentence. You should not use the same words over and over to introduce source material. Try using different words—for example, *points out, observes, comments, notes, remarks,* and *concludes.*

> <u>According to the article "Children and Television Vio-
> lence,"</u> "Children often behave differently after they've
> been watching violent programs on television."

"Children often behave differently after they've been watching violent programs on television," <u>observes one Pennsylvania State University study</u>.

"Children often behave differently," <u>claim researchers in a study reported by the American Psychological Association</u>, "after they've been watching violent programs on television."

6 Watching Out for Plagiarism

As a rule, you must document any words or ideas from an outside source that are not **common knowledge**, factual information widely available in reference works. When you present information from another source as if it is your own (whether you do it intentionally or unintentionally), you commit **plagiarism**—and plagiarism is theft. You can avoid plagiarism by understanding what you must document and what you do not have to document.

For information on documentation, see B10.

FOCUS **Avoiding Plagiarism**

You should document

■ Word-for-word quotations from a source
■ Ideas from a source that you put in your own words
■ Tables, charts, graphs, or statistics from a source

You do not need to document

■ Your own ideas
■ Common knowledge
■ Familiar quotations

When you consult a source to get ideas for your writing, be careful to avoid the errors that commonly lead to plagiarism. The following paragraph from Brian Siano's essay "Frankenstein Must Be Destroyed: Chasing the Monster of TV Violence" and the four rules that follow will help you understand and correct these common errors.

ORIGINAL

Of course, there are a few crazies out there who will be unfavorably influenced by what they see on TV. But even assuming that somehow the TV show (or movie or record) shares some of the blame, how does one predict what future crazies will take for inspiration? What guidelines

ESL Tip
Ask students whether any culture they are familiar with defines plagiarism differently. Use this as a springboard to a discussion of the conventions of plagiarism. Make sure students understand that in American culture, plagiarism is not acceptable.

Teaching Tip
Go over the issue of plagiarism versus paraphrasing, giving students lots of practice material.

■ Computer Tip
Keep track of material that you download from the Internet. Make sure you do not accidentally commit plagiarism by cutting and pasting such information into your paper without identifying it as quoted material.

would ensure that people write, act, or produce something that *will not upset a psychotic?* Not only is this a ridiculous demand, it's insulting to the public as well. We would all be treated as potential murderers in order to gain a hypothetical 5 percent reduction in violence.

1. Document Ideas from Your Sources

PLAGIARISM

> Even if we were to control the programs that are shown on television, we would only decrease violence in society by perhaps 5 percent.

Even though the writer does not quote Siano directly, she must still identify him as the source of the paraphrased material.

CORRECT

> According to Brian Siano, even if we were to control the programs that are shown on television, we would only decrease violence in society by perhaps 5 percent (24).

2. Place Borrowed Words in Quotation Marks

PLAGIARISM

> According to Brian Siano, there will always be a few crazies out there who will be unfavorably influenced by what they see on television (24).

Although the writer cites Siano as the source, the passage incorrectly uses Siano's exact words without quoting them. The writer must either quote the borrowed words or rephrase the material.

CORRECT (BORROWED WORDS IN QUOTATION MARKS)

> According to Brian Siano, there will always be "a few crazies out there who will be unfavorably influenced by what they see on TV" (24).

CORRECT (BORROWED WORDS REPHRASED)

> According to Brian Siano, some unstable people will commit crimes because of the violence they see in the media (24).

3. Use Your Own Phrasing

PLAGIARISM

> Naturally, there will always be people who are affected by what they view on television. But even if we agree that television programs can influence people, how can we really know what will make people commit crimes? How can we be absolutely sure that a show will not disturb someone who is insane? The answer is that we cannot. To pretend that we can is insulting to law-abiding citi-

zens. We cannot treat everyone as if they were criminals just to reduce violence by a small number of people (Siano 24).

Even though the writer acknowledges Siano as her source, and even though she does not use Siano's exact words, her passage closely follows the order, emphasis, sentence structure, and phrasing of the original. In the following passage, the writer uses her own wording, quoting one distinctive phrase from her source.

CORRECT

> According to Brian Siano, we should not censor a television program just because "a few crazies" may be incited to violence (24). Not only would such censorship deprive the majority of people of the right to watch what they want, but it will not significantly lessen the violence in society (24).

● **Writing Tip**
Even though the paragraph ends with documentation, the quotation requires its own citation.

4. Distinguish Your Ideas from the Source's Ideas

PLAGIARISM

> Any attempt to control television violence will quickly reach the point of diminishing returns. There is no way to make absolutely certain that a particular television program will not cause a disturbed person to commit a crime. It seems silly, then, to treat the majority of people as "potential murderers" just to control the behavior of a few (Siano 24).

In the preceding passage, it appears that only the quotation in the last sentence is borrowed from Siano's article. In fact, the ideas in the second sentence are also Siano's. The writer should use an identifying phrase (such as "According to Siano") to acknowledge the borrowed material in this sentence and to show where it begins.

CORRECT

> Any attempt to control television violence will quickly reach the point of diminishing returns. According to Brian Siano, we cannot be absolutely certain that a particular television program will not cause a disturbed person to commit a crime (24). It seems silly, then, to treat the majority of people as "potential murderers" just to control the behavior of a few (24).

● **Writing Tip**
Each quotation requires its own separate parenthetical documentation.

7   **Drafting a Thesis Statement**

After you have taken notes, review the information you have gathered, and draft a thesis statement. Your **thesis statement** is a single sentence that states the main idea of your paper and tells readers what to expect. After

For more on thesis statements, see 12D.

reviewing her notes, Allison Rogers came up with the following thesis statement for her paper on media violence.

Thesis Statement

> For most adults, no amount of onscreen violence is an excuse for violent behavior; when it comes to young children, however, violent movies present a real danger.

8 Making an Outline

For more on outlining, see 12E.

Once you have drafted a thesis statement, you are ready to make an outline. Your outline, which covers just the body paragraphs of your paper, can be either a **topic outline** (in which each idea is expressed in a word or a short phrase) or a **sentence outline** (in which each idea is expressed in a complete sentence). After reviewing her notes, Allison Rogers wrote the following sentence outline for her paper.

I. Teenagers claim the movie Natural Born Killers made them commit murder.
  A. According to John Grisham, the movie inspired the teenagers to commit their crimes.
  B. Grisham says that several murders have been committed by teenagers who say they were influenced by the movie.
II. The idea that movie violence causes violent behavior is not supported.
  A. Other factors could have influenced the teenagers.
  B. No clear link between media violence and aggressive behavior has been discovered.
III. Anecdotal evidence supporting the link between "copycat crimes" and media violence has two problems.
  A. Movies are seldom definitively linked to crimes.
  B. Anecdotal evidence is not representative.
IV. The right of the majority to watch movies and television shows of their choice should not be limited because some unbalanced people may commit crimes.
 V. Still, young children should be protected from media violence.
  A. Parents should protect young children.
    1. Parents should monitor what children see on television and in the movies.
    2. Parents should discuss the content of movies and television shows with their children.
  B. The media should do more to protect young children.

1. Movie theaters should enforce rating systems.
2. Violent programs should not be shown on stations whose audience is primarily children.

9 Writing Your Paper

Once you have decided on a thesis and written an outline, you are ready to write a draft of your paper. Begin with an **introduction** that includes your thesis statement. Usually, your introduction will be a single paragraph, but sometimes it will be longer.

In the **body** of your research paper, you support your thesis statement, with each body paragraph developing a single point. These paragraphs should have clear topic sentences so that your readers will know exactly what points you are making. Use transitional words and phrases to help readers follow your ideas.

Finally, your **conclusion** should give readers a sense of completion. Like your introduction, your conclusion will usually be a single paragraph, but it could be longer. It should reinforce your thesis statement and should end with a memorable sentence.

Remember, you will probably write several drafts of your paper before you hand it in. You can use the Self-Assessment Checklists on pages 132 and 133 to help you revise and edit your paper.

Allison Rogers's completed paper on media violence begins on page 642.

> **● Writing Tip**
> Use a thesis-and-support structure to organize your research paper. (See 12A.)

For more on introductions and conclusions, see 13A and 13B.

> **● Writing Tip**
> Check carefully to make sure you have not committed plagiarism. (See Appendix B, section 6.)

10 Documenting Your Sources

When you **document** your sources, you tell readers where you found the ideas that you used in your paper. The Modern Language Association (MLA) recommends the following documentation style for research papers. This format consists of *parenthetical references* within the paper that refer to a *Works Cited* list following the paper.

Parenthetical References in the Text

A parenthetical reference should include just enough information to lead readers to a specific entry in your Works Cited list. A typical parenthetical reference consists of the author's last name and the page number (Grisham 2). If you use more than one work by the same author, include a shortened form of the title in the parenthetical reference (Grisham, "Killers" 4). Notice that there is no *p* or *p.* before the page number.

Whenever possible, introduce information from a source with a phrase that includes the author's name. (If you do this, include only the page number in parentheses.)

As John Grisham observes in "Unnatural Killers," Oliver Stone celebrates gratuitous violence (4).

Place documentation so that it does not interrupt the flow of your ideas, preferably at the end of a sentence.

In three special situations, the format for parenthetical references departs from these guidelines.

1. When You Are Citing a Work by Two Authors

Film violence has been increasing during the past ten years (Williams and Yorst 34).

FOCUS **Formatting Quotations**

- **Short quotations**   Quotations of no more than four typed lines are run in with the text of your paper. End punctuation comes after the parenthetical reference (which follows the quotation marks).

  According to Grisham, there are "only two ways to curb the excessive violence of films like Natural Born Killers" (576).

- **Long quotations**   Quotations of more than four lines are set off from the text of your paper. Begin a long quotation ten spaces (or one inch) from the left-hand margin, and do not enclose it in quotation marks. Do not indent the first line of a single paragraph or part of a paragraph. If a quoted passage has more than one paragraph, indent the first line of each paragraph (including the first) three additional spaces (or one-quarter inch). Introduce a long quotation with a complete sentence followed by a colon, and place the parenthetical reference one space *after* the end punctuation.

  Grisham believes that eventually the courts will act to force studio executives to accept responsibility for the effects of their products:

  > But the laughing will soon stop. It will take only one large verdict against the likes of Oliver Stone, and his production company, and perhaps the screenwriter, and the studio itself, and then the party will be over. The verdict will come from the heartland, far away from Southern California, in some small courtroom with no cameras. (577)

2. When You Are Citing a Work without a Listed Author

```
Ever since cable television came on the scene, shows
with graphically violent content have been common
("Cable Wars" 76).
```

3. When You Are Citing an Indirect Source

If you use a statement by one author that is quoted in the work of another author, show this by including the abbreviation *qtd. in* ("quoted in").

```
When speaking of television drama, Leonard Eron, of the
University of Illinois, says "perpetrators of violence
should not be rewarded for violent acts" (qtd. in Siano
23).
```

FOCUS **Preparing the Works Cited List**

- Begin the Works Cited list on a new page after the last page of your paper.
- Number the Works Cited page as the next page of your paper.
- Center the heading *Works Cited* one inch from the top of the page; do not underline the heading or place it in quotation marks.
- Double-space the list.
- List entries alphabetically according to the author's last name.
- Alphabetize unsigned articles according to the first major word of the title.
- Begin typing each entry at the left-hand margin.
- Indent second and subsequent lines five spaces (or one-half inch).
- Separate each division of the entry—author, title, and publication information—by a period and one space.

The Works Cited List

The Works Cited list includes all the works you cite (refer to) in your paper. Use the guidelines in the box above to prepare your list.

The following sample Works Cited entries cover the situations you will encounter most often. Follow the formats exactly as they appear here.

Books

Book by One Author

List the author, last name first. Underline the title. Include the city of publication and a shortened form of the publisher's name—for example, *Prentice* for *Prentice Hall* or *Bedford* for *Bedford/St. Martin's*. Use the abbreviation *UP* for *University Press,* as in *Princeton UP* and *U of Chicago P.* End with the date of publication.

● **Writing Tip**

For more examples of MLA documentation style, see the *MLA Handbook for Writers of Research Papers,* 5th ed. (New York: MLA, 1999) or the MLA Web site <http://www.mla.org>.

Brown, Charles T. <u>The Rock and Roll Story</u>. Englewood
     Cliffs: Prentice, 1983.

Book by Two or Three Authors

List second and subsequent authors, first name first, in the order in which they are listed on the book's title page.

Coe, Sophie D., and Michael D. Coe. <u>The True History of
     Chocolate</u>. New York: Thames, 1996.

Book by More Than Three Authors

List only the first author, followed by the abbreviation *et al.* ("and others").

Sklar, Robert E., et al. <u>Movie-Made America: A Cultural
     History of American Movies</u>. New York: Random, 1999.

Two or More Books by the Same Author

List two or more books by the same author in alphabetical order according to title. In each entry after the first, use three unspaced hyphens (followed by a period) instead of the author's name.

Angelou, Maya. <u>Even the Stars Look Lonesome</u>. New York:
     Bantam, 1997.

---. <u>I Know Why the Caged Bird Sings</u>. New York: Bantam,
     1985.

Edited Book

Dickinson, Emily. <u>The Complete Poems of Emily Dickinson</u>.
     Ed. Thomas H. Johnson. New York: Little, 1990.

Translation

García Márquez, Gabriel. <u>Love in the Time of Cholera</u>.
     Trans. Edith Grossman. New York: Knopf, 1988.

Revised Edition

Gans, Herbert J. <u>The Urban Villagers</u>. 2nd ed. New York:
     Free, 1982.

Anthology

Kirszner, Laurie G., and Stephen R. Mandell, eds.
     <u>Patterns for College Writing</u>. 8th ed. New York:
     Bedford, 2001.

Essay in an Anthology

Grisham, John. "Unnatural Killers." <u>Patterns for College
     Writing</u>. Ed. Laurie G. Kirszner and Stephen R.
     Mandell. 8th ed. New York: Bedford, 2001. 566-75.

More Than One Essay in the Same Anthology

List each essay separately with a cross-reference to the entire anthology.

Grisham, John. "Unnatural Killers." Kirszner and Mandell
     566-75.

Kirszner, Laurie G., and Stephen R. Mandell, eds.
     <u>Patterns for College Writing</u>. 8th ed. New York:
     Bedford, 2001.

● **Writing Tip**

MLA recommends that you underline book titles, not put them in italics.

● **Writing Tip**

When the abbreviation *ed(s)*. follows a name, it means "editor(s)"; when the abbreviation *Ed.* comes before a name, it means "edited by."

```
Stone, Oliver. "Memo to John Grisham: What's Next--
     'A Movie Made Me Do It'?" Kirszner and Mandell
     576-79.
```

Section or Chapter of a Book

```
Gordimer, Nadine. "Once upon a Time." "Jump" and Other
     Stories. New York: Farrar, 1991. 23-30.
```

Periodicals

Article in a Journal with Continuous Pagination throughout an Annual Volume

Some scholarly journals have continuous pagination; that is, one issue might end on page 234, and the next would then begin with page 235. In this case, the volume number is followed by the date of publication in parentheses.

```
Allen, Dennis W. "Horror and Perverse Delight:
     Faulkner's 'A Rose for Emily.'" Modern Fiction
     Studies 30 (1984): 685-96.
```

Article in a Journal with Separate Pagination in Each Issue

For a journal in which each issue begins with page 1, the volume number is followed by a period and the issue number and then by the date. Leave no space after the period.

```
Lindemann, Erika. "Teaching as a Rhetorical Art." CEA
     Forum 15.2 (1985): 9-12.
```

Article in a Monthly or Bimonthly Magazine

If an article does not appear on consecutive pages—for example, if it begins on page 43, skips to page 47, and continues on page 49—include only the first page, followed by a plus sign.

```
O'Brien, Conor Cruise. "Thomas Jefferson: Radical and
     Racist." Atlantic Monthly Oct. 1996: 43+.
```

Article in a Weekly or Biweekly Magazine (Signed or Unsigned)

```
Miller, Arthur. "Why I Wrote The Crucible." New Yorker
     21 Oct. 1996: 158-63.

"Real Reform Post-Enron." The Nation 4 Mar. 2002: 3.
```

Article in a Newspaper

```
Gelles, Jeff. "New Tool to Aid Identity-theft Victims."
     Philadelphia Inquirer 6 Feb. 2002, late ed.: D01.
```

Editorial or Letter to the Editor

```
"Support for the Saudi Struggle." Editorial. New York
     Times 28 Feb. 2002, late ed.: A26.
```

Internet Sources

When citing Internet sources appearing on the World Wide Web, include both the date of electronic publication (if available) and the date you accessed the source. (Some of the following examples include only the date of access; this indicates that the date of publication was not available.) In addition, include the electronic address (URL) enclosed in angle brackets.

Professional Site

> <u>Words of the Year</u>. American Dialect Society. 18 Jan.
> 2002 <http://www.americandialect.org/woty.html>.

Personal Site

> Lynch, Jack. Home page. 21 Dec. 2001 <http://
> andromeda.rutgers.edu/~jlynch>.

Article in an Online Reference Book or Encyclopedia

> "Croatia." <u>The World Factbook 2001</u>. 30 Mar. 2002.
> Central Intelligence Agency. 30 Dec. 2002
> <http://www.odci.gov/cia/publications/factbook>.

> "Empire State Building." <u>Britannica Online</u>. Vers.
> 98.1.1. Nov. 1997. Encyclopaedia Britannica. 8 Mar.
> 1999 <http://www.eb.com>.

Article in a Newspaper

> Lohr, Steve. "Microsoft Goes to Court." <u>New York
> Times on the Web</u> 19 Oct. 1998. 9 Apr. 1999
> <http://archives.nytimes.com/archives/search/
> fastweb?search>.

Editorial

> "Be Serious." Editorial. <u>Washington Post</u> 25 Mar. 1999.
> 9 Apr. 1999 <http://newslibrary.Krmediastream.com/
> cgi-bin/search/wp>.

Article in a Magazine

> Nobel, Philip. "Head for the Hills." <u>Metropolis
> Magazine</u> Feb. 2002. 20 Feb. 2002 <http://
> www.metropolismag.com/html/content_0202/far/
> index.html>.

Posting to a Listserv or Newsgroup

Be sure to include the phrase "Online posting."

> Thune, W. Scott. "Emotion and Rationality in Argument."
> Online posting. 23 Mar. 1997. CCCC/97 Online. 11
> Nov. 1997 <http://www.missouri.edu/HyperNews/get/
> cccc98/proplink/12.html>.

Other Nonprint Sources

Television or Radio Program

> "Prime Suspect 3." Writ. Lynda La Plante. Perf. Helen
> Mirren. <u>Mystery</u>! WNET, New York. 28 Apr. 1994.

Videotape, Movie, Record, or Slide Program

> Updike, John. Interview. "<u>Comments on 'A&P'</u>." Dir. Bruce
> Schwartz. Videocassette. Harcourt, 1997.

Personal Interview

> Garcetti, Gilbert. Personal interview. 7 May 2000.

Material Accessed through a Computer Service

When citing information from a commercial computer service such as CompuServe, America Online, or Prodigy, include the name of the computer service (America Online, for example), the date you accessed the material, and the keyword you entered to find the material.

> Glicken, Natalie. "Brady Defends Gun Law in Court."
>   <u>Congressional Quarterly</u>. America Online. 10 Oct.
>   1996. Keyword: CQ.

If instead of entering a keyword, you followed a series of topic labels, indicate the path you used.

> <u>Yiddish King Lear, The</u>. America Online. 2 July 2002.
>   Path: Research and Learning; Arts; Films and
>   Movies; Internet Movie Database; King Lear.

If the material you are citing has appeared in print, include the print publication information before the electronic information. Use the abbreviation *n. pag.* ("no pagination") if no pages are given.

Material Accessed on a CD-ROM or a DVD

In addition to the publication information, include the medium (CD-ROM), the vendor (UMI-Proquest, for example), and the date you accessed the information.

> Braunmiller, A. R., ed. <u>Macbeth</u>. By William Shakespeare.
>   CD-ROM. New York: Voyager, 1994.

Teaching Tip
Refer students to a handbook for additional models.

Sample Research Paper in MLA Style

Following is Allison Rogers's completed essay on the topic of media violence. The essay follows the conventions of MLA documentation style. Note that it has been reproduced in a narrower format than a standard (8½″ × 11″) sheet of paper.

Rogers 1

Allison Rogers
English 122-83
Essay 3
8 April 2001

Violence in the Media

Introduction

Mickey and Mallory, two characters in Oliver Stone's film <u>Natural Born Killers</u>, travel across the Southwest, killing a total of fifty-two people. After watching this movie, two teenagers went on a crime spree of their own and killed one person and wounded another, paralyzing her for the rest of her life. At their trial, their defense was that watching <u>Natural Born Killers</u> had made them commit their crimes and that Hollywood, along with the director of the movie, Oliver Stone, was to blame. As creative as this defense is, it is hard to accept.

Thesis statement

For most adults, no amount of onscreen violence is an excuse for violent behavior; when it comes to young children, however, violent movies present a real danger.

Paragraph combines quotation and paraphrase from Grisham article with Allison's own observations

According to John Grisham, Oliver Stone's <u>Natural Born Killers</u> "inspired" two teenagers "to commit murder" (5). Grisham goes on to say that since the movie was released, several murders have been committed by troubled young people who claimed they were "under the influence" of Mickey and Mallory (5). This type of defense keeps reappearing as the violence in our everyday lives increases: "I am not to blame," says the perpetrator. "That movie (or television show) made me do it."

Paragraph combines clearly documented paraphrases of Stone and Siano articles with Allison's own conclusions

The idea that violence in the media causes violent behavior is not supported by the facts. When we look at Ben and Sarah, the two teenagers who supposedly imitated Mickey and Mallory, it is clear that factors other than

Rogers 2

<u>Natural Born Killers</u> could have influenced
their decision to commit murder. Both young
adults had long histories of drug and alcohol
abuse as well as psychiatric treatment (Stone
39). In addition, no clear experimental link
between violent movies and television shows and
aggressive behavior has been established. Many
studies have shown that after watching violent
television shows, children tend to act aggres-
sively, but after about a week they return to
their normal pattern of behavior (Siano 22).

What, then, are we supposed to make of
crimes that seem to be inspired by the media?
As Siano points out, a body of anecdotal evidence supports the link between these "copycat
crimes" and media violence (24). Two problems
exist with this type of "evidence," however.
The first problem is that in most cases, the
movie or television show is never definitely
linked to the crime. For example, after the
movie <u>The Money Train</u> was released, a clerk in
a New York City subway token booth was set on
fire in much the same way a subway token clerk
was in the movie. Naturally, it appeared as if
the movie had inspired the crime. But at the
time of the crime, several newspapers reported
that the violent act shown in the movie had
occurred at least twice in the year before the
movie's release. So the question remains: Did
the movie cause the violence, or did it simply
reflect a kind of violent behavior that was
already present in society? The truth is that
we cannot answer this question.

The second problem with anecdotal evidence
is that it is not representative. Crimes that
are inspired by the media--killers imitating
the characters in slasher movies, for example--
are unusual. As Siano says, most people who

Phrase "As Siano points out" introduces
Allison's summary of source's ideas

No documentation necessary for
common knowledge

Rogers 3

watch violent movies do not go out and commit crimes (24). Only a few people will have such extreme reactions, and because they are mentally unbalanced, we cannot predict what will set them off. It could be a movie like <u>Natural Born Killers</u>, but it could also be a Bugs Bunny cartoon or a Three Stooges movie. The point is that society should not limit the right of the majority to watch the movies and television shows they want to see just because a few unbalanced individuals might go out and commit crimes.

Even if the link between media violence and violent behavior is not clear, most people agree that young children are easily influenced by what they see. One study has shown that young children who watch violent movies and television shows behave differently from those who do not (American Psychological Association). For this reason, young children should be protected. First, parents need to understand their responsibility for monitoring what their children see on television and in the movies. Second, as the American Psychological Association suggests, parents should take the time to discuss the content of movies and television shows with their children. Parents should be sure to teach their children what is real and what is not real and what is right and what is not right.

The media have already taken steps to protect children. For example, rating systems now in place can help. These give parents the ability to judge the content of movies before children go to see them and to evaluate television shows before they are turned on. Clearly, however, more needs to be done to protect young children. For one thing, these rating systems

The two paragraphs on this page combine paraphrases from an article with Allison's own observations

Rogers 4

must be enforced. If an R movie is being shown
at a theater, for example, the management must
require proof of age. In addition, movies or
television shows containing violence should not
be shown on stations whose audience is primarily children, such as the Disney Channel, even
at night. The time of day should not matter.
When we think of Disney, Mickey Mouse should
come to mind, not Dirty Harry (American Psychological Association).

There is no doubt that violence is learned
and that violent media images encourage violent
behavior in young children. It is not clear,
however, that violent movies and television
shows will actually cause an adult to commit a
crime. Placing the blame on the media is just
an easy way to sidestep the hard questions,
such as what is causing so much violence in
our society and what can we do about it. If we
prohibit violent programs, we will only deprive
many people of their right to view the programs
of their choice, and we will prevent artists
from expressing themselves freely. In the
process, these restrictions will also deprive
society of a good deal of worthwhile entertainment.

Conclusion

This paragraph needs no documentation
because it represents Allison's own ideas

Rogers 5

Works Cited

American Psychological Association. "Children
    and Television Violence." <u>School Violence
    Virtual Library</u> 6 June 1997. 19 Oct. 2001
    <http://www.uncg.edu/edu/ericcass/
    violence/index.htm>.

Grisham, John. "Unnatural Killers." <u>The Oxford
    American</u> Spring 1996: 2-5.

Siano, Brian. "Frankenstein Must Be Destroyed:
    Chasing the Monster of TV Violence." <u>The
    Humanist</u> Jan.-Feb. 1994: 20-25.

Stone, Oliver. "Memo to John Grisham: What's
    Next--'A Movie Made Me Do It'?" <u>LA Weekly</u>
    29 Mar.-4 Apr. 1996: 39.

Answers to Odd-Numbered Exercise Items

Chapter 15

◆ PRACTICE 15-1, page 214

Answers: **(1)** Complete subject: Derek Walcott **(3)** Complete subject: Walcott's early years; simple subject: years **(5)** Complete subject: His early poems; simple subject: poems **(7)** Complete subject: Walcott **(9)** Complete subject: the renowned poet; simple subject: poet **(11)** Complete subject: the sixty-two-year-old Caribbean poet; simple subject: poet

◆ PRACTICE 15-2, page 215

Possible answers: **(1)** pets **(3)** Pets **(5)** Social workers/ Nurses/Doctors **(7)** patients **(9)** dogs

◆ PRACTICE 15-3, page 215

Answers: **(1)** Sixteen nations; plural **(3)** Living quarters; plural **(5)** They; plural **(7)** Russia and the United States; plural **(9)** An international crew; singular

◆ PRACTICE 15-4, page 217

Answers: **(1)** Prepositional phrases: With more than 27 percent, of the vote, in history; subject: Theodore Roosevelt **(3)** Prepositional phrases: Until Roosevelt, of votes; subject: candidate **(5)** Prepositional phrases: For example, of the Progressive Party, about 16 percent, of the vote, in the 1924 race; subject: Robert M. LaFollette **(7)** Prepositional phrases: In 1980, of the vote; subject: John B. Anderson **(9)** Prepositional phrases: In 2000, with the support, of many environmentalists, for the presidency; subject: Ralph Nader

◆ PRACTICE 15-5, page 219

Answers: **(1)** see **(3)** offers **(5)** enters; wins **(7)** realizes **(9)** enjoy

◆ PRACTICE 15-6, page 220

Answers: **(1)** are **(3)** is **(5)** is **(7)** becomes **(9)** are

◆ PRACTICE 15-7, page 220

Answers: **(1)** wrote **(3)** is; seems **(5)** lives **(7)** dies **(9)** works

◆ PRACTICE 15-8, page 222

Answers: **(1)** Complete verb: had become; helping verb: had **(3)** Complete verb: had become; helping verb: had **(5)** Complete verb: would get; helping verb: would **(7)** Complete verb: did cause; helping verb: did **(9)** Complete verb: would remain; helping verb: would

Chapter 16

◆ PRACTICE 16-1, page 227

Answers: **(1)**, and **(3)**, and **(5)**, and **(7)**, so/and **(9)**, for

◆ PRACTICE 16-2, page 227

Answers: **(1)**, for **(3)**, or **(5)**, but **(7)**, for **(9)**, and

◆ PRACTICE 16-3, page 228

Possible edits: Diet, exercise, and family history may account for centenarians' long lives, but this is not the whole story. Recently, a study conducted in Georgia showed surprising common traits among centenarians. They did not necessarily avoid tobacco and alcohol, nor did they eat low-fat diets. In fact, they ate relatively large amounts of fat, cholesterol, and sugar, so diet could not explain their long lives. They did, however, share four key survival characteristics. First, all of the centenarians were optimistic about life, and all of them were positive thinkers. They were also involved in religious life and had deep religious faith. In addition, all the centenarians had continued to lead physically active lives, and they remained mobile even as elderly people. Finally, all were able to adapt to loss. They had all experienced the deaths of friends, spouses, or children, but they were able to get on with their lives.

◆ **PRACTICE 16-4, page 229**

Answers will vary.

◆ **PRACTICE 16-5, page 230**

Answers: **(1)** Sometimes runners-up are better remembered than winners; the triumphant are forgotten. **(3)** Robert Falcon Scott was a British naval officer; Roald Amundsen was a Norwegian explorer. **(5)** Amundsen's men buried food along the trail; Scott's men left food in only a few locations. **(7)** Amundsen's men made it to the Pole in December 1911; Scott's party arrived in January 1912. **(9)** Scott's exhausted party could not get to their scarce provisions; none of the men survived the trek to the Pole.

◆ **PRACTICE 16-6, page 231**

Answers will vary.

◆ **PRACTICE 16-7, page 234**

Answers: **(1)** Andrew F. Smith, a food historian, wrote a book about the tomato; subsequently, he wrote a book about ketchup. **(3)** The word *ketchup* may have come from a Chinese word; however, Smith is not certain of the word's origins. **(5)** Ketchup has changed a lot over the years; for example, special dyes were developed in the nineteenth century to make it red. **(7)** Ketchup is now used by people in many cultures; still, salsa is more popular than ketchup in the United States. **(9)** Some of today's ketchups are chunky; in addition, some ketchups are spicy.

◆ **PRACTICE 16-8, page 234**

Possible edits: **(1)** *Time* selects the Man of the Year to honor the person who has most influenced the previous year's events; consequently, the choice is often a prominent politician. **(3)** During the war years, Hitler, Stalin, Churchill, and Roosevelt were all chosen; in fact, Stalin was featured twice. **(5)** In 1956, The Hungarian Freedom Fighter was Man of the Year; then, in 1966, *Time* editors chose The Young Generation. **(7)** In 1975, American Women were honored as a group; nevertheless, the Man of the Year has nearly always been male. **(9)** The Man of the Year has almost always been one or more human beings; however, the Computer was selected in 1982 and Endangered Earth in 1988.

◆ **PRACTICE 16-9, page 235**

Possible Answers: **(1)** Living at home gives students access to free home-cooked meals; in contrast, dorm residents eat dining hall food. **(3)** Being at home means the commuters get to take part in family life; however, they may also miss out on social activities on campus. **(5)** At most colleges, commuters have access to social activities such as dances, clubs, and games; in fact, many campuses have their own commuter social groups. **(7)** Commuter students might have to help take care of younger or older family members; for example, the student might baby-sit for a younger brother or sister. **(9)** Commuters are always under the watchful eye of their parents; moreover, their parents are likely to be stricter than the dorm counselor.

◆ **PRACTICE 16-10, page 237**

Answers will vary.

Chapter 17

◆ **PRACTICE 17-1, page 243**

Answers: **(1)** Independent clause **(3)** Dependent clause **(5)** Independent clause **(7)** Independent clause **(9)** Dependent clause

◆ **PRACTICE 17-2, page 244**

Answers: **(1)** Independent clause **(3)** Independent clause **(5)** Dependent clause **(7)** Dependent clause **(9)** Independent clause

◆ **PRACTICE 17-3, page 246**

Possible Answers: **(1)** When/As **(3)** Although **(5)** Because **(7)** Even though **(9)** wherever

◆ **PRACTICE 17-4, page 247**

Possible edits: **(1)** Although professional midwives are used widely in Europe, in the United States, they usually practice independently only in areas with few doctors. **(3)** Stephen Crane powerfully describes battles in *The Red Badge of Courage* even though he never experienced a war. **(5)** After Jonas Salk developed the first polio vaccine in the 1950s, the incidence of polio began to decline rapidly in the United States. **(7)** Before the Du Ponts arrived from France in 1800, American gunpowder was inferior to the kind manufactured by the French. **(9)** Because Thaddeus Stevens thought plantation land should be distributed to freed slaves, he disagreed with Lincoln's peace terms for the South.

◆ **PRACTICE 17-5, page 249**

Answers: **(1)** This image is reinforced by a television show that started several years ago. **(3)** During one episode, Hyota was wandering through the streets, which were full of people, looking for someone to help him. **(5)** This television program, which teaches American street expressions to Japanese viewers, is very popular. **(7)** The English they learn, which is of little use in the real world, is not enough to protect them from street hustlers. **(9)** For example, a sixteen-year-old Japanese exchange student who did not understand the command "freeze" was shot.

◆ **PRACTICE 17-6, page 251**

Possible Answers: **(1)** MTV's very first music video, which was performed by a group called the Buggles, made the claim "Video Killed the Radio Star." **(3)** Recording executives, who had been suspicious of MTV at first, soon realized the power of music videos in selling records. **(5)** The Cars' "You Might Think" won best video at the first MTV Music Awards telecast, which aired in September 1984. **(7)** The fashion program *House of Style* became popular in 1989 partly because of supermodel Cindy Crawford, who was its first host. **(9)** That same year, Arkansas governor Bill Clinton, who would soon be elected president, met with young voters on *Rock the Vote*.

◆ **PRACTICE 17-7, page 252**

Answers will vary.

Chapter 18

◆ **PRACTICE 18-2, page 260**

Answers: **(1)** Adverb: sometimes; edited sentence: Sometimes, job applicants feel tongue-tied when asked even simple questions. **(3)** Adverb: however; edited sentence: However, there are strategies that can control jitters during job interviews. **(5)** Adverb: then; edited sentence: Then, they should understand that a simple mistake does not have to ruin the entire interview. **(7)** Adverb: surprisingly; edited sentence: Surprisingly, experts advise applicants to think of the interviewer as a close friend. **(9)** Adverb: usually; edited sentence: Usually, visualizing a calm and beautiful landscape can help one relax.

◆ **PRACTICE 18-3, page 262**

Answers will vary.

◆ **PRACTICE 18-4, page 262**

Answers: **(1)** Prepositional phrase: during World War II; edited sentence: During World War II, many male factory workers became soldiers. **(3)** Prepositional phrase: in the war's early years; edited sentence: In the war's early years, the U.S. government encouraged women to take factory jobs. **(5)** Prepositional phrase: in unprecedented numbers; edited sentence: In unprecedented numbers, they entered the industrial workplace. **(7)** Prepositional phrase: with their efforts; edited sentence: With their efforts, productivity rose and quality improved. **(9)** Prepositional phrase: for the first time; edited sentence: For the first time, many women felt comfortable wearing pants.

◆ **PRACTICE 18-5, page 263**

Answers will vary.

◆ **PRACTICE 18-6, page 264**

Answers: **(5)** After graduation, these professors can also write letters of recommendation for them. **(7)** In addition, the study recommends that students study in groups and that they take courses that require writing, preferably several short papers rather than one long one. **(9)** Throughout their college careers, students should give themselves a chance to become involved in outside activities.

◆ **PRACTICE 18-7, page 265**

Possible edits: **(7)** In fact, one coach is rumored to have placed bounties on rival players. **(9)** Of course, the fans also share the blame for the violence of football.

◆ **PRACTICE 18-8, page 267**

Answers: **(1)** Growing up in the slums of London, Charlie Chaplin began his acting career in vaudeville shows. **(3)** Turning to writing and directing, Chaplin made his first famous film, *The Tramp* in 1915. **(5)** Continuing to play the little tramp in other silent films, Chaplin starred in *The Kid* (1921) and *The Gold Rush* (1925). **(7)** Charming audiences in *City Lights*, the little tramp was last seen in *Modern Times* (1936). **(9)** Departing from Hollywood in the 1950s, Chaplin settled in England.

◆ **PRACTICE 18-9, page 268**

Answers will vary.

◆ **PRACTICE 18-10, page 269**

Answers: **(1)** Captured as a young girl by a rival tribe, Sacajawea was later sold into slavery. **(3)** Hired by the explorers Lewis and Clark in 1806, Charbonneau brought his pregnant wife along on their westward expedition. **(5)** Guided by Sacajawea's knowledge of the rugged terrain, the expedition also benefited from her familiarity with native food plants. **(7)** Protected by the presence of a Shoshone woman and her infant, Lewis and Clark encountered little hostility from the tribes they met. **(9)** Celebrated for many years as an American hero, Sacajawea recently received an additional honor.

◆ **PRACTICE 18-11, page 271**

Answers will vary.

◆ **PRACTICE 18-12, page 272**

Answers: **(1)** American tourists and foreign visitors flock to Orlando's theme parks. **(3)** At the Magic Kingdom, the roller coaster Space Mountain and the Pirates of the Caribbean ride draw large crowds. **(5)** Children and adults enjoy having their pictures taken with Mickey Mouse. **(7)** Three-dimensional films and simulated disaster rides can surprise first-time theme park visitors. **(9)** Admission to the parks and the food sold there can be quite expensive.

◆ **PRACTICE 18-13, page 273**

Answers: **(1)** Despite his lack of formal education, Edison had a quick mind and showed a talent for problem solving. **(3)** Edison patented the earliest phonograph in 1878 and created the first practical light bulb the following year. **(5)** Edison later developed an electric railroad and produced one of the first batteries to store long-term power. **(7)** His early experiments with sound pictures were surprisingly successful and would eventually lead to talking pictures. **(9)** Edison carried out much of his work in New Jersey and had laboratories there in West Orange and Menlo Park.

◆ **PRACTICE 18-14, page 275**

Answers: **(1)** These college presidents and their supporters want to improve the academic performance of college athletes. **(3)** A second proposal requires athletes to earn a certain number of credits every year and mandates a minimum grade point average for them. **(5)** Many Big East coaches believe standardized test scores are biased and want their use in screening student athletes banned. **(7)** According to supporters, however, many athletes under the current system fail to advance academically and often finish their eligibility fifty or more hours short of graduation. **(9)** In the supporters' view, poor supervision by athletic directors and lack of support for academic excellence are to be blamed for the poor performance of student athletes.

◆ PRACTICE 18-15, page 276

Answers: **(1)** A playwright who wrote the prize-winning *A Raisin in the Sun*, Lorraine Hansberry, was born in Chicago in 1930. **(3)** Hostile neighbors there were responsible for throwing a brick through a window of their house, an act Hansberry never forgot. **(5)** Lena Younger, the mother of the family, is about to receive a ten-thousand-dollar insurance payment following her husband's death. **(7)** Her dream for the family, a house with a yard her grandson can play in, leads her to purchase a home in a white neighborhood. **(9)** One of their new white neighbors has offered to pay the Younger family a bribe not to move into the neighborhood, an offer Walter now decides to accept.

◆ PRACTICE 18-16, page 278

Possible edits: Kente cloth is made in western Africa and produced primarily by the Ashanti people. It has been worn for hundreds of years by African royalty, who consider it a sign of power and status. Many African Americans wear kente cloth because they see it as a link to their heritage. Each pattern on the cloth has a name, and each color has a special significance. For example, red and yellow suggest a long and healthy life, while green and white suggest a good harvest. Although African women may wear kente cloth as a dress or head wrap, African-American women, like men, usually wear strips of cloth around their shoulders. Men and women of African descent wear kente cloth as a sign of black pride; in fact, it often decorates college students' gowns at graduation.

Chapter 19

◆ PRACTICE 19-1, page 283

Answers: **(1)** Parallel **(3)** They also admit that cigarettes are expensive, smelly, and dangerous. **(5)** Being happy in life is more important to me than making a lot of money. **(7)** Judges must care about justice, uphold the laws, and treat defendants fairly. **(9)** Love is blind, but hate is blinder.

◆ PRACTICE 19-2, page 285

Answers will vary.

◆ PRACTICE 19-3, page 286

Answers: **(1)** Pasadena, Claremont, and Pomona are major cities in the valley. **(3)** Watching the big Tournament of Roses parade is more exciting than viewing the Macy's Thanksgiving parade. **(5)** Judges rate the rose-covered floats on their originality, artistic merit, and overall impact. **(7)** The Rose Bowl game is not only America's oldest collegiate championship but also the country's most popular bowl game. **(9)** Visitors come to play challenging skill games and enjoy various ethnic foods.

Chapter 20

◆ PRACTICE 20-1, page 292

Answers: **(1)** three fifty-watt bulbs; coal oil; baking bread **(3)** wooden table; unfinished game of checkers; apple-tree stump

◆ PRACTICE 20-2, page 293

Answers will vary.

◆ PRACTICE 20-3, page 293

Answers will vary.

◆ PRACTICE 20-4, page 295

Possible edits: **(1)** Adult children can become frustrated because their parents seem to treat them as if they were not capable of making their own decisions. **(3)** When this happens, the children may begin to whine childishly or even throw a temper tantrum although such behavior only reinforces their parents' attitude. **(5)** To get parents to stop being critical, an adult child might turn the tables and encourage his or her parents to talk about their own childhoods. **(7)** Adult children might also explain that while they value their parents' opinion, they are still going to make their own decisions. **(9)** Although parents may have been telling these stories the same way for years, the child may have a very different perspective on the event.

◆ PRACTICE 20-5, page 297

Possible edits: **(1)** Clichés: working like a dog; living high on the hog. Many people think that a million-dollar lottery jackpot allows the winner to stop working long hours and start living a comfortable life. **(3)** Cliché: hit the jackpot. For one thing, lottery winners who win big prizes do not receive their winnings all at once; instead, payments—for example, $50,000—are usually spread out over twenty years. **(5)** Clichés: with their hands out; between a rock and a hard place. Next come relatives and friends who ask for money, leaving winners with difficult choices to make. **(7)** Cliché: Adding insult to injury. Even worse, many lottery winners have lost their jobs because employers thought that once they were "millionaires," they no longer needed to draw a salary. **(9)** Cliché: In their hour of need. Faced with financial difficulties, many would like to sell their future payments to companies that offer lump-sum payments of forty to forty-five cents on the dollar.

◆ **PRACTICE 20-6, page 298**

Answers will vary.

◆ **PRACTICE 20-7, page 299**

Answers will vary.

◆ **PRACTICE 20-8, page 301**

Answers: **(1)** Many people today would like to see more police officers patrolling the streets. **(3)** The attorneys representing the plaintiff are Geraldo Diaz and Barbara Wilkerson. **(5)** Travel to other planets will be a significant step for humanity.

Chapter 21

◆ **PRACTICE 21-1, page 308**

Answers: **(1)** Run-on **(3)** Run-on **(5)** Run-on **(7)** Correct **(9)** Correct **(11)** Correct

◆ **PRACTICE 21-2, page 310**

Possible edits: **(1)** Nursing offers job security and high pay; therefore, many people are choosing nursing as a career. **(3)** The Democratic Republic of the Congo was previously known as Zaire; before that, it was the Belgian Congo. **(5)** Millions of Jews were killed during the Holocaust; in addition, Catholics, Gypsies, homosexuals, and other "undesirables" were killed. **(7)** Japanese athletes play various positions on American baseball teams; however, until recently all Japanese players were pitchers. **(9)** Père Noel is the French name for Santa Claus; he is also known as Father Christmas and St. Nicholas.

◆ **PRACTICE 21-3, page 311**

Possible edits: **(1)** Harlem, which was populated mostly by European immigrants at the turn of the last century, saw an influx of African Americans beginning in 1910. **(3)** Many African-American artists and writers created a settlement in Harlem during the 1920s, which led to a flowering of African-American art. **(5)** When scholars of the era recognize the great works of the Harlem Renaissance, they point to the writers Langston Hughes and Countee Cullen and the artists Henry Tanner and Sargent Johnson. **(7)** Because Harlem was an exciting place in the 1920s, people from all over the city went there to listen to jazz and to dance. **(9)** While contemporary African-American artists know about the Harlem Renaissance, it is still not familiar to many others.

◆ **PRACTICE 21-4, page 312**

Possible edits: In the late nineteenth century, Coney Island was famous; in fact, it was legendary. Every summer, it was crowded, and people mailed hundreds of thousands of postcards from the resort on some days. Coney Island, which was considered exotic and exciting, even had a hotel shaped like an elephant. Although some people saw Coney Island as seedy, others thought it was a wonderful, magical place. It had beaches, hotels, racetracks, and a stadium; however, by the turn of the century, it was best known for three amusement parks. These parks were Luna Park, Steeplechase, and Dreamland. Even though gaslight was still the norm in New York, a million electric lights lit Luna Park. While Steeplechase offered many rides, its main attraction was a two-mile ride on mechanical horses. At Dreamland, people could see a submarine; in addition, they could travel through an Eskimo village or visit Lilliputia, with its three hundred midgets. Today, the old Coney Island no longer exists. Fire destroyed Dreamland in 1911, and Luna Park burned down in 1946. In 1964, Steeplechase closed. The once-grand Coney Island is gone. Still, its beach and its boardwalk endure. Its famous roller coaster, the Cyclone, still exists, and its giant Ferris wheel, the Wonder Wheel, keeps on turning. Now, a ballpark has been built for a new minor league baseball team. The new team is called the Brooklyn Cyclones.

Chapter 22

◆ **PRACTICE 22-1, page 317**

Answers: **(1)** Add a verb. **(3)** Add a subject and a verb. **(5)** Add a subject and a verb. **(7)** Add a verb. **(9)** Add a subject.

◆ **PRACTICE 22-2, page 318**

Answers: Items 2, 4, 6, and 7 are fragments. *Rewrite:* Sara Paretsky writes detective novels, such as *Burn Marks* and *Guardian Angel*. These novels are about V. I. Warshawski, a private detective. V. I. lives and works in Chicago, the Windy City. Every day as a detective, V. I. takes risks. V. I. is tough. She is also a woman.

◆ **PRACTICE 22-3, page 319**

Answers: **(1)** Most scholars agree that the United States flag was designed by Francis Hopkinson, a New Jersey delegate to the Continental Congress. **(3)** The first flag may have been sewn by Betsy Ross, a Philadelphia seamstress. **(5)** The Pledge of Allegiance was first recited during a ceremony in 1892, the four-hundredth anniversary of Columbus's arrival in the New World. **(7)** In 1814, Francis Scott Key composed "The Star Spangled Banner" during a fierce naval battle, an attack by a British warship on Fort McHenry in Baltimore's harbor. **(9)** When "The Star Spangled Banner" was proposed as the National Anthem in 1929, some people argued for other songs, such as "America" or "America the Beautiful."

ANSWERS TO
ODD-NUMBERED
EXERCISE ITEMS

◆ **PRACTICE 22-4, page 321**

Answers: **(1)** First-born children are reliable, serious, and goal-oriented in most cases. **(3)** Only children have personality characteristics like those of first-borns in larger families. **(5)** Second-born children may compete with their older sibling but more often pursue different interests in terms of academics and other activities. **(7)** In large families, middle-born children often form close personal relationships among themselves or with friends outside of the family. **(9)** Youngest children can be charming and funny but sometimes manipulative in their relationships with other family members.

◆ **PRACTICE 22-5, page 322**

Answers will vary.

◆ **PRACTICE 22-6, page 325**

Answers will vary.

◆ **PRACTICE 22-7, page 326**

Answers will vary.

◆ **PRACTICE 22-8, page 327**

Answers: **(1)** Prior to the 1990s, most animated films were hand-drawn, requiring painstaking skill. **(3)** Some people object to computer animation, criticizing it as too mechanical. **(5)** The first full-length animated film was Walt Disney's *Snow White and the Seven Dwarfs,* released originally in 1937. **(7)** Disney's conventional animation reached its peak with *Beauty and the Beast,* considered by many the equivalent of a great live-action feature. **(9)** DreamWorks studios has become Disney's main competitor, producing such hits as *Antz* and *Shrek.*

◆ **PRACTICE 22-9, page 328**

Answers: **(1)** Emergency medical technicians receive intensive training. This training is meant to prepare them for saving lives. **(3)** Retailers often locate frequently purchased items at the back of their stores. They do this to increase customer traffic. **(5)** Japan's Tokyo Zoo is closed for two months each year. This is done to give the animals a vacation from visitors. **(7)** More and more, people rely on e-mail to keep in touch with family and friends. **(9)** Early telephone users said "Ahoy" instead of "Hello" to greet incoming calls.

◆ **PRACTICE 22-10, page 331**

Possible edits: **(1)** Many homeless people are mentally ill. **(3)** People disagree about the effects of violent video games. **(5)** Competition for athletic scholarships increased. **(7)** Pizza is high in fat. **(9)** Something is likely to change.

◆ **PRACTICE 22-11, page 333**

Answers will vary.

Chapter 23

◆ **PRACTICE 23-1, page 341**

Answers: **(1)** know **(3)** include **(5)** sell; top **(7)** surprises; gives **(9)** hosts; draws

◆ **PRACTICE 23-2, page 342**

Answers: **(1)** write **(3)** supervise **(5)** give **(6)** contain **(7)** put; read **(9)** hates

◆ **PRACTICE 23-3, page 342**

Answers: **(1)** fill **(3)** survey **(5)** plays **(7)** smell **(9)** greets

◆ **PRACTICE 23-4, page 344**

Answers: **(1)** have **(3)** has **(5)** do **(7)** is **(9)** has

◆ **PRACTICE 23-5, page 346**

Answers: **(1)** Prepositional phrase: in the painting; subject: cupids; verb: symbolize **(3)** Prepositional phrase: in the kitchen; subject: appliances; verb: make **(5)** Prepositional phrase: of skis and poles; subject: set; verb: costs **(7)** Prepositional phrase: in the city; subject: Workers; verb: pay **(9)** Prepositional phrase: including people like my father; subject: Volunteers; verb: help

◆ **PRACTICE 23-6, page 348**

Answers: **(1)** has **(3)** wants **(5)** takes **(7)** seems **(9)** is

◆ **PRACTICE 23-7, page 350**

Answers: **(1)** Subject: Bering Straits; verb: are **(3)** Subject: twins; verb: are **(5)** Subject: this; verb: has **(7)** Subject: people; verb: are **(9)** Subject: reasons; verb: are

◆ **PRACTICE 23-8, page 351**

Answers: **(1)** Subject: story; verb: has **(3)** Subject: narrator; verb: has **(5)** Subject: Madeline; verb: lives **(7)** Subject; vault; verb: is **(9)** Subject: Roderick; verb: is

Chapter 24

◆ **PRACTICE 24-1, page 356**

Answers: **(1)** When Beverly Harvard became the chief of the Atlanta police force, she was the first African-American woman ever to hold that title in a major U.S. city. **(3)** Now, more than half the department is African-American, and women make up about a quarter of the force. **(5)** Her husband even agreed to pay her $100 if she made it onto the force. **(7)** In fact, when she entered the police academy, she did not really plan to be a police officer; she just wanted to prove her husband wrong and to win the $100 bet. **(9)** When her promotion was announced, some veteran officers criticized her appointment as police chief, but most younger officers praised the choice.

◆ **PRACTICE 24-2, page 358**

Answers: **(1)** Young people who want a career in the fashion industry do not always realize how hard they will have to work. **(3)** In reality, no matter how talented he or she is, a recent college graduate entering the industry is paid only about $22,000 a year. **(5)** A young designer may receive a big raise if he or she is very talented, but this is unusual. **(7)** Employees may be excited to land a job as an assistant designer but then find that they color in designs that have already been drawn. **(9)** If a person is serious about working in the fashion industry, he or she has to be realistic.

◆ **PRACTICE 24-3, page 359**

Possible edits: **(1)** According to recent studies, a juror may have his or her mind made up before the trial even begins. **(3)** This unfounded conclusion often depends on which attorney makes his or her initial description of the case the most dramatic. **(5)** Jurors with poor decision-making skills are also not likely to listen to challenges to their opinions when the full jury comes together to deliberate. **(7)** Correct **(9)** For example, one juror argued that a man being tried for murder was acting in his own defense because the victim was probably carrying a knife, but no knife was mentioned during the trial.

◆ **PRACTICE 24-4, page 362**

Answers: **(1)** A local university funded the study, and Dr. Alicia Flynn led the research team. **(3)** Two-thirds of the subjects relied on instinct alone and only one-third used logical analysis. **(5)** Many experts read the report, and most of them found the results surprising.

Chapter 25

◆ **PRACTICE 25-1, page 367**

Answers: **(1)** Present participle modifier: Tracing their origins to the late 1700s; modifies: organizations **(3)** Present participle modifier: Focusing on academics; modifies: fraternities **(5)** Present participle modifier: Evolving out of these; modifies: fraternities and sororities **(7)** Present participle modifier: Reflecting members' interests; modifies: fraternities and sororities **(9)** Present participle modifier: Taking various forms; modifies: hazing

◆ **PRACTICE 25-2, page 369**

Answers: **(1)** Past participle modifier: The best-preserved fossil ever found; modifies: it **(3)** Past participle modifier: excited by the find; modifies: hunters **(5)** Past participle modifier: Supported by previous rulings; modifies: judge **(7)** Past participle modifier: Questioned by the press; modifies: hunters **(9)** Past participle modifier: Shocked by the ruling; modifies: dealer

◆ **PRACTICE 25-3, page 370**

Answers will vary.

◆ **PRACTICE 25-4, page 372**

Answers will vary.

◆ **PRACTICE 25-5, page 374**

Answers: **(1)** Frightened by a noise, the cat broke the vase. **(3)** Lori looked at the man with red hair sitting in the chair. **(5)** People are sometimes killed by snakes with their deadly venom. **(7)** I ran outside in my bathrobe and saw eight tiny reindeer. **(9)** Wearing a mask, the exterminator sprayed the insect.

Chapter 26

◆ **PRACTICE 26-1, page 382**

Answers: **(1)** owned **(3)** browsed **(5)** turned; wanted **(7)** insisted **(9)** kicked

◆ **PRACTICE 26-2, page 384**

Answers: **(1)** broke **(3)** beat **(5)** let; felt **(7)** kept; took **(9)** hurt; lost **(11)** left; came

◆ **PRACTICE 26-3, page 386**

Answers: **(1)** Correct **(3)** were; Correct **(5)** were **(7)** Correct; Correct **(9)** was **(11)** was

◆ **PRACTICE 26-4, page 388**

Answers: **(1)** could **(3)** will **(5)** could **(7)** would **(9)** could

Chapter 27

◆ **PRACTICE 27-1, page 393**

Answers: **(1)** started **(3)** appeared **(5)** expanded **(7)** consumed **(9)** changed

◆ **PRACTICE 27-2, page 396**

Answers: **(1)** found **(3)** drawn **(5)** seen **(7)** gotten; grown **(9)** begun

◆ **PRACTICE 27-3, page 397**

Answers: **(1)** become **(3)** come; found **(5)** Correct; made **(7)** spoken; Correct **(9)** Correct

◆ **PRACTICE 27-4, page 399**

Answers: **(1)** have been **(3)** named **(5)** had **(7)** adopted **(9)** have given

◆ **PRACTICE 27-5, page 399**

Answers: **(1)** have presented **(3)** developed **(5)** has become **(7)** have begun

◆ PRACTICE 27-6, page 401

Answers: **(1)** had left **(3)** had arrived **(5)** had lied **(7)** had decided **(9)** had been

◆ PRACTICE 27-7, page 403

Answers: **(1)** surprised; preapproved **(3)** designed; inscribed **(5)** stuffed **(7)** concerned **(9)** acquired

Chapter 28

◆ PRACTICE 28-1, page 409

Answers: **(1)** headaches (regular) **(3)** feet (irregular) **(5)** deer (irregular) **(7)** brides-to-be (irregular) **(9)** loaves (irregular) **(11)** beaches (regular) **(13)** sons-in-law (irregular) **(15)** wives (irregular) **(17)** elves (irregular) **(19)** catalogs (regular)

◆ PRACTICE 28-2, page 410

Answers: **(1)** friends **(3)** husbands-to-be; catches; senses **(5)** Correct; personalities; lives **(7)** sexes; species.

◆ PRACTICE 28-3, page 411

Answers: **(1)** I **(3)** they; I **(5)** she; I **(7)** it

◆ PRACTICE 28-4, page 413

Answers: **(1)** Antecedent: campuses; pronoun: they **(3)** Antecedent: students; pronoun: their **(5)** Antecedent: Joyce; pronoun: she **(7)** Antecedent: friends; pronoun: them

◆ PRACTICE 28-5, page 413

Answers: **(1)** they **(3)** it **(5)** He **(7)** It

◆ PRACTICE 28-6, page 415

Answers: **(1)** Compound antecedent: Larry and Curly; connecting word: and; pronoun: their **(3)** Compound antecedent: Laurel and Hardy; connecting word: and; pronoun: their **(5)** Compound antecedent: *MASH* or *The Fugitive*; connecting word: or; pronoun: its **(7)** Compound antecedent: film or videotapes; connecting word: or; pronoun: their **(9)** Compound antecedent: popcorn and soft drinks; connecting word: and; pronoun: their

◆ PRACTICE 28-7, page 417

Answers: **(1)** Indefinite pronoun antecedent: Either; pronoun: its **(3)** Indefinite pronoun antecedent: Everything; pronoun: its **(5)** Indefinite pronoun antecedent: Neither; pronoun: her **(7)** Indefinite pronoun antecedent: Several; pronoun: their **(9)** Indefinite pronoun antecedent: Anyone; pronoun: his or her

◆ PRACTICE 28-8, page 418

Possible edits: **(1)** Everyone has the right to his or her own opinion. **(3)** Somebody forgot his or her backpack. **(5)** Someone in the store has left his or her car's lights on. **(7)** Each of the applicants must have his or her driver's license. **(9)** Either of the coffeemakers comes with its own filter.

◆ PRACTICE 28-9, page 419

Answers: **(1)** Collective noun antecedent: company; pronoun: its **(3)** Collective noun antecedent: government; pronoun: its **(5)** Collective noun antecedent: family; pronoun: its **(7)** Collective noun antecedent: team; pronoun: its **(9)** Collective noun antecedent: gang; pronoun: its

◆ PRACTICE 28-10, page 419

Answers: **(3)** Correct **(5)** its; their **(7)** his or her **(9)** its; Correct **(11)** his or her

◆ PRACTICE 28-11, page 422

Answers: **(1)** Subjective; Possessive **(3)** Objective; Possessive; Possessive **(5)** Subjective; Subjective; Possessive; Objective **(7)** Objective; Subjective; Possessive **(9)** Possessive

◆ PRACTICE 28-12, page 425

Answers: **(1)** me **(3)** him **(5)** I **(7)** Correct; me **(9)** They

◆ PRACTICE 28-13, page 425

Answers: **(1)** she [is] **(3)** she [does] **(5)** we [have] **(7)** they [serve] **(9)** [it fits] me

◆ PRACTICE 28-14, page 426

Answers: **(1)** who **(3)** who **(5)** who **(7)** whoever **(9)** who

◆ PRACTICE 28-15, page 428

Answers: **(1)** themselves **(3)** himself **(5)** yourself **(7)** itself **(9)** themselves

Chapter 29

◆ PRACTICE 29-1, page 435

Answers: **(1)** poorly **(3)** truly **(5)** really **(7)** specifically **(9)** important; immediately

◆ PRACTICE 29-2, page 436

Answers: **(1)** good **(3)** good **(5)** good **(7)** well **(9)** good

◆ PRACTICE 29-3, page 438

Answers: **(1)** more slowly **(3)** healthier **(5)** more loudly **(7)** more respectful **(9)** wilder

◆ **PRACTICE 29-4, page 439**

Answers: **(1)** largest **(3)** most successful **(5)** most powerful **(7)** most serious **(9)** most popular

◆ **PRACTICE 29-5, page 440**

Answers: **(1)** better **(3)** better; worse **(5)** better **(7)** best **(9)** better

Chapter 30

◆ **PRACTICE 30-1, page 446**

Possible edits: **(1)** When the first season of the reality show *Survivor* aired, it was an immediate hit. **(3)** For a while, *Survivor* became a cultural phenomenon—probably because it was seldom in bad taste. **(5)** It was surprising to see the controversial shows that suddenly appeared on the air. **(7)** A recent poll asked viewers: "Do you enjoy reality TV, or has it gone too far?" **(9)** It turns out that reality TV is nothing new.

◆ **PRACTICE 30-2, page 448**

Possible Answers: **(1)** By the 1700s, there were thirteen British colonies in North America. **(3)** The Revolutionary War went on for eight years. **(5)** For the first congress, the colonies sent representatives to Philadelphia in 1787. **(7)** One of their goals was to protect the rights of individuals. **(9)** The Constitution works because it was written to allow additions or amendments.

◆ **PRACTICE 30-3, page 450**

Answers: **(1)** species; sharks **(3)** Sharks **(5)** No plural nouns **(7)** sharks; meat-eaters; species; people **(9)** 1950s; sharks

◆ **PRACTICE 30-4, page 452**

Answers: **(1)** Count: approaches **(3)** Noncount **(5)** Count: shortages **(7)** Count: individuals **(9)** Count: systems

◆ **PRACTICE 30-5, page 454**

Answers: **(1)** every **(3)** A few violent **(5)** their **(7)** Many **(9)** some

◆ **PRACTICE 30-6, page 457**

Answers: **(1)** the; a **(3)** No article needed **(5)** the; the; the; No article needed **(7)** No article needed **(9)** a **(11)** a; No article needed; No article needed; the

◆ **PRACTICE 30-7, page 459**

Answers: **(1)** Question: Is converting metric measurements to English measurements difficult?; Negative statement: Converting metric measurements to English measurements is not difficult. **(3)** Question: Was that family very influential in the early 1900s?; Negative statement: That family was not very influential in the early 1900s. **(5)** Question: Has the winner of the presidential election always been the candidate who got the most votes?; Negative statement: The winner of the presidential election has not always been the candidate who got the most votes. **(7)** Question: Can the prosecutor verify the accuracy of the witness's story?; Negative statement: The prosecutor cannot verify the accuracy of the witness's story. **(9)** Question: Have customs officers at the border been requiring motorists to show proof of citizenship?; Negative statement: Customs officers at the border have not been requiring motorists to show proof of citizenship.

◆ **PRACTICE 30-8, page 463**

Answers: **(1)** is being [is] **(3)** are knowing [know] **(5)** are having [have] **(7)** are changing [Correct]; are becoming [Correct] **(9)** was showing [showed]; are [Correct]

◆ **PRACTICE 30-9, page 464**

Answers: **(1)** a brand-new high-rise apartment building **(3)** numerous successful short-story collections **(5)** the publisher's three best-selling works **(7)** a strong-willed young woman **(9)** an exquisite white wedding gown

◆ **PRACTICE 30-10, page 468**

Answers: **(1)** in; in **(3)** in; at; to **(5)** in; in; in **(7)** to; in; with; from; to; with; with **(9)** with; at; of **(11)** on; on **(13)** to

◆ **PRACTICE 30-11, page 471**

Answers: **(1)** Some people who have dreams of going to college have to set them aside for a variety of reasons. **(3)** Correct **(5)** "Distance learning" takes place when a teacher and student are separated by physical distance, and technology hooks them up. **(7)** Correct **(9)** Teachers can distribute assignments, and students can hand them in by fax or e-mail.

Chapter 31

◆ **PRACTICE 31-1, page 480**

Answers: **(1)** A talented musician, he plays guitar, bass, and drums. **(3)** Correct **(5)** The remarkable diary kept by young Anne Frank while her family hid from the Nazis is insightful, touching, and sometimes humorous. **(7)** Most coffins manufactured in the United States are lined with bronze, copper, or lead. **(9)** California's capital is Sacramento, its largest city is Los Angeles, and its oldest settlement is San Diego.

◆ **PRACTICE 31-2, page 482**

Answers: **(1)** In recent years, many Olympic athletes have been disqualified because they tested positive for banned drugs. **(3)** Correct **(5)** Banned by the rules of the Olympics, these drugs still appeal to athletes because they supposedly enhance performance. **(7)** Often called dietary supplements, these alternative chemicals are supposed to enhance athletic performance in the same way steroids supposedly do. **(9)** Instead of enhancing performance, they often cause considerable damage to the body.

◆ **PRACTICE 31-3, page 483**

Answers: **(1)** For example, the African-American celebration of Kwanzaa is less than forty years old. **(3)** By the way, the word *Kwanzaa* means "first fruits" in Swahili. **(5)** This can, in fact, be demonstrated in some of the seven principles of Kwanzaa. **(7)** The focus, first of all, is on unity (*umoja*). **(9)** In addition, Kwanzaa celebrations emphasize three kinds of community responsibility (*ujima, ujamaa,* and *nia*).

◆ **PRACTICE 31-4, page 484**

Answers: **(1)** Traditional Chinese medicine is based on meridians, channels of energy believed to run in regular patterns through the body. **(3)** Herbal medicine, the basis of many Chinese healing techniques, requires twelve years of study. **(5)** Correct **(7)** Nigeria, the most populous country in Africa, is also one of the fastest-growing nations in the world. **(9)** The Yoruban people, the Nigerian settlers of Lagos, are unusual in Africa because they tend to form large urban communities.

◆ **PRACTICE 31-5, page 487**

Answers: **(1)** Correct **(3)** Correct **(5)** The Japanese had just landed in the Aleutian Islands, which lay west of the tip of the Alaska Peninsula. **(7)** As a result, they made them work under conditions that made construction difficult. **(9)** In one case, white engineers who surveyed a river said it would take two weeks to bridge. **(11)** Correct

◆ **PRACTICE 31-6, page 488**

Answers: **(1)** The American Declaration of Independence was approved on July 4, 1776. **(3)** At 175 Carlton Avenue, Brooklyn, New York, is the house where Richard Wright began writing *Native Son*. **(5)** Correct **(7)** The Pueblo Grande Museum is located at 1469 East Washington Street, Phoenix, Arizona **(9)** St. Louis, Missouri, was the birthplace of writer Maya Angelou, but she spent most of her childhood in Stamps, Arkansas.

◆ **PRACTICE 31-7, page 490**

Answers: **(1)** The capital of the Dominican Republic is Santo Domingo. **(3)** Chief among these are sugarcane, coffee, cocoa, and rice. **(5)** Correct **(7)** Tourists who visit the Dominican Republic remark on its tropical beauty. **(9)** Correct

◆ **PRACTICE 32-1, page 496**

Answers: **(1)** We're all trying hard to watch our diets, but it's not easy. **(3)** Maybe we shouldn't be so tempted, but it's hard to resist the lure of the fast-food chains and their commercials. **(5)** When we're away from home and hungry, it's the picture of that burger that pops into our minds. **(7)** It shouldn't be so hard to find a fast, healthy meal. **(9)** It's still not the perfect meal for a dieter, but it isn't too bad.

◆ **PRACTICE 32-2, page 498**

Answers: **(1)** the singer's video **(3)** the writer's first novel **(5)** the players' union **(7)** the children's bedroom **(9)** everyone's dreams

◆ **PRACTICE 32-3, page 499**

Answers: **(1)** Parents; theirs **(3)** its; weeks **(5)** Ryans; years **(7)** classes; Correct; your **(9)** tests; Correct

◆ **PRACTICE 33-1, page 506**

Answers: **(1)** Midwest; Lake Michigan; Chicago; O'Hare International Airport; nation's **(3)** north; Soldier Field; Chicago Bears; Wrigley Field; Chicago Cubs; American League; baseball team **(5)** John Kinzie **(7)** United States; Mrs.; cow **(9)** mother; Aunt Jean; Uncle Amos

◆ **PRACTICE 33-2, page 509**

Answers: **(1)** "We who are about to die salute you," said the gladiators to the emperor. **(3)** "The bigger they are," said boxer John L. Sullivan, "the harder they fall." **(5)** Lisa Marie replied, "I do." **(7)** When asked for the jury's verdict, the foreman replied, "We find the defendant not guilty." **(9)** "Yabba dabba doo!" Fred exclaimed. "This brontoburger looks great."

◆ **PRACTICE 33-3, page 510**

Answers: **(1)** Essayist Simone de Beauvoir wrote, "One is not born a woman; one becomes one." **(3)** "Tribe follows tribe," said Suquamish Chief Seattle in 1854, "and nation follows nation." **(5)** Abolitionist Sojourner Truth said, "The rich rob the poor, and the poor rob one another." **(7)** Former slave Harriet Tubman said, "When I found I had crossed that line, I looked at my hands to see if I was the same person." **(9)** "No man chooses evil because it is evil," wrote Mary Wollstonecraft in 1790. "He only mistakes it for happiness."

◆ **PRACTICE 33-4, page 512**

Answers: **(1)** *Plan Nine from Outer* **(3)** *Born to Sing;* "You Don't Have to Worry"; "Time Goes On"; "Just Can't Stay Away" **(5)** *The Weakest Link; Friends; Law and Order*

◆ **PRACTICE 33-5, page 513**

Answers: **(1)** Sui Sin Far's short story "The Wisdom of the New," from her book Mrs. Spring Fragrance, is about the clash between Chinese and American cultures in the early twentieth century. **(3)** Interesting information about fighting skin cancer can be found in the article "Putting Sunscreens to the Test" that appeared in the magazine Consumer Reports. **(5)** Ang Lee has directed several well-received films, including Crouching Tiger, Hidden Dragon. **(7)** The title of Lorraine Hansberry's play A Raisin in the Sun comes from Langston Hughes's poem "Harlem."

◆ **PRACTICE 33-6, page 514**

Answers: **(1)** New Orleans has two nicknames: the "Crescent City" and the "City that Care Forgot." **(3)** The French Quarter is famous for several attractions: its unique buildings, its fine food, its street musicians, and its wild nightlife. **(5)** The Square—a gathering place for artists and other merchants—centers on a monument to Andrew Jackson. **(7)** Its popular beignets (pronounced ben-*yeas*) are deep-fried pastries covered with sugar. **(9)** New Orleans visitors—people from all over the world—particularly enjoy the laid-back atmosphere of the city.

Chapter 34

◆ **PRACTICE 34-1, page 522**

Answers: **(1)** weigh; Correct **(3)** Correct; deceive; believing **(5)** Correct; veins; Correct **(7)** Their; Correct; grief **(9)** variety; foreign

◆ **PRACTICE 34-2, page 523**

Answers: **(1)** unhappy **(3)** preexisting **(5)** unnecessary **(7)** impatient **(9)** overreact

◆ **PRACTICE 34-3, page 524**

Answers: **(1)** lonely **(3)** revising **(5)** desirable **(7)** microscopic **(9)** ninth **(11)** effectiveness **(13)** fortunate **(15)** argument **(17)** advertisement **(19)** careless

◆ **PRACTICE 34-4, page 525**

Answers: **(1)** happiness **(3)** denying **(5)** readiness **(7)** destroyer **(9)** fortyish **(11)** cried **(13)** business **(15)** spying **(17)** livelihood **(19)** joyful

◆ **PRACTICE 34-5, page 526**

Answers: **(1)** hoped **(3)** resting **(5)** revealing **(7)** unzipped **(9)** cramming **(11)** appealing **(13)** referring **(15)** omitted **(17)** fatter **(19)** repelled

◆ **PRACTICE 34-6, page 528**

Answers: **(1)** effects; already **(3)** buy; Correct **(5)** Correct; Correct **(7)** by; effects **(9)** Correct; affect

◆ **PRACTICE 34-7, page 529**

Answers: **(1)** here; every day **(3)** Correct; conscience **(5)** conscious; its **(7)** here; Correct; it's **(9)** hear; Correct

◆ **PRACTICE 34-8, page 531**

Answers: **(1)** past; knew **(3)** peace; Correct **(5)** Correct; laid **(7)** passed; Correct **(9)** know; Correct; mind

◆ **PRACTICE 34-9, page 533**

Answers: **(1)** plane; quite **(3)** supposed; quiet **(5)** principal; Correct **(7)** plain; quite **(9)** Correct; quiet

◆ **PRACTICE 34-10, page 534**

Answers: **(1)** There; Correct **(3)** threw; Correct **(5)** to; they're **(7)** Correct; through **(9)** Correct; used

◆ **PRACTICE 34-11, page 535**

Answers: **(1)** whose; Correct **(3)** where; Correct **(5)** Correct; whether; Correct **(7)** who's; your **(9)** you're; where

Index